KARL MARX'S THEORY OF REVOLUTION

This volume is dedicated
to
those who sow
though they will not reap.

> *Some seed the birds devour,*
> *And some the season mars,*
> *But here and there will flower*
> *The solitary stars . . .*
>
> A.E.H.

KARL MARX'S THEORY OF REVOLUTION

by Hal Draper

VOLUME II
THE POLITICS
OF SOCIAL CLASSES

MONTHLY REVIEW PRESS
NEW YORK AND LONDON

Library of Congress Cataloging in Publication Data
Draper, Hal.
    Karl Marx's theory of revolution.
    Includes bibliographies and index.
    CONTENTS: 1. State and bureaucracy. 2. v. 2.
    Politics and social classes. 1. Marx, Karl, 1818-1883—Political science
Collected works. 2. Revolutions—Collected works.
I. Title.
JC233.M299D7   301.5'92   76-40467
ISBN 0-85345-566-X

10 9 8 7 6 5 4 3 2 1

CONTENTS

APPENDICES

FOREWORD:
HOW NOT TO QUOTE MARX

The Foreword to Volume 1 took up a number of overall problems faced by any attempt to present Marx's views, particularly by an attempt at "a full and definitive treatment" of Marx's political thought. One of these problems can be usefully discussed again from another angle, taking inspiration from an article by Engels called "How Not to Translate Marx."

I explained why this work has taken the route of presenting a large number of passages from Marx and Engels themselves, instead of merely offering the hundred-and-nth "interpretation" of their views, and I contrasted this method with "quotation-mongering." Of course, quotation-mongering, being a pejorative, means any kind of quoting you don't like; but instead of pinning a definition to the mat, I offer a more positive contribution. What are the booby traps to look for in quoting from Marx and Engels?

The answer naturally applies in generalized form to anyone else. But nothing compares with marxology as the natural habitat of tendentious quotation. Ronald L. Meek put it mildly when he wrote: "All too often, writers seem to assume that when dealing with Marx it is permissible to relax academic standards to a degree which they themselves would regard as quite illegitimate if they were dealing with any other economist."[1] As usual, the main problem is not dishonesty. To be sure, there is a minor sector of the field, the gutter school of marxology, where anything goes; but this need not concern us here.

The main problem is what I would call, if pressed to invent a pseudoscientific nomenclature, Marxolalia. (Better, Marxophasia; but I prefer the sound of the first.) It may be defined as the propensity to garble Marx. The victim of this disorder cannot reproduce Marx's

1

thought in a form that Marx would recognize. Of the many causes of this disorder, I want to concentrate on one that is remediable.

There are few writers or thinkers in history whose every word and grunt has been examined by hostile critics so minutely as Marx's has. This is quite in order, provided that the words and grunts are evaluated with ordinary common sense and decency. Marx came into the world to challenge all the established authorities, governmental authorities and intellectual authorities, and he can hardly complain if the authorities react with some hostility. They seize on the useful fact that every scrap of his correspondence has been published somewhere; unpublished as well as published manuscripts have been exhumed and reprinted; unfinished fragments have been solemnly published and annotated; workbooks and notes have been scoured; scraps of paper have been fished out of wastebaskets, as it were, and given to the world; volumes of real and alleged conversations have been put into circulation.

It may seem unnecessary to point out that all this material exists on several levels of reliability, and investigators who want to be trusted must always ask themselves what exactly they are quoting from. Yet hundreds of times, over and over, I have seen remarks by Marx that were hastily dashed off in a letter to a friend, or a few words jotted down in a note, solemnly quoted (without identification) as if they were long-pondered programmatic statements every syllable of which had been thought out for its exact scientific meaning—indeed, even without regard to other statements on the subject of greater reliability. I wonder how many figures would come through such a working-over, done with a view to discreditment. In any case, several dozen "interpretations" of Marx can be fabricated, with little difficulty, through proper exegesis of the proper "quotations" thus wrenched off; and this has been going on industriously for a hundred years.

I repeat that I am not referring to garden-variety types of disingenuous or out-of-context quoting, but to a more elusive sort of Marxolalia. Thus, one sentence quoted from Marx's *Grundrisse* (economic workbooks) is just as quotable as any other sentence, isn't it? But the so-called *Grundrisse* is a peculiar nonbook: it consists of notebooks kept by Marx with no thought of publication—notes and jottings toward the eventual writing of a work on political economy. Each sentence represents a thought that popped into Marx's mind at the time—unreviewed, unrevised, uncriticized, often ungrammatical, and sometimes undecipherable. If it turned out to be badly formulated,

Marx had no obligation to add a footnote to the notes for the guidance of future sharpshooters. Not only that: these thoughts and notes were often scribbled late at night and when Marx was suffering from carbuncles, gastrointestinal illness, headaches, and assorted dyspepsias. Everyone knows Marx's jocular remark, on finishing *Capital,* that "I hope the bourgeoisie will remember my carbuncles all the rest of their lives," [2] but quoters should remember them too.

I have just taken an important work as example, but all kinds of quoting operations are undertaken also on the most ephemeral sources.

Let us consider this systematically, by drawing up a list of the types of writings and documents by Marx or Engels that are used for quoting or quotation-mongering, in descending order of reliability. At the top of the list are naturally:

1. Books and major essays that were published under the control of the writer, with the usual opportunity for correction, revision, etc. (Most of Marx's or Engels' major works will come to mind as examples.)

2. Articles published under the control of the writer.

a. Articles composed as political statements, for a political audience, and signed; in short, intended for the purpose they are used for.

b. Articles in which remarks on issues occur only in passing, often elliptically.

c. Journalistic articles, written as hack work, perhaps not even signed.

3. Articles published not under the control of the writer. Perhaps the most extreme case is that of *New York Tribune* articles that were rewritten or added to at will by the editors.

4. Unpublished manuscripts.

a. Unfinished or fragmentary, often never reviewed or revised—unfinished for various possible reasons, including dissatisfaction with the work.

b. Finished—but unpublished for various possible reasons, including dissatisfaction.

5. Letters. The circumstances of a letter, including its addressee, must always be taken into account. When writing to Engels, Marx takes much for granted and does not have to phrase his thoughts as they come to the pen in order to avoid ignorant or malicious misinterpretation. Some letters to others are diplomatizing. All letters are time-bound: opinions expressed (for example, about people) may change.

Letters are prime examples of ad-hoc writings that cannot be usefully quoted until the context is evaluated.

a. Circular letters. These are very like political statements, more like considered articles than casual correspondence.

b. "Educational" letters. Written to strangers in some cases, to party leaders in others, these are written with some conscious effort to set down a view; but even so, without the responsibilities entailed by publication.

c. Intimate letters, where all is "thinking aloud" and no effort is made to avoid possible misunderstandings by a third party. Most of the correspondence between Marx and Engels comes under this head. Very often, general-sounding statements have specific contexts and meanings.

d. Casual or ad-hoc letters, perhaps hastily dashed off, given little or no consideration of any kind.

6. Private notes, notebooks, and workbooks. These were not only not written for publication but were often written in a personal "shorthand," or in a telegraphic and allusive style, intended only for the writer's eyes. The aforementioned *Grundrisse* is an example of a long work in this style; Marx's "Conspectus of Bakunin's Book &c." is a shorter and more fragmentary case.

This list does not touch on other lines of variation, such as the difference between the early Marx and the mature Marx. Whatever one's views on this score, I do not understand how anyone can quote one of Marx's *Rheinische Zeitung* articles of 1842—written before he was even a socialist—as if it were as valid a statement of "Marxism" as anything later, without even alerting the reader. The same is still true about (say) the first year in which Marx adopted socialism and started working out his theory and method; for example, in writing the so-called *Economic and Philosophic Manuscripts of 1844.* And it is still true in every later case where we know that the formation of Marx's theory of society is *in process.* The opposite theory of quotation-mongering has it that "Marxism" is something that comes into the world integral and homogeneous: chip anything off this monolith (whether in 1842 or 1882, from a book or from a carbuncular grunt) and you have a "specimen" of Marxism which needs only to be put under the microscope to show anything you want to know, like a specimen pebble from a Precambrian stratum.

And we have not even mentioned the peculiar difficulties added by translations—difficulties from one standpoint, opportunities from another. In English books it is translations that are being quoted most of the time. But we cannot go into this here.

"I AM NO MARXIST," SAID HE

A number of examples of How Not to Quote Marx occur incidentally in the present volume, in the course of other expositions. Let us take an additional example, typical of its species, which we would not otherwise discuss, but which crops up frequently for easily understood reasons.

Professor George H. Sabine's *History of Political Theory* begins its chapter on "Communism" with the following information:

> Karl Marx once said of himself that he was not a Marxist. This remark referred in part to his own comparative indifference to the doctrinal completeness of his social philosophy and the misgivings with which he and Engels in their later life regarded the dogmatism of some of their disciples. It referred also to the wide variety of influences both theoretical and practical that flowed from his thought.[3]

Of the three things Marx is said to have referred to by this statement, at least two are fictional: Professor Sabine simply made them up. This is a space-efficient method of "interpretation," since it wastes no time on presenting what Marx may have said on the subject. Countless other marxological authorities have quoted Marx's *jeu d'esprit*, "I am no Marxist," to prove other imaginative interpretations, including the thesis that there is no such thing as Marxism at all. Marx himself said so, didn't he?

Indeed, the citing of Marx's revelation of his non-Marxism seems to have accelerated in recent decades, if I am not mistaken—partly feeding on itself, and partly perhaps reflecting a cyclical shift from refuting Marx to defusing him, in that movement which swings from seeing him as a terrorist ogre to painting him as a tame pussycat. I ask the reader's indulgence, therefore, for taking this space to present an assemblage of the facts, since this desperate recourse has never been taken before.

To begin with, it all stems from a pointed quip by Marx which we know of only because Engels mentioned it incidentally on four occasions, mostly in letters. By a pointed quip I mean a remark which is made in jocular form in order to soften a serious point. It follows that it is precisely the form, the literal wording, which is intended to be taken good-humoredly. The marxological transmogrification of this *boutade* (to use Longuet's later expression) into a programmatic declaration for the ages is one of the monuments to marxological prestidigitation.

It is first mentioned by Engels in a letter written while Marx is still alive and a neighbor of his. Writing to Bernstein in 1882, Engels poohpoohs the assertion of a French Possibilist (reformist) that "Marxism" is discredited in France (Engels quote-marks the term because it was used in the assertion), but he goes on to indicate that he does not think much of this French "Marxism" himself.

> Now to be sure, so-called "Marxism" in France is an altogether peculiar product, so much so that Marx said to Lafargue: *ce qu'il y a de certain c'est que moi, je ne suis pas Marxiste* [what is certain is that, as for me, I am no Marxist] .[4]

At the risk of overkill in explaining a joke—always a lugubrious thing to do—it must be pointed out that evidently Engels has not the slightest idea of the profound meanings that will be read into this. (This does not bother the marxologists, for it is one of the common tenets of the fraternity that Engels always got Marx all wrong, whatever he wrote.)[5]

Marx had to tell Lafargue face to face that he, a leader of the French movement, did not understand his own theory and politics—not in a quarrel but in a perfectly friendly fashion. This is the usual context of the pointed quip in civilized society. We know that this fits the background of Marx's relations with his son-in-law and disciple, for there is plenty of evidence of Marx's dim view of Lafargue's theoretical-political capacity and his frequent state of exasperation with the Frenchman's mistakes and inadequacies. The relationship can be seen even better in Engels' voluminous correspondence with Lafargue, which continually verges on cordial irritation with the shortcomings and immaturity of the entire French party leadership; it is not only a question of Lafargue himself. (This is not the first time that Marx and Engels lament the incapacity of would-be disciples to understand their ideas, and it will not be the last.)[6] In the other three places where Engels mentions the same quip, this and nothing else is the content.

Let us set these passages down for the full record. They all occur in 1890: in two letters written in August and in a published article a month later. In a letter to Schmidt, Engels deplores the quality of a book review by Moritz Wirth:

> . . . little Moritz is a calamitous friend. The materialist conception of history too has a lot of such friends today, to whom it serves as a pretext for *not* studying history. Just as Marx said about the French "Marxists" of the late seventies: *"Tout ce que je sais, c'est que je ne suis pas Marxiste"* [All I know is that I am no Marxist].[7]

Three weeks later Engels recalls this again, writing to Lafargue himself. The subject here is the faction of intellectuals in the German party called the "Jungen," which is discussed below in Chapter 17:

> These gentlemen all go in for Marxism, but of the kind you were familiar with in France ten years ago and of which Marx used to say: *"tout ce que je sais c'est que je ne suis pas marxiste moi!"* And he would probably have said of these gentlemen what Heine said of his imitators: I sowed dragons and I reaped fleas.[8] [This entire letter is in French.]

In a few days Engels has to write a public reproof of the "Jungen" faction, for publication in a party paper. Marx's saying is still in his mind, and his open letter includes the following:

> Marx foresaw also these disciples when, toward the end of the '70s, he said of the then prevailing "Marxism" of certain Frenchmen: *"tout ce que je sais, c'est que moi, je ne suis pas marxiste"*—"all I know is that *I* am no 'Marxist.' "[9]

This is the first time it appears in print.*

---

* There is another, thirdhand source that dates back to September 1883. G. A. Lopatin, the Russian Populist translator of *Capital,* had a talk with Engels and wrote a friend the next day with a report of the conversation, which included this:

> Do you remember, as I said, that Marx himself had never been a Marxist? Engels related that during the struggle of Brousse, Malon and Co. against the others, Marx once laughingly said: "I can say only one thing, that I am *no Marxist!* . . ." [Retranslated from the German][10]

The "struggle of Brousse, Malon and Co. against the others" (the Marxists) took place in 1881-1882, culminating in the split which saw the formation of a Possibilist party versus a more-or-less Marxist party. It was, then, a recent event when Lopatin talked with Engels. It had been even fresher when Engels wrote his first

In short, all facts indicate we have a perfectly ordinary situation in which Marx—in order to tell a comrade and friend (and son-in-law) that in all frankness he does not know his class from his elbow—uses a time-honored method of taking the edge off a blunt criticism: *If what you people are putting out is "Marxism," then I'm no Marxist.* This sort of thing has been done several thousand times with less brouhaha.

But isn't it odd for Marx to "deny" he is a Marxist, even jocularly? On the contrary, it would have been odd if he had reacted any other way, when the term began to show up. All historical figures who are fated to be suffixed with *-ist* (or, worse still, *-ite*) abjure it to begin with; for these tags almost always begin by being used as epithets by enemies. The reason is simple: labeling a set of ideas or policies with an individual's name makes it seem "personal" and cliquish; and this is often the conscious intent of the labeling.

Robert Owen devised a dozen labels for his ideas and organizations, but never "Owenite." Proudhon said: "I am told that somewhere or other there are people who call themselves Proudhonists; they must be imbeciles . . ."[12] John Wilkes, hearing someone fulsomely praise his speeches to his face, retorted: "Sir, surely you don't suppose me to be a Wilkite?"[13] Closer to our times, Trotsky wrote polemics to prove that "Trotskyism" was nothing but an invention of the Stalinists, whereas he preferred to call his views "Bolshevik-Leninism"even though his own followers called themselves Trotskyists quite freely; and while Stalin by exception promoted the use of the term *Stalinism* as an

---

letter about it to Bernstein in 1882. Yet in two of the 1890 loci, Engels had referred to the late 1870s—perhaps a lapse of memory. While Lopatin's testimony is not decisive per se, his dating (reporting Engels) fits the pattern of events better than the "late seventies," especially if we look at the content of Engels' letters to Lafargue during those years before 1880. —One more comment on Lopatin: although he states very plainly that Marx said it "laughingly," his first sentence is peculiar, as if he is trying to make something of it. For as a Populist it would be right up his street to believe that Marx was no more a Marxist than . . . Lopatin. If this is what he is getting at, then the jugglery with Marx's "laughing" quip started with the first one who had the proper ax to grind, and its later career stands in bold relief. —Finally, let us mention Marx's other French son-in-law, Charles Longuet, who included a rather vague reference in 1900 in his preface to Marx's *Civil War in France:* ". . . well known is his witty sally [*boutade*] apropos of certain applications or concretizations of his doctrine: *'Toujours est-il que moi, je ne suis pas marxiste.'* " (Still and all, *I* am no Marxist.) The words are now distorted by approximate memory, and Longuet is too discreet even to mention that Marx was talking about the French. The context suggests that Longuet would like to juggle with the quotation but he does not do it explicitly.[11]

honorific at home, his followers abroad commonly took the label as a Trotskyite slander on a leader who was merely an unhyphenated Leninist—a term Lenin eschewed. So it goes. The initial indignant rejection of conferred *-isms, ists,* and *ites* is so standard in political history that one wonders how it escaped the attention of the marxologists who work wonders with Marx's innocent quip.

As usual, the term *Marxist* was invented by enemies. Even so, it took some time to show up. As soon as Marx came on the scene as the proponent of a particular approach to socialism, rivals pointed fingers at the "Marx tendency." It is hard to see how one can denounce a viewpoint without putting a name to it. Marx might want to call his views "scientific socialism" or by some other nonpersonal designation, but an enemy has no inhibitions about personalizing things immediately.

"Marx tendency" or "Marx group" translates into German as *Partei Marx* (which does not mean "Marx party" in our current sense). It is *Partei Marx* that first showed up, along with *Partei Everybody Else.* It was probably used during the 1846 dispute with Weitling and Kriege. Hess, temporarily distressed by the "Circular Against Kriege," wrote to Marx: "with your party I will have nothing more to do."[14] What *Partei*? Well, the Circular had charged in its first lines that Kriege had compromised the "communist party." Kriege himself retorted that "the 'party' that Marx allegedly represents does not exist." Hess just as freely referred to the "Kriege 'Partei' " in a letter.[15] I also think that the tag *Partei Marx* was used for the *Neue Rheinische Zeitung* group in 1848-1849—by others, not by Marx's collaborators.[16] All this was standard operating procedure, and not very relevant, since it was so common.

Partei Marx was spread over the whole German press in 1852 when the Prussian government organized its frame-up trial of the Cologne Communists and featured the designation in the official indictment, along with *Partei Willich-Schapper.*[17] The split in the Communist League in September 1850 had produced these two factions or groups, and the government's case revolved around them. Marx's pamphlet for the defense, *Revelations on the Communist Trial in Cologne,* discussing the alleged evidence, was peppered with references to both of the group labels—but with a typical difference. *"Partei Marx"* almost always appeared in quote-marks; not so *Partei Willich-Schapper.*[18] The tag popped up contemporaneously in a letter by Mrs. Jenny Marx and one by Engels.[19] But in fact Marx's name had not yet been converted into an ism.*

This contribution—the invention of the terms *Marxian* and *Marxist*—seems to have taken place in 1872 as the struggle in the International heated up before the Hague Congress. It was made by Bakunin and his bore-from-within clique, in particular his first lieutenant James Guillaume. Characteristically, the new labels were *not* applied to Marxists (in any sense we would recognize) but to the majority on the General Council which was opposed to Bakunin, and which thus was accused of being Marx's creatures.

The first appearance, as far as we know, was in a faction-organizing letter sent by Bakunin to Italy, dated January 23, charging that "the Jewish-Teutonic, or Marxian, group which still dominates the General Council" wants to convert the International into a kind of state, and so on. His attack on "the Marxians in the General Council" offers Bakunin's common mix of anti-Semitism, racialism, and slander, as he denounces "the hatred of Marx and the Marxians against us . . . That is the way Germans and especially German Jews combat their opponents."[21] Bakunin uses *marxien,* in more or less the same way he uses *mazzinien* in dealing with Mazzini.

A few months later, the Bakuninists published letters of protest against the General Council's pamphlet *The Alleged Schisms in the International,* written by Marx and Engels. Bakunin's letter, dated June 12, denounced *"la politique marxienne"* along with the "German and Russian Jews" who were Marx's "agents," particularly "the little Russian Jew" (N. Utin) who was Bakunin's chief opponent in Geneva, all of them being accused of holding dangerous ambitions, "both personal and racial," implying a Jewish conspiracy.[22] A broadside by Guillaume dated June 10 likewise exposed "M. Marx's Jewish lackeys," but these lackeys were not called "Marxists" until his next letter of June 15. Among the imprecations that drip off his libertarian pen against the *"socialistes hébraïsants"* were, first, "the dynasty of

---

* The adjective form *Marxsche* turned up just as naturally, as when the leading Cologne paper referred to "some people of the *Marxschen Sekte,"* or a writer attacked the *"Marxschen Partei."*[20] But this is a standard way of making an adjective out of any name, and should not be equated with an ideologizing suffix like *-ist, -ian, -ite,* and the like.

Marxides," then the "Marxist conspiracy," and finally the "Marxists" *tout court.*[23] In this way, the first labels for the "Marxists" were born, like the first land animals, in a sea of mud.

Now one can be sure that the terms *Marxist* and *Marxism* would have eventually come into use by supporters of Marx, as well as by more or less objective historians; this usually happens with the passage of time and the subject's death, to answer a need. The role of enemies seems to be to shortcut the process, for the reasons already mentioned. At any rate, *Marxism* did not come into accepted use in Marxist circles during Marx's lifetime.*

That Marx himself would reject the term *Marxist* was always beyond doubt. That his most intimate collaborators eschewed it also, up to a relatively late date, only underlines their natural reluctance to "personalize" a historic theory which made its way by rising above mere cliques and individual sects. Death removes not only the person but also the "personal" stigma of an ism, and so there was no really good reason for Engels and for Marx's friends to keep quote-marking the term. Still less reason for tendentious marxology to make a fuss about it.

We look forward to the time when Marx's quip will cease to be the favorite quotation of the quotation-mongers.

---

* One very minor exception has been pointed out: at the end of 1877 the French Guesdist organ *Egalité* published an unsigned article on German political economy which incidentally stated that "Lassalle adopts the Marxist theories"[24] —a statement certain to disgruntle Marx. In France *Marxist* came to be used to label the Guesdists as a current distinct from the Possibilists and Blanquists (these latter two labels being likewise endowments by others). The Possibilist leader Paul Brousse, a Bakuninist who had gone over to right-wing socialism, published a brochure entitled *Le Marxisme dans l'Internationale* in 1882.[25] After Marx's death, Engels' letters occasionally reflected this common use of *Marxist* for the French group, like everyone else; he usually, but not invariably, enclosed it in quotes.[26] In his own mind the usage was secondhand, as we know from his explanation to Paul Lafargue: "We have never called you anything other than 'the *so-called* Marxists' and I would not know how else to designate you." The trouble was, he explained, that the group had no short usable name that was clear to readers elsewhere.[27] Writing to Laura Marx Lafargue, Engels remarked that "we have proved to the world that almost all Socialists in Europe are 'Marxists' (they will be mad they gave us that name!) . . ."[28] In 1893 Laura quipped, in a jocular French-language note to Engels: "As for me, my dear General, you know that it's enough to be *marxiste et engelsiste* to stay young forever!"[29] It is to be hoped that Laura will not go down in marxological history as the Founder of Engelsism.

ABOUT THE PRESENT VOLUME

First, there are two reminders that need repeating from the Foreword to Volume 1. (1) The little superscript numbers that pepper these pages, pointing to the reference notes in the back, should be ignored by the general reader. These reference notes *never* add to the line of thought, being strictly confined to giving sources and other technical information. (2) An unorthodox sign is used here to indicate that certain quoted passages or words are in English in the original: the degree mark. A double degree mark (°°) at the beginning of a quotation means that the whole passage was originally written in English. Inside a quotation, words or phrases originally in English are marked off using the symbol like quotation marks, °as here.° In both forms, the device has been used only where there was reason to signal the fact, not in every case.

To my original remarks on extant translations, add this. It does a reader little good to be given a reference source that can be checked only with great difficulty, such as some out-of-print edition of a work by Marx obtainable only in research libraries. Sometimes there is no choice; but for this reason I have tried to confine my references to English versions as much as possible to easily accessible editions, whether or not those versions were actually used for citation. The new English edition of the Marx-Engels *Collected Works* (ME:CW) would be the ideal solution, not because of the quality of its translations (which is very spotty), but because it should remain in print and generally available for a long time, and because it is inclusive. Unfortunately, only the first seven volumes are out as this is written. Still, wherever possible I have given the ME:CW location of a passage. This lacking, I have used, as the second in order of preference, the Marx-Engels *Selected Works in Three Volumes* (ME:SW). In these and other cases, the reference is bracketed if it was not actually used for quotation but is merely given for information. Forthcoming ME:CW volumes will continue to be used in this way as the English-language hitching post.

The tentative outline of Volume 2 which appeared in the first volume listed two chapters which have since been moved. The planned chapter on the women's rights movement has been returned to its original position in a later volume, along with the subject of Marx's views on women's emancipation in general. The chapter listed as "Nationalism and revolution" will be treated as part of a larger subject without which it does not make sense: Nationalism, internationalism, and foreign policy. In order to gain adequate space for this very extensive subject, and for two or three other subjects which will be crowded out of Volume 3, our present plan—in agreement with the publisher—calls for a fourth volume.

H. D.

September 1977

I | THE PROLETARIAT AND PROLETARIAN REVOLUTION

1 | PATTERNS OF REVOLUTION

By 1843-1844 Marx had come to look on the proletariat as the moving force of the coming revolution. By the writing of *The German Ideology* Marx and Engels were quite clear that the revolution they advocated was a *proletarian revolution.* What did this mean to them, and what did it entail?

They spent the rest of their lives answering these questions; and by the same token it will take the rest of this work to present their answers. But we can usefully start with some basic aspects of Marx's developed conceptions, especially in the borderland between terminology and idea.

1. REVOLUTION—SOCIAL AND POLITICAL

The word *revolution* is most commonly used as either a bogy or a banality, depending on whether it is seen as a sinister plot or reduced to a mere synonym for change. When the word becomes respectable, as ferocious words do when coopted, then not only is every detergent advertised as "new and revolutionary," but every new political device is advertised as in tune with some fashionable "revolution," such as the Revolution of Rising Expectations. More seriously, the word is also used historically to denote deep-going social change, as when the medieval invention of the horse collar is called an economic revolution, or in such terms as the Industrial Revolution. This is not said to object to such usages, but to differentiate them from those encountered in the framework of Marx's theory.

In a more specific sense, a revolution is seen as a transfer of governmental power. But this still covers a host of ambiguities. Transfer of power from whom to whom, or from what to what? As popularly used, it may simply be a matter of a change in personnel: this set of colonels in the Government Palace instead of that set of politicians; the substitution of one clique or faction for another. The term is activated especially if directly forceful methods are used instead of constitutional forms. It may make no more difference than the substitution of one set of political manipulators for another by any other means—for example, by more or less corrupt elections, or even honest ones.

The case becomes more interesting if one faction represents not merely a different set of pockets or Swiss bank accounts, but a different stratum or group interest—even if still within the ruling class. Marx's analysis of Bonapartism brought up many examples of this. Or, as we also saw in that analysis, the new wielders of political power may represent not a different social stratum of the ruling class but merely a different political policy, with or without a different ideological orientation. Or, perhaps most likely of all, both may be true: a different social stratum acts as the bearer of a different policy or ideology. Certainly the historical tendency is toward such a combination. But history exhibits various permutations within these boundaries, the boundaries being set by the range of possibilities for a given social system and its ruling class.

Within these boundaries, one very important type of difference may involve changes in political structure, in state forms. In modern history most of these cases involve shifts from more or less democratic state forms to antidemocratic ones (military dictatorship, fascism) or the other way round. It is such transformations in governmental forms that especially tend to get called revolutions. These are the most highly visible forms of transfers of governmental power. All of these involve political revolutions.

Political revolution, then, puts the emphasis on the changes in governmental leadership and forms, transformations in the superstructure. But if such a revolution involves a change in social stratum even within the ruling class, a social element is plainly entailed. Political revolutions run the gamut, from those involving almost no social side, to those with a very important social element, even if it is within the class boundaries we have assumed.

If these social boundaries are burst by the impact of the change, then we have a different sort of revolution, which is of special importance to Marx's theory. As Marx explained to a Cologne jury in 1849: the development of insoluble contradictions within the society "prepares the way for *social crises,* which burst out in *political revolutions.*"[1] The outcome is a revolution involving the transference of political power to a new class; and this change in ruling class tends to entail a basic change in the social system (mode of production). It is this kind of revolution which is most properly called a *social* revolution.

Unfortunately this does not end the terminological problem, as we weave our way through the voluminous literature that talks about revolution. If we decide to define social revolution as a basic transformation in the social system involving its class base, then it is apparent that such a sweeping change cannot be conceived as a mere act or event, but as a process, more or less extended in time. The transformation from capitalism to socialism is envisaged by Marx as such a historical process (as we shall see in Volume 4). Moreover, it is clear that in some cases in the past, social systems have changed basically, and classes have risen and fallen, in a secular movement of history which can be described as a social revolution—at least in historical retrospect, even though no one may have been aware that a revolution was going on.

It would be convenient if such a long-term or secular transformation in society, however achieved, had a tag of its own, so that one could discuss its relationship to other things called revolutions. There is no such agreed-on label; we must take the desperate recourse of inventing one. Let us call this a *societal revolution,* meaning that it denotes a change from one type of society to another, keeping in mind that for Marx's theory a society is not simply a cultural but a socioeconomic whole.

We can now narrow our focus to what tends to be called a social revolution in Marx's theory. It is most clearly used for a political revolution that expresses a social-revolutionizing drive toward the transference of state power to a new class. It is "a political revolution with a social soul," in Marx's earliest (1844) formulation.[2] By the same token it points in the direction of a societal revolution, regardless of when changes in the social system actually begin to take place. It does this by establishing a new constellation of sociopolitical forces, with new historic potentialities. The societal revolution is the realization of these potentialities. "Every real revolution," wrote Engels, "is a social one, in that it brings a new class to power and allows it to remodel society in its own image."[3]

Our aim is not to make a hard-and-fast distinction between political revolutions and social revolutions but, if anything, the reverse: to recognize how often they are mingled in given revolutionary situations, so that the two elements must be distinguished by analysis. For, especially in modern times, revolutionary events tend to blend both in varying proportions. The purely political revolution, involving a change in factions only, is likely to be a mere palace revolution, that is, one in which the upset takes place only on top without drawing in any sector of the people as actors on the scene. It is increasingly limited to socially backward areas. The modern tendency is for political revolution, however narrowly initiated, to waken the elements of social revolution from dormancy or to raise them to new levels. Thus the relationship between political and social revolution is not static. All this has been true of bourgeois revolutions since the first stirrings of the bourgeoisie, and it will provide important background for our chapters on that subject (Chapters 7-10 below). In terms of Marx's development, it was the revolution of 1848–1849 that was the proving ground.

For Marx, then, revolution is defined by the nature of the change involved, by sociopolitical relations. In the popular mind, where "the ruling ideas are the ideas of the ruling class," and therefore in journalistic terms, revolution and revolutionary developments are seen primarily in terms of particular means: force and violence, as departures from the political methods prescribed by the established powers. We shall devote considerable attention, in Volume 3, to Marx's conception of the relationship between social revolution and the means to effect it; suffice to say that the relationship emerges from a social historical analysis—it is not one of definition. Just as revolutionary change obviously did not always involve violent action ipso facto, so also violent outbreaks are by no means necessarily revolutionary, even if this term is stretched to include counterrevolutionary. Time and again, right up to today, it has taken violent methods ("revolutionary" actions in the eyes of the status quo) to gain simple reforms. Indeed, political revolution (of some limited sort) is not a rare road to social reforms. A related conception identifies revolution with the technique of the coup d'état: revolution suggests seizing the radio station, telephone exchange, local Winter Palace, and so on. This crude myth was by no means invented by Hollywood, which took it over from the respectable literature where it was already entrenched.

These ruling ideas about revolution are typically bourgeois conceptions, class-conditioned distortions of the social reality. They represent the other side of the coin of a ruling class's built-in dread of revolutionary violence, on the one hand, and on the other, its unwillingness and inability to conceive of revolution as a social upheaval from below. A putsch by an armed gang is something it can handle, and also something it can dismiss as banditry or pathology; in neither case need it face the social reality of mass revolution, which often comes as a surprise. The definition of revolution in terms of means (violent, illegal) is a characteristic of bourgeois ideology just as much as its opposite, namely, the insistence that social change must be limited to nonviolent means. This bourgeois approach provides a spectrum from the most pacifistic reform to the most violent putschism; and no part of it has anything to do with Marx's theory, which stands outside of this obsession with the dichotomy of violence or nonviolence.

The revolution that concerns Marx is defined by the nature of the social change it entails, by the class relationships in that change. It is a political revolution which is the immediate manifestation of a social revolution.

2. CLASS POLITICAL POWER

Proletarian revolution is, then, a short form for proletarian social revolution—transference of state power to a new ruling class, the proletariat.

This raises the problem of the class nature of the new political power. In principle this problem is no different from that of analyzing the class nature of any other political institutions, including those of the established society; this is what we discussed under the head of the theory of the state, in Volume 1. The difference is that in a revolutionary context everything is in flux, and does not meekly stand still for leisurely examination. The difficulties thus created are immense.

Marx offered no political formulas on this subject, nor could he do so. The totality of a social (class) analysis is at stake. Marx had to take up more than once the nature of given political movements that aspired to power or were moving to seize it. He had to analyze stated declarations, claimed intentions, programmatic documents, articulated ideologies and unarticulated biases, the correspondence of word and deed, objective socioeconomic linkages, and everything else bearing on the totality of the class configuration, not only at a given moment but over a period of experience. This refers us back to the social theory on which politics (including Marx's politics) is based. Working this problem out in a concrete case tests a theory of society's laws of motion.

The *Communist Manifesto* raised this problem in a discussion of what it called feudal socialism. Its interest lies in this: it identifies a type of "socialism" which conceals its real class character behind an appeal to the proletariat's interests:

> Owing to their historical position, it became the vocation of the aristocracies of France and England to write pamphlets against modern bourgeois society. . . .
>
> In order to arouse sympathy, the aristocracy were obliged to lose sight, apparently, of their own interests, and to formulate their indictment against the bourgeoisie in the interest of the exploited working class alone . . .
>
> In this way arose feudal Socialism . . . half echo of the past, half menace of the future; at times, by its bitter, witty and incisive criticism, striking the bourgeoisie to the very heart's core; but always ludicrous in its effect, through total incapacity to comprehend the march of modern history.

The problem of exposure is first solved with a flourish:

> The aristocracy, in order to rally the people to them, waved the proletarian alms-bag in front for a banner. But the people, so often as it joined them, saw on their hindquarters the old feudal coats of arms,* and deserted with loud and irreverent laughter.[4]

But the section ends with a more concrete sociopolitical analysis of

---

* This image is taken from Heine's then-recent satire *Germany, A Winter's Tale* (Caput 3), where he ridicules the introduction of the spiked helmet for the Prussian cavalry:

It suggests medieval nobles and squires,
Knights errant and lords superior,
Who bore true faith upon their breast,
Coats of arms upon their posterior.

Heine too had the serious aim of combating trends that looked back to pre-bourgeois times.

what betrays feudal socialism as antiproletarian. More important, we shall see in Chapter 9 below that Marx and Engels did in fact have to write a great deal more to analyze the nature of this alien socialism— alien to the proletariat as a class.

But analysis does not end the matter; the proof of the pudding is in the eating; the class nature of revolution is tested by what the new class in power does. Social revolution means that the new class in power does not limit itself to change within the framework of the old social system, but tends to put its new state power into basic conflict with the former ruling strata. And the conflict must be resolved more or less quickly in favor of the new or the old; the new political power must proceed to revolutionize the socioeconomic foundation, or else it will be destroyed by the rooted power of the latter. In either case, by revolution or counterrevolution, congruence will eventually be reestablished between the political and socioeconomic institutions.

The conflict may be seen by both sides only in embryo. This is what happened when, four months after the February revolution of 1848, the Paris workers rose up against the new republican regime. In the midst of these June Days, Marx wrote about the difference:

> None of the innumerable revolutions of the French bourgeoisie since 1789 was an assault on *order*, for they left standing class rule, the slavery of the workers, the *bourgeois order*, no matter how often the political form of this rule and this slavery changed. June has impugned this *order*. Woe to June![5]

Marx had to make this analysis in the flux of struggle. After all, the problem of the class nature of a new or aspiring political power does not exist only for uninvolved observers or distant historians. The problem is itself part of the political and social struggle going on, and it may not be resolvable by theory but only in the course of the struggle itself. The ongoing struggle, especially in critical phases, provides tests —tests of who represents what. Part of the struggle is on convincing the proletariat not only of who represents what (passive formulation) but of whom to act through and with. It is not merely a matter of registering a verdict post hoc.

3. THE GUIDING AIM OF REVOLUTION

It is insufficiently appreciated that, from early on, Marx and Engels habitually stated their political aim not in terms of a desired change in social system (socialism) but in terms of a change in class power (proletarian rule).

The two could not be assumed to be synonymous. The aim of proletarian rule, to be sure, commonly assumed socialism or communism as the corresponding societal form; but the reverse by no means worked automatically. Marx and Engels took as their governing aim not the aspiration for a certain type of future society, but the position of a social class as an embodiment of humanity's interests; not an abstract ideology of change (socialist ideas) but a class-conditioned perspective, what they called the proletarian outlook. In this context, the term *proletarian outlook* does not mean the outlook of a proletariat taken statically (for there is no such single outlook) but rather the outlook on society corresponding to the basic interests of the proletariat.

After Marx's initial period of exploration in 1843-1844,[6] the joint view of Marx and Engels on this issue was clearly stated in *The German Ideology*. Struggles over political forms, "all struggles within the state, the struggle between democracy, aristocracy, and monarchy, the struggle for the franchise, etc., etc., are merely the illusory forms . . . in which the real struggles of the different classes are fought out among one another."

> Further, it follows that every class which is striving for dominance, even when its dominance, as is the case with the proletariat, presupposes the abolition of the old form of society in its entirety and of domination in general, must first conquer political power in order to represent its interest in turn as the general interest [of society], which in the first moment it is forced to do.[7]

Behind the ideology of change is the class representing change: "The existence of revolutionary ideas in a particular period presupposes the existence of a revolutionary class . . ."[8]

This emphasis in *The German Ideology* is tied up closely with the view of the revolution not simply as a certain transformation of society but above all as a transformation of people. Socialism as the "revolution in humankind" (which will be discussed in Volume 4) was not an afterthought for Marx but the conception with which he began.

Only the proletarians of the present day, who are completely shut off from all self-activity, are in a position to achieve a complete and no longer restricted self-activity, which consists in the appropriation of a totality of productive forces and in the development of a totality of capacities entailed by this.[9]

The socioeconomic arrangement (socialism) was the means; the revolutionary target was something else, which merely required socialism:

In all appropriations up to now, a mass of individuals remained subservient to a single instrument of production; in the appropriation by the proletarians, a mass of instruments of production must be made subject to each individual, and property to all. Modern universal intercourse cannot be controlled by individuals unless it is controlled by all.

The revolution changes people, not simply by its ultimate effects, but in its course:

This appropriation [as described above] is further determined by the manner in which it must be effected. It can only be effected through a union which by the character of the proletariat itself can again only be a universal one, and through a revolution in which, on the one hand, the power of the earlier mode of production and intercourse and social organization is overthrown and, on the other hand, there develops the universal character and the energy of the proletariat, which are required to accomplish the appropriation, and the proletariat moreover rids itself of everything that still clings to it from its previous position in society.[10]

In this whole passage Marx has his eye on what the revolution means for humankind. He proceeds to discuss what the philosophers have meant by *der Mensch* as a social abstraction, how they substituted this social abstraction for the actual individuals of given social classes, and thus transformed history into a "process of consciousness" instead of a development of class-conditioned social entities. By ignoring the individuals' subjection to the distortions of class society (the division of labor), the philosophers worked a sleight-of-hand: "the average individual of the later stage was always foisted on to the earlier stage, and the consciousness of a later age on to the individuals of an earlier."[11] This later stage, or age, is still to be won; that is what the revolution has to do.

It is important to establish that this order of priority continued to govern Marx's and Engels' statements of the meaning of revolution, even when they were not directly discussing the issue. Thus Engels in 1847:

> In all civilized countries the necessary consequence of democracy is the political rule of the proletariat, and the political rule of the proletariat is the first presupposition of all communist measures.[12]

The same priority was embodied in the basic statements of the *Communist Manifesto*:

> If the proletariat during its contest with the bourgeoisie is compelled, by the force of circumstances, to organize itself as a class; if, by means of a revolution, it makes itself the ruling class, and, as such, sweeps away by force the old conditions of production, then it will, along with these conditions, have swept away the conditions for the existence of class antagonisms and of classes generally, and will thereby have abolished its own supremacy as a class.[13]

Thirty-five years later Engels referred back to this passage in a letter giving a summary statement of the aims of revolution, in which, as usual, he states the "ends of the social revolution of the future" in terms of proletarian power; the matter of socialist reorganization of society is not even mentioned, though assumed.[14] There is no question of counterposing one to the other; it is the governing priority which is exhibited. Elsewhere he would couple the two, while maintaining the same order:

> The revolution which modern socialism strives to achieve is, briefly, the victory of the proletariat over the bourgeoisie, and the establishment of a new organization of society by the destruction of all class distinction.[15]

The point can perhaps be sharpened by posing an occasionally mooted question: what is it that *defines* the crux of Marxism? The problem has been pointed up by the fact that one or another Marxist has rejected this or that theory of Marx's, say, "dialectical materialism," or the labor theory of value. There can be little doubt about the answer given by Marx and Engels, and it would not be pitched in terms

---

* An example of a proposed answer in terms of a set of ideas is that put forward in 1933 by S. Hook, who posed the question explicitly: "it can be categorically stated that it is Marx's theory of the state which distinguishes the

of a set of ideas.* Their ism must be basically defined, in terms of class power, as *the theory and practice of the proletarian revolution.*

In point of fact, both Marx and Engels seldom raised a question in terms of definition. One case in which Engels did this occurred in 1846, shortly after the completion of *The German Ideology.* He described in a letter his debates with the followers of True-Socialism in a German workers' club in Paris:

> I therefore defined the objectives of the Communists in this way: (1) to achieve the interests of the proletariat in opposition to those of the bourgeoisie; (2) to do this through the abolition of private property and its replacement by community of goods; (3) to recognize no means of carrying out these objectives other than a democratic revolution by force.[19]

The order of priority goes to the heart of the matter in the following sense. Before and after Marx, most varieties of socialism or communism defined themselves in terms of a desired transformation in socio-economic organization, and adopted a working-class orientation (if they did so at all) in order to effectuate this program.[20] For Marx, this relationship of means and ends was reversed. The revolutionary program is defined in terms of a new class ascendancy; the need for a reorganization of society is the consequence. While Marx's well-known reluctance to concern himself with the forms of future socialist society has been ascribed to an overreaction against utopianism, a contributing element is the fact that it is not the form of organization of future society that is in the center of his theory of revolution.

There is still another aspect of this question of priority. From Marx's standpoint, what made his theory revolutionary was that it looked to a literal *overturning:* not simply an overthrow, the deposition of established power, but a turning-over of the social corpus itself, as "the lowest stratum of our present society" stirs, heaves up, with "the whole superincumbent strata of official society being sprung into the air," as

---

true Marxist from the false."[16] His context is how to distinguish "liberal" Marxism, that is, Bernsteinian reformism. However, a social reactionary can hold a class theory of the state similar to Marx's, merely choosing a different class side. To be sure, the theory may have to be clandestine, as may have been illustrated by a certain German case.[17] This is true even more often of Marx's economic theory; for example, N. F. Danielson and G. A. Lopatin, who translated *Capital* into Russian, largely agreed with its contents but were far from being Marxists, whereas Karl Liebknecht disagreed with Marx's economic theory.[18]

the Manifesto pictured it vividly. This is the revolution; the revolution is not the adoption of a certain social schema. It was only the revolution of the exploited majority that could do this, in Marx's view; therefore the revolution from below had to be a proletarian revolution, and the proletarian ascendancy to power had to be a revolution from below.

4. PROLETARIAN AND BOURGEOIS REVOLUTION

In presenting the proletariat as the ruling class to be, Marx often stressed that in this respect the proletariat would only be doing what other classes had done before it throughout the history of the world. Most explicit was an analogy with the bourgeoisie, which also dominated a historic era by its struggle for the conquest of political power. The bourgeois revolution was the social revolution of the past, the proletarian revolution is the social revolution of the future: this is a common note. In both cases, a lower class organizes itself politically to conquer state power.

But the analogy between bourgeois and proletarian revolution holds only up to a point, like most analogies. The differences in the classes entail equally basic differences in the revolutions they bear. Some of these differences will best be discussed under other heads, especially differences in perspective (abolition of classes and state, for example). Here let us note three that are of immediate consequence for the course of the revolution itself.

The first two are already set forth in the *Communist Manifesto*.

(1) All previous revolutions have been in the interest of one form of private property over another form of private property. The proletarian revolution breaks out of this cycle, for it is the revolution of a propertyless class. The Manifesto puts it this way:

> All the preceding classes that got the upper hand sought to fortify their acquired status by subjecting society at large to their conditions of appropriation. The proletarians cannot become masters of the productive forces of society except by abolishing their own previous mode of appropriation, and thereby also every other previous mode of appropriation. They have nothing of their

own to secure and to fortify; their mission is to destroy all previous securities for, and insurances of, individual property.[21]

This fact is of enormous moment not simply for the aims of the revolution but for its accomplishment. For one thing, as we have seen, the bourgeois revolution had the advantage of offering the deposed ruling class a new lease on property-holding life, even if on less advantageous terms.[22] This was a factor in blunting the bitterness of defeat as well as in infiltrating the enemy. The proletariat has nothing of this sort to offer.

(2) The proletarian revolution differs from the bourgeois in that it proposes to put political power in the hands, not of another minority class to exploit the producers in a new way, but of a class representing the exploited majority. This was strongly stated in the Manifesto as part of the "upheaval from below" aspect stressed in the preceding section:

> All previous [historical] * movements were movements of minorities, or in the interest of minorities. The proletarian movement is the [self-conscious] * independent movement of the immense majority, in the interest of the immense majority. The proletariat, the lowest stratum of our present society, cannot stir, cannot raise itself up, without the whole superincumbent strata of official society being sprung into the air.[24]

These two differences will also be important in connection with the perspective of abolishing classes and the state.

(3) The third difference is partly an outgrowth of the first. The bourgeoisie, a property-owning class, was able to build up its social relations gradually within the womb of feudal society and to attain effective control of economic power within the framework of the old society, before it was able to take political power and change the class nature of the state. Its economic power developed with the inevitability of gradualness (this is where the phrase applies)—even with the aid of the still feudal or absolutist state. The latter not only could not resist this process but was compelled to desire it. Secure in their economic power, the bourgeois could use this position of strength as a fortress from which to press further toward the acquisition of decisive political power.

If any class was ever in a position to bring about its transformation

---

* The bracketed words were added in the Moore-Engels English translation of the Manifesto.[23]

of society gradually and without upheavals, it was certainly the bourgeoisie. But history shows us that this process had its limits in the sphere of political power. Within the old state, the bourgeoisie was certainly able to achieve considerable quantitative increase in political weight (political "power" in the colloquial sense of influence), but the state continued to be basically controlled by an alien (prebourgeois) class force which merely bent to the new pressure. The old ruling classes did not release their death-clutch on the state levers except after a definite period of political revolutionary action, which unblocked the development of the bourgeois social transformation.

The proletariat cannot emulate this pattern, because it differs basically from previous ruling classes in that it is not a property-owning class; in fact it develops as a class insofar as the producers are separated from ownership of means of production. The proletariat cannot build up a class economic power within the shell of capitalist society, as a prelude to overwhelming that society by its economic strength, in some fashion comparable to the pattern of bourgeois revolution.

Some contrary conceptions, looking to the rise of a proletarian "economic power" of some sort within the womb of bourgeois society, will concern us in Volume 3 in connection with socialist reformism. Here let us mention three aspects of the problem in order to highlight it. (1) Individual workers may own property—a home, for example, not to speak of clothes and toothbrush—but these are items of personal property of which they are the direct consumers; these things are not the private property which functions as means of production in the economic power structure. All the worker-owned homes in the country give the proletariat no economic leverage in the system and no political leverage of social significance. (2) It was once believed in some reform circles that the organization of cooperatives provided a proletarian analogue to the bourgeois experience; and Marx had to argue against this as an illusion.[25] This tendency has almost disappeared today even as a type of socialist reformism; for one thing, producers' cooperatives have failed to develop in the fashion predicted. (3) Another sense in which a sort of proletarian economic power has been seen as growing up within the womb of capitalism, to eventually take it over, is the view that trade-unionism has this historic role. This often plays on the colloquial use of economic power that has been mentioned: it is influence or pressure that is meant, the need to be reckoned with, not the institutionalized power of property.* Trade-unionism is a modern form of the same economic power that every exploited class has had in history: the power to threaten by its struggle the revenues and perquisites of the possessing classes and thereby to obtain concessions. The view that sees trade-unionism literally as the womb-form of socialism is *classical syndicalism,* which will be touched on in the last section of Chapter 5 below.

In sum: for Marx, the working class (unlike the bourgeoisie) cannot inseminate its own system of economic power within the old one, thereby establishing a plateau of power from which to gain the political heights. The order necessarily is the reverse. The proletariat—through the organization of its political movement, like every other aspiring class—must first conquer political power and then begin the process of socioeconomic transformation. For the bourgeoisie, political power was finally plucked as the ripe or overripe fruit of its socioeconomic power, its power as a possessing class. For the proletariat, political power is needed as the engine with which to bring a new social order into existence.

As a consequence of the comparison between bourgeois and proletarian revolution, the question has been mooted: which one is "easier"? Marx has made remarks on both sides of this question, with dubious applicability. In *The Eighteenth Brumaire* he has an explicit comparison, although by bourgeois revolutions he really has 1789 in mind, and by proletarian revolutions, or "the revolution of the nineteenth century," he has the June 1848 uprising in Paris before him.

> The social revolution of the nineteenth century cannot draw its poetry from the past, but only from the future. It cannot begin with itself before it has stripped off all superstition in regard to the past. Earlier revolutions required recollections of past world history in order to drug themselves concerning their own content. In order to arrive at its own content, the revolution of the nineteenth century must let the dead bury their dead. There the phrase went beyond the content; here the content goes beyond the phrase.[26]

This may be taken as a warning against imitation of past patterns on the

---

* In this connection we must again point out that Marx and Engels used terms like *political power* from time to time in the same colloquial way as everyone else; the context must be examined.

ground of sheer analogy or in sheer parroting of watchwords and formulas. Marx goes on to this:

> Bourgeois revolutions, like those of the eighteenth century, storm swiftly from success to success; their dramatic effects outdo each other; men and things seem set in sparkling brilliants; ecstasy is the everyday spirit; but they are short-lived; soon they have attained their zenith, and a long crapulent depression lays hold of society before it learns soberly to assimilate the results of its storm-and-stress period. On the other hand, proletarian revolutions, like those of the nineteenth century, criticize themselves constantly, interrupt themselves continually in their own course, come back to the apparently accomplished in order to begin it afresh, deride with unmerciful thoroughness the inadequacies, weaknesses and paltrinesses of their first attempts, seem to throw down their adversary only in order that he may draw new strength from the earth and rise again, more gigantic, before them, recoil ever and anon from the indefinite prodigiousness of their own aims, until a situation has been created which makes all turning back impossible, and the conditions themselves cry out: *Hic Rhodus, hic salta!* Here is the rose, here dance![27]

This is an interesting résumé of revolutionary patterns, but the flat counterposition of bourgeois and proletarian revolutions with respect to these patterns is not as historically general as the language implies.

In *Capital* Marx emphasizes an advantageous aspect of the change to socialism:

> The transformation of scattered private property, arising from individual labor, into capitalist private property is, naturally, a process incomparably more protracted, violent, and difficult than the transformation of capitalistic private property, already practically resting on socialized production, into socialized property. In the former case, we had the expropriation of the mass of the people by a few usurpers; in the latter, we have the expropriation of a few usurpers by the mass of people.[28]

There are obviously things to be said on both sides of the calculus of difficulty, if that rather unprofitable enterprise is undertaken. The important point for present purposes is simply the fact of difference itself. The luring analogies between bourgeois and proletarian revolutions, or among all revolutions for that matter, are not without interest; but in the last analysis the patterns of proletarian revolution are as unique as the class it reflects.

2 | THE SPECIAL CLASS

A discussion of the political problems of proletarian revolution requires some clarification on a number of points in Marx's social theory. The following summary covers a number of controversial questions by stating Marx's view.

We have used *proletariat* so far with the broad meaning of wage-workers, especially in order to differentiate it from the early history of the word.[1] It is necessary now to be more exact, not so much for the sake of scientific accuracy as in order to dispense with some common misunderstandings of the political import of proletarian revolution. Marx's attitude toward precise definition in political terminology was typical of his day in being relatively permissive as compared with contemporary standards; but he grew more inclined to precision at least in the field of economic science. We saw this reflected in his increased care to distinguish between *proletariat* and *working class* on at least one occasion.[2]

Part of the problem was that, although *proletarian* was already in use as a term broader than *worker*,[3] Marx came to assign a narrower scope to it by a terminological outcome of his economic theory. Over the span of Marx's life, socialist literature attached a whole spectrum of meaning to the word. A good example of the broad end of the spectrum was in a programmatic statement of the Communist League, probably written by Schapper, shortly before the *Communist Manifesto:* "In present-day society proletarians are all those who cannot live on their capital, the worker as well as the men of learning, the artist as well as the petty-bourgeois . . ."[4] Behind this unworkably broad usage, as also the usage by others,[5] was the strong honorific coloration that the word was intended to convey in these circles. Actually the real sense was a negative: all who were not idlers. Terminologically it raised the banner of a united front by disparate social elements against the ruling minority. Although the origins of this kind of honorific aura around *proletarian* are pre-Marxist and non-Marxist,* its effects linger on in Marxist literature.

1. ECONOMIC DEFINITION

In Marx's theory, the proletariat is the working class peculiar to capitalist relations of production. It does not comprise all who work for a living, or who do useful or necessary work. It consists of workers whose livelihood depends on a wage relationship with employers of labor power, and who therefore produce surplus value in the process of commodity production.

Thus the term *proletariat* is not coterminous with a number of other expressions that are often used synonymously.

• The proletariat does not include all wage-workers. For example, it does not include wage-workers employed by government—road-building workers, in one example by Marx[6]—since strictly speaking they do not produce surplus value in the course of commodity production.

• The proletariat does not consist only of industrial workers (whatever that descriptive term is taken to comprise). Surplus value is produced in the course of other types of commodity production.

• The proletariat does not consist only of manual workers. There is a whole sphere of intellectual or mental labor which is as proletarian as any other. (We will return to this in Chapter 16.)

• The proletariat does not consist only of workers "at the point of production" (again, however that phrase is interpreted). For example, transportation may contribute to the surplus value of the transported commodity; and a truck driver may be as proletarian as an assembly-line hand.

• The proletariat does not consist only of workers engaged in producing tangible commodities. Producers of services (nonmaterial commodities) may also be producing surplus value. To take an example

---

* Contrast Marx's emphasis that the term "productive laborer" (as against unproductive) was *not* honorific but a reflection of capitalist conditions (discussed in Chapter 16 below).

which combines this and a previous point: a salaried teacher in a privately owned school that is run as a profit-making enterprise is producing surplus value for the employer.

Some of the above points restrict the technical coverage of the term more than is commonly realized. There is a final point to be made which expands it significantly.

• The basic unit of the proletariat in capitalist production, considered structurally, is not any individual but the *collective laborer*. This term of Marx's refers to the ensemble of workers whose labor taken together is necessary to produce a given commodity. It may be a small number (rarely one!) or a very large collectivity; but, more important, it commonly unites both manual and intellectual (mental) labor specialties, both labor at the point of production and away from the factory, both labor expended directly on the product and labor indirectly associated with the necessities of production (like floor-sweeping). It also includes supervisory labor of any type necessary to the production of the commodity. No one of this collectivity is responsible for the value embodied in the commodity; all of them are collectively. There is no basis for distinguishing between proletarian and nonproletarian constituents of the collective laborer; all of them are members of the proletariat.

The bourgeois-proletarian antagonism on which Marx bases the modern class struggle is, then, not represented by the dichotomy between dirt-splattered, horny-handed, blue-collared toilers and clean-shirted, chair-warming paper manipulators. The latter is a bourgeois conception, that is, it arises from class conceptions of social antagonisms that are cherished by the ruling class as a self-serving stereotype or caricature of the real world. This remains true even when it is inverted, that is, when the horny-handed lower-class image is idealized by alienated bourgeois who wish to break with their class.

2. WORKING-CLASS CIRCLES

One present importance of emphasizing the narrow economic meaning of *proletariat* to Marx is to shake up common misunderstandings. Thus, it is true that, technically, an editorial supervisor of the *Encyclopaedia Britannica* may be a proletarian while a Navy Yard shipfitter is not. But marginal consequences of this extreme sort are not typical of the sociopolitical role played by proletarian elements as against non-proletarian strata. The example calls attention to the need for the next step: a concrete examination of the relationship between an economic stratum as such and its social role, and hence the tendency of its relationship to the political class struggle.

Obviously the encyclopedia editor, even if technically a proletarian, will tend to react socially and politically quite differently from a factory hand. Marx's conception of revolution simply puts forward the following proposition. Objective class status is the most important single determinant of sociopolitical role in the long run; and of the various class situations, that of the proletariat tends to drive most consistently toward a break with bourgeois relations.

> Not in vain does it [the proletariat] go through the stern but steeling school of *labor.* It is not a question of what this or that proletarian, or even the whole proletariat, at the moment *regards* as its aim. It is a question of *what the proletariat is,* and what, in accordance with this *being,* it will historically be compelled to do. Its aim and historical action is visibly and irrevocably fore-shadowed in its life situation as well as in the whole organization of bourgeois society today.[7]

This was written before the young Marx had got very far with his economic investigation of "the whole organization of bourgeois society." But it already roots the revolutionary role of the proletariat in its life situation, the objective relations that condition its social existence. Engels said no more when, much later, he described the proletariat as "a class whose conditions of life necessarily drive it to social revolution."[8]

A social analysis of the relation between classes and politics will, however, not normally show a simple duel situation. The duel pattern implies a highly polarized conjuncture such as commonly occurs at the end of a development, not at its beginning. For a better schema, let us resort to the metaphor implied by the phrase *social circles.* You are invited to think of a system of concentric circles, with surrounding areas. Here the main body of the proletariat is to be seen as a core group, occupying a central position with relation to the revolutionary drives within society.

In the accompanying schematic diagram, one aim is to illustrate the

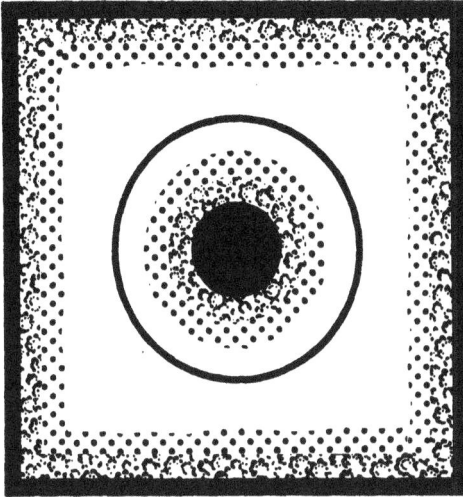

In this bare schema, the whole circular area in the center represents the *working classes.*

• *Proletariat:* the two central circles—the solid black core and its penumbra. The core represents the *industrial proletariat*; the penumbra, all other proletarian workers.

• *Other wage-workers:* represented by the dotted-area circle.

• *Working petty-bourgeoisie (traditional petty-bourgeoisie):* represented by the last, all-white circle. It comprises artisans, shopkeepers, etc., in the towns, peasantry in the countryside, depending on self-employed labor and small-property ownership. The significance of including these strata among the working classes is discussed in Chapter 11.

The bourgeoisie is represented by the outer strips running in a square; the three differently shaded strips suggest the small, middle and big bourgeoisies. No significance is to be attached to other features of the schematic sketch.

The "middle classes" (in the residual sense) are suggested by the irregular white area lying vaguely between the working-class circles and the bourgeoisie's square. For the use of the term *middle classes*, see Chapter 11.

fact that revolution entails the setting into motion of ever-expanding circles of society. The strategic position to set these circles into motion is occupied by the proletariat: such is Marx's view—"the proletarians created by large-scale industry assume leadership of this movement and carry the whole mass along with them . . ."[9]

The relations among classes, class strata, and class elements in revolution involve, of course, far more than the bare bones of class definition. The underlying demarcations of class merely provide a framework for their social interactions. From this standpoint our emphasis will be on the main body of the proletariat *plus* those sections of the population whose life situations in society tend to be similar. (This consideration will be concretized in subsequent chapters.) It is this combination which tends to be called the working classes, or even the working class, in Marx's writings—a term, therefore, which is best regarded as not narrowly technical-economic but as a socially extended penumbra around the proletariat. Let us specify now that when Marx leaves the specific ground of economic science in his discussions, and especially when the context is political affairs, the terms *proletariat, workers,* or *working class* tend to denote this same combination.

3. VANGUARD AND ALLIES

When Marx wrote in the *Communist Manifesto* that the proletarian revolution, unlike the bourgeois, was the "movement of the immense majority," it was an anticipative formula. In almost all countries, insofar as the proletarian revolution was the movement of a majority, it could not be the movement of the proletariat only but of the proletariat and its allies, namely, those social circles it could set in motion. "The class exclusively dependent on wages all its life is still far from being a majority of the German people," wrote Engels in 1870. "It is, therefore, also compelled to seek allies."[10] And he proceeded to weigh the worth of various class elements as allies. We shall do so in Part II.

In 1848–1849 the gravamen of Marx and Engels' policies in the revolution was the problem of allies, as we shall see. The revolutionary movement collapsed over this problem, over "the incoherence, incongruence and apparent contradiction which prevailed in that movement" as a consequence of the crisscrossing pulls of the various social sectors:

°°When interests so varied, so conflicting, so strangely crossing each other, are brought into violent collision; when these contending interests in every district, every province, are mixed in different proportions; when, above all, there is no great centre in the country . . . what else is to be expected but that the contest will dissolve itself into a mass of unconnected struggles, in which an enormous quantity of blood, energy, and capital is spent, but which for all that remain without any decisive results?[11]

What was lacking in this failed revolution was precisely the pattern of a vanguard class successfully drawing all its allies after it.

This standpoint provides a very important qualification to the bird's-eye view embodied in the *Communist Manifesto*'s vivid picture that "Society as a whole is more and more splitting up into two great hostile camps, into two great classes directly facing each other: bourgeoisie and proletariat."[12] This picture emphasizes the long-term trend toward increasing polarization. But in shorter-range terms, a decisive problem of each polar class is to attract and hold class allies and to neutralize others. The proletarian revolution depends not on the proletariat alone, but on the hegemony of the proletariat among the revolutionary forces.

A one-sided dogmatization of this Manifesto aphorism was turned by the Lassallean movement into the watchword that, relative to the working class, "all other classes are only one reactionary mass." Both Marx and Engels ridiculed this apparently "radical" assertion and denounced it as politically reactionary. It meant the defeat of revolution by excluding allies. (This issue will be discussed at large in Chapter 11.)

The social revolution would not be made by the proletariat *solus*, and there was no need to wait until the development of society had made the proletariat a majority by itself, nor even to expect that such an extreme point might be reached. To be sure, the social revolution was possible only where the proletariat had come to occupy "at least an important position among the mass of people," Marx wrote,[13] but this was so because only such a proletariat could hope to head a revolutionary class alliance. It was the proletarian-dominated alliance which he expected to be the mass basis of the social transformation.

4. WHY THE PROLETARIAT?

What is there in the life situation of the working class that causes Marx to regard it as the historically nominated hard core of modern revolution?

The answer has nothing to do with idealizing workers as such; it does not depend on regarding workers as somehow better, or more clever, courageous, or humanitarian than other people. Nor is it relevant to prove, as can be done with ease, that workers often follow reactionary courses and leaders and by no means show an invariable affinity for progressive causes. They are at least as capable of being misled and deceived as any other section of society (including intellectuals). They are filled with selfish aspirations and unworthy prejudices like everyone else. If this were the sort of thing involved, the case would not only be closed—it could never have been opened.

Taking workers person for person as individuals, the question whether they are better than others because they belong to an anointed class is quite alien to Marx's method of inquiry. In general Marx does not view social conflicts as contests between Good People and Bad People. The capitalists pilloried in *Capital* for their callous disregard of the suffering caused by brutal exploitation were just as likely to be kind parents and generous friends as the next person, and not given to trampling down children in the street. People act one way as individual atoms in the social fabric; they often act quite differently as part of a class collectivity. The bourgeois explanation is "Business is business"—which means that one must make a sharp distinction between an individual-human role and a class-constrained role. The life situation of capitalists also determines a class role, with class characteristics that cannot be deduced simply from the sum total of individual psychologies.

Like every other class and organic social group, the proletariat is more than the sum of its individual atoms. The working class is *atomized* when it is unorganized. Class organization brings class characteristics to the fore, and, as a function of organization, class characteristics increasingly take precedence over merely individual reactions, the greater the scale of class involvement. Then, in a feedback effect, class reactions can also reshape and reeducate individual reactions. Thus class-consciousness develops. When Marx was in a mind for Hegelian phraseology, the atomized class was a "class in itself" (*an sich*) but became a "class for itself" (*für sich*) insofar as it organized into a social entity and achieved consciousness of its social and political role in the course of struggle.*

All this, for Marx, is a historical process, not a static mystique. "Revolutionariness" does not reside in the substance of the proletariat like sanctity in the Holy Ghost; the notion that every proletarian is immanently more revolutionary than the unanointed at any given time or place has no more to do with Marx than muttering a paternoster. The conditions of existence of the working class provide the connection between the economic position of the class and its political tendencies; "the proletariat is revolutionary in accordance with its whole [social] position . . ."[15]

The historical advantages possessed by the working class for the role of revolutionary vanguard may be summarized as follows.

1. *The conditions of life of the working class lead it to organize, to produce a more and more homogeneous movement.*

Its class propensity to organize is outstanding. The model and pioneer in this respect is the capitalist class itself, whose own class-consciousness and sense of class solidarity have often been inspirations to its workers. But then, the capitalists are the other urban class organized by modern industry. Agrarian populations are unable to rival the achievements of the urban classes, by reason of their own conditions of existence. "The dispersion of the rural laborers over larger areas breaks their power of resistance while concentration increases that of the town operatives," observes Marx in *Capital*.[16] A similar contrast obtains for the landed possessing classes.

Workers are taught organization not by their superior intelligence or by outside agitators, but by the capitalists. Concentrated geographically in urban areas, workers are further organized in factory gangs, assembly lines, work shifts, labor teams, and so on—that is, by the organization of the division of labor, to which capitalism has contributed so mightily. Capitalism has no choice about teaching its workers the wonders of organization and labor solidarity, because without these the system cannot operate. Capital "assembles the bourgeois and the proletarians

---

* This distinction is made mainly in three or four of Marx's earlier writings (up to 1852).[14] It has been widely distorted into the claim that for Marx a class exists only in the form of conscious organization. For Marx's last use of this bit of Hegelese, see below, Chapter 12, §9.

in large cities, in which industry can be carried on most profitably, and by this herding together of great masses in *one* spot makes the proletarians conscious of their power."[17] It expounds the need for discipline, and at the same time involuntarily demonstrates the defects of bureaucratic discipline. It enforces centralization of effort, and glorifies the advantages of combined labor and the subordination of individual self-interest to group needs. It socializes masses of workers in one place and subjects them to simultaneous resentments. The working class can say: "The *organization* you teach me I will execute, and it shall go hard but I will better the instruction."

It is evident that these lessons are not taught equally to all workers, even apart from the usual individual differences. There are differences in working-class life situations, too. For example, the lessons are plainer to assembly-line workers than to an office secretary who works "with" a boss rather than with fellow workers. We will touch on other reasons later.

2. *The interests of workers, as a group organized by capital, lead them to struggle.*

To engage in class struggle it is not necessary to "believe in" the class struggle any more than it is necessary to believe in Newton in order to fall from an airplane. (In the latter eventuality, however, it is advisable to believe in parachutes.) The working class moves toward class struggle insofar as capitalism fails to satisfy its economic and social needs and aspirations, not insofar as it is told about struggle by Marxists. There is no evidence that workers like to struggle any more than anyone else; the evidence is that capitalism compels and accustoms them to do so.

Not only their leaders but workers as a whole begin by preferring class peace and social tranquility, for excellent reasons. But if that ended the matter, it would be impossible to account for the fact of class organization. The basic function of class organization is struggle, present or potential, reality or threat. The very notion of an organization, like a trade union, which is inherently hospitable to members of one class only, and which is inherently weakened until it achieves the organization of the entire class as such, is a notion that fits no bourgeois ideology.

3. *The thrust of the proletariat's organized struggle persistently tends to go outside the framework of bourgeois institutions and ideas.*

The operative contradiction is between the rights of private property, capitalism's juridical idol, and the organized proletariat's inevitable insistence on *social responsibility* for all vital aspects of life, including the economic. The inherent claim of capitalist private-property relations is that the whole area of economic life, in which one has to earn a living, is withdrawn from the hegemony of society and handed over to the unilateral power of capital as its birthright. The inherent claim of an organized proletariat is that it must have a say in this. This contradiction reflects Marx's proposition that the basic contradiction of capitalism is that between social production and private appropriation.

In the course of working out the contradiction, capitalism accepts many compromises; for example, it yields to state intervention in the name of social responsibility, and even demands intervention, especially for subsidies, strikebreaking, and so on. But it is in the nature of the organized working class that it can never win enough of the substitution of social responsibility for private corporative control; and it is in the nature of capital that it always seeks to subordinate partial and distorted forms of social responsibility to the continued reality of capital's claim to social hegemony. This opposition is a basic one.

There is a spectrum in demands for social responsibility too. More or less radicalized workers may raise demands for price and profit controls, regulation, even nationalization; in intense class struggles, sit-in strikers have taken over factories without a qualm about the rights of private property. But even conservative workers and their unions, taking class collaboration for granted, tend to support social-control proposals which do not impress them with having immediate anti-capitalist implications: controls over prices, health insurance, offshore oil, and many other citadels of property. Capital is usually more class-conscious than that; hence it denounces the insistence on social responsibility versus private-property rights as "creeping socialism." This charge reflects a reality.

Samuel Gompers used to argue that his simple slogan for the labor movement—"More!"—was more revolutionary than the socialist program. The answer need not deny the real revolutionary implications of his slogan, which Gompers had no intention of carrying through. "More!" is an implicitly revolutionary program if one obvious condition is added: that labor consistently and unremittingly press for it *regardless of all capitalist considerations*, that is, even when "more" is incompatible with capitalist needs and interests. Obviously, "more" is not revolutionary if it is raised only when it does not incommode capital; Gompers did not confess to this limitation, which was his actual regulating principle. His appeal was a class appeal, to be sure, therefore inherently discommoding to capital; it need only be applied unremittingly. As labor presses for more—including more social responsibility, more control over its conditions of existence—the class drives the logic of its own life situation outside the bounds of the capitalist framework and tends to create the conditions for exploding that framework.

None of this happens automatically; hence the complications discussed in many chapters. A potentiality is set up. But this potentiality does not obtain equally for other classes and social strata. The working class is not the only class or group alienated, at one time or another, by the operations and depredations of capitalism; the capitalist class has despoiled middle-class strata, bankrupted petty-bourgeois property owners, embittered an intelligentsia, plundered a peasantry, and so on. Radicalized movements and parties based on these social resentments have not been rare. But the political programs they tend to adopt as they move into opposition to the status quo are likely to remain within the bounds of the capitalist system. Hence they tend to concentrate on mere political reform, on economic nostrums like money manipulation, on demagogic attacks on the Bank Octopus or Interest Slavery or some other excrescence of the system; they do not tend to come out for abolition of the capitalist system. Historically and on a worldwide scale, the latter conclusion is associated with the working class, when *it* moves left. This is the content of Engels' much-compressed aphorism: "who says proletariat, says socialism." [18]

4. *The proletariat's conditions of existence not only impel it toward organized antibourgeois struggle, but push it into a persistent boldness and militancy which is well-nigh unique to this class at critical stages of struggle.*

This points to the largely unexplored terrain of the social psychology of classes. For we are concerned with this as a class phenomenon, not as individual characteristics. This difference is important.

For example: one of the best-known stereotypes of timidity is that of the Timid Professor—the Hollywood caricature of the pince-nez'd, harrumphing, mousy scholar who blends out of sight among the library books. When the individual faculty members of a large American university are examined nowadays, this stereotype hardly seems to exist, and maybe it never did. In fact, more and more professors are achieving the personalities of vacuum-cleaner salesmen. Yet the organized picture is altogether different. Put these aggressive personages together in the collective form of an Academic Senate and the result is a peak of pusillanimity that would blow the fuse on a sociological computer, even at times when indignation and resentment at Trustees or Regents are sweeping their stout hearts.

In many sociological surveys, as has been set forth to the nearest sigma, well-paid workers, who may live in $40,000 houses and send their children to college, register answers to questionnaires that stamp them as indistinguishable from middle-class mentalities. So also librarians (to take another occupation I know something about). Yet striking labor aristocrats—say, printers—can if necessary break company windows, rampage on picket lines, beat up scabs, and outrage other forms of gentility, without arousing enough surprise to generate the size of headlines reserved for three-person "student riots." On the other hand, underpaid librarians tend to be uneasy about actually accepting a leaflet about the idea of organizing.

If workers on a picket line have to be restrained from bashing a strikebreaker in an access of indignation, this does not necessarily gainsay the fact that their thinking is "middle class" and "respectable" in some sense; but obviously they are less constrained by the norms of bourgeois respectability. Their militancy reflects not an immediate state of consciousness, but the fact that they are more alienated from bourgeois society than the questionnaires show. It reflects an objective class position that may sooner or later tend to mold their behavior in class-patterned situations more decisively than do their consciously held social views—especially in the context of organization and struggle. In turn, and in time, class-struggle action tends to remold consciousness; it reeducates.

Militancy, taken as a collective and not merely as an individual phenomenon, is in principle an index to the degree of alienation characteristic of a social group, corresponding to its life situation—its objective relationship to the productive process and to the resulting social hierarchy and pressures. This principle is not confined to class questions. Oppressed national or ethnic minorities tend to be more militant than their counterparts in the dominant society, likewise because they are more alienated from the "ruling ideas of the ruling class" which define the respectable limits of oppositional postures. In the case of the proletariat, the roots of this alienation lie in the capitalist mode of production.*

It is quite true that the peasantry and (say) the petty-bourgeoisie are entirely capable of explosions of violent rage when driven to desperation; in fact, it is precisely these classes that offer the best, or worst, cases of spasms of mindless destructiveness. Few episodes can rival the peasant Jacqueries or the ravages of a "petty-bourgeoisie in a frenzy" for brutal ferocity, with or without the instigation of cooler reactionary heads. This is the typical paroxysm of blind-alley desperation; it is a confession of impotence, not an assertion of strength. There is a great historical difference between bold militancy and going berserk. It was to the former that Engels referred when he contrasted the behavior of the still undeveloped working-class forces in the 1848 revolution with the petty-bourgeois. The workers, he asserted, distinguished themselves from the middle class "in showing upon every occasion, that revolutionary boldness and readiness for action, in which any party, headed by and composed principally of petty tradesmen, will always be deficient."[20]

5. *The proletariat is the only class that has the social weight and power to carry through the abolition of the old order and to build a new society.*

Contributing to this claim are the four characteristics of the proletariat already considered. But this point is primarily concerned with another factor, which also goes beyond the arithmetic of mere numbers. This is the strategic role of the indispensable services performed

---

* Alienation of labor under capitalism, in Marx's mature theory, will be touched on again in Volume 4. For present purposes it may be sufficient to point to the following line of thought in *Capital*:

> . . . all means for the development of production transform themselves into means of domination over, and exploitation of, the producers; they mutilate the laborer into a fragment of a man, degrade him to the level of an appendage of a machine, destroy every remnant of charm in his work and turn it into a hated toil; they estrange from him the intellectual potentialities of the labor process in the same proportion as science is incorporated in it as an independent power; they distort the conditions under which he works, subject him during the labor process to a despotism the more hateful for its meanness; they transform his life-time into working-time, and drag his wife and child beneath the wheels of the Juggernaut of capital.[19]

For the beginnings of this view, see *KMTR* 1, Chapter 7, section 8.

by the proletariat in keeping society going. "Of all the instruments of production, the greatest productive power is the revolutionary class itself," wrote Marx.[21] By the same token, this class is at the levers of economic power not by conscious decision but by its objective conditions of existence. The conscious decision concerns its willingness to put its hands on the levers; this is indisputably a question of great moment, but it arises because no other class has the choice.

A qualification to this claim is the situation of the technological-scientific employees of a sector of the economy, insofar as they are considered to be outside the working classes (untrue for most of them, from Marx's standpoint) or insofar as they are taken as a separate class by themselves (a view even harder to justify). In any case, the type of argument that can be made for this stratum and its potentiality only underlines the case for the working class as a whole. Experience shows that the whole of society quivers when the working class stirs; when a substantial sector of it undertakes a large-scale battle, the authorities react as to civil war; and this is true even on terrain far from revolution. It is true in spite of all the theses broadcast about the alleged fading away of the working class. So far the periodic announcements that the working class is obsolete, having been displaced by technology, automation, and so on, have not been reflected in the realities of social struggle.*

Behind all of the foregoing considerations is a generalized formulation which needs to be stated. It is perhaps most closely related to the third point. Marx's theory asserts that *only the proletariat, by the conditions of its existence, embodies a social program pointing to an alternative to capitalism.*

However desperate a peasantry or a petty-bourgeoisie may become, these classes cannot give society a lead in a new direction, not simply because of social-psychological constraints, but because there is no social solution that effectively corresponds to these classes' interests while at the same time corresponding to the interests of society in general, including the preservation of the social fabric in time of dissolution and crisis. In contrast, the working class, as the bottom layer of the class system, cannot stir without objectively pointing to a program, even when it consciously rejects it: namely, the assumption of

---

* For further discussion of this point, see Special Note A, "On the Abolition of the Proletariat by Automation."

social responsibility by a democratically organized people, regardless of private interest—a program which, concretized, means the abolition of capitalism.

In his "Letter to the Labour Parliament" meeting in Manchester in 1854, Marx summarized in a sentence why "the working classes of Great Britain, before all others, are competent and called for to act as leaders" in the movement to emancipate labor. "Such they are from the conscious clearness of their position, the vast superiority of their numbers, the disastrous struggles of their past, and the moral strength of their present." [22]

By the same token, these and other characteristics are preconditions for the role of class leadership; as long as they are not present, the class is not fit to rule, as we shall see in the next chapter. In this light, it is not a question of how the proletariat can be deceived, betrayed, seduced, bought, brainwashed, or manipulated by the ruling powers of society, like every other class. The basic point is that it is the proletariat that it is crucial to deceive, seduce, and so on.

In the same light, it is not a question of guarantees of victory, assurances of optimism, and other irrelevancies. Marx points: *here,* not there, is the arena of decision, the direction of hope.

3 | ANATOMY OF THE PROLETARIAT

The question just discussed, the ground for Marx's orientation toward the proletariat, has a negative counterpart. There were popular views about the proletariat that Marx rejected, including certain grounds for pro–working-class sympathies.

To begin with, Marx had to reject the pervasive philanthropism of the early socialists, who, as the *Communist Manifesto* eventually explained, "are conscious of caring chiefly for the interests of the working class, as being the most suffering class. Only from the point of view of being the most suffering class does the proletariat exist for them." This was not primarily a sociological observation; in the case of the early socialists the proletariat "offers to them the spectacle of a class without any historical initiative or any independent political movement."[1] Pity and do-goodism, excellent attributes for charitably inclined ladies and gentlemen, stand in antithesis to the perspective of revolution: the desire to do good for the people is counterposed against the need for the people to do it themselves.

1. THE REJECTION OF ILLUSIONS

Equally important was the fact that the revolutionaries' historical analysis relieved them of the natural impulse to harbor comforting illusions about the individuals or strata making up the chosen class, as if the latter was truly a chosen people.

During Marx's youth, the propagandistic elocution about The People that emanated from the bourgeois revolutionary tradition of '89 and '93 had been transmogrified in the early socialist movement into

49

philanthropic-humanitarian rhetoric about the suffering proletariat. It can be read in great quantity, in perhaps its most attractive guise, in English Chartist literature; it can be seen in its most repulsive form in Eugène Sue's "socialistic" romances like *The Mysteries of Paris*. Idealization of "proletarians" (really artisanal workers for the most part) in the French communist clubs was reflected in the roseate glow of Marx's first reaction to meeting circles of genuine workers in Paris.[2] It was the development of his historical and theoretical analysis that freed him to be as tough-minded as necessary about the ignorance, backwardness, or venality of sections of the working class as it is, along with seeing their capacity for militancy, sacrifice, heroism, and other laudable qualities. This analysis, with the help of educational experience, also gave him another context: the capacity of the bourgeoisie and its intelligentsia to be outdone by no one in ignorance, backwardness, and venality, with less excuse.

In fact, in another year Marx had disposed of this traditional approach. In *The Holy Family* he answered Bruno Bauer's diatribes against the masses in this way: "When socialist writers ascribe this [revolutionary] world-historic role to the proletariat, it is not at all, as Critical Criticism [Bauer] pretends to believe, because they regard the proletariat as *gods*. Rather the contrary."[3] The contrary was a great deal of overemphasis on the "dehumanization" of the proletariat, serving to underline the factors of objective necessity. The proletariat "cannot emancipate itself without abolishing the conditions of its own life. It cannot abolish the conditions of its own life without abolishing *all* the inhuman conditions of life of society today which are summed up in its own situation."[4]

The mythology that makes White Knights out of horny-handed workers or Galahads out of certified proletarians was later elaborated by radical literati out slumming; but it has nothing to do with Marx. His correspondence, particularly with Engels, can yield a thick anthology of uninhibited damnations against workers and workers' groups, as well as against all other known classes, groups and creeds, for behaving like asses, sheep, knaves, traitors, clowns, reactionaries, and renegades—all of which proves his impartial cantankerousness.* During the American Civil War, Marx could offhandedly write Engels that "England has

---

* There seems to be a special problem about calling workers *asses*. For one marxological view, see Special Note H.

disgraced herself more than any other country, the workers by their christian slave nature, the bourgeois and aristocrats by their enthusiasm for slavery,"[5] and later rebound to enthusiasm for English workers' support to the North. In a letter to Marx, Engels commented on the education of the Chartist leftist Ernest Jones:

> . . . without our doctrine he . . . would never have found out how on the one hand the instinctive class hatred of the workers against the industrial bourgeoisie, the sole possible basis for the reorganization of the Chartist party, can not only be retained but even widened, developed and made to serve as the foundation of enlightening propaganda, and how on the other hand one can be progressive all the same and oppose the reactionary cravings of the workers and their prejudices.[6]

To call the proletariat a revolutionary class is a condensation: it means a class with the historical potential of making a revolution; it is a label for a social drive; it is not a description of current events. This revolutionary class begins, like everybody else, by being filled with "reactionary cravings" and prejudices: otherwise the proletarian revolution would always be around the corner. Marx's theory looks on the proletariat as an objective agency of social revolution in the process of becoming. In this respect his conception of the proletariat as the historically revolutionary class is similar to his reiterated view that the bourgeoisie was such a revolutionary class in a previous era, in spite of its well-known timidity and narrow-mindedness.

One of the illusions, therefore, that Marx combats is the illusion of the Instant Revolution. Put crudely it goes: *If the proletariat is by nature revolutionary, then why doesn't it go and make a revolution?* This unhistorical ultimatism crops up frequently in socialist history, but not as an outcome of Marx's theory; it typically reflects the impatience of bourgeois intellectuals who cannot afford to wait.

Such was the case with the ultraleftists in the Communist League after the failure of the revolution to sweep Europe in 1849. One of them wrote Marx in 1851: "Your warning that one should not harbor any illusions about the proletariat was really very well taken by me." Thereupon this fire-eater, who had been impatient for a good insurrection the year before, repudiated socialism in another year and wound up life as a minister of the kaiser.[7]

The proletariat is a part of bourgeois society; it is born and raised in the same slough. The problem of revolution begins there, it does not end. As Laura Marx once put it, in a letter to Engels: "The rottenness of our society breaks out, there is no denying it, as well among the workmen as the Wilsons [referring to a French deputy symbolizing corruption] and a revolution is badly needed to sweep the world clean."[8] Over a long life Engels observed the corruption of workers, including revolutionary workers, by bourgeois society under various pressures. Commenting on the rife corruption of the Social-Democracy's bourgeois intellectual parliamentarians in the 1880s, he thought back to a comparison with an old practical problem:

> The necessarily more or less bourgeois parliamentarians [of the Social-Democratic party] are an inevitable evil just like the case of workers who are blacklisted by the bourgeoisie, hence left jobless, and who are saddled on the party as professional propagandists. The latter case was already rife in 1839–1848 among the Chartists and I was able to observe it at that time. Give them a per-diem allowance and they will go over to the dominant bourgeois and petty-bourgeois or "educated" deputies. But all that will be overcome. My confidence in our proletariat is just as unqualified as my mistrust of the wholly rotten German philistinedom is unbounded.[9]

How will it be overcome?

2. THE PROLETARIAT AS PROCESS: MATURATION

So far we have often referred to the proletariat as if it constituted a homogeneous whole. All such global statements are approximations at best. Most of the problems of proletarian revolution stem from the massive role of divisions, disproportions, and disparities within the working classes, among its different sectors, and among its individuals. The process of overcoming these diversities and discords is a key part of the road to proletarian revolution.

One can view this process as one of maturation. Maturation has several sides (physical, intellectual, emotional, and so on) even in the simple case of an individual; so also in the case of a class, which is a more complex phenomenon. To mention a few prominent aspects:

1. There is the process of maturation of the objective conditions

under which the proletariat develops, that is, the maturation of the economic system itself.

2. This is closely connected with a process of homogenization in the conditions of existence of different sectors of the working class (though this process is never complete). There are innumerable subdivisions of this problem, from the effect of labor aristocracies to the radicalizing (or alienating) effect of different occupations; we will have occasion to mention some in the course of illustrations.

3. In explaining Marx's theory of the state and social evolution, there is inevitable emphasis on the "ruling ideas of the ruling class," the decisive effect of bourgeois domination on social outlooks. The working class, of course, is as subject to this effect as the rest of society; in fact, it is the chief target. The process of maturation is, in these terms, the process in which the working class frees itself from the impact of bourgeois power, propaganda, and socioeconomic pressures. But all other differences aside, that part of the working class which is always under the strongest pressure from the bourgeois world is its leadership. As the interface between the proletariat and its dominators, working-class leaders take the brunt of this pressure, and (like earth strata suffering from slippage) it is this layer that is most easily deformed by the resulting stresses and strains. The process of maturation demands an eye on the relation between the class and its leadership or representatives.

4. Finally, maturation is closely associated with the self-organization of the class; in fact, the latter can be viewed as the measuring rod of the former. Insofar as organization is the barometer of maturation, some of the problems of maturation will come up concretely below in Chapters 4 and 5 on trade-unionism.

We begin here with the first and basic aspect of the question. The maturation of the proletariat goes hand in hand, if not step by step, with the level of development of the capitalist economy itself. There cannot be a strong proletariat without widespread or intensive industrialization. Contrariwise, weak development of industry and commerce implies an underdeveloped proletariat. In addition, disparities will arise in the stage of social development of the working class within a country and between countries.

When the 1848 revolution broke out, Engels noted, both the bourgeoisie and the proletariat of Germany were more backward than the

French and English. ("Like master, like man.") The different stages of development induce different reactions to the revolutionary wave.

> °°The working-class movement itself never is independent, never is of an exclusively proletarian character until all the different factions of the middle class [that is, the bourgeoisie] and particularly its most progressive faction, the large manufacturers, have conquered political power . . .[10]

The big bourgeoisie, the "large manufacturers," are more progressive in the basic economic sense that, by developing industry on a large scale, they also develop the social conditions for the growth, organization, and education of a modern proletariat: that is, they produce their own gravediggers.

> Now, in Germany the mass of the working class were employed, not by those modern manufacturing lords of which Great Britain furnishes such splendid specimens, but by small tradesmen, whose entire manufacturing system is a mere relic of the Middle Ages. And as there is an enormous difference between the great cotton lord and the petty cobbler or master tailor, so there is a corresponding distance from the wide-awake factory operative of modern manufacturing Babylons to the bashful journeyman tailor or cabinet-maker of a small country town, who lives in circumstances and works after a plan very little different from those of the like sort of men some five hundred years ago.[11]

The lack of modern economic conditions (continues Engels) means "a pretty equally general absence of modern ideas." In the Germany of 1848 a large part of the working class actually raised the cry for a return to the medieval guild system. Only a "mere minority" were even capable as yet of thinking in terms of their emancipation as a class. But after all, it was only four years before, with the uprisings of the Silesian and Bohemian textile workers, that a working-class movement had come into existence in Germany at all![12]

Some thirty years later, by the 1880s, the picture in Germany was vastly different, and still changing. In letters Engels used to give the German party's editor, E. Bernstein, a sort of correspondence course in this question. In the immediate background was the problem of disparities within the working-class movement, in the first place of opportunistic currents in the party, and of the relationship between radicalization and impoverishment in the mass. In one such letter Engels began by expressing his joy that "The center of gravity of the movement has shifted from the semirural districts of Saxony into the *big industrial cities*":

The mass of our people in Saxony consists of hand-weavers, who are doomed to extinction by the steam loom, and only drag out an existence on starvation wages through side jobs (gardening, toy carving, etc.). These people are in an economically reactionary situation and represent a declining stage of production. Therefore they are, to say the least, not the natural-born representatives of revolutionary socialism to the same extent as the workers in large-scale industry. They are not on that account reactionary by nature (as, for instance, the remnants of the hand-weavers here [in England] finally became—the hard core of the "Conservative Working Men"), but they are unreliable in the long run. Especially also because of their terribly miserable condition, which makes them far less capable of resistance than the urban workers, and because of their dispersion, which makes it easier to enslave them than the people of the big towns. In view of the facts given in the *Sozialdemokrat,* the heroism with which these poor devils have still held out in such numbers is indeed to be admired.

But misery and militancy do not add up to the historic mission of the proletariat:

But they are not the right kind of nucleus for a great national movement. Under certain circumstances—as from 1865 to 1870—their misery makes them more immediately responsive to socialist views than the big-city people. But the same misery also makes them unreliable. A drowning man grasps at every straw, and cannot wait for the rescuing boat to cast off from shore. The boat is the socialist revolution; the straw is the protective tariff and [Bismarckian] state-socialism. It is indicative that in our old districts it is almost only the Conservatives that have any chance against us. And if Kayser [opportunist Social-Democratic deputy] could perpetuate such an absurdity as the protective-tariff business, without the others daring to come right out against it, the trouble lies (as Bebel himself wrote me) nowhere else than among the voters, especially Kayser's!

Now everything is different. Berlin, Hamburg, Breslau, Leipzig, Dresden, Mainz, Offenbach, Barmen, Elberfeld, Solingen, Nuremberg, Frankfurt, Hanau, *plus* Chemnitz and the Erzgebirge districts—that provides an entirely different foothold. The class which is revolutionary because of its economic position has become the nucleus of the movement.[13]

The last sentence emphasizes that objective social situation is the basic factor conditioning the revolutionary maturation of the proletariat, though other elements may bring about conjunctural radicalization (misery, for example). The unstable radicalism of the old declining crafts was also one of the chief weaknesses of the First International in Britain, since the International's base lay more among these crafts than in heavy industry.[14]

Engels was often more interested in the political consequences of these patterns than in the theory of development; it should not be thought that the problem was simply abstract.

We cannot draw the mass of the nation over to us without this mass gradually developing itself. Frankfurt, Munich, Königsberg cannot suddenly become as pronouncedly proletarian as Saxony, Berlin, the mining-industry districts. The petty-bourgeois elements among the leaders will temporarily find in the masses, here and there, the background they lacked hitherto. What has hitherto been a reactionary current among individuals can now reproduce itself as a necessary element of development—locally—among the masses. This would make change in tactics necessary, in order to lead the masses farther along without thereupon leaving the bad leaders on top.[15]

All this emphasizes the objective side of the development. But the social-historic process is naturally accompanied by changes in consciousness (social psychology). Another way of looking at both aspects is suggested by the concept of bourgeoisification.

3. BOURGEOISIFICATION: MODERNIZING ASPECT

The term *bourgeoisification* may suggest the image of a virginally uncorrupted proletariat being debauched by a pathological process. The historical reality is not that simple-minded.

The proletariat comes into the world in an already bourgeoisified milieu; and outside this milieu the main alternatives are simply more reactionary prebourgeois conditions and ideas. But the proletariat does not arrive panoplied in full modernity any more than does the bourgeoisie; it evolves over a historical era from more backward conditions, trailing the old consciousness as well. As society itself is bourgeoisified, so too is the proletariat—that is, developed into the modern working class typical of bourgeois society. At this stage, bourgeoisification also means progress and maturation.

For a whole transitional era, complained Marx and Engels, German society—all classes, hence also the proletariat—remained under the sign of the pigtail, symbol of prebourgeois backwardness. As Engels explained: °°"A country cannot pass through 200 years like what 1648–1848 were for Germany without leaving a small impression of the philistine even on the working class. Our revolution of 48/49 was too short and too incomplete to wipe that out altogether."[16] As the proletariat, pushed forward by its social situation, emerges from this miasma, elements still bound to the past stand in the way, even inside the movement, says Engels:

> From the outset we have fought to the utmost against the petty-bourgeois philistine mentality within the party, because this mentality, developed since the Thirty Years War, has taken hold of *all* classes in Germany, and become a hereditary German evil, sister of servility, of the spirit of subservience and of all hereditary German vices. This is what has made us [Germans] ridiculous and contemptible abroad. It is the main cause of the flabbiness and weak character predominating among us. It reigns on the throne as often as in the cobbler's lodge. Only since a *modern* proletariat has been formed in Germany—only since then has a class developed there that is hardly at all affected by this hereditary German plague, and that has shown a free outlook, energy, humor, tenacity in struggle. And shouldn't we fight against every attempt to artificially inoculate this healthy class, the only healthy class in Germany, with the old hereditary poison of philistine narrowmindedness and philistine slackness?[17]

It happens that Engels' target here is the reformist leadership of the Social-Democratic Party itself, but he is not describing them as merely bearers of bourgeoisification; for the bourgeois intelligentsia, like the bourgeoisie, was also infected with "the hereditary German plague." Under German conditions, the debilitating consciousness they promoted derived also from earlier influences, as did the flabbiness of the German bourgeoisie itself in face of the Bismarckian state.

A distinction must be made therefore: a *modernized* proletariat develops along with the bourgeoisification of society, but whether this means a bourgeoisified proletariat (in the pejorative sense) is another matter; for this modern proletariat arrives in struggle with the bourgeoisie.

In another letter directed against the reformist leadership, Engels likewise counterposed the influence of modernizing forces on the proletariat against the narrow backwardness of social relations in the country:

> I never concealed the fact that in my opinion the masses in Germany are much better than the gentlemen [who are their] leaders . . . Germany is an atrocious country for people who have little will-power. The narrowness and pettiness of civil as well as political conditions, the small-town character of even the big cities, the small but constantly increasing pettifoggeries in the struggle with police and bureaucracy—all this enervates instead of spurring on to resistance; and so in this "big children's nursery" [as Heine put it] many become childish themselves. Petty conditions beget petty outlooks, so that it takes great understanding and energy for anyone living in Germany to see beyond the immediate, to keep one's eye on the large-scale interconnection of world events, and not to fall into that self-complacent "objectivity" which sees no further than its nose and precisely for that reason is the most narrowminded subjectivity even when it is shared by thousands of such subjects.
> . . . [This trend] must be fought resolutely. And here the mass of workers themselves furnish the best point of support. They alone live in Germany under approximately modern conditions; all their afflictions big and small are centered on oppression by *capital*, and whereas all other struggles in Germany, both social and political, are petty and trivial and revolve around trivialities which elsewhere have long been settled, their struggle is the only one with grandeur, the only one that is up to the mark of the times, the only one that does not enervate the fighters but supplies them with ever new energy.[18]

The same pattern could be seen in France, though it was more modernized than Germany. There the mass legacy from the prebourgeois past was the peasantry, and sectors of the proletariat were continuously being recruited from this source. A worker did not become a modern proletarian the day after he left the farm in the Franche-Comté and got a job in a Paris workshop. This could be seen on a big scale especially when Bonaparte's prefect for Paris, Haussmann, carried through an urban renewal project in Paris involving much building and boulevard construction, work that gave new employment to building-trades workers, thus buying them off as supporters of the Second Empire. This was the source of "the imperialistic [Bonapartist], Haussmannist building-trade proletariat stemming from the peasants, which Bonaparte created in the big towns," wrote Engels.[19] These new-minted proletarians were yesterday's peasants, therefore peasants still in consciousness, and a more easily manipulated base than an experienced working class.

England, the most modern society in Europe, was also notoriously encrusted with traditionalism in thought as well as customs. In any case the process of organizing the proletariat (reaching full maturation) was also a process of eliminating "traditional prejudices":

> This workers' party is only just being formed [in England]; its elements are still occupied with casting off traditional prejudices of every sort—bourgeois, old trade-unionist, and even doctrinaire-socialist—so that they may finally be able to get together on a basis common to all of them.[20]

There is still another complication, a countervailing factor arising from prebourgeois conditions. While big industry is still developing, therefore still dislocating the status quo, and bringing unaccustomed problems and evils, there is a special impetus given to struggle by the newly proletarianized masses.

> The class struggles here in England, too [wrote Engels to an American], were more turbulent during the *period of development* of large-scale industry and died down just in the period of England's undisputed industrial domination of the world. In Germany, too, the development of large-scale industry since 1850 coincides with the rise of the socialist movement, and it will be no different, probably, in America. It is the revolutionizing of all traditional relations by industry *as it develops* that also revolutionizes people's minds.[21]

It is the flux, the climate, of instability—the feeling that if so much can change, anything else can—that provides this factor.

> Our great advantage is that with us [in Germany] the indus-
> trial revolution is only now in full swing, whereas in France and
> England it is settled in the main. . . . The great mass of the people
> grow up in the conditions in which they have later to live; they
> are accustomed to them; even the fluctuations and crises have
> become something they take almost for granted. Then there is the
> remembrance of the unsuccessful attempts of previous move-
> ments. With us, on the other hand, everything is still in full
> flow.[22]

This thought appeared in another letter to Germany, but in a wider
context:

> In England and France the transition to large-scale industry is
> thus pretty much completed. The conditions under which the
> proletariat exists have already become stable . . . for a new revolt
> against capitalist production a new and more powerful impulse is
> required, say, the dethronement of England from its present
> dominance in the world market, or a particular revolutionary
> situation in France.[23]

In this passage one gets a view of the three stages involved: the stage
of *transition* (to full bourgeoisification of society) which we have been
discussing in this section; the stage of relative *stability* of the system;
and the stage of *downturn*, which, for England, was to be marked
especially by its loss of hegemony in the world market.

4. BOURGEOISIFICATION: "SHARING THE FEAST"

It was in the middle stage of bourgeois society that a proletariat
could most easily be bourgeoisified. It is an expensive business: the
capitalist class must first be able to afford it. From a short-term view,
periods of prosperity are most conducive, since there is more to trickle
down.

The upswing of the Bonapartist regime was an example for Engels:

> With the temporary prosperity and the prospect for the *gloire de
> l'empire*, the [French] workers seem to be clean bourgeoisified

after all. It will take a harsh chastisement by crises if they are *soon* to become capable of anything again.[24]

The effects of the Second Empire's economic changes far outlasted the emperor:

°° The transformation of Paris into a Luxusstadt [luxury city] under the second empire could not help taking [effect] on the working class too. But any serious movement will shake off a good deal of that. The effect upon the intellect of the masses, I am afraid, will be more lasting.[25]

In England, during the doldrums of the 1850s, the liberal bourgeois "are making use of the prosperity or semi-prosperity to buy the proletariat," with an ex-socialist acting as broker.[26] We often find that such comments by Engels on the bourgeoisification of proletarian consciousness have to do with parliamentary politics: the workers follow the bourgeois parties. In the 1860s: "Everywhere the proletariat is the °tag, rag and bobtail° of the official parties," and it is the Tories rather than the Liberals who have gained from the increase in the urban workers' vote. This has its good side—

But it remains a desperate certificate of poverty for the English proletariat all the same. The *parson* has shown unexpected power, and so has cringing before °respectability.° Not a single working-class candidate had a ghost of a chance, but °mylord Tom Noddy° or any parvenu snob could have the workers' votes with pleasure[27]

Even in the 1890s, when this sad state of affairs was changing rapidly, Engels was as ready to express his impatience at the English workers "with their sense of fancied national superiority, with their essentially bourgeois ideas and views, with the narrowmindedness of their 'practical' outlook, with their leaders who are strongly infected with parliamentary corruption," though he immediately added: "But things are moving forward for all that."[28] For the old-line trade-unionists were now being overshadowed by the militant New Unionism; and when Engels rejoiced over "the defeat of the *bourgeois labor party,*" this term means the bourgeois-minded tendency in the trade-union movement, not a political party.[29]

In America, the relative absence of a feudal past is part of the reason why the pressure to think like a bourgeois is so strong:

... there are the special American conditions: the ease with which the surplus population is drained off to the farms, the necessarily rapid and rapidly growing prosperity of the country, which makes bourgeois conditions look like a *beau idéal* to them, and so forth.[30]

Especially with regard to England, there was a long-term factor that overshadowed the short-term pattern of boom and bust. This, as Engels emphasized many times over several decades, was England's economic monopoly position on the world market, the profits of which trickled down to its working class and muted its struggle. As early as 1856 Engels had noted this effect in the specific case of Ireland: "Ireland may be regarded as the first English colony ... and one can already notice here that the so-called liberty of English citizens is based on the oppression of the colonies."[31] As he and Marx were to reiterate later, the loss of Ireland could be decisive for precipitating the whole of English society into crisis.

Colonies were a special form of superexploitation, but economically England's industrial superiority levied an exploitive toll on the whole world. As England headed into a new upswing, Engels recognized this as a long-term factor of bourgeoisification:

... the English proletariat is actually becoming more and more bourgeois, so that this most bourgeois of all nations is apparently aiming ultimately at the possession of a bourgeois aristocracy and a bourgeois proletariat *alongside* the bourgeoisie. For a nation which exploits the whole world this is of course to a certain extent justifiable.[32]

In this letter to Marx, Engels was adding a certain heightened color to the formulation; but he was going to repeat the essential ideas both in articles and letters.[33] The absence of a "separate working-class political party" in England, he wrote in 1874, "is understandable in a country in which the working class has shared more than anywhere else in the advantages of the immense expansion of its large-scale industry. Nor could it have been otherwise in an England that ruled the world market ..."[34] He looked forward to America's encroachment on English-dominated trade:

°°The fact cannot be longer shirked that England's industrial monopoly is fast on the wane. ... But what is to become of the "hands" when England's immense export trade begins to shrink down every year instead of expanding? ...

It will do one great thing: it will break the last link which still binds the English working class to the English middle class. This link was their common working of a national monopoly. That monopoly once destroyed, the British working class will be compelled to take in hand its own interests, its own salvation, and to make an end of the wages system. Let us hope it will not wait until then.[35]

We see it was not a question of fatalistic resignation but of looking facts in the face (as he stressed in the same article). It was also a question of accounting for reality as well as facing it: in the midst of a report on the antics of the English socialist sects, he explained that "apart from the unexpected, a really general workers' movement will come into existence here [in England] only when the workers feel that England's world monopoly is broken. Participation in the domination of the world market was and is the economic basis of the political nullity of the English workers."[36]

And this reality shows up ideologically as bourgeoisification:

You ask me what the English workers think about colonial policy. Well, exactly the same as they think about politics in general: the same as the bourgeois think. There is no workers' party here, you see, there are only Conservatives and Liberal-Radicals, and the workers gaily share the feast of England's monopoly of the world market and the colonies.[37]

"Sharing the feast" is a key idea. Insofar as the proletariat does get a sufficient share of the feast, the class struggle will be muted, Marx expected. But it is not only a question of the class as a whole. We have already mentioned that the proletariat's interface with the bourgeoisie, its leadership, is inevitably under the greatest social pressure. On a somewhat less ideological level, it must also be stressed that it is much easier for the bourgeoisie to "share the feast" with a restricted sector of the working class than with the whole. This understandable strategy applies to several such sectors (especially the labor aristocracy, as we shall see) but it applies most forcibly to that thin section of the proletariat which is both indispensable and specially exposed: leaders.

It would be a mistake to see this solely in cash terms, a worse mistake to see the problem as simple bribery. Such cases, while frequent enough, are least interesting. Even where money is directly involved, its power can be exerted publicly or semipublicly. When Engels wrote that "The leaders [of the English movement] are almost all petty unreliable fellows . . . while the two big bourgeois parties stand there, purse in hand, on the lookout for someone they can buy,"[38] he was referring to the purchase of labor leaders by financing their candidacy for Parliament. If elsewhere he describes trade-union leaders as "venal" (*verkäuflich*),[39] the word is more social than moral: it means *ready to be bought off.*

But the more profound respect in which a labor leadership is bought off is not by money at all, but by social cooptation (which naturally may be accompanied by perquisites). Marx called the turn on two trade-union leaders who were still active in the General Council of the International when he observed (to Engels) that they "are both pos✔ sessed with a mania for compromise and a thirst for respectability."[40] When both openly embraced bourgeois respectability, after the to-do of the respectables over the Paris Commune, it was not because they were being paid in money. The trade-union candidates coopted by the Liberals, wrote Engels, are "so-called workers' representatives, that is, those people who are forgiven their being members of the working class because they themselves would like to drown their quality of being workers in the ocean of their liberalism . . ."[41]

Even where Engels refers broadly to the working class he often has the leadership more specifically in mind:

> The most repulsive thing here [in England] is the bourgeois "respectability" which has grown deep into the bones of the workers. The division of society into innumerable strata, each recognized without question, each with its own pride but also its inborn respect for its "betters" and "superiors," is so old and firmly established that the bourgeois still find it fairly easy to get their bait accepted. I am not at all sure, for instance, that John Burns is not secretly prouder of his popularity with Cardinal Manning, the Lord Mayor, and the bourgeoisie in general than of his popularity with his own class. . . . And even Tom Mann, whom I regard as the best of the lot, is fond of mentioning that he will be lunching with the Lord Mayor. If one compares this with the French, one realizes what a revolution is good for after all.[42]

This sort of thing does not happen because a John Burns is more corruptible than any other John, for it is only workers' leaders who get invited to lunch with lord mayors; they are in the exposed positions. As it happened, a few years later Burns broke with socialism and rose rapidly to become a Liberal nonentity, today footnoted in history only because of the past he repudiated; on the other hand, Tom Mann later got better acquainted with his lordship's jails than with his cuisine. As Engels had remarked in another connection,* "unfortunately it seems to be a law of the proletarian movement that everywhere a section of the workers' leaders necessarily goes bad . . ."[44]

In the last analysis, it is misleading to consider something called bourgeoisification as an independent phenomenon. It is a useful term especially for the more extreme manifestations of a bourgeois mentality and of cooptation to a bourgeois lifestyle, but at bottom the characteristics and pressures it denotes are mainly the negative side of the proletariat's maturation toward class-consciousness. In a bourgeois society, everything is more or less bourgeoisified.** *Debourgeoisification* is the negative way of saying revolutionization. Marx's comment on that subject in 1863 was pitched in terms that he also applied to revolution as the "locomotive of history":

> How soon the English workers will free themselves from their apparent bourgeois infection one must wait and see. . . . Only the small German petty-bourgeois . . . would imagine that in developments of such magnitude twenty years are more than a day—though later on days may come again in which twenty years are embodied.[46]

---

* The connection is worth mentioning. The *Bee-Hive*, the only labor paper of the time, 1869, was being taken over by thoroughly bourgeois elements. Some months later, Engels wrote:

> It is really lucky that the *Bee-Hive* now shows its bourgeois colors both impudently and stupidly. . . . This cringing before Gladstone, and the whole bourgeois-patronizing-philanthropic tone, must soon break the paper's neck and make a real workers' paper a necessity. It is very good that, just at the moment when the workers are rousing from their Liberal intoxication, their only paper is becoming more and more bourgeoisified.[43]

** Engels included; so he pointed out in 1857. Hailing the onset of economic crisis as a political ice-breaker, he informed Marx that

> I feel in mighty good spirits amidst this °general breakdown.° The bourgeois filth of the last seven years had stuck to me to some extent after all; now it is being washed away, and I am beginning to feel like a new person again. The crisis will do me good physically like a sea bath, I already see that.[45]

5. INTERNAL DIVISION

The splitting up of the working class into antagonistic fractions, and the overcoming of this split, are crucial to the process leading to proletarian revolution. A survey of differences inside the working class would show a very long list of important points of short-term and long-term conflict inside the class—about as much as beset the capitalist class.[47] All of them are rooted in, and some concern only, intra-class competition for livelihood. Marx stated this pattern very early, as the basis for a long-range view of proletarian development:

> Competition separates individuals from one another, not only the bourgeois but still more the workers, in spite of the fact that it brings them together. Hence it is a long time before these individuals can unite, apart from the fact that for the purpose of this union—if it is not to be merely local—the necessary means, the big industrial cities and cheap and quick communications, have first to be produced by large-scale industry. Hence every organized power standing over against these isolated individuals, who live in conditions daily reproducing this isolation, can only be overcome after long struggles. To demand the opposite would be tantamount to demanding that competition should not exist in this definite epoch of history, or that the individuals should banish from their minds conditions over which in their isolation they have no control.[48]

Many of these areas of competition are more important as trade-union problems than for present purposes; but the type of internal conflict which we take for illustration here is also one that traditionally has racking political effects. This is the antagonisms among different groups (taken by ethnic or national origin, color, creed, or other division) within the proletariat of a single country. This question has a long dark history; we will give a couple of brief illustrations.

1. *Irish workers in England.* Marx saw this problem as intimately linked to the need for Ireland's liberation from English rule, which, by draining Ireland economically, forced its surplus labor into the English market, and "thus forces down wages and lowers the moral and material condition of the English working class":

> And most important of all! Every industrial and commercial center in England now possesses a working class *divided* into two *hostile* camps, English proletarians and Irish proletarians. The

ordinary English worker hates the Irish worker as a competitor who lowers his standard of life. In relation to the Irish worker he feels himself a member of the *ruling* nation and so turns himself into a tool of the aristocrats and capitalists of his country *against Ireland,* thus strengthening their domination *over himself.*[49]

From these economic sources bloom the poison flowers of national hatreds. The English worker's attitude toward the Irish

> is much the same as that of the "poor whites" to the "niggers" in the former slave states of the U.S.A. The Irishman pays him back with interest in his own money. He sees in the English worker at once the accomplice and the stupid tool of the *English rule in Ireland.*

From these national hatreds, the bourgeoisie gains a comfortable position for exploiting both of them:

> This antagonism is artificially kept alive and intensified by the press, the pulpit, the comic papers, in short, by all the means at the disposal of the ruling classes. This *antagonism* is the *secret of the impotence of the English working class,* despite its organization. It is the secret by which the capitalist class maintains its power. And that class is fully aware of it.[50]

As a consequence of this analysis, one of the main fields of activity of the International in England, under Marx's leadership, was the struggle of the Irish workers, who were well represented in the General Council. There were successes; reporting an important demonstration, held in spite of a police ban, Engels related:

> This is the first time an Irish demonstration has been held in Hyde Park; it was very successful ... It is also the first time the English and Irish sections of our population have united in friendship. These two elements of the working class, whose en- · mity towards each other was so much in the interests of the Government and wealthy classes, are now offering one another the hand of friendship; this gratifying fact is due principally to the influence of the last General Council of the International, which has always directed all its efforts to unite the workers of both peoples on a basis of complete equality.[51]

The ethnic antagonism, rooted in economic competition, could be dissolved only by joint struggle, which was the road to maturation.

2. *Black workers in the United States.* Irish workers were the

"niggers" of England, as we have seen Marx mention above, but it was the American case that provided the biggest arena for this pattern of exploitation. It is in the U.S. melting pot that the widest variety of racial and national conflicts have been kept boiling; the effect was to split the proletariat and corrupt the socialist movement, which was also shot through with anti-Chinese racism as the importation of Chinese cheap labor undercut working conditions.

Our concern here is not with justice for the oppressed, but something else. Just as the liberation of Ireland was a necessity for *English* freedom from capitalist rule, so also Marx saw the special oppression of black labor in the United States as a life-and-death problem of the class struggle of the entire working class:

> In the United States of North America, every independent movement of the workers was paralyzed so long as slavery disfigured a part of the Republic. Labor with a white skin cannot emancipate itself where labor with a black skin is branded. But out of the death of slavery a new life at once arose. The first fruit of the Civil War was the eight hours' agitation . . .[52]

During the Civil War one of the bases for Marx's support to Northern victory was the thesis that the enslavement of blacks also meant the superexploitation of white workers. If slavery spread to new states, argued Marx in 1861, then—

> The slave system would infect the whole Union. In the Northern states, where Negro slavery is in practice unworkable, the white working class would gradually be forced down to the level of helotry. This would accord with the loudly proclaimed principle that only certain races are capable of freedom, and as the actual labor is the lot of the Negro in the South, so in the North it is the lot of the German and the Irishman, or their direct descendants.[53]

In the United States, the English-Irish antagonism became intertwined with native-immigrant and black-white antagonisms in one cluster of internecine hatreds that was the bulwark of the Democratic Party, to which Marx referred as "this conservative and °blackleg° element."[54] In the first place, Marx linked transatlantic tension between England and America with the latter's growing Irish population: "The English and American governments (or the classes they represent) play on these feelings in order to perpetuate the covert struggle be-

tween the United States and England." This tension also provides
England with a pretext for maintaining "a *big standing army*, which, if
need be, as has happened before, can be used against the English
workers after having done its military training in Ireland."[55] In the
United States, the Irish made their way up over the backs of the blacks.
When, in the 1862 elections after the Republicans had finally come out
for the abolition of slavery, the Democrats made gains in New York and
elsewhere, Marx pointed to some elements in the ethnic pattern:

> The *city* of New York, mightily torn apart by the Irish mob,
> actively involved in the slave trade up to recent times, the seat of
> the American money market, and full of owners of mortgages on
> Southern plantations, was from time immemorial decisively
> "Democratic," just as Liverpool is still pro-Tory today. . . .
> . . . The Irishman sees in the Negro a dangerous competitor.
> The sturdy farmers of Indiana and Ohio hate the Negro in second
> place after the slaveholder. To them he is a symbol of slavery and
> the debasement of the working class, and the Democratic press
> daily threatens them with an inundation of their territories by the
> "nigger."[56]

The Democratic Party, the bulwark of black oppression in this
period, flourished especially on the basis of pullulating ethnic antagonisms splitting the working class. The German and Irish workers whom
Marx had referred to in 1861 were succeeded by immigrant waves of
Italians, East Europeans, Chinese, and others, and the melting pot
became a steaming cauldron of ethnic hostilities as each stratum was
educated to trample on the lower in accordance with the American Way
of Life. Engels offered a summary view in 1892:

> Your great obstacle in America, it seems to me, lies in the
> exceptional position of the native workers. Up to 1848 one could
> only speak of the permanent working class as an exception: the
> small beginnings of it in the cities in the East always had still the
> hope of becoming farmers or bourgeois. Now a working class has
> developed and has also to a great extent organized itself on
> trade-union lines. But it still takes up an aristocratic attitude and
> wherever possible leaves the ordinary badly paid occupations to
> the immigrants, of whom only a small section enter the aristo-
> cratic trades. But these immigrants are divided into different
> nationalities and understand neither one another nor, for the
> most part, the language of the country. And your [U.S.] bour-

geoisie knows much better even than the Austrian government how to play off one nationality against the other: Jews, Italians, Bohemians, etc., against Germans and Irish, and each one against the other, so that differences in the standard of life of different workers exist, I believe, in New York to an extent unheard-of elsewhere. And added to this is the total indifference of a society which has grown up on a purely capitalist basis, without any comfortable feudal background, towards the human beings who succumb in the competitive struggle: "there will be plenty more, and more than we want, of these damned Dutchmen, Irishmen, Italians, Jews and Hungarians"; and, to cap it all, John Chinaman stands in the background who far surpasses them all in his ability to live on next to nothing.

In such a country, continually renewed waves of advance, followed by equally certain setbacks, are inevitable. [57]

A year later Engels made the same point in the course of explaining to a correspondent why the American movement was still so backward. Besides the two-party system and the influence of economic prosperity:

Then, and more especially, immigration, which divides the workers into two groups: the native-born and the foreigners, and the latter in turn into (1) the Irish, (2) the Germans, (3) the many small groups, each of which understands only itself: Czechs, Poles, Italians, Scandinavians, etc. And then the Negroes. To form a single party out of these requires quite unusually powerful incentives. Often there is a sudden violent élan, but the bourgeoisie need only wait passively, and the dissimilar elements of the working class fall apart again. [58]

There is an especially big gap in this area between the relative simplicity of theory and the difficulties of practice. Marx's theory points to vitally important problems and choices for a proletarian movement, but the theoretical role of ethnic antagonisms is the least mystery of all.

6. A CLASS FOR ALL CLASSES

We saw that in the course of the young Marx's development, the adoption of an orientation toward the proletariat as the revolutionary class first had to solve the problem posed by Hegel's position, which counterposed classes with particular (selfish) interests against a universal class which stood for the general interests of society against all particularism. Marx not only rejected the notion that the state bureaucracy was such a universal class, but also the idea that any class embodied society's universal interest in some eternal way. The universal class, in a given historical context, was one whose own interests were such as to coincide with the transformation needed by society as a whole. In this sense, he nominated the proletariat as the universal class of the coming era, hence the class agent of revolution.[59]

Although the formulation later became less Hegelian, the basic idea did not change for Marx in subsequent writings, and reappeared in virtually every stage of his theoretical formation. In the period leading up to the *Communist Manifesto* it is restated several times. In the Paris manuscripts, the aim is the emancipation of the workers, "not that *their* emancipation alone is at stake, but because the emancipation of the workers contains universal human emancipation—and it contains this, because the whole of human servitude is involved in the relation of the worker to production . . ."[60] Likewise in *The Holy Family* and *The German Ideology:*

> When the proletariat is victorious, by no means does it thereby become the absolute side of society, for it is victorious only by abolishing [transcending] itself and its opposite.[61]
>
> If [self-] interest properly understood is the principle of all morality, then the point is for men's private interest to coincide with the interest of humanity.[62]
>
> [Class divisions] cannot be abolished until a class has formed which no longer has any particular class interest to assert against the ruling class.[63]
>
> [A revolutionary class must] present its interest as the communal interest of all members of society . . . it must give its ideas the form of universality . . . [It] comes forward from the outset . . . not as a class but as the representative of the whole society, it makes its appearance as the whole mass of society confronting the one ruling class.[64]

The *Communist Manifesto* put it that, in conquering political power, the proletariat must raise itself to the position of "the national class" (changed in the Moore-Engels English version to "the leading class of the nation" to avoid misunderstanding); it "must constitute itself as the nation," thus "it is itself still national, though not in the sense of the bourgeoisie."[65] Two years later: the proletariat is "a class in which the revolutionary interests of society are concentrated."[66] Formulations of this idea keep cropping up,[67] and merge into the well-known conception about the eventual abolition of all class distinctions in the new society ushered in by proletarian victory.

In all this Marx and Engels were emphasizing that they did not become partisans of the proletarian revolution because they had become partisans of the proletariat as a particular class, or of the class interests narrowly peculiar to it. This is a distinction which has to be understood with some precision. It will help to counterpose Marx's approach to two others which he rejected.

1. Marx rejected the kind of pro-worker sympathy which limits its horizon to the narrow, class-bound, corporative interests of the proletariat as it exists today under capitalism. The latter approach may lead to pure-and-simple trade-unionism or bread-and-butter reform, on the one hand, or on the other, to the kind of "professional proletarianism" (*ouvriérisme*) which became prominent in the syndicalist movement, counterposing proletarian interests to universal social concerns.[68]

2. Equally alien to Marx is the apparently opposite approach, which sees only the ideal goal of universal human emancipation, divorced from the actual class struggle, and held by high-minded Men of Good Will untainted by class considerations.

In short, Marx's theory aims to integrate proletarian class interests and universal social interests. This integration is possible only for the revolutionary class of the era. It is necessary in order to broaden the social base of proletarian revolution.

7. REVOLUTIONIZING
THE REVOLUTIONARY CLASS

There is a final problem Marx had to solve, the solution to which is the capstone of his theory of revolution.

The young Marx began, like all other socialists of the time, with the proletarian seen as victim. Emphasizing, and at first exaggerating, the proletariat's total estrangement from the rest of society, he rang changes on its "dehumanization" as part of a Hegelian pattern whereby only complete dehumanization can negate itself into complete realization of humanity, and so forth.[69] This was suitable for philosophic theses, but the Hegelian dialectic had no solution for the political difficulty this talk creates. It makes a workable argument for intellectuals denouncing the system for brutifying the people, but—can one expect these poor brutes to make a revolution, let alone build a new society?

Even if the exaggerated language is dropped, it is still true, not only of the proletariat but of the upper classes and scornful intellectuals, that all strata of the population under a stultifying system are mentally crippled by the ruling ideas they absorb, are cramped by tradition and habit into patterns of acquiescence. *You expect these wretches to make a revolution?*

Marx's answer is: no. These people as they are cannot make a revolution or build a new world. They will have to be changed and transformed before they are fit to take power or wield it. But they will not be changed by preachments, books, leaders, or commands. They will become fit to rule only through their own struggle—a course of struggles against intolerable conditions, to change the conditions and thus change themselves.

On the one hand, then, it is important for Marx to point to the goal of proletarian revolution now, not waiting until a new and fit generation has arisen, since no such happy result will ever eventuate if the struggle is not begun *before* it has a possibility of being consummated. On the other hand, the same principle shows how a revolutionary can maintain an objective and cold-eyed view of the defects and inadequacies of the class, without illusions, since only such an attitude comprises the need for change. The principle is so basic that even before he was a socialist, Marx knew that if a child is told not to walk until it is able to walk, it will never be able to walk.[70]

As in so many other questions, the first suggestions of this view appear dimly in *The Holy Family* and then come out fullblown in *The German Ideology.* The former made tentative efforts to get out of the dilemma without quite hitting the point dead-center. Thus:

> To use an expression of Hegel's, it [the proletariat] is, in its abasement, the *revolt* against this very abasement, a revolt to which it is necessarily driven by the contradiction between its human *nature* and its life situation which is the open, decisive and comprehensive negation of that nature.[71]

It does a little better later, by noting the relation between self-change and organization against opposition.*

In *The German Ideology* the new principle is present in clear statements. We have already quoted one such passage in Chapter 1.[74] Then even more forcefully:

> Both for the production on a mass scale of this communist consciousness, and for the success of the cause itself, the alteration of men on a mass scale is necessary, an alteration which can only take place in a practical movement, a *revolution;* the revolution is necessary, therefore, not only because the *ruling* class cannot be overthrown in any other way, but also because the class *overthrowing* it can only in a revolution succeed in ridding itself of all the old crap and become fitted to found society anew.[75]

The point is made yet again, this time against a challenge by Max Stirner: "a society cannot be made new," said Stirner, "so long as those of whom it consists *and* who constitute it remain as of old." This is the old static dilemma. Marx replies that the communist proletarians do not remain as of old.

The tireless propaganda work carried on by these proletarians,

---

* This comes up almost accidentally as a retort to the Bauerites, who aver that a spiritual mode of being cannot be elevated without being changed, and to be changed it must be subjected to extreme opposition. Marx replies: if the Bauerites "were better acquainted with the movement of the lower classes," they would know "that the extreme opposition they have been subjected to from practical life is changing them every day." Literature by workers shows "that the lower classes know how to elevate themselves intellectually [*geistig*] " even without the help of the Bauerites. How? By organization, the "organization of the masses" of which the Bauerites talk abstractly but which is actually accomplished by bourgeois conditions themselves.[72] There is another passage which is really more to the point, though bogged down in the philosophic jargon typical of the book. The Bauerites proclaim the mass of people as the main enemy, and Marx replies:

> The enemies of progress *outside* the mass are precisely those *products* of *self-debasement, self-rejection* and *self-alienation* of the *mass* which have been endowed with independent being and a life of their *own*. The mass therefore aims against its *own* deficiency when it aims against the independently existing *products* of its *self-debasement,* just as man, turning against the existence of God, turns against his *own religiosity*. But as those *practical* self-alienations of the mass exist in the real world in an outward way, the mass must fight them in an *outward* way. It must by no means regard these products of its self-alienation as merely *ideal* phantasmagoria, mere *alienations of self-consciousness*, and must not wish to abolish *material* estrangement by a purely *inward spiritual* action.[73]

their daily discussions among themselves [in the communist clubs], sufficiently prove how little they themselves want to remain "as of old" and how little they in general want people to remain "as of old." ... they know too well that only under changed circumstances will they cease to be "as of old," and therefore they are determined to change these circumstances at the first opportunity. In revolutionary activity the changing of oneself coincides with the changing of circumstances.[76]

Marx then calls it "this great dictum": revolutionary activity changes you as you change conditions. Marx and Engels held it up as a measuring-rod in the first days after the outbreak of the revolution of 1848.

In Berlin the people who made the March 18 revolution were soon quieted by the king's promises. This, wrote Engels, is the clearest proof that revolutionary struggle was needed, to educate people so easily duped. "Not only the state, its *citizens* too had to be revolutionized. Their submissiveness could only be shed in a sanguinary liberation struggle."[77] The revolution gave the people new liberties and arms, but—

> That, however, is not yet the main result. The people that fought and won on the barricades is an altogether different people from the one that assembled before the castle on March 18 to be enlightened about the meaning of the concessions obtained, by the attacks of the dragoons. It is capable of altogether different things, it has an altogether different stance with relation to the government. The most important conquest of the revolution is *the revolution itself*.[78]

Engels shortly found that the Berliners had not changed so drastically so quickly. The principle was still the measuring rod of the limitations of the March revolution: "Its greatest shortcoming is that it has not revolutionized the *Berliners*."[79]

This, it turned out, was the epitaph of the revolution in Germany. Summing up the events in France, in 1850, Marx buried illusions with the statement that the workers were still incapable of accomplishing their tasks; conditions would become ripe only when the proletariat was pushed to the van in England, which dominated the world market:

> The revolution, which finds here not its end but its organizational beginning, is no short-winded revolution. The present generation

is like the Jews whom Moses led through the wilderness. It has not only a new world to conquer, it must go under in order to make room for the men who are equal to coping with a new world.[80]

Praising an economic study by a working tailor, Marx made the point: "Before the proletariat wins its victory on the barricades and battle lines, it announces the coming of its rule by a series of intellectual victories."[81] Among the conquests on the road to revolution is the development of working-class intellectuals (to use a later phrase). Later that year Engels echoed the view at a Chartist banquet where the continental émigrés were urged to unite:

> Engels, in replying to this speech [writes Schoyen], made plain his and Marx's view that revolution would come only as the "result of a long struggle, consummated by a new generation of men"—a belief which smacked of apostasy to the majority of the emigration, still desperately dreaming of imminent action.[82]

Two decades later, Engels had a similar point to make about the still-backward Spanish working class, leading, however, to an affirmative perspective in politics. The new republican government in Madrid called for elections to a Constituent: "what position was the International to take?"

> Spain is so backward a country industrially that *immediate* complete emancipation of the working class is still entirely out of the question. Before it gets that far, Spain must pass through various preliminary stages of development and clear away quite a number of obstacles. The republic offered an opportunity to compress the course of these preliminary stages into the shortest possible period of time, and to rapidly eliminate these obstacles. But this opportunity could be made use of only through the active *political* intervention of the Spanish working class. The mass of workers felt this; everywhere they pressed for participation in the event, insisting that the opportunity be utilized to take action, instead of leaving the field free to the action and intrigues of the possessing classes, as heretofore.[83]

The maturation of the proletariat was not a detached process, like the training of plants in a greenhouse before being exposed to the rigors of weather. This maturation took place only by getting into struggle; it was hastened by political storms. But it could not be simply skipped.

The anarchist policy of abstention from politics (immediate revolution or nothing) assured disaster. One of the schools of revolution was class politics independent of the ruling classes and parties.

8. TO BECOME FIT TO RULE

The "great dictum"—that revolutionary struggle changes the revolutionary—was Marx's solution to the old static dilemma. In 1848–1849 the revolution had proved that the working class was not yet ready to cope; but it had also shown the difference between revolutionary and prerevolutionary days. Struggle was the school in which the education took place; revolution speeded up the curriculum and enriched the course.

> ... in this vortex of movement [in the revolution], in this torment of historical unrest, in this dramatic ebb and flow of revolutionary passions, hopes, and disappointments, the different classes of French society had to count their epochs of development in weeks where they had previously counted them in half centuries. A considerable part of the peasants and of the provinces was revolutionized.[84]

The peasants were revolutionized as disillusionments overwhelmed them "with revolutionary speed." At this point Marx adds another great dictum, italicized: *"Revolutions are the locomotives of history."*[85]

From this standpoint the failed revolution was not simply a negative fact. Defeats—"the disastrous struggles of their past"[86]—were a precondition for class leadership. The revolution of 1848 was a landmark in the process of self-changing and self-education that was equivalent to the production of a proletariat fit to rule.

But only socialists with such a theory of revolution could look on it that way. Most óf the Forty-eighters faded away as the ground cooled, with more or less bluster. More rather than less bluster characterized the group in the Communist League which broke with Marx at this time on the ground that one either made a revolution right away or went to sleep. Either way there was no question of a long-term perspective in which a class was fitted to cope.

Well before this split, Marx had stated more than once that the time dimension of the revolutionary development had to be a lengthy one. Even in his "Address to the Communist League of March 1850," written while he still thought that the international revolutionary situation was continuing, he had warned that "the German workers are not able to attain power and achieve their class interests without completely going through a lengthy revolutionary development," in the course of which they had the task of "clarifying their minds as to what their class interests are."[87] We have also seen what he had written in his series of articles *The Class Struggles in France*. But a minority group in the Central Committee of the league led by Schapper and Willich (supported by a majority of the London membership) had absorbed little of Marx's conception of revolution. For them, power boiled down to an act of will. There was nothing unexpected about this, since this was the traditional mind-set of the old Jacobin-style revolutionism (sometimes called Blanquism after its best-known representative). It was the pre-Marx revolutionism of the European movement. These revolutionaries had no need for a lengthy period of self-change in the movement since they did not really expect the class as such to move at all: the rule of the revolutionary band would be imposed by a *coup de main*, and a period of educational dictatorship would follow.

This trend was brought out virulently by the stresses of émigré disappointments after a failed revolution; the concluding debate took place at a meeting of the league's Central Committee on September 15, 1850. In a speech Marx formulated the issue around the "great dictum":

> In place of the critical outlook the Minority substitutes a dogmatic one; in place of the materialist, an idealist one. Instead of the actual conditions, *pure will* becomes the drive-wheel of the revolution for them. Whereas we tell the workers: "You have fifteen, twenty, fifty years of civil wars and peoples' struggles to go through, not only to change the conditions but in order to change yourselves and make yourselves fit for political rule," you say on the contrary: "We must come to power right away, or else we might as well go to sleep."*

---

* This is how Marx quoted himself "verbatim" in an account written in 1852.[88] He was presumably correcting the corresponding passage in the minutes of the meeting, or quoting from his own notes. The minutes give the passage in slightly different form:

Instead of the materialist outlook of the Manifesto, the idealist outlook

On the practical side, this principle on how the proletariat becomes "fit for political rule" also makes the revolutionary fit for waiting out and working through periods of nonrevolutionary struggles. Marx had to refer to it again in writing on two subsequent defeats of the French working class, each of which ushered in a difficult period for the socialists. In his study of Bonaparte's accession to power, reviewing the 1848 period Marx dwelt on the gap between the limited bourgeois-democratic aims of the February revolution and the advanced social stamp which the fighting ability of the proletariat had put on it.

> There was thus indicated the general content of the modern revolution, a content which was in most singular contradiction to everything that, with the material available, with the degree of education attained by the masses, under the given circumstances and relations, could be immediately realized in practice.[90]

A week after Bonaparte's coup d'état, Engels had written Marx with his thoughts on why the proletariat had not intervened to fight (a subject on which he later wrote an extensive article). He was very sure that the working class would not be ready for "a new revolution until it gathers new strength by spending a few years of wretchedness under the rule of maximum order."

> ... it cannot be denied in the least that when the revolutionary party [tendency, not organization] in a revolutionary development allows affairs to take decisive turns without any say of its own or, if it does interfere, without emerging victorious, one may be fairly certain that for some time it is to be considered as done for.[91]

The new revolution did come eventually, and new strata were indeed revolutionized; but in 1871 Marx had to write with the "great dictum" in mind as before:

> °°The working class did not expect miracles from the Commune. ... They know that in order to work out their own emancipation, and along with it that higher form to which pres-

---

was emphasized. Instead of the actual conditions the *will* was emphasized as the main thing in the revolution. Whereas we tell the workers, "You have fifteen, twenty, fifty years of civil war to go through in order to change the conditions, to make yourselves fit for ruling," this is what is said instead: "We must come to power *right away*, or else we may as well go to sleep."[89]

ent society is irresistibly tending by its own economical agencies, they will have to pass through long struggles, through a series of historic processes, transforming circumstances and men.[92]

The mere overthrow of an oppressive rulership by its (untransformed) victims does not necessarily "transform circumstances" at all. On the contrary, a common historical pattern has been that of the "servant become master," who may be even more obnoxious than a more traditional ruler—as Marx noted in another connection.[93] Others before Marx had called it "the slave on the throne."

On the theoretical side, the "great dictum" emphasized that not only the proletarian revolution but the proletariat itself is a historic process. This begins as a process of maturation, first of all in terms of the social system. It ends as an educational and transforming process. Marx's theory is about the proletariat as a revolutionary class *in posse;* revolution makes it a revolutionary class *in esse.*

4 | TRADE UNIONS AND CLASS

A key to the nature of Marx's conception of proletarian socialism is a seldom noted fact: Marx was the first leading figure in the history of socialism to adopt a position of support to trade unions and trade-unionism, on principle.

This position was not difficult to take in later decades, after the trade-union movement had entrenched itself; its success was not hard to recognize by that time. What Marx recognized in advance was the basic relationship of trade unions as an institution to the proletariat as a class and to the social revolution as a goal.

1. THE LITMUS-TEST

Before Marx, there were some individual socialists, at least in England, who took a positive and favorable view of these new-fangled workers' "combinations," and they too have received insufficient attention.* In fact, their point of view now has to be exhumed from history, precisely because they did not make a lasting impress on the ongoing movement—unfortunately.

But of the recognized socialistic tendencies proliferating in the 1840s as well as in the preceding quarter of a century, all were hostile to the beginnings of trade unions to one degree or another, and from

* Above all, William Thompson, who is now noticed in histories of socialism almost only because of his first work, *Inquiry into the Principles of the Distribution of Wealth;* but his subsequent *Labor Rewarded* gave a pioneer analysis of a socialist basis for supporting trade unions.[1] Another outstanding individual exception was James Morrison, editor of the trade-union paper *The Pioneer;* but typically Morrison's socialism was of a mild sort, as his paper shows.

varying standpoints. The extreme form of one line was represented by P. J. Proudhon, the "father of anarchism": he not only condemned trade unions and strikes on principle but vigorously approved gendarmes' shooting down strikers as enemies of society, that is, enemies of small property.*

Quite different but also hostile was the standpoint of Chartist left-wingers like Ernest Jones, who rejected trade-unionism as a "fallacy," not only useless but positively an evil, since it distracted workers from really revolutionary struggle.[5] This was an authentic expression of that leftist type of sectarianism which would long remain a powerful trend even in movements that were nominally Marxist. Typically, Jones's attitude toward trade unions softened into support as he himself became more and more favorable to reform politics. In general, the future division between reformist rightism and sectarian leftism—both equally alien to Marx's approach—was most clearly prefigured on the issue of the socialist attitude to this class organization.

Marx had occasion to assert his claim to historical priority in a letter in 1869, in connection with his book against Proudhon: "in 1847, when all the political economists and all the Socialists concurred on one single point—the condemnation of *Trade-Unions,* I demonstrated their historical necessity."[6] Less than three decades later, so far forgotten was this earlier period that Engels had to explain to Bebel:

> . . . Marx's assertion is true of *all* socialists who made their appearance up to that time (with the exception of us two, who were unknown in France) insofar as they had occasion to deal with combinations—with *Robert Owen* leading the procession.*

* Marx quoted from and commented on this statement of Proudhon's in an essay on anarchist anti-politics.[2] Marx's first discussion of Proudhon's opposition to trade-unionism is in the last section of his *Poverty of Philosophy.*[3] In 1851 Engels jotted down notes analyzing another of Proudhon's works; here he clearly pinpointed Proudhon's basic support to small property and merchant profit (in spite of his fame for the aphorism "Property is theft"), and, in addition, showed how Proudhon's denunciation of trade-unionism related to his admiration for "the soul of the peasant" (Proudhon's expression). Engels ended this section of his notes as follows: "His criterion was that of small Parisian industry, instead of seeing the need for associations [unions] in the development of large-scale industry . . ."[4]

* This reference to Owen is accurate. But in *Anti-Dühring* (repeated in *Socialism Utopian and Scientific*) in the course of glowing praise for Owen, Engels

The same applies to the Owenists and among the French to Cabet. As there was no right of combination in France this question was little touched upon there. But since before Marx there existed only feudal, bourgeois, petty-bourgeois and utopian socialism, and socialism blended from various of these elements, it was clear that all of these socialists, each of whom claimed to possess a definite panacea and stood outside the real working-class movement, portrayed *every* form of the real movement, hence also combinations and strikes, as a false path which diverted the masses from the only way that leads to salvation, the way of the true faith.[9]

Why was Marx the first leading thinker to embrace trade-unionism, even in its first elementary forms, in his conception of the process leading to social revolution? The short answer is: because only Marx developed a socialist theory about the primary role of *class organization as such*. All other kinds of socialism looked to a much broader or much narrower constituency: in one case, all of The People, if not all of Humanity, or at least all of the people who were not "idlers"; in the other, an elite band of revolutionists, or a somewhat less elite party of the Enlightened. These other socialisms might seek or claim a special orientation toward the proletariat as a recruiting ground or other convenience,[10] but in no case was the class line in organization the basic road to their revolution.

This indeed is another way of explaining how Marxism defines itself as proletarian socialism, as the socialism of a class, and not a socialism derived from a predilection for or a vision of a future social order. It also explains why the trade-union question has been one of the most reliable litmus-tests of the real nature of a given socialist tendency, that is, of its view of the relationship between socialism and the proletariat.

---

mentions that "He was president of the first congress at which the Trade Unions of England united in a single great trade association."[7] This may mislead: Owen's semi-accidental and transitory connection with the early trade-union movement only ended by highlighting his basic hostility to it.[8] However, there were trade-union militants who considered themselves Owenites, that is, socialists; their spokesmen, such as James Morrison, had to break with Owen himself.

2. EARLY CONSIDERATIONS

Marx's ideas on trade-unionism, because of the nature of the subject, go through a steady course of development over the decades, not because of changes in underlying conceptions but because concrete experience was necessary to flesh out generalities. There are two kinds of experience involved here: Marx's own, and the developing reality of trade unions themselves.

There was no trade-union movement in the Rhineland for the young Marx to encounter. In the Paris to which he moved next, it was only a nascent phenomenon. Even in England, where Engels first found that trade unions were already a power, they had been flourishing for only two decades when the young German visitor was writing his book on *The Condition of the Working Class*. In the 1850s, especially in dispatches to the *New York Tribune*, Marx followed trade-union struggles and strike movements closely; in 1853 his articles were filled with strike news; but it was all necessarily observed from the outside. It was with the organization of the International that Marx began to work closely with a number of trade-unionists in England, and then, as unions were established in Germany and elsewhere, widened his experience. Finally, it was after his death that English trade-unionism took the heartening turn he had been anticipating, and so it was Engels alone who had the opportunity to learn from the "New Unionism," as well as to follow the movement on the Continent.

It was the young Engels who undoubtedly played the initiatory role in this field, as also in turning Marx's attention to political economy. Certainly, Engels' *Condition of the Working Class in England*, which he began writing toward the end of 1844, is already quite clear in its attitude toward "[t]hese different sections of workingmen, often united, often separated, Trade Unionists, Chartists, and [Owenite] Socialists."[11] When we today read his chapter on "Labor Movements," the first half of which is devoted to a sympathetic account of the then trade-union movement, its friendly tone is so familiar to us that it is hard to grasp how extraordinary it was for the socialism of the day. "Engels," wrote Ryazanov, "was the first who endeavored to give a theoretical exposition of the course of trade-union development among the workers,"[12] but, more than that, his book was the first important attempt to do this within the framework of a revolutionary socialist standpoint. It was the first influential product of socialist thought that rejected the two prevalent attitudes—the opinion that trade-unionism was useless or harmful to socialism, and the belief that it was all-sufficient for workers' interests, in short, sectarianism and reformism— in order to assume the *integration* of trade-unionism into the socialist perspective of revolution.

As we have seen,[13] Engels' theoretical outlook is here far from generalized as yet, but it is quite clear that what is important to him about trade unions is their character as the movement of a class. Shortly after publication of the book (and after moving to Brussels to live near Marx), Engels explained to readers that "I was chiefly concerned to describe the position of the bourgeoisie and the proletariat in relation to each other and the necessity of struggle between these two classes; and that I attached especial importance to proving how completely justified the proletariat was in waging this struggle . . ."[14]

Up to this point, Marx's writings had paid little or no attention to trade unions. In the Paris manuscripts of 1844 there is a passing reference at the beginning that merely echoes Adam Smith.[15] In *The Holy Family* a reference to English and French workers' associations is buried in philosophic fuzz.[16] In *The German Ideology*, the first work of close collaboration with Engels, a generally favorable attitude toward trade unions shines weakly through two passages of polemic against Stirner. The references are incidental, but suggestive. Stirner, the proto-anarchist, has announced that the workers need only cease work to win all power. (The illusion of the victorious General Strike with Folded Arms arose as one of the infantile notions of radicalism.) Marx and Engels reply that

> even a minority of workers who combine and go on strike very soon find themselves compelled to act in a revolutionary way—a fact he could have learned from the 1842 uprising [general strike] in England and from the earlier Welsh uprising of 1839, in which year the revolutionary excitement among the workers first found comprehensive expression in the "sacred month," which was proclaimed simultaneously with a general arming of the people.[17]

Engels' *Condition of the Working Class* had already expressed a similar sense of the limitations of trade-union action.

In *The German Ideology*, however, the positive side of trade-unionism gets emphasized in another sally against Stirner many pages away. Stirner sees the workers only in connection with his talk about "seizing employers by the throat" and similar fustian, while he thinks that workers who demand higher wages are treated as criminals. Marx and Engels point out that, unlike Stirner's universe (Prussia), in England, America, and Belgium workers who act for higher wages are by no means necessarily treated as criminals but "on the contrary quite often actually succeed in obtaining higher wages." They ridicule the tall talk about "seizing by the throat," as if this had any meaning short of revolution; the workers would gain nothing, "or at any rate much less than through associations and strikes." [18]

The first fruits of Marx's economic studies do not appear until his *Poverty of Philosophy* in 1847; the closing chapter is on "Strikes and Combinations of Workers." Here we get the first clear statement of his view of trade unions in the context of his theory on the relationship of socialism and class.

Workers' unions grow along with modern industry; the degree of unionization is index to a country's rank on the world market; thus England has "the biggest and best organized combinations." Not only partial and temporary combinations formed ad hoc for a strike: "Permanent combinations have been formed, °*trades unions*,° which serve as bulwarks for the workers in their struggles with the employers." This goes on simultaneously with the organization of a workers' political movement by the Chartists.

> The first attempts of workers to *associate* among themselves always takes place in the form of combinations.
> Large-scale industry concentrates in one place a crowd of people unknown to one another. Competition divides their interests. But the maintenance of wages, this common interest which they have against their boss, unites them in a common thought of resistance—*combination*. [19]

It acquires a "double aim," not only to stop competition among the workers, but to "carry on general competition with the capitalist."

> If the first aim of resistance was merely the maintenance of wages, combinations, at first isolated, constitute themselves into groups as the capitalists in their turn unite for the purpose of repression, and in face of always united capital, the maintenance of the association becomes more necessary to them than that of wages. This is so true that English economists are amazed to see the workers sacrifice a good part of their wages in favor of associations, which, in the eyes of these economists, are established solely in favor of wages. In this struggle—a veritable civil

war—all the elements necessary for a coming battle unite and develop. Once it has reached this point, association takes on a political character.[20]

Marx then summarizes the class meaning of this development:

Economic conditions had first transformed the mass of the people of the country into workers. The domination of capital has created for this mass a common situation, common interests. This mass is thus already a class as against capital, but not yet for itself. In the struggle, of which we have pointed out only a few phases, this mass becomes united, and constitutes itself as a class for itself. The interests it defends become class interests. But the struggle of class against class is a political struggle.[21]

We have already explained the Hegelese term "class for itself."[22] By organizing, in the course of struggle, an atomized class becomes a self-conscious class, and the interests of proletarian individuals are generalized into class interests. Why "the struggle of class against class is a political struggle" will be touched on in Chapter 5.

3. "THE REAL CLASS ORGANIZATION"

The same line of thought is summarized in the *Communist Manifesto*, more neatly but less vividly. Due to the growth of industry, the increase in the proletarian mass, and their increasing insecurity,

the collisions between individual workmen and individual bourgeois take more and more the character of collisions between two classes. Thereupon the workers begin to form combinations (Trades' Unions)* against the bourgeois; they club together in order to keep up the rate of wages; they found permanent associations in order to make provision beforehand for these occasional revolts.

Victories are only temporary. "The real fruit of their battle lies, not in the immediate result, but in the ever-expanding union [unification] of the workers." The development of communication technology serves also to centralize the local struggles that break out, "into one national

---

* The parenthetical explanation was inserted in the Moore-Engels translation of 1888.

struggle between classes." The authors then add: "But every class struggle is a political struggle."[23]

"This organization of the proletarians into a class, and consequently into a political party"[24] is for Marx the basic fact of the road to social revolution. Special emphasis must be placed on two words.

First, it is the *organization* of workers on a classwide scale that tends to politicize the struggle. The working class needs organization only in order to carry on its struggle; in order to submit it needs no organization at all. The special function of class organization is class struggle, present or potential, reality or threat. This is not gainsaid by the fact that the established powers try to persuade the class organization to think in terms of class collaboration. If trade unions "are not made to fight against the encroachments of capital what are they made for?" challenged Engels.[25]

Second, *class:* it is the role of trade unions in the beginnings of this process that makes them the class organizations of the proletariat par excellence. This view has always put Marx's theory at loggerheads with those socialists who considered themselves too revolutionary to bother with such unenlightened organizations as trade unions.

The point was sharpened in Germany, where a trade-union movement started developing only after a socialist group was already in existence and desirous of heading off a rival. This was the attitude of the Lassallean organization, headed by J. B. von Schweitzer. Marx condemned it as soon as it showed itself. Schweitzer realizes, wrote Marx, "that with the development of a *real* workers' organization in Germany based on trade unions, his artificial league of sectarians °would soon be nowhere.°" Engels agreed, in the same terms.[26]

The growth of the *real* class organizations did in fact undermine the league of sectarians, so much so that the Lassalleans were forced in a few years to accept unity with the pro–trade-union socialists led by Bebel and Liebknecht. When this unity took place at the Gotha congress in 1875, among the many defects of the proposed party program which Marx and Engels attacked was its remnant of a Lassallean attitude toward the trade unions. Engels stormed:

> . . . there is a not a word [in the program] about the organization of the working class as a class by means of the trade unions. And that is a very essential point, for this is the real class organization of the proletariat, in which it carries on its daily struggles with capital, in which it trains itself . . .[27]

Since the trade union is "the real class organization of the proletariat," Marx liked to show that bourgeois fears of trade-unionism
corresponded to this basic class character. He did this in some detail in
his reports on English strike movements for the *New York Tribune;* it is
also piquant to see how he did this with respect to a very early stage in
the story. A chapter in *Capital* on the history of anti-working-class
legislation ends with the episode of the Le Chapelier law of 1791,
passed by the French revolutionary Assembly to ban trade-unionism in
the name of Liberty, Equality, and Fraternity. This law "by means of
State compulsion, confined the struggle between capital and labor
within limits comfortable for capital . . ." Marx writes with indignation:

> "Granting," says Le Chapelier, the reporter of the Select Commit-
> tee on this law, "that wages ought to be a little higher than they
> are . . ." yet the workers must not be allowed to come to any
> understanding about their own interests, nor to act in common
> and thereby lessen their "absolute dependence, which is almost
> that of slavery"; because, forsooth, in doing this they injure
> "the freedom of their ci-devant masters, the present
> entrepreneurs" . . .[28]

This early bourgeois fear of trade unions was not simply a characteristic
of the Third Estate deputy Le Chapelier; Marx points also at Robespierre himself. In 1865, when there was talk in Prussia of abolishing the
anti-trade-union law, Marx commented:

> *En passant:* the Prussian anti-trade-union-law, like all the Conti-
> nental laws of the kind, stems from the decree of the *Assemblée*
> *Constituante of 14 June 1791* [the Le Chapelier law], in which
> the French bourgeois very severely punished °anything of the
> sort,° including workers' associations of every kind—for example,
> by loss of civil rights for a year—under the pretext that this was
> *restoration of the guilds* and in contradiction with constitutional
> liberty and the "Rights of Man." It is very characteristic of
> Robespierre that, at a time when it was a crime punished by the
> guillotine to be "Constitutional" in the sense of the Assemblée of
> 1789, he kept in force all of its laws *against* the workers.[29]

Yet in 1791 the number of modern wage-workers to be repressed was
small. The proletariat as a class was in the egg, and so was class
organization. But the class's built-in drive to organize was enough to
draw the lightning.

From 1791 through the nineteenth century, the fears of the bourgeoisie were an index to the class character of even far from class-conscious trade unions. In 1853 Marx informed his *Tribune* readers of the meaning of the strike wave by quoting the English bourgeois press: "The agitation at present," wrote the *Weekly Times*, "is limited to a series of independent skirmishes, but there are indications that the period is not very distant when this desultory warfare will be turned into a systematic and universal combination against capital." [30]

4. ENGELS LAYS THE BASIS

The workers' propensity for trade-union organization was something of an economic mystery, during most of the nineteenth century, for the bourgeois economists and also for most of the socialists. Both proved very handily, over and over, that the workers could never gain anything by strikes and trade-union struggles; therefore it all made no sense. The economists concluded that the workers should rely on sweet harmony with their employers; the socialists concluded that only their own favorite political sect had anything to offer. Despite these near-unanimous assurances, the working class of England—followed in time by the Continental workers—organized unions more and more solidly, and engaged in strike movements in waves, at considerable sacrifice.

Marx did not fully work out his economic theory on this subject until shortly before the publication of *Capital*; a key component was clarified only about 1865. Yet, as we have seen, Marx took a positive view of trade-unionism long before this, and Engels even before him. On what ground?

The answer appears most clearly from Engels' early work, which accepts the prevalent view that trade unions cannot improve workers' economic conditions for the class as a whole, because of "the economic law according to which wages are determined by the relation between supply and demand in the labor market. Hence the Unions remain powerless against all *great* forces which influence this relation." This echoes the position of the left Chartists and Owenites as well as of the bourgeois world. But Engels urges a significant qualification: unions do have power when dealing with "minor, single influences," presumably meaning capitalists who are out of line; and unless resisted, capitalists would "gradually reduce wages to a lower and lower point . . . and wages would soon reach the minimum." This tendency "is, *under average conditions*, somewhat restricted by the opposition of the workingmen."[31]

Still, Engels concedes here to the consensus of the authorities that unions are powerless to affect the overall forces and patterns of the labor market, and that time and again their struggles end in disastrous sacrifices.* He then asks the question that people like Ernest Jones failed to ask:

It will be asked, "Why, then, do the workers strike in such cases, when the uselessness of such measures is so evident?" Simply because they *must* protest against every reduction, even if dictated by necessity; because they feel bound to proclaim that they, as human beings, shall not be made to bow to social circumstances, but social conditions ought to yield to them as human beings; because silence on their part would be a recognition of these social conditions, an admission of the right of the bourgeoisie to exploit the workers in good times and let them starve in bad ones. Against this the workingmen must rebel so long as they have not lost all human feeling, and that they protest in this way and no other, comes of their being practical English people, who express themselves in *action*, and do not, like German theorists, go to sleep as soon as their protest is properly registered . . .[33]

So goes the humanistic motivation. Then there is a passing reference to economic motive which does not outlast the sentence, followed once more by subjective considerations of class-consciousness:

The active resistance of the English workingmen has its effect in holding the money-greed of the bourgeoisie within certain limits, and keeping alive the opposition of the workers to the social and

---

* But it is a measure of the brilliance of *The Condition of the Working Class* that its analysis of the trade-union question is substantially more balanced than that reached by Marx even at the end of 1847, when he was preparing a series of lectures on political economy published two years later as *Wage-Labor and Capital*. In unpublished notes for a lecture on wages and unions, Marx accepted without qualification the bourgeois economists' objections to the economic rationale of unions and strikes, proposing only socialist revolutionary motivations for supporting trade-unionism,[32] which will be cited in the next section. The difference was due to Engels' closeness, in England, to the real movement. In fact, by the 1850s, after Marx moved to England, and in the midst of a strike wave, Marx began reflecting considerations similar to those that Engels had anticipated in 1844–1845. So much for theory without practice.

political omnipotence of the bourgeoisie, while it compels the admission that something more is needed than Trades Unions and strikes to break the power of the ruling class. But what gives these Unions and the strikes arising from them their real importance is this, that they are the first attempt of the workers to abolish competition.[34]

Unions try first to abolish competition among workers, that is, one-sidedly; but competition is "the vital nerve of the present social order"; therefore workers are led "to abolish not only one kind of competition, but competition itself altogether, and that they will do."[35]

Finally, trade-union struggle is a training for the class war. "The incredible frequency of these strikes proves best of all to what extent the social war has broken out all over England." The strikes are skirmishes. "They are the military school of the workingmen in which they prepare themselves for the great struggle which cannot be avoided . . . And as schools of war, the Unions are unexcelled."[36]

The weak side of this explanation, once we are beyond the partial economic motivation suggested, is that it explains why socialists should support these trade-union struggles from their own standpoint (and this is uppermost for Engels, to be sure), but it does not really explain why the mass of non-socialist and non–class-conscious workers persist in their allegedly irrational course. But this problem, which could be answered only by a more sophisticated theory of capitalist economy, is not in the center of Engels' thinking. The strong side of his approach, and its important contribution, is that it clearly projects trade unions as the organizations of elementary resistance of the class, pointing from elementary resistance on to final class power.

5. THE ROLE OF TRADE-UNIONISM
IN MARX'S THEORY

Let us now summarize what the trade-union movement means in terms of Marx's mature theory. Much of the foregoing, of course, still holds.

1. *Elementary resistance.* The formulation by Engels in the preceding section is still the most compact, and should not be neglected

simply because it is rarely converted into a theoretical statement. Workers are human beings before they are proletarians. Some critics have called *Capital* a "jeremiad" against the bourgeoisie, in derogation of its scientific objectivity (confusing objectivity with nonpartisanship). The kernel of truth is that Marx did not conceal the fact that the socialist animus against capitalist society is not solely based on the cold truths of political economy, which demonstrate that the animus is historically meaningful. In fact, Marx cut loose along these lines even more in his reportage on England for the *New York Tribune* and the German socialist press.

The point can be illustrated from the negative side by contrasting the anti–trade-union viewpoint of Lassalle, who fossilized the economic derogation of trade-unionism into a dogma based on an "iron law of wages." Lassalle wrote: "The trade-union struggle of the worker is the futile struggle of the commodity Labor to act as a human being."[37] Presumably because it was futile, Lassalle condemned the struggle. But because it *was* a struggle for humanness, Marx and Engels sought to integrate it into the road to social revolution.

2. *Defense of immediate economic interests.* An important codicil to his original acceptance of the bourgeois economists' case against trade unions was suggested by Marx in 1853, as he explained the current strike wave in England: "Under certain circumstances, there is for the workman no other means of ascertaining whether he is or [is] not paid to the actual market value of his labor, but to strike or to threaten to do so."[38]

But it was not until the 1860s that Marx completed his theory of wages, and hence of the economic basis of trade-unionism. He first wrote it up when he had to debate an Owenite member of the General Council of the International who maintained the old thesis that trade unions were positively harmful.[39] Marx's presentation of the question* sought to establish that there *was* an area within which trade-union struggle could determine the economic conditions of the workers involved, that is, to overturn the dogma held by virtually all socialists

---

* It was published posthumously, in English as *Value, Price and Profit*, in German with the more suitable title of *Wages, Price and Profit*. —The evolution of Marx's theory of wages, as well as its relationship to the mythical theory of "increasing misery" that he is alleged to hold, is the subject of an extensive literature, which is outside our present purview.[40] I plan to take up the "increasing misery" myth in another volume.

who considered themselves revolutionists and many who did not.

It is true, Marx argued, that "the general tendency of capitalistic production is ... to push the *value of labor* more or less to its *minimum limit,*" but

> is this saying that the working class ought to renounce their resistance against the encroachments of capital, and abandon their attempts at making the best of the occasional chances for their temporary improvement? If they did, they would be degraded to one level mass of broken wretches past salvation. I think I have shown that their struggles for the standard of wages are incidents inseparable from the whole wages system, that in 99 cases out of 100 their efforts at raising wages are only efforts at maintaining the given value of labor, and that the necessity of debating their price with the capitalist is inherent in their condition of having to sell themselves as commodities. By cowardly giving way in their every-day conflict with capital, they would certainly disqualify themselves for the initiating of any larger movement.[41]

In notes for this lecture, he originally intended to summarize the positive side of trade-unionism in the following succinct sentences:

> °°Trades' Unions work well as far as they counteract, if even temporarily, the tendency to a fall in the general rate of wages, and as far as they tend to shorten and regulate the time of labour, in other words, the extent of the working day. They work well as far as they are the means of organising the working class as a class.[42]

Marx did not return to the trade-union question as such in what we have of *Capital,** but in 1881 Engels dealt with it in a series of popular articles for English workers. This presented a compact summary of why trade unions "are a necessity for the working classes in their struggle

---

* In the first volume, trade-unionism is glancingly mentioned as the means whereby the workers "try to organize a regular cooperation between employed and unemployed in order to destroy or weaken the ruinous effects" of the capitalist law that the pressure of the relative surplus-population regulates competition in the labor market.[43] This was plainly one of the many subjects that Marx postponed to the unwritten volumes. Of course, *Capital* has other material bearing on the theory of wages in general. —A basic passage on the economic role of trade-unionism is among the "isolated fragments" in Marx's manuscript "Results of the Immediate Process of Production," appended to Ben Fowkes's new translation of Volume 1 of *Capital* (Pelican Marx Library), pages 1069-70.

against capital," specifically, of the area within which trade-union struggle can be effective. To cite only some essential sentences:

> The average rate of wages is equal to the sum of necessaries sufficient to keep up the race of workmen in a certain country according to the standard of life habitual in that country. That standard of life may be very different for different classes of workmen. The great merit of Trades Unions, in their struggle to keep up the rate of wages and to reduce working hours, is that they tend to keep up and to raise the standard of life. . . .
>
> The law of wages, then, is not one which draws a hard and fast line. It is not inexorable with certain limits. There is at every time (great depression excepted) for every trade a certain latitude within which the rate of wages may be modified by the results of the struggle between the two contending parties. . . .
>
> The law of wages is not upset by the struggles of the Trades Unions. On the contrary, it is enforced by them.[44]

That is, as Engels goes on to say, the law of wages is "elastic," and the problem is to define its limits of elasticity.[45]

3. *Development of class consciousness and organization.* We have seen that this was the motivation with which Marx and Engels started, apart from the economic problems just discussed. For example, in the aforementioned 1847 notes for a lecture on wages, after accepting the economists' strictures on trade unions, Marx replies that all this is "correct only from their viewpoint." He counterposes a socialist viewpoint which amounts to this:

> But they [trade unions] are the means for the unification of the working class, the preparation for the overthrow of the whole old society together with its class antagonisms. And from this standpoint the workers rightly laugh at the clever bourgeois pedants who count up what these civil wars [strikes] cost them in dead and wounded and in financial sacrifices. He who would beat the opponent will not discuss the cost of the war with him.[46]

This should be read, not as the reply of the workers laughing at the bourgeois pedants, but as Marx's reply to virtually all other socialist circles of the time, most particularly those who thought of themselves as revolutionaries.

This fact comes close to the surface in what is perhaps Marx's most effective polemic along these lines. This is—again—from the year 1853, in the midst of the strike wave and after Marx had been in England long enough to grasp the full meaning of a modern trade-union movement. It occurs in a *Tribune* article much of which is given over to long excerpts from Ernest Jones's speech at a Chartist demonstration, exemplifying Jones's strongest side, the side that endeared him to Marx, his role as a tribune of the people. But, as we have mentioned, this same Jones was also writing strong denunciations of trade-unionism in his press. And so in the first part of this *Tribune* article, Marx inserts a direct refutation of Jones's views on trade unions without mentioning his name in this connection, merely politely stating that it applies to some socialists. I suggest it should be read as a summary of what Marx was in fact telling Jones and his similars around the Chartist movement:

°°There exists a class of philanthropists, and even of socialists, who consider strikes as very mischievous to the interests of the "workingman himself" . . . I am, on the very contrary, convinced that the alternative rise and fall of wages, and the continual conflict between masters and men resulting therefrom, are, in the present organization of industry, the indispensable means of holding up the spirit of the laboring classes, of combining them into one great association against the encroachments of the ruling class, and of preventing them from becoming a pathetic [*sic:* apathetic?], thoughtless, more or less well-fed instruments of production. In a state of society founded upon the antagonism of classes, if we want to prevent Slavery in fact as well as in name, we must accept war. In order to rightly appreciate the value of strikes and combinations, we must not allow ourselves to be blinded by the apparent insignificance of their economical results, but hold, above all things, in view their moral and political consequences. Without the great alternative phases of dullness, prosperity, over-excitement, crisis and distress, which modern industry traverses in periodically recurring cycles, with the up and down of wages resulting from them, as with the constant warfare between masters and men closely corresponding with those variations in wages and profits, the working-classes of Great Britain, and of all Europe, would be a heart-broken, a weak-minded, a worn-out, unresisting mass, whose self-emancipation would prove as impossible as that of the slaves of Ancient Greece and Rome. We must not forget that strikes and combinations among the serfs were the hot-beds of the mediaeval communes, and that those communes have been in their turn, the source of life of the now ruling bourgeoisie.[47]

No doubt Marx was also telling Jones that the strike wave was in process of changing the working class. Writing in the *Tribune,* he leaped ahead as usual: "In 1853, there have waned away the false pretences on the part of the masters and the silly illusions on the part of the men. The war between these two classes has become unmitigated, undisguised, openly avowed and plainly understood."[48] The adjectives, of course, were premature; there was a long zigzag road ahead. But, as Engels emphasized in connection with American labor, class-consciousness could come "only through practical experience. Hence it must begin with trade unions, etc., if it is to be a mass movement, and every step forward must be forced upon them by a defeat."[49]

It is not only consciousness that "must begin with trade unions"; elementary organization too. Here, as in much else, it is the capitalists who show the way—and then denounce their workers for following their example. In Manchester, an association of manufacturers, complete with a central committee, was organized to resist unionization, but

> They will not allow the machinery set up by and for themselves to be counterbalanced by a similar machinery set up by their men [reported Marx for *Tribune* readers]. They intend fortifying the monopoly of capital by the monopoly of combination. They will dictate terms as an associated body. But the laborers shall only dispute them in their individual capacity. They will attack in ranged battle, but they will not be resisted, except in single fight.[50]

But as the factory lords mounted their "Anti-Labor League" (reported Marx a little later), the workers found that the only way to resist "this English Capital League" was by their own union.[51]

4. *The training school.* Already in *The Condition of the Working Class* Engels had twice described the trade unions as schools: "the military school of the workingmen," "schools of war." So also, a quarter century later, Marx praised the significance of "the guerilla fights between capital and labour—we mean the strikes which during the last year have perturbed the continent of Europe." This was in a report for the General Council to a congress of the International.[52]

The trade-union movement is a school or training ground of the proletariat in a less warlike sense too, including that of preparing cadres of workers capable of administering society. Engels pointed out that "the working people, in the management of their colossal Trade Societies" also prove themselves "fit for administrative and political work."[53] This applies not only to the training of union officials—who sometimes become fit only to administer a labor market—but, in a larger sense, to the growth in organizational and administrative know-how that permeates far down into the ranks of a union with an actively participating membership.

There is still another consequence of trade-unionism that goes beyond any of the above points. While we will consider the conscious participation of trade unions in politics in the next chapter, Marx had occasion to point out that the mere existence of a trade-union movement had a meaning with relation to the state. This was particularly evident in the case of an authoritarian regime like Bismarck's, and Marx took care to point it out precisely to the Lassallean socialists, the representatives of "Royal Prussian Government socialism." When he publicly broke with this group, he lectured its chieftain Schweitzer that

> Combinations, together with the °trades unions° growing out of them, are of the utmost importance not only as a means of organization of the working class for struggle against the bourgeoisie—this importance being shown by the fact, *inter alia,* that even the workers in the United States cannot do without them despite voting rights and the republic—but in addition, in Prussia and Germany generally, the right to organize is a breach in police rule and bureaucratism ... in short, it is a measure to make "subjects" come of age ...[54]

The reference to Bismarck's Prussia was a little fuller in another letter around the same time: the government would not concede the complete abolition of the anti–trade-union laws "because that would involve making a breach in the bureaucracy, would make the workers legally of age," and would weaken the Junkers' control over agricultural labor—"which Bismarck could never allow and which was altogether incompatible with the Prussian *bureaucratic* state."[55]

In liberalized states and under favorable economic conditions, the tension between trade-union movement and state could be eased, as long as the system could afford it; but it always posed a problem. A quarter century later, Engels still found it necessary to lecture the German party that "Nowhere more than in Germany does the right of combination need to be made secure as against the *state* too," and not only as against the capitalist class.[56]

6. LIMITATIONS OF TRADE-UNIONISM

The historical problem in the socialist movement was seeing the positive side of trade-unionism; there was never any lack of denunciation of the limitations, deficiencies, and faults of trade unions. The socialist orthodoxy that Marx overturned leaned exclusively on the latter. This pressure ensured that Marx and Engels scarcely ever took up the question without adequate reminders that the trade-union movement was not the end of the road for the working class.

To reflect this side of their views, we select three passages of special interest.

The first is a draft resolution on "Trade Unions—Their Past, Present and Future" which Marx drew up for the 1866 congress of the International. At first blush it seems to be a very inclusive statement, for it contains the positive side too; but in fact Marx had to pull this punch. It was the first formal challenge in the International as a whole to the old anti–trade-union prejudices that were still rife, especially in the French section controlled by the Proudhonists. When Marx had drafted the Inaugural Address of the International two years before, any mention of trade unions had been a touchy point. Progress had been made, but now mention of strikes was the sore point.* This document is therefore not a statement that fully reflects where Marx's thinking was by 1866; it included only as much as Marx thought could be adopted at this juncture by the International congress.

With this reservation, it is worth citing almost complete, for it is the first international statement that effectively linked trade-unionism with socialism as part of a revolutionary program.

°°TRADES' UNIONS
THEIR PAST, PRESENT AND FUTURE
(Marx's draft)

(a) Their past.

Capital is concentrated social force, while the workman has only to dispose of his working force [labor power]. The *contract*

---

* Only two years later, at the Brussels congress of 1868, after Proudhonist influence had waned, it became possible to adopt a resolution entitled "Trades' Unions and Strikes," in which it was "Resolved—1. That strikes are not a means to the complete emancipation of the working classes, but are frequently a necessity in the actual situation of the struggle between labour and capital."[57] By this time, there were other problems, as we shall see.

between capital and labour can therefore never be struck on equitable terms, equitable even in the sense of a society which places the ownership of the material means of life and labour on one side and the vital productive energies on the opposite side. The only social power of the workmen is their number. The force of numbers, however, is broken by disunion. The disunion of the workmen is created and perpetuated by their *unavoidable competition amongst themselves.*

Trades' Unions originally sprung up from the *spontaneous* attempts of workmen at removing or at least checking that competition, in order to conquer such terms of contract as might raise them at least above the condition of mere slaves. The immediate object of Trades' Unions was therefore confined to everyday necessities, to expediencies for the obstruction of the incessant encroachments of capital, in one word, to questions of wages and time of labour. This activity of the Trades' Unions is not only legitimate, it is necessary. It cannot be dispensed with so long as the present system of production lasts. On the contrary, it must be generalised by the formation and the combination of Trades' Unions throughout all countries. On the other hand, unconsciously to themselves, the Trades' Unions were forming *centres of organisation* of the working class, as the mediaeval municipalities and communes did for the middle class. If the Trades' Unions are required for the guerilla fights between capital and labour, they are still more important as *organised agencies for superseding the very system of wages labour and capital rule.*

(b) Their present.

Too exclusively bent upon the local and immediate struggles with capital, the Trades' Unions have not yet fully understood their power of acting against the system of wages slavery itself. They therefore kept too much aloof from general social and political movements. Of late, however, they seem to awaken to some sense of their great historical mission . . . [English and U.S. examples are then cited.]

(c) Their future.

Apart from their original purposes, they must now learn to act deliberately as organising centres of the working class in the broad interest of its *complete emancipation.* They must aid every social and political movement tending in that direction. Considering themselves and acting as the champions and representatives of the whole working class, they cannot fail to enlist the non-society men into their ranks. They must look carefully after the interests of the worst paid trades, such as the agricultural labourers, rendered powerless by exceptional circumstances. They must convince the world at large that their efforts, far from being narrow and selfish, aim at the emancipation of the downtrodden millions.[58]

A year before this, Marx had included a stronger statement on the limitations of trade unions at the close of his presentation on "Wages, Price and Profit":

At the same time, and quite apart from the general servitude involved in the wages system, the working class ought not to exaggerate to themselves the ultimate working of these everyday struggles. They ought not to forget that they are fighting with effects, but not with the causes of those effects; that they are retarding the downward movement, but not changing its direction; that they are applying palliatives, not curing the malady. They ought, therefore, not to be exclusively absorbed in these unavoidable guerilla fights incessantly springing up from the never-ceasing encroachments of capital or changes of the market. They ought to understand that, with all the miseries it imposes upon them, the present system simultaneously engenders the *material conditions* and the *social forms* necessary for an economical reconstruction of society. Instead of the *conservative* motto, *"A fair day's wage for a fair day's work!"* they ought to inscribe on their banner the *revolutionary* watchword, *"Abolition of the wages system!"*
... Trades Unions work well as centres of resistance against the encroachments of capital. They fail generally from limiting themselves to a guerilla war against the effects of the existing system, instead of simultaneously trying to change it, instead of using their organised forces as a lever for the final emancipation of the working class, that is to say, the ultimate abolition of the wages system.[59]

Engels began his aforementioned series of popular articles for English workers[60] with a critique of the "Fair Day's Wage" watchword, and included discussion of trade-unionism's limits. But a less known passage on the same subject may be of interest here. The question came up as a side issue in a polemic with the German economist Lujo Brentano in 1891, that is, after bourgeois economics had been convinced that there *was* a positive point to trade-unionism after all. Since the workers had not heeded their wise counsel to eschew union organization as a waste of time and substance, the economists had now turned around to use the reform-minded unions as a dead cat with which to belabor the socialists' insistence on fundamental change. Whereas once socialists had had to explain that there was a point to workers' unionization, now Engels had to explain that trade unions could not solve all of the workers' problems.

> Herr Brentano's continually repeated statement that workers' protective legislation and trade-union organization lend themselves to the improvement of the condition of the working class is not in the least his own discovery. From *The Condition of the Working Class in England* and *The Poverty of Philosophy* to *Capital* and to my most recent writings, Marx and I have said this a hundred times, but with very considerable qualifications. Firstly, the favorable effects especially of workers' resistance organizations are limited to times of average and brisk trade; in periods of stagnation and crisis they regularly bog down. Herr Brentano's assertion that they "are able to paralyze the disastrous effects of the reserve army" is ridiculous bombast. And secondly —aside from other, less important qualifications—neither the protection given by legislation nor the resistance of the unions abolishes the main thing that has to be eliminated: the capital-labor relationship, which the antagonism between the capitalist class and the wage-working class always generates anew. The mass of wage-workers remain condemned to life-long wage-labor, the gulf between them and the capitalists becomes ever deeper and wider, the more modern large-scale industry takes over all branches of production. But since Herr Brentano would like to make the wage-slaves into *contented* wage-slaves, he has to enormously overstate the advantageous effects of labor protective laws, trade-union resistance, social-patchwork legislation, etc.; and since we are so misguided as to confront this overstatement with simple facts—hence his wrath.[61]

These and similar explanations are pitched in terms of any trade union, any resistance organization limited to economic issues, therefore even the best unions, even the best possible ones. But precisely because Marx took a positive stand for trade-unionism, it became necessary to differentiate between better and worse, unlike the sectarians who needed only to damn them all. Marx had to concern himself with the issues of policy and program inside the trade-union movement, like any other supporter.

We shall be concerned here with the large-scale issues in this area, and in particular with the largest one: the kind of trade-unionism that tends to a tunnel vision focused only on narrow and short-sighted goals, hence self-sterilizing in the long run, versus the kind of trade-unionism that best facilitates the movement's contribution to the long-term advancement of the class.

7. BUSINESS UNIONISM

The kind of trade-unionism that Marx opposed had been strongly enough criticized in the International resolution of 1866: the kind that systematically kept its efforts "narrow and selfish" in the interest of specially favored sectors and enclaves of the working class; the kind that remained "too exclusively bent upon the local and immediate struggles with capital," and increasingly detested struggles of any sort; above all, the kind that rejected political involvement and repudiated any program of "complete emancipation" as being an interference with its own pursuit of narrow privileges. This kind of unionism has been given various labels, such as "pure-and-simple unionism." Its central characteristic is that it regards the trade union as merely a haggler over the sale of labor power within the high walls of the capitalist system, a merchant of labor. From this point of view, business unionism is an apt description, though its use postdates Marx. (Engels often called it simply "conservative" unionism, as we shall see.)[62]

By the mid-1870s, the International dead, the English trade unions were in full flight to the most philistine forms of business unionism. "For a number of years past," Engels wrote to his German comrades in 1879, "the English working-class movement has been hopelessly describing a narrow circle of strikes for higher wages and shorter hours, not, however, as an expedient or means of propaganda and organization but as the ultimate aim." It is divided into Tories and Liberals. "One can speak here of a labor movement only insofar as strikes take place here which, whether they are won or not, do not get the movement one step further." He advised the party press: "No attempt should be made to conceal the fact that at present no real labor movement in the Continental sense exists here . . ."[63] A labor movement "in the Continental sense" meant a movement that took itself seriously as a representative of the organized class—not a mere job trust or corporative guild.

Engels linked this difference to the "sense of theory" traditional to German workers:

> What an incalculable advantage this is may be seen . . . from the indifference to theory which is one of the main reasons why the English working-class movement crawls along so slowly in spite of the splendid organization of the individual trades . . .[64]

Business unionism needed little theory; bourgeois political economy provided more than enough for its purposes. It existed entirely within the confine of the ruling ideas of the ruling class. As a bourgeois enterprise, it took on the same shortsighted, blinkered concentration on considerations of immediate advantage that historically distinguished its masters.[65]

One of the self-defeating forms of business unionism was the guild-like job trust. Many unions were shackled not only by bourgeois traditions but also by "[w]orkingmen's traditions, inherited from their first tentative efforts at independent action, such as the exclusion, from ever so many old Trade Unions, of all applicants who have not gone through a regular apprenticeship; which means the breeding, by every such union, of its own blacklegs [scabs]."[66] The London dockers bred their own blacklegs by closing their lists to all new members; in addition they refused essential cooperation with another union; and "Then the dockers are raising an outcry against the immigration of foreign paupers (Russian Jews)."[67] The result of these reactionary policies was that another old-line union rapidly lost its base. In Manchester, another striking union was handcuffing itself by restrictive guild practices: "they still plainly have some old trade-union traditions in their heads, that they will work only on this or that machine and only in a certain customary way; but they will soon drop this crap."[68]

> In a country with such an old political and labor movement there is always a colossal heap of traditionally transmitted rubbish which has to be got rid of by degrees. There are the prejudices of the skilled unions . . . the petty jealousies of the various trades, which become accentuated in the hands and heads of leaders into outright hostility and battles behind the scenes; there are the clashing ambitions and intrigues of the leaders [and so on] . . .[69]

In the 1880s Engels trusted that the coming depression would "make an end of the old trade unions here, let us hope," for the "craft character which stuck to them from the first . . . is becoming more unbearable every day."

> The fools want to reform society to suit themselves but not to reform themselves to suit the development of society. They cling to their traditional superstition, which does them nothing but harm, instead of getting quit of the rubbish and thus doubling their numbers and their power and really becoming again what at present they daily become less—associations of all the workers in a trade against the capitalists. This, I think, will explain many things to you in the behavior of these privileged workers.[70]

8. THE LABOR ARISTOCRACY

Engels' reference to "privileged workers" reflects a long-standing problem occupying the attention of socialists concerned with the trade-union movement. The guild-like and job-trust aspects and forms of conservative trade-unionism did indeed suggest the pattern of privileged enclaves of better-off workers inside the bourgeois order; and this had fed the lively suspicion of the early socialists that trade-unionism was an evil to be fought.

Among the many internal divisions of the working class, one of the most visible—touched on in Chapter 3 above[71]—was the stratification of low-paid and high-paid workers in whole trades and sectors of the class. This gave rise to terms like *aristocracy of labor*, no doubt first as a metaphor.[72]

There was a mutually reinforcing tendency for the skilled trades to be more easily organized, and for the unionized trades to enforce higher wages. Therefore there was a tendency for trade-unionist narrowness and trade-union successes to be linked by critics of the movement, themselves taking a narrow view. Thus, in a key article opposing trade unions per se, Ernest Jones, in the name of the revolutionary wing of Chartism, also denounced the "aristocracy of labor":

> . . . it is said I am setting the laborers against the skilled mechanics—the low-paid trades against the high-paid.
>
> Do we fight against class-government? Well, then? there is class-government in our own ranks, and we ought to fight against it too. Do we fight against aristocratic privilege? Well then—there

is aristocratic privilege of the vilest die among the high-paid trades, and we ought to fight against it too. Truth is the best policy. THE ARISTOCRACY OF LABOR MUST BE BROKEN DOWN, the same as any other aristocracies. *If you don't,* when you have established democracy, *these men will carry the Re-action.*[73]

In the Continental movement, similar reproaches and fears were directed at the cooperatives, the trade unions being still underdeveloped.* In England, Jones also directed his shafts at the cooperatives, which "increased the numbers of the most dangerous class—the aristocrats among their own body."[75]

While Marx disagreed with Jones's blanket opposition to trade-unionism, it was in this period of the early 1850s that he regarded Jones, for all his defects, as the best representative of left Chartism. Marx's first use of the "aristocracy" figure comes along in 1850 in the context of a passage on Chartism. Reviewing the past period, he notes that the Chartist organization is declining:

> The petty-bourgeois who still belong to the party, allied with the aristocracy of the workers, form a purely democratic wing whose program is limited to the People's Charter and some other petty-bourgeois reforms. The mass of workers living under really proletarian conditions belong to the revolutionary wing of the Chartists.[76]

The term is used here much as the left Chartists were using it, as a descriptive analogue. It occurs in the same way in *Capital.* There the passing reference is simply to the effects of crises on "the best-paid part of the working class, its aristocracy," without coloration.[77] But as the

---

* This talk came to a head at the Lausanne (1867) congress of the International, which was dominated by the French and Belgian Proudhonists. A formal report and full-length discussion dealt with the proposition that the existing workers' associations, specifically the cooperative movement, tended to produce a "fourth estate" (a higher-paid stratum of workers) at the expense of the formation of a "fifth estate" (depressed low-paid workers) whose conditions were so much the worse. (This danger had been suggested to the International from a rightward standpoint by the bourgeois-democratic radical philosopher Ludwig Büchner.) The reporter, C. de Paepe, counterposed "mutualist" (Proudhonist) associations to cooperatives which operated simply as profit-making enterprises within the present system. If the latter spread, it would mean "the creation of a new class composed of cooperative members who share these profits," a sort of middle class intermediate between the bourgeoisie (third estate) and the depressed proletariat (new fifth estate).[74]

higher-paid and trade-unionized sectors of the English working class fossilized into business unionism and adopted the self-protective devices of the job trust, deepening the gulf between themselves and underpaid unskilled labor, the descriptive figure took on more importance. From the early 1870s on, the conception plays a more important role, in historical fact and in Marx's and Engels' writings about the fact.

At the London Conference of the International in 1871, in the course of a discussion to which we will return,[78] the minutes report Marx's opinion on the state of the trade unions:

> . . . in England, the trade unions have existed for a half century, and the great majority of the workers are outside of the trade unions, [which] are an aristocratic minority. The poorest workers do not belong to them; the great mass of workers whom economic development daily drives out of the countryside into the cities remain outside the trade unions for a long time and the wretchedest [part of the] mass never gets into them. . . . The same goes for the workers born in the East End of London: one out of ten belongs to the trade unions. Peasants and day-laborers never join these [trade-union] societies.[79]

During the preparations for the conference, Engels had written to an Italian comrade along the same lines. In England—

> The trade-union movement, among all the big, strong and rich trade unions, has become more an obstacle to the general movement than an instrument of its progress; and outside of the trade unions there are an immense mass of workers in London who have kept quite a distance away from the political movement for several years, and as a result are very ignorant. But on the other hand they are also free of the many traditional prejudices of the trade unions and the other old sects, and therefore form excellent material with which one can work.[80]

There soon followed a public falling-out with the trade-union leaders collaborating with Marx in the International, as we shall see. For the next two decades Marx and Engels repeatedly pointed to "aristocratic" stratification inside the proletariat as part of the explanation for the fossilization of the trade-union structure, until the "New Unionism" shook that structure.

In the middle of the 1880s Engels stressed that there had been a permanent improvement in conditions "for two 'protected' sections only of the working class." One was the factory hands; the other was "the great Trades Unions" organizing male adults only or mainly.

> They form an aristocracy among the working class; they have succeeded in enforcing for themselves a relatively comfortable position, and they accept it as final. They are the model working men of Messrs. Leone Levi and Giffen [bourgeois economists], and they are very nice people indeed nowadays to deal with, for any sensible capitalist in particular and for the whole capitalist class in general.[81]

But, added Engels, "the great mass of the working people" are as poor as ever and the East End is still a pool of misery.

Visiting America in 1888, Engels replied to an interview question about English socialism in the same spirit, emphasizing the contrast between "the proletarian consciousness of the *masses*" and the workers' organizations which, "like the aristocracy of the workers in general, go along with Gladstone and the liberal bourgeoisie." He added that "The official workers' organizations, the °Trade-Unions,° which here and there are threatening to become reactionary," are hobbling behind in the rearguard.[82]

When the "New Unionism" erupted not long afterwards, the contrast which Engels had steadfastly pointed to amidst the apparent wasteland turned out to be the key to the new development. And Engels continued to use the "labor aristocracy" concept in the new period.

9. COOPTATION OF TRADE-UNIONISM

Another development accompanied the growing importance of the labor aristocracy, and reinforced its influence.

It is the pattern in all countries that, as soon as the bourgeoisie reconciles itself to the fact that trade-unionism is here to stay, it ceases to denounce the institution as a subversive evil that has to be rooted out with fire and sword in order to defend God, country, and motherhood, and turns instead to the next line of defense: domesticating the unions, housebreaking them, and fitting them into the national family as one of the tame cats.

In an essay comparing conditions in 1885 with the old days of 1845,

Engels pointed to this change. The manufacturers were maturer and wiser about unions, and also aware of how badly their "great Liberal Party" needed workingmen's votes.

> Trades Unions, lately considered inventions of the devil himself, were now petted and patronised as perfectly legitimate institutions and as useful means of spreading sound economical doctrines amongst the workers. Even strikes, than which nothing had been more nefarious up to 1848, were now gradually found out to be occasionally very useful, especially when provoked by the masters themselves, at their own time.[83]

In fact, by this time the manufacturers had virtually taken over the program of the Chartists. What, in a different social context, had been the program of revolutionaries was now not only respectable but a necessity for bourgeois advance.

A factor making this possible (as Engels pointed out in an 1892 preface to his old book of 1845) was the great advance in industrial development and profits. The *scale* of profits had changed. The really big capitalists no longer found it worthwhile to practice "petty thefts upon the workpeople" in order to eke out their takings, and so became "apparently moralized." It was only the petty tradesmen who had to pick up a penny here and there in that way. Thus a number of reforms became possible, including the Ten Hours Bill.

But these very reforms—which seemed to be concessions to the working class, and were so in part—were tied to another process taking place in the capitalist structure. Their effect operated "in favor of the giant capitalist in his competition with his less favored brother." The big capitalists even began

> to discover in strikes—at opportune times—a powerful means to serve their own ends. The largest manufacturers, formerly the leaders of the war against the working class, were now the foremost to preach peace and harmony. And for a very good reason. The fact is that all these concessions to justice and philanthropy were nothing else but means to accelerate the concentration of capital in the hands of the few, for whom the niggardly extra extortions of former years had lost all importance and had become actual nuisances; and to crush all the quicker and all the safer their smaller competitors, who could not make both ends meet without such perquisites.[84]

The bigger the enterprise, the greater was the loss and inconvenience of labor conflicts, hence the greater the desire to avoid "unnecessary squabbles." All this explains why a huge corporation can often exhibit an apparently more enlightened labor policy than a twopenny capitalist scrabbling for a living in a sweatshop; but the other side of this meant that, when conflict does break out, it tends more rapidly to assume the proportions of civil war.

This relationship could go on most smoothly when big capital was dealing with relatively limited sections of privileged workers, and so the pattern reinforced tendencies toward "aristocratic" stratification in the proletariat—as long as capital could afford it.

10. BREAKTHROUGH: THE "NEW UNIONISM"

By the 1880s the English union movement was covered over with a bureaucratic crust that looked invincible, even though—or because—only some ten percent of the working class were organized. Engels' interest lay in looking beyond this encrustation, toward the forces that would break through it; above all, he did not identify the crust with the class, nor the leaders with the labor movement as such, nor its bourgeoisified bureaucrats with the proletariat. He had long been pointing to the potentialities of the unorganized mass, who "form excellent material" precisely because they are free of the prejudices that had grown on the established movement like fungi.[85]

On the eve of the first breakthrough, he was writing to a comrade that

> here [in England] an instinctive socialism, which fortunately resists any definite formulation according to the dogma of one or another socialist organization and hence will accept it all the more easily from a decisive event, is getting more and more of a hold on the masses. It need only start somewhere or other and the bourgeois will marvel at the latent socialism that will break out and be manifest then.[86]

In another letter written the same day, he thought he saw the working class being ever "more penetrated by the Socialist leaven."[87] The point is not to exhibit Engels' prescience—he was ever sanguine—but rather to stress the direction in which he kept looking. In particular, he kept reminding that, in all periods of encrustation, a molecular movement went on underneath, eventually precipitating the outburst which others would greet as sudden and startling, precisely because it came from the invisible lower depths.

In this case, the "light jostle needed for the entire avalanche to move"[88] came in July 1888 from the workingwomen of a match factory, stimulated to organization by socialists. Then the gasworkers, another sector of presumably unorganizable underpaid workers, were organized by socialists, including Eleanor Marx, and won a resounding victory. Eleanor Marx became one of the leaders of the resultant Gas Workers and General Laborers Union, which was in the vanguard of the "New Unionism." The Dockworkers Union was the next and decisive step; and a new era of unionism opened up. (It may be compared to the later rise of the CIO in the United States.)

> In short, anyone who sees only the surface would say it was all confusion and personal squabbles. But *under* the surface the movement is going on; it is seizing ever broader strata, and for the most part precisely among the hitherto stagnant *lowest* masses; and the day is no longer far off when this mass will suddenly *find itself*, when it dawns upon it that it is this colossal self-moving mass; and when that day comes short work will be made of all the rascality and squabbling.[89]

The new movement was "utterly different from that of the *old* trade unions: the skilled laborers, the labor aristocracy." The new people "are drawing far greater masses into the struggle, shaking up society far more profoundly, and putting forward much more far-reaching demands . . ."[90]

> °°These new Trades Unions of unskilled men and women are totally different from the old organisations of the working-class aristocracy and cannot fall into the same conservative ways; they are too poor, too shaky and too much composed of unstable elements, for anyone of these unskilled people may change his trade any day. And they are organised under quite different circumstances—all the leading men and women are Socialists, and socialist agitators too. In them I see the *real* beginning of the movement here.[91]

The new impulse came out of London's "stagnant pool of misery," the East End—"mostly small, *unskilled* Unions and therefore despised by the haughty Trades Council of the aristocracy of labour . . . *It is the*

East End which now commands the movement and these fresh elements, unspoiled by the 'Great Liberal Party,' show an intelligence" similar to that of "the equally unspoiled German workmen." They insist on socialists as their leaders.[92]

> ... the movement spreads and seizes one layer of the workers after another. It has now shaken out of their torpor the unskilled laborers of the East End of London, and we all know what a splendid impulse these fresh forces have given it in return.[93]

The East End, shaking off misery and despair, "has returned to life, and has become the home of what is called the 'New Unionism,' that is to say, of the organization of the great mass of 'unskilled' workers." This unionism is essentially different, for it does not take the wage system as fixed and given, and its leaders are socialists.

> ... the masses, whose adhesion gave them strength, were rough, neglected, looked down upon by the working-class aristocracy; but they had this immense advantage, that *their minds were virgin soil,* entirely free from the inherited "respectable" bourgeois prejudices which hampered the brains of the better situated "old" Unionists. And thus we see now these new Unions taking the lead of the working-class movement generally, and more and more taking in tow the rich and proud "old" Unions.[94]

This upheaval was important to Engels not because it meant that the revolution was around the corner—he was not *that* sanguine—but because it showed the irrepressible class forces at work. In fact, the modern labor and socialist movement dates from this development. It was a question of the direction of the movement:

> ... the masses are on the move, and there is no holding them back any more. The longer the stream is dammed up, the more powerful will be the breakthrough when it comes. And these unskilled are very different chaps from the fossilized brothers of the old trade unions; not a trace of the old pettifogging spirit, of the craft exclusiveness of the engineers, for instance; on the contrary, a general cry for the organization of *all* trade unions into *one* brotherhood and for direct struggle against capital.[95]

In an article for the German press on the 1890 May Day celebration in London, Engels went over many of the ideas we have been quoting from his correspondence; in addition there was special emphasis on the new unions' rejection of the old guild attitudes:

> The old ones [trade unions], which admit none but "skilled" workers, are exclusive; they bar all workers who have not been trained according to the statutes of the guild concerned, and thereby even expose themselves to competition from those not in the guild; they are rich, but the richer they become, the more they degenerate into mere sick-funds and burial clubs; they are conservative and they steer clear above all of that ". . ." socialism, as far and as long as they can. The new "unskilled" unions, on the other hand, admit *every* fellow-worker; they are essentially, and the Gas Workers even exclusively, strike unions and strike funds.[96]

All layers of the working class would be affected, up to the old labor aristocracy and down to the borders of the lumpenproletariat:

> I am happy I have lived to see this day. If *this* stratum can be organized, that is a big fact. . . . the lowest stratum of East End workers enters the movement and then the upper strata must follow their example . . .
>
> Furthermore: for lack of organization and because of the passive vegetative existence of the real workers in the East End, the lumpenproletariat* has had the main say there so far; it behaved like *and was considered* the very type and representative of the million of starving East Enders. That will now cease. The peddler and those like him will be forced into the background, the East End worker will be able to develop his own type and make it count by means of organization; and this is of enormous value for the movement. . . . a new section enters the movement, new troops . . . Hurrah![98]

---

* In this passing reference to the lumpenproletariat, it is not altogether clear what East End elements are meant. The example of the peddler which is immediately given points to marginal and itinerant elements outside the proletariat, in accordance with the analysis below, in Chapter 15. But this has nothing to do with Engels' emphasis elsewhere on the success of the New Unionism in organizing the most depressed layers of the working class; in fact, here Engels counterposes the lumpenproletariat to "the East End worker." Similarly, in a letter to a union organizer (perhaps Eleanor Marx) Engels wrote:

> If these poor downtrodden men, the dregs of the proletariat, these odds and ends of all trades, fighting every morning at the dock gates for an engagement, if *they* can combine, and terrify by their resolution the

The upheaval had a "stunning effect" on the bourgeoisie and the general public, commented Engels in the same letter. No doubt it especially stunned authorities on the labor movement. It was not only the socialist sectarians who were incapable of grasping the main feature of the trade-union movement, namely, the fact that here in the elementary class organization of the proletariat was an irrepressible reservoir of elemental class struggle.

---

mighty Dock Companies, truly then we need not despair of any section of the working class. This is the beginning of real life in the East End, and if successful will transform the whole character of the East End. There—for want of self-confidence, and of organisation among the poor devils grovelling in stagnant misery—*lasciate ogni speranza* ... If the dockers get organised, all other sections will follow . . .⁹⁷

The transformation to the dockworkers of today—a revolutionization of human-kind on a partial scale—was achieved by class struggle, not welfarism.

5 | TRADE UNIONS AND POLITICS

While it became common to speak of the trade unions as the *elementary* organization of class struggle, this did not mean that its struggle had to remain on a primitive and rock-bottom level of consciousness. On the contrary, Marx emphasized the need to urge the trade unions on to higher levels of activity and struggle, in a line of progress culminating in commitment to independent political action. A socialist trade-unionist who considered himself advanced beyond bread-and-butter unionism had internal responsibilities; political revolutionists outside the union structure had proposals to urge. In any case, Marx had definite ideas on what made a trade union better or worse, effective or weak, from the standpoint of its basic class role.

1. PROGRESSIVE UNIONISM

These proposals for effective trade-unionism can be summarized from the material in the preceding chapter, for they all stem from Marx's view of the relationship between trade unions as an organizational form and the proletariat as a potentially revolutionary class. We list five main points.

1. *Class-struggle policy and militancy.* In one of his popular articles for trade-unionists in 1881, Engels wrote:

> The struggle of the labourer against capital, we said. That struggle does exist, whatever the apologists of capital may say to the contrary. It will exist so long as a reduction of wages remains the safest and readiest means of raising profits; nay, so long as the wages system itself shall exist. The very existence of Trades

Unions is proof sufficient of the fact; if they are not made to fight against the encroachments of capital, what are they made for? There is no use in mincing matters. No milksop words can hide the ugly fact that present society is mainly divided into two great antagonistic classes . . .[1]

The objective role of trade unions in the class struggle is one thing; the conscious policy of a given union leadership is another. We will be concerned here not with the problems of generalship, but only with the conceptions held by the leadership and membership.

A class-struggle policy by a union does not mean one consciously embracing a revolutionary goal or ideology (whatever that may be taken to mean) or one that adopts a socialist program, whether or not the union is in fact led by socialists. A class-struggle policy may be defined as one that defends the interests of the workers as such, against the employers as such, regardless of the consequences of this struggle for the capitalists, for their system, or for the government, without drawing back out of consideration for any interests other than those of the embattled class.

A great number of class struggles, even large-scale strikes, have been fought by workers and directed by leaders who held nothing but immediate bread-and-butter aims, yet maintained consistent loyalty to class interests in the face of considerable pressure. They may even have held views approving of the capitalist system and rejecting socialism; this bespeaks their level of consciousness; but what matters is whether these views were subordinated to the needs of the class struggle, or whether they came to supersede the latter.

Contrariwise, a class-collaboration policy takes the widely heralded "harmony of interests of labor and capital" not simply as a consciously held opinion or wish but as the *determinant* of trade-union policy in action. The crux is, again, not whether specific trade-unionists "believe in" this harmony, any more than whether they believe in capitalism; the crux is whether in fact they derive trade-union policy from these ideas, instead of from their response to the felt needs of their class. Thus a trade-unionist may be altogether nonrevolutionary in subjective opinion, yet capable of following a class-struggle policy in action. Indeed, a worker who is advancing in class-consciousness normally goes through such a transitional phase. The worker's version of a "belief in" capitalism contains vital elements that are operationally hostile to the *capitalist's* version of a belief in capitalism. The difference between these two modes of procapitalism is itself a reflection of the class-struggle reality, and it is brought to the surface, to consciousness, in the course of struggle. In this sense, a class-struggle policy tends to produce a socialist consciousness, through experience, even though it does not start with it.

So much for generalization. In practice, an activist translation of a theoretical statement about class-struggle policy may appear as *militancy*.

More concrete discussion of trade-union policies is outside our purview, but it may be useful to point to some specific cases in which Engels reacted to special problems of class-struggle policy. We cite Engels, rather than Marx, because it was he who lived on into the period when problems of socialist policy in trade unions began to loom large.

In 1891 twenty thousand Ruhr miners exploded in a strike for higher wages and eight-hour shifts. The government broke the strike with soldiery, but the fight marked a stage in the organization and radicalization of the miners. The German Social-Democratic leadership had believed the moment unfavorable for battle and had warned the miners against premature action—probably correctly. The party leaders also feared that the government wanted an outbreak that could be put down by force and turned to political capital against the socialists—again probably correctly. There was an acute problem of generalship involved. Yet the way in which the party press dealt with the strike provoked one of the few occasions when Engels intervened on a matter of internal policy. He wrote to both Bebel and Kautsky with obvious disquiet.

Engels did not question that it would have been wiser tactics for the miners to have held back. But how should socialists react when the proletariat goes into battle against their better judgment? He wrote first to Kautsky:

> Our people in Berlin [party leaders] see everything only from *their* standpoint. So too they often forget that they cannot assume the miners have the kind of discipline that was drilled into the *old* soldiers of the party by the Anti-Socialist Law; and that *every* new group of workers *will be driven toward us* in the course of unwise, necessarily unsuccessful but, under the circumstances, inevitable strikes of angry passion . . . One cannot have only the pleasant sides of the movement, one must also accept the momen-

tarily disagreeable things. Besides, the rigid discipline of a *sect* cannot continue to exist in a *big party*, and that also has its good side.[2]

To Bebel:

> The ill-advised strike of angry passion is, as matters stand, the usual way that large new strata of workers are brought in our direction. *These* facts seem to me to have been given too little consideration in the treatment by *Vorwärts*. Liebknecht [its editor] knows no shadings, he is either all black or all white; and if he thought he was duty-bound to prove to the world that our party did not egg on this strike, and even calmed it down, then God have mercy on the poor strikers—for them less than a desirable amount of concern has been shown, to see that they come to us soon.[3]

The underlying issue was loyalty to the class movement, regardless of the immediate consequences for the narrower interests of the party.

If the German leadership was perturbed when the class struggle did not flow through party channels in a properly disciplined way, the problem with the French movement was just the opposite. There the trade unions remained weak and impotent; there was not enough proletarian discipline to win a strike or build an organization even under favorable conditions; it was much easier to indulge in the favorite game of "r-r-revolutionary" windbagging. Writing to his Paris contact (Marx's daughter Laura), Engels advised, apropos of a situation in 1886:

> ... strike discipline is very useful for the French workers; the first condition for the success of such a struggle is scrupulous regard for legality, and all revolutionary bragging and outbursts of passion lead inevitably to defeat. This discipline, which is the first condition for a successful and firm organization, is what the bourgeoisie fears most.[4]

The immediate trade-union objective in France, Engels explained, was to force the government to treat strikes as *legal* acts. Where in Germany the party leadership had an overbureaucratic conception of how to react to spontaneous militancy, in France the leaders still had to learn that the workers' movement does not live by spontaneous spasms alone.

"Scrupulous regard for legality"—so Engels had cautioned the French in this juncture, as a matter of generalship. The relativity of militancy will be illuminated from another direction if we turn to a problem involving the most law-abiding people on earth, the English. After a tense confrontation in London, Marx reported to Engels:

> Here the government has nearly produced a revolt. The Englishman first needs a revolutionary education, of course, and two weeks would be enough for that if [Police Commissioner] Sir Richard Mayne had absolute control.... One thing is certain, these thick-headed John Bulls, whose brainpans seem to have been specially manufactured for the constables' bludgeons, will never get anywhere without a really bloody encounter with the ruling powers.[5]

Marx had reacted similarly when the *Sunday Times* once admonished the strike movement that "The demands of the working people may be submitted to when urged in a respectful manner." He retorted in an article:

> °°Has any one ever heard of the price of coffee rising at Mincing Lane when "urged in a *respectful* manner!" The trade in human flesh and blood, being carried on in the same manner as that of any other commodity, give it at least the chances of any other.[6]

2. *Against sectism.** We saw that Engels, writing to Kautsky, implied that the German party was mistakenly taking the narrow view of the sect, with its "rigid discipline," instead of the attitude of a class party. A sect counterposed its special views (which might be very good in themselves) to the interests of class development as a whole. What seemed like a momentary failing of the German party was, however, the systematic character of other groups: in particular, the "Marxist" group in England (repudiated by Marx) called the Social Democratic Federation and led by H. M. Hyndman, as well as another group called the Socialist League, associated with William Morris.

The silly standoffishness of these two repositories of an alleged revolutionary socialism was a continual affliction to Engels especially as the explosive development of the "New Unionism" opened up new possibilities for socialism. The case was similar with the American group, the Socialist Labor Party. Writing to an American correspon-

---

* The more usual term is *sectarianism*; but this commonly implies the pursuit of certain policies, whereas I am concerned here with the adoption of the sect as a form of organization, apart from the policies pursued by the sect. This question—sectism, as well as party organization generally—will be discussed more basically in Volume 3.

dent, Engels expressed his hope that the S.L.P. would kindly liquidate itself in the interest of socialist progress, and turned to the English example:

> Over here it is being proved that a great nation simply cannot be tutored in a doctrinaire and dogmatic fashion, even if one has the best of theories . . . The movement *is* under way now at last and, I believe, for good. But not directly socialist, and those among the English who have understood our theory best remain outside it: Hyndman because he is incurably jealous and intriguing, [E. Belfort] Bax because he is a bookworm.[7]

These personal characterizations were justified, but not sufficient to explain the self-defeating policies of the sectists. Experience showed that what was involved was a conceptualized dogma about the relationship between the enlightened elite of the vanguard and the benighted body of the class. In a letter a few months later, Engels generalized a little more, but still focused on style of operation. He raged at the bad attitude of

> the Socialist League, which looks down on everything that is not directly revolutionary (which means here in England as in your country: all who do not limit themselves to making phrases and otherwise doing nothing), and the [Social Democratic] Federation, which still behaves as if all except themselves were asses and bunglers, although it is precisely owing to the new impetus lent to the movement that *they* have succeeded in getting some following again.[8]

Indeed, some of the best organizers of the new unions began as S.D.F. members but had to break with the sect in order to do effective work as trade-union militants. Engels generally supported such organizers against the sect. In a published interview he repudiated the S.D.F. on the ground of its sectism, and gave an example:

> It is an exclusive body. It has not understood how to take the lead of the working-class movement generally, and to direct it towards socialism. It has turned Marxism into an orthodoxy. Thus it insisted upon [dockers' leader] Johns Burns unfurling the red flag at the dock strike, where such an act would have ruined the whole movement, and, instead of gaining over the dockers, would have driven them back into the arms of the capitalists.[9]

The sectism of the Hyndman group, like its similars, suggested a fossilized sort of ultimatism, as if it were saying to the class it purported to represent: Either you obey my certified-correct Revolutionary Program, or else I will punish you by withdrawing my benediction on your existence and will refuse to be contaminated by further association with your unsanctified activities. Marx implemented a basically different conception of the relation of socialists to trade unions. Socialists should act as a loyal left wing of the class movement, not an alternative counterposed to it; they should start with the working class as it is and where it is, in order to change it; they should be a part of its real class organizations no matter how backward the mass might be from their standpoint; and they should become the best militants for the limited aims of the movement-as-is. But at the same time, and through this association, they seek to push the whole movement upward to higher levels of class-struggle commitment and consciousness by means of the lessons of experience, all without giving up or hushing their own full views or ceasing to criticize mistaken and ineffective policies.

We have just paraphrased the *Communist Manifesto,* whose words apply fully to the trade-union arm of the proletariat: "In the various stages of development which the struggle of the working class has to pass through, they [the Communists] always and everywhere represent the interests of the movement as a whole"; and "The Communists fight for the attainment of the immediate aims, for the enforcement of the momentary interests of the working class; but in the movement of the present, they also represent and take care of the future of that movement." It is in this sense that the Manifesto explains that "The Communists do not form a separate party opposed to other working-class parties [*read:* other arms of the working class]," that "They have no interests separate and apart from those of the proletariat as a whole," and that, finally, "They do not set up any sectarian principles of their own, by which to shape and mould the proletarian movement." [10] The operative word in the last sentence is *sectarian.*

3. *Organizing the unorganized.* This requires no special discussion here. We have seen that this task was one of the great differences between the "New Unionism" and the old, and one of the features of the former that excited Engels' enthusiasm. An allied question is the organization by the trade-union movement of the unemployed, especially in depression periods. No policy question is more closely related to the basic class character of the movement, indicating whether a trade

union operates as an exclusive guild or job trust rather than an arm of the class.

4. *Trade-union democracy.* Programmatic insistence on the democratic control of a union by its membership does not stem simply from abstract concern with the values of democracy in general. It is, rather, an important antidote to the pressures of bourgeoisification and co-optation that we have discussed. Assuming that leaders as individuals are no more venal or corrupt than rank-and-file members, it is still true that leadership and official position puts an individual under the pressure of employers in particular and bourgeois society in general. These pressures come from two directions. One is the obvious allurement of rewards and blandishments from above, whether these are direct or indirect bribes or merely the enticements of social cooptation. Another is the fact that trade-union officials become *ex*-workers; they cease to live the same life as their fellow workers, even with the best of intentions, to a small or great degree; the conditions of existence change, and a change of consciousness may follow. Trade-union democracy maximizes the counterpressure of the working-class ranks on them. The institutions of proletarian democracy are also an indispensable school for training working-class cadres in the administration and surveillance of society itself, for making the class fit to rule, as we have discussed.[11] Nor do these considerations exhaust the case for trade-union democracy as a vital part of Marx's program.

Marx had occasion to raise the issue of trade-union democracy directly when the German Lassallean organization was setting up its party-controlled trade unions in 1868 (on which, more later). In a letter to its leader, J. B. von Schweitzer, Marx (writing as the German secretary of the International) objected to the system of internal "dictatorship" being established.*

> As for the draft Rules, I consider them erroneous in principle, and I believe I have had as much experience in the trade-union field as any of my contemporaries. Without going further into details, I only want to remark that *centralist* organization, although very useful for secret societies and sectarian movements, goes against the nature of trade unions. Even if it were desirable— I state outright that it is impossible—it would not be possible; and least of all in Germany. Here where the worker's life is

---

* For an incidental view of the Lassallean party dictatorship imposed on controlled trade unions, see Special Note B.

regulated from childhood on by bureaucracy and he himself believes in the authorities, in the bodies appointed over him, he must be taught before all else to walk by himself.[12]

In this letter Marx pointed specifically to that part of the Rules which placed the office of the president (Schweitzer himself) above the membership. "And to have this now in a trade-union movement! The latter revolves largely around money questions and you will soon discover that here all dictatorship comes to an end." This prediction was true in Schweitzer's case.

5. *Independent political action.* Finally, Marx considered it essential that the trade-union movement progress from a narrow preoccupation with economic, or bread-and-butter, issues alone, to the larger issues of society, in short, the field of politics in the broadest sense. In Marx's view, this was a necessity from the standpoint of the trade unions' own practical considerations in the long run; for the effectiveness of pure-and-simple unionism begins to dwindle as it develops and as it encounters more complicated problems. Marx thought that one of the single biggest accomplishments of the International was that "We have succeeded in drawing into the movement the one really big workers' organization, the English *'Trades-Unions,'* which formerly concerned themselves *exclusively* with wage questions."[13]

The orientation toward politicalization followed in part from his analysis of the limitations of trade-unionism, in particular the limits of economic gains. He remarked in the *New York Tribune* during the 1853 strike wave, when he expected the unions to learn from their failures:

> ... should, as I suppose, the depression prove lasting, the work people will soon get the worst of it, and have to struggle—very unsuccessfully—against *reduction* [of wages]. But then their activity will soon be carried over to the *political field,* and the *new organization of trades, gained in the strikes, will be of immense value to them.*[14]

The strikes would not be able to gain their immediate economic objectives, he thought, because of the economic circumstances under which they had been launched.

> But they have done their work. They have revolutionized the industrial proletariat, and, stirred up by dear food and cheap labor, the consequences will show themselves in due time. Already the idea of a Parliament of Labor, which, in fact, means

nothing but a general reassembling of the workingmen under the banners of Chartism, evokes the fears of the middle-class press.[15]

"In due time" the unions did turn to political action, though not on Marx's schedule. It was a question of establishing the direction. A quarter century later, Engels' series of popular articles for workers still had to point the direction, for it was to be another decade before English labor moved definitively into politics. His articles were peppered with arguments for independent political action. The central passage, in an article entitled "A Working Men's Party," makes a point we have not yet mentioned.

Engels begins by recalling that "The working class has interests of its own, political as well as social," but English workers leave their political interests in the hands of the capitalist class's parties. Many Continental countries are ahead of them in this respect. But there is a widespread feeling that this course is now obsolete and impractical:

> Thinking men of all classes begin to see that a new line must be struck out, and that this line can only be in the direction of democracy. But in England, where the industrial and agricultural working class forms the immense majority of the people, democracy means the dominion of the working class, neither more nor less.[16]

Then let that working class prepare itself for its ruling responsibilities. The best way is "to use the power already in their hands, the actual majority they possess in every large town," and thereby send workers into Parliament.

> Moreover, in England a real democratic party is impossible unless it be a working men's party. Enlightened men of other classes (where they are not so plentiful as people would make us believe) might join that party and even represent it in Parliament after having given pledges of their sincerity.... But no democratic party in England, as well as elsewhere, will be effectively successful unless it has a distinct working-class character. Abandon that, and you have nothing but sects and shams.[17]

His series of articles had already argued that the trade unions must orient toward achieving a new socialist society. Now he is pointing out that even within the cadre of the old society, it is only a working-class party that can move society "in the direction of democracy," the direction whose final station lies beyond the borders of the present system.

While urging a socialist perspective, neither Engels nor Marx confronted the trade unions with the ultimatistic demand that they must adopt socialism as their political banner or else suffer the slings and arrows of sect denunciation. The five points listed would fit the unions for broader societal tasks; they point a direction to be urged, beginning with the most elementary activities of economic defense, and ending (in due time) with the trade-unionists' conscious adoption of a workers' state as their programmatic aim. This defines a spectrum of trade-union consciousness, and it provides the framework for helping to move the trade unions along the road to political awareness.

For Marx, this is the trade-unionism of the revolutionary; but it is not the "revolutionary unionism" that arose out of the sects outside the Marxist movement.

2. CLASS STRUGGLE AND POLITICS

In the language of the movement, it became standard to speak of the trade unions as the economic arm of the working class, the proletarian party as the political arm; and we have already used this two-armed metaphor in the preceding section. It is, however, misleading in suggesting that the two arms are merely coordinate, of equal standing. In Marx's view, this is not so, as we will see in section 6 below. There is another possible misunderstanding to be cleared up as well.

In a couple of statements we have quoted, Marx seems to be blurring the difference between economic and political action. The *Communist Manifesto* said that "every class struggle is a political struggle," repeating a formulation that had appeared the year before in Marx's polemic against Proudhon.[18] What does this mean? Is every trade-union struggle —say, one over wages—a political struggle? There are two parts to the answer.

In the first place, this aphoristic formula of 1847–1848 is still tinged with Marx's early views. Marx always looked on the trade-union movement as a process in the class struggle, on various levels. In the course of maturation the working class moved nearer the goals set by society's evolution. On the highest level the working class confronted society-wide responsibility. In the politico-philosophic language of the milieu in which Marx's thinking first developed, it was society-wide (or human-community–wide) tasks that defined the word *political.** This broad usage—much broader than the *political* we are used to—still conditions the language we have quoted.

Secondly, the statement takes on the air of an aphorism by dint of drastic condensation (which is one of the characteristics of the Manifesto in general). It is not simply making the point that a *class-wide* struggle tends to turn to overtly political action, though this is true. The struggle is implicitly political, impinging on political power, even before the proletariat may actually go over to open political activity. When a class war reaches a high level, it is already a political struggle insofar as such a struggle no longer merely involves concessions by a ruling class to a subject class but, rather, objectively raises the question of which class will rule society. At this level, the stakes are state power, whether the combatants know it or not.

As it happens, a quarter century later Marx had occasion to go over this ground again, in a letter to a German socialist in America. Here he emphasizes the class-wide and generalized nature of the struggle.

> The political movement of the working class has as its ultimate object, of course, the conquest of political power for this class, and this naturally requires a °previous organization° of the working class developed up to a certain point and arising precisely from its economic struggles.
>
> On the other hand, however, every movement in which the working class comes out as a *class* against the ruling classes and tries to coerce them by °pressure from without° is a political movement. For instance, the attempt in a particular factory or even in a particular trade to force a shorter working day out of individual capitalists by strikes, etc., is a purely economic movement. On the other hand the movement to force through an eight-hour, etc. *law* is a *political* movement. And in this way, out of the separate economic movements of the workers there grows up everywhere a *political* movement, that is to say, a movement of the *class*, with the object of enforcing its interests in a general

---

* This was explained in our first volume.[19] It must be remembered that this broad use of *politics* or *state* characterized not only Hegel but also those who broke with his conclusions but stayed inside his conceptual framework; it was the language of a whole milieu. At the opposite pole is the contemporary tendency to narrow *political* to electoral activity.

form, in a form possessing general, socially coercive force. While these movements presuppose a certain degree of previous organization, they are in turn equally a means of developing this organization.[20]

This explanation was written under the pressure of the Bakuninist campaign to prohibit the International from engaging in political activity; Marx has to explain that politics has a broader social horizon than electoral politics. At about the same time Marx was still putting the same thought with the former conciseness, by writing that Bakunin "has not even seen that every class movement *as* a class movement, is necessarily and was always a *political* movement."[21]

Just as economy that is studied on a society-wide scale (not microeconomics) cannot but be political economy, so economic struggle on a class-wide scale merges into political struggle.

> ... a struggle between two great classes of society [wrote Engels in 1881] necessarily becomes a political struggle. So did the long battle between the middle or capitalist class and the landed aristocracy; so also does the fight between the working class and these same capitalists. In every struggle of class against class, the next end fought for is political power....[22]

The original flat equation, *class struggle = political struggle*, has now been restated more carefully in terms of a *tendency*.

3. THE EXPERIMENT IN THE INTERNATIONAL

As trade unions move toward independent political action, problems are raised about the relationship of two currents: trade-unionists who are reaching out toward the broader realm of social and political issues in order to implement their economic aspirations, and political revolutionists who look to the trade-union movement as a means of effectuating their aims. These two currents may overlap in personnel, or merge in the case of individuals, but they tend to exist separately as movements, that is, as autonomous arms of the working-class movement.

The International, however, was an early experiment in hybrid organization, combining trade-union organizations with political (and other) organizations under one structural roof. This experiment had not been so planned; it happened that way, out of the first coming together of the French Proudhonists and the English trade-unionists in the St. Martin's Hall mass meeting that launched the International in 1864. The statutes (Rules) as well as the Inaugural Address, and the structure that developed, were all tailored to that reality. But in the long run the combination proved to be unviable; it necessarily led to intolerable strains; and after this experience the working-class movement had to proceed with the two-arm pattern.

The situation was helped by the fact that, fortunately, Proudhonism as a theory and a movement was declining by this time; but time was still needed to bring its representatives toward tolerance of union organization and strikes. Symbol of the initial situation was the fact that Marx had to leave the very mention of trade unions out of the Inaugural Address. For this and other reasons, the International did not provide a model for a solution of the two-current problem; it only made a beginning; and this limitation must be kept in mind.

Marx's essential role in the General Council of the International was working out the framework of collaboration between the mixture of Continental revolutionaries and semirevolutionaries on the one hand, and, on the other, a heterogeneous group of English trade-unionists, including many who were essentially reform-minded, others averse to politics of any kind, and some averse to independent politics and inclined to immersion in Liberalism. From the beginning he had to guide the strained alliance through a series of whirlpools and dangerous rapids. This task could have been accomplished only by someone who stood outside and above the various narrow viewpoints, and saw a farther goal.

It should be clear from the preceding chapter why Marx had no compunction whatsoever about collaborating in this way—the pejorative term is hobnobbing—with that section of the trade-union officialdom which in the conditions of the time was playing a progressive role. There would be a reason to devote a section of this chapter to a detailed presentation of Marx's amazingly successful and fruitful work with these trade-union leaders over a number of years; without this material the emphasis in this section is skewed, for we will put the spotlight on the eventual negative outcome rather than on the positive practical work, which was of considerable value to the British working-class movement. Fortunately, this job is done in an excellent book, *Karl Marx and the British Labour Movement*, by Collins and Abramsky.

Reading it is the equivalent of a *very* long Special Note appended to this volume.

The alliance broke up when its trade-union wing ceased to move in a progressive direction. To be sure, it was rocked by the Paris Commune and the daring position which the International was led by Marx to take on this heinous subversion of civilization (so described by the bourgeois press). But, more decisively, it began falling apart as the British trade-unionists moved into another kind of politics—bourgeois politics. It was not Marx but the trade-unionist wing that became restless and finally fractious because of the direction in which the International was steadily developing.

The question of support to the Paris Commune did not at first enter as a divisive issue. When Marx read his address on *The Civil War in France* to the General Council, it was adopted unanimously and without a murmur of dissent.[23] To be sure, the subsequent blast of horror-stricken denunciation in the press made weak knees tremble and reinforced pre-existing tendencies; but for some time after, the most schismatic of the reformists (John Hales in particular) put on a left face by ganging up with the Bakuninists against Marx. In short, the split between Marx and the British trade-unionists was not brought about because Marx insisted on lining the International up on the side of an unpopular radical issue in France. While it was not Marx who decided that the progressive alliance called the International had to be broken, he had to recognize when the strain of rightward drift became intolerable.[24]

Marx had seen the signs even before the Commune crisis. Less than a year before, soon after the Franco-Prussian War had started, he wrote his French friends that the English workers were right in saying "A plague on both their houses" and in opposing designs by the "English oligarchy" to support war against France, and he added:

> °°For my own part, I do everything in my power, through the means of the *International,* to stimulate this "Neutrality" spirit and to baffle the *"paid"* (paid by the "respectables") leaders of the English working class who strain every nerve to mislead them.[25]

Two years later, a letter by Engels indicated that he (and Marx, of course) realized how the General Council was breaking down; the letter spoke of a key figure's demoralization "by his dealings with English

agitators and °trading politicians and Trades-Unions paid secretaries,°
who here nowadays are all bought up, or begging to be bought up, by
the middle class . . ."[26]

Marx brought the break out into the open a few months later, at the
Hague congress of the International. It was apparently precipitated
semi-accidentally, on a side issue. Two of the British labor leaders who
were in process of going over to Liberal politics, Hales and Mottershead,
questioned the credentials of one Maltman Barry (who was expected to
vote with Marx) on no stated ground whatever. Instead of giving
reasons, Mottershead made the sniping remark that Barry was not a
workers' leader in England. This fired Marx. According to the minutes:

> Marx says that whom a section elects is no one else's concern;
> moreover, it redounds to Barry's honor that he does not belong
> among the so-called leaders of the English workers, since these
> people are more or less bought up by the bourgeoisie and the
> government; Barry was attacked only because he would not serve
> as Hales's tool. *

Marx's outspoken denunciation formalized the end of the two-
current alliance for a whole period, as the trade-union leaders shifted
their alliance to an entirely different current. The labor movement was
entering into an era of bureaucratic encrustation which lasted until the
"New Unionism." Marx and Engels later referred back to this break
only with satisfaction at having done their duty. Shortly after the
Hague Congress, Hales tried to stir up the General Council against Marx
because of the latter's disrespectful remarks about labor leaders, but his
efforts only boomeranged against him.[32] At the end of the year, Engels

---

* So in a set of minutes certified by Cuno and Sorge and sent to Marx.[27] There
are three other versions, without essential differences. In another set of minutes,
which was published in 1958, the wording is almost the same.[28] Barry himself
wrote up the congress for the London *Standard*, and related the incident as
follows:

> He (Mottershead) asserted that Barry was not a recognised leader of
> English working men. . . . Marx said no fault had been found in Barry, and
> the validity of the mandate had not been contested. The question of fitness
> was one for the section making the appointment. As to the accusation that
> Barry was not a recognised leader of English working men, that was an
> honour, for almost every recognised leader of English working men was
> sold to Gladstone, Morley, Dilke, and others.[29]

Bakunin's lieutenant Guillaume wrote it up long afterward in his characteristically
distorted fashion.[30] The accuracy of Marx's view of the financial links between
the trade-union leaders and the Liberal Party machine has been established in
some detail by Royden Harrison.[31]

noted that there were various parliamentary exercises being undertaken by some people: "And what people? With a few exceptions, they consist of the labor leaders whom Marx branded as corrupt at The Hague!"[33] Two years later, the issue was a retrospective one for Marx:

> In England . . . the industrial workers must above all get rid of their present leaders. When I denounced these fellows at the Hague Congress, I knew that I would thereby let myself in for unpopularity, slander, etc., but such consequences have always been immaterial to me. Here and there it is beginning to be realized that in making that denunciation I was only fulfilling a duty.[34]

Writing to a Communard in 1876, Marx mentioned that "the rascals, so-called workers' leaders (Englishmen) whom I exposed at the Hague Congress" were still getting money from the Liberal politicians. "These workers' leaders, Mottershead, etc., are the same curs with whom it was impossible to organize a meeting against the executioners of the Commune."[35] The English labor movement "has decayed into petty-minded trade-union stuff and the so-called leaders, including Eccarius, dangle after the liberal bourgeoisie," reported Engels.[36] Marx's wife Jenny was no doubt reflecting the family consensus when she wrote a friend:

> About English workers à la Mottershead, Eccarius, Hales, Jung, etc., let me say nothing. They are all arch-rascals, up for sale and bought and sold, and chasing after an honest shilling °by hook and by crook.° A really pitiful crew![37]

Marx looked back in a letter of 1878 and summed up the past period:

> The English working class has been gradually becoming more and more deeply demoralized by the period of corruption since 1848 and had at last got to the point when it was nothing more than the tail of the Great Liberal Party, i.e., of its *oppressors*, the capitalists. Its direction had passed completely into the hands of the venal trade-union leaders and professional agitators. These fellows shouted and howled behind the Gladstones, Brights, Mundellas, Morleys and the whole gang of factory owners, etc., *in majorem gloriam* [to the greater glory] of the Tsar as the emancipator of nations, while they never raised a finger for their own brothers in South Wales, condemned by the mine-owners to die of starvation. Wretches![38]

In 1887, referring back to such labor leaders and their parliamentary aspirations, Engels wrote that "We had to fight them since the founding of the International."[39] But "we" had also had to work with them—up to a point, and with certain preconditions.

And so the organizational formula of the International proved itself to be an enlightening experiment by failing. At the International's 1871 conference, the resolution on political action had said that "in the militant state of the working class, its economical movement and its political action are indissolubly united."[40] United in one organization? This form of unity was very dissoluble indeed. And yet unity in some form was vital to the success of both arms of the movement.

Separation into two autonomous arms raised its own problems. In England the trade-union movement (before and after the International, and outside of it) grew up for decades without any workers' political movement in existence; in Germany the socialist movement came into existence first, and was instrumental in creating the economic organizations. From these different directions, there was always the problem of cohabitation.

In the former type of case—trade unions without a political movement alongside—it was a question of establishing the missing arm. This is what Engels told his trade-union readers in his article series of 1881:

> This knowledge [that the fundamental evil is the wages system itself] once generally spread amongst the working class, the position of Trades Unions must change considerably. They will no longer enjoy the privilege of being the only organisations of the working class. At the side of, or above, the Unions of special trades there must spring up a general Union, a political organisation of the working class as a whole.[41]

There was a similar problem in the United States, which typically could not be grasped by the sectist minds of the Socialist Labor Party groups there. In 1891 the New York section of the S.L.P. decided to affiliate to the Central Labor Federation of the city (as if the latter were the International), and the American Federation of Labor under Gompers refused to charter the city federation because of the socialist affiliation. Engels gave the opinion that the socialist sect was in the wrong for insisting. The A.F.L. was an association of trade unions only; hence it had the "formal right" to reject non–trade-union bodies. "I cannot judge from here, of course," added Engels, "whether it was *propagandistically* advisable to expose oneself to such a rejection. But it was beyond question that it had to come, and I, for one, cannot blame Gompers for it."[42]

The two-arm pattern conformed to practical needs, and seemed to be fixed. But not before Marx had to deal with another attempt at fusing the two arms, this time in Germany.

4. EXPERIMENT IN PARTY-CONTROLLED TRADE UNIONS

In Germany, where political organization had pre-empted the field, could the indissoluble unity of the two arms be ensured by simply making trade-unionism an arm of the political party? The same sectist mentalities that had led the Socialist Labor Party of America in this direction also dominated the Lassallean organization in Germany.

The first socialist group in Germany, founded by Lassalle, had arisen entirely within the tradition of hostility to trade unions that was characteristic of all pre-Marx socialism. But in the 1860s, trade unions started forming without the Lassalleans' permission. By 1868, the Lassallean organization, now led by J. B. von Schweitzer, was faced with the threat of a congress, called for Berlin, which was going to consider setting up a broad trade-union movement. The majority of the Lassalleans were in favor of a point-blank hostile attitude to the trade-union congress, as an enemy encroachment on their turf. Schweitzer, however, jammed through a more flexible tactic to achieve a similar end: his party organization would not kill but rather take over the rival movement, and then make sure it remained a creature of the political leadership without real autonomy. Its constituent trade unions would be controlled, by statute and in a formal manner, by the leadership of the party—that is, by Schweitzer. Thus his way of scotching the danger of an independent trade-union movement was to make it an appendage to his political empire.

Marx set his face strongly against this course: the trade unions must be built on the basis of organizational autonomy in order to perform their basic functions in a healthy manner. Then this autonomous movement would have to decide, soon or late, its own relationship to the political movement of the class, with the socialists within it pressing for their own position on this like everyone else.

This, to Marx, meant "the development of a *real* workers' organization in Germany based on trade unions." Schweitzer (wrote Marx to Engels) was afraid that in this case "his artificial league of sectarians °would soon be nowhere.°"[43] Engels agreed that the Berlin congress must be "a *real* workers' congress, not simply a duplicate of the [Lassallean] congress" with no one but Lassalleans in its ranks.[44] Furthermore, wrote Engels, it appears from the Lassallean paper that Schweitzer would like to carry over the "rigid structure" of his party organization to the trade-union movement; and this, Engels thought, was unlikely to succeed since the workers would not stand for dictatorship over their economic livelihood.[45] Once he lost his tight organization and was no longer able to "play at dictator," the change would be fatal to him.[46] Marx was of the same opinion: ". . . Schweitzer thinks he can simply replace his dictatorship over the [Lassallean] G.G.W.A. with a dictatorship over the German working class. This is very naive."[47]

As the issue came to a head Marx prepared to state his views to Schweitzer in explicit terms. He told Engels in advance that he was going to attack Schweitzer's position that "two organizations can only be harmful" and that the trade-union organization must give way to the political. Schweitzer wanted "his own workers' movement," but Marx's letter would "make clear to him that he must choose between the 'sect' and the 'class.' "[48] This Marx did some days later, in an important letter from which we have already quoted his views on party democracy.[49] The main burden of the letter was insistence on the autonomy of the burgeoning trade unions from party dictatorship. As planned, this was cast in the form of insistence on the independence of the movement of the "class" (trade unions) from the "sect" (the Lassallean party).

Lassalle, explained Marx, made the mistake of founding a sect: "instead of looking among the genuine elements of the class movement for the real basis of his agitation, he wanted to prescribe the course to be followed by this movement according to a certain doctrinaire recipe." What defines a sect? In this letter Marx put it as follows: "The sect sees the justification for its existence and its point of honor not in what it has in *common* with the class movement but in the *particular shibboleth* which *distinguishes* it from the movement."

The rise of the trade unions as real workers' organizations (continued Marx) gave the Lassallean sect the opportunity "to merge in the class movement and make an end of all sectarianism." Its political content would then be carried into the broader movement "as an element enriching it." Instead, "you [Schweitzer] actually demanded of the class movement that it should subordinate itself to the movement of a particular sect." Therefore the suspicion arises that "whatever happens you want to preserve your 'own workers' movement.' " Instead of collaborating with other socialists in connection with the Berlin trade-union congress, you Lassalleans simply took over control; as for the others, "you only left them the alternative of either *joining* you or *opposing* you," and gave the congress the appearance of a mere "enlarged edition" of the preceding Lassallean party congress.[50]

Such "enlarged editions" of a controlling party later became known as front organizations. This is what Engels had in mind in writing to Marx a few days later. The Lassallean sectarians intend that their political organization

> will play the same role in the new trades unions (only publicly) as our old secret league [Communist League] did in the public workers' associations. The trades unions will form only the exoteric section of the Only True Lassallean Church, but the latter remains the Only True Church.[51]

In 1847–1848 the Communist League, in London and elsewhere, organized the German Workers Educational Association as such an "exoteric section" (front organization), as a broader recruiting and agitational arena and as the legal front of a movement which might be outlawed. While no longer conspiratorially organized, the League still recognized the need for secrecy: this was one difference from the Lassalleans' situation. Secondly, a real trade-union movement, as the elementary movement of the working class, could not be regarded in the same light as an ordinary club or a social-fraternal-educational society; the comparison showed what was wrong with the sectarian conception of the Lassalleans.*

---

* In 1875 a letter by Engels contained a peculiar formulation which seems to bear on this question. Writing to the German party about the defects of the Gotha program, he noted the necessity of including mention of trade-unionism,[52] and added:

> Considering the importance which this [trade-union] question has attained also in Germany, it would be absolutely necessary in our opinion to mention it in the program and if possible to leave open a place for it in the party organization.[53]

Leave open a place for *what* in the party organization? A place for the trade

5. THE PRIMACY OF
THE POLITICAL MOVEMENT

Insistence on the organizational autonomy of the trade unions, however, does not settle the problem of the relationship between the two arms of the class; it only makes a healthy solution possible. It could not be an end in itself for Marx, or for anyone who denied that the trade-union struggle by itself could emancipate the proletariat, and who believed that the class struggle in its generalized form tended to become a political struggle. The general war had to be led by a general staff that was conscious of the general political tasks and organized around these tasks.

For Marx, therefore, the political movement is primary, that is, it should assume the overall leadership of the class. In the light of Marx's controversy with Schweitzer among other enlightening episodes, this primacy of the political movement can be spelled out as follows: The political organization of revolutionists which aspires to be accepted as leader of the class-in-movement has the job of convincing the autonomous trade-union movement to follow its counsels and policies. This is its essential trade-union work.

Moreover, we must now add that the picture has been considerably oversimplified by talking about only *two* arms of movements of labor. Already in Marx's and Engels' time there were other arms of the labor movement developing: cooperatives, cultural and educational organizations, an independent as well as a party press, special protective funds, and so on. If the needs of the struggle required that there be a certain amount of coordination and congruence among the lesser and greater arms of the labor movement, Marx—and most others—had no doubt that the political movement was in the best position to provide such leadership and guidance. This was not a very controversial question in most quarters. The problem was how this task of the political organization should be carried out, not to speak of by whom.

For Marx, certain elementary considerations are dictated by his approach to the problem. By its nature the trade-union movement consists—and should consist—of workers at quite different stages and

---

unions *in*—literally inside—the party organization would go beyond even Schweitzer's practice; this cannot be the meaning. Engels may have had in mind a place in the party organization for the direction of the party's trade-union cadres and their work.

degrees of class-consciousness, trade-union consciousness, and political consciousness. Considered as a school, it has an infinite number of grades, or gradations, from primitive wage-consciousness all the way to full agreement with a revolutionary socialist program. As they approach the latter end of the spectrum, workers will tend to join the political party of socialism, perhaps recruited by fellow workers who have gone before them. They in turn may seek to recruit their brothers and sisters in the unions. Thus the trade unions are in part a recruiting ground for the political movement. Where could it want a better one? asked Engels. Writing of the desirability of getting a big A.F.L. delegation from the United States to come to the International Socialist Congress at Brussels in 1891, he remarked, "They would see many things there that would disconcert them in their narrowminded trade-union stand-point—and besides, where do you want to find a recruiting ground if not in the trade unions?"[54] Twenty years before, in a letter offering general advice to the American section of the International, Marx spelled this out: "The Trades Union you must try to win °at all costs.°"[55]

But the trade-union movement is not merely a recruiting ground from Marx's standpoint, since it has its own elementary functions whether there is a political movement or not. Since it is also an arena of continuing struggle, the political party will not aim to "graduate" its trade-union recruits out of their unions (in the usual meaning of recruitment), but rather will be interested in forming a consciously revolutionary cadre of socialist trade-unionists inside this basic class movement, to fructify and leaven its work along the lines discussed in section 1 of this chapter. In fact, recruitment does not chiefly mean gaining members but making adherents; short of that, bringing as many trade-unionists as possible nearer political agreement. In a word, the ability of a political party to lead and guide the trade unions would be decided by its ability to develop a framework of socialist members and supporters inside the economic arm.

Thus a type of unity between the two arms could be established which would be entirely different in operation and in consequences from Schweitzer's simple mechanism of party dictatorship. In 1878—after the Lassallean group had disappeared by merger into the German Social-Democracy and after the Bebel-Liebknecht policy of autonomous trade unions had triumphed—Engels praised the German movement for the symbiotic relationship of mutual reinforcement that had taken shape:

> °°A great advantage to the German movement is that the Trades' organization works hand in hand with the political organization. The immediate advantages offered by the Trades' organization draw many an otherwise indifferent mass into the political movement, while the community of political action hold[s] together, and assures mutual support to, the otherwise isolated Trades Unions.[56]

In seeking to give political guidance to the trade unions, a proletarian political movement differs in no way formally from the bourgeois parties, particularly the bourgeois liberal parties which have traditionally sought to make the labor movement part of its own entourage and recruit its forces and energies for the liberals' political fortunes. Marx, as we have seen, was in a position to watch this working out, as his former trade-unionist colleagues of the General Council went over to the Liberal Party and then—seeing the world turned left to right in their new ideological mirrors—bitterly accused socialists of "meddling" in their unions as outside agitators. Indeed, it became a tradition that the same trade-union bureaucracy which systematically used its own apparatus inside the unions to subordinate them to bourgeois politics, indignantly denounced efforts by a workers' party to reach the membership as somehow illegitimate if not downright subversive.*

The view that the political struggle is primary was not in the least peculiar to Marx, nor to socialism. Inside the socialist movement, however, an alternative view—that it is the trade-union movement that should be regarded as sufficient for the road to socialism—cropped up occasionally and crystallized as *syndicalism;* it will be discussed in the last section of this chapter.

---

* The Social-Democratic form of this tradition did not become prominent inside the socialist movement until after Engels' death, although three years before that, Carl Legien, who was to become the chief of trade-union reformism in Germany, had enunciated the principle that trade unions must be "neutral" in party politics.[57] It was in 1906 that the issue came to a head in the German party, in the context of the rise of Bernstein's "Revisionism." The alleged principle of "trade-union neutrality" was the formula by which reformists sought to prevent a trade-union movement from deciding to support *socialists;* where the trade unions were supporting bourgeois politicians and functioning as political appendages of bourgeois parties, the reformists swung happily into line. While the later Second International debates on "trade-union neutrality" are outside our purview, we

6. FORMS OF LABOR POLITICAL ACTION

For Marx the exact form of the relationship to be established between the trade unions and a workers' party was an open question, depending on the development of both movements in a particular country and time. It was neither necessary nor possible to establish prefabricated models or molds. Writing to Spanish workers on behalf of the General Council and hence also of Marx, Engels explained:

> Experience has everywhere proved that the best means of liberating the workers from this domination of the old parties is to found in each country a proletarian party with its own policy, a policy clearly distinguished from that of other parties, since it has to express the conditions of emancipation of the working class. The details of this policy may vary according to the particular circumstances in each country. . . .[58]

Even more, the details of organizational form would be sure to vary. We have touched on the different pattern of development in Germany and England; let us sketch Marx's reaction to events in these countries.

In 1869 Wilhelm Liebknecht—after long prodding by Marx—was finally impelled by events to break with his long-standing policy of opportunist alliance with a bourgeois liberal party; he went along with the founding of a new socialist party that offered an alternative to the Lassallean sect. This party, founded at Eisenach, was based largely on trade-unionists—from the trade-union wing of the Lassalleans breaking with the Schweitzer dictatorship, and from independent trade unions that had been founded with Bebel's help on an autonomous model. But the new "Eisenacher" party was not based on the trade unions in its organizational structure (in the way that the British Labor Party is today), nor did it aim at being so constituted. Such an organic relationship might have stunted the development of both arms.

Marx greeted this step as a positive one, and supported the Eisenacher party. This did not lead him to believe that this German pattern was a model for England.

In England the politicalization of labor was going through painful stages. Far behind was the Chartist period, when voteless workers

---

must note that this slippery formula had nothing whatever to do with Marx's view about the organizational autonomy of trade unions with relation to political parties.

barged into the political process as a revolutionary force from the outside. As the workers received the ballot, it became worth the while of the bourgeois parties to take them in tow. The Reform Bill of 1867, by the same token, made it possible for labor leaders to think of rising to heights commensurate with their ambitions. Two prerequisites were votes and money; the former could be traded for the latter. The votes were to come from workers; the money had to be begged from the Liberal moneybags, such as the industrialist Samuel Morley, a leading political broker. The labor leader George Howell, having left the General Council of the International in 1869, plaintively wrote to a bourgeois politician: "Cannot something be done to pave the way for a few working men to go into the House? Some of us have to stand in the character of obstructives [inside the trade unions] because we will not consent to the revival of the old Chartist Practice, that of opposing all parties except those pledged to labour questions." [59] He pointed in alarm to the fact that proposals for "direct representation of labour" were cropping up "in a most unpleasant manner."

"Nobody holds it against the 'labor leaders' that they would have liked to get into Parliament," wrote Engels in the German press after the 1874 elections. "The shortest way would have been to proceed at once to form anew a strong workers' party with a definite program . . ." But instead—

> In order to get into Parliament the "labor leaders" had recourse, in the first place, to the votes and money of the bourgeoisie and only in the second place to the votes of the workers themselves. But by doing so they ceased to be workers' candidates and turned themselves into bourgeois candidates. They did not appeal to a working-class party that still had to be formed but to the bourgeois "great Liberal Party."

To further their careers in bourgeois politics, they set up a Labor Representation League, and, under the guidance of the Liberal industrialist, "drew up a 'labor program' to which any bourgeois could subscribe and which was to form the foundation of a mighty movement to chain the workers politically still more firmly to the bourgeoisie and, as these gentry thought, to get the 'founders' into Parliament." [60]

The case was better when unions went for "direct representation"; in the 1874 election, miners' unions got two union secretaries into Parliament. "At any rate," wrote Engels, "the ice has been broken and two workers now have seats in the most fashionable debating club of Europe ..." They would not be able to play a role in Parliament, he added, but still "the elections of 1874 have indisputably ushered in a new phase in English political development."[61]

These were halting efforts and half-way forms as compared with the step that Marx advocated, an openly independent workers' party; and indeed he and Engels criticized publicly and privately the inadequacy of the ways in which the labor leaders were moving into politics. At the same time they exhibited the objectively progressive meaning of what was actually happening, for they were not victims of the later mystique according to which anything tagged "progressive" must be advocated and supported. It was by criticism, not approval, that they sought to move the advanced elements of the class beyond the bourgeoisified forms in which they were still imprisoned.

One of the progressive consequences of the new steps taken by the labor leaders in pursuit of their political ambitions was—these leaders' self-exposure. Such exposure as the outcome of experience was one of the most important processes in the education of a class. Just before the 1874 election Engels had written to a German comrade that he hoped the ambitious bureaucrats *would* get elected:

> Here the whole mass of labor leaders paid by the bourgeoisie, especially by [Samuel] Morley, put themselves forward with all their strength *to be elected to Parliament as °working men's candidates°* BY THE BOURGEOIS. But they probably won't be successful, much as I would wish the whole gang to get in, on the same ground that I am glad of the election of Hasenclever and Hasselmann [in Germany] ...[62]

For these people would expose their real politics before their proletarian constituencies, just as (Engels continued) Schweitzer had "ruined himself" in the Reichstag.

A decade later, Engels was still observing new steps forward in this process, always slower than his hopes.

> ... a new period will date from the next elections, even if this does not show itself with all speed. There will be workers in Parliament, in growing numbers, and each one will be worse than the other. But that is necessary here [in England]. All the scoundrels who played the role of bourgeois-radical philistines here in the International's day must show themselves in Parlia-

ment just as they are. Then the masses will become socialist here too. Industrial overproduction will do the rest.[63]

In fact it took more than three decades for events to approximate this rough scenario. But in another decade, things were at least on the move. The form of "direct representation" (trade-union campaigns for trade-union candidates) was putting more and more workers into Parliament. Engels hailed the fact that there was increasing support for direct representation from, for example, the textile workers:

> ... and a Manchester labor newspaper calculated that the Lancashire textile workers might control twelve seats in Parliament in this county alone. As you see, it is the trade union that will enter Parliament. It is the branch of industry and not the class that [as yet] demands representation. Still, it is a step forward. Let us first smash the enslavement of the workers to the big bourgeois parties; let us have textile workers in Parliament just as we already have miners there. As soon as a dozen branches of industry are represented, class-consciousness will arise of itself.[64]

Direct representation was a "step forward" to the establishment of a political party that carried this form to its logical conclusion, as the formation of the Labor Party did later. With this background, the organizational form of the workers' party in England became quite different from the German exemplar.

The English model—a workers' party based on the organizational structure of the trade unions—was also probably expected by Marx in that other country where unionization had preceded a mass socialist organization: the United States. Interviewed by an American newspaperman, Marx was quoted as saying: "Upon Trades-Unions, in many countries, have been built political organizations. In America the need of an independent Workingmen's party has been made manifest. They can no longer trust politicians . . ."[65] This statement is in line with other indications of Marx's views, as well as Engels'; it is acknowledgment of a possibility, one that would be welcomed, but not prescribed. The road to a workers' party by *structurally* founding it on the organized trade-union movement was one alternative, but only one, under given historical circumstances. That was as far as Marx was concerned to press the issue.

7. "REVOLUTIONARY UNIONISM" AND SYNDICALISM

Marx's conception of the place of trade unions in the class struggle makes it clear that he gave short shrift to the notion of "revolutionary trade unions" as an ultimatistic demand. The subject requires some comment only because of later developments.

This notion has already come up in two connections. Although we have emphasized the Lassalleans' taste for party-controlled unions, it will come as no surprise to learn that the Lassalleans themselves put the matter in other terms: they wanted to ensure the socialist character and ideological purity of the trade unions. Party domination was the means of enforcing this revolutionary requirement. The case of the Socialist Labor Party in the United States was similar, even though these American Lassalleans (often called Marxists) did not have as big a movement to operate on as their German congeners did.

In both these cases, and in many others to come, Marx's view of the trade union as the elementary organ of class struggle was rejected in favor of the traditional ultimatum of the sect: *If you workers do not adopt the Only True Faith, we hereby read you out of the proletariat.*

Such theories of "revolutionary unionism" leave no room for the existence of autonomous arms of the class; one must pre-empt the others. If the Lassalleans saw a role only for the political party, this exclusiveness suggested its own mirror image, which came to be called syndicalism.* The trade union is substituted for the political party as the overall organizer of workers' power and the future society. The trade union, in effect, takes on all political roles (while rejecting the term *political* as inapplicable). The trade union, therefore, becomes the revolutionary vanguard, that is, an advanced portion of the class, and is no longer the elementary and broad organizer of workers as yet unclass-conscious. From Marx's standpoint, when the trade union takes the place of political organization, nothing takes the place of the trade union, whose role in the class struggle is left a vacuum.

This fatally narrowed conception of trade-unionism existed only in embryonic form in Marx's time; it cropped up only sporadically in the

---

* So in English; but since *syndicalisme* is simply the French word for trade-unionism, the less ambiguous term *revolutionary syndicalism* is common in Continental languages.

International. Impetus to ideas of this sort came especially out of the Proudhonist antipathy to political action per se; such antipoliticism lay behind some disputes in the movement.

A primitive expression of this notion came up at the 1868 Brussels congress of the International in connection with the war question on the agenda; the answer proposed was a general strike as the reply to a declaration of war. Since "it would suffice for the working men to strike work to render war impossible," the resolution recommended that the workers "cease work in case a war be declared in their country." This resolution, pushed by the Belgian delegates and supported by the French, was actually adopted.[66] Marx was apparently unaware of its adoption when he read about the proposal in Eccarius' *Times* report of the congress; he wrote Engels that Eccarius "ascribed to the Germans and English the Belgian nonsense, °to *strike against war*.°"[67] (The German delegates had proposed a different resolution, and it is not clear from the minutes how the Belgian version came to be adopted, since this seems to have taken place at an administrative session.)[68]

The proposal was "nonsense" to Marx because such a general strike could only precipitate an all-out confrontation with the state power for control over society—commonly called a revolution. The Belgian resolution, therefore, was not about a very big strike but was a modest proposal that a revolution should be proclaimed by resolution.

In early 1869 the Belgian leader De Paepe reformulated his Proudhonist conceptions into what we can now recognize to be a definitely syndicalist proposal: the future social order, he argued, must be based on the International's own institutions, especially trade unions. He put these ideas forward at the Basel Congress; they were echoed by the Swiss and Spanish Bakuninists; and in Geneva, even J. P. Becker, a friend of Marx's with congenitally unstable politics, began to repeat the talk about substituting trade unions for political organization. Engels wrote wonderingly to Marx:

> Old Becker must have gone clean out of his head. How can he decree that the °Trades Union° *has* to be the real workers' association and basis of all organization, and that the other forms of organization *have* to remain only provisional alongside it, etc. All this in a country where proper °trades unions° still don't even exist. And what a complicated "organization."[69]

In fact, syndicalist notions often flourished where "proper trade unions" had not yet developed, that is, where the concept of the trade union was not yet that of a real class organization but mostly a theoretical construct. It is clear that Marx and Engels dismissed out of hand such ideas as Becker had started to develop. In 1870, assuming that these ideas were emanating from Bakuninist circles, Marx, writing to a friend, pointed to them as one example of the poverty of Bakunin's "theoretical baggage." According to this view, he wrote, °°"The working class must not occupy itself with *politics*. They must only organise themselves by trades-unions. One fine day, by means of the *Internationale* they will supplant the place of all existing states. You see what a caricature he has made of my doctrines!"[69a] At this point Marx plainly did not think the notion needed refutation. *

At the International's London Conference of 1871, similar ideas came out of a murky discussion of the proposal by French delegate Delahaye to favor the formation of international federations of trade unions which would be, inter alia, models of "the real commune of the future."[70] In the ensuing discussion Marx and Engels both summarized reasons why the trade unions are necessarily limited in their tasks and possibilities, and especially stressed that even in England the trade unions had not organized most workers. We have cited some of their remarks in another context.[71] On this question their purpose was to explain why it was not the trade unions that could be viewed as the structural basis of socialist society; in this connection the scant minutes record only the following:

> He [Marx] denies that it is the commune of the future because [this] project rests on the division of labor, principal cause of the slavery of the workers. It may ameliorate the lot of the workers a little, but it cannot be offered as an ideal.[72]

Objections from other delegates pointed out that the adoption of the Delahaye scheme would leave no reason for existence for the International itself, as for any political movement. The Delahaye resolution was defeated.

The substance of the syndicalist idea was encountered from an

---

* In spite of all, syndicalistic notions have been attributed to Marx on the sole basis of a certain conversation with an obscure German trade-unionist named Hamann, which took place shortly after the above-quoted correspondence about Becker. Since references to this conversation with Hamann keep popping up, the facts are set forth in Special Note B.

unexpected source a few years later: Professor Dühring, who wanted to found a school of socialism of his own, made it an accusation against socialists in general. In *Anti-Dühring* Engels quotes Dühring's statement that the conception of "collective ownership" is unclear because "this conception of the future always gives the impression that it means nothing more than corporative ownership by groups of workers." Engels dismisses this as simply a baseless falsehood.[73]

That Dühring had plucked the notion out of the air at all showed that it was floating around. A caution is necessary. Because of the later association of syndicalism with anarchism, violence, revolutionary phrases, and so on, it has a literary aura of revolutionism about it; but this should not be antedated. During the years we are concerned with, radical views that sought to replace political action with trade-union organization were more than likely to be reformist-oriented, a flight from the revolutionary task of directly confronting state power. (In fact, this also conditions the later history of syndicalism, but that is another story.)

Thus, against various socialist alternatives, Marx had to make clear his own distinctive view of the relationship between the economic movement of the trade unions and the political movement of a party or party-like organization. Trade unions were training grounds of the class, as well as its first line of defense, but the goal of the training was still a political and social revolution.

6 | THE PRINCIPLE
OF CLASS SELF-EMANCIPATION

We have emphasized in several ways that Marx's socialism was above all a *class socialism*—a theory about the social struggle of a class, embedded in a theory of societal dynamics—and that this is what was unique about it. The main difficulty with grasping this notion is that it appears to be so simple and transparent, when in fact it is neither—as the history of Marxist sects proved while Marx and Engels were still alive. The same is true of another famous phrase associated with their class socialism: *the self-emancipation of the proletariat.*

1. FROM CHARTISM
TO THE INTERNATIONAL

Praise for the idea of self-emancipation is usually as obligatory as hatred of sin, respect for motherhood, and hopes for the Good Life. Only a certain British aristocratic household has dared to revel in the family motto, *"Tout d'en haut,"* which describes the practical politics of the world.[1] Like all laudable aspirations, talk of self-emancipation goes back very far—it was probably already well known in Olduvai Gorge—especially under the label of *self-help.* The inculcation of self-help has always been popular among the people who would otherwise be obliged to provide the help, and who therefore easily recognize it as a virtue of the poor. In England the bourgeoisie made a contribution of this sort to legitimizing the idea of self-emancipation among the working classes.

The literature of the Chartist movement fused self-emancipation with the idea of political struggle. The principle of self-emancipation, as an invocation to rely only on proletarian forces for proletarian goals, was a platitude in the Chartist movement, above all on the left, while Marx was still in school. It did not take a Marx to invent it; on the contrary, it probably arose spontaneously out of the facts of class mistrust, wherever the pattern of the class struggle enforced its lessons. It gave rise to attitudes repudiating the sanctity of charity, the Lord-is-my-shepherd hosannas, fidelity to the Master, and a host of other virtues beloved of ruling classes: "To us there is nothing so hateful, so detestable, so offensive, as a patronising, mendacious magnanimity," wrote an English workers' paper.[2]

The idea of self-emancipation was so common in the Chartist left that it is easy to suppose that the German émigrés in its midst heard it as often as anyone, as well as knowing all the German self-help saws. A few months before the *Communist Manifesto*, Marx's associate Wilhelm Wolff wrote an article in the Communist League's paper in which he exhorted: "in truth no one will or can free us proletarians if we do not do it *ourselves.*" Typically he introduced this with a German proverb, *"Selbst ist der Mann"* (roughly: Let George do it but you yourself are George), which breathes the old air of self-help.[3]

So when Marx wrote the aphoristic formulation of the principle into the first clause of the International's *Rules:*

> CONSIDERING, That the emancipation of the working classes must be conquered by the working classes themselves . . .[4]

it was the embodiment of a long-standing and widely used idea, though it is from this source that the formula became so famous that it was repeated by various elements who did not believe a word of it. This use also gave it sufficient prominence to come to the attention of academic historians of socialism who had no idea what it meant. Thus, the eminent Belgian historian Emile de Laveleye—one of those who, Engels rightly remarked, spread nothing but "lies and legends" about the history of the International[5]—wrote in 1881, in a much republished book:

> The International also affirmed that "the emancipation of the laborers must be the work of the laborers themselves." This idea seemed an application of the principle of "self-help"; it enlisted for the new association, even in France, the sympathies of many distinguished men who little suspected how it was to be interpreted later on. This affords a new proof of the fact, frequently

observed, that revolutionary movements always go on increasing in violence. The originators of the movement . . . are replaced by the more fanatical, who, in their turn, are pushed aside, until the final abyss is reached to which wild revolutionary logic inevitably leads.[6]

In contrast to this learned liberal, the reactionary historian of the International, Villetard, understood very quickly that the militants of the International were so wildly fanatical as to believe exactly what the principle of self-emancipation said. "No idea, without excepting perhaps their hatred of capital," he charged, "entered more passionately into their heads and hearts." He quotes a French militant of the International who expressed these heinous sentiments: "We have proclaimed . . . that we no longer wanted deliverers, that we no longer wished to serve as instruments . . ."[7]

The principle of self-emancipation figured not only in the Rules of the International but also on the back of the individual's membership card, where it led off the brief statement of principles condensed from the Rules.[8] Documents of the International not written by Marx or Engels freely appealed to the same concept.* It must be remarked, however, that in two cases that come easily to hand the concept is seen emerging from the old self-help idea like Michelangelo's "Prisoners" from the rough marble. Thus, an address calling for an independent labor press drafted by some members of the General Council started with Poor Richard himself: "Benjamin Franklin is reported to have said, 'If you want a thing done, and well done, do it yourself,' and this is precisely what we must do . . . we must take the work of salvation into our own hands . . ."[12] And the Address of the Land and Labour League, which historian Royden Harrison thinks was partly written

---

* Aside from the manifestos, the General Council was made unaccustomedly sensitive to the question of *who* acted in their name. A small but symbolic point was worked out in the General Council meeting that adopted its well-known address to Abraham Lincoln: who was to present the document to the U.S. embassy? The minutes relate:

> A long discussion then took place as to the mode of presenting the address and the propriety of having a M.P. with the deputation; this was strongly opposed by many members who said working men should rely on themselves and not seek for extraneous aid.[9]

The motion that was passed limited the delegation to Council members. Marx reported to Engels:

> . . . *part* of the Englishmen on the Committee wanted to have the deputation introduced by a member of Parliament since it was customary. This

under the influence of Marx, exhorts: "There is one, and only one, remedy. Help yourselves."[13]

Later on, Engels rightly predated the conception to "the very beginning," before it had been adopted in the International: "our notion, from the very beginning, was that 'the emancipation of the working class must be the act of the working class itself,'" he wrote in a preface to the *Communist Manifesto*.[14] (This varies slightly the canonical formulation, as did Marx in another work.)[15] The *very* beginning has already been described in our Volume 1,[16] that is, the course of Marx's and Engels' development toward the conception before their own programmatic ideas had crystallized. The context indicates that Engels was thinking of the period around 1847 when the Manifesto was in preparation.

2. THE SIN OF CHARITY

By 1847 (as far as we can make out from published articles) the idea of self-emancipation merged in Marx's thinking with his view of the class struggle as the crux of socialist policy. The resultant fusion was expressed several times that year by both Marx and Engels. The immediate target was the bourgeoisie's best known alternative to working-class struggle. To be sure, all alternatives offered by society were efforts to convince the people that they need not act for themselves—"but the greatest of these is charity."

Peter had explained it long ago: "for charity shall cover the multitude of sins." It had also been explained in the Old Testament: "For the poor shall never cease out of the land: *therefore* I command thee, saying, Thou shalt open thine hands wide ..."[17] The holy injunction is given a very practical reason, we see. This sociological strategy of Christianity has often been the butt of radicals' denunciation. Marx took his turn in 1847, in a burst of indignation at a pious Prussian who

---

hankering was defeated by the majority of the English and the unanimity of the Continentals, and it was declared, on the contrary, that such old English customs ought to be abolished.[10]

There were other symbolic tests. In 1865 the General Council announced it had refused the proposal of a rich English lord who had offered an annual subsidy to be the organization's "protector."[11] The question of "Tory gold" was going to be an issue touching on Self-Emancipation all through the century.

had sermonized that "If only those whose calling it is to develop the social principles of Christianity do so, the Communists will soon be put to silence." Marx replied with some passion:

The social principles of Christianity have now had eighteen hundred years to develop and need no further development by Prussian Consistorial Councillors.

The social principles of Christianity have justified the slavery of antiquity and glorified medieval serfdom, and in case of need likewise acquiesce in defending the oppression of the proletariat, even though putting a doleful face on it.

The social principles of Christianity preach the necessity of a ruling and an oppressed class, and all they have for the latter is the pious wish the former will be charitable.

The social principles of Christianity assign the Consistorial compensation for all infamies to heaven and thereby justify the continuation of these infamies on earth.

The social principles of Christianity declare all vile acts of oppressors against the oppressed to be either just punishment for original sin and other sins, or trials that the Lord in his infinite wisdom imposes on the redeemed.

The social principles of Christianity preach cowardice, self-contempt, abasement, submissiveness, meekness, in short, all the qualities of *canaille;* and the proletariat, which is not willing to be treated as *canaille,* has need of its courage, its self-reliance, its pride and its sense of independence even more than of its bread.

The social principles of Christianity are cringing, and the proletariat is revolutionary.

So much for the social principles of Christianity.[18]

The article had already made the point that "the proletariat expects help from no one but itself."[19]

This was not Marx's first sally against philanthropism. In an earlier article he had said one of his purposes was to refute

the idea of the philanthropic bourgeois that it is only a question of providing a little bread and a little education for the proletarians, and that only the worker is stunted by the present state of society but otherwise the existing world is the best of all possible worlds.[20]

But Engels had so far outdone him in this line. In *The Condition of the Working Class in England* Engels had authentically reflected the

English left's attack on the charity system—"your self-complacent, Pharisaic philanthropy" which gives the victims a hundredth part of what has been plundered from their labor:

> Charity which degrades him who gives more than him who takes; charity which treads the downtrodden still deeper in the dust, which demands that the degraded, the pariah cast out by society, shall first surrender the last that remains to him, his very claim to manhood, shall first beg for mercy before your mercy deigns to press, in the shape of an alms, the brand of degradation upon his brow.[21]

By 1847 Engels was more inclined to put it politically, as when he attacked the French moderate republicans for their program of restricted democracy which emphasized "philanthropic charity" instead: "measures of pure charity, that is, measures to soften down the revolutionary energies of the proletarians." Welfare charity "is far from being based upon fraternity, whilst at the same time it is an insolent and very impotent denial of equality."[22] Such sentiments were familiar in the Chartist organ that published this article, but less so in the German paper which, about the same time, published his long criticism of the literature of the then prominent "True Socialist" tendency. This starts with a thrust at one Karl Beck's "Songs of the Poor Man," which begins with a poem addressed to the House of Rothschild.

> It is not the destruction of Rothschild's real power or the social conditions on which it is based that the poet threatens; no, he wishes only it should be used in a humanitarian way. He laments that the bankers are not socialistic philanthropists, not sentimental visionaries, not benefactors of humanity, but just bankers. Beck sings the praises of this cowardly, petty-bourgeois *misère*, of the "poor man," the *pauvre honteux*, with his poor, pious and contradictory desires, the "little man" in all his forms —not of the proud, menacing and revolutionary proletarian.[23]

About the same time, in his *Poverty of Philosophy*, Marx included a pungent page devoted to

> the *humanitarian school*, which ... seeks, by way of easing its conscience, to palliate even if slightly the real contrasts; it sincerely deplores the distress of the proletariat, the unbridled competition of the bourgeois among themselves; it counsels the workers to be sober, to work hard and to have few children; it

advises the bourgeois to put a judicious ardor into production. . . .

The *philanthropic* school is the humanitarian school carried to perfection. It denies the necessity of antagonism; it wants to turn all men into bourgeois . . . The philanthropists, then, want to retain the categories which express bourgeois relations, without the antagonism which constitutes them and is inseparable from them. They think they are seriously fighting bourgeois practice, and they are more bourgeois than the others.[24]

The *Communist Manifesto* repeats this more concisely, under the head of "bourgeois socialism," by which it means bourgeois social reform (for *social-ism* was then a common label simply for reformatory concern with the Social Question). Besides Proudhon--

> To this section belong economists, philanthropists, humanitarians, improvers of the condition of the working class, organizers of charity, members of societies for the prevention of cruelty to animals, temperance fanatics, hole-and-corner reformers of every imaginable kind.[25]

A little further the Manifesto points out that utopian socialism, despite its positive "critical" content, tends to degenerate into this kind of socialism too. "Only from the point of view of being the most suffering class does the proletariat exist for them." And "the proletariat, as yet in its infancy, offers to them the spectacle of a class without any historical initiative or any independent political movement." In contrast, the Manifesto's message is that the proletarian movement is "the self-conscious, independent movement of the immense majority, in the interests of the immense majority."[26]

Only a movement of the immense majority, in its own interests, could be a movement of self-emancipation. This moves out of the sphere of charity versus self-help, to become a basic determinant of the nature of socialism.

3. SHEEP AND SAVIORS

The principle of self-emancipation has this in common with the Golden Rule, that it is venerated as a maxim and violated to the maximum. Just as literal adherence to the Golden Rule would bring down present-day society, so conformity with the self-emancipation principle would dissolve most of the socialist sects that have existed. What self-emancipation meant to Marx and Engels is evident particularly in their criticisms of other socialisms of the time, as well as in their critique of ruling ideologies. One was as likely as the other to praise the vision of sheep following a Good Shepherd.

In a polemic by Engels against the "True Socialist" current, he gave an example of the sort of socialistic sentimental poetizing that deserved contempt. A True-Socialist versifier had burbled as follows (italics added by Engels):

> And yet at last will come
> The day . . .
> People shall sit together, hand in hand,
> Like *children* in the great hall of the heavens.
> Once more a chalice, a chalice shall pass around,
> Love's chalice at the *love* feast of the nations.[27]

The invocation of Love (which should be capitalized to indicate it has little to do with love) was often associated with such *Schwärmerei;* a political history of this empyreal Love as an instrument of mastery would be useful. Another celebrant of political-mystical Love whom Marx had to attack was Hermann Kriege, who departed European shores as a member of the Communist Correspondence Committee which Marx had fostered, and in America's greener pastures turned his "communism" into a petty-bourgeois radicalism that was discrediting to his former associates. Marx and Engels collaborated on a circular explaining to their American friends why Kriege was not a communist. The first part of this statement is devoted to Kriege's "Transformation of Communism into Love-Mongering." Other passages point to Kriege's pattern of treating political disciples as pious sheep. The point was not simply Kriege's religiosity, but how he put it to political use. According to Kriege, explained the circular, once the idol Mammon is overthrown the Reign of Joy begins:

> . . . and when this overthrow is accomplished, then come the prophets, the "we," who "teach" the proletarians what remains to be done. These prophets "teach" their disciples—who here appear to be singularly ignorant about their own interests—how they "should work and enjoy in common" . . .[28]

In the course of the 1848–1849 revolution, there was no lack of politicians who were anxious only to do the people good as long as the people refrained from doing it themselves. In one of his articles in the *Neue Rheinische Zeitung,* Engels found a parable. Praising the resistance of the Poles to Prussian conquest, he related a touching anecdote about a practical philanthropist, picked up from a biography of the priest Joseph Bonavita Blank. The holy man was frequented by birds that hovered on and about him; and the people wondered mightily to see this new St. Francis. No wonder: he had cut off the lower half of their beaks, so that they could get food only from his own charitable hands. Engels adds the moral:

> The birds, say his biographer, *loved* him *as their benefactor.*
> And the shackled, mangled, branded Poles refuse to love their Prussian benefactors! [29]

Or one could look to France for the same edifying pattern, where Bonaparte as emperor "intended to turn the French people into á flock of sheep, only fit for the shears, or to be led to nibble in silence under the shade of an enervating security."[30] Or to England, where Marx commented on the doings of the House of Lords: "The sentimental lords, who please themselves in treating the workingmen as their humble clients, feel exasperated whenever that rabble ask for rights instead of sympathies."[31]

The socialist sects could for the most part be divided between those whose leaders posed as messiahs and saviors and those who were engaged in seeking a messiah-savior. Of the former, Marx had experience with Lassalle and Weitling. Of the latter, Engels, writing to Marx from Paris, reported on the Louis Blanc type of socialists there:

> Like the wagon-driver in the fable, they seek the Hercules who is to pull the social cart out of the muck for them. [But] the Hercules resides in their own arms.[32]

A few months before, when Engels had visited Louis Blanc himself, "the little Great Man" had made a better impression temporarily: "he seems to have dropped the habit of taking a patronizing attitude with regard to the workers," Engels' letter reported.[33]

Marx was especially sensitive to the German pattern that he labeled *obrigkeitliche Sinn,* the mentality submissive to authority on high. We have in passing seen his reaction to this when it came up, as in his remark (cited in the preceding chapter) that "Here [in Germany] where the worker's life is regulated from childhood on by bureaucracy and he himself believes in the authorities, he must be taught before all else to walk by himself."[34] It was in the same connection—the case of Schweitzer—that Marx commented:

> For the German working class the most necessary thing of all is for it to cease conducting its agitation under the by-your-leave of higher authority. Such a bureaucratically schooled race must go through a complete course in "self-help."[35]

A year later, he ran across a passage in a Defoe novel that he had to share with Engels. Defoe, dealing with Gustavus Adolphus' 1630 intervention "in the German crap," wrote that the German Protestant princes "would have been very glad to have had the work done at another man's charge; but like true Germans they were more willing to be saved, than to save themselves, and therefore hung back . . ."[36] Marx underlined these words for his friend's benefit, as if chortling at the characterization of "true Germans." He might have recalled his first published article of 1842, in which he had deplored the fact that "Germans are by nature very submissive, excessively obedient and deferential."[37]

This sheep-and-savior pattern was highly visible in Germany for historical reasons, but it was by no means confined to that country. Ruling classes fostered it everywhere. In a manifesto written for the International, Marx dealt with recent Belgian massacres of strikers. The Belgian capitalist, he observed, was so liberty-loving that he rejected factory laws encroaching on his liberty.

> He shudders at the very idea that a common workman should be wicked enough to claim any higher destiny than that of enriching his master and natural superior. He wants his workman not only to remain a miserable drudge, overworked and underpaid, but, like every other slaveholder, he wants him to be a cringing, servile, broken-hearted, morally prostrate, religiously humble drudge. Hence his frantic fury at strikes. With him, a strike is a blasphemy, a slave's revolt, the signal of a social cataclysm.[38]

At a General Council meeting Marx put it sententiously, in a speech attacking English policy in Ireland: "The old English leaven of the conqueror comes out in the [government's] statement: we will grant but you must ask."[39] Old English leaven, German *obrigkeitliche Sinn*, French bureaucratic rigidity—this was the pattern inculcated by every exploitive society. For a thousand years or so, writers have repeated that the walls of Jericho fell before Joshua's trumpet, even though the Bible twice states that they fell when "the people shouted with a great shout."[40]

4. EMANCIPATION FROM BELOW

It is characteristic of a generality like the principle of self-emancipation that it can be understood concretely only through its application to problems of revolutionary policy which Marx dealt with under other heads; that is, through its relevance to other parts of this work. Still, it is useful to see how he, along with Engels, generalizes on this basic conception in various contexts. Let us look at some typical cases in which they insistently point to the movement of the people from below as the crux of revolution.

One of the chief reasons why the interest of these generalities is severely limited is that invocations of the People Rising Like Lions After Slumber are so common in socialist literature, or even outside of it—dripping off the pens of ideologists who really expect the people to rise like tame circus lions and jump through their hoops. As Marx remarked, on the refusal of the English bourgeoisie to give the vote to all the people: thus "they confess they are striving to replace the old aristocracy with a new one. To counter the existing oligarchy they would like to speak *in the name of the people,* but at the same time avoid having the people appear in their own person when their name is called."[41]

Consider, for example, a passage in Marx's 1847 polemic against the same pious Prussian who had glorified "the social principles of Christianity" (seen in section 2 above). He had also appealed for "a monarchy relying on the support of the people," and so Marx addressed himself to this early version of the Social Monarchy:

> We wish to make only a few kindly remarks to those gentlemen who would like to save the alarmed Prussian monarchy by a *salto mortale* [daring leap] into the people.
> Of all political elements the people is the most dangerous for a king ... [For] the real people, the proletarians, small peasants, and populace—this is, as Hobbes says, *puer robustus, sed maliti-*

osus, a sturdy and ill-natured lad, and will not let either thin kings or fat ones make game of him.

This people would, above all else, wrest from His Majesty a constitution together with universal suffrage, freedom of association, freedom of the press, and other unpleasant things.[42]

As he wrote this, Marx was naturally unaware that two decades later the Social Monarchy would be the goal of the founder of the German Social-Democracy in his pourparlers with Bismarck. But these kindly remarks would have been wasted on Lassalle, who was as ready as anyone to celebrate the *puer robustus*—in order to make game of him himself.

The case is somewhat different when the context of the generalities is a period when deeds speak, as during revolutions. In the revolution of 1848–1849 Marx's paper had no lack of occasions to make the point that victory depended on fully unleashing the people's struggle from below. Political freedom entailed self-emancipation. "In Germany," wrote Engels, "there are no longer any 'subjects,' ever since the people became so free as to emancipate themselves on the barricades."[43] In an article on the crimes of the Hohenzollerns, Marx closed with a peroration:

> But there is still one power which the gentlemen in Sans Souci [royal palace] give little heed, to be sure, but which nevertheless will speak with a thunderous voice. The PEOPLE—the people who, in Paris as on the Rhine and in Silesia as in Austria, foaming with anger, await the moment of the uprising, and—who knows how soon—will give all the Hohenzollerns and all overlords and underlords what they deserve.[44]

Behind this rhetorical generality, however, was more than simple elocution: in fact, over a year of dealing with day-to-day revolutionary problems, such as will be partially described in Chapters 8 to 10 below.

In his book on the 1848 revolution in France, Marx recurs to a characteristic metaphor of the theater (as in "theater of war"): in this case, not the contrast between above and below, but rather between the active participants on the stage of history and the passive onlookers in the pit or in the balconies. He writes, on the first phase of the revolution:

> Instead of only a few factions of the bourgeoisie, all classes of French society were suddenly hurled into the orbit of political

power, forced to leave the boxes, the stalls and the gallery and to act in person upon the revolutionary stage![45]

Similarly on the peasantry when they were momentarily set in motion, to give Bonaparte his election victory of December 10, 1848:

> For a moment active heroes of the revolutionary drama, they could no longer be forced back into the inactive and spineless role of the chorus.[46]

It is, to be sure, only a metaphor, a useful way of thinking of the revolutionary process as drama.* Less figuratively, in another passage of the same work, Marx explains why the French working class was still incapable of self-emancipation:

> As soon as it is risen up, a class in which the revolutionary interests of society are concentrated finds the content and the material for its revolutionary activity directly in its own situation: foes to be laid low, measures dictated by the needs of the struggle to be taken; the consequences of its own deeds drive it on . . . The French working class had not attained this level; it was still incapable of accomplishing its own revolution.[48]

The French working class had not become fit to rule; no mere exhortations could overcome this lack of maturation.

5. LITERATURE AND REVOLUTION

Another approach to this question is provided by the image of "the People" in literature. A writer, to be sure, is not making a revolution, but is creating a literary work, which is certainly different, and all the more under the creator's own control. In the few cases where we see Marx or Engels making literary judgments on contemporaneous works, the present question figures prominently. Here are two cases in point.

In response to Margaret Harkness' novel *City Girl*, Engels' letter to

---

* The same metaphor peeps out of Marx's peroration to his "Address to the National Labor Union of the United States," on behalf of the International:

> On you, then, depends the glorious task to prove to the world that now at last the working classes are bestriding the scene of history no longer as servile retainers, but as independent actors, conscious of their own responsibility . . .[47]

the author was very laudatory, but suggested a criticism. While he specifically refused to judge a novel by its social or political content--its "tendency"--he objected that Harkness' treatment of the mass of workers was simply untrue to life:

> °°In the "City Girl" the working class figures as a passive mass, unable to help itself and not even showing (making) any attempt at striving to help itself. All attempts to drag it out of its torpid misery come from without, from above. Now if this was a correct description about 1800 or 1810, in the days of Saint-Simon and Robert Owen, it cannot appear so in 1887 to a man who for nearly fifty years has had the honour of sharing in most of the fights of the militant proletariat. The rebellious reaction of the working class against the oppressive medium which surrounds them, their attempts—convulsive, half conscious or conscious—at recovering their status as human beings, belong to history and must therefore lay claim to a place in the domain of realism.[49]

Or perhaps, he added, the author was merely concentrating on "the passive side of working-class life, reserving the active side for another work." He was willing to admit that London's East End, the scene of the novel, showed this passive side—workers "passively submitting to fate"—more than anywhere else. His objection had to be pitched in apparently general terms, based on the past, that is, on experience; but it was in the same East End, only three months after this letter, that the turbulent "New Unionism" flamed up in a match factory, as we saw in Chapter 4.

Our second case is provided by Ferdinand Lassalle's sortie into belles lettres with his poetic drama *Franz von Sickingen,* on the alliance of the knights under Sickingen and Hutten with Luther in the wars of the German Reformation. Lassalle requested a critique from both Marx and Engels, and the exchange of correspondence is enlightening. Whereas in *The Peasant War in Germany* Engels had turned center stage over to Thomas Münzer and his revolt from below as well as to the peasant rebellion, Lassalle chose to focus on and idealize the obsolete figures of the knightly class who were defending a moribund social stratum. Even more significantly: throughout Lassalle's drama, Sickingen is spoken of literally as the Savior, the "people's shepherd," and in other similar terms; the masses are openly viewed by Sickingen in the same way as his creator Lassalle viewed his own flock of sheep:

. . . The masses are a child
That must be first drilled, educated
Before their better sense can have free play.
What else can we expect as the result
Of priestly oppression and besotment? [50]

Marx's and Engels' criticisms politely and diplomatically explained to Lassalle why the drama failed of its tragic effect. For our present purposes they especially emphasized the mistake (literary and historical) in concentrating on the upper-class rebels. Marx counseled: you concentrated all interest in the *"noble* representatives of the revolution —behind whose watchwords of unity and liberty there still lurked the dream of the old empire and of club-law," instead of making the revolutionary elements of the city and countryside an important part of the background. Engels made the same point in several ways, adding that Lassalle had missed the real tragedy represented by these two hero-figures, Sickingen and Hutten, who had placed themselves in the void between the nobility and the peasantry, that is, "the tragic collision between the historically necessary postulate and the practically impossible execution." Marx, furthermore, did not conceal the Sickingen-Lassalle identity: "Have you yourself not fallen to a certain extent into the diplomatic error, like your Franz von Sickingen, of placing the Lutheran-knightly opposition above the plebeian-Münzerian opposition?" [51] Marx was less diplomatic when he later wrote to a friend characterizing Lassalle as a "quack savior." [52]

As Engels had occasion to say about another man (an ex-Communard): "he would usher in the social republic *par ordre du mufti*"—by orders from above by the powers-that-be. [53]

6. THE COMMUNE'S CRIME

As in 1848, as in all revolutions, the experience of the Paris Commune brought the idea of self-emancipation out of the manifestos and into the stream of reality. Marx's views on the Commune will be considered at large in a later volume but an anticipatory note is in order here.

Shortly before the Commune, in the International's second Address on the Franco-Prussian War, Marx already pointed to the feature about the newly formed republic of liberal politicians that excited "misgivings." It was the fact that this regime had been engineered from above; that Bonapartism had not been *subverted*—which literally means, overturned from below—but only replaced by the Third Republic:

> That Republic has not subverted the throne, but only taken its place become vacant. It has been proclaimed, not as a social conquest, but as a national measure of defence.[54]

The great thing about the Commune, for Marx, was that the case was just the opposite: the working masses of Paris took over.

> °°It is a strange fact. In spite of all the tall talk and all the immense literature, for the last sixty years, about Emancipation of Labor, no sooner do the working men anywhere take the subject into their own hands with a will, than uprises at once all the apologetic phraseology of the mouthpieces of present society . . .[55]

In Marx's first draft for *The Civil War in France*, which was longer and more discursive, Marx asked: what is it that is *new* about this revolution, in terms of previous French revolutions? True, the workers have borne the brunt, but that was always so. Likewise, "That the revolution is made in *the name* and confessedly *for* the popular masses, that is, the producing masses, is a feature this Revolution has in common with all its predecessors." Here is the answer:

> °°The new feature is that the people, after the first rise [rising], have not disarmed themselves and surrendered their power into the hands of the Republican mountebanks of the ruling classes, that is, by the constitution of the *Commune*, they have taken the actual management of their Revolution into their own hands and found at the same time, in the case of success, the means to hold it in the hands of the People itself, displacing the State machinery, the governmental machinery of the ruling classes by a governmental machinery of their own. This is their ineffable crime! Workmen infringing upon the governmental privilege of the upper 10,000 and proclaiming their will to break the economical basis of that class despotism which for its own sake wielded the organised State-force of society! This is it that has thrown the respectable classes in Europe as in the United States

into the paroxysm of convulsions and accounts for their shrieks of abomination, [yelling that] it is blasphemy . . .[56]

There follows the statement: "But the actual 'social' character of their Republic consists only in this, that workmen govern the Paris Commune!"—which was expanded in the final version.

"Some patronising friends of the working class," writes Marx,* ask sympathy for the Commune because it did not undertake any "socialist enterprises," any utopian projects. Marx replies:

> These benevolent patronisers, profoundly ignorant of the real aspirations and the real movement of the working classes, forget one thing. All the socialist founders of Sects belong to a period in which the working class themselves were neither sufficiently trained and organised by the march of capitalist society itself to enter as historical agents upon the world's stage, nor were the material conditions of their emancipation sufficiently matured in the old world itself.[58]

But (he goes on to say) the Commune was right in not setting up a Fourierist phalanstery or a little Icaria à la Cabet. What it did set up was the condition of its own emancipation, "no longer clouded in utopian fables"—for

> the government by the working class can only save France and do the national business, by working for its *own emancipation,* the conditions of that emancipation being at the same time the conditions of the regeneration of France.[59]

*   *   *

The principle of self-emancipation has often been praised as a democratic conception: people taking their own destiny in hand. This is

---

* Marx means the followers of Comte, called Positivists. The English Positivists, especially Prof. Edward Beesly, did defend the Commune against the press slander campaign, in spite of their own antisocialism. In a caustic paragraph just before this, Marx had distinguished the English Comtists from their French "co-religionists," and attacked Comtism as follows:

> Comte is known to the Parisian workmen as the prophet in politics of Imperialism [Bonapartism] (of personal *Dictatorship*), of capitalist rule in

true enough. What is sometimes overlooked is that this principle under-lines the *revolutionary* (literally: subversive, overturning) nature of Marx's view of socialism. Nothing is more revolutionary in its thrust than this principled rejection of all "gracious patronage from above" (to use an expression of Engels').[60] All the more so because it is double-edged, pointed against both the established powers and classes and against the proponents of socialism from above.

So if Marxism, as we have explained, can be briefly defined as the theory and practice of proletarian revolution, it was equally the theory and practice of the self-emancipation of the working class. Only a movement looking to class struggle from below could be a genuinely proletarian revolutionary movement; for it was the proletariat that was *below*—"the lowest stratum of our present society," which "cannot stir, cannot raise itself up, without the whole superincumbent strata of official society being sprung up into the air."[61]

The principle of self-emancipation is illuminated by its opposite, which, as we have seen, Marx had to discuss from time to time: the "revolution from above."[62] Whether this was a palace-revolution or a Bonapartist coup,* it was a danger. Marx commented on the revolution-from-above pattern in the course of the draft address on the Commune which we have already cited. In pre-Bismarck Prussia, the Stein-Hardenberg reforms had been carried through in order to rally popular support against Napoleon; in Russia the czar's emancipation of the serfs had been engineered from the top. Marx wrote:

> °°In both countries the social daring reform was fettered and limited in its character because it was octroyed from the throne and not (instead of being) conquered by the people.[64]

---

political economy, of hierarchy in all spheres of human action, even in the sphere of science, and as the author of a new catechism with a new pope and new saints in place of the old ones.[57]

This passage did not appear in the final version.

* Or both: a Bonapartist palace-revolution. Engels saw a possibility of this in the 1850s if the emperor were assassinated in one of the many *attentats;* he remarked in a letter to Marx that he hoped the old scoundrel would *not* be done in. For in that case the Bonaparte clique would merely make a deal with the Orleanist royalists and go right on:

> Before the workers' districts could think about it, Morny [Bonaparte's heir apparent] would have made his palace-revolution, and although a revolu-tion from below would be thereby postponed only briefly, yet its basis would be a different one.[63]

Octroy is a rare word in English, but it deserves to be more widely used.* It reeks of the handing-down of largesse from the Master, the imposition of change from on high, from the savior to his sheep, from the lord to his lackeys. *Octroyal revolution* is revolution from above—the polar opposite of self-emancipation. Corresponding to it we can put *octroyal socialism*, as a generic term for the many varieties of radicalism that have looked for an elite band to hand down their new social order to a suitably grateful and docile people.

---

* In German the word entered political language (from the French) during the revolution of 1848, as a political weapon of the left against the Prussian Crown's "octroyed" constitution. The right denounced it as an "evil foreign word." [65] Marx picked it up with enthusiasm in his *Neue Rheinische Zeitung* during the revolution, as we shall see.

II | SOCIAL CLASSES IN REVOLUTION

7 | THE BOURGEOISIE AND BOURGEOIS REVOLUTION

When Marx first confronted the problem of changing society, the revolution that loomed large was not the proletarian revolution but the bourgeois revolution: the revolutionary change needed to abolish the legacy of feudalism and the regime of absolutism, and to put the bourgeoisie* in direct control of the state. Our discussion of Bonapartism[2] has already raised some questions about the revolutionary role of the bourgeoisie in this, its own revolution. In this chapter we will be particularly concerned with the relation between the bourgeois revolution and the proletarian socialist revolution. This is a complex of problems on which Marx's theory of revolution went through a number of alterations as it developed. It can be understood only step by step.

This question was fated to be one of the most controversial of the ensuing century; and so the nature of Marx's views is often obscured by the dust of later disputes. The reader is urged to resist a common tendency to view Marx's ideas through the prism of the discussions on permanent revolution and bourgeois-democratic revolution that raged in the Russian socialist movement in the first two decades of the twentieth century. All of the Russian-born theories—Trotsky's on permanent revolution, Lenin's on "democratic dictatorship of the

---

* Marx usually used *bourgeoisie* and *capitalist class* interchangeably, without a definite distinction. It would be useful to make a terminological demarcation, with *capitalist* narrowly reserved for the strictly economic relationship of exploitation, and *bourgeois* for the broader and more varied social relationships that cluster around the capitalist class. In this sense the bourgeoisie would be viewed as a social penumbra around the hard core of capitalists proper, shading out into the diverse social elements who function as servitors or hangers-on of capital without themselves owning capital. I suggest this distinction *not* because it was followed by Marx but to alert the reader to the need for interpreting different cases from their context. —Marx often used *middle class* for *bourgeoisie*, explained below.[1]

proletariat and peasantry," and the Mensheviks' on bourgeois–revolution–first—appealed to Marx's authority as usual; but it is doubtful that any of them fully grasped Marx's views. Besides, it is useful to repeat that phrases and formulations used a half century apart, under differing social conditions, do not necessarily have exactly the same content; a concrete examination must be made.

The twentieth-century controversy is outside our purview, but out of these disputes came a common marxological myth. The myth had it that only in a momentary aberration in 1850 did Marx discount the revolutionary character of the bourgeoisie in this type of historical situation. In point of fact, Marx, along with many other revolutionaries of the day, started out in 1843 with a rejection of the bourgeoisie's revolutionary potentiality.

For this we must go back to the essay in which he first identified the proletariat as the bearer of the socialist revolution, his introduction to a critique of Hegel's political thought.[3]

1. MARX'S STARTING POINT IN 1843

In this early article Marx raised a question that had to be resolved before nominating the proletariat as the revolutionary class: *what about the bourgeoisie?* After all, it was a question of absolutist Germany, where the bourgeoisie was not in power and suffered from the rule of obsolete classes. Whatever one thought of the potentiality of the proletariat, wasn't the bourgeoisie a revolutionary class in its own way and for its own aims?

Marx's answer here is no. In fact, his argument closely links his thesis that the proletariat is *the* revolutionary class with the opinion that the bourgeoisie is not revolutionary at all. He does not yet seem to consider that there may be more than one revolutionary class, on different levels.

He does recognize that the bourgeoisie was the revolutionary class in the France of 1789, but thinks this is no longer so since it now holds political power in that country. The French pattern (on which he has just been reading widely) as well as the English suggests that backward Germany may be slated to go through the same stages. It is to this suggestion that Marx firmly answers no: the German bourgeoisie has already missed its historic opportunity to be the revolutionary class of the nation. Clearly involved in Marx's argument is a concept of "uneven and combined development" (to use a later term).

He sees the German bourgeoisie as virtually inert. It has negated its historic revolutionary role through timidity and cowardice. He notes that "other nations dared to carry out a revolution" but "our rulers were afraid" to do so; while we do not enjoy the benefits of others' revolutions, we do suffer from their counterrevolutions. Running through all of German society are the legitimation of baseness, the ancestral knout, despicable phenomena of all sorts, wretchedness in government.[4]

In France and England this problem is posed in a modern way, because a partial emancipation has already taken place there: industry and wealth (the bourgeoisie) have emancipated themselves from the old political world, from semifeudal absolutism. "In France and England, then, it is a matter of abolishing monopoly [*understand:* capitalism] that has proceeded to its final consequences [*at any rate, to bourgeois political power*]; in Germany it is a matter of going on to the final consequence of monopoly. There it is a question of solution, and here [in Germany] it is first a question of collision."[5]

But, continues Marx's argument, if that were all there was to it, then Germany's perspective would be like Russia's: no revolutionary prospect at all as yet. But in fact Germany's development has been uneven: "they are about to begin in Germany with what France and Germany are about to end." For "the *total* German development goes beyond the *political* German development." For example, the theoretical conceptions that have become rife in Germany, mainly in philosophic guise, are the fruit not merely of the backward German conditions but of the advanced European conditions to the west. Thus there is a force at work, theory, which is a part of the total German development, for "theory too becomes a material force as soon as it grips the masses."[6]*

---

* Marx also makes clear in this article, however, that German theory takes on a philosophic guise because of German backwardness.[7] Fifteen years later he made the same point less philosophically:

°°The middle class [,] still too weak to venture upon active movements, felt themselves compelled to march in the rear of the theoretical army led by Hegel's disciples against the religion, the ideas and the politics of the old world.... The power of philosophy during that period was entirely owing to the practical weakness of the bourgeoisie; as they could not assault the antiquated institutions in fact, they must yield precedence to the bold idealists who assaulted them in the region of thought.[8]

But will it be possible to bridge the "enormous discrepancy" between theory and social reality in Germany? "The question is posed: can Germany attain a practice" which is on a level with its best theory, can it make a revolution which will raise it not only to the height already attained by France and England "but to the *human height* which will be the immediate future of these nations"? That is: can it make not merely a partial (bourgeois-democratic) revolution but the basic "radical revolution" which will go even beyond the bourgeois stage reached in France and England? [9]

Marx is aware that posing this possibility should give one pause: "But Germany has not climbed up to the intermediate stages of political emancipation along with the modern nations. ... How can it, with a *salto mortale* [daring leap], jump not only over its own limitations but at the same time over the limitations of the modern nations ...?" The premises for such a "radical revolution" appear to be lacking. [10]

To help make the leap, Marx points to another element of uneven and combined development in the total German picture: Germany, to be sure, has not had its share of modern political struggles, but it *has* "shared the *sufferings* of that development, without sharing its gratifications and partial satisfactions."

> So one day Germany will find itself on the level of European decadence before it ever stood on the level of European emancipation. It will be comparable to a *fetish worshiper* who languishes away from the diseases of Christianity.

Hence the German regimes

> are driven to combine the *civilized defects* of the *modern political world,* whose advantages we do not possess, with the *barbarous defects* of the *ancien régime,* which we enjoy in full ...

It is this combined development which brings about the peculiar situation that this backward Germany naively "shares all the illusions of the constitutional political system without sharing its realities." This "eclecticism" (Marx's label for this combination of unevenly developed elements) "will reach a height undreamed of before," as is shown by the case of Prussia's king "who proposes to play all the roles of monarchy, feudal and bureaucratic, absolute and constitutional, autocratic and democratic" at the same time in his own person. [11]

The conclusion:

Germany, representing the defect of the political present erected into a whole world of its own, will not be able to break down the specifically German limitations without breaking down the general limitation of the political present.

That is the first flat statement: Germany will not be able to get rid of its absolutist holdovers from feudalism without at the same time going further.

It is not the *radical* revolution that is a utopian dream for Germany, not *general human* emancipation, but rather the partial, the *merely* political revolution, the revolution that leaves the pillars of the house standing.

This partial, merely political revolution would mean only the emancipation of "part of civil society" (the bourgeoisie), whereas Marx is directing the argument to the necessity of "the general emancipation of society."[12]

At this point we get one of the better-known passages: only that class can emancipate the whole of society which is identified as the general representative of all of society. Marx continues:

> But every particular class in Germany lacks the consistency, incisiveness, courage, and ruthlessness that could stamp it as the negative representative of society. Not only that, but every rank of society likewise lacks that breadth of soul that identifies itself, if only for the moment, with the soul of the people . . .[13]

Most particularly the German bourgeoisie lacks these qualities, which once made the French bourgeoisie the revolutionary representative of its society. In contrast, in Germany

> even the opportunity for playing a great role is always already past before it is present, and every class is involved in the struggle against the class below it as soon as it begins a struggle against the class above it. Hence the princes get into a struggle against the monarchy, the bureaucrats against the nobility, and the bourgeoisie against all of them, while the proletariat is already beginning to get into a struggle against the bourgeoisie. The middle class hardly dares to conceive the idea of emancipation from its own standpoint when the development of social conditions along with the progress of political theory pronounces that standpoint itself to be antiquated or at least problematic.

That is another flat statement that the bourgeoisie cannot make its own revolution, qualified at the end ("at least problematic"). But the qualification fades as Marx contrasts France with Germany:

> In France partial emancipation is the basis of universal emancipation. [*That is, the already accomplished bourgeois revolution is the basis for the coming universal one.*] In Germany universal emancipation is the conditio sine qua non of any partial emancipation. [*That is, here a complete social revolution is the condition for winning even bourgeois political democracy.*] In France it is the reality, in Germany it is the impossibility, of stage-by-stage liberation that must give birth to complete freedom.[14]

We now have the assertion of a flat impossibility. It is on the basis of this line of thought that Marx goes on to the more famous passage in which he first points to the proletariat as the class that can do *what the bourgeoisie cannot do*.[15] This despite the fact that "The proletariat is just beginning to come into existence in Germany only now as a result of the rising *industrial* movement." (Not even the Silesian weavers' revolt has yet taken place.) The conclusion is:

> In Germany *no* kind of bondage can be broken without breaking *every* kind of bondage. *Fundamental-minded* Germany cannot revolutionize without revolutionizing *from the foundation up.*

And then a last sentence expects that this revolution will begin in France and subsequently arouse Germany.[16]

While Marx thus started with what was essentially a primitive theory of permanent revolution, we will see that he proceeded to go through a complex course of rethinking in the course of experience, first circling away from this view, before coming squarely back to it in a more sophisticated form, as the outcome of the revolution of 1848–1849. In all this Engels' role was more important than is usually realized.

2. DEMOCRACY AND COMMUNISM

Marx's view, that the coming revolution in Germany could only take place under the aegis of the proletariat, was amended in the course of the 1840s. One factor was not merely some theoretical deduction about the bourgeoisie, but the bourgeoisie's own behavior.

The image held by Marx in 1843 of the German bourgeoisie as an inert class had been largely true until about 1840.[17] This was one reason why the early socialists tended to dismiss it as a potentially revolutionary force. "The year 1840 was a turning-point in the history of Germany," Marx and Engels wrote later.[18] By 1843 there had already been some significant oppositional stirrings of liberalism; still, by the middle forties the bourgeoisie was clearly showing how timid it was for all that. In contrast, in June 1844 the first attention-compelling workers' revolts took place in Germany (Silesia and Bohemia). In the midst of these events, therefore, the picture was blurry. It was not until 1846–1847 that the movement of bourgeois liberalism got moving quite visibly.* Let us keep this time sequence in mind as we trace Marx's and Engels' view of the question. Their ideas on the subject did not evolve simply in their skulls, but in reaction to events whose meaning was not immediately plain.

In the spring of 1845 Engels was assuming, like Marx, that the "imminent" social revolution (coming "in a very short time," too) could not be stopped by any bourgeois advances, and that it would go right through to the goal of "the Community system" ("communism").[20] In the fall, when, as we have seen,[21] Engels became quite clear that it was the proletariat that would have to carry through the social revolution, he embodied this view in a context which left no room for a first-stage bourgeois revolution:

> °°... we do not count on the middle classes at all. The movement of the proletarians has developed itself with such astonishing rapidity, that in another year or two we shall be able to muster a glorious array of working [-class] Democrats and Communists—for in this country [Germany] Democracy and Communism are, as far as the working classes are concerned, quite synonymous.[22]

And he contrasts "the movement" with the bourgeois-liberal agitation for merely constitutional rights.

Engels' blanket identification of "Democracy and Communism" is the keynote here. It asserts the *telescoping* of the two tasks before Germany: the establishment of democratic institutions and the aboli-

---

* Marx later (autumn 1850) sketched an economic analysis of the rhythm of prosperity and depression which conditioned the development of the liberal opposition in the '40s.[19]

tion of capitalism along with absolutism. At the end of 1845 Engels enlarges on this theme in an important statement which begins by pointing to the "social" (not merely political-democratic) side of the French Revolution:

> The French Revolution was from beginning to end a social movement, and since then a purely political democracy has altogether become an impossible chimera.
> *Democracy nowadays is communism.* Any other democracy can still exist only in the heads of theoretical visionaries who do not bother their heads about what is really happening, for whom principles are not developed by men and circumstances but arise out of themselves. Democracy has become the proletarian principle, the principle of the masses. . . . The democratic masses can be confidently counted in when reckoning up the communist forces. And when the proletarian parties of the various nations get together, they are entirely right in inscribing the word "Democracy" on their banners, for, with exceptions that don't count, all European Democrats in the year 1846 are more or less clear communists.[23]

It is vital to understand that at this time "Democracy" did not mean only certain political ideas or "values" or procedures, but rather primarily a political *movement* or *tendency*, aiming to put power in the hands of the People in one sense or another.* In the socialist language of the day, a "pure democracy" meant a pure-and-simple democracy, a purely political democracy, which might give the bourgeoisie what it wanted but offered nothing to satisfy the social aspirations of the masses; hence "Democracy" must be a social movement too, a movement for deeper social change.

This is an "algebraic" conception: the Democratic x was given one meaning by the petty-bourgeois Democracy, who might even call it *social*-ism; but for Engels this Democratic x had to be nothing less than communism. What he called the "Democratic Revolution"[26] had also to be the communist revolution.

---

* For the variable meanings of *democracy* in this period, see Volume 1 of this work.[24] It is particularly important at this point to put the spotlight on the phrase *the Democracy.* This was not the label of a set of ideas, but of a movement of the people, of the broad masses (in whatever sense, including vague ones). In fact, *the Democracy,* as used by the left in the nineteenth century, was very like another vague term popular in the twentieth, *the Masses.* A Democrat (capitalized or not) was one of the supporters of or participants in this movement, whatever their

3. STAGES OF THE REVOLUTION

By 1846, for the reasons already given, we first find Engels conceding that the bourgeoisie is going to play a revolutionary role to some extent at least. Now we get a two-stage view of the course of the revolution: in the first stage the bourgeoisie wins political power for itself; in the second stage, which follows immediately, the working class proceeds to overthrow the bourgeoisie. But there is no stopping point between the two stages; they flow into each other continuously.

Here is how Engels puts it in March 1846. First he explains very clearly the difference between democracy as conceived and practiced by the bourgeoisie, which makes democratic rights dependent on wealth, and the democratic conceptions of the proletarian movement. Then:

°°in all countries, during the time from 1815 to 1830, the essentially democratic movement of the working classes, was more or less made subservient to the liberal movement of the bourgeois. The working people, though more advanced than the middle classes, could not yet see the total difference between liberalism and democracy—emancipation of the middle classes and emancipation of the working classes; they could not see the difference between liberty of *money* and liberty of *man*, until money had been made politically free, until the middle class had been made the exclusively ruling class. . . . In all countries the middle classes were, from 1815 to 1830, the most powerful component, and, therefore, the leaders of the revolutionary party. The working classes are necessarily the instruments in the hands of the middle classes, as long as the middle classes are *themselves revolutionary* or progressive. The distinct movement of the working classes is, therefore, in this case always of secon-

---

views on democracy in today's sense. *The Democracy* often appeared as a capitalized noun, especially in the Chartist press, but there was no consistency, and we may expect that one meaning shades into the other, depending on context. Not only the Chartists: in an 1852 article in the *New York Tribune* Marx attacked the Whig leader Lord John Russell's demagogic use of democratic rhetoric. Russell had said, "The people of this country are, in other words, the Democracy of the country." Marx then exerted himself to show that Russell's explanations of the label emptied it of all meaning.[25] —This historical usage affects my own use of the term, where I have capitalized Democracy or Democrat to distinguish it from today's sense. In German, of course, there is no distinction, since all nouns are capitalized; interpretative capitalization is due to the translator.

dary importance. But from that very day when the middle classes obtain full political power—from the day on which all feudal and aristocratic interests are annihilated by the power of *money*— from the day on which the middle classes *cease* to be progressive and revolutionary, and become stationary themselves, from that very day the working class movement takes the lead and becomes the *national movement.*[27]

"Democracy"—the goal of *the Democracy,* the social program of the masses—is still equated with the proletarian revolutionary movement and not with the bourgeois movement, which is "liberalism." This has not changed. But the revolution is now envisaged as going through a necessary stage in which the "progressive and revolutionary" bourgeoi- sie exhausts its progressiveness by winning power, so that the revolution must *continue on* beyond this stage in order to gain real Democracy, which is "the liberty of *man,"* not of money—that is, communism.

So Engels; no reliable expression of Marx's thinking on this subject at this time is extant.* However, since the spring of 1845 Marx and Engels had worked together closely in Brussels, not only on their joint literary work but also as movement activists. Their organizational activity was simultaneously on three levels: building a communist polit- ical center (first the Communist Correspondence Committee, later the Communist League); building the German Workers Educational Union, a broader proletarian club; and building the left-wing Democratic move- ment (the International Democratic Union in Brussels, then the Demo- cratic Association, and cooperating with the Fraternal Democrats organized by the London left Chartists).

---

* There are two partial exceptions. In August 1844 Marx inserted in the Paris *Vorwärts* an excerpt from a letter written by his wife Jenny, already quoted in Volume 1.[28] Jenny, writing from Trier, commented on a recent assassination attempt that it showed that "in Germany a political revolution is impossible, but for a social revolution all the seeds are present"—the germinal idea of permanent revolution.[29] Karl had not yet put the idea down on paper, as far as we know. There is a report from a more dubious source. After being badly bested by Marx in a political confrontation on March 30, 1846, Weitling reported Marx's views in a letter which is full of distortions; and according to this unreliable letter Marx had said that "As for the realization of communism, there can be no talk of it to begin with; the bourgeoisie must first come to the helm."[30] No doubt Marx did say something like this; forty-odd years later Engels thought Marx's "main thesis" was "clear enough" in this part of Weitling's letter,[31] but the exact formulation is another matter.

This organizational pattern should be seen from the vantage point of Engels' explanations about the relationship of Democracy and Communism. The Democratic organizations involved were definitely not bourgeois-liberal in political character; rather, they united Communists, revolutionary workers, and nonproletarian Democrats who were willing to go at least part of the way with the Communists. In 1845-1846 the Communist group around Marx in Brussels was signing itself the "Democratic Communists,"[32] and a Brussels police report on Marx identified him as a "dangerous Democrat and Communist."[33]

By 1847 the Prussian bourgeoisie had forced a sort of constitution out of the king, and the convocation of the Diet had accelerated the pace of events. In March, Engels (also Marx later in the year) had no doubt that the bourgeoisie was going to take political power in short order. They "are almost forced by circumstances to change the governmental system" in spite of their "indolence." Engels added: "There is, besides, no doubt, that, under present circumstances, the people will support the middle classes, and by their pressure from without, which indeed is very much wanted, strengthen the courage and enliven the energies of those within." The economic distress of the people would ensure this. Outside of this greater emphasis on the bourgeoisie's playing out its revolutionary role, Engels' picture of the course of the revolution remained unchanged. The "Democratic movement" and the "Democratic party" were still counterposed to the movement of the bourgeoisie, not identified with it.

°°From the moment, however, the middle classes establish their own government, identify themselves with a new despotism and aristocracy against the people, from that moment democracy takes its stand as the only, the exclusive movement party; from that moment the struggle is simplified, reduced to two parties, and changes, by that circumstance, into a "war to the knife."[34]

4. IN REACTION TO "FEUDAL SOCIALISM"

We must now take into account a new factor which gave Marx and Engels a considerable push toward increased emphasis on the revolutionary role of the bourgeoisie, that is, the expectation that it would play a leading part in overthrowing absolutism and its old ruling classes.

They found they had to combat a dangerous tendency among the petty-bourgeois socialists—encouraged by the regime—to utilize the antibourgeois hatred of the workers *in order to mobilize them on the side of the more reactionary class still in power.* Concentrating on the new evils brought by bourgeois development and exploitation, this tendency pointed to the bourgeoisie as the enemy, and told the workers: *The enemy of your enemy is your friend.* * As Engels wrote in his draft for the Manifesto: "From the ills of present-day society this group draws the conclusion that feudal and patriarchal society should be restored because it was free from these ills." [40] This was not the first, and would not be the last, time that this ploy was worked in order to mobilize support for a more reactionary force against a more immediate exploiter.

This "reactionary socialism," or "feudal socialism," came especially from a tendency calling itself the "True Socialists." In the spring of 1847 Engels wrote a pamphlet against this tendency, but only two sections of his manuscript are extant. In one of them he argues that the absolute monarchy can be overthrown only by the bourgeoisie, and not by petty-bourgeois elements who are in the tow of the feudalists. [41] In this connection he has a significant paragraph about the German working class. For the first time he states clearly that, in its present socioeconomic stage of development, it cannot *as yet* take over the leadership role in the revolution.

There are two counts against it, he writes. It is too "split up" into different economic sectors, and it is too thinly scattered over the big country, with few concentration points. These characteristics make it

---

* Marx pointed more than once to the same pattern in another form, that is, where the proletariat is used as troops for the bourgeoisie, also in order to combat the enemy of its enemy. The *Communist Manifesto* refers to the undeveloped stage where "the proletarians do not fight their enemies, but the enemies of their enemies, the remnants of absolute monarchy ..." [35] In an article on the June 1848 uprising in Paris, Marx says of the February overthrow of the Louis Philippe monarchy: "What they [the people] instinctively hated in Louis Philippe was not Louis Philippe, but the crowned rule of a class, capital on the throne. But, magnanimous as always, they fancied they had destroyed their enemy after overthrowing the enemy of their enemies, the *common* enemy." [36] The same problem naturally cropped up in England too, when hatred of the bourgeoisie among (say) the Chartists led to illusions about the role of the Tory aristocracy, simply because the latter too were antibourgeois in their own way. In 1852 Engels wrote of the left-wing Chartist leader Ernest Jones, who was combating this tendency: "without our doctrine he would never have hit the right tack and

difficult for it "to constitute itself into *one* class," that is, to constitute itself into one united class political movement. "So little is the mass of workers in Germany prepared to take over leadership in public affairs."[42]

Thus the issue is posed that will be the main subject of this and the following three chapters, as well as of innumerable basic disputes in the socialist movement.

A couple of months later, Engels brought out another reason why the stage of bourgeois power must be gone through first:

> Only when a *single* class--the bourgeoisie—stands forth as the exploiter and oppressor; only when poverty and misery can no longer be written down to the account of one social estate now and another one at another time, or simply of the unlimited monarchy together with its bureaucrats: only then ensues the last decisive struggle . . . between the bourgeoisie and the proletariat.[43]

The conception here is that the evils of the old system overlay and obscure the new evils of the bourgeois order, and must first be abolished in order to be able to concentrate all the forces of progress against the new ruling class, which now can no longer throw the blame for things on its own enemy, absolutism.

There were other blasts the same year against the socialists who sought to channel anticapitalism into support for the "enemy of our enemy." Early in the year Engels worked on, but did not finish, an attack on a number of True-Socialist littérateurs; among other things it castigated indifference to bourgeois "political revolutions" and to other political issues of interest to the bourgeoisie.[44] Another was

---

would never have found out how on the one hand the instinctive class hatred of the workers against the industrial bourgeoisie, the sole possible basis for the reorganization of the Chartist party, can not only be retained but even widened, developed and made to serve as the foundation of enlightening propaganda and how on the other hand one can be progressive all the same and oppose the reactionary cravings of the workers and their prejudices."[37] Jones had to combat his own tendency in this same direction.[38] "It was entirely natural," thought Engels, "particularly at the beginning of the industrial revolution, that the workers, engaged as they were in direct struggle against only the industrial bourgeoisie, should ally themselves to the aristocracy and other sections of the bourgeoisie, who did not exploit them directly and who were also opposing the industrial bourgeoisie." Entirely natural, like a disease, but still dangerous: "this alliance contaminated the working-class movement with a considerable influx of reactionary elements" and with other deleterious influences.[39]

written by Marx's close friend of the Communist League, Wilhelm Wolff: "Such questions and such views can come only from those among us who are blinded by an otherwise quite justified hatred of the bourgeoisie . . ." We certainly aim to destroy the bourgeoisie— "However, are we proletarians in Germany ready to completely transform the social disorder, in our own interests, i.e., can we throw out the bourgeoisie right away and put the principles of communism into practice?" Wolff explained why the bourgeoisie must first get rid of the absolutist regime, and argued that political freedoms and democratic processes are vital for the proletarian struggle to overthrow the bourgeoisie itself.[45]

The same month that Wolff's article appeared, September, Marx entered the lists with an article directed against a government organ which had tried to capitalize on the line of the "True Socialists." The title of this article, "The Communism of the *Rheinische Beobachter*," indicated the problem: this organ of the reactionaries was pretending to a certain anticapitalism in order to deflect popular discontent to the bourgeoisie rather than to the regime. Marx, in the name of "the most revolutionary of all the revolutionary parties in Germany," declared roundly that "the Communists have nothing in common" with either the profeudal socialists or the profeudal government organs that pushed this political line.

The government paper had argued that the liberal bourgeoisie only wants to use the people as "cannon fodder" in order to seize state power for itself. Yes, answered Marx, we know that the bourgeoisie pursues only its own interests, but it is false to conclude that the popular movement is therefore "exploited by the liberal bourgeoisie for its own ends."

> The people—or, to replace this loose and variable expression with a definite one, the proletariat—reasons altogether differently . . . The proletariat does not ask whether the people's welfare is the main consideration or a secondary one to the bourgeoisie, whether they *want* to use the proletariat as cannon-fodder or not. The proletariat does not ask what the bourgeoisie merely *want* but rather what they *must* do.* It asks whether it is the present

---

* Compare this key sentence (which we will return to) with what Marx had written in *The Holy Family* about the proletariat: "It is not a question of what this or that proletarian, or even the whole proletariat, at the moment *regards* as its aim. It is a question of *what the proletariat is*, and what, in accordance with this *being*, it will historically be compelled to do."[46]

political state of affairs, the rule of the bureaucracy, or the one which the liberals strive for, the rule of the bourgeoisie, that will offer it more means to attain its own ends. . . . the rule of the bourgeoisie not only puts entirely new weapons in the hands of the proletariat for the struggle *against* the bourgeoisie but also obtains an entirely different status for the proletariat, a status as a recognized party.[47]

The "new weapons" which the proletariat will know how to use are such institutions as "freedom of the press and freedom of association." The gentlemen of the *Rheinische Beobachter* "imagine that the proletariat wishes to be helped; it does not occur to them that the proletariat expects help from no one but itself."[48]

The proletariat (Marx goes on) attacks the bourgeois liberals who dominate the Prussian Diet from quite a different side:

The proletariat blames the Diet for being on the defensive, for not attacking, for not going ten times farther. It blames the Diet for not coming out decisively enough to make possible the proletariat's participation in the movement. . . . a Diet that demands trial by jury, equality before the law, abolition of serf labor, freedom of the press, freedom of association, and a real representative system—a Diet that has broken with the past once for all and establishes its demands in accordance with the needs of the times rather than with antiquated laws—such a Diet could count on the strongest support by the proletariat.[49]

The article ends with a vigorous attack on the idea of supporting "a monarchy relying on the support of the people," discussed in our previous chapter.[50]

5. MARX POSES THE DILEMMA

Like Engels earlier in the year, Marx explained why the proletariat was not yet ready to take the place of the bourgeoisie in the overthrow of absolutism. He did this in a polemic against a democratic liberal named Heinzen, in October-November. On this point it was the most thorough statement to date.

. . . if the proletariat overthrew the political rule of the bourgeoisie, its victory would be only transitory, only an incident in the service of the *bourgeois revolution,* as in the year 1794, so long as in the course of history, in its "movement," the material conditions have not yet been created which render necessary the abolition of the bourgeois mode of production and therefore also the definitive overthrow of bourgeois political rule. Accordingly, the Reign of Terror in France necessarily served only the purpose of sweeping away the remnants of feudalism from French soil with its powerful hammer-blows. The timidly overcareful bourgeoisie would not have completed this job in decades. The bloody action of the people therefore only cleared the way for it. Similarly the overthrow of the absolute monarchy would be simply a thing of the moment if the economic conditions for the rule of the bourgeois class have not yet attained maturity....

The property question, which is a world-historical question in "our time," therefore takes on meaning only in the *modern bourgeois society.* The more developed this society is, the more therefore the bourgeoisie has developed economically in a country, and the more state power has assumed a bourgeois expression, then the more stridently does the *social* question come to the fore . . .[51]

But why should the German workers prefer "the *direct rule of the bourgeoisie* to the brutal oppression of the absolute government"? Essentially Marx gave the answers we have already seen.* This passage ended as follows:

They [the workers] know that their own struggle with the bourgeoisie can only get started on the day the bourgeoisie has been victorious. For all that, they do not share Mr. Heinzen's bourgeois illusions. They can and must treat the *bourgeois revolution* as a condition for the *workers' revolution.* But not for a moment can they consider it their *final goal.*[53]

We see, then, that Marx was echoing Engels' insistence on the continuance of the struggle "on the day the bourgeoisie has been victorious."

This article also devoted some emphasis to the reluctance of the bourgeoisie to fight for fear of the class struggle below it. In this

---

* On this point, compare also Marx's briefest formulation, given in the course of a lecture on free trade in January 1848. The English workers, he said, are not duped by the illusions and lies of the free-traders,

and if, in spite of this, the workers made common cause with them against the landowners, it was in order to destroy the last remnants of feudalism and to have only a single enemy left to deal with.[52]

connection, Marx points all the way back to his own article of 1843–1844, with which we began this chapter:

> As I have already pointed out in [that article], Germany has a Christian-Germanic blight of its own. Its bourgeoisie was so retarded that it is beginning its struggle with the absolute monarchy and seeking to establish its own political power at a time when in all developed countries the bourgeoisie is already engaged in the sharpest struggles with the working class and its political illusions are already outlived in the consciousness of Europe. In this country where the political squalor of the absolute monarchy still exists together with a whole retinue of decayed semifeudal social orders and relations, yet on the other hand—partially indeed as a result of industrial development and Germany's dependence on the world market—there exist the modern antagonisms, between bourgeoisie and working class and the struggle that arises therefrom: for example, the workers' revolts in Silesia and Bohemia. Therefore the German bourgeoisie already finds itself in a position of antagonism to the proletariat before it has yet constituted itself politically as a class.[54]

This lays the basis for what was actually going to happen in the coming revolution, though Marx does not yet see the full import of his own point. Here is another passage from Marx's exposition:

> They [the bourgeoisie] know better [than Heinzen] where the shoe pinches. They know that in revolution the *rabble* becomes impertinent and starts to grab. Therefore the gentlemen of the bourgeoisie try as much as possible to change the *absolute* monarchy into a *bourgeois* monarchy in an amicable way without a revolution.
>
> But in Prussia, as previously in England and France, the absolute monarchy does not let itself be bourgeoisified amicably. It does not abdicate amicably. Besides their personal prejudices, the princes have their hands tied by a whole civil, military and clerical bureaucracy—components of the absolute monarchy which by no means want to change their status as rulers for one as servants with respect to the bourgeoisie. For another thing, the feudal orders hold back; for them it is a question of To-be-or-not-to-be, that is, property or expropriation. It is clear that the absolute monarchy, in spite of all the servile genuflections of the bourgeoisie, perceives its real interests to lie on the side of these feudal orders.[55]

This predicted quite accurately what the 1848 revolution was soon going to show. But Marx did not resolve the implied dilemma, or even continue to discuss it here. If the bourgeoisie is afraid of making its own revolution, and the regime cannot otherwise be overthrown, and the proletariat is not yet ready to do the job, what happens to the bourgeois revolution, let alone the prospect of an immediately succeeding more radical Democratic revolution?

6. THE BLOC OF DEMOCRATIC CLASSES

It was about this time, autumn 1847, that Engels started sketching the outline of a more complex approach to the problem of the coming revolution.*

He had already pointed out that the German proletariat was still split up, scattered, and small. This put a question mark over the proletariat's ability not only to carry out the revolution against absolutism but even to achieve the second-stage revolution against the bourgeoisie—by itself. In a polemic against the same Heinzen, Engels developed a conception of the revolutionary Democracy as a *bloc of lower classes led by the proletariat, mobilized against the bourgeoisie as well as against absolutism, on the basis of a transitional type of program.*

What are the tasks of the Democracy? asks Engels.

> . . . its task is to make clear the oppression of the proletarians, small peasants and petty-bourgeoisie—for in Germany these constitute the "people"—by the bureaucracy, nobility and bourgeoisie . . .

Note that the bourgeoisie, as before, is listed on the other side of the barricades, even though absolutism still has to be overthrown.

> Its [the revolutionary Democracy's] task is to demonstrate that the conquest of political power by the proletarians, small peasants and petty-bourgeoisie is the first condition for carrying out these means.

---

* As we shall see in the rest of this chapter, it is not clear whether at this point Marx worked with Engels in developing this approach or whether he even agreed with it as yet. Certainly the available documentation indicates that it was Engels who pushed ahead more boldly on this issue.

Political power is now to be conquered not by the proletariat alone but by a bloc of classes—proletariat, small peasantry and petty-bourgeoisie.

> Furthermore its task is to examine to what extent one can count on the early attainment of Democracy, what means are available to the party, and with what other parties it must combine as long as it is too weak to stand alone.[56]

But (argues Engels) Heinzen is wrong in orienting toward the small peasants, who are least capable of revolutionary initiative. For six hundred years all progressive movements have stemmed from the towns. "The industrial proletariat of the towns has become the copestone of all modern democracy; the petty-bourgeois and still more the peasants are completely dependent on its initiative." Denominating the proletariat as the copestone of modern democracy means assigning it the *hegemony* of the Democratic bloc.

But the program of this Democratic revolution cannot begin by being the complete Communist program. Another kind of program is necessary for this stage, a transitional program.* This is the program which all the Democrats (Communist Democrats or non-Communist Democrats) are prepared to support—even Heinzen, for his social-reform proposals "are such as the *Communists* themselves propose as preparation for the abolition of private property." But for the Communists these measures are preparatory only:

> They are possible as preparations, as intermediate steps transitional to the abolition of private property, but not otherwise.[58]

The gulf between the Communists and Heinzen is that, for the latter, these measures are final; they are the end, not the means; they are "not intended for a revolutionary situation but for a peaceful bourgeois situation." On the contrary, these measures are impossible for a stable bourgeois situation, and the bourgeois economists who oppose these measures are right in maintaining this as long as they remain within the framework of the private-property system. But the economists' objections "lose all force as soon as one views these social reforms as pure *mesures de salut public,* as revolutionary and transitional measures."

---

* The concept of a transitional program—a plan for the passage from present-day society to the new social order—was already well known in the socialist movement; this term itself had been prominently used by Cabet, Heinzen, and others.[57]

Engels then repeats this latter point: these measures must be considered

> not as final measures but as transitional *mesures de salut public*
> flowing out of the transitional struggle of the class itself.
>
> For Mr. Heinzen they are without rhyme or reason, since they
> are put forward as wholly arbitrary, artificially concocted, phil-
> istine do-gooder enthusiasms . . .[59]

This makes Heinzen a bad Democrat; and, adds Engels, we do not
attack him because he is not a Communist—we attack him because he is
a bad Democrat.

Finally, an important statement on the bloc of Communists and
Democrats:

> The Communists, far from starting unprofitable quarrels with
> the Democrats under present conditions, rather come out at this
> time in all practical party questions as Democrats themselves. In
> all civilized countries, Democracy has the political rule of the
> proletariat as its necessary result, and the political rule of the
> proletariat is the first presupposition of all Communist measures.
> As long as Democracy has not yet been won, so long therefore do
> Communists and Democrats fight together, and so long are the
> interests of the Democrats likewise those of the Communists. Till
> then the differences between the two parties are purely theoret-
> ical in nature and can very well be discussed theoretically without
> thereby disturbing their common action in any way. It will even
> be possible to come to an understanding on many measures to be
> undertaken immediately after the attainment of Democracy in
> the interest of the hitherto oppressed classes, e.g., the operation
> of the big industries and railways by the state, education of all
> children at state expense, etc.[60]

It is to be noted that Engels has quite got over his earlier naive
opinion that "with exceptions that don't count, all European Democrats . . . are more or less clear Communists."[61] It is now a question of a
united front between different tendencies ("parties")—a more complicated problem. Also, Engels now believes that the transitional period of
the revolution starts with a mixed-class state power ("the attainment of
Democracy") which is not yet definitively committed to establishing
Communism. And finally: the state power is committed only to certain
measures, to a transitional program which, from the Communist standpoint, is merely preliminary to a Communist society, but which, to be
carried out, objectively necessitates going over to Communism.

The formulation of this transitional program goes through various drafts in the next few months, and winds up as the ten-point program at the end of Part II of the *Communist Manifesto.*

Engels' conception of a limited bloc between the proletarian movement and the radical petty-bourgeoisie must, however, be distinguished from another view that still existed in the minds of the Communist League membership. The month before Engels' article, this old concept had been embodied in the leading article in the *Kommunistische Zeitschrift*, probably written by Schapper. It views a coalition of proletariat and petty-bourgeoisie as natural simply because it does not see a *class* difference between the two strata, or sees it only dimly. Reflected here is still the mentality of the artisanal workers, who have not quite reconciled themselves to the proletarian condition of propertylessness. Schapper wrote:

> In present-day society proletarians are all those who cannot live on their capital, the worker as well as the man of learning, the artist as well as the small bourgeois; and even if the small bourgeoisie still possesses some property, yet it is obviously approaching with giant strides the condition which will wholly put it on a par with the rest of the proletarians. Therefore we can already count it in our ranks, for it has as great an interest in guarding against a condition of complete propertylessness as we have to emerge from that condition. Let us unite, therefore, and both sectors can be helped.[62]

Would-be Communists like Schapper had not yet established the *independence* of the proletarian standpoint from that of the petty-bourgeoisie. Engels' program started from differences between the two classes, and asked whether they can march together for a while, and how far.

7. THE REVOLUTIONARY DEMOCRACY
AND THE PROLETARIAT

The transitional program for the victory of the Democracy in the coming revolution, in Engels' view, went right up to the outbreak of the revolution itself. He did not cease to insist that Democracy had to mean Communism *in the end.*

But not everything that was called "democratic" was of a piece with this Democracy, and he was at pains to keep the line clear. In November of 1847 he discussed the civil war going on in Switzerland between the reactionary "Sonderbund" cantons and the more modern Swiss regions. Old Switzerland (*Urschweiz*, the original High Alps cantons) and Norway, he comments, are two of the most backward regions of Europe, yet both are "democratically organized."

> But there are democracies of various sorts, and it is very necessary for the Democrats of the civilized countries finally to reject responsibility for the Norwegian and Old Swiss democracy.
> The Democratic movement in all civilized countries is, in the last instance, striving for the political rule of the proletariat. . . .
> The Democracy of the civilized countries, *modern* Democracy, therefore has absolutely nothing in common with the Norwegian and Old Swiss democracy.[63]

For it is only the revolutionary Democracy that represents "modern Democracy."*

Now who are these other, non-Communist but revolutionary, Democrats who are to constitute the allies in the coming victory of Democracy? For one thing, Marx and Engels are at this very time working hand in hand with a group of them in Brussels.[65] But since Belgium is not expected to be the center of the revolution, France is more to the point. For this country, Engels points explicitly to the political movement around the left-Democratic (or Social-Democratic) organ *La Réforme*, whose leader is Ledru-Rollin. In January 1848 Engels once again repeats his view that

> °°all modern democracy is based upon the great fact, that modern society is irreparably divided into two classes—the bourgeoisie . . . and the proletarians . . . [And] the acknowledged tendency of modern Democrats in all countries is to make political power pass from the middle classes [bourgeoisie] to the working classes, these latter constituting the immense majority of the people . . .[66]

---

* Compare the statement included in a *Kommunistische Zeitschrift* article (probably written by Schapper) summarizing reasons why workers should reject Cabet's plan to build experimental communities: "because for the Communists, who recognize the principle of personal freedom . . . a community of goods is impossible without a transitional period, indeed a Democratic transitional period, during which personal [that is, private] property is first gradually changed into social property—as impossible as a harvest without sowing for a farmer."[64]

and his article identifies these forces in France as Ledru-Rollin's movement around *La Réforme:*

> °°It has saved the honour, independence, and the strength of French Democracy as a distinct party. It has maintained the principle of the Revolution ... It has asserted the rights of the working classes in opposition to middle-class encroachments. It has unmasked these bourgeois radicals—who would make the people believe that no class oppression exists—who will not see the frightful civil war of class against class in modern society,— and who have nothing but vain words for the working people.[67]

Even immediately after the February revolution, Engels still continued to regard the *Réforme* group as representatives of the workers and "Communists without knowing it."[68] How disillusioned Marx and Engels were later to become with Ledru-Rollin's politics is to be read in Marx's *Class Struggles in France.* But the workers who looked to Ledru-Rollin—that is, likewise had illusions about him—were those who made the February and June insurrections in Paris.

In their relations with these French revolutionary Democrats, Marx and Engels regarded themselves as representing the revolutionary Democracy across the border. For example, in the autumn of 1847 Engels contacted Louis Blanc as a representative of "the London, Brussels, and Rhineland Democracy," and in this capacity informed the Frenchman that "You can regard M. Marx as the leader of our party (i.e., of the most advanced section of the German Democracy . . .) and his recent book against M. Proudhon as our program."[69] This makes very clear that there was no question about hiding socialist views behind a façade; for, on the one hand, Blanc was himself a leading French socialist, and on the other, the program embodied in Marx's *Poverty of Philosophy* openly advocated the revolutionary overthrow of the bourgeoisie by the proletariat. The point is that the revolutionary Democracy was conceived as an umbrella movement uniting conscious socialists or Communists with those who were "Communists without knowing it."

On the eve of the revolution, in an article published January 23, 1848, Engels summarized the prerevolutionary period of 1847. He still believes that a compromise is no longer possible between the bourgeoisie and the regime; "a life-and-death struggle" between these opponents will end with the victory of the liberals.[70] But then the united forces of the Democrats and Communists will move:

We are no friends of the bourgeoisie, as is well known. But this time we do not grudge them their [coming] triumph. We can calmly smile at the haughty airs with which they look down, especially in Germany, on the apparently tiny band of Democrats and Communists.

... The gentlemen actually believe that they are working in their own behalf.... And yet nothing is more obvious than that they are only paving the way everywhere for *us*, the Democrats and Communists; that they will gain at most a few years of uneasy enjoyment of victory, to be forthwith overthrown in turn. Everywhere the proletariat stands at their rear ... in France and Germany, silent and reserved but on the quiet preparing the downfall of the bourgeoisie ...[71]

Then, with a visible assumption of brashness in the face of the "haughty airs," Engels addresses the bourgeoisie rhetorically: You are working in our interest; fight on and clear the social ground for us; and

As a reward for that, you shall be allowed to rule for a short time ... but do not forget: "The executioner stands at the door."[72]

8. TRANSITION TO THE "SECOND REVOLUTION"

The *Communist Manifesto* came off the press a few days afterward. But before taking it up, we have to go back a little way, to Engels' draft for the Manifesto, written at about the same time as the polemics against Heinzen. The draft is clearer on this issue than the more circumspect Manifesto is going to be.

A good deal of the draft needs no detailed review now, since it only repeats what we have already seen. In the coming "decisive struggle" between the bourgeoisie and absolutism, the Communists want the bourgeoisie to win, and as quickly as possible, "in order as soon as possible to overthrow them again." And "from the day when the absolute governments fall, comes the turn for the fight between bourgeois and proletarians." The "reactionary socialists" are identified as the antibourgeois but profeudal elements we have already discussed.[73]

The answer to Question 17 states that it will not be possible for the coming proletarian revolution to abolish private property "at *one* stroke." The reason, however, is not simply that realistically this process will take some time. Rather, the proletarian revolution will "be able to abolish private property only when the necessary quantity of the means of production has been created." One of the tasks of proletarian rule itself is to bring this about.[74]

This is the context for Question 18: "What will be the course of this revolution?" The answer is in terms of a specific kind of transitional period.

> *Answer:* In the first place it will inaugurate a *democratic constitution* and thereby directly or indirectly the political rule of the proletariat.

Indirectly in a country like Germany—

> where the majority of the people consists not only of proletarians but also of small peasants and petty-bourgeois, who are only now being proletarianized and in all their political interests are becoming more and more dependent on the proletariat and therefore soon [*N.B.: not now*] will have to conform to the demands of the proletariat. This will perhaps involve a second fight, but one that can end only in the victory of the proletariat.

This is a very enlightening consideration: in effect, there may have to be a "second revolution." During the contemplated transitional period, in fact, there is a question mark left hanging over the reality of "proletarian rule," at least in a country like Germany. What gives this transitional period its specific transitional character is this: (1) it is based on a bloc of classes—proletariat, small peasantry, and petty-bourgeoisie—under the hegemony of the proletariat; (2) it is a transition not from proletarian rule to the realization of socialism, but rather it is a transition to definitive proletarian rule itself, out of a revolutionary Democratic regime which is more ambiguous in character.

Hence the answer continues as follows with regard to the transitional period, the name of which is Democracy:

> Democracy would be quite useless to the proletariat if it were not immediately used as a means of carrying through further measures directly attacking private ownership and securing the means of subsistence of the proletariat.

And a twelve-point program then follows to concretize this.

In the last paragraph of the answer, we are given to understand that the realization of the program will develop not so much in accordance merely with technical possibilities (as would be true of any workers' state) but in accordance with a programmatic evolution: "the proletariat will see itself compelled to go always further," to carry through more radical onslaughts on private property, through the logic of socioeconomic needs. [75] It is in this process, clearly, that the Democratic (non-Communist) allies will come to see that they have to come along in the direction of consistent Communism—or else make the "second fight" necessary.

In the answer to Question 19 we are told that "The communist revolution . . . will be a revolution taking place simultaneously in all civilized countries, that is, at least in England, America, France and Germany." But its further evolution in these different countries is not expected to be uniform. "In each of these countries it will develop more quickly or more slowly" depending on the degree of industrialization already attained. "It will therefore be slowest and most difficult to carry out in Germany . . ." [76]

Clearly, this revolution is *continuing on* over a period of time, as it proceeds uninterruptedly from one phase to the next.

In the answer to Question 24, which distinguishes different kinds of socialists, we gather that, on the political side, the transitional period implies the joint power of the Communists and the tendency of "democratic socialists." This latter tendency—the social-reform wing of the Democracy—"in the same way as the Communists desire part of the measures listed in Question [18] not, however, as a means of transition to communism but as measures sufficient to abolish the misery of present society and to cause its evils to disappear." It is these allies who will have to be brought along as the revolutionary regime has to make more and more radical inroads on private property. They are mixed in class basis: some are "proletarians who are not yet sufficiently enlightened regarding the conditions of the emancipation of their class," and some "are members of the petty-bourgeoisie, a class which, until the winning of Democracy and the realization of the socialist measures following upon it, has in many respects the same interest as the proletariat." [77]

"Until the winning of Democracy"—and afterward? One gathers that the "democratic socialists" will sort themselves out as the revolution continues its course, with the Communists winning over enough to consolidate a majority for the uninterrupted continuation of the revolution.

9. THE *COMMUNIST MANIFESTO*

In contrast, the final text of the Manifesto by Marx avoided a definite statement on many of the problems we have been mooting, or referred to them in an open-ended way. There was more than one reason.

In the first place, most of the document viewed the problems of social evolution from a great historical height where the immediate issues of a country like Germany dwindled from sight. When it said that "the bourgeoisie has at last, since the establishment of Modern Industry and of the world market, conquered for itself, in the modern representative State, exclusive political sway,"[78] it was making a statement that was then applicable to only two European countries at most—and the word *exclusive* was an exaggeration for both of them.[79] It was because the Manifesto took the long view that it survives so well. But for 1848 it took up "what is to be done" only in the very brief Part IV.

Secondly, it is sometimes forgotten that the Manifesto was written not as an exposition of Marx's and Engels' personal opinions but as a program to be accepted and signed by an organization.* Clear-cut statements on immediate political perspectives were bound to be more controversial than a long-term theoretical statement, both inside and outside the Communist League. In addition, as we have already suggested, it is possible that Marx at this point may have had less decided views on the matter than Engels.

In any case, it is only on the last page of the Manifesto that the

* While Engels was planning to revise his own draft of the Manifesto, he wrote Marx: "What I have here has not yet all been submitted for endorsement, but, apart from a few quite minor details, I mean to get it through in a form in which there will at least be nothing contrary to our views."[80] Writing in 1860 about the history of the Communist League, Marx recalled that, through its early years, the League's doctrines "ran through all the varieties of French and English socialism and communism, plus their German variations. . ." At the second congress of the League in November–December 1847, there was a lively discussion, and "after vehement debates over several weeks, the *Manifesto of the Communist Party* written by Engels and me was accepted . . ."[81] This indicates that Marx and Engels might have been willing to omit from the official document points on which there was no consensus, but not that they included anything they disagreed with. While it is true that, as Engels wrote toward the end of his life, the Manifesto "marked the merger of the two currents" represented by the worker-artisans who formed the League and by the Marx-Engels circle,[82] it is not true that Marx and Engels wrote the document as a "compromise," except in the above-stated limited sense. (This type of problem is further discussed in Special Note E, section 1, below.)

political issue of the coming German revolution is taken up at all, though it had already entered obliquely into the discussion of the various socialist schools in Part III, with two extensive attacks on the profeudal socialist tendencies. It is on this last page that we find that in Germany the bourgeoisie has conquered no sway at all but "is on the eve of a bourgeois revolution." The political perspective is formulated with an escape clause:

> In Germany they [the Communists] fight with the bourgeoisie whenever it acts in a revolutionary way, against the absolute monarchy, the feudal squirearchy, and the petty-bourgeoisie.

The statement is circumspect ("whenever it acts in a revolutionary way") and makes no prediction on whether it will so act. The stress is on the long view even here, hostility to the bourgeoisie—

> in order that the German workers may straightway use, as so many weapons against the bourgeoisie, the social and political conditions that the bourgeoisie must necessarily introduce along with its supremacy, and in order that, after the fall of the reactionary [pro-absolutist] classes in Germany, the fight against the bourgeoisie itself may immediately begin.
> ... the bourgeois revolution in Germany will be but the prelude to an immediately following proletarian revolution.

The idea of immediacy is stressed three times. The revolution is to move uninterruptedly from the bourgeois state into the proletarian revolution.[83]

"In France the Communists ally themselves with the Social-Democrats," that is, with the group around Ledru-Rollin's *La Réforme;* and organizational alliances are also spelled out for England, America, Switzerland, and Poland, but not for Germany.[84]

What in Engels' draft had been a fairly clear view of the course of the revolution, through a transitional period marked by the victory of the Democracy, leaves its mark on the Manifesto only in passing references, which are suitably noncommittal. The most obvious of these is the formulation that

> the first step in the revolution by the working class, is to raise the proletariat to the position of ruling class, to win the battle of democracy [*die Erkämpfung der Demokratie*].[85]

So goes the standard (Moore-Engels) translation done forty years later.

In terms of our present discussion, the last phrase—literally, "the winning of Democracy"—means: the attainment of the stage marked by the political power of the Democracy.* It is, in German as in English, a rather hazy way to put it, which leaves open—probably intentionally—whether this winning refers to the victory of the Democratic bloc over the reaction or to the victory of the proletariat at the head of the Democracy. Here this victory is flatly equated with establishing the proletariat as the ruling class, without any more explanation than this issue receives elsewhere in the Manifesto.

The ten-point program that follows[88] echoes many of the previous versions of the transitional program; but—again—it is not presented in that context, nor as a program for a bloc of Communists and other revolutionary forces, even though such blocs are envisaged in Part IV.

Another reticence of the Manifesto concerns its treatment of the class composition of the Democracy: there is no treatment. We have seen that, repeatedly and vigorously, articles by Engels had included the petty-bourgeoisie as a constituent of the antibourgeois bloc of the Democracy. This was to be a bloc of the proletariat, small peasantry, and petty-bourgeoisie: so Engels had explained in his article against Heinzen and in his draft of the Manifesto. But this conception nowhere appears in the Manifesto itself.

On the contrary, where the petty-bourgeoisie is characterized, it is dismissed as reactionary and worse: "In Germany the *petty-bourgeois* class, a relic of the sixteenth century . . . is the real social basis of the existing state of things."[89] This hostile formulation is contained not in the section on "Petty-Bourgeois Socialism" but in the following section on "True Socialism." In fact, this helps to explain what is involved. For it is in polemics against "True Socialism" that the harshest indictments of the petty-bourgeoisie are found. The main danger seen is the effort to mobilize a petty-bourgeois socialistic (reform) movement to support the obsolete ruling classes against the coming bourgeois revolution. This apprehension exists even for Engels, at the very same time that he is advocating the Democratic bloc of proletariat, small peasantry, and

---

* The only translation of the Manifesto that clearly indicated this meaning was the French version by Laura (Marx) Lafargue, revised by Engels, and published in Paris in 1886: *"la conquête du pouvoir politique par la démocratie,"* the conquest of political power by the democracy.[86] This meaning was possibly also intended by the 1850 Macfarlane translation, "the conquest of Democracy," in view of the capitalization of the last term.[87]

petty-bourgeoisie. In his 1847 unfinished pamphlet, he had sought to counter the "True Socialist" faith in the absolutist-bureaucratic status quo with the argument that the line of social progress involves the bourgeoisie's accession to power. In line with this emphasis he argues that no other class—not the petty-bourgeoisie, not the peasantry—can play this progressive social role today. "The petty-bourgeois," he writes, "is conservative so long as the ruling class merely gives a few concessions; the bourgeois is revolutionary, until he himself rules."[90] Thus there is a tendency for the petty-bourgeoisie to be taken in tow by the feudal elements.

But Engels makes clear that this pattern of the past is no longer quite valid. His analysis is more up-to-date than the flat hostility that Marx wrote into the Manifesto shortly afterward. The petty-bourgeoisie, Engels goes on to say, is squeezed between the political power of the nobility and the bureaucratic state, on the one hand, and the economic power of the bourgeoisie, on the other; but more and more even its reactionary sectors see the advantages of lining up with the bourgeoisie. Germany, he writes, has just about arrived at the stage where the petty-bourgeoisie under pressure "is taking the heroic resolve of abandoning the nobility and throwing itself on the bosom of the bourgeoisie," and is daily coming more and more under the hegemony of that class.[91]

In contrast, the Manifesto seems to leave no room for a positive approach to the petty-bourgeoisie. It even ends with a passage that speaks of fighting in Germany "with the bourgeoisie whenever it acts in a revolutionary way" against the monarchy, nobility, *and the petty-bourgeoisie,* this class being lumped with the counterrevolution.[92] Part I too had lumped the petty-bourgeoisie with the prebourgeois reaction in a list of classes which the proletariat fights as "the enemies of their enemies."[93] Thus, whereas Engels had been listing the petty-bourgeoisie as part of the Democratic alliance for revolution, the Manifesto listed it on the other side of the barricades, as nothing more than an ally of the absolutist-feudal reaction. What this reflects is the fact that at this point Marx saw petty-bourgeois Feudal Socialism and True Socialism looming very large as a dangerous obstacle to the revolution.

But this totally negative approach to the petty-bourgeoisie, which is a peculiarity of the Manifesto, did not last beyond it. A month after it had come off the press, and with the revolution already breaking out, the two authors put out a flysheet containing the "Demands of the

Communist Party [Tendency] in Germany," which—for the first time in an official way—came out foursquare in favor of the Democratic bloc of proletariat, small peasantry, and petty-bourgeoisie exactly as *Engels* had been writing about it.

For the sake of convenience, let us anticipate the next chapter by looking at some leading features of this brief document, which was issued as a supplement to the Manifesto and used as such.

While the Manifesto was laconic and noncommittal on the immediate political program in the leading countries, this subject required concrete attention as soon as the revolution broke out. When Berlin erupted on March 18, Marx, Engels, and a Communist League group were in Paris, and drew up the flysheet of demands in preparation for activity in Germany. These seventeen demands constituted an adaptation of the ten-point program suggested in the Manifesto as the first steps of proletarian rule. Besides the fact that proletarian rule was not yet here, that ten-point list had been abstractly drafted for disparate countries, and before the onset of a directly revolutionary situation. The new list of seventeen "Demands" is specifically directed to Germany, and is tailored to the uncertain circumstances that obtained at the end of March.

The flysheet contained no general political discussion or perspective, for the members of the League were supposed to use it in conjunction with the Manifesto itself,[94] which thereby provided its political context. Directed to Germany, the new demands were formulated to be less thoroughgoing than the Manifesto's ten points, which had had England and France very prominently in mind. For example, inheritance is to be limited, not abolished. Although a number of inroads into bourgeois economic power were still proposed in the Demands, including a number of nationalizations, the greater thrust was against the royal power and the landowners; and in explanation of the demand (no. 10) for a state bank to replace all private banks, it is even written that "this measure is necessary in order to bind the interests of the conservative bourgeoisie to the cause of the revolution."* This is the clearest indication of continued willingness to "fight with the bourgeoisie whenever it acts in a revolutionary way."[96]

---

* Engels cites most of the demands in his 1885 history of the Communist League, but this statement is not one of those included. From the later perspective it no doubt looked like one of the naivetés of 1848.[95]

Finally, the Demands definitely dropped the Manifesto's view of the petty-bourgeoisie as counterrevolutionary; rather, it includes this class in the united front of potentially revolutionary forces: "It is to the interest of the German proletariat, the petty-bourgeoisie and the small peasantry to support these demands with all possible energy."[97] This united front pointedly excludes the bourgeoisie itself. In other words, on this issue it turned out that the view embodied in the Manifesto was a temporary aberration. From this time on, it was the conception developed by Engels that became the joint view of the partnership.

*   *   *

While it is true that the Manifesto was not written as a guide to immediate political problems in a particular country, its lacunae and unclarities in this field suggest how moot many of these problems were on the eve of the revolution. In any case, the revolution came on the heels of the Manifesto's publication, and all bets were off. Fifteen years later, Marx would remark in a letter to his friend: "the easy-going delusions and the almost childish enthusiasm with which, before February 1848, we greeted the era of revolution have gone to the devil."[98] Certainly, it was during the thirteen months of their participation in the revolution in Germany itself, and then during the following years of reflection on the events, that Marx and Engels worked out their more mature views on the questions which, before 1848, could be raised but not successfully answered.

These questions above all concerned the relationship between the bourgeois revolution of the day (the revolution of the Democracy) and the proletarian revolution. The motto for this inquiry might be taken from *The German Ideology*:

> . . . all struggles within the state, the struggle between democracy, aristocracy, and monarchy, the struggle for the franchise, etc., etc., are merely the illusory forms . . . in which the real struggles of the different classes are fought out among one another . . .[99]

To these illusory and real struggles we now turn.

8 | PERMANENT REVOLUTION IN 1848

Although the *Communist Manifesto* was reticent on a number of programmatic issues, it stated very positively that "the bourgeois revolution in Germany will be but the prelude to an immediately following proletarian revolution," and it repeatedly made clear that the coming revolution was expected to move uninterruptedly from the bourgeois stage into an antibourgeois phase.[1] This was a very widespread, though by no means unanimous, view among the radicals of the time; and it had a tag: the "revolution in permanence," or permanent revolution. The idea figures much more prominently than the term.

Like "dictatorship of the proletariat," this term is now so thoroughly wrapped in later controversies that one must make a strenuous effort to see what it meant in 1848, even though (or because) what it meant then was quite simple and uncomplicated. In addition, for English-speaking people there is an extra difficulty: the word *permanent* in this expression retains its specifically French and Latin meaning. It does not mean perpetual or never stopping, but rather *continuing, uninterrupted.**

A *revolution in permanence* describes a situation in which there is more than one phase or stage in the revolutionary process—for example, a bourgeois-liberal and a proletarian Communist stage, or a national-

---

* Marx plays on the term in his *Eighteenth Brumaire*, when he mentions that the French National Assembly had adjourned both in 1849 and 1850 and each time left behind a Permanent Commission (which means a *temporary* continuations committee of the assembly). He then puns: "the party of Order declared itself in permanence against the revolution. This time [1850] the parliamentary republic declared itself in permanence against the President [Bonaparte]."[2] There is a similar punning usage in a letter by Marx to Engels, in which Marx jocularly says he could not "declare myself in permanence at Schärttners with a pot of beer."[3]

Johann Peter Hasenclever (1810-1853)   From the Öffentliche Sammlung,
Arbeiter und Magistrat   Münster-in-Westfalen, Germany

In 1853 Marx recommended to his readers in the *New York Tribune* that they view this painting, then on exhibition in America, for an insight into the atmosphere of the Revolution of 1848. His suggestion is appended to an article, headed "Financial Failure of Government" etc., in the issue of August 12, 1853:

> Those of your readers who, having read my letters on German Revolution and Counter-Revolution, written for *The Tribune* some two years ago, desire to have an immediate intuition of it, will do well to inspect the picture by Mr. *Hasenclever*, now being exhibited in the New-York Crystal Palace, representing the presentation of a workingmen's petition to the magistrates of Düsseldorf in 1848. What the writer could only analyze, the eminent painter has reproduced in its dramatic vitality.

Marx's reference is to the series of articles, now usually called *Revolution and Counterrevolution in Germany*, which was drafted by Engels. The picture presents a dramatic interplay between the scene in the foreground—the city burghers on the right, grouped around the council table with an interesting similarity to the Last Supper; the workers' delegation on the left, obviously far from united but led by a staunch spokesperson—and the partially seen revolutionary demonstration in the marketplace outside, under a turbulent sky.

liberation and a social-revolutionary stage. (Both cases apply to the revolution of 1848.) The term implies that the movement of revolution goes on from one phase to the next with no lasting interruption, in a continuous process, without halting for a historical period in which one stage stabilizes itself. There may be pauses, but no stabilization. The second stage is seen as emerging more or less organically out of the first. It is this relationship that Marx and Engels have been emphasizing, in different ways, well before the outbreak of the revolution.

In all likelihood, the term *permanent revolution* came out of the literature of the French Revolution; certainly this was true of the concept, or consciousness of the pattern, whatever term was actually used. It was the escalation of the French Revolution from the tentative anti-absolutist protests of the Estates General in May 1789 to the left-wing club movement of 1793, passing through a series of ascendant political currents, that was the historical model.

> In the first French Revolution the rule of the *Constitution-alists* is followed by the rule of the *Girondins* and the rule of the *Girondins* by the rule of the *Jacobins.* Each of these parties relies on the more progressive parties for support. As soon as it has brought the revolution far enough to be unable to follow it further, still less to go ahead of it, it is thrust aside by the bolder ally that stands behind it and sent to the guillotine. The revolution thus moves along an ascending line.[4]

So Marx explained in *The Eighteenth Brumaire*, without putting a label on the ascending line. Engels likewise made the linkage more than once.[5]

This was the pattern of permanent revolution in the actual course of the French Revolution. The term could also be applied to the political outlook of the militants to the left of the Jacobins' main body—Marat and especially the sans-culotte spokesmen called the Enragés—who sought to push the revolution beyond the bounds of bourgeois interests into a further stage dimly seen as a social transformation penetrating more deeply into the class structure. The idea was to keep the revolution going farther: ongoing, hence (with a Gallic accent) *permanent.* As more and more radical strata of the revolutionary population came to dominate the scene, finally the springs of society, overloaded by the strain, snapped back to make the revolution conform to the historical possibilities.

In the first two times that Marx used the term *permanent revolution,* in 1843 and 1844 (and no prior uses by anyone else are known), the context was clearly the French Revolution.*

1. THE TERM IN 1848

When we first meet *permanent revolution* in 1848, it is not simply a historical reference but a current programmatic slogan. But it is clearly not a slogan distinctive of the extreme left, let alone of Marx and Engels alone, but rather one understood to be widely accepted by the Democracy, that is, by everyone to the left of the bourgeois republicans.

Engels, in an unpublished article about the December 10 election in France, is discussing the split between the two wings of the pre-February "revolutionary Democracy" or "Socialist-Democratic party." There is a right wing, representing the petty-bourgeois radicals, which is running Ledru-Rollin, and a left wing, representing the "socialist workers," which is running Raspail. What is the difference between them?

> Ask the papers of the Montagnards, *La Réforme, La Révolution* [the right wing], and they will tell you that they themselves cannot figure it out; that the Socialists [the left wing] put forward literally the same program—the permanent revolution, progressive tax and inheritance tax, organization of labor—that the Mountain has put forward; that absolutely no quarrel over principles exists . . .[6]

Clearly this "permanent revolution" is not some extreme Blanquist invention but figures casually as one of the many socialistic phrases that are on the lips of anyone aspiring to be thought leftish.

This will not be surprising if we forget modern marxological myths and focus on the political issues of 1848. A programmatic demarcation exists between two camps that come forward as different varieties of republicanism. On the right are the "pure" republicans, that is, those who want a purely bourgeois republic. On the left are the "social

* For more information on the uncertain origin of the term, and in particular Marx's first uses of it, see Special Note C. This also discusses the myth that the term was Blanquist in origin.

republicans," the advocates of the "Social Republic," or "Social and Democratic Republic," that is, a republic that undertakes social, not merely political, measures answering the needs of the working masses; a republic that is therefore expected to go beyond the class interests of the bourgeoisie, necessarily coming into conflict with the bourgeoisie and its political representatives. This means carrying through the revolution from its merely political phase (defeat of the monarchist-aristocratic state) to the "social" phase. This is what gives it its antibourgeois bite.

The term *permanent revolution* turns up so casually because it is only a way of asserting the aim of the Social Republic beyond the bounds of such republican institutions as would satisfy the bourgeoisie. What the Ledru-Rollin radicals of the Montagnard wing are saying is simply this: *We too are in favor of going on to the Social Republic, we are not merely for bourgeois republicanism;* or in more modern language: *We claim to be for socialism, not simply bourgeois democracy.* And Engels' comment was: *That's what they say but they don't mean it in action*—as was eventually proved, when it was only the revolutionary left that continued to advocate pushing beyond the bounds of bourgeois democracy, that is, to advocate the permanence of the revolution. It was at this later point that permanent revolution became an "extremist" position.

This interpretation is confirmed by two other references to permanent revolution that crop up in 1849.

In an article published in January, Engels is enthusiastic about the Hungarian uprising:

> . . . we again find the uprising en masse, national manufacture of weapons, assignats, short shrift to anyone obstructing the revolutionary movement, the revolution in permanence—in short, all the main features of the glorious year 1793 . . .[7]

This bridges the gap between permanent revolution as historical reference and as contemporaneous revolutionary fact.

In July, during the dispersal after the defeat of the revolution, Engels writes from Switzerland to Jenny Marx, assuring her that if Marx is unsafe in Paris he would be "entirely safe here in Vaud. Even the government calls itself red and *partisan de la révolution permanente.* In Geneva, it's the same."[8] These two cantons of French Switzerland were known as the most progressive in the country,[9] but their leaders were not even socialists, let alone extreme revolutionaries. James Fazy, the Bonapartist "dictator of Geneva" (as Marx called him), was a Radical party demagogue who had no objection to wielding vaguely radical phrases that were currently fashionable.[10] It would seem that *permanent revolution* was one of these.

When Engels wrote about this period thirty-five years later, the term still came to his pen in connection with the French Revolution. We of the *Neue Rheinische Zeitung,* he related, "unconsciously imitated the great model" set by Marat in his paper *L'Ami du Peuple,* for "he, like us, did not want the revolution declared finished but continued in permanence." This remark followed right after a good summary of the concept of permanent revolution:

> To us, February and March [the Paris and Berlin uprisings in 1848] could have had the significance of a real revolution only if they had not been the conclusion but, on the contrary, the starting point of a long revolutionary movement in which, as in the Great French Revolution, the people would have developed further through its own struggles and the parties become more and more sharply differentiated until they had coincided entirely with the great classes, bourgeoisie, petty-bourgeoisie and proletariat, and in which the separate positions would have been won one after another by the proletariat in a series of battles.[11]

It should be plain that if this contemporaneous meaning of the term is understood, there is little sense to the myth that has Marx and Engels repudiating the permanent revolution concept after 1850. The revolution of 1848 was just getting under way when Marx made a speech including these words: "The Jacobin of 1793 has become the Communist of our day."[12] He was not portraying himself as merely a time-transplanted Jacobin. He was saying the same thing that Engels had already written more than once: *today revolutionary Democracy means Communism.*

2. ALTERNATIVES TO PERMANENT REVOLUTION

Although the phrase *permanent revolution* was widely accepted, not every advocate of the Social Republic held a permanent revolution perspective. For present purposes, here are two types of contemporaneous radicals who rejected this outlook—for opposite reasons—whether or not the phrase was used.

First, there was the radical who advocated the Social Republic in some sense for some time in the future, but who expected the liberal bourgeoisie to come to power first for a whole historical period. In Marx's book these were the petty-bourgeois Radical Democrats, standing on the left wing of bourgeois republicanism. What this political type advocated was halting the revolution at the bourgeois-democratic phase.

Typical of this current were the French radicals of Ledru-Rollin's social-democratic school (who were recorded by Engels as actually accepting permanent revolution as a slogan or catchword). In their case they left no doubt of their real politics because they had the misfortune of temporarily coming to power. Although they continued to use socialistic language, they set the achievement of a bourgeois-democratic republic as their acceptable goal for the period, confining themselves to prodding the bourgeoisie into doing its liberal duty. They therefore figured prominently in Marx's subsequent analysis, *The Class Struggles in France.*[13]

A variant on this theme was represented by one Andreas Gottschalk, who for a while opposed Marx's tendency inside the Cologne workers' movement. Gottschalk was a philanthropic physician to the poor who had become a leader of the Cologne Workers Association before Marx arrived, and who completely discredited himself in that organization in the course of the next year. His politics was essentially that of the "True Socialists," spiced with demagogic use of radical catchwords, sometimes oscillating between an opportunistic acceptance of democratic revolution as the goal, and a sectarian rejection of anything outside the proletarian bailiwick (which he viewed as his fief). But for the most part his politics oriented to the "red monarchy" (the "Social Monarchy"), that is, dependence on the old state to do the workers good. In April 1849 the Workers Association denounced his "despotic mentality [which] violates the most elementary democratic principles," and particularly attacked his "red monarchy" outlook.[14]

What Gottschalk's politics never included was precisely the permanent revolution concept, whether he was supporting "red" monarchism against bourgeois constitutionalism or boycotting support of Democratic candidates in the name of *ouvriériste* isolation. Yet he, too, seems to have played with the phrase *permanent revolution*, like the French radicals.*

Second: there was a way of rejecting the permanent revolution perspective that was the opposite of that of the petty-bourgeois radicals, the other side of the coin. This was to deny the need or possibility of a bourgeois revolution even for the first stage of the revolutionary process; that is, to insist that the revolution must *begin* as a communist revolution, bypassing the Democratic phase altogether. This was precisely one difference between the Blanquist and the Marxist approaches to the problem, as Spitzer explains:

> . . . while Marx and his successors were concerned with transforming a middle-class [bourgeois] revolution, Blanqui was attempting, when all of the conditions for this revolution were present, to anticipate it.
>
> This crucial aspect of his political thought is expressed in these sentences: "if socialism is not its [the revolution's] author it will not be its master. It must make it, not allow it to be made. The morrow belongs only to the victor." In short, for a revolution to end in socialism, it had to be begun by socialists.[19]

Blanqui's aim was to forestall the bourgeois revolution, not to drive through it onward to socialism.

The contrast was strongly made by Engels in 1852, writing on the revolution in Germany. It was the Willich-Schapper group that exemplified the Blanquist type of adventurism he is discussing:

---

* An article by B. Nicolaievsky says that the term *permanent revolution* "kept popping up again and again" in Gottschalk's publications.[15] In the Marx biography by Nicolaievsky and Maenchen-Helfen, Gottschalk's use of the term is mentioned only in connection with a vitriolic attack on Marx which he published after he had lost support among the Cologne workers.[16] In this "open letter" Gottschalk not only foams over with slanders but also expostulates that Marx does not "believe in the permanence of the revolution," whereas he, Gottschalk, thinks "a permanent revolution" is a possibility.[17] He seems to be using it only as a general catchword for revolution *tout court*; it is not some special concept. But Gottschalk's use was not peculiar, since the term kept popping up for decades in the writings of political figures who were not concerned with its special relation to the problems of bourgeois revolution. For example, in 1873 Engels in passing recorded its appearance in the literature of the Spanish Bakuninists.[18]

°° [The Marxist] party never imagined itself capable of producing, at any time and at its pleasure, that revolution which was to carry its ideas into practice. . . . The practical revolutionary experience of 1848–49 confirmed the reasonings of theory, which led to the conclusion that the democracy of the petty traders must first have its turn, before the Communist working class could hope to permanently establish itself in power and destroy that system of wages-slavery which keeps it under the yoke of the bourgeoisie. Thus the secret organization of the Communists could not have the direct purpose of upsetting the *present* governments of Germany. Being formed to upset not these, but the insurrection-ary government [of the bourgeoisie], which is sooner or later to follow them, its members might, and certainly would, individu-ally lend an active hand to a revolutionary movement against the present status quo in its time; but the *preparation* of such a movement, otherwise than by secret spreading of Communist opinions by the masses, could not be the object of the Association.

This is why, Engels continues, they had to split with "some [who] tried to turn it into a conspiracy for making an *ex tempore* revolution."[20]

In this explanation Engels counterposed the basic view of permanent revolution to the traditional Blanquist strategy. Blanquism was one type of radicalism that did not want to continue uninterruptedly (that is, in permanence) from the bourgeois to the proletarian revolution, but rather wanted to jump over the former.

3. FIRST RESPONSE TO THE REVOLUTION

Revolutionary theories are tested in revolution. The first such labo-ratory for Marx and Engels was the revolution of 1848–1849. For thirteen months they actively participated in it in Germany, while following its vicissitudes from day to day in the adjoining countries. These thirteen months were the real crucible of the largest portion of the revolutionary theory which they were going to develop over the next decades, until another revolution supervened in 1871.*

* What Lenin wrote in 1907 was quite true: "In the activities of Marx and Engels themselves, the period of their participation in the mass revolutionary struggle of 1848–1849 stands out as the central point. This was their point of

If Engels was able to say some years later (in the passage just quoted) that "The practical revolutionary experience of 1848–49 confirmed the reasonings of theory," this was true only with an important qualification: the practical experience also changed and refashioned their theoretical views.

As the revolution of 1848 gets under way before hitting Germany, it is important to note two articles published by Engels in which the emphasis is on the executioner waiting at the door, that is, on the proletarian revolution standing behind the bourgeoisie. An article published on February 20 says that the predicted triumph of the bourgeoisie is being fulfilled by the overthrow of three absolute monarchies in two weeks (Denmark, Naples, Sardinia—the Paris uprising is two days ahead).

> The Germans are the last because their revolution will be altogether different from the Sicilian revolution [that is, not simply bourgeois]. The German bourgeois and philistines know very well that behind them stands a proletariat which is growing daily and which, on the day after the revolution, will present quite different demands than they themselves would like. The German bourgeois and philistines therefore behave in a cowardly, indecisive, vacillating way; they fear a collision no less than they fear the government.
>   . . . A Neapolitan revolution has automatically attained its goal as soon as decisive bourgeois institutions have been won; a German revolution has just got well started as soon as it has gone that far.
>   Therefore the Germans must first be thoroughly compromised before all other nations, they must become the laughing-stock of all Europe to an even greater extent than they are now, they must be *compelled* to make the revolution. But in that event it will also be the uprising not of the cowardly bourgeois but of the German workers; they will rise up, to put an end to the whole squalid mess of the official German establishment and restore German honor by a radical revolution.[22]

The last paragraph, which is also the end of the article, strikes an

departure when determining the future pattern of the workers' movement and democracy in different countries. It was to this point that they always returned in order to determine the essential nature of the different classes and their tendencies in the most striking and purest form. It was from the standpoint of the revolutionary period of that time that they always judged the later, lesser, political formations and organizations, political aims and political conflicts."[21]

uneasy note which, while not new, points ahead to what is going to be the decisive problem of this revolution.

A week later, Engels celebrates the February revolution in Paris by emphasizing even more strongly the perspective of the coming *proletarian* revolution. The workers were "the *only* ones who erected barricades" and fought aggressively. They "were not inclined to fight merely for" the big bourgeoisie. "They continued the struggle" even while the bourgeois were celebrating on the boulevards.

> The bourgeoisie has made its revolution; it has overthrown Guizot and with him the exclusive rule of the big stock-exchange men. But now, in the second act of the struggle, no longer does one section of the bourgeoisie confront another, but the proletariat confronts the bourgeoisie.

There follows a paean to the French proletariat:

> It has given the world a shock that every country will feel one after the other; for the victory of the republic in France is the victory of the Democracy in all of Europe.
> Our era, the era of the Democracy, is opening. The flames of the Tuileries and the Palais Royal are the dawn of the proletariat. Bourgeois rule will now smash up or be smashed up everywhere.
> Hopefully, Germany will now follow.[23]

It is clear that, as before, "the Democracy" means the *antibourgeois* bloc of classes led by the proletariat.

4. THE LINE OF THE *N.R.Z.*

When a mid-March uprising in Berlin hurled Germany into the revolution, Marx and Engels together with a group of close comrades went to Cologne, the scene of Marx's first political activity and still the most advanced center of the Rhineland. There on June 1 they launched a daily paper called the *Neue Rheinische Zeitung,* which became the extreme left-wing organ of the revolution.

Its subtitle was *"Organ der Demokratie."* This is usually translated as "Organ of Democracy," and grossly misinterpreted. The paper was the "Organ of *the Democracy"* in the sense that Marx had already worked out. And as we have seen, "the Democracy" did not include the bourgeoisie. From the beginning the *N.R.Z.* acted as the organ of the

Democratic bloc of lower classes that had been envisaged before the revolution, and it was directed against the liberal bourgeoisie in power, as represented by the Camphausen and Hansemann ministries.

A programmatic statement by Marx in the second issue not only arrayed it against the "gentlemen" of the "circumspect and moderate bourgeoisie" but also made clear that *this* organ of the Democracy looked even on the "Democratic party" itself with a dubious eye.* With regard to the former, Marx wrote: the bourgeois liberals in power want to limit the movement to carrying out only "their own political system"; they stick at a middle-of-the-road position between the Democratic party on the left and the absolutists on the right. While they are progressive with relation to the absolutist regime, they are "reactionary —as against the Democracy."

And with regard to the Democratic party: we warn it (wrote Marx) against its illusions on the situation; so far it has proclaimed principles but not acted on behalf of them.

> We must squarely warn against those hypocritical friends who declare that they agree with the principle, to be sure, but doubt that it can be carried out, since the world is not yet ripe for it . . . These people are dangerous.[25]

The *N.R.Z.*, as the political center for Marx's operation, therefore assumed a double task: mobilizing the proletariat, small peasantry, and

---

* "Democratic party" was a much-used expression but of course there was no organization with this name. As we have explained, *party* meant a political tendency, even if unorganized. We shall see Engels writing, later, about *joining* the Democratic party; this meant announcing adherence to a certain wing of politics. What Marx actually became a member of was the local Democratic Association in Cologne (as well as becoming a member of the Workers Association). Later the local Democratic Associations got so far as to meet regionally and nationally and to elect executive committees for coordination. In the legislatures, a "party" meant at most a parliamentary caucus. The club movement in the revolution should not be confused with modern party structures. —A good place in the *N.R.Z.* to see this meaning of "party," and also the above-explained meaning of *Organ der Demokratie,* is a business announcement which boasted: "Through their personal connections with the heads of the Democratic party in England, France, Italy, Belgium and North America, the editors are in a position to reflect the politico-social movement abroad for their readers more correctly and clearly than any other paper. In this regard the *Neue Rheinische Zeitung* is the organ not simply of the German but of the European Democracy."[24] That is, it is the organ of a movement (the Democracy) and not simply of a concept (democracy).

petty-bourgeois Democrats (the bloc of the Democracy) against bourgeois liberalism, against the party of the bourgeoisie; and functioning as the extreme left wing of the Democracy itself.

As an article by Engels later in the year said:

> We have never coveted the honor of being an organ of any parliamentary left. On the contrary, with respect to the often disparate elements out of which the Democratic party in Germany was formed, we have considered it imperatively necessary to keep a sharp eye on no one more closely than on the Democrats.[26]

Six months after that, Marx remarked in an article that "The March revolution in Berlin, that weak echo of the revolution in Vienna, never filled us with enthusiasm," that is, not for the elements that led it and their limited aims.[27] And about four decades later, Engels summarized it this way:

> °°When we returned to Germany in Spring 1848, we joined the Democratic Party as the only possible means of gaining the ear of the working class; we were the most advanced wing of that party, but still a wing of it. . . . I think all our practice has shown that it is possible to work along with the general movement of the working class at every one of its stages without giving up or hiding our own distinct position and even organisation.[28]

In point of fact, Marx and Engels "joined" the Democratic party not merely as a "means of gaining the ear of the working class," but also because they had a theoretical concept of the Democracy as the leader of the coming radical revolution.

In line with this political outlook, the group of Communist co-workers around Marx in Cologne adopted a simple division of labor, to begin with. On the basis of the same political position, some (especially Schapper and Moll) concentrated their activity in the Cologne Workers Association, which had been founded only in April. Others, headed by Marx, initially concentrated on making the *N.R.Z.* a political force inside the movement of the Democracy, becoming active members of the city Democratic Association, as well as of the Workers Association. (The two associations, moreover, usually worked together—when Gottschalk's intrigues were not setting them at loggerheads.) When the American journalist Albert Brisbane visited Cologne on his journey through the revolution, he found that Marx was "the leader of the popular movement."[29]

This division of labor in Marx's group of Communist activists has been usually ignored in interpretations.* In fact, Marx's influence in the Workers Association—not only in the Democratic Association—grew steadily despite his arduous work in putting out a daily, and despite the bitter opposition of the Gottschalk clique; later in the year, Marx was even elected president of the Workers Association.[30] This association had its own organ, which carried its news and reports, whereas the N.R.Z. was oriented toward the Democratic movement nationally. Although published in Cologne, its impact was directed outward; more radical papers elsewhere reprinted from its columns.

5. THE *N.R.Z.* AND THE WORKERS' MOVEMENT

It is now necessary to dispose of a myth that has become almost standard in the literature of marxology. The subtitle of the *N.R.Z.*, translated as "Organ of Democracy," is understood to mean "organ of bourgeois democracy," and, on top of this, the claim is made that the columns of the paper ignored the working class and its issues, at least for months. We have seen that the first part of this picture is a mistake; the second part is false.**

* Marxological enterprises likewise generally ignore Marx's campaign for the establishment of workers' associations in Germany *before* he returned to Cologne, in the two-and-a-half-month period between the March revolution in Berlin and the first issue of the *N.R.Z.* on June 1. Marx and the Communist League under his direction sent organizers through Germany to establish new workers' associations and to bring new and old ones together in a central national body. This unsuccessful campaign for workers' associations, well before Marx and his friends got involved with the Democratic Associations in Germany, has been largely dropped down the Memory Hole because it gainsays the myth, touched on in this chapter, that Marx's *N.R.Z.* line ignored the workers' movement. While the subject of organizational policies will be taken up at large in Volume 3, the main facts about Marx's campaign for a broad German workers' movement in April-May 1848 are presented in Special Note J.

** The main source of this tale is the biography of Marx by Nicolaievsky and Maenchen-Helfen, which states flatly that "During the first months it [the *N.R.Z.*] avoided anything that might possibly disturb the united front [of the Democracy]. Not a word was spoken of the antagonism between proletarian and non-proletarian, bourgeois or petty-bourgeois democracy."[31] Not a word of this statement is true.

One need only read Marx's and Engels' articles during the first month, June, to confirm Engels' later statement that the *N.R.Z.* "represented the standpoint of the proletariat within the Democratic movement of the time,"[32] or his description of the *N.R.Z.* line as "our proletarian Democracy."[33] To be sure, these later summary statements were worded on the basis of a memory conditioned by later developments, but they are essentially accurate, as when he writes that the "banner" of the *N.R.Z.* "could only be that of the Democracy, but of a Democracy that everywhere emphasized in detail the specific proletarian character which it could not yet inscribe once for all on its banner."[34] What this means is that the paper presented a proletarian (communist) version of the Democratic program but not a full proletarian program.

To begin with, the *N.R.Z.* clearly analyzed current events in terms of class struggles, counterposing the interests of the bourgeoisie to those of the "people" and the workers. Here is one brief example, among many, of how this was done: in a June 7 article on the clash of economic interests in the Berlin assembly in connection with the foreign trade in wool, Engels explained that the wool producers were almost all big landowners of the aristocracy whereas "the wool manufacturers are mostly big capitalists, gentlemen of the big bourgeoisie." Hence the issue, he explained to the new readers, had to do with "class interests, whether the big landed aristocracy would fleece the big bourgeoisie, or vice versa." He adds, "For us Democrats" the only interest of this case is to reveal the relation between the "merely conservative class" (the bourgeoisie) and the "reactionary class" (the aristocracy).[35] Another typical article, on June 14, directed against the bourgeois liberals in the government, counterposed the "big bourgeoisie" to "the people, that is, the workers and the democratic citizenry [*Bürgerschaft*]."[36]

Such articles appeared in the first few days of the paper's existence. No doubt Marx would have preferred to take it easy at the beginning on controversial class questions, at least *suaviter in modo*. But before the first month was up, there was the June uprising of the Paris workers—"the most colossal event in the history of European civil wars," as Marx called it four years later.[37] The *N.R.Z.* reacted instantly with stormy article after article as a militant defender of proletarian revolution. It cannot be overemphasized that this was done, furthermore, in face of an almost unanimous journalistic hysteria over the specter of revolution in France. Not to speak of the bourgeois liberals, there was scarcely a single organ even of the "Democratic party" anywhere in Germany that came out in support of the Paris workers.*

In the teeth of this storm the *N.R.Z.*, less than a month old, not only gave total support to the Paris uprising, in numerous articles with detailed reportage, but highlighted the fact that it was the revolt of the proletariat against the bourgeoisie, not a Democratic party movement. Since this was done in massive detail, a few examples will suffice.

In the very first account of the Paris battle, Engels' first sentence was: "The uprising is a purely working-class uprising." The theme of the article was that "The decisively proletarian character of the uprising stands out in all its details."[39] In his next long article giving more of the story as information was received, Engels wrote typically: "The June revolution is the first that really splits the whole society into two great enemy camps," and "The workers of Paris fought all alone against the armed bourgeoisie," and so on, over and again.[40]

The next day Marx's major article on "The June Revolution" dots some *i*'s. It too is written so completely in terms of proletariat versus bourgeoisie that it is hardly necessary to cite more than its first paragraph:

> The Paris workers have been *suppressed* by superior force, [but] they have not *succumbed* to it. . . . The momentary triumph of brute force has been bought at the cost of destroying all the illusions and fancies of the February revolution, of disintegrating the whole old-Republican party, of splitting the French nation into two nations, the nation of owners and the nation of workers. The tricolor republic now wears only *one color* . . . It has become the *red republic.*[41]

Marx proceeds to hammer home the fact that what has been the Democratic party has broken up, and that all its nonproletarian components (including *La Réforme,* which is named) have gone over to the

---

* Even in Cologne itself, the other local Democratic paper, *Wachter am Rhein,* repudiated the Paris workers' struggle. Engels reminisced in 1884: "we had the satisfaction of being the only paper in Germany, and almost in Europe, that held aloft the banner of the crushed proletariat at the moment when the bourgeois and petty-bourgeois of all countries were overwhelming the vanquished with a torrent of slander." However, aside from the big press, the organ of the Cologne Workers Association followed the *N.R.Z.*'s lead, and so did the organ of the Berlin Workers Association; the Berlin leader Stephan Born was then considerably influenced by Marx and the *N.R.Z.*[38]

side of the oppressors. The *fraternité* of the classes has turned into *"civil war,* civil war in its most terrible form, the war of labor and capital."[42]

It is scarcely surprising if (as Engels related later[43]) most of the radical-Democratic shareholders pulled out of the *N.R.Z.* as a result, undeterred by the fact that Marx made clear the paper advocated a similar revolution *in Germany* not immediately but only in the stage still to come. They did not find this reassuring.

Engels introduced a direct invocation of the theme of the *Communist Manifesto.* The Paris uprising, he wrote, is

> the greatest historical crisis that has ever broken out . . . the *class struggle of the bourgeoisie and the proletariat.*
> . . . How much . . . bloody sweat has flowed in the *struggle of classes,* in the struggle of free men and slaves, patricians and plebeians, lords and serfs, capitalists and workers![44]

In July, the second month of operation, Marx applied the same class-struggle terms to German affairs, in this case a proposed bill for a citizens' militia. He pointed out the built-in class distinction, designed "to dig a bottomless abyss between the *bourgeois* of the militia and the *proletarians* of the militia."[45] In an article about a speech by Proudhon in the French assembly on July 31, Marx concluded that, although Proudhon presented himself as a representative of the proletariat versus the bourgeoisie—

> What we attack in Mr. Proudhon was the "utopian science" with which he wanted to smooth over the antagonism between capital and labor, between proletariat and bourgeoisie.[46]

Since the myth applies to the first months of the *N.R.Z.*, we need not go further; the later period is beyond question. (For example, it was in the *N.R.Z.* that Marx's *Wage-Labor and Capital* was first published as a serial.)

The political function of the myth about the *N.R.Z.* will become clearer below, for its role is to lay the basis for another and coordinate myth, that of Marx's fictional "Blanquist aberration" of 1850; this will be considered in its place, in Chapter 10. Now our main interest is in making clear the mutually reinforcing character of the two aspects of the *N.R.Z.*'s policy: to act as the left wing of the Democracy itself, pushing for expansion of the revolution, and (to use Engels' word again) to represent the standpoint of the proletariat within the Democratic movement. The real problem was: how long could the *N.R.Z.* try to ride these two horses, and under what conditions?

Before turning to this fateful issue of the revolution, let us summarize the policy with which Marx *began* operations in Cologne. First of all, there was the two-platoon division of labor already mentioned. As a matter of policy the Marx political center aimed to build two cooperating movements, the Democratic club movement and the Cologne Workers Association. The role of the paper was to deal with the overall politics of the revolution, as a guide to both movements. In this context:

1. The *N.R.Z.* was the organ of the extreme left (proletarian) wing of a Democratic movement which was itself envisaged as a bloc of lower classes (proletariat, small peasantry, petty-bourgeoisie) arrayed against the "big bourgeoisie" represented politically by bourgeois liberalism.*

2. This is not to say that it presented itself as the organ of a workers' movement, let alone a workers' organization; it did not. As mentioned, the Cologne workers' organization had its own organ, which Marx and his friends supported; there was no competition between this paper and the *N.R.Z.* From the standpoint of the *N.R.Z.*, the workers' associations of the various cities, like their Democratic Associations, were *parts* of the general Democratic movement or "Democratic party."

3. The *N.R.Z.* was an agitational newspaper, not a theoretical magazine, though it often stopped to explain political ideas, especially in

---

* Marx and the *N.R.Z.* typically spoke of the "big" bourgeoisie as the class behind bourgeois liberalism in order to differentiate it from the petty-bourgeoisie whose real interest lay in the transformation of society. For the social distinction between the not very big bourgeoisie of the time (the bourgeoisie proper) and the petty-bourgeoisie, see the beginning of Chapter 11, below. —Regarding the progressive bloc of classes: Marx expounded his view on August 4, 1848, at a meeting of the Cologne Democratic Association. Unfortunately this speech is known only through an unreliable newspaper report, which probably reflects its content as through a glass darkly. Marx was attacking a previous talk given by Weitling, who had advocated a "dictatorship . . . as the most desirable constitutional form." The report summarized Marx's argument against this proposal as follows:

> . . . since the state power cannot be established by a single class, the idea of putting into effect a system of dictatorship under a single head deserves to be called nonsense; on the contrary, the governmental power must be put together, like the Provisional Government in Paris, out of the most heterogeneous elements, which thereupon have to unite through an interchange of ideas on the most suitable kind of governmental administration.[47]

major articles by Marx. It agitated for the revolution of the Democracy. It did not agitate for communism (or socialism) in Germany but explained, as in connection with the June uprising, that it did not believe that communism was as yet on the order of the day for Germany.[48] As a political center the Marx group did carry on educational work for communism to train a vanguard, but this educational work was carried on particularly in and through the Workers Association.

Marx was quite aware that widespread public propaganda for communism at this stage might scare the pith out of the already quite pithless bourgeoisie. This brings us back to the central dilemma that became increasingly clear as the revolution stumbled on. If the bourgeoisie was so easily panicked, could it really be depended on to do its duty and make its *own* revolution, as Marx and Engels had so confidently expected?

6. THE BOURGEOISIE REFUSES TO "DO ITS DUTY"

We have seen with what assurance Marx and Engels had predicted that the bourgeoisie had no alternative to carrying through a political revolution that would put it in power and introduce a constitutional-liberal regime. We have seen that they were quite aware of how fainthearted this bourgeoisie was and how much it feared the threat of the proletariat behind it; but this did not yet lead them to conclude that the bourgeoisie might refuse to carry out its historical task. It did suggest to them that the initial task of the proletariat (or "the people") might be to push the bourgeoisie from behind. But one way or the other, the outcome was going to be "not what the bourgeoisie merely *want* but rather what they *must* do."[49]

It was only in the course of the revolution itself that they found out that the bourgeoisie did not recognize the "must." Some decades later, Engels wrote as if that was to have been expected. Reviewing the 1848-1849 period, he first stated the historic issue:

> The question is, who is to rule: the forces of society and state grouped around the absolute monarchy—big feudal landowners, army, bureaucracy, clerical crew—or, rather, the bourgeoisie. The

still nascent proletariat has an interest in the struggle only insofar as through the bourgeoisie's victory it gets air and light to nourish its own development, elbow-room to carry on the struggle in which it will one day gain the victory over all other classes.

But the bourgeoisie did not "do its damned duty":

> But the bourgeoisie, and the petty-bourgeoisie along with it, remains inactive and inert when the hostile government attacks it in the very seat of its power, disperses its parliament, disarms its militia, and subjects it itself to martial law. Then the Communists step into the breach, and appeal to the bourgeoisie to do its damned duty. As against the old feudal society, both of them—bourgeoisie as well as proletariat—constitute the new society, both of them stand together. The appeal, of course, remains fruitless . . .[50]

This essay does not proceed to discuss why this happened but goes on to other matters. The "of course" could be written only in hindsight.

At the time in 1848, Engels confessed surprise at the refusal of the bourgeoisie even to defend its specific bourgeois interests against the old ruling class. The context is the clash between the bourgeois manufacturers and the aristocratic landowners over the wool trade which we have already mentioned:

> For us Democrats, the matter is of interest only because Herr Hansemann [bourgeois-liberal minister] takes the side of the defeated party [the absolutist aristocracy], because he supports not the merely conservative class [bourgeoisie] but the reactionary class. We confess we did not expect this from the bourgeois Hansemann.[51]

This was written only a week after the *N.R.Z.* had started publishing; already the scenario was not being followed.

What had happened? Engels wrote, a week later, that the bourgeoisie had concluded a general social alliance with the "defeated" party of absolutism instead of doing its duty of overthrowing the latter's power completely. The bourgeoisie, through the Hansemann ministry, might be running the government but "the revolution was not completed."

> The big bourgeoisie, antirevolutionary as always, concluded a defensive and offensive alliance with the Reaction, out of fear of the people, i.e., of the workers and the Democratic citizenry. . . .
> Thus the revolution was really called in question, and it could

be called in question because it was only a half-revolution, only the beginning of a long revolutionary movement.

It is clear he understood that this raised a big question-mark over the whole theory of the revolution:

> Here we cannot go into why and to what extent the rule of the big bourgeoisie in Prussia is at the present moment a necessary transitional stage to Democracy, and why the big bourgeoisie went over to the side of the Reaction immediately after its own accession to the throne. For the present we only report the fact.[52]

All this in the first two weeks of the *N.R.Z.* As early as June 4 Marx had raised a tentative question about the course of the revolution, in order to indicate that "the revolution was put in question, that the interest of the revolution was not the interest of the class that had attained mastery or of its political representatives."[53] By June 18 Engels added something to his previous statement that the bourgeoisie had disavowed the very existence of the revolution:

> It is through a second revolution that it [the revolution] will evidence its existence.
> The events of June 14 [when Berliners stormed the arsenal] are only the first lightning flashes of the revolution . . .[54]

To be sure, even before 1848 Engels had written of the "second revolution" idea as a potentiality.[55] Now such talk about a "second revolution" pointed to the need for a revised perspective.

7. WHY THE BOURGEOISIE PREFERRED REACTION

Why had it turned out that there was no historic compulsion on the bourgeoisie to "do its damned duty" and carry through the ousting of the old ruling classes from the seats of state power? There are three points to be made.

1. The most basic consideration is that Marx and Engels found they were wrong in their original belief that the direct capture of state power was the only road for the bourgeoisie to the modernization and industrialization of the economy, to its bourgeoisification. The alternative

was what Marx later analyzed as Bonapartism. This is also why Bismarckian Bonapartism was the "revolution from above," as against the revolution from below by the Democracy which he advocated. It was the substitute revolution.

The bourgeois liberal leaders did not think it out that way in 1848-1849. What consciously pushed them along this line was a negative: fear of the revolution itself. It is true that Marx and Engels had been aware of this factor long in advance—after all, even in his very first article of 1842 Marx had already taken a slap at "the natural impotence of a half-liberalism," referring to the bourgeois-liberal representation in the Rhenish Diet.[56] But they had not believed that this fear could or would outweigh everything else for the bourgeoisie.

2. In general, the bourgeoisie's fear included a mortal dread of anything that created upsets, disturbance, agitation, turbulence, and instability—all bad for business.*

To the outbreak of the revolution the bourgeoisie reacted with "that eternal outcry for order and tranquillity, which has everywhere seized this class after violent commotions and consequent derangement of trade."[59] In the *N.R.Z.* Engels wrote contemptuously:

> But we [Germans] were philistines and we remain philistines. We have made a couple of dozen revolutions, little and big, of which we ourselves got scared before they were ever brought to completion. After talking real big, we carried out nothing at all. . . . All questions were handled with the most timorous, obtuse and narrowminded philistinism . . .[60]

Toward the end of 1848 Marx wrote scathingly of the bourgeoisie's "wretched, jittery, narrowminded egoism," which filled it with fear as soon as a finger was laid on property anywhere. Its main slogan was restoration of confidence and the credit system; that is why every

---

* This fear can be seen transmuted through the mind of an intellectual—not a businessman—in the words of David Friedrich Strauss. Strauss, though never a political rebel, had been influential in the beginnings of German new thought with his 1835 rationalist version of the *Life of Jesus*; this book exercised a radicalizing influence on the young Engels and led him to Hegelianism.[57] But the revolution of 1848 brought out a typical reaction in Strauss: "To a nature like mine," he wrote, "it was much better under the old police state, when we had quiet on the streets and were not always meeting with excited people, new-fashioned slouch hats, and beards."[58] *Beards?* This subversive role of beards should make it obvious that the Great Hair Question is not a new source of commotion. For a *Plus ça change* note on this burning issue, see Special Note D.

stirring had to be suppressed, not only among the proletariat but in every social stratum that had interests different from the bourgeoisie. The Hansemann ministry set out to strengthen the state power in order to restore confidence and credit, but it only strengthened a state power that restored confidence in itself through bullets, since it lacked all credit. Therefore its activity boiled down to police work, and it "represented nothing but the *old,* refurbished *police- and bureaucratic state."*[61]

This remained a frequent theme in Marx's writings, as he kept on emphasizing that the revolution of 1848 failed because "at that time the bourgeois preferred peace-and-quiet accompanied by servitude rather than the mere *prospect* of struggle [even if] accompanied by freedom . . ."[62] In 1850 Engels summed up the character of the German bourgeoisie: it

> is infinitely more fainthearted than the English or French, and insofar as even the slightest chance of returning anarchy shows up, that is, really decisive struggle, it shudders and withdraws from the arena.[63]

A decade after the revolution Marx explained to his *New York Tribune* readers that politics in Prussia must be understood in terms of the pusillanimity of the bourgeoisie. While they do not like "moderate solvency" on the part of debtors, their watchword is "moderate liberty." This sector, "whose political creed may be characterized as *liberalismus vulgaris,* is anything but heroical."

> Then there is before their eyes and in their hearts the still fresh remembrance of the revolution; and, lastly, the Prince Regent must not be frightened out of his new constitutionalism. So one liberal hero admonishes the other, to do him the good service which the husband asked from his wife on her being insulted in the open street by a military officer. "Keep me back," cried the gallant fellow, "or I shall take revenge, and there will be bloodshed."

This bourgeoisie knows, Marx continued, that if its local liberalism goes beyond very narrow limits, "it must roll back or resolve itself into a general continental movement. The fear of the latter is shared alike by the higher middle class and by the Prince Regent."[64] The "Constitution-mongers" of the bourgeoisie, he wrote in another article, are firmly resolved to accept any humiliation "to gain a nominal Constitution, whatever its contents, to ascend by cringing in the dust."[65]

3. Of course, this cowardice and congenital dread of disorder had very material roots, which we have already seen indicated: fear of the proletariat pressing in the rear. In 1848 this fear took on flesh and blood. The *Communist Manifesto* had ended: "Let the ruling classes tremble at a Communistic revolution." They did. Not because of the Manifesto or of literary productions from any quarter; they began trembling even before the June uprising in Paris.[66]

Only a month had elapsed since the March days in Berlin when Engels, writing from his home town, Barmen, described the change that had come over the radical bourgeois whom he had once expected to be revolutionary. They had moved sharply to the right, while the workers had begun to organize. His brother-in-law Emil Blank,

> who is still the best of the lot, has in practice become a bourgeois; the others even more so, ever since they have got themselves established and have come into collision with the workers. . . . The point is, at bottom, that even these radical bourgeois here see us as their main enemy in the future, and that they don't want to put any weapons in our hands which we would very soon turn against them themselves.[67]

He was later going to write about "the Rhenish liberal philistines, who had suddenly become reactionary."[68] The June uprising in Paris sent the German bourgeoisie stampeding in terror into the arms of the Crown and the aristocracy, even though nothing of the sort was happening in Germany. Marx wrote in the *N.R.Z.* on June 29 that the French bourgeoisie had had to put an end to the threat from below:

> Factually and actually in practice, the thing must be decided. Did you canaille make the February Revolution for *yourselves* or for *us?* The bourgeoisie posed the question in such a way that it had to be answered in June—with bullets and barricades.[69]

The example held for the Germans; they too had to end the threat from below before it grew too menacing. The French government's bloody suppression of the June uprising was inspiring. The pattern was next brought home to Marx by the debacle in Austria as the bourgeoisie "betrayed" Vienna:

> In France it [the bourgeoisie] came forward as a despot and made its own counterrevolution. In Germany it came forward as a

slave-girl and made the counterrevolution its own despot. In France it won out, in order to humble the people. In Germany it humbled itself, in order to keep the people from winning. All history shows nothing more *ignominious and mean-spirited* than the German bourgeoisie.[70]

Just before the revolution, Engels had brashly told the bourgeoisie: "do not forget: 'The executioner stands at the door.'"[71] The revolution itself said the same thing even more forcefully. So the bourgeoisie refused to open that door.

8. ANALYZING THE COUNTERREVOLUTION

The original scenario for permanent revolution had had the bourgeoisie making an alliance with the Democracy to overthrow the old ruling classes. What Marx saw in the course of 1848 was that the bourgeoisie had turned in the other direction, making an alliance with the trinity of Crown-aristocracy-bureaucracy on which the old state rested.

This was spelled out in a major four-part article by Marx in December, "The Bourgeoisie and the Counterrevolution." The two camps, rivals for state power, had made a deal:

The Crown would sacrifice the nobility for the bourgeoisie; the bourgeoisie would sacrifice the people for the Crown. Under these conditions the monarchy becomes bourgeois and the bourgeoisie becomes monarchist.[72]

The bourgeoisie was intoxicated by the delusion that "the ruling powers of the old state" would really subordinate themselves to bourgeois political domination. Thus—

It was clear. The Prussian bourgeoisie had only one task, the task of establishing itself snugly in its rule, of getting rid of the troublesome anarchists [revolutionary people], of restoring "calm and order" and bringing back the revenues that had gone lost during the March upheaval. . . . The weapons that the Prussian bourgeoisie had been forced to avail itself of, in its struggle against the feudal society and its monarchy—right of association, freedom of the press, etc.: must they not be shattered in the hands of a people carried away by folly, which no longer needed to wield them *for* the bourgeoisie and showed signs of a suspicious hankering to use them *against* the bourgeoisie?

Obviously only one obstacle stood in the way of a deal between the bourgeoisie and the Crown ... a single obstacle, the people—*puer robustus sed malitiosus* [sturdy but wicked lad], as Hobbes put it.* The *people* and the *revolution!*

The *revolution* was the *people's legal title;* it was on the revolution that its turbulent claims were based. The revolution was the bill it had drawn on the bourgeoisie. It was by the revolution that the bourgeoisie had attained to rule. The day it attained to rule was also the day this bill fell due. The bourgeoisie had to enter a *protest* against the bill.[74]

Not long afterward, the German bourgeoisie publicly avowed what Marx had charged.**

Soon after the end of the revolutionary period, Engels produced his historical study on *The Peasant War in Germany,* which was explicitly presented as a parable for 1848: "The classes and fractions of classes which everywhere betrayed 1848 and 1849 are to be found in the role of traitors as early as 1525, though on a lower level of development."[76] In a later preface to this work, Engels summarized the question we are now discussing. He noted that he had been wrong in writing in 1850 that "the modern big bourgeois" were "rapidly getting [the Austrian and Prussian monarchies] under their yoke by means of the national debt. And behind the big bourgeois stand the proletarians."[77] (Even in 1850 he still had illusions that the bourgeoisie was going to "do its damned duty," if only in another form.) Writing two decades later, he

---

* Marx is echoing his 1847 reference to Hobbes's *puer robustus.*[73]

** Hammen, as anti-Marxist a chronicler as one could desire, writes as follows in this connection:

> The "betrayal of the bourgeoisie," as Marx and Engels called it, was at work. Actually, it was a refusal by the liberal bourgeoisie and many Democrats to continue the fight ... after it became evident that many revolutionists were exploiting the situation for other purposes. Here and there the red flag had supplanted the Black-Red-Gold. ...
>
> Already on May 11 [1849], the *Kölnische Zeitung* reported that the presence of many "impure elements in the German movement" which threatened the "lives of the citizens and the free expression of their views" was producing a revulsion of feeling in favor of the governments. A private letter of ... a Rhineland liberal ... [said that] All people with property "will prefer the absolute monarchy to a red republic" ... By May 13 the paper conceded unhappily that ... "The intelligent propertied class of citizens, the kernel and center of the nation" was beginning to waver, even to retreat to a counterrevolutionary position.[75]

recognized that "the mass of the bourgeoisie . . . does not *want* to rule. It still has 1848 in its bones."[78] That is, its decisive motivation is still fear of the proletariat.

This was the link between the bourgeoisie's dread of the permanent revolution and the phenomenon of Bonapartism. Engels sets it forth in an important passage. In two decades the German bourgeoisie has developed economically, but "How, then, is it possible that the bourgeoisie has not conquered political power as well, that it behaves in so cowardly a manner towards the government?"

> It is the misfortune of the German bourgeoisie to have arrived too late, as is the favorite German manner. The period of its florescence is occurring at a time when the bourgeoisie of the other West European countries is already politically in decline. In England, the bourgeoisie could get its real representative, Bright, into the government only by an extension of the franchise, whose consequences are bound to put an end to all bourgeois rule. In France, where the bourgeoisie as such, as a class in its entirety, held power for only two years, 1849 and 1850, under the republic, it was able to continue its social existence only by abdicating its political power to Louis Bonaparte and the army. And on account of the enormously increased interaction of the three most advanced European countries, it is today no longer possible for the bourgeoisie to settle down to comfortable political rule in Germany after this rule has outlived its usefulness in England and France.[79]

This is the pattern of uneven and combined development at work.

It is a peculiarity of the bourgeoisie, in contrast to all former ruling classes, that there is a turning point in its development after which every further expansion of its agencies of power, hence primarily of its capital, only tends to make it more and more unfit for political rule.* *"Behind the big bourgeois stand the proletarians."* As the bourgeoisie develops its industry, commerce and means of communications, it produces the proletariat. At a certain point—which need not be reached everywhere at the same time or at the same stage of development—it begins to

---

* This is an excellent example of Engels' penchant for "making large generalizations, not all of them properly qualified," to which I have already referred.[80] He has not given evidence for this "turning point" theory, nor will he return to it. I think the evidence shows the peculiarity of the bourgeoisie is that it is "unfit for political rule," as compared with former ruling classes, at all stages of its existence, that this characteristic is inherent in the nature of the class, as I have discussed in Volume 1.[81]

notice that its proletarian double is outgrowing it. From that moment on, it loses the strength required for exclusive political rule; it looks around for allies with whom to share its rule, or to whom to cede the whole of its rule, as circumstances may require.

This is all a generalization from the experience of the revolution of 1848–1849. He applies it specifically to Germany:

> In Germany this turning point came as early as 1848. To be sure, the German bourgeoisie was less frightened by the German proletariat than by the French. The June 1848 battle in Paris showed the bourgeoisie what it ought to expect; the German proletariat was restless enough to prove to it that the seed that would yield the same crop had already been sown to German soil, too; from that day on the edge was taken off all bourgeois political action. The bourgeoisie looked round for allies, sold itself to them regardless of the price—and even today [1870] it has not advanced one step.
>
> These allies are all reactionary by nature. There is the monarchy with its army and its bureaucracy; there is the big feudal nobility; there are the little cabbage-Junkers and there are even the priests. With all of these the bourgeoisie made pacts and bargains, if only to save its dear skin, until at last it had nothing left to barter. And the more the proletariat developed, the more it felt as a class and acted as a class, the more fainthearted did the bourgeois become.[82]

In 1850 Marx had written that:

> If the [defeat of the] June insurrection raised the self-assurance of the bourgeoisie all over the Continent and caused it to league itself openly with the feudal monarchy against the people, who was the first victim of this alliance? The Continental bourgeoisie itself. The June defeat prevented it from consolidating its rule . . .[83]

The bourgeoisie was indeed prevented from consolidating its political rule, but, in the sequel under Bismarckian Bonapartism, it went ahead to consolidate its economic rule nevertheless. The same factors that negated the path of permanent revolution *in the form envisioned by Marx and Engels in 1848* also pushed the bourgeoisie along the path of Bonapartism.

This in turn had to engender, and did engender, a later and revised form of the concept of permanent revolution.

9 | PERMANENT REVOLUTION: FINAL VERSION

Around the latter part of 1848 and early 1849, Marx gave up the expectation that the bourgeoisie might come through after all.

This was not an easy conclusion to come to, since—in the absence of a crystal ball to foresee alternative roads—it suggested that in Germany the road of progressive economic modernization might be closed or long delayed. Marx did not adopt the conclusion on some given day; on the contrary, there are many signs of groping and oscillation, as might be expected of militants who were trying to understand an unexpected development, not in a library carrel a hundred years later but in the hurly-burly of revolutionary events.

1. WRITING OFF THE BOURGEOISIE

Even as early as July 1848 there was already an element of ambiguity in the following passage in an article by Marx:

> The [Hansemann ministry] wants to establish the rule of the bourgeoisie while at the same time striking a compromise with the old police- and feudal state. In this two-sided and contradictory task, at every turn it sees the still-to-be-established rule of the bourgeoisie and its own existence frustrated by the reactionary forces of the absolutist, feudal type—and it will succumb to the latter. The bourgeoisie cannot fight it out for its own rule without temporarily taking the people as a whole as its ally, hence without coming out more or less democratically.[1]

There is the direct statement that "it will succumb," but the next implication is that "it will succumb *unless* . . ." The second view, in fact, remained the operative line for months.

A month before, in the eloquent article in which Marx defended the June uprising of the Paris workers, his bitterness toward the bourgeois executioners of the revolt did not prevent him from asking, toward the end of the article, whether this "deep gulf that has opened before us" should lead one to think that the fight for a democratic constitution makes no difference, that the difference between a democratic state form and the absolutist state form is only "empty, illusory, nil." His answer is a vigorous *no*. The struggles arising out of social development have to be fought to their conclusion:

> The best form of the state is that in which social antagonisms are not blurred, are not forcibly—hence only artificially, only illusor-ily—fettered. The best form of the state is that in which they come to a free fight and thereby to a solution.[2]

Therefore the *N.R.Z.* group pushed for everything that would fur-ther a democratic-constitutional government, a complete democratiza-tion of the state. But increasingly a question mark had to be put over the issue: what social force could achieve this aim?

The answer was not worked out by meditation in the offices of the *N.R.Z.* It came in response to a series of shocks. In September a watershed event cast a bright light. An uprising broke out in the Frankfurt area, fought "by the workers of Frankfurt, Offenbach and Hanau, and by the peasants of the surrounding region," Engels re-ported. The bourgeois elements opposed the movement, and it was suppressed by the government with the help of Prussian, Austrian, and Hessian troops. Engels' article on the uprising looked at the class alignment and generalized: why the victories of the counterrevolution all over Europe?

> Because all sides know that the struggle that is looming in all civilized countries is an entirely different one, an infinitely more important one, than all previous revolutions: because in Vienna as in Paris, in Berlin as in Frankfurt, in London as in Milan, it is a question of the *overthrow of the political rule of the bourgeoisie*, of a transformation whose imminent consequences already fill all comfortable and puzzled citizens with dismay.
>
> Is there any revolutionary center in the world where the red flag, the battle symbol of the fraternizing European proletariat, has not waved over the barricades in the last five months?

In Frankfurt too, the parliament of the united Junkers and bourgeois was combated under the red flag.

It is because the bourgeoisie is threatened by every uprising breaking out now—threatened directly as to its political existence and indirectly as to its social existence: this is the reason for all these defeats. The mostly unarmed people have to fight not only against the forces of the organized bureaucratic and military state which have been taken over by the bourgeoisie, but also against the armed bourgeoisie itself. Confronting the unorganized and badly armed people stand the joint forces of the other classes of society, well organized and well equipped. And that is why the people have been beaten so far, and why they will continue to be beaten till their opponents are weakened—whether because the troops get involved in war or because they have an internal split—or until some big event drives the people into desperate struggle and demoralizes their opponents.[3]

Engels' article then points to looming events in France as the hope of renewed revolutionary élan in Europe.

At the end of August Marx, on a visit to Vienna, spoke before the Democratic Association there, and seems to have expressed an opinion about the Austrian situation that he had not yet applied to Germany. "Herr *Marx*," said the Viennese press report, "opined it made no difference *who* was Minister, for now here too—as in Paris—it was a question of the struggle between the bourgeoisie and the proletariat."[3a]

By December the pattern was clear enough for the publication of Marx's major programmatic article, "The Bourgeoisie and the Counterrevolution," which (as we have seen) indicted the bourgeoisie for going over to the counterrevolution. It contains the most powerful flagellation yet of the bourgeoisie's incapacity. A key passage, from the second part, is a good example of Marx's "thunderer" style as well as of the political interpretation he is developing:

The German bourgeoisie had developed so sluggishly, cravenly and slowly that at the moment when it menacingly confronted feudalism and absolutism, it saw itself menacingly faced by the proletariat and by all sections of the citizenry [*Bürgertum*, burghers; not bourgeois] whose interests and ideas were related to the proletariat. And it not only saw a class *behind* it but all of Europe hostilely arrayed *before* it. The Prussian bourgeoisie was not, as the French bourgeoisie of 1789 had been, the class that represented the *whole* of modern society vis-à-vis the representatives of the old society, the monarchy and the aristocracy. It had sunk down to a kind of *social estate* just as clearly distinct from the Crown as from the people, eager for opposition to both, irresolute before either taken individually, because it always saw both of them either before or behind; inclined from the outset to betray the people and to compromise with the crowned representative of the old society, because it itself already belonged to the old society; representing not the interests of a new society against an old one but newly revived interests inside an obsolescent society; at the helm of the revolution not because the people stood behind it but because the people pushed it on before; in the van not because it represented the initiative of a new era of society but only the rancor of an old one; a stratum that had not broken through under the old state but which now was heaved up to the surface of the new state by an earthquake; without faith in itself, without faith in the people, grumbling at those above, trembling at those below, egoistic toward both sides and conscious of its egoism, revolutionary vis-à-vis the conservatives, conservative vis-à-vis the revolutionaries, distrustful of its own catchwords, given to phrases instead of ideas, intimidated by the international storm, exploiting the international storm;—no energy in any direction, plagiarism in all directions; common because it was not original, original in its commonness;—haggling over its own aspirations, without initiative, without faith in itself, without faith in the people, without a world-historical mission;—a damned old codger who found himself condemned to lead and mislead the first youthful currents of a sturdy people into the channels of his own senile interests;—sans eyes, sans ears, sans teeth, sans everything;—in such wise did the *Prussian bourgeoisie* find itself at the helm of the Prussian state after the March revolution.[4]

It would seem that after all this strong language Marx was writing the liberal bourgeoisie off as any kind of revolutionary force.

2. "SOCIAL REPUBLIC"
OR COUNTERREVOLUTION

If not the bourgeoisie, what social force was the alternative to the restoration of absolutist power?

Marx points to the class bloc we have already described: proletariat, petty-bourgeoisie, small peasantry. This time the peasantry is featured more prominently than before, for the government has just made clear, by its bill on the abolition of feudal burdens on the land, that it is impotent to attack feudal property on the land for fear of awakening ideas about bourgeois property. Bourgeois "egoism" has blinded it "to the point where it drove away its own *indispensable allies*—the class of *peasantry.*"*

The French bourgeoisie began with the emancipation of the peasantry. With the peasants it conquered Europe. The Prussian bourgeoisie was so wrapped up in its own *narrow*, immediate interests that it even alienated this ally and made it a tool in the hands of the feudal counterrevolution.[5]

Conclusion:

The history of the Prussian bourgeoisie, as in general that of the German bourgeoisie from March to December, proves that in Germany a purely *bourgeois revolution* and the establishment of *bourgeois rule* under the form of *constitutional monarchy* are impossible, and that only the feudal absolutist counterrevolution is possible or else the *social-republican revolution.*[6]

This—counterrevolution or Social Republic—is an important new formulation of the revolutionary alternatives.

As we have seen,[7] the slogan of the Social Republic (or Social and Democratic Republic) was already in common use to indicate a democratic republic that takes social measures beyond the interests of the bourgeoisie. At the time, "social institutions" meant in a general way what we might now call "socialistic" institutions. For example, in the *N.R.Z.* for September 1, 1848, Engels wrote that

the democratic-social republic must first be proclaimed [in France], the French proletariat must first stand over its bourgeoisie with its foot on its neck, before the lasting victory of Democracy is thinkable in Italy, Germany, Poland, Hungary, etc.[8]

This is also the meaning of Marx's counterposition, in his 1850 *Class Struggles in France,* of the "bourgeois republic" to the "republic with social institutions." The republic that was actually set up by the Constituent Assembly in May was, says Marx, "not the republic with social institutions, not the vision that hovered before the fighters on the

---

* The peasantry, which became increasingly important to Marx in the next months, will be closely examined in Chapter 13 below.

barricades." It was "no revolutionary weapon against the bourgeois order, but rather . . . the political reconsolidation of bourgeois society, in a word, *a bourgeois republic."* True, the government "was forced by the immediate pressure of the proletariat to announce it as a *republic with social institutions"* but in fact "the Paris proletariat was still incapable of going beyond the bourgeois republic otherwise than in its *fancy* . . .'"[9] Engels wrote later that "a *pure,* bourgeois republic in Germany was outstripped by events before it came into existence."[10]

The slogan of the Social Republic remained a popularized and agitational (because open-ended) way of referring to a government that takes a socialistic direction, right up to the time of the First International and after.* In 1848 it lent itself very well to designate the idea of the *transitional* regime which was no longer bourgeois but not yet Communist, based on a bloc of progressive classes.

At the point we are at now (end of 1848), Marx's concept of this bloc is broad indeed. How broad may be seen from the sentence that follows immediately after the above-quoted invocation of "the social-republican revolution":

> But this itself must rearouse the viable part of the bourgeoisie out of its apathy; this is guaranteed us above all by the *fearful reckoning* with which the counterrevolution will surprise it in the spring . . .[12]

Clearly Marx is hoping that at least a more progressive section ("viable part") of the bourgeoisie itself will decide that, for them, the Social Republic is a lesser evil to absolutist counterrevolution, and therefore go along willingly with a regime based on the broad bloc of classes lying to the left of the main mass of the bourgeoisie.

---

* This was brought out specifically by Marx in 1871 in his *Civil War in France:*

The cry of "social republic," with which the revolution of February [1848] was ushered in by the Paris proletariat, did but express a vague aspiration after a Republic that was not only to supersede the monarchical form of class rule, but class rule itself. The Commune was the positive form of that Republic.[11]

3. END OF THE LINE

The following month, January 1849, posed the problem on the plane of immediate tactics. An election—based on a two-stage and quite undemocratic electoral system with a restricted franchise—was scheduled in Prussia for the 22nd. Should the Workers Association run its own candidates, on the platform of the Social Republic, against the "plain Democrats" who, as advocates of a bourgeois republic, were also enemies of the old regime?

This led to the last phase of Marx's persistent attempt to support the bourgeois opposition against absolutism. His statement of policy was paraphrased as follows in the report in the Workers Association organ on the Executive's discussion:

> ... at the moment it is not a question of doing something along the lines of our principles but of putting up opposition to the government, absolutism and feudal rule; sufficient for this, however, are plain Democrats—so-called liberals—who are likewise not satisfied by a long shot with the present regime. One must take the situation as it is for once. Since the important thing now is to put up the strongest possible opposition to the existing absolutist system, then, if it is understood that the principles we ourselves hold cannot be put across in the elections, good sense requires us to unite with another party which likewise is putting up opposition, in order not to let our common enemy, the absolute monarchy, win.[13]

The association, in fact, decided to support candidates of the Democracy on the condition that they opposed the constitution "octroyed" (handed down) by the Prussian king.

On the basis of experience Marx was later going to dispute the simple "good sense" of this policy. In any case, this was not a question of choosing between good bourgeois candidates and bad ones, but rather of choosing between supporters of two different social systems, one progressive and the other historically reactionary.*

---

* This is the basic difference between the problem faced by Marx and the later issue it resembles, namely, the social-democratic "lesser evil" policy of supporting liberal bourgeois candidates against right-wing bourgeois candidates. In addition, the issue as posed in January 1849 was influenced by two immediate factors: (1) Because of the electoral laws only a fraction of the workers had the right to vote; hence any electoral policy was not mainly directed to a proletarian constituency. (2) The group that opposed support to Democratic candidates and advo-

On the eve of the election a two-part article by Marx went all-out in an appeal not only to the Democracy but especially to the bourgeois opposition to defeat absolutism, and in particular to defeat the octroyed constitution. It deserves notice as a milestone in Marx's political development, for never again will he invest such expectations in the bourgeoisie.

Cologne's leading paper, the *Kölnische Zeitung,* had charged that the opponents of the octroyed constitution were proponents of a red republic; it was necessary to broaden opposition to the constitution if this scare propaganda were to be countered. Marx answered: that is not the issue—not a red republic or any republic. The only issue is this:

> Do you want the old *absolutism* together with a newly refurbished estates system—or do you want a bourgeois *representative system?* . . . it is not at all a question of a struggle against bourgeois property relations, such as is taking place in France and is under preparation in England. It is rather a question of a struggle against a political constitution which endangers *"bourgeois* property relations," by surrendering the helm of state to the representatives of the *"feudal* property relations" . . .[15]

The main appeal of the article is systematically pitched in terms of the interests of the bourgeoisie itself: "does the bourgeoisie gain a state form in which it can freely conduct the common affairs of its class, the interests of commerce, industry and agriculture . . . ?"[16]

> Bourgeois industry *must* burst the fetters of absolutism and feudalism. A revolution against both means only that bourgeois industry has reached a pinnacle where it must conquer a state form suitable for it or else go under.[17]

(This reverts to the old conviction that one "does not ask what the bourgeoisie merely *want* but rather what they *must* do.")[18]

Addressing himself to the Democracy, Marx explains:

> We are surely the last to want the rule of the bourgeoisie. We were the first in Germany to raise our voices against it . . .
> But we appeal to the workers and petty-bourgeoisie: Better to

---

cated workers' candidates only, the Gottschalk clique in the Cologne Workers Association, took off from a *reactionary* standpoint, one that looked to an accommodation with a "social monarchy" as against alliance with the Democracy.[14] In any case, in 1850 Marx decided in hindsight that this policy was mistaken even for 1849, as we shall see.

put up with modern bourgeois society, which through its industrialization creates the material means for establishing a new society which will emancipate all of you, than turn the clock back to an outlived form of society which, on the pretext of saving your class, thrusts the whole nation back into medieval barbarism![19]

If the Crown's constitution is against the class interests of the Prussian bourgeoisie, why is this bourgeoisie in favor of it? Marx's first answer:

> The commercial and industrial sector of the bourgeoisie throws itself into the arms of the counterrevolution out of fear of the revolution. As though the counterrevolution were anything else than the overture to revolution.

His appeal to the bourgeoisie, then, is: restoration of the absolutist power will make a revolution more certain, not less. (The bourgeoisie was not convinced, with good reason.) Next, Marx points to that sector of the bourgeoisie "which, indifferent to the collective interests of its class, pursues a special interest of its own, a separate interest which is even hostile to the others."[20] This sector includes "the financial barons, the public creditors, bankers and rentiers" plus government-business contractors and their intellectual and professional hangers-on. But these cannot account for the bourgeoisie as a whole.

The election results showed that, while in the Rhineland the Democratic candidates nosed out the opposition, in Prussia as a whole the bourgeoisie continued moving right. The end of the line was near.

In mid-February Marx put all this behind him, though without backtracking:

> We like firm attitudes. We have never flirted with a parliamentary party.* The party that *we* represent, the party of the people, exists in Germany only in elementary form. But where it is a struggle against the *existing government,* we ally ourselves even with our enemies. We take as a fact the official Prussian opposition, just as it emerges out of the miserable German cultural conditions obtaining to the present day, and hence we have allowed *our* own views to stay in the background during the electoral struggle. Now, *after* the election, we again affirm our old relentless standpoint not only as against the government but also as against the official opposition.[22]

---

* Likewise a little later: "the *Neue Rheinische Zeitung* has never presented itself as the organ of a parliamentary party."[21]

From here on, Marx moved more and more away from participation in the Democratic movement as such, toward emphasis on the primacy of the workers' organizations and toward mobilization of the peasantry of the region. On April 14 the break was made definitive: Marx and three close collaborators announced their resignation from the Rhineland committee of the Democratic Association, and publicly stated that the objective should be the organization of workers' associations instead.[23] Thus Marx returned the goal of workers' class organization to the top of the agenda, as explained at the end of Special Note J. However, the project for a national congress of workers' associations died, as the revolution itself was repressed throughout the country in the next period.

This resignation marked the formal end of a period of experimentation in Marx's theory of revolution and in his practice.

4. SECOND VERSION
OF PERMANENT REVOLUTION

The line that Marx pursued in the Prussian election of January 1849 had served to keep alive the initial version of the permanent revolution concept. But if we follow the line from his December article on "The Bourgeoisie and the Counterrevolution" to his resignation from the Democratic Association committee in April, we can distinguish a second version of permanent revolution to which he moved.

The first version had envisaged the following uninterrupted stages: (1) the bourgeoisie takes political power from absolutism; (2) the Democracy, as a bloc of proletariat, petty-bourgeoisie, and peasantry, moves in to take over from the bourgeoisie.

The second version involves a simple change: since the bourgeoisie refuses to take political power, the Democracy must strive to capture political power directly for itself. What remains unchanged is this: the perspective is still to accelerate bourgeois economic development (modernization and industrialization) under the aegis of the new revolutionary power to the point where the next stage—proletarian power—goes onto the order of the day. The bourgeois-democratic stage is to be telescoped under a political power which is not that of the bourgeoisie itself. (Looking ahead, we can see an analogy: under Bonapartism the bourgeois stage is also going to be carried out under a political power which is not that of the bourgeoisie itself.)*

This does not involve the illusion that communism itself is on the immediate social agenda for backward Germany, but it does involve skipping the stage of the "pure," or bourgeois, republic and going over directly to the Social Republic. It also pushes to the fore the slogan of a second revolution.

To be sure, an article had already referred to the second revolution during the very first month of the *N.R.Z.*[26] Now it was more pressing. Marx used a well-publicized occasion to give it prominence—his defense speech before a Cologne jury in February, which ends as follows:

> In conclusion, I repeat that only the first act of the drama has been concluded. The struggle of the two societies, medieval society and bourgeois society, will be carried on anew in political forms. . . .
>
> But whatever the road the new National Assembly may take, the necessary result can be nothing else than this: *complete victory of the counterrevolution* or *a new victorious revolution!* Perhaps the victory of the revolution is possible only after the counterrevolution has been consummated.[27]

The last sentence, qualified with a "perhaps," writes off the bourgeoisie as a revolutionary force, this time for good.

The aim of a democratic constitution as the goal of the struggle was not at all affected. Right after the first-stage election, Marx returned to

---

* Readers concerned with the Russian analogy mentioned in Chapter 7[24] may note the resemblance between this second version of permanent revolution and Lenin's formula "democratic dictatorship of the proletariat and peasantry." Trotsky argued—rightly, I think—that there was no necessary incompatibility between Lenin's formula and his own theory of permanent revolution; the former, he maintained, "in large measure bore an intentionally algebraic character." But I do not think Trotsky understood that the basic conception of permanent revolution is itself an "algebraic" formula, that is, it can be concretized by different policies. Trotsky's brief references to Marx in this connection—about going over to "socialist measures," and about "the bourgeois revolution of '48 as the direct introduction to the proletarian revolution"—are relevant only to Marx's final variant.[25] He was probably familiar mainly with the content of Marx's "Address to the Communist League" of 1850, to be discussed in the next chapter. Also, needless to say, the preponderant role of the agrarian question and the peasantry in Russia introduced a big difference from Marx's situation. For these and other reasons, it is unwise to equate the general concept of permanent revolution with any single application of it to a given historical situation.

the charge against the octroyed constitution with heavy emphasis on the Democratic class lineup:

> Can the petty-bourgeois and peasants, and the proletarians in addition, find a better state form for the representation of their interests than the democratic republic? Aren't these precisely the classes that are the most radical and the most democratic in the whole society? Isn't the proletariat precisely the specifically *red* class? [28]

As a matter of fact, the last phase of the German revolution acted this out. In May, what Engels later wrote up as "The German Campaign for the Reich Constitution" broke out with armed uprisings in the Rhineland and South Germany; on the 16th the Prussian government presented Marx with an expulsion order; on the 19th the *N.R.Z.* appeared for the last time, in a special red-ink issue, in which the editors said of themselves: "Their last word everywhere and always will be: *Emancipation of the laboring class!*" [29] Engels went to fight with the insurrectionary forces.

Engels' essay on this last flare-up of the revolution, written soon afterwards, summarized the class lineup as follows, thereby also explaining the movement's hapless futility:

> The soul of the whole movement was the class of the *small bourgeoisie,* called by preference the *middle class* [*Bürgerstand*], and this indeed is the predominating class in Germany, especially in the South. . . .
>
> Behind the small bourgeoisie everywhere, however, stand other classes, which take up the movement . . . give it a more definite and energetic character, and wherever possible try to take it over: the *proletariat* and a large part of the *peasants,* which the advanced section of the petty-bourgeoisie generally joined for a while, in addition.
>
> These classes, with the proletariat of the larger towns at the head, took the solemnly affirmed assurances of support for the Constitution more seriously than the petty-bourgeois agitators liked. . . . [Everyone understood] that after victory the petty-bourgeoisie would have to defend this same constitution against these very same proletarians and peasants. These classes pushed the small bourgeoisie to an open break with the existing state power. [30]

The "viable" or "progressive" sector of the bourgeoisie (recall the expectation in Marx's "The Bourgeoisie and the Counterrevolution") was around too—if only "at the beginning of the movement":

> Besides, at the beginning of the movement, the more resolute section of the big and middle bourgeoisie likewise joined with the petty-bourgeoisie, just as we see in all previous petty-bourgeois movements in England and France. The bourgeoisie never rules as a whole; leaving aside the feudal castes that have still retained some part of their political power, even the big bourgeoisie, as soon as it has defeated feudalism, splits into a governing party and an opposition party, which are usually represented on the one hand by the bank and on the other by the manufacturers. The oppositionist, progressive section of the big and middle bourgeoisie then has common interests with the petty-bourgeoisie as against the ruling section, and it unites with the petty-bourgeoisie for a common struggle.[31]

The right wing of the movement was fighting for national unification under the Black-Red-Gold constitution of the Reich; the Democratic left wing fought for a "red republic" (Social Republic). But the revolution never got a chance to become permanent, that is, to start the expected class shifts toward the left as a result of the defeat of the old regime; for the Democratic uprising was suppressed.

5. THE INTERNATIONAL MEANING OF PERMANENT REVOLUTION

Marx had never expected the movement to win in backward Germany alone, if confined to German forces only. He looked on Germany as one battlefield in a European war (the revolution), and usually a secondary one at that.

This adds another dimension to the concept of permanent revolution; for it views the course of the revolution on a European-wide scale, proceeding "in permanence" (in ongoing waves) from one country to another. There are two aspects to this country-to-country interaction: the role of the more advanced (more industrialized) countries in relation to others where the bourgeoisie had not yet won political power; and the role of oppressor countries in relation to oppressed nationalities.

To be sure, this internationalism of the revolution had been a part of

Marx's thinking from the outset; the best-known early expression in Marx is the last sentence of his introduction to a critique of Hegel in 1844: "When all the inner conditions are fulfilled, the *German resurrection day* will be announced by the *crowing of the Gallic cock.*"[32] (He kept on expressing this very opinion through 1848.) More important, this international perspective became a basic ingredient of permanent revolution especially through the experience of 1848–1849. Here too, the origin of the term *permanent revolution* in the French Revolution played a conditioning role. We may recall Marx's early remark that Napoleon had substituted "permanent war for permanent revolution."* The historical significance of the Napoleonic wars was that they spread the bourgeois revolution to other parts of Europe, that is, they made the revolution "permanent" (ongoing) on an international scale even while limiting the revolution at home. The elements of European war and European revolution were inextricably mingled.

Even more than in Napoleonic days, the revolution of 1848–1849 presented the spectacle of the *contagious revolution,* flaring up in ongoing waves in one country after another, with an interacting impact. For the first time on such a big scale, internationalism was not merely an aspiration, a "moral value," a daydream, or a philosophic notion, but a practical, matter-of-fact social force.

It was also the answer in terms of political theory to the impossibilities of the German revolution. Could one really believe that this backward country, with its small proletariat, petty-bourgeois Democracy, timid bourgeoisie, under an overbearing bureaucratic state, could carry through the permanent revolution even as far as a Social Republic? Not on the basis of German forces, thought Marx.

The article in which Marx laid out this line of thought in systematic form appeared in the *N.R.Z.* at the beginning of the new year, 1849. It has sometimes been misinterpreted through failure to understand that in it "world war" means *revolutionary war on a world-wide scale,* on the analogy of the Napoleonic "permanent revolution."**

The article begins for contrast, with the elocutionary declamations

---

* For this, see Special Note C, page 595.

** This usage is spelled out quite explicitly in an article by Engels later in June: "The European, the *people's war* . . . the European war of liberation is for Germany a civil war at the same time . . . the great struggle for liberty which is spreading through all Europe . . ."[33]

with which the leaders of Europe acknowledged the internationalism of the revolution: "The pope consecrated it ritually; Lamartine's Aeolian harp quavered weakly with tinkling philanthropic airs, set to words about *fraternité,* the brotherhood of social sectors and nations," and so on.[34] Marx's internationalist thesis is presented in the last section of the article:

> The defeat of the working class in France [in June] and the victory of the French bourgeoisie meant at the same time that the nationalities that had responded to the crowing of the Gallic cock [the February revolution in Paris] with heroic strivings for liberation were again stifled. Poland,* Italy and Ireland were once again ravaged, despoiled and massacred by Prussian, Austrian and English myrmidons. The defeat of the working class in France and the victory of the French bourgeoisie was at the same time the defeat of the middle classes in all European countries where the middle classes, temporarily united with the people, had responded to the crowing of the Gallic cock with a bloody insurrection against feudalism. Naples, Vienna, Berlin! The defeat of the working class in France and the victory of the French bourgeoisie was at the same time the victory of the East over the West, the defeat of civilization by barbarism. In Walachia began the suppression of the Romanians by the Russians and their tools, the Turks; in Vienna, the Croats, pandours, Czechs, Jellachich's redcoats, and similar riffraff strangled German freedom, and at the same time the czar is omnipresent in Europe. The overthrow of the bourgeoisie in France, the triumph of the French working class and the emancipation of the working class in general—this is therefore the battlecry of European liberation.

But it was on England that the revolutionary wave broke:

> England rules the world market. A transformation of the relations of political economy in every land of the European continent, on the whole of the European continent, is a tempest in a teapot without England. The relations of industry and commerce inside every country are ruled by their intercourse with other countries, and are conditioned by their relation on the world market. But

---

* Compare Engels' reference, a couple of years later, to the national element in the international extension of the revolution: "The revolution of 1848 calling forth, at once, the claim of all oppressed nations to an independent existence, and to the right of settling their own affairs for themselves, it was quite natural that the Poles should at once demand the restoration of their country . . ."[35]

England rules the world market, and the bourgeoisie rules England.

The liberation of Europe, whether in an uprising by the oppressed nationalities for independence or the overthrow of feudal absolutism, is therefore conditioned on a victorious uprising of the French working class. But every social upheaval in France is necessarily wrecked on the rock of the English bourgeoisie, of the industrial and commercial world domination by Great Britain. Every partial social reform in France, and on the European continent in general, is and remains an empty pious wish insofar as it aspires to end there [without involving England].

What then can be the positive outcome? Marx's analysis continues:

And old England will be overthrown only by a *world war*, which alone can offer the Chartist party, the organized English workers' party, the conditions for a successful uprising against its giant oppressor. The Chartists at the head of the English government: only at this point does the social revolution leave the realm of utopia for the realm of reality. But every *European war* in which England is involved is a world war. It will be carried on in Canada as well as in Italy, in the East Indies as well as in Prussia, in Africa as well as on the Danube. And European war will be the first consequence of a victorious workers' revolution in France. As in Napoleon's day, England will be in the van of the counterrevolutionary armies, but through the war itself it will be hurled forward to the van of the revolutionary movement [given the victory of Chartism] and will expiate its crime against the revolution of the eighteenth century.

Revolutionary uprising of the French working class, world war: this is the agenda for the year 1849.[36]

England's importance for the international scale of the revolution had also been eagerly asserted by Engels back in April 1848, when he wrote of his certainty that the Chartists would take power in two months.[37] But these statements should not be regarded primarily as predictions—the expression of high confidence is always expected while a struggle is in progress—but as analyses of the conditions under which the European convulsion could have a positive revolutionary outcome.

Marx's insight into the international meaning of permanent revolution was embodied several times in his *Class Struggles in France* in 1850. It applied to France as well as to backward Germany. Taking it a little ahead of order, let us see how Marx stressed it in this work, in hindsight:

> Just as the workers thought [after the February revolution] they would be able to emancipate themselves side by side with the bourgeoisie, so they thought they would be able to consummate a proletarian revolution within the national walls of France, side by side with the remaining bourgeois nations. But French relations of production are conditioned by the foreign trade of France, by her position on the world market and the laws thereof; how was France to break them without a European revolutionary war, which would strike back at the despot of the world market, England?[38]

Then, after the suppression of the June uprising:

> . . . with the victories of the Holy Alliance, Europe has taken on a form that makes every fresh proletarian upheaval in France directly coincide with a *world war*. The new French revolution is forced to leave its national soil forthwith and *conquer the European terrain*, on which alone the social revolution of the nineteenth century can be accomplished.
>
> Thus only the June defeat has created all the conditions under which France can seize the *initiative* of the European revolution. Only after being dipped in the blood of the *June insurgents* did the tricolor become the flag of the European revolution—the *red flag!*[39]

In France, writes Marx, the working class fights for the program of the petty-bourgeoisie, not its own:

> In France it [the proletarian revolution] is not accomplished; in France it is proclaimed. It is not accomplished anywhere within the national walls;* the class war within French society turns into a world war, in which the nations confront one another. Accomplishment begins only at the moment when, through the world war, the proletariat is pushed to the van of the people that dominates the world market, to the van of England. The revolution, which finds here not its end, but its organizational beginning, is no short-lived revolution.[41]

---

* It is interesting that at this point the editors of the Marx-Engels *Werke* append a note in which they take this passage to be an advance attack on Stalin's theory of "socialism in one country," and present a refutation of it as such.[40]

It was only this international standpoint that provided a realistic political basis for Marx's concept of permanent revolution.

There was also a politico-military side that deserves notice. It was, naturally, Engels who took it up. In the late spring of 1849, he wrote in 1876,

> All could still have been won if the [Frankfurt] parliament and the leaders of the South German movement had only had courage and resolution. A parliamentary decree calling the Baden and Palatinate army to the defense of the Assembly would have sufficed. The Assembly with one blow would have thereby won back the confidence of the people. The defection of the Hesse-Darmstadt troops and the adhesion of Württemberg and Bavaria to the movement could then be expected with assurance; the small states of middle Germany would likewise have been drawn in; Prussia would have had its hands full at home, and in the face of so powerful a movement in Germany, Russia would have been forced to pull back its troops in Poland, troops which thereafter were effectively used in Hungary. Hungary could therefore have been saved in Frankfurt; and besides there was a present probability that, given a victoriously advancing revolution in Germany, the daily expected eruption in Paris would not have ended up with the defeat without a struggle that was the fate of the radical petty-bourgeois on June 13, 1849.
>
> The chances were as favorable as could be. The advice to call on the Baden-Palatinate forces was given in Frankfurt by all of us [of the *N.R.Z.* group]; the advice to march on Frankfurt without any call was given in Mannheim [Baden] by Marx and myself. But neither the Baden leaders nor the Frankfurt parliamentarians had the courage, energy, understanding or initiative.[42]

The first sentence quoted above may be viewed as an example of Engels' tendency to "be swayed a little too much by the military aspect of things" at times (as Marx had occasion to caution him).[43] The sociopolitical imperatives were stronger than anyone's "courage and resolution," and were primary in the permanent revolution pattern. But within this framework, the military reverberations of revolutionary action could also be a political force.

6. THIRD AND FINAL VERSION

The drive of events soon made the second version of permanent revolution as untenable as the first. By April 1849 at least, Marx no longer believed that the leading elements of the Democracy could make a revolution any more than could the bourgeoisie proper. It was in this month that he resigned from the leadership of the Democratic Association, as we have seen, and it was also in this month that he began publishing *Wage-Labor and Capital* in his paper.

Although we now read *Wage-Labor and Capital* only as a work on political economy, it was introduced to the readers of the *N.R.Z.* with the first formal announcement of a political turn. Marx set down a new thesis: direct counterposition of *proletarian* revolution to absolutism.

Current history, he writes, has proved that the subjugation of the working class in the course of the revolution simultaneously meant the defeat (by absolutism) of its class opponents, "the bourgeois republicans in France and the bourgeois and peasant classes which were fighting feudal absolutism throughout the continent of Europe."

> The June struggle in Paris, the fall of Vienna, the tragicomedy of Berlin's November 1848, the desperate exertions of Poland, Italy and Hungary, the starving of Ireland into submission—these were the chief factors which characterized the European class struggle between bourgeoisie and working class and by means of which we proved that every revolutionary upheaval, however remote from the class struggle its goal may appear to be, must fail until the revolutionary working class is victorious, that every social reform [that is, reformation] remains a utopia until the proletarian revolution and the feudalistic counterrevolution measure swords in a *world war*.[44]

This is a momentous conclusion for Marx to come to. The alternatives are no longer Social Republic or counterrevolution; the elastic formula of the Social Republic is replaced outright by the proletarian revolution.

Along the same lines, a month later, Engels advises the German workers not to allow themselves to be used to "pull the chestnuts out of the fire" for the bourgeoisie and its ministry.

> The question is posed whether they are willing to be used for this purpose at a time when in the whole of Germany *civil war* stands

at the door and when perhaps there will soon be occasion for them *to come forward with their own demands.*[45]

In his account of "The German Campaign for the Reich Constitution" written more than a year later, Engels concludes with a review of the three class patterns. The turn that Marx had announced in April had been verified by the course of the armed campaign: this is what Engels explains.

> The campaign for the Reich constitution was wrecked by its own halfway character and inner *misère*. Ever since the defeat of June 1848, the question before the civilized part of the European continent was posed as follows: either the rule of the revolutionary proletariat or the rule of the classes that held sway before February. No halfway house is possible any longer. Especially in Germany has the bourgeoisie shown itself incapable of ruling; it could maintain its rule over the people only by turning the rulership back to the nobility and the bureaucracy. The petty-bourgeoisie, in alliance with the German ideology, sought through the Reich constitution to arrive at an impossible equilibrium of forces, which they hoped would postpone the decisive conflict. The attempt had to fail: those who were serious about the movement were not serious about the constitution, and those who were serious about the constitution were not serious about the movement.
>
> But for all that, the campaign for the Reich constitution had important results nonetheless. Above all, it simplified the situation. It cut off an endless series of conciliation attempts; now that it has lost, victory can go only to the somewhat constitutionalized feudal-bureaucratic monarchy or else to the real revolution. And the revolution in Germany can no longer come to a conclusion other than with the complete rule of the proletariat.[46]

The third, and final, form of permanent revolution, then, affirms that the political revolution against the old power can be made not by the liberal bourgeoisie, not by the petty-bourgeois Democracy, but only under the hegemony of the proletariat—not the weak German proletariat by itself but as a part of the European proletarian revolution. The opportunity for the proletariat to play this final role would come as an ongoing revolution shifted to the left, from domination by the bourgeoisie to the ascendancy of the petty-bourgeois left. As Engels summarized it later, referring to the *N.R.Z.* group in 1849:

We openly proclaimed that the people of the tendency we represented could enter the struggle for the attainment of our real party aims only when the most extreme of the official parties existing in Germany came to the helm; then we would form the opposition to it.[47]

10 | BOURGEOIS AND PROLETARIAN REVOLUTION: BALANCE SHEET

When Marx went to England around the end of August 1849, followed by Engels less than three months later, he was of the opinion that the European revolutionary situation that had started in 1848 was not yet closed out; the defeats of 1849 had produced a lull, but a new upsurge was around the corner, probably in France. He maintained this prognosis for about a year. Around July 1850 his economic studies—as well as the course of events—persuaded him that the return of industrial prosperity meant an end to the ongoing continental crisis, and that the movement now had to reorient. The task ahead was now preparation—preparing for the next revolutionary crisis, rather than planning immediate tactics and their execution.

A joint article explained this turn in economic analysis and its political consequences in the new London-based magazine edited by Marx, the *Neue Rheinische Zeitung, Politisch-ökonomische Revue* (for short, *N.R.Z.-Revue* to distinguish it from the Cologne newspaper).[1] Marx concluded: "With this general prosperity . . . there can be no talk of a real revolution," which is possible only when the productive forces again come in collision with the bourgeois forms of production. And he added in italics: *"A new revolution is possible only in consequence of a new crisis. It is, however, just as certain as this crisis."*[2]

This adjustment to the termination of the European crisis was, of course, an important policy decision, and on its basis Marx reoriented his practical work and priorities. But the change of prognosis did not itself affect his political-theoretical analysis of revolutionary problems. Looking back from 1895, Engels made this point sharply in his introduction to a new edition of *The Class Struggles in France*, after mentioning that Marx's change in estimate took place between Parts I–III and Part IV of that work. He quotes the italicized statement, and adds:

> But that was the only essential change which had to be made. There was absolutely nothing to alter in the interpretation of events given in the earlier chapters, or in the causal connections established therein . . .[3]

This applies also to the invocation of permanent revolution in Part III.

To be sure, the interval between revolutionary crises was going to be more than a few years, despite the usual sanguine expectations. Engels optimistically referred in 1851 to "the probably very short interval of rest which is allowed us before the close of the first and the beginning of the second act of the movement," and Marx signed his name to the article containing this statement.[4] And in the following year Engels thought there might be a new revolutionary upsurge in France in a matter of months.[5] Through the 1850s Marx expected Bonaparte's difficulties to lead to an explosion.[6] But the theory of permanent revolution, like any thought-out political theory, did not depend on the date of an expectation. In fact, experience had shown that it was more important to get revolutionary conceptions clear before a revolution than during it, when it might be too late.

In the immediate post-revolution period, Marx and Engels wrote three important works in which they addressed themselves to the overall lessons of the experience they had just gone through. All of them are permeated with the third and final view of permanent revolution, whether written before or after the change in prognosis. These were, in chronological order:

• *The Class Struggles in France 1848–1850*: written by Marx as a series of articles for the *N.R.Z.-Revue*. As mentioned, the change in prognosis came before Part IV, which was introduced by its explanation.

• *Address of the Central Committee to the Communist League*, March 1850: written by Marx and Engels after discussions in the group. Its drafting coincides with the writing of Part III of the *Class Struggles in France*.

• *Revolution and Counterrevolution in Germany*: this series of articles for the *New York Tribune* was written, or drafted, by Engels, but it went through Marx's hands and was published under his signature. We can assume that he revised it at will whenever he thought necessary. Its writing covered more than a year, beginning August 1851.

The first of these considered the revolution in France; the third, the revolution in Germany. The second was composed in general terms as an overall programmatic guide, and we will take it up last.

1. DECLARATION OF
THE PERMANENT REVOLUTION

Marx's *Class Struggles in France* stresses above all the hegemony in the revolution of the "proletariat round which petty-bourgeois and peasants grouped themselves more and more . . ."[7] He counterposes this proletarian hegemony to the leadership of the petty-bourgeois Democracy—which by now (1850) is calling itself by the label Social-Democracy, freely using the amorphous term socialism, and invoking the "Red Republic." In France these elements have been pushed to the left, rhetorically speaking, by the pressure of events; but their socialistic rhetoric is for the Greek kalends.

The course of the revolution, as Marx describes it, presented a pattern of *polarization*. On the one hand, the reaction denounced the slightest reform as "socialism." On the other hand—

> So swiftly had the march of the revolution ripened conditions that the friends of reform of all shades, the most moderate claims of the middle classes, were compelled to group themselves round the banner of the most extreme party of revolution, round the *red flag*.[8]

Gradually the "peasants, petty-bourgeois, the middle classes in general" had had to line up alongside the proletariat, under the blows from their right. Now Marx lays the greatest stress not on the common interests of this bloc but on its heterogeneity. It

> is no less a coalition of different interests than the *Party of Order* [the Right]. From the smallest reform of the old social disorder to the overthrow of the old social order, from bourgeois liberalism to revolutionary terrorism—as far apart as this lie the extremes that form the starting point and the finishing point of the party of "Anarchy" [so called by the Right].[9]

All of the very different socialisms professed by these disparate elements purported to aim at the "emancipation of the proletariat." In its own way this testified to the hegemony of the proletariat in the bloc, regardless of the sincerity of the professions: "just as in the party of *Order* the *finance aristocracy* necessarily took the lead, so in the party of *'Anarchy'* the *proletariat.*" And "the different classes, united in a revolutionary league, grouped themselves round the proletariat . . ."[10] This thought is repeated in a dozen ways especially in Part III of Marx's work.

It is as a part of this analysis that the term *permanent revolution* appears again, linked directly to the perspective of the capture of state power by the *proletariat,* not merely by the Democratic (or Social-Democratic) bloc.

As against the various petty-bourgeois and bourgeois socialisms pullulating on the left, as against all the utopian doctrinaires of the movement who sought to do away with the revolutionary class struggle, as against all these ideologists,

> the *proletariat* rallies more and more round *revolutionary socialism,* round *Communism,* for which the bourgeoisie has itself invented the name of *Blanqui.* * This socialism is the *declaration of the permanence of the revolution,* the *class dictatorship* of the proletariat as the necessary transit point to the *abolition of class distinctions generally,* to the abolition of all the relations of production on which they rest, to the abolition of all the social relations that correspond to these relations of production, to the revolutionizing of all the ideas that result from these social relations.[11]

The "permanence of the revolution" means its ongoing character, its continuation without a halt (even if with pauses) until the rule ("class dictatorship") of the proletariat has been achieved. The rule of the petty-bourgeois Democracy may be a phase through which the revolution will pass, but it is not a stage at which the revolution will rest. The permanent revolution concept *counterposes* the aim of proletarian revolution against any regime under the hegemony of "petty-bourgeois socialism"; the latter, the characteristic politics of the Democracy, is incapable of moving òutside the framework of the bourgeois social order.

This analysis entails a corresponding change in terminology. Since

* For the significance of Blanqui's name in this statement, see Special Note C, page 592.

Marx and Engels no longer view the proletariat as the left wing of a movement dominated by a different class force, they no longer use the term *the Democracy* to mean a coalition that includes the proletariat. From now on, this label is used only for the petty-bourgeois Democratic movement, which lies—or sprawls—between open reaction and open social revolution.

This new usage, we may say parenthetically, was not peculiar to Marx at this time. For example, there was an explicit explanation of this change in terminology, regarding the use of the term *Democracy* in France and Germany, in an article series published in the left Chartist paper published by Ernest Jones. The articles were titled "The Working Classes in Germany," by "One of Their Exiled Leaders," the writer being probably one of Marx's friends in London, perhaps Eccarius. In 1852 Marx referred to the use of the term in England, in *New York Tribune* articles. The bourgeois liberals of the Manchester school, he wrote, constitute a party which "in other countries, would be called *democratic.*" When the Whig leader Lord John Russell came out as a proponent of the Democracy, Marx quoted him at some length and commented: "Thus, then, Democracy is nothing but the claims [demands] of the Bourgeoisie . . ."[12]

For that matter, as we know, the term *permanent revolution* was not confined to Marx.* But, with or without the term, the concept came frequently from Marx's pen. While writing *The Class Struggles in France*, Marx also did a review of English affairs, which presented the following prospect. When the imminent crisis came, the Whigs would fall from power; then—

> A short-lived Tory ministry may follow them at first, but the ground will quake under its feet, all the opposition parties will

---

* The phrase "maintaining the revolution in permanence" also appeared in the brief programmatic statement adopted in April 1850 by a *Société Universelle des Communistes Révolutionnaires,* signed by Communist League representatives (Marx, Engels, Willich), one left Chartist, and two Frenchmen of the Blanquist tendency in the London emigration. This was an attempt at a united front of revolutionary groups; it existed, on paper only, till the autumn.[13] We will return to this united-front effort in Volume 3. —The phrase *permanent revolution* also appeared about this time in a "Red Catechism for the German People" drafted by Moses Hess around the end of 1849, published anonymously in 1850. Marx had nothing to do with this statement, and did not even know who had put it out. It is quite likely that Hess (who had been heavily influenced by Marx in a revolutionary direction as long as a revolution was going on) had picked up the term and the idea from the two places it had already appeared as a programmatic watchword, namely, the articles constituting *The Class Struggles in France* and the

unite against it, the industrialists at their head. . . . [The Tories] will be forced at least to go as far as a parliamentary reform. This means that they will inescapably assume political power under conditions that will open the doors of Parliament to the proletariat, place its demands on the order of the day in the House of Commons and hurl England into the European revolution.[15]

This is the typical concept of a permanent revolution pattern: the ongoing left shift that screws a crisis up to the point of explosion. This passage was written in the spring of 1850, hence while Marx was still expecting an imminent return to an overt revolutionary situation, but while this fact conditions the time coefficient of events, it does not change the concept.

2. TOWARD A "REVOLUTION OF THE MAJORITY"

In adopting the view that the revolution must continue on to the proletarian revolution without bogging down in a bourgeois-democratic phase, Marx was not cutting the proletarian left loose from class allies. The need for a class alliance is unchanged; but he is reversing the relation of hegemony. It is still true, as much as before, that the old regime can be overthrown only by the united strength of the bloc of disaffected classes: "But this time the *proletariat was at the head of the revolutionary league,*" writes Marx in *The Class Struggles.*[16]

Marx's 1850 version of permanent revolution has nothing in common with the Blanquist-type putsch, with which it is sometimes coupled by the marxological myth. It has nothing to do with the old dream of a seizure of power by an elite conspiratorial minority. Marx's conception is that, while the "second revolution" must of course be supported by a majority of the people, it can be successful only if this revolutionary mass is *led* by the proletarian (Communist) vanguard.

March address to the Communist League, plus discussions with League members, no doubt. In view of this, it is interesting that Hess gives strong emphasis to the international aspect of permanent revolution. The red flag, says his Catechism, means "the permanent revolution until the complete victory of the working classes in all civilized countries—the red republic." And the "red republic" is to be achieved "through a revolution which must be continued on until the workers of all civilized countries have taken over political power." For if the workers win in one country they must immediately go to the aid of their comrades in other countries, since they cannot rule in a single country in the long run: so says the Catechism.[14]

This is what Engels underlined in his introduction to the 1895 republication of Marx's *Class Struggles in France.* Looking back, Engels pointed out that "After the defeats of 1849 we in no way shared the illusions of the vulgar Democracy" about a speedy victory of the "people." On the contrary, "we looked to a long struggle, after the removal of the 'tyrants' [of the Right], among the antagonistic elements concealed within this 'people' itself." The perspective was "that the great decisive combat had commenced, that it would have to be fought out in a single, long, and vicissitudinous period of revolution, but that it could only end in the final victory of the proletariat."[17] This 1895 statement describes the concept of permanent revolution as clearly as anything written in 1850.

All previous revolutions, continued Engels, have been by "small minorities": "if we disregard the concrete content in each case, the common form of all these revolutions was that they were minority revolutions." Even here, to be sure, there was a permanent revolution pattern:

> As a rule, after the first great success, the victorious minority divided; one half was satisfied with what had been gained, the other wanted to go still further, and put forward new demands . . . In individual cases these more radical demands were actually forced through, but often only for the moment . . . In reality, however . . . the achievements of the first victory were only safeguarded by the second victory of the more radical party; this having been attained, and, with it, what was necessary for the moment, the radicals and their achievements vanished once more from the stage.

This, for example, was the permanent revolution pattern of the left currents in the Great French Revolution. Was it not also applicable to the proletariat in 1848? True, the workers lacked any consciousness of the revolutionary road to be taken—

> And yet the movement was there, instinctive, spontaneous, irrepressible. Was not this just the situation in which a revolution had to succeed, led, true, by a minority, but this time not in the interest of the minority, but in the veriest interest of the majority?

If in the past minorities could take and hold power with *false* promises to the masses, why couldn't a proletarian-revolutionary minority take power now on the basis of *really* satisfying the interests "of the great majority itself"? Finally, and decisively important: since the big bourgeoisie held all real power,

> and, on the other hand, had grouped all the other social classes, peasantry as well as petty-bourgeoisie, round the proletariat, so that, during and after the common victory, not they but the proletariat grown wise by experience had to become the decisive factor—was there not every prospect then of turning the revolution of the minority into a revolution of the majority? [18]

History proved, to be sure, that this prospect was premature in 1848, that the society and the proletariat were not yet ripe for socialist revolution, that is, for "a revolution of the majority"; but it is clear what a gulf there is between this aspiration to find a way to achieve "a revolution of the majority" and the Blanquist goal of the seizure of power by a band of conspirators. In *The Class Struggles in France* Marx set forth the clear idea of a majority which is led by a class:

> The French workers could not take a step forward, could not touch a hair of the bourgeois order, until the course of the revolution had aroused the mass of the nation, peasants and petty-bourgeois, standing between the proletariat and the bourgeoisie, against this order, against the rule of capital, and had forced it to attach itself to the proletarians as their protagonists. [19]

3. THE LESSON FROM GERMANY

While Marx covered France, it was Engels who, in 1851–1852, drafted the historical summary of the revolutionary experience in Germany. He has a vivid paragraph summarizing the permanent revolution pattern in a generalized form, taking off from the initial unanimity of classes in the March 1848 upheaval:

> °°But it is the fate of all revolutions that this union of different classes, which in some degree is always the necessary condition of any revolution, can not subsist long. No sooner is the victory gained against the common enemy, than the victors become divided among themselves into different camps and turn their weapons against each other. It is this rapid and passionate development of class antagonism which, in old and complicated social organisms, makes a revolution such a powerful agent of social and political progress; it is this incessantly quick upshoot-

ing of new parties succeeding each other in power which, during those violent commotions, makes a nation pass in five years over more ground than it would have done in a century under ordinary circumstances.[20]

We are reminded of Marx's aphorism that "Revolutions are the locomotives of history," or a method of "condensing" historical development into a short period.[21]   As a matter of fact, in Germany the components of the Democratic camp "divided among themselves" without the petty-bourgeois Democracy ever even coming to power. It was not the accession to power that exposed them this time, but rather their paralysis before the prospect of power.

°°The Proletarian, or really revolutionary party, succeeded only very gradually in withdrawing the mass of the working people from the influence of the democrats, whose tail they formed in the beginning of the revolution. But in due time the indecision, weakness and cowardice of the democratic leaders did the rest, and it may now be said to be one of the principal results of the last years' convulsions, that wherever the working class is concentrated in anything like considerable masses, they are entirely freed from that democratic influence which led them into an endless series of blunders and misfortunes during 1848 and 1849.[22]

This says from another direction what Marx had written in *The Class Struggles in France*, that the coming revolution has to be fought by the proletariat independently of the Democratic leadership—in fact, that one of its first tasks is to fight off the imposition of the Democrats' leadership on the revolutionary struggle. The petty-bourgeois Democrats talked big but were aghast at the very idea of really taking power; for "in case of victory, were they not sure to be immediately turned out of office and see their entire policy subverted by the victorious proletarians who formed the main body of their fighting army?"[23]

The working-class vanguard elements in the towns, writes Engels, had this perspective:

to bring matters to a crisis, by which either the nation was fairly and irresistibly launched in the revolutionary career, or else the *status quo* before the revolution restored as near as possible, and thereby a new revolution rendered unavoidable.[24]

It was the "Marx party" around the *N.R.Z.* that had this perspective.

4. THE MARCH 1850 ADDRESS

Toward the end of March 1850 Marx and Engels drafted a circular letter to the membership of the reorganized Communist League, to prepare for the revolutionary upturn which they then still expected imminently. While Marx was coevally writing Part III of *The Class Struggles in France* as a historical analysis, this circular was written as a concise outline of revolutionary strategy in a permanent revolution situation. It was the two men's most systematic and generalized summing up of the lessons of 1848–1849, including what they now considered their mistakes. For this reason this circular has been the target of the most persistent efforts by marxologists to discredit it as an expression of Marx's views; Special Note E shows how baseless this campaign is, and also the importance which both Marx and Engels ascribed to the document.

One of the main elements in this "Address [communication, or circular] of the Central Committee to the Communist League" is its recognition that the Communist vanguard group in Cologne, organized around the *N.R.Z.* as its political center and under Marx's leadership, had made a central mistake which provides the Address with its leitmotif. This mistake concerned *independence:* the inviolable independence of the revolutionary proletarian vanguard in organization and policy, the maintenance of the independence of the proletariat—"the only decidedly revolutionary class"[25]—from the bourgeois and petty-bourgeois movements.

At the very beginning we learn that it had been a mistake to shelve the organization of the Communist League, to allow the connections of branches and center "to become loose and gradually dormant."*

---

* We shall return to this self-criticism in connection with the problem of party organization, in Volume 3; here we are interested in the more general political issue. We may mention, in anticipation, that it has been hotly mooted whether Marx actually had the League *formally* dissolved at the outset of the 1848 revolution or only consigned it to the shelf. (In the March Address, as also elsewhere,[26] he says the latter was true.) The evidence is inconclusive; but, more important, the issue is of third-rate significance, for what is beyond question is that during the revolution Marx did *not* consider it necessary to have a political vanguard group organized on a membership basis, as distinct from the political center represented by the *N.R.Z.* operation. The reasons for this view and its relation to Marx's later opinions can be discussed usefully only in the more general context of Marx's organizational theory.

> Consequently, while the Democratic party, the party of the petty-bourgeoisie, organized itself more and more in Germany, the workers' party lost its only firm foothold, remained organized at most in separate localities for local purposes and in the general movement thus came completely under the domination and leadership of the petty-bourgeois Democrats.[27]

Note that it is not just the organizational policy that is criticized; a larger political mistake is pointed to. The conclusion follows: "An end must be put to this state of affairs, the independence of the workers must be restored." To this end,

> the workers' party, therefore, must act in the most organized, most unanimous and most independent fashion possible if it is not to be exploited and taken in tow again by the bourgeoisie as in 1848.[28]

There is reiterated emphasis on the need for complete independence of workers' organizations in relation to the Democratic movement (which, remember, now regularly means the political movement of the pink petty-bourgeoisie, not including the proletarian left). There is also emphasis on that independence which comes with the self-arming of the workers. And in view of the electoral question that Marx had encountered in January 1849, there is a special passage on the question of independent workers' candidates in elections. Here Marx and Engels recognize in very strong words that their policy in the Prussian election had been wrong. The penultimate sentence of the Address comes back, for the nth time, to the basic importance of "the independent organization of the party of the proletariat."[29]

From first page to last, the refrain of the March Address is: independence—the independent action of the proletariat—and no compromising of the total independence of the proletarian movement either organizationally or politically; most especially, independence as a precondition for any alliance.

This theme of independence needs concretizing. Here it is particularly applied to the issue which we have watched Marx grapple with over a period of years: the relation of the proletarian Communist movement to the movement of the putatively revolutionary bourgeoisie and petty-bourgeoisie, under conditions where the state power is held by the common enemy of all three classes, absolutism. The standpoint of the Address is, of course, that of the third (final) version of permanent revolution; the revolution is seen as continuing uninterruptedly until the proletarian revolution clearly asserts itself as the only possible alternative to a return to absolutism. The expectation is that this course will go through a phase in which the petty-bourgeois Democracy will temporarily grasp the ascendancy as the revolution shifts leftward.

The most striking element in the Address is a new realization about this perspective. It concerns the view taken of the petty-bourgeois Democracy (now calling itself the Social-Democracy). During the revolution Marx had slowly and quite reluctantly come to the conclusion that this Democracy was impotent as a friend of the revolution. Now the experience of the period has convinced him of a more far-reaching proposition: when this petty-bourgeois Democracy comes to power, it will not merely be a feeble friend—it will be the most dangerous enemy of the social revolution.*

The Address recalls that in 1848 it was the liberal bourgeoisie that unmade the revolution—

> And the role, this so treacherous role which the German liberal bourgeois played in 1848 against the people, will in the impending revolution be taken over by the Democratic petty-bourgeois, who at present occupy the same position in the opposition as the liberal bourgeois before 1848. This party, the Democratic party, which is far more dangerous to the workers than the previous liberal one, consists of three elements . . .

These three elements include "the most advanced sections of the big bourgeoisie" which still want to overthrow absolutism, as well as the various (left or right) elements of the petty-bourgeoisie. These coalesced elements, which now "call themselves Republicans or Reds, just

---

* It is this thesis, not the trumped-up charge of "Blanquism," that has made this Address so scandalous a document in the eyes of Marx's critics. When Eduard Bernstein invented the "Blanquism" charge, it was a substitute for openly attacking the thesis that hit him close to the bone: the prediction that social-reformism was not merely wrong but bound to be the most dangerous enemy of the revolution in a crisis. But Marx's thesis is not to be found in Blanqui or the actual Blanquist movement. For Blanqui the enemy was absolutism first and last, despite denunciations of the bourgeoisie; and in fact, as bourgeois democracy took over later in the century, the Blanquist movement itself merged with reformism. The opinion that Blanquist-type putschism or adventurism is incompatible with social-reformism has no basis either in theory or in historical experience. Reformism as a socialist tendency will be taken up at large in Volume 3; but we may mention that Engels reiterated the present thesis about social-reformism very strongly in letters to Bebel in 1884.[30]

as the republican petty-bourgeois in France now call themselves social-ists," are, in phrases if not in deeds, united against the main body of the bourgeoisie-cum-absolutism.

Marx makes clear that "the petty-bourgeois Democratic party" is petty-bourgeois as defined by its politics, but that its class composition is naturally much more heterogeneous, including other social strata that subordinate themselves to the petty-bourgeois character of the move-ment.

> The petty-bourgeois Democratic party in Germany is very powerful; it comprises not only the great majority of the bour-geois inhabitants of the towns, the small people in industry and trade and the guild masters; it numbers among its followers also the peasants and the rural proletariat, insofar as the latter has not yet found a support in the independent urban proletariat.[31]

What defines this coalition as petty-bourgeois, scientifically speak-ing, is the way in which the boundaries of its political program coincide with the boundaries of the social interests and outlook of the petty-bourgeoisie as a class, its demands being oriented toward "a change in social conditions by means of which existing society will be made as tolerable and comfortable as possible for them."[32] (The specific de-mands will be considered in Chapter 11.)

The central question of revolutionary strategy that the Address works out is this: how to prepare the independent working-class forces, before as well as during the expected ascendancy of the petty-bourgeois Democracy, for the critical showdown with this final enemy of the revolution. The Address sought to spell out a battle plan against the expected enemy; or, as Marx wrote a year later, it was "a plan of war against the Democracy."[33]

The Address advises:

> The relation of the revolutionary workers' party to the petty-bourgeois Democracy is this: it marches together with the latter against the camp which it aims at overthrowing [bourgeoisie-cum-absolutism] ; it opposes the Democrats in everything whereby they seek to consolidate their position in their own interests.[34]

But, warns Marx, the proletarian camp must not limit itself to the political terrain of the Democracy.

> [The demands of the Democracy] can in no wise suffice for the party of the proletariat. While the Democratic petty-bourgeois

wish to bring the revolution to a conclusion as quickly as possible, and with the achievement, at most, of the above demands,
it is our interest and our task to make the revolution permanent,
until . . .

"Permanent until" introduces the equivalent of a definition:

. . . until all more or less possessing classes have been forced out
of their position of dominance, until the proletariat has conquered state power, and the association of proletarians, not only
in one country but in all the dominant countries of the world, has
advanced so far that competition among the proletarians of these
countries has ceased and that at least the decisive productive
forces are concentrated in the hands of the proletarians.[35]

This passage can be taken as a classic statement of Marx's developed
view of the permanent revolution, including its international component.

5. THE BATTLE PLAN

How should the proletarian camp be prepared *now,* while the petty-
bourgeois Democracy is still oppressed by the common enemy, to fight
the Democracy on the day when it gets the upper hand? Marx's "plan
of war" is given in considerable detail for such a concise statement. Its
highlights are these.

1. Today the Democrats present a sweet face of unity to the
workers, because they

strive for the establishment of a large opposition party which will
embrace all shades of opinion in the Democratic party, that is,
they strive to entangle the workers in a party organization in
which general Social-Democratic phrases predominate, behind
which their special interests are concealed and in which the
particular demands of the proletariat may not be brought forward
for the sake of beloved peace.

This type of all-inclusive reform party, as Marx describes it, should not
be confused with a party that simply permits and encourages "all
shades of opinion." The point of this Democratic-front type of party is
that it inhibits and chokes off revolutionary views on the left on the

traditional ground that these are divisive and hence a blow against party unity. It is democratically tolerant only to its right. It has good reason for this one-sidedness, since, if the proletarian left did push its own program obstinately, the petty-bourgeois and bourgeois leadership and sectors of this party *would* be alienated and scared off. Therefore—

> Such a union would turn out solely to their [the Democrats'] advantage and altogether to the disadvantage of the proletariat. The proletariat would lose its whole independent, laboriously achieved position and once more sink down to being an appendage of official bourgeois democracy. This union must, therefore, be most decisively rejected.

Instead, the proletarian vanguard must insist on an independent political movement of the workers, above all independent of the Democracy:

> Instead of once again stooping to serve as the applauding chorus of the bourgeois democrats, the workers, and above all the [Communist] League, must exert themselves to establish an independent, secret and public organization of the workers' party alongside of the official Democrats and make each section [of the League] the central point and nucleus of workers' societies in which the attitude and interests of the proletariat will be discussed independently of bourgeois influences.[36]

2. Does complete independence from the Democrats exclude collaboration with them? No, such collaboration is in order; it means marching together—under separate commands—in a temporary united front of action:

> In the case of a struggle against a common adversary no special union is required. As soon as such an adversary has to be fought directly, the interests of both parties, for the moment, coincide, and, as previously, so also in the future, this connection, calculated to last only for the moment, will arise of itself.[37]

3. Then, as soon as the petty-bourgeois Democracy has won the victory (mainly through the self-sacrificing courageous fight of the workers), it "will call upon the workers to maintain tranquillity and return to their work, will guard against so-called excesses and bar the proletariat from the fruits of victory." The message of the Address is that the Communist vanguard must, on the contrary, press the workers to take the opposite direction—not toward winding the revolution down, but raising it to higher levels; must make sure that the masses are

armed; must press them to leave the compromised and compromising Democrats behind, and prepare them for the inevitable counter-revolutionary role that the Democrats will play as their left flank is turned.

> In a word, from the first moment of victory, mistrust must be directed no longer against the conquered reactionary party, but against the workers' previous allies, against the party that wishes to exploit the common victory for itself alone.

The experience of the revolution had taught that the Democrats needed no manifesto to remind *them* to turn their mistrust "no longer against the conquered reactionary party" but against their own "previous allies," the workers. Marx is emphasizing that the workers should be as clear-headed about the realities of class power.

4. The Democrats will use their ascendancy to try to cut down the workers' opposition on their left. Therefore:

> Destruction of the influence of the bourgeois democrats upon the workers, immediate independent and armed organization of the workers, and the enforcement of conditions as difficult and compromising as possible upon the inevitable momentary rule of the bourgeois democracy—these are the main points which the proletariat and hence the League must keep in view during and after the impending insurrection.[38]

5. After discussing a number of important strategic issues of revolutionary policy (which will be taken up in Volume 3), the last paragraph summarizes:

> [The workers] must do the utmost for their final victory by clarifying their minds as to what their class interests are, by taking up their position as an independent party as soon as possible and by not allowing themselves to be seduced for a single moment by the hypocritical phrases of the Democratic petty-bourgeoisie into refraining from the independent organization of the party of the proletariat. Their battle-cry must be: The revolution in permanence.[39]

While it is the last sentence that has captured attention, it is the preceding sentence that sums up the main message of the Address, and for that matter also epitomizes the content of the battle-cry *permanent revolution.*

6. THE THESIS OF INCAPACITY

It was primarily on the experience of the 1848–1849 revolutionary period that Marx founded a view that henceforth was to be a basic component of his theory of revolution. This was his view of the incapacity of the latter-day bourgeoisie to emulate the English of the seventeenth century and the French and American bourgeoisies of the eighteenth century by making its own revolution, the bourgeois-democratic revolution against absolutism. This conclusion was a precondition for the development of his theory of Bonapartism and the nature of the Bonapartist state, and it has already played a part in our discussion of Bonapartism in Volume 1.[40] We have already mentioned *inter alia* Marx's and Engels' statement ten years after the revolution:

°°When the volcanic upheavings of 1848 suddenly threw before the eyes of the astonished liberal middle classes of Europe the giant specter of an armed working class, struggling for political and social emancipation, the middle classes, to whom the safe possession of their capital was of immensely higher importance than direct political power, sacrificed this power, and all the liberties for which they had fought, to secure the suppression of the proletarian revolution.[41]

This remark was directed to all Europe, but it was most especially about the German bourgeoisie that Marx emphasized the thesis of incapacity. A typical statement from 1856 dealt with Prussia:

°°The middle class, who betrayed the revolution of 1848, have now the satisfaction, even while they are accomplishing their social triumph by the unrestrained accumulation of capital, of seeing themselves politically annihilated. . . . If at times their choking anger breaks through their fears, if they occasionally muster enough courage to threaten, from their seats in the Chamber, the Junkers with a coming revolution, they are sneeringly answered that the revolution has as heavy an account to settle with them as with the nobility.

Indeed, the higher middle class [big bourgeoisie] is not likely to find itself again, as in 1848, at the head of a Prussian revolution.[42]

In 1879 a *Chicago Tribune* interviewer quoted Marx as follows on the German capitalist class:

This modern capitalistic system, you must recollect, is quite new in Germany in comparison to other States. Questions were raised which had become almost antiquated in France and England, and political influences to which these States had yielded sprang into life when the working classes of Germany had become imbued with Socialistic theories. Therefore, from the beginning almost of modern industrial development, they have formed an Independent Political Party. They had their own representatives in the German Parliament.* There was no party to oppose the policy of the Government, and this devolved upon them. To trace the course of the party would take a long time, but I may say this: that, if the middle classes of Germany were not the greatest cowards, distinct from the middle classes of America and England, all the political work against the Government should have been done by them.[43]

Looking back on the Cologne Communist witch-hunt trial of 1852, Marx saw the bourgeoisie content to strengthen the old police state rather than fight for a risky democratization. The Prussian government

> found the anti-Communist witchhunt worthwhile only as an introduction to a reactionary crusade against the liberal bourgeoisie; and the bourgeoisie itself sharpened the edge of the main weapon of this reaction, the political police, through the condemnation of the workers' representatives . . .

And the pattern has led to "the unlimited rule of the political police in the new Holy Prusso-German Empire" run by Bismarck.[44]

Engels likewise pointed frequently to "the weakness, irresolution, servility and cowardice so characteristic of all middle-class movements in Germany," and not only in Germany.[45] In one of his surveys of the 1848 days, he wrote:

> The German bourgeoisie, which had only just begun to establish its large-scale industry, had neither the strength nor the courage to win for itself unconditional domination in the state, nor was there any compelling necessity for it to do so. . . . Terrified not by what the German proletariat was, but by what it threatened to become and what the French proletariat already was, the bourgeoisie saw its sole salvation in some compromise, even the most cowardly, with monarchy and nobility . . .

Consequently it was the workers that had to fight for democratic rights in society—"rights which the bourgeoisie, in the interest of its own rule,

---

* The interviewer is telescoping several decades in reporting the conversation: socialist deputies entered the North German Diet in 1867.

ought to have fought for, but which it itself in its fear now began to dispute, as far as they concerned the workers."[46]

Emphasis on the outcome of 1848 did not mean that the pattern had been initiated only that year. On another occasion Engels linked it to a much earlier period:

> In Germany philistinism is the outcome of a shipwrecked revolution, of an interrupted, repressed development. The abnormally prominent traits characteristic of it—cowardice, narrowmindedness, helplessness and inability to take the initiative—are a result of the Thirty Years War and the period following it, precisely the period of rapid rise of almost all other great peoples. This character still clung to it when Germany was again swept into the historical movement.[47]

Engels frequently compared the German bourgeoisie, to its discredit, with the French and English, who after all *had* made something of a revolution. In contrast—

> Our German bourgeoisie is stupid and cowardly; it has not even been able to seize and hold the political power the working class won for it in 1848; in Germany the working class must first sweep away the remnants of feudalism and of patriarchal absolutism, which our bourgeoisie should have eradicated long ago.[48]

So "the German bourgeoisie has never had the ability to lead and represent the nation as its ruling class," while the French bourgeoisie has lost this ability and the British may be in process of following suit.[49] The emphasis on the German bourgeoisie's pre-eminence in social cowardice did not leave the English and French off the hook. True, Prussia's was "the most cowardly of all bourgeoisies," but still—

> In the best of cases the bourgeoisie is an unheroic class. Even its most brilliant victories—in England in the seventeenth century or in France in the eighteenth—had not been won by it itself but had been won for it by the plebeian masses of people.[50]

In England too, the bourgeoisie pulled its punches out of fear of class struggle from below. Recent events, Marx wrote in 1857, bear witness to "the lassitude of the British middle classes, and their longing for compromises with the oligarchs, in order to escape concessions to the proletarians."[51] Marx explained more fully in an article on "The English Middle Class" (meaning, as usual, the bourgeoisie):

°°Whatever other shapes this social struggle [between capital and labor] may hereafter assume, we have seen only the beginning of it. It seems destined to nationalize itself and present phases never before seen in history: for it must be borne in mind that though temporary defeat may await the working classes, great social and economical laws are in operation which must eventually insure their triumph. . . . Just as the middle class inflict blows upon the aristocracy, so will they receive them from the working classes. It is the instinctive perception of this fact that already fetters the action of that class against the aristocracy. The recent political agitations of the working classes have taught the middle class to hate and fear overt political movements. In their cant, "respectable men don't join them, Sir." The higher middle classes ape the aristocracy in their modes of life, and endeavor to connect themselves with it. The consequence is that the feudalism of England will not perish beneath the scarcely perceptible dissolving processes of the middle class; the honor of such a victory is reserved for the working classes. When the time shall be ripe for their recognised entry upon the stage of political action, there will be within the lists three powerful classes confronting each other—the first representing the land; the second, money; the third, labor. And as the second is triumphing over the first, so, in turn, it must yield before its successor in the field of political and social conflict.[52]

In the less developed European countries, things were naturally no different. "The sentimental bourgeoisie have everywhere sacrificed the revolution to their god called Property," wrote Marx in the midst of a report on Austria.[53] In Italy even the Mazzini republican nationalists "have at last convinced themselves that, even in the case of national insurrections against foreign despotisms, there exists such a thing as class-distinctions, and that it is not the upper classes which must be looked to for a revolutionary movement in modern times."[54] Discussing the vicissitudes of the Spanish revolutionary movement, Marx generalized in 1856:

°°This furnishes a new illustration of the character of most of the European struggles of 1848–49, and of those hereafter to take place in the Western portion* of that continent. On the one hand

---

* Here Marx cautiously leaves room for Russia to be an exception. The ensuing decades established the permanent revolution pattern for Russia too, under conditions we have discussed in part.[55]

there are modern industry and trade, the natural chiefs of which, the middle classes, are averse to the military despotism; on the other hand, when they begin the battle against this same despotism, in step the workmen themselves, the product of the modern organization of labor, to claim their due share of the result of victory. Frightened by the consequences of an alliance thus imposed on their unwilling shoulders, the middle classes shrink back again under the protecting batteries of the hated despotism. This is the secret of the standing armies of Europe, which otherwise will be incomprehensible to the future historian.[56]

So while the bourgeoisie did advance its own interests, it was only slowly and cautiously. Under this class, history inched into the future looking fearfully over its shoulder.

7. A CALCULUS OF DIFFICULTY

The refusal of the latter-day bourgeoisie to do its bourgeois-democratic duty by overthrowing absolutism could be looked on in various ways from the standpoint of the question: *Does this help or hinder the prospect of proletarian revolution?*

Implicit in the first reaction of Marx and Engels, during the revolutionary years, was the view that the cowardly German bourgeoisie was doing the revolution a disservice, that its failure to act would be a historical impediment. This opinion subsequently went through some modifications, but considerations of the problem tend to be distorted by conjunctural impressions. In any case, rosier views were possible.

We have an example of Engels' effort to look on the bright side of the development, in 1853 as he wrote encouragingly to a friend. We see him putting it not in terms of the proletariat taking over the field of democratic demands but rather of having those demands taken off its hands:

All the socialist stupidities that still had to be championed in 1848 as against the pure Democrats and South German republicans, Louis Blanc's nonsense [National Workshops], etc., even things that *we* were compelled to put forward in order to obtain support for our views in the confused German situation—all that is now championed by our opponents—Ruge, Heinzen, Kinkel, et al. The preliminaries of the proletarian revolution, the measures that prepare the battleground and clear the way for us, such as a single and indivisible republic, etc., things that *we* had to champion then *against* the people whose natural, normal job it should have been to achieve or, at least, to demand them—all that is now taken for granted. The gentlemen [of the petty-bourgeois Democracy] have learned. This time we start right off with the Manifesto . . .[57]

It is true that when the German socialist movement rallied in the next decade, it did start right off with the essential content of the Manifesto (or a Lassallean facsimile thereof); to this extent Engels' ebullience was justified. But there is an implication in the letter that turned out to be historically unwarranted. It was not true that the proletarian socialist movement was relieved of the task of championing those democratic demands that constitute the "preliminaries of the proletarian revolution." On the contrary, one of the decisive features of combined development in Germany was that the socialists had to champion both sets of demands—the completion of the bourgeois-democratic revolution and the establishment of a new social order—and the problem of how to combine them was going to be fateful for the movement. This historical development offered a great potential for either help or hindrance.

The advantageous side of the pattern impressed itself on Marx and Engels after the 1850s. The permanent revolution pattern put an extra thrust behind the proletarian movement, in that it was now pressed forward not merely by workers' needs but by the unfulfilled democratic needs of the whole society. More than ever, the proletariat assumed the position of representing the universal interests of society, not merely the narrow interests of a particular class. Besides, the pattern seemed to offer the possibility of a short-cut, a way of bypassing at least part of the long process of bourgeois political development.

This thought showed up in the published report of a talk given by Marx to a German workers' society in London in 1867. It is the second of the considerations adduced as grounds for hope in the German proletariat: "they did not need to pass through a long-drawn-out bourgeois development like the workers of other countries."[58] Still, it is hard to deduce Marx's line of thought from these few words in a secondhand report. As it happens, a similar remark by Engels also comes to us secondhand. On his last New Year's Eve, as 1894 ended, Engels chatted with a Russian visitor, Vera Zasulich, who reported the conversation in a letter to Plekhanov. Zasulich paraphrased Engels as follows:

> Fortunately for Germany, the political bourgeois revolution has been so delayed there that an already awakened working class was involved in it. That would prevent the German working class from being caught up in a purely occupational [economic] struggle like the English and would further its social-political interests. This piece of good luck is also in store for Russia: according to what we say, the working class there reads, it is awakening, and consequently plays a conscious part in the [movement for] political emancipation.[59]

The question is closely related to the concept of combined development in social history. A broader way of posing the issue involves not merely the fact of the German bourgeoisie's timidity, but the larger picture of the consequences of industrial backwardness in Germany. In a letter to Kautsky in 1884, Engels sought to explain why the movement was forging ahead in Germany precisely because of the consequences of combined development. First, the unexpected fact:

> Strange. What helps us advance the most is precisely the retarded industrial situation of Germany. In England and France the transition to large-scale industry is pretty much completed. The conditions under which the proletariat exists have already become stable ... The political or directly socialistic movements that arose during the period of industrial revolution—immature as they were—have collapsed and have left behind discouragement rather than encouragement: bourgeois capitalist development has shown itself stronger than the revolutionary counterpressure. For a new revolt against capitalist production a new and more powerful impulse is required, say, the dethronement of England from its present dominance in the world market, or a particular revolutionary situation in France.[60]

The consequences for Germany:

> In contrast, in Germany large-scale industry dates back only to 1848 and is the biggest legacy of that year. The industrial revolution is still going on, even under the most unfavorable conditions. Home-industry based on small, free, or tenant landholding is still constantly struggling against machinery and steam; the founder-

ing small peasant grabs onto home-industry as his final sheet-anchor; but he hardly gets industrialized before he is again crushed by steam and machinery. . . . Along with this goes the direct transformation of all conditions of life in the industrial centers through the powerful advance of large-scale industry. Thus all Germany—with the possible exception of the Junker-ridden Northeast—is swept into the societal revolution, the small peasant is drawn into industry, the most patriarchal of districts are hurled into the movement and thereby revolutionized much more basically than England or France. This societal revolution, which results in the end in the expropriation of the small peasant and artisan, is being carried out, however, at a time when it happened to fall to a German, Marx, to work out in theoretical terms the results of the English and French historical development practically and theoretically, to make clear the whole nature of capitalist production and therewith its final historical destiny; and moreover to give the German proletariat a program such as its British and French predecessors never possessed. More basic revolutionization of society on one hand, greater clarity of mind on the other—this is the secret of the irresistible advance of the German workers' movement.[61]

Engels wrote along the same lines to Bebel about the same time.[62]

The problem may be usefully regarded not as one of determining which pattern was preferable—the advanced English model or the retarded German model—but simply as an exploration of the advantages and disadvantages of each. The socialists themselves did not have a choice to make; history presented *faits accomplis*. The real problem for the socialists was how best to realize the revolutionary potential of either pattern.

8. CAN THE REVOLUTION GO TOO FAR?

Another problem raised by the permanent revolution pattern emerges from an interesting discussion by Engels of the French Revolution. Even in this classic case of bourgeois revolution, wrote Engels, the bourgeoisie was incapable of making its own revolution under its own steam:

> . . . it becomes plain that the bourgeoisie in this case as always was too cowardly to stand up for its own interests; that from the

[taking of the] Bastille on, the plebs had to do all the work for it; that without the plebs' intervention on July 14 and October 5-6 [1789] till August 10 and September 2 [1792], etc., the bourgeoisie would have succumbed to the Ancien Régime every time; that the [European] Coalition in alliance with the [French] Court would have crushed the revolution, and that therefore it was only these plebeians who carried through the revolution; that this, however, would not have happened if these plebeians hadn't read a meaning into the revolutionary demands of the bourgeoisie they didn't have, if they hadn't pushed equality and fraternity to extreme conclusions turning the bourgeois meaning of these catchwords on its head, because this meaning, driven to the extreme, changed over to just its opposite; that this *plebeian* equality and fraternity had to be a pure dream at a time when it was a question of establishing the *very opposite*, and that as always—irony of history—this *plebeian* conception of the revolutionary catchwords became the mightiest lever for accomplishing this opposite: *bourgeois* equality—before the law, and fraternity— in exploitation.[63]

In this case, then, the permanent revolution drove outside the bourgeois framework and beyond its historical possibilities, but this was not simply a matter of unrealistic revolutionism, as the common philistine outlook had it. Rather, this apparently unrealistic extremism was the only way in which, objectively, the realistic limits of the bourgeois framework could be attained in fact. The revolution had to pass the bounds of practicality in order to reach them; it had to go too far in order to go as far as possible.

This aspect of the permanent revolution pattern is not as paradoxical as it may sound. A tinsmith knows that sheet metal must be bent well beyond ninety degrees in order to snap back to the desired right angle. Or, to change the image: the revolution haggles with history, raising the price to an extravagant high in order to settle for the going rate.

Engels later saw that something like this had happened in 1848- 1849 too. We have already quoted his retrospective generalization: "the achievements of the first victory ... were only safeguarded by the second victory of the more radical party; this having been attained, and, with it, what was necessary for the moment, the radicals and their achievements vanished once more from the stage."[64] This indispensable historical role of "extremism" is one of the reasons why hardheaded feet-on-the-ground types—meaning people with limited horizons—may show up as unrealistic dogmatists under revolutionary conditions; for they are now beyond their depth. Revolution changes the standards of practicality along with much else, since much becomes practical for the first time. Thus people tagged as "fanatic extremists" astonish historians by producing results where sensible burghers fail in time of revolution.*

We may compare Marx's remark in 1852 that °°"the British Bourgeois are not excitable Frenchmen. When they intend to carry a Parliamentary reform they will not make a Revolution of February."[66] That is to say, the February revolution of 1848 in Paris, taken in its bourgeois limitations, showed the use of revolutionary methods to effect nothing more than the equivalent of a parliamentary reform. Yet, in terms of historical realism, the reform could not have been achieved except by revolution.

Engels summed up in 1892, starting with the unexcitable British of 1649:

> ... had it not been for that [British] yeomanry and for the *plebeian* element in the towns, the bourgeoisie alone would never have fought the matter out to the bitter end, and would never have brought Charles I to the scaffold. In order to secure even those conquests of the bourgeoisie that were ripe for gathering at the time, the revolution had to be carried considerably further— exactly as in 1793 in France and 1848 in Germany. This seems, in fact, to be one of the laws of evolution of bourgeois society.[67]

This analysis may be compared with the superficiality of historians who regard Cromwell as the only realistic bourgeois-revolutionary figure of the period, as against the noble-hearted but nubble-headed visionaries to his left like the Levelers, who therefore were justly suppressed—the view taken by Eduard Bernstein in his best-known historical work.[68] In general, the philistine mentality fails to see that the middle of the road is defined only by the extremes. Possibilism becomes impractical when revolution changes the bounds of realism.

---

* James Connolly put it this way, at the end of a discussion of practicality in politics: "Revolution is never practical—until the hour of revolution strikes. *Then* it alone is practical, and all the efforts of the conservatives and compromisers become the most futile and visionary of human imaginings."[65]

9. LIMITED EXPECTATIONS

It should not be supposed that Marx turned a blind eye to the slow advances made by the bourgeoisie in its own cowardly way. Alongside the passages cited above are others in which Marx duly acknowledged what was happening, if only at a snail's pace. In England, for example, the coalition ministry was squeezing out concessions to the "Manchester school," that is, to bourgeois liberalism:

°°What do these concessions prove? That the industrial bourgeoisie, weakly represented as it is in the House, are yet the real masters of the situation, and that every Government, whether Whig, Tory, or Coalition, can only keep itself in office, and the bourgeoisie out of office, by doing for them their preliminary work. Go through the records of British legislation since 1825, and you will find that the bourgeoisie is only resisted politically by concession after concession financially. What the Oligarchy fail to comprehend is the simple fact that political power is but the offspring of commercial power, and that the class to which they are compelled to yield the latter, will necessarily conquer the former also. Louis XIV himself, when legislating through Colbert in the interest of the manufacturers, was only preparing the revolution of 1789, when his *"l'état c'est moi"* was answered by Sieyès with *"le tiers état est tout."*

The "Manchester men" were satisfied with the financial concessions as the price of their alleged principles. "They are in the commercial habit of pocketing the present profits, and of letting principles shift for themselves," wrote Marx mockingly.[69]

And it should not be supposed that the bourgeoisie, though incapable of carrying through the bourgeois-democratic revolution to its end, was incapable of participating in the initiation of a new revolutionary upsurge, though it might turn timid in the crunch. In correspondence with Marx in 1851, Engels was glad that even the Cologne bourgeoisie's journalistic voice "now daily sermonizes that *il faut passer par la mer rouge* [it is necessary to go through the red sea, that is, through revolution] and admits all the mistakes of the Constitutionals of 1848."[70] Days later, referring to "the philistine Democracy of the larger towns," he opines that "this petty-bourgeois ordinary-type Democracy . . . is itself much too much squeezed and oppressed not to come around, together with the big bourgeoisie, to the need to *passer par la mer rouge.*" He adds ironically:

> The fellows [Democrats] will more and more resign themselves to the necessity of a momentary terroristic rule of the proletariat—after all this can't last long, for the positive content of the document [the March Address] is really so nonsensical there can be no question of the permanent rule of such people and the ultimate carrying out of such principles![71]

He expects that

> In any case . . . the Democratic hullabaloo and scandalmongering will soon be in full swing again and [they] will go hand in hand with the Communists. And we have long known that the fellows will be playing dirty tricks on us anyhow on the day after the movement is over, and this cannot be prevented by any diplomacy.[72]

Engels expressed similar grounds for optimism in 1863: "A European movement seems very likely to me, since the bourgeois has now again lost all fear of the Communists, and if need be would again get going with a will."[73]

Marx had expressed the conviction in 1852 that the British bourgeoisie would have to perform the same service:

> °°During all the time, from 1846 to 1852, they [the British bourgeoisie] exposed themselves to ridicule by their battlecry: Broad principles and practical (read *small*) measures. And why all this? Because in every violent movement they are obliged to appeal to the *working class.* And if the aristocracy is their vanishing opponent the working class is their arising enemy. They prefer to compromise with the vanishing opponent rather than to strengthen the arising enemy, to whom the future belongs, by concessions of a more than apparent importance. Therefore, they strive to avoid every forcible collision with the aristocracy; but historical necessity and the Tories press them onwards. They cannot avoid fulfilling their mission, battering to pieces Old England, the England of the Past . . .[74]

Up to the last lines, this passage seems to be reiterating Marx's lack of expectations from the bourgeoisie. The final qualification, however, is not inconsistent. "They, cannot avoid fulfilling their mission" has the ring of Marx's earlier (1847) assurance that one need "not ask what the bourgeoisie merely *want* but rather what they *must* do."[75] But it is now quite different. The difference lies in what the limits of the ineluctable mission are conceived to be, in the 1850s as against 1847. The bourgeoisie no longer has the mission of carrying through the Democratic revolution, but Marx certainly expects still that its progressive strivings will enter into the process of "historical necessity" by which Old England and Old Europe will be battered to pieces. We should remember, for example, Marx's continued expectation that the French bourgeoisie would move to revolt against Bonapartism.[76]

10. "PROGRESSIVE AS AGAINST . . ."

Marx's conclusions about the historical incapacity of the bourgeoisie still allow, we see, for the continued opinion that this class's struggle for liberal democratization, however limited and however cowardly, remains *progressive as against* the old regime of absolutism and the political remnants of feudalism, as against the aristocratic governing classes, the Crown, the big landowners' special privileges, and so on.

To fully understand his position, we must see how it was distinguished from two others that arose in opposition. One was the reincarnation of the old profeudal socialism in the Lassallean movement. The other was the reincarnation of "petty-bourgeois socialism" in the post-1848 Social Democracy. From the standpoint of Marx's views counterposed to both, these are to be seen as bisymmetric errors.

On the first: the most detailed explanation of Marx's views was set forth in 1865 in a popular pamphlet, written by Engels and closely checked and amended by Marx, *The Prussian Military Question and the German Workers Party*. The first two parts of this booklet dealt with the "military question," which then meant the issue of popular militia versus standing army. Behind this issue of the day was the question of political support to the Bismarck regime, whose parliamentary opponent was the liberal bourgeoisie. How should the workers' party line up with regard to this ongoing struggle? This was the subject of the third and last part of the booklet.

Engels' target here was the politics of Lassalle (who had died only the year before, precipitating a crisis in his organization). Lassalleanism took off from a virulent hatred of bourgeois liberalism, and oriented toward an alliance with Bismarckian absolutism against their joint enemy. This reactionary position was anathema to Marx and Engels, who had been fighting such tendencies in the working-class movement since 1847.[77] They constantly denounced the Lassallean variant as "Royal Prussian socialism," along with its mentor, the "would-be workers' dictator" Lassalle. The argument in the 1865 pamphlet goes as follows.*

In a country like England, where the whole mode of production has been transformed, the proletarian "has directly to do only with *one* social class that confronts him as an enemy, that exploits him: with the class of capitalists, the bourgeois." But not so in a country like Germany, where the industrial revolution is still in process, where "out of the earlier feudal and postfeudal conditions a lot of social elements have remained behind which, so to speak, muddy the social waters." Here, alongside modern capitalists and workers, there are also "the most wonderful antediluvian living fossils wandering about: feudal lords, patrimonial tribunals, cabbage-Junkers, cane thrashing . . . guilds, jurisdictional conflicts," and so on. And all these fossil elements are in league against the bourgeoisie.[78]

As soon as the working class begins to stir, both sides seek its support. "The feudal and bureaucratic representatives of the dying society appeal to the workers to strike jointly with them against the bloodsuckers, the capitalists, the sole enemies of the workers; the bourgeoisie points out to the workers that they both together represent the new social era and therefore in any case have the same interests as against the *old* form of society that is dying." Since the proletariat's own aim is "conquest of political power through direct universal suffrage" on the road to achieving socialism, "what attitude should the workers' party take with regard to the contenders?" Since "neither the feudal-bureaucratic party, which is usually called the *Reaction* for short, nor the liberal-radical bourgeois party will grant these demands voluntarily," the proletariat builds its strength by establishing its own independent workers' party, and asks, "From which side can the workers obtain the biggest concessions?"

The Reaction stands for "undoing or at least inhibiting modern

---

* The following account of *The Prussian Military Question and the Workers Party* is given in some detail since this important pamphlet has been generally ignored in the literature of Marxism.

social development." But the workers do not want to change back "into guildsmen or peasant smallholders, half enserfed or wholly enserfed" under the control of the masters and "gracious lords." Besides, it is impossible to turn back the clock in history. Modern machinery, steam power, railways, and so on, "permit no such absurd retrogression; on the contrary, they gradually and inexorably destroy all remnants of feudal and. guild conditions and dissolve all the little social contradictions handed down from earlier times into the one world-historical contradiction between capital and labor."

> To the same degree that this simplification of the social class contradictions takes place, the power of the bourgeoisie grows, but to a much greater extent there grows also the power, the class consciousness, the capacity for victory of the proletariat; only through this increase in power of the bourgeoisie does the proletariat gradually get to the point of becoming the majority, the preponderant majority, in the state, as it is already in England but not at all as yet in Germany, where peasants of all kinds on the countryside and small craftsmen and small tradesmen, etc., in the towns still hold it back.

Therefore every victory for Reaction's side inhibits this social development and postpones the day of the proletariat's victory. But every bourgeois victory over the Reaction contributes to the eventual overthrow of the bourgeoisie itself, by furthering the building of the workers' movement. True, the Reaction can make concessions to the workers—at the expense of the bourgeoisie, like the English Ten Hours Law—but it will not make *political* concessions, it will "neither extend voting rights nor give freedom of press, organization and assembly, nor restrict the power of the bureaucracy." In any case, these concessions "are obtained without any return-favor on the part of the workers" since the Reaction uses them as a thrust against the bourgeoisie; hence "the workers owe them no thanks, nor do they ever thank them." [79]

The aristocracy and bureaucracy do not need parliamentary representation to maintain their power:

> Therefore the whole parliament business can go to the devil as far as they are concerned.
>   In contrast, the bourgeoisie and the workers can exercise a really organized political power only through parliamentary representation; and this parliamentary representation is worth something only if it has a say and decision-making power—in

other words, if it can control the pursestrings. But this is precisely what Bismarck avowedly wants to prevent. We ask: is it in the interest of the workers that this parliament be deprived of all power—this parliament whose doors they themselves hope to force open by winning direct universal suffrage and in which they hope one day to form the majority?[80]

Not that such universal suffrage by itself means political power, as has been shown under French Bonapartism. Besides, in Germany two-thirds of the working people are on the land and presently under the power of the landowners—hence nothing will change till the rural proletariat is drawn into movement.

Furthermore, the labor movement under present conditions is only *tolerated* by the government. "From the moment when this movement develops the workers into an independent power, when they thereby become dangerous to the government, the thing will immediately be put a stop to." The government will not cut its own throat by allowing freedom of the press, organization, and assembly, and without these freedoms "no labor movement is possible."

> And if it should happen that the Reaction throws some apparent political concessions to the German proletariat, then hopefully the German proletariat will answer with the proud words of the old song of Hildebrand: *"With the spear shall ye take gifts, spearhead pointed against spearhead."*[81]

On the other hand, what can the proletariat expect from the bourgeoisie? The answer is not in terms of concessions but of the objective effect of bourgeois victories over the old regime, in "getting rid of the rubbish left over from an earlier period." True, the proletariat has its own score to settle with the bourgeoisie later, "but this struggle cannot be fought out till they confront each other alone." First the "old junk" has to be thrown overboard to clear the ship for battle—"only this time the battle will be fought out not between two ships but on board the one ship between officers and crewmen." Meanwhile, in today's Germany, the objective consequences of bourgeois victories over the old ruling class is summarized as follows:

> The bourgeoisie cannot fight for its political rule, nor express this political rule in a constitution and laws, without at the same time putting weapons in the hands of the proletariat. . . . Consistently, therefore, it must demand direct universal suffrage,

freedom of the press, organization and assembly, and abolition of all discriminatory laws against particular classes of the population. But this is all that the proletariat need demand of it. The proletariat cannot demand that the bourgeoisie cease to be a bourgeoisie but rather that it carry through its own principles consistently. . . .

It is therefore in the interests of the workers to support the bourgeoisie in its struggle against all reactionary elements, *so long as the bourgeoisie remains true to itself.*[82]

This seems to take us back to the formulation of the *Communist Manifesto,* to "fight with the bourgeoisie whenever it acts in a revolutionary way, against the absolute monarchy,"[83] and similar statements viewing the bourgeois struggle as a prelude to workers' victory.*

However, this time Engels asks the next question: "But what if the bourgeoisie becomes untrue to itself and betrays its own class interests and the principles that flow from them?" Furthermore, this is not merely a supposition, for "This case will always come about, since the bourgeoisie, through its lack of political courage, will everywhere be untrue to itself from time to time."

Engels' answer is that the alternative open to the workers' movement (assuming it does not simply abdicate) is "to push the bourgeoisie forward against its own will, and compel it as far as possible to extend the suffrage, to unshackle press, organization and assemblies, and

---

* This idea had been stated by Marx and Engels more than once after the Manifesto; for example, in 1850: "The real revolutionary movement can begin in England only when the Charter has been realized, just as in France the June battle became possible only when the republic had been won." Here the Charter stands for the attainment of complete bourgeois-democratic rights for the working-class mass. This is a strong statement because it seems to make this stage a *necessary* precondition for proletarian victory. Its weaker form is the idea that the bourgeoisie wants to, or would prefer to, bring about a thorough bourgeois democracy, as is indeed stated in the same article: "the sole state form in which our European capitalists have confidence is the *bourgeois republic.* In general there is only one expression for bourgeois confidence in any state form: *its quotation on the stock exchange.*" But for precisely this reason the ensuing experience of Bonapartism put many question marks over the expectation. In still another form, the idea emphasized is that the bourgeois attainment of democratic institutions brings the working class into the political arena; for example: "The English Freetraders are radical bourgeois who want to break radically with the aristocracy, in order to rule without limitation. What they overlook is that, despite themselves, they thus bring the people onto the stage and into power." Other aspects of this question were taken up in our first volume.[84]

thereby set up an arena for the proletariat in which it can act freely and organize itself." But he cannot leave it there, for experience has already shown that the bourgeoisie may refuse to be "compelled":

> Even in the most extreme case that the bourgeoisie out of fear of the workers crawls away and hides under the petticoats of Reaction and appeals for protection from the workers to the power of that element which is its own enemy—even in this case the workers' party will not be behindhand in going ahead with the agitation which has been betrayed by the bourgeoisie, for civil liberties, freedom of the press, assembly and organization, in spite of the bourgeoisie. Without these freedoms the workers' party itself cannot act freely; in this struggle it is struggling for its own life-element, for the air which it needs to breathe.[85]

So it is clear that at bottom the workers' fight for democratic rights and freedoms is not on behalf of *bourgeois* democracy but is a necessity for workers' democracy, for workers' power; it is a fight not for bourgeois rights but for workers' rights.

"It goes without saying," adds Engels, that in all this there must be a completely independent workers' party opposing the bourgeoisie, "and in the next revolutionary storm—and these storms now recur as regularly as business cycles and equinoctial tempests—it will be ready to act."[86] Thus the whole strategic policy is put into the context of preparation of the independent proletarian movement for the revolutionary situation.

11. THE CRITERION OF PROGRESSIVENESS

What now of the bisymmetric opposite of the policy just discussed? Where the Lassalleans looked to an alliance with the Bismarckian monarchy against the liberal bourgeoisie, the petty-bourgeois Democracy (Social-Democracy) reversed the terms of the alliance. But it did not simply opt for an alliance with, rather than against, the liberal bourgeoisie: it aimed to *subordinate* itself and workers' interests to this alliance.

For the Democracy, bourgeois liberalism was not simply "progressive as against" the old ruling class: it was historically progressive in a more basic sense. The Democracy oriented toward becoming a part of the left wing of bourgeois democracy, not simply as a policy in one phase of the revolution but as the overall strategy for the whole historical period. At bottom, it represented that wing of bourgeois democracy that wanted to "remain true to itself," that is, true to bourgeois democracy more consistently than the others. It was, for example, more insistent in advocating the elimination of the semifeudal "living fossils" in the interest of the bourgeoisie itself. As a type of reformism this tendency will come under consideration under that head in Volume 3; here we focus on Marx's view of this approach to bourgeois liberalism.

In a book published in 1860, *Herr Vogt,* Marx had to rediscuss his views on "the relationships among the aristocracy, bourgeoisie and proletariat," for an ignorant critic had written as if Marx merely wanted to "drive the aristocracy from power." No, was the reply, that would be "the most ordinary bourgeois liberalism" and nothing more.[87] And he cited a number of passages from his published writings in which he had linked the overthrow of the aristocracy and the bourgeoisie's accession to power with the historical process leading to the overthrow of the bourgeoisie itself. (Unfortunately, not all of his references are accurate, some of them apparently being made from memory.)[88] An example—an accurate one—is his citation of a passage from *The Class Struggles in France* which begins: "The development of the industrial proletariat is, in general, conditioned by the development of the industrial bourgeoisie . . ." and ends: "Only *its rule* [the rule of the bourgeoisie] tears up the material roots of feudal society and levels the ground *on which alone a proletarian revolution is possible."* (Emphasis added by Marx in the 1860 book.) After some other citations, Marx adds: "Therefore in countries where the aristocracy in the Continental sense . . . must first be 'driven out of power,' there is lacking, in my opinion, the first premise of a proletarian revolution, namely, an *industrial proletariat* on a national scale."[89]

Let us tie this up with a question we have only touched on up to now:[90] the force of the label *progressive.* For Marx this label never achieved the all-sanctifying power it later had in some parts of the socialist movement; above all, he did not assume that *progressive* meant *to be supported politically.* He could write, "Rent of land is conservative, profit is progressive,"[91] without suspecting that this might be thought to imply support of the profit system. He wrote elsewhere: under capitalism "anarchy of production, which is the source of so much misery, is at the same time the source of all progress."[92] This bourgeois "anarchy of production" is a motive force of bourgeois progress, no more. It was quite possible for Marx to recognize that A is "progressive as against" B *in some specific context, within the terms of a given analysis,* without equating such a judgment with the programmatic determination that A is historically progressive in the basic relations of an era.

The difference lies not in the magic of the label *progressive* but in the criterion underlined by Marx in the above-cited passage from *Herr Vogt,* which in turn lies behind the analysis in *The Prussian Military Question and the Workers Party.* The criterion is: does the ground *still* have to be leveled "on which alone a proletarian revolution is possible"?—in particular, by the production for the first time of "an industrial proletariat on a national scale." Have the socioeconomic conditions already been attained that make proletarian socialism historically possible for the first time?

In the section of the *Communist Manifesto* beginning "The bourgeoisie, historically, has played a most revolutionary part . . ."[93] capitalism is treated as historically progressive up to this point. Bourgeois liberalism, which was traditionally the cutting edge of bourgeois development against absolutist restrictions, plays a historically progressive role as long as there is *still* ground that needs to be leveled to make proletarian revolution possible. Once this role has been accomplished, once the social conditions are in existence for the proletariat's own bid for power, the progressiveness of the bourgeois movement in this large-scale sense must be considered in a basically altered context. (To be sure, there may always be progressive *elements* in certain relationships, as subordinate and far from decisive considerations, especially where these subordinate elements are "progressive as against . . .")

But even where a formation or relationship is indubitably progressive from Marx's standpoint, this fact did not mechanically determine his political support. Political support is a choosing of sides in a class struggle; whether it is accorded or not involves much more than the label of progressiveness. We have already seen an example of this in the attitude of Marx and Engels toward "progressive despots" like Napoleon.[94] Let us take a more elementary example.

Marx's formulation in *Herr Vogt* must recall the process that Marx describes indignantly in *Capital,* on the primitive accumulation of capital. This so progressive capital comes into the world "dripping from head to foot, from every pore, with blood and dirt," its birth "heralded by a great slaughter of the innocents," feeding on "the capitalized blood of children," recruiting its forces "by undisguised looting, enslavement, and murder"—and so on.[95] All this—including the driving of the peasantry off the land by the enclosures movement and the superexploitation of the new proletarians in the warrens of the Industrial Revolution—"tears up the material roots of feudal society and levels the ground on which alone a proletarian revolution is possible," producing "an industrial proletariat on a national scale," and other preconditions. This development is therefore progressive—an indisputably historical manifestation of the progressive role of capitalism. What follows politically?

This objective historical fact was of great importance for Marx, especially in evaluating antibourgeois trends that looked backward to outlived conditions. But, to put it mildly, this consideration did not lead him to give political support to the governments and leaders and ideologists at the head of this historically progressive movement. On the contrary, he advocated the building of a proletarian movement to fight against these "progressive" leaders. It was the petty-bourgeois Democracy, which he cordially despised, that implicitly or explicitly followed the policy, "This bourgeoisie is historically progressive, *therefore* our political role is to form the left wing of this progressive movement."

The grim era of the accumulation of capital and the Industrial Revolution was the best that could be done by the capitalist system, which is inherently destructive of human values, even when it was historically progressive as against the old society it was rooting out. *But it was not progressive as against the class struggle of the workers it exploited.* The bourgeois development was progressive insofar as· it cleared the ground of *pre*capitalist encumbrances to the proletarian revolution; but the process of proletarian revolution does not begin with revolution. It begins with the elementary class struggle against this same progressive bourgeoisie—a class struggle that begins not on the day when all the ground has already been cleared but long before then, indeed with the first breath of the new working class.

In short: since bourgeois development is progressive only insofar as it clears the ground for the development of the proletarian class struggle, it can never be progressive as against the proletarian class struggle itself.

This question sometimes merges with another one, on the basis of a standpoint equally alien to Marx's thinking. This is the view that the movement for proletarian revolution should not begin until there is a present possibility of victory, before which time it is "utopian" and "unrealistic." Since the movement for proletarian revolution begins with the elementary class struggle, this viewpoint means that the class struggle is to be discouraged—in reality, repressed—until some suitable late date. Among the many assumptions of this standpoint is the belief that the class struggle can be turned on and off by some manipulationist leadership. From Marx's view, this is a typical reflection of ruling-class ideology, which habitually views slaves as tools; and this would be clear even if the Manifesto had not remarked of the proletariat that "With its birth begins its struggle with the bourgeoisie."[96] In any case, there is no way of determining when the historical possibility of victory has arrived in this sense: *on s'engage et puis on verra.* Anyone could see that proletarian revolution was premature in 1848, if one waits a half century; and when Engels wrote this opinion down in 1895[97] he was not under the impression it was a great revelation. This 20-20 hindsight was for some—not Engels—a condemnation of the Forty-eighters for failing to possess a crystal ball.

The most important consideration is this: for a class to begin its class struggle, on cue, only when the proletarian revolution is stamped *possible*—even if this elitist fantasy were possible—is to ensure that the possibility will not turn into reality for a very long time. Unless class struggle develops long before this point, a revolutionary class cannot organize in any way, let alone in the advanced political forms necessary for victory; and this is a long process. Without class struggle, a revolutionary class cannot develop its own leadership and experienced cadres. Without class struggle, the class cannot attain the political and ideological level necessary to aspire to victory in revolution, let alone gain the victory.

The revolutionary class struggle—considered in 20-20 hindsight— begins with the historical certainty of defeats, at best of mixed defeats and partial victories. "Now and then the workers are victorious, but only for a time. The real fruit of their battles lies, not in the immediate result, but in the ever-expanding union of the workers."[98] It is only through defeats that a revolutionary class gains the experience to build an effective movement and learns how to be successful. The history of every class aspiring to political power is necessarily a history of educational defeats crowned by only one lasting victory.

11 | THE PETTY-BOURGEOISIE IN REVOLUTION

As a step in economic analysis, for methodological reasons, Marx often treated society as if it were simplified down to the polar classes, bourgeoisie and proletariat, often plus the landowning class. Even in these contexts he did not neglect to caution that he was not examining "the actual composition of society, which by no means consists only of two classes, workers and industrial capitalists."[1] But this methodological simplification is seldom of use in political analysis; here other classes and class elements play a role that cannot be neglected.

The role of the petty-bourgeoisie in the revolutionary process has already come in for notice in the course of the last four chapters, but there is a good deal to be added. In the first place, we must be sure to understand whom Marx meant by the petty-bourgeoisie. As with other class terms, we have to differentiate between popular usage and strict (scientific) definitions.

1. DEFINITIONS

Strictly speaking, the petty-bourgeoisie comprises those who make their living primarily by the exercise of their own labor with their self-owned means of production (tools) or other property (like a shop). They are, typically, self-employed small producers or tradespeople: carpenters working in their own shops, tailors working for their own customers, small merchants, and so on; in short, largely self-employed artisans and shopkeepers.*

* In an 1865 pamphlet Engels remarked of the petty-bourgeoisie that "It finds its place less in production than in the distribution of commodities; retail trade is

They are property owners, albeit in a small way. (We are concerned not with personal property but productive property, property used in the process of production.) But although property owners, they are not capitalists, that is, not employers living primarily by the extraction of surplus labor from wage-workers.

This points to a basic distinction between bourgeoisie and petty-bourgeoisie, a distinction which the similarity in name tends to obscure.* The petty-bourgeoisie is not the same as the small bourgeoisie, even though it may shade into the latter. The distinction centers on the degree to which wage-labor figures in the enterprise. The petty-bourgeoisie earn their living by dint of their own labor and their own property; the bourgeoisie live on earnings from the labor of others.

Inevitably the petty-bourgeois sector shades off in two directions. Successful artisans or shopkeepers may begin to employ hired help, even though they themselves continue to work longer and harder than their "hands." Further expansion may turn them into primarily employers of wage-laborers, even though they continue to manage the

---

its main occupation."[2] But this must be taken as a statistical description referring to Germany in 1865, not as a definition. The characteristic picture of the petty-bourgeoisie is conveyed less technically in a passing vignette: "the German burgher can lightheartedly ponder over his plans for honest acquisition of a small property and his hopes for the elevation of the lower classes of the nation."[3] The key phrase here is "small property." In a longish sociological description of the petty-bourgeoisie set down in an unfinished pamphlet in 1847, Engels emphasized this class's localism, among other things: "The petty-bourgeois represents internal-domestic and coastwise trade, handicrafts, manufacture based on hand labor—branches of industry carried on in a limited terrain, requiring small amounts of capital, with a slow rate of turnover, giving rise only to local, sluggish competition." And: "With its petty local interests, even in its days of greatest glory in the later Middle Ages it managed to arrive only at local organizations, local struggles, and local advances . . ."[4] Here Engels' aim is to compare it unfavorably with the bourgeoisie.

* The similarity exists in English and French more than in German, where the corresponding terms are usually *Bourgeoisie* and *Kleinbürgerschaft* (or *-tum*)— usually, but not invariably. However, especially in the case of Marx and Engels when they are thinking in an English or French context, even this common German usage tends to be influenced by the term *petty-bourgeoisie*, with its etymological relation to *bourgeoisie;* as a result there are contexts where *kleine Bourgeoisie* (small or petty bourgeoisie) is not clearly distinguished from *Kleinbürgerschaft*. And besides, the problem is not merely terminological: the *Kleinbürgerschaft* does in fact, in life, shade off into the *kleine Bürgerschaft* or *Bourgeoisie*. All of this constitutes a warning that in many cases only the context confirms the meaning.

business personally. Thus they may become, in effect, small bourgeois (petty capitalists) combining three roles as capitalist, manager, and laborer. In the opposite direction, the petty-bourgeois may once have been, or in adversity may sink back to being, a journeyman or assistant laboring in another's establishment—that is, may sink into the ranks of the proletariat. There is a continuum from the young apprentice or wage-worker, through the self-employed tradesperson, to the more affluent employer-manager.

Scientifically speaking, there is also a rural petty-bourgeoisie: the peasantry, who work their own land with their own labor. As peasants shade off into employers of hired labor, like their urban counterparts, they may divide into small peasants, big peasants, middle peasants, in accordance with agreed-on limits. To be sure, etymologically the term *petty-bourgeoisie* suggests only inhabitants of "burgs" or towns; and it is common enough to speak of the petty-bourgeoisie *and* the peasantry, as we (following Marx) have done in previous chapters; but analytically it is important to see the common social position of both the urban and agrarian sectors of this class. However, specific discussion of the peasantry is reserved for the following chapters.

Another ambiguity is caused by the confusion of *petty-bourgeoisie* and *middle class*. Whereas the former denotes a specific class that can be rigorously defined, *middle class* or *middle classes* has no fixed meaning whatever; this term takes on a meaning only from its context and the declared intention of the user. Especially in historical usage, it may refer to several different classes or combinations of classes.

In their English-language writings and letters, Marx and Engels most often followed the common British practice of using *middle class* to mean the bourgeoisie proper, including the big bourgeoisie.[5] In this way the bourgeoisie is seen in the middle between the landed aristocracy as upper class and the lower orders. This usage carried over by custom even to the United States and the U.S. press, even though it did not correspond to American reality. In the plural, *middle classes,* like as not, included also the petty-bourgeois strata, thus embracing various classes seen in the middle between the aristocracy and proletariat. In German, Marx and others were likely to use a term like *Mittelstand* as a common broad label for social elements intermediate between bourgeoisie and proletariat, without pinpointing a specific class.[6] All this should be considered suggestive and admonitory, not exhaustive.

Thus, statements about Marx's views on the "middle class(es)," made without further specification, are often like essays on the Quiddity of What. This affects the alleged theory of the "disappearance of the middle classes" along with other quiddities.*

2. THE JANUS CLASS

Here we are particularly concerned with the sociopolitical characteristics of the petty-bourgeoisie that are of importance in the process of revolution. These characteristics flow from its class position. This class is inherently Janus-like.

In his manuscript for the fourth volume of *Capital,* Marx made a special economic analysis of the petty-bourgeoisie. He asks, "What then is the position of independent handicraftsmen or peasants who employ no laborers and therefore do not produce as capitalists?" His first answer (omitting details) is the elementary one: "they are producers of commodities. But their production does not fall under the capitalist mode of production." Then he suggests an interesting way of looking at this.

These noncapitalist producers are operating within a framework in which capitalist relations predominate. A social order has a tendency to assimilate alien elements to itself; under feudalism, for example, even nonfeudal relations are given a feudal form; so too, capitalism. From this standpoint—

> The independent peasant or handicraftsman is cut up into two persons. As owner of the means of production he is capitalist; as laborer he is his own wage-laborer. As capitalist he therefore pays himself his wages and draws his profit on his capital; that is to say, he exploits himself as wage-laborer, and pays himself, in the surplus-value, the tribute that labor owes to capital. Perhaps he also pays himself a third portion as landowner (rent), in exactly the same way . . .
> . . . The means of production become capital only insofar as they have become separated from the laborer and confront labor as an independent power. But in the case referred to, the producer—the laborer—is the possessor, the owner, of his means of production. They are therefore not capital, any more than in relation to them he is a wage-laborer. Nevertheless, they are looked on as capital, and he himself is split in two, so that *he,* as capitalist, employs himself as wage-laborer.[7]

* For this mythical theory, see Special Note F.

This analysis also applies to the shopkeeper, if the merchant capitalist is taken as one of the "two persons."*

In this double vision, the petty-bourgeois represent a living duplex, a class amalgam with an internal class struggle of their very own, a social schizoid ("cut up into two persons").

The petty-bourgeois Janus faces two ways. On one side the petty-bourgeois confront the capitalist, on the other side the worker. Two different lines of demarcation run through them: (1) If a line is drawn between property owners and the propertyless, then they are property owners; and as such they can rejoice in their identity with millionaires and thrill to orations on the Rights of Property. (2) If a line is drawn between those who live by their own labor and those who live by others' labor, then the petty-bourgeois belong with the former, and they are workers; and as such they can appreciate the grievances of the working classes, including the proletariat.

The petty-bourgeois are therefore pulled in two directions. On the basis of the first demarcation, they can be taken in tow by the bourgeoisie. On the basis of the second, they have a community of interest, especially in the long run, with the proletariat as against the evils of the capitalist system.

> Through the small amount of capital it owns, it [the petty-bourgeoisie] shares in the conditions of existence of the bourgeoisie; through the insecurity of its existence, in the conditions of the proletariat.[9]

They are also victims of a squeeze from both directions. From above, they are crowded out by the pressure of more efficient capitals and oppressed by the policies of a government interested in the expansion of big industry rather than the tribulations of the local tailor. The "honest labor [of the petty-bourgeois] —even if it is only that of his workmen and apprentices—is daily more and more depreciated in value by the competition of large-scale production and machinery," wrote

---

* To be sure, even a capitalist may have a minor aspect as a (self-employed) wage-worker, in a sense explained by Marx: "Any labor of superintendence by a capitalist is included in wages. In this aspect he is the wage-worker, even though not of another capitalist but of his own capital."[8] The crux concerns the weight of the wage-worker aspect; in the typical capitalist it is not only very small but limited to the labor of superintendence, for both reasons socially inoperative, unlike the case of the petty-bourgeois. The peasant's case, discussed in the next chapter, is like the petty-bourgeois.

Engels, with a parenthetical inclusion of the small employer (small bourgeois or petty capitalist).[10] Marx had his share of being squeezed by shopkeepers but could see their side, as in an exasperated letter to Engels:

> These lousy small shopkeepers are a pitiful class . . . A large—the largest—part of these shopkeepers suffer all the miseries of the proletariat, plux "anxiety" [Angst] and "enslavement to respectability," but without the compensating self-reliance of the better workers.[11]

On the other hand, from below the petty-bourgeois enterprisers may be harassed by the "laziness" of their apprentices, shop assistants, or other hired help, who will not share their enthusiasm for self-sweating. They may be especially vulnerable to "labor troubles" as small employers, for the poor mini-capitalist is driven to supersweating in order to extract from the labor of employees that which is needed to balance the advantages of a bigger competitor. They will resent the consumers who prefer the chain store to the corner grocery. Apart from these specific abrasions, the "lower classes" always loom before their consciousness as the social abyss into which they and their families will fall in case of economic failure.

3. THE PETTY-BOURGEOIS AS CONTRADICTION

It follows that the petty-bourgeoisie is a clot of contradictions, a mixture that cannot jell, a focus of social eclecticism. When it is a question of ideology, the contradictions may become logical ones, but in the first place they are social contradictions. Marx more than once took Proudhon as the very type, as in this early case:

> From head to foot M. Proudhon is the philosopher and economist of the petty-bourgeoisie. In an advanced society the *petty-bourgeois* necessarily becomes from his very position a socialist on the one side and an economist [i.e., bourgeois economist] on the other; that is to say, he is dazed by the magnificence of the big bourgeoisie and has sympathy for the sufferings of the people. He is at once both bourgeois and man of the people. Deep down in his heart he flatters himself that he is impartial and has found

the right equilibrium, which claims to be something different from the golden mean. A petty-bourgeois of this type glorifies *contradiction* [in his theorizing] because contradiction is the basis of his existence. He is himself nothing but social contradiction in action. He must justify in theory what he is in practice, and M. Proudhon has the merit of being the scientific interpreter of the French petty-bourgeoisie—a genuine merit, because the petty-bourgeoisie will form an integral part of all the impending social revolutions.[12]

A year later, in his 1847 book on Proudhon, Marx emphasized the eclecticism of the type. Proudhon sees that "Every economic relation has a good and a bad side . . . He sees the good side expounded by the [bourgeois] economists; the bad side he sees denounced by the socialists." He becomes "the man in search of formulas" by which to criticize both capitalism and communism, but fails "to rise, be it even speculatively, above the bourgeois horizon."

> He wants to be the synthesis—he is a composite error.
> He wants to soar as the man of science above the bourgeois and the proletarians; he is merely the petty-bourgeois, continually tossed back and forth between capital and labor, [bourgeois] political economy and communism.[13]

In a sketch of Proudhon eighteen years later, Marx again stressed the element of eclecticism:

> . . . the petty-bourgeois is composed of on-the-one-hand and on-the-other-hand. This is so in his economic interests and *therefore* in his politics, in his religious, scientific and artistic views. So in his morals, in everything. He is a living contradiction. If, like Proudhon, he is in addition a clever man, he will soon learn to play with his own contradictions and develop them according to circumstances into striking, spectacular, now scandalous, now brilliant paradoxes.[14]

Proudhon, of course, makes an excellent specimen because of his notorious enthusiasm for self-contradiction combined with his often overt admission "that his ideal is the petty-bourgeoisie." He wants to dissolve both "extremes" of society, bourgeoisie and proletariat, into "the golden mean," which is the petty-bourgeoisie—so comments Marx after reading Proudhon's 1852 idealization of Bonaparte's coup d'état.[15]

In general, hostility to both the bourgeoisie and the proletariat is a characteristic feature of the petty-bourgeois mentality; but in a society which is in fact dominated by the former, the balance can be maintained chiefly in phrases. Normally the petty-bourgeois *thinks* like a bourgeois even in order to formulate resentments against the bourgeoisie. There is a contradictory mixture, to be sure, but the bourgeois side of the contradiction tends to be uppermost. Petty-bourgeois Democrats, writes Marx,

> who deny not merely the class struggle but even the existence of classes, only prove that, despite all their blood-curdling yelps and the humanitarian airs they give themselves, they regard the social conditions under which the bourgeois rules as the final product, the *non plus ultra* of history, and that they are only the servitors of the bourgeoisie.[16]

The petty-bourgeois ideologist arrives at the bourgeois standpoint in a "roundabout way," through internalization of bourgeois standards as "eternal verities" of a nonclass nature.*

---

* I am here paraphrasing and somewhat generalizing another of Marx's comments on Proudhon: on "How in this roundabout way he arrives once more at the standpoint of bourgeois economy."[17] To bring out the *bourgeois* side of the typical petty-bourgeois ideology is not to negate the difference between these class mentalities. This helps to explain—but not justify—the element of confusion introduced by a passage of the *Communist Manifesto* where Proudhon is put forward as the representative of "bourgeois socialism," a social-reformism that seeks to preserve bourgeois society by "redressing social grievances."[18] This is preceded by two sections on "petty-bourgeois socialism" in which Proudhon is not mentioned.[19] One may wonder: does Marx interpret Proudhon as a "bourgeois socialist" (as in the Manifesto) or as a "petty-bourgeois socialist" (as in most of his writings before and after the Manifesto)? The Manifesto treatment is ill-advised, if only because of the formal contradiction, but it is not altogether invalid. It stresses, perhaps overstresses, that side of Proudhon which Engels also emphasized in *The Housing Question* and *Anti Dühring:* Proudhon, like Dühring, "wants existing society, but without its abuses." Both want to abolish the abuses of bourgeois society on the basis of the same laws of capitalist production that give rise to those abuses.[20] This is close to the definition of "bourgeois socialism" given in the Manifesto. We should also remember that the reference to Proudhon in the Manifesto is specifically to the book by Proudhon that Marx had attacked the year before in his *Poverty of Philosophy.* Engels eventually had occasion to remark that "Marx's *Poverty of Philosophy* appeared several years before Proudhon put forward his practical proposals for social reform" in an 1851 work.[21] Perhaps at the time of writing the Manifesto Marx was less clear on the trend of Proudhon's thinking, although he had already characterized it as petty-bourgeois.

4. INSTABILITY INSTITUTIONALIZED

The same pattern that makes the petty-bourgeoisie self-contradictory also makes it vacillating and changeable, "constant in nothing but inconstancy." This is merely contradictoriness expressed in time, but it deserves special mention. "While the old [medieval] burgherdom was the most stable class of society, the modern petty-bourgeoisie is the most changeable," wrote Engels; "bankruptcy has become an institution with it."[22]

Marx and Engels had plenty of opportunity to see this characteristic in action in the revolutionary years of 1848–1849, both in Germany and France. In Paris, soon after the February revolution, Engels observed the following about the party of Lamartine and *Le National*:

> The petty-bourgeoisie play a mediating but very miserable role. . . . They, and with them the Provisional Government, vacillate very much. The quieter everything gets, the more the government and the petty-bourgeois party incline toward the big bourgeoisie; the more disturbed things get, the more they side with the workers. . . .
>
> The biggest misfortune is that the government must, on the one hand, make promises to the workers and, on the other, be unable to keep them, since it does not have the courage to assure itself the necessary financial means by taking revolutionary measures against the bourgeoisie . . . The *La Réforme* people are allowed to make promises, and then, by the most inept and conservative decisions, it is made impossible for them to make good on what they have promised.[23]

The elements of the petty-bourgeoisie may be viewed as iron filings pulled by opposite poles, that is, by the polar classes; revolution whips up a magnetic storm.

In the following passage from his account of the German campaign of 1849, Engels treats the small bourgeoisie and the petty-bourgeoisie interchangeably:

> If it depended on the small bourgeoisie, it would hardly abandon the juridical basis of legal, peaceful and well-behaved struggle and take up muskets and paving-stones instead of so-called moral weapons. In Germany, as in France and England, the history of all political movements since 1830 shows us that this class is always boastful, full of big talk, and here and there even

extreme in its phraseology, as long as it sees no danger; faint-hearted, cautious and mealy-mouthed as soon as the slightest danger approaches; dumbfounded, worried and vacillating as soon as the movement it stirred up is seized on by other classes and taken seriously; betraying the whole movement for the sake of its petty-bourgeois existence as soon as things get to the point of struggle with arms in hand—and finally, as a result of its indecisiveness, always eminently duped and maltreated as soon as the reactionary party wins.[24]

This same teeter-totter between crowing and cowering was likewise what Marx observed of the petty-bourgeoisie in time of crisis:

... the revolutionary threats of the petty-bourgeois and their Democratic representatives are mere attempts to intimidate their antagonist. And when they have run into a blind alley, when they have sufficiently compromised themselves to make it necessary to give effect to their threats, then this is done in an ambiguous fashion that avoids nothing so much as the means to the end and tries to find excuses for succumbing. The blaring overture that announced the contest dies away in a pusillanimous snarl as soon as the struggle has to begin, the actors cease to take themselves *au sérieux,* and the action collapses completely, like a pricked bubble.

And he links this with the fact that the petty-bourgeoisie is an *Übergangsklasse* (transition class), that is, an in-between class, a class shading off into the bourgeoisie or the proletariat—one "in which the interests of the two classes are simultaneously mutually blunted." In consequence the petty-bourgeois "imagines himself elevated above class antagonism generally."[25]

Volatility is especially characteristic of what has been called "the petty-bourgeoisie in a frenzy," that is, when this class is driven to the wall by forces beyond its control (as always) and beyond its understanding (as usual). The French petty-bourgeoisie had been active in the February revolution of 1848 along with the working class in the coalition entitled "the People," but afterwards it found itself with empty hands. Something had gone wrong. Its discontent, which might have been dangerous to the bourgeois Provisional Government, was siphoned off into fury against a scapegoat, against the boondoggling of the so-called "national workshops," which were supposed to be a working-class concession. And so "they sought the reason for their misery" in the workers' movement. Marx explains: "no one was more fanatic about the alleged machinations of the Communists than the petty-bourgeoisie, who hovered helplessly on the brink of bankruptcy."[26]

5. PORTRAIT BY ENGELS

A detailed political portrait of the petty-bourgeoisie winds through Engels' history of the German revolution of 1848–1849.

First, an identification of the class, repeating some of the matter we have already covered Engels' language here is adapted for the readers of the *New York Tribune*.

°°The small trading and shopkeeping class is exceedingly numerous in Germany, in consequence of the stinted development which the large capitalists and manufacturers, as a class, have had in that country. In the larger towns it forms almost the majority of the inhabitants; in the smaller ones it entirely predominates, from the absence of wealthier competitors or influence. This class, a most important one in every body politic, and in all modern revolutions, is still more important in Germany, where, during the recent struggles, it generally played the decisive part. Its intermediate position between the class of larger capitalists, traders, and manufacturers, the bourgeoisie properly so-called, and the proletarian or industrial class, determines its character. Aspiring to the position of the first, the least adverse turn of fortune hurls the individuals of this class down into the ranks of the second.

Its vacillatory instability is next emphasized:

Thus eternally tossed about between the hope of entering the ranks of the wealthier class, and the fear of being reduced to the state of proletarians or even paupers; between the hope of promoting their interests by conquering a share in the direction of public affairs, and the dread of rousing, by ill-timed opposition, the ire of a Government which disposes of their very existence, because it has the power of removing their best customers; possessed of small means, the insecurity of the possession of which is in the inverse ratio of the amount,—this class is extremely vacillating in its views. Humble and crouchingly submissive under a powerful feudal or monarchical Government, it turns to the side of Liberalism when the middle class is in the ascendant; it becomes seized with violent democratic fits as soon as the middle class has secured its own supremacy, but falls back into the abject despondency of fear as soon as the class below itself, the proletarians, attempts an independent movement. We shall by and by [in this history] see this class, in Germany, pass alternately from one of these stages to the other.[27]

Engels acidly exhibits the chasm between phrases and deeds for these elements; but it must not be supposed that the apparent hypocrisy which results is merely a moral defect. This hypocrisy, besides being as always the sincere homage vice pays to virtue, is an honest reflection of the *social* predicament of the petty-bourgeois. Impelled toward valiant resistance to evil, they speak accordingly; incapable of militant implementation in action, they act accordingly.

°°This class had always been more forward in its demands than the Liberal-Monarchico-Constitutional bourgeoisie; it had shown a bolder front, it had very often threatened armed resistance, it was lavish in its promises to sacrifice its blood and its existence in the struggle for freedom; but it had already given plenty of proofs that on the day of danger it was nowhere, and that it never felt more comfortable than the day after a decisive defeat, when everything being lost, it had at least the consolation to know that somehow or other the matter *was* settled.[28]

And so "our valiant Democratic shopkeepers" swore to "spill their last drop of blood"—with the usual dénouement.

Engels draws an interesting parallel between the petty-bourgeoisie's pattern in business and in revolution:

°°The petty bourgeoisie, great in boasting, is very impotent for action and very shy in risking anything. The *mesquin* [shabby-mean] character of its commercial transactions and its credit operations is eminently apt to stamp its character with a want of energy and enterprise; it is, then, to be expected that similar qualities will mark its political career.[29]

The petty-bourgeoisie fails "by showing in politics the same short-sighted pusillanimous, wavering spirit, which is characteristic of its commercial operations."[30]

The upshot was seen in the armed campaign of 1849:

Accordingly, the petty bourgeoisie encouraged insurrection by big words and great boasting as to what it was going to do; it was eager to seize upon power as soon as the insurrection, much against its will, had broken out; it used this power to no other purpose but to destroy the effects of the insurrection. Wherever an armed conflict had brought matters to a serious crisis, there the shopkeepers stood aghast at the dangerous situation created for them; aghast at the people who had taken their boasting appeals to arms in earnest; aghast at the power thus thrust into their own hands; aghast, above all, at the consequences for themselves, for their social positions, for their fortunes, of the policy in which they were forced to engage themselves. Were they not expected to risk "life and property," as they used to say, for the cause of the insurrection? Were they not forced to take official positions in the insurrection, whereby, in case of defeat, they risked the loss of their capital? And in case of victory, were they not sure to be immediately turned out of office and see their entire policy subverted by the victorious proletarians who formed the main body of their fighting army? Thus placed between opposing dangers which surrounded them on every side, the petty bourgeoisie knew not to turn its power to any other account than to let everything take its chance, whereby, of course, there was lost what little chance of success there might have been, and thus to ruin the insurrection altogether. Its policy, or rather want of policy everywhere was the same, and, therefore, the insurrections of May, 1849, in all parts of Germany, are all cut out of the same pattern.[31]

All this is required reading for a course on How Not to Make a Revolution.

6. PETTY-BOURGEOIS AS ANTI-SEMITE

The swing role of the petty-bourgeoisie goes all the way from an instrument of the Democracy to an instrument of the reaction, depending on the historical position. Before 1848 the German petty-bourgeoisie had already shown a fat reactionary streak; this was the side that Marx had one-sidedly generalized in the Manifesto. The revolutionary period tumbled it pell-mell to the left, as a vacillating component of the Democracy. The ensuing period of rapid industrial development muted social antagonisms temporarily. Then the sharp economic crisis of 1873 revealed the full extent to which the old *Mittelstand* had been undermined, by the powerfully developing bourgeoisie on the one hand, and the powerfully growing working-class movement on the other.

In 1878 came a two-pronged attack on the socialist proletariat: Bismarck put through the Anti-Socialist Law, illegalizing the Social-Democratic Party; and his court chaplain Stoecker launched an attempt at a rival mass movement, the Christian Social party. After a brief unsuccessful experiment in appealing to workers, Stoecker reoriented to aim squarely at the mass of petty-bourgeois elements with a program of political anti-Semitism and social demagogy. But it was with the rise of a racialist and pseudoradical (oppositionist) movement of organized anti-Semitism that the petty-bourgeoisie really came into its own as the mass reservoir for this tendency; for this movement reflected its social contradictions as it was ground between hammer and anvil.[32]

Engels saw the social roots of this movement in the *pre*capitalist elements of society, the elements that were being crowded out by the bourgeoisie without being proletarianized. "Anti-Semitism is the mark of a backward culture," Engels begins in a letter:

> In Prussia it is the lower aristocracy, the Junkers, who take in 10,000 marks and spend 20,000 and therefore become forfeit to usurers, that deal in anti-Semitism; and in Prussia and Austria it is the petty-bourgeois, the guild artisan and small shopkeeper who have met ruin through big-capitalist competition, that form their chorus and scream along with them. But if capital is annihilating *these* classes of society, which are reactionary through and through, it is performing its function, and is doing good work, regardless of whether it is Semitic or Aryan, circumcised or baptised; it helps backward Prussia and Austria to go forward, finally to arrive at the modern standpoint where all the old social differences are merged into the one big antithesis of capitalists and wage-workers. Only where this is not yet the case, where no strong capitalist class exists yet, therefore also no strong class of wage-workers, where capital is still too weak to take control of the whole of national production and hence has the Stock Exchange as its main theater of activity, where therefore production is still in the hands of peasants, lords of the manor, artisans and similar classes inherited from the Middle Ages—only there is

capital particularly Jewish and only there does anti-Semitism arise.

But in America and England (continues Engels) where the capitalists are far richer than the Rothschilds, and also in the Rhineland, the capitalists are not Jewish.

> Anti-Semitism therefore is nothing else than a reaction of medieval, declining social strata against modern society, which essentially comprises capitalists and wage-workers, and therefore anti-Semitism serves only reactionary ends under a speciously socialistic cover; it is a variety of feudal-socialism, and with that we can have nothing to do.[33]

This dealt with the anti-Semitic movement then arising in Germany. How the social role and basis of anti-Semitism was later manipulated by more modern rulers is of course another story.

7. AT ARM'S LENGTH

Whatever revolutionary noises may emanate at times from petty-bourgeois circles, a consistent and independent revolutionary leadership cannot be expected to emerge from it: on the contrary, "the petty-bourgeoisie can preserve a revolutionary attitude toward the bourgeoisie only as long as the proletariat stands behind it." This was Marx's conclusion from the experience in France: the petty-bourgeois Republican party (Ledru-Rollin's group around La Réforme) helped the government suppress the proletariat in 1848–1849, and "Thus they themselves blasted the background against which their party stood out as a power . . ."[34] They pulled the rug from under their own feet.

Petty-bourgeois parties have played significant roles in politics in various countries, but typically not leading roles. They can act as a front—prominent but not dominant.

> The small farmers and the petty-bourgeois [wrote Engels about America] will hardly ever succeed in forming a strong party: they consist of elements that change too rapidly . . . but to make up for it they are a splendid element for politicians, who speculate on their discontent in order to sell them out to one of the big parties afterward.[35]

It follows that the role of petty-bourgeois elements inside the working-class movement must be viewed with caution, if not apprehension, as we have already mentioned. Marx and Engels urged time and again that they be held at arm's length.

> The accession of petty-bourgeois and peasants [wrote Engels to Bebel in 1879] is indeed a sign of the rapid progress of the movement, but also a danger for it, as long as one forgets that these people have to come over and come over only *because* they have to. Their accession is an indication that the proletariat has really become the leading class. But since they come over with petty-bourgeois and peasant conceptions and aspirations, one should not forget that the proletariat would forfeit its historical leading role if it made concessions to these conceptions and aspirations.[36]

This question will recur in connection with the role of intellectuals (in Chapter 18) and of reformism (in Volume 3).

Engels read a similar lecture to Paul Lafargue when the latter got inflated notions on the subject. Lafargue and Guesde had just won acquittal by a bourgeois jury on the charge of making "inflammatory" speeches, after a principled defense expounding the political meaning of the speeches in question. Lafargue, carried away by euphoria, thought the court victory indicated "a big step" toward winning bourgeois adherents: "It shows, to some extent, that the bourgeoisie is ready for some part of our theories." On the other hand, Laura Marx Lafargue (who had a better political head than her husband) rather thought that the jury's verdict reflected the resentment of small bourgeois against finance capital.

Engels strongly agreed with Laura. In the ensuing correspondence it will be noted that the discussion refers to the small bourgeoisie and the petty-bourgeoisie interchangeably; these social circles shaded from one into the other.

Engels makes two complementary points. The verdict *was* a significant victory—significant especially for what it showed about the useful conflicts inside the bourgeoisie's lower ranks:

> °°The bourgeoisie, from the moment it is faced by a conscious and organised proletariat, becomes entangled in hopeless contradictions between its liberal and democratic general tendencies *here,* and the repressive necessities of its defensive struggle against the proletariat *there.* A cowardly bourgeoisie, like the German and Russian, sacrifices its general class tendencies to the momentary advantages of brutal repression. But a bourgeoisie with a

revolutionary history of its own, such as the English and particularly the French, cannot do that so easily. Hence that struggle within the bourgeoisie itself . . .

But "Paul exaggerates the significance of the Paris verdict in so far as it is a symptom of the accessibility of the industrial bourgeoisie for socialist ideas."

> The struggle between usurer and industrial capitalist is one within the bourgeoisie itself, and though no doubt a certain number of petty bourgeois will be driven over to us by the certainty of their impending expropriation *de la part des boursiers* [by the stock exchange operators], yet we can never hope to get the mass of them over to our side. Moreover, this is not desirable, as they bring their narrow class prejudices along with them. In Germany we have too many of them, and it is they who form the dead weight which trammels the march of the party.

And he continues with a prescient view of how petty-bourgeois recruits deform the ideas of socialism in the act of embracing them:

> It will ever be the lot of the petty bourgeois—as a mass—to float undecidedly between the two great classes, one part to be crushed by the centralization of capital, the other by the victory of the proletariat. On the decisive day, they will as usual be tottering, wavering, and helpless, *se laisseront faire* [will let themselves be led without resistance], and that is all we want. Even if they come round to our views they will say: of course communism is the ultimate solution, but it is far off, maybe 100 years before it can be realised—in other words: we do not mean to work for its realisation neither in our, nor in our children's lifetime. Such is our experience in Germany.[37]

The "experience in Germany" figured in a book Engels published the following year. He pointed to "petty-bourgeois socialism" as a tendency in the Social-Democratic Party, especially in the parliamentary fraction, and characterized it as follows:

> . . . while the fundamental views of modern socialism and the demand for the transformation of all the means of production into social property are recognized as justified, the realization of this is declared possible only in the distant future, a future which for all practical purposes is quite out of sight. Thus, for the present one has to have recourse to mere social patchwork, and sympathy can be shown, according to circumstances, even with

the most reactionary efforts for so-called "uplifting of the laboring class." The existence of such a tendency is quite inevitable in Germany, the land of philistinism *par excellence,* particularly at a time when industrial development is violently and on a mass scale uprooting this old and deeply rooted philistinism.[38]

No language is richer than German in words for philistines and philistinism. In this case Engels uses *Spiessbürgertum,* which has a social coloration not prominent in the English term; it often implies pettybourgeois Babbitry rather than bourgeois philistinism.*

8. THE POSITIVE SIDE

The preceding pages have sufficiently emphasized the negative aspects of the petty-bourgeoisie in politics, as seen by Marx, but, like any Janus, its other side demands attention too. As our iron-filings metaphor indicated, the human components of this class could be drawn in different directions. They were pulled in a reactionary direction insofar as they sought to turn back the clock of social development; they turned in a progressive direction insofar as they allied themselves with the proletarian movement for a joint battle against joint enemies.

It is true that most of Marx's and Engels' remarks in this area were heavily tinged with caveats and cautions against relying on the revolutionary noises emanating from petty-bourgeois sources. This negative coloration was primarily derived not from theory but from sad experience.

In Chapter 7 we followed their thinking on the subject, the inclusion of the petty-bourgeoisie in the Democratic revolutionary alliance, up to the outbreak of revolution; here the negative cast derives strongly from the role played by Feudal Socialism and its variations such as "True Socialism." Still, after some backing and filling especially on Marx's

---

* This is virtually explicit in a book review by Marx and Engels, which ends with the thought that the culture of the petty-bourgeoisie, which flourished in medieval Nuremberg, is now falling to pieces along with the petty-bourgeoisie itself. The review continues: "Whereas the decline of earlier classes, such as the knighthood, could offer material for splendid tragic works of art, the *Spiessbürgertum* can quite appropriately get no further than impotent expressions of a fanatic maliciousness and a collection of Sancho Panza maxims and wiseacreisms."[39]

part, they went into the first months of the revolution with considerable expectations from the Democratic petty-bourgeoisie. In the subsequent chapters we saw, weaving through the account of their developing views on the class basis of permanent revolution, a mounting disillusionment with the revolutionary potentialities of this class, as well as with the bourgeoisie. We saw that they were not overeager to accept the evidence as it piled up, and that even after expressing considerable awareness of the Democracy's default, Marx was still willing to exert his influence on the Cologne left to swing it to support the petty-bourgeois Democracy in the election of January 1849.[40] Their fingers were burnt again; the smart persisted.

The political end-product of this disillusionment, however, was never the rejection of alliance with petty-bourgeois elements but rather the hardening of conditions for such an alliance.

A month *before* the January 1849 election, Engels formulated a general attitude in an article written about the coming election in France—written for the *Neue Rheinische Zeitung* but not published.

> The Radical petty-bourgeois are socialistic simply because they clearly see before their eyes their own ruin, their transit to the proletariat. It is not as petty-bourgeois, as owners of a small capital, but as future proletarians that they got enthusiastic about the Organization of Labor [the current socialistic slogan] and revolutionizing the relations of capital and labor. Give them political power and they will soon forget all about the Organization of Labor. Political power, indeed, gives them—at least in the first moments of intoxication—the prospect of acquiring capital, of escaping the ruin that threatens. It is only when the armed proletarians stand right behind them, with bayonets fixed forward, that they will remember their allies of yesterday.[41]

This was immediately followed by a reference to Germany also: "That is how they acted in February and March"—March being shorthand for the outbreak of revolution in Berlin—

> and Ledru-Rollin as their leader was the first to act in this way. If they are now suffering from disappointment, does that change the attitude of the workers toward them? If they emerge repentant, do they have the right to demand that the workers, under altogether different circumstances now, should once again fall into the trap?

Engels proceeded to answer his own question: No, the petty-bourgeois radicals (and the small bourgeoisie too, thrown in here interchangeably) do not have the energy to carry through social-revolutionary measures.[42]

The attitude that Engels expressed in this unpublished article became the attitude of the whole "Marx party" around the *N.R.Z.* during 1849. We saw, in Chapter 10, that it hardened into the "plan of war" against the petty-bourgeois Democracy that was written into the Address to the Communist League of March 1850. Even this battle plan for a revolutionary situation seen as immediately approaching did not exclude collaboration: it provided for marching together in a temporary united front of action.[43] Mainly, its concern was proletarian hegemony in an alliance.

But of course, as soon as the perspective shifted to the long-range political haul rather than immediate revolution, the strategic approach to petty-bourgeois radicalism had to shift too. The changeableness of the petty-bourgeoisie enforced changing tactics with respect to it. In the face of revolution, reformism exhausts its positive role. In "normal" times, which means in nonrevolutionary times, reformism still has a halfway role to play. In the programmatic pamphlet on *The Prussian Military Question and the German Workers Party* that Engels wrote in 1865 with Marx's help, the generalizations about the role of the petty-bourgeoisie were suited to the time.

"Its political situation is as contradictory as its social existence," said the pamphlet, and it proceeded to acknowledge the positive side of its political trend:

> . . . in general, however, "pure-and-simple democracy" is its most accurate expression. Its political vocation is to push the bourgeoisie forward in their struggle against the remnants of the old society and especially against their own weakness and cowardice, and to help fight for those freedoms—freedom of the press, organization and assembly, universal suffrage, local self-government—which a timid bourgeoisie, in spite of the bourgeois nature of these demands, can do without, but without which the workers could never win their emancipation.[44]

From time to time it was important to see that reaction in power not only increased the oppression of workers but also alienated intermediate strata—as when in 1890 Engels noted that the German government was losing support because of the tax burden, the high cost of living, military conscription, and the fear of war: "all this has done its work in alienating from the Government the peasant, the small trades-man, the workman, in fact the whole nation, with the exception of the few who profit by the State-created monopolies."[45] All this increased the number of disadvantaged social strata and elements whom a revolu-tionary proletariat could hope to lead eventually toward revolution. But the main strategic lesson remained fixed: the volatile petty-bourgeoisie, and petty-bourgeois radicalism in particular, could be won over to the leadership of a revolutionary proletariat not by making concessions to its halfheartedness but by standing up against it, by steadfast opposition.

This was still the main lesson Engels drew, for the edification of the German movement of the 1880s, as he reviewed the experience of 1848–1849:

> ... we everywhere opposed also the Democratic petty-bour-geoisie when it tried to gloss over its class antagonism to the proletariat with the favorite phrase: after all, we all want the same thing; all the differences rest on mere misunderstandings. But the less we allowed the petty-bourgeoisie to misunderstand our proletarian democracy, the tamer and more amenable it became towards us. The more sharply and resolutely one opposes it, the more readily it ducks and the more concessions it makes to the workers' party. Of that we have become convinced.[46]

9. THE "ONE REACTIONARY MASS" FORMULA

From Marx's standpoint, it is important to understand the mixed-up factors at war in the political soul of the intermediate class strata, because this situation suggests a diversity of possibilities for their relationship to the proletarian revolutionary movement, rather than a predetermined negation.

To be sure, the diversity has limits—the limits of radicalization for petty-bourgeois souls—but we have seen that Marx and Engels never left this unstressed. They were never in danger of becoming overoptimistic about this side of the petty-bourgeois Facing-Both-Ways.

Both the petty-bourgeoisie and the peasantry (the urban and rural sectors of the class) are "classes that are on the decline and *reactionary* in relation to the proletariat as soon as they aspire to maintain themselves artificially," wrote Engels.[47] But they are not reactionary under all social conditions; not all sectors of the class are equally reactionary under the same conditions; different sectors and groups might vary widely on different issues; and last but not least, the difference must always be borne in mind between parties and groups based on this class and the possibilities of recruiting the rank and file of the class or of parts of it, in a fight against their own parties. In other words, we enter the realm of intelligent political leadership of a broad revolutionary movement that is striving to reach out, without compromising its own politics, as against the wooden drill of a self-pickling sect.

Among the many differences that expressed the gulf between Marx and the Lassallean sect at the inception of the German socialist movement was their counterposed views on the question before us: the attitude of proletarian socialists toward the intermediate class strata. Whereas Marx and Engels after 1849 can hardly be considered soft on the petty-bourgeoisie, it remained for the Lassalleans to announce the discovery that, relative to the working class, "all other classes form only one reactionary mass."[47a]

The "one reactionary mass" theory was going to have a prosperous career among various socialist sects, but Marx denounced it as soon as it showed up. The formula was embodied in the draft of the "Gotha program" which was written in 1875 to unify the Eisenacher party of Bebel and Liebknecht with the Lassallean organization, to form the German Social-Democracy. Marx attacked it as "nonsense" in his *Critique of the Gotha Program*, one section of which was devoted to this issue.

A blanket formula like the "one reactionary mass" phrase meant that the working class had no possibility of gaining allies. It was doomed to isolation from other oppressed sections of the people, not simply for revolution but indeed for any significant social struggles. Moreover, the concept condemned in advance any effort to gain such allies as unprincipled. For this reason it sounded very revolutionary, very leftist and uncompromising. But in fact it was a formula for restricting the proletarian movement to its own corner of society. It is a classic example of a reactionary-sectarian concept taking an ultraleft form as disguise. As such, it was hard to handle, and extraordinarily well suited to promote all-around confusion.

It is easy to see how it fitted in with the Lassalleans' predilections, which were the opposite of Marx's. Lassalle, despite the radical phrases about all upper classes, looked to an alliance also; but his longed-for alliance was not with the progressive bourgeois movement against the old regime, but rather, with the Bismarckian monarchy against its progressive bourgeois opposition. For this purpose it was useful to denounce all nonproletarian elements as an undifferentiated "reactionary mass," since this threw the bourgeois liberals and their aims into the same bag with the feudo-aristocracy and the Bismarckian bureaucracy. All cats became black in this murk. Flirting with, or maneuvering in alliance with, one or another wing of the "reactionary mass" became simply a tactical question of practical expedience; it was no more discreditable to line up with Bismarck against bourgeois democracy than vice-versa. Marx put this down in so many words when he explained that Lassalle's motivation was "to put a good color on his alliance with absolutist and feudal opponents against the bourgeoisie." The formula, he remarked with ironic restraint, is "indeed not at all displeasing to Herr Bismarck."

Marx pointed challengingly to the gap between the swaggering revolutionism of the formula and the actual electoral policy of the Lassalleans:

> Has one proclaimed to the artisans, small manufacturers, etc., and *peasants* during the last elections [to the Reichstag in 1874] : Relatively to us you, together with the bourgeoisie and feudal lords, form only one reactionary mass?[48]

The answer, of course, was no—the Lassalleans did not conceive their "one reactionary mass" theory as a guide to political action, but only as a rationalization for manipulation of their working-class constituency in a hoped-for deal with the antibourgeois reaction.

It was embarrassing that the Lassalleans claimed to derive their reactionary formula from the *Communist Manifesto* itself. We saw (in Chapter 7) why this was possible: one of the weaknesses of the Manifesto was that it tended to treat the petty-bourgeoisie flatly as a part of reaction and not as a possible ally of the proletariat; nowhere did it recognize the character of petty-bourgeois politics as a form of reformism. This peculiarity of the Manifesto, submerged for a quarter century, now popped up to plague its authors.

In his *Critique of the Gotha Program* Marx mentioned that "Lassalle knew the *Communist Manifesto* by heart, as his faithful followers know the gospels written by him," but—claimed Marx—by inventing the "one reactionary mass" formula Lassalle "has falsified it grossly." This was essentially true, since the Manifesto loudly and repeatedly stressed the progressiveness of the bourgeoisie as against the old order. The Manifesto was not ambiguous with respect to the differentiation of *bourgeois* progressiveness from absolutist reaction; it was ambiguous only in respect to the petty-bourgeoisie. And, of course, the Lassalleans were specially intent on throwing the bourgeoisie, not the petty-bourgeoisie, into the "one reactionary mass."

Marx was therefore justified in arguing, in this Critique, that the Lassallean formula falsified the message of the Manifesto. Citing one of the passages of the Manifesto (not very aptly, by the way, but there were many such passages to choose from), Marx continued:

> The bourgeoisie is here [in the Manifesto] conceived as a revolutionary class—as the bearer of large-scale industry—as against the feudal elements and intermediate strata [*Mittelständen*] that desire to maintain all social positions created by obsolete modes of production.* Therefore they do not form only one reactionary mass *together with the bourgeoisie.*[50]

Not "together with the *bourgeoisie,*" true. But in this very refutation, we see that Marx has again bracketed the feudal elements and the *Mittelstände.*

However, his next paragraph sets out to show that the *Communist Manifesto* said the same about the intermediate elements, and here he is on shaky ground. The Manifesto, writes Marx, "adds that the 'intermediate elements . . . (become) revolutionary . . . in view of their impending transfer into the proletariat.' " And he claims that "therefore it is again nonsense to say that they [the intermediate strata] 'form only one reactionary mass' as against the working class, 'together with the bourgeoisie' and the feudal elements into the bargain."

But here his quotation from the Manifesto is truncated and by no means reflects what that document said about the petty-bourgeoisie (which surely makes up a prominent part of the intermediate strata, the *Mittelstände*). The Manifesto, in the passage he quotes, had more to say about it:

> The intermediate strata, the small industrial, the small merchant, the artisan, the peasant, all these fight against the bour-

---

* A much-used English translation of this passage is misleading by making this clause nonrestrictive: ". . . relatively to the feudal lords and the lower middle class, who desire to maintain . . ."[49] I think this somewhat changes the meaning.

geoisie, to safeguard their existence from ruin as intermediate strata. They are therefore not revolutionary, but conservative. Nay more, they are reactionary, for they try to roll back the wheel of history. If they are revolutionary, they are so in view of their impending transfer into the proletariat;* they thus defend not their present but their future interests; they desert their own standpoint to place themselves at that of the proletariat.[51]

The Lassalleans could point to the flat statement, "they are reactionary," even if Marx could point to the clear expectation that they could be led to "desert their own standpoint ..." More important, the Manifesto contained other dismissals of the petty-bourgeoisie as reactionary, as already explained.

The Lassallean claim that the "one reactionary mass" formula was based on the Manifesto might well have been confusing at the time, but it is not too hard to sort out now. The case is different with the confusions introduced by Engels' discussions of the issue.

10. ENGELS ON "ONE REACTIONARY MASS"

Shortly before Marx sent his critique of the Gotha program to the German party leadership, Engels sent an advance letter along the same lines. This letter likewise objects to accepting "Lassalle's high-sounding but historically false phrase" that "in relation to the working class all other classes are only one reactionary mass." But his main line of argument is a remarkable blunder.**

---

* Here again the Moore-Engels standard translation of the Manifesto made changes that confuse matters as soon as an unanticipated query comes up. It inserted two phrases: "If *by chance* they are revolutionary, they are so *only* in view of ..." I have translated this passage, above, from the original text. (For more examples of problems with the Moore-Engels version, see Special Note G.)

** One part of Engels' remarks on this issue is not a mistake but may be very misleading to modern readers. "If in Germany, for instance, the democratic petty-bourgeoisie belonged to this reactionary mass," asks Engels, how could your party (Eisenacher party) have collaborated with the South German People's Party for so many years, and how could your paper have taken "almost the whole of its political contents" from the petty-bourgeois *Frankfurter Zeitung?*[52] This challenging question was not an approval of Liebknecht's opportunist policy of adaptation to the South German petty-bourgeois radicals, but rather a sharp thrust against it; both Engels and Marx had been criticizing this course for some

"This proposition," writes Engels, "is true only in a few exceptional cases: for instance, in a revolution of the proletariat, like the Commune ..."[53] On the contrary, the Paris Commune was an outstanding example of just the opposite pattern: widespread support to the revolutionary side by the intermediate classes and elements, including even some elements of the small bourgeoisie, and even some of their representative organizations in Paris itself. Marx had laid very great stress on precisely this aspect in his *Civil War in France.*[54]

The difference between Engels' statement and the historical reality that was well known to him is so great that it raises the question of what he could have had in mind. The obvious answer—though hardly a justificatory one—was the reactionary solidarity of all political elements in the Versailles assembly, that is, on the counterrevolutionary side of the struggle; this "reactionary mass" extended even to the Proudhonists who were ex-leaders of the International, like Tolain. As in all revolutionary situations, a polarization took place: in Paris the tendency was for all political currents to rally around the Commune (the bourgeois exceptions fleeing to Versailles); on the other side of the barricades, open reaction formed the center of the coalition that extended down to a petty-bourgeois radical wing. On one side "one revolutionary mass," on the other "one reactionary mass" (in Versailles). But this is not the same "one reactionary mass" figuring in the Lassallean formula. And even the Versailles reaction had shadings. In short, this statement of Engels' falls to pieces as soon as it is examined.

The second of the "exceptional cases" adduced by Engels is this: "... or in a country where not only the bourgeoisie has molded state and society in its own image but where in its wake the democratic petty-bourgeoisie, too, has already carried out this remolding down to its final consequences."[55] This seems to mean: in a country where bourgeois democratization has been carried out to its final limits— hence, *not* in Germany. This works as an argument against the application of the Lassallean formula to Germany; but does it work for the more advanced capitalist countries? Does it mean that, in a completely bourgeoisified democratic republic (say, the United States), everybody except the proletariat becomes "reactionary" and the final struggle

---

time. Engels is pointing out: now, after a long opportunist relationship with the People's Party, you are making a 180-degree flipflop in rhetoric, consigning yesterday's partner to the same "one reactionary mass" as the right-wing reactionaries, thus replacing an opportunist policy with a sectarian phrase.

takes place with the proletariat fighting alone? Without question Engels would reject this bizarre conclusion, but it is implied by his confused argument against the "one reactionary mass" formula.

The trouble probably is that Engels is thinking not about a polarization of classes (people) but of *parties*. The distinction is vital in revolution. Engels might have meant to say that, as revolution comes on the agenda, all nonproletarian parties tend to go over to the other side; it is the mass of the supporters of these parties, especially in the intermediate strata, that can be won over by a victoriously advancing revolution. *This* pattern has been seen time and again in history.

That this is the source of the confusion—the shifting of the question to the fate of parties, not people and class groups—becomes likely when we find that in later discussions Engels made this interpretation explicit more than once. For example, seven years later he criticized an article that advocated putschism and the old Jacobin-conspiratorial game as the proper response to Bismarck's Anti-Socialist Law.* He commented as follows on the writer's ultraleftist conception of how a proletarian revolution takes place:

> This [conception] at last is the dreamed-of realization of the phrase "one reactionary mass." All the official parties united in one lump *here*, just like all the Socialists in one column *there*— great decisive battle; victory all along the line at one blow. In real life things do not happen so simply. In real life . . . the revolution begins the other way round, by the great majority of the people and also of the official parties rallying *against* the government, which is thereby isolated, and overthrowing it; and it is only after those of the official parties whose existence is still possible have mutually, jointly, and successively accomplished one another's destruction that Vollmar's great division takes place, bringing with it the last chance of our rule.[56]

It is quite clear that the "great division" that takes place even at the end is the polarization of *parties*. But a revolution can be successful only if the masses can be won away from the parties they followed. Engels concludes: "If, like Vollmar, we wanted to start straight off with the *final act* of the revolution, we should be in a terribly bad way." In the "final act of the revolution" all other parties have exhausted their

---

* The author was G. von Vollmar who, not long after this ultraleftist escapade, became an extreme right-winger in the Social-Democracy.

roles, and "we" can come to power precisely because a substantial section of the intermediate strata can be detached.

The question cropped up again in 1891 when the "one reactionary mass" formula appeared in Kautsky's draft for the Erfurt program of the German party. Engels wrote him about his "great astonishment" at once more seeing this "agitational" and "extremely one-sided phrase." He objects to it even though it is a question of parties in "one reactionary mass." The phrase should be thrown out because it takes a "historical tendency" and enunciates it as an "accomplished fact."

> The moment the social revolution starts, all other parties *appear* to be a reactionary mass vis-à-vis us. Possibly they already *are* such, have lost all capacity for any progressive action whatsoever, although not necessarily so. But at the *present moment* we cannot say so, at least not with the certainty with which we proclaim the other programmatic principles. Even in Germany conditions may arise under which the left parties, despite their miserableness, may be *forced* to sweep away part of the colossal antibourgeois, bureaucratic and feudal rubbish that is still lying there. And in that event they are simply no reactionary mass.[57]

And, continues Engels, if the proletariat is not yet ready to take power, the phrase is even more misleading, because it divides the nation into "a reactionary majority and an impotent minority." He offers three relatively recent examples of reform work done by bourgeois parties to show the hollowness of characterizing all of them indiscriminately as "*one* reactionary mass." The formula applies least of all to England:

> . . . in England, for instance, this tendency will *never* become an absolutely complete fact. When the overturn comes here the bourgeoisie will still be ever ready for every manner of reform in detail. Only there is no longer any sense in insisting on reforming in detail a system that is being overthrown.

It was in Germany after the First World War, not in England, that history was going to show that the revolution could be defeated only because "one reactionary mass" did *not* exist, that is, because the leftmost bourgeois parties separated themselves from the reactionary right in order to absorb the impact of the crisis.

"The Lassallean phrase," concludes Engels, "is justified *under certain circumstances* in agitation, although with us it is enormously abused."[58] He does not indicate what the justificatory circumstances might be.

In an 1895 letter about France, Engels seems to be thinking of the formula in terms of "a coalition of all the bourgeois parties against socialism, a mass which always forms at a time of danger and then dissolves again into its various and mutually opposed interest groups."[59] This makes it not a phenomenon of the "final act" but an on-and-off characteristic of the class struggle in general: an interpretation tending to empty it of any significant content. But the same letter goes on to agree that, on "the day of the crisis," "we shall have a compact mass confronting us." A compact mass of *parties?* We end with another ambiguity.

In short, the Lassallean phrase—which hung on in the German movement as a bit of verbal bravado—was productive of nothing but confusion from its beginning to its end.

Writing less than two months after the last-cited letter, in his 1895 introduction to Marx's *Class Struggles in France*, Engels was concerned to emphasize a quite different side of the question. In the 1848 revolutions "all sections of the people" sympathized with the insurrections—"one revolutionary mass" in our previous phrase—but this "will hardly recur." He warns against an overoptimistic illusion:

in the class struggle all the middle strata will probably never group themselves round the proletariat so exclusively that in comparison the party of reaction gathered round the bourgeoisie will well-nigh disappear.[60]

It would have been better to advise dropping all talk of the sort exemplified by "one reactionary mass" and concentrate on the question of class alliances. When the above passage was written, Engels had just finished his most important programmatic article on a question of class alliance which could determine the fate of revolutions: socialist political policy with respect to the peasantry. To this question we now turn.

12 | THE PEASANT QUESTION: SOCIAL SETTING

Much of the preceding chapter necessarily applies also to the agrarian sector of the petty-bourgeoisie, that is, to intermediate social strata on the land, which means primarily the peasantry.

The peasantry stands apart from other intermediate classes in two important respects: (1) its size—its preponderance in numbers and in area covered, not only in the world at large but also in Europe, including most of the countries of Western Europe in Marx's time; (2) the particularity of its conditions of life, which are rural rather than urban, and tend to be socially more homogeneous than any class in urban society. Outside of the two polar classes, it is the peasantry that has historically been most important to the fate of socialist revolution on a world scale.

One of the hoariest of the myths of marxology is the belief that Marx and Engels simply dismissed the peasantry as rural troglodytes without interest—the "Marx against the peasants" legend.* In fact, they wrote more voluminously on the peasant question than on many important aspects of the working-class movement.

Marx's views on the politics of the peasant question are naturally based on his economic analysis of the impact of capitalist development on agriculture. In this work, where the economics of the agrarian question as such is outside our purview, we can only explain some of

---

* *Marx Against the Peasants* is the title of a book by D. Mitrany, a Romanian peasant champion; it traditionally figures in marxological bibliographies to represent the peasant question—apparently because of its title, for only about seventeen pages near the beginning of the book contain even scattered mentions of Marx's or Engels' views.[1] (Its subject is really Lenin and the Russian Revolution.) Most of the mentions refer to agrarian economic theory; there is little indication that Mitrany was even acquainted with the considerable writings of Engels as well as Marx on the political and programmatic aspects of the peasant question.

his conclusions, especially where these importantly condition the political issues.[2]

It is by no means true that Marx's or Engels' political views, in this or any other field, were merely deductions from economic premises. Marx's agrarian economics provides limits and signposts for an investigation of the political problems. The political conclusions are affected also by a complex of other social conditions, which in turn are based on economic drives outside the field of agriculture altogether. Furthermore, Marx and Engels came to some political conclusions on the basis of history and experience before working out the economic theory, which in turn acted to test, modify, condition and suggest new developments in the political arena.

1. TWO FORMS OF AN EVIL

A basic economic consideration is the relative unproductiveness of small holdings in agriculture, analogous to the problem of small units in industry. The existence of a landowning peasantry fosters a tendency counter to the fullest utilization of the modern forces of production in technology and organization.

> This mode of production presupposes parcelling [division into small parcels] of the soil, and scattering of the other means of production. As it excludes the concentration of these means of production, so also it excludes cooperation, division of labor within each separate process of production, the control over and the productive application of the forces of Nature by society, and the free development of the social productive powers. It is compatible only with a system of production and a society moving within narrow and more or less primitive bounds. To perpetuate it would be, as Pecqueur rightly says, "to decree universal mediocrity." At a certain stage of development it brings forth the material agencies for its own dissolution.[3]

This passage occurs in a chapter of *Capital* on the "Historical Tendency of Capitalist Accumulation" which presents a highly telescoped summary of the effects of capitalism, and it refers to the artisans and urban petty-bourgeoisie as much as to the peasantry. It is primarily a description not of the future but of the past, the capitalist destruction of "the old social organization" of late feudalism.

In his *Class Struggles in France* Marx summarized the reasons why the French peasantry groaned under the burden of mortgage debt:

> Now the fruitfulness of land diminishes in the same measure as land is divided. The application of machinery to the land, the division of labor, major soil improvement measures, such as cutting drainage and irrigation canals and the like, become more and more impossible, while the *unproductive costs* of cultivation increase in the same proportion as the division of the instrument of production itself. All this, regardless of whether the possessor of the small allotment possesses capital or not. But the more the division increases, the more does the parcel of land with its utterly wretched inventory form the entire capital of the small allotment peasant, the more does investment of capital in the land diminish, the more does the cotter lack land, money and education for making use of the progress in agronomy, and the more does the cultivation of the soil retrogress.[4]

This refers concretely to a specific scale of land ownership, the division of the land among the peasantry after the French Revolution, and its subsequent tendency to parcellization. This conditions the thesis that large-scale production is economically superior to such small-scale production.

It is clearly a non sequitur to push this thesis into the ground with two other alleged deductions: (1) that therefore any large-scale enterprise is automatically superior to any small-scale enterprise; and (2) that the larger the scale the greater the efficiency in a smooth curve up to infinity.* The issue was the economic consequences of the peasant mode of production as a historical reality.

As for the first deduction: Marx's critique of the economic consequences of peasant (small-holding) agriculture is only half the picture. *Marx did not counterpose large-scale agriculture to small-scale as his*

---

* A reviewer of D. Mitrany's book in the *Political Science Quarterly* pointed out:

> The same protective instinct [for the peasant] leads Mr. Mitrany to beg some vital questions of economic theory. To dispose, for example, of the Marxist analysis of the economics of the small holding, by stating it in terms of the crude formula "the larger the scale the greater the efficiency" (pp. 108-109), is a failure to face up to the real question: Is the ideal of the "sound" 25-35 acre peasant holding compatible with the *optimum* scale of production possible . . . ?[5]

economic good. The consequences of the former were deleterious also, as long as private property in land was maintained.

Since this half of the question is seldom brought out, here is a relevant passage from *Capital,* which provides the real context for the critique of both:

> Here, in small-scale agriculture, the price of land, a form and result of private ownership, appears as a barrier to production itself. In large-scale agriculture and large estates operating on a capitalist basis, ownership likewise acts as a barrier, because it limits the tenant farmer in his productive investment of capital, which in the final analysis benefits not him but the landlord. In both forms, exploitation and squandering of the vitality of the soil (apart from making exploitation dependent upon the accidental and unequal circumstances of individual producers rather than the attained level of social development) takes the place of conscious rational cultivation of the soil as eternal communal property, an inalienable condition for the existence and reproduction of a chain of successive generations of the human race. In the case of small property, this results from the lack of means and knowledge of applying the social labor productivity. In the case of large property, it results from the exploitation of such means for the most rapid enrichment of farmer and proprietor. In the case of both, through dependence on the market-price.
>
> All critique of small landed property resolves itself in the final analysis into a criticism of private ownership as a barrier and hindrance to agriculture. And similarly all counter-criticism of large landed property. In either case, of course, we leave aside all secondary political considerations. This barrier and hindrance, which are erected by all private landed property vis-à-vis agricultural production and the rational cultivation, maintenance and improvement of the soil itself, develop on both sides merely in different forms, and in wrangling over the specific forms of this evil its ultimate cause is forgotten.[6]

The two "specific forms of this evil" are small-scale agriculture and large-scale agriculture *on the basis of private property in land.* This is equally forgotten in "wrangling over" Marx's views on the peasant question.

In *Capital* Marx continues with the explanation that, if small landed property presupposes a backward state of economic development, large landed property vitiates the quality both of the land itself and of social conditions on and off the land, in the towns as well as on the countryside.[7]

> While small landed property creates a class of barbarians standing halfway outside of society, a class combining all the crudeness of primitive forms of society with the anguish and misery of civilized countries, large landed property undermines labor-power . . . on the land itself. Large-scale industry and large-scale mechanized agriculture work together. If originally distinguished by the fact that the former lays waste and destroys principally labor-power, hence the natural force of human beings, whereas the latter more directly exhausts the natural vitality of the soil, they join hands in the further course of development in that the industrial system in the countryside also enervates the laborers, and industry and commerce on their part supply agriculture with the means for exhausting the soil.[8]

Marx's central interest, then, is not in championing large-scale production against small-scale, but in counterposing socialized production to the evils of both "specific forms" of private ownership of land. Indeed, this was already true in his very first essay in economic analysis.* This does not gainsay the fact that socialized agriculture for the most part presupposes a scale of production beyond the peasant family farm.

In *Capital* there is a passage in which Marx even seems to be complimenting peasant economy, after a discussion of the impact of capitalism on agriculture:

> The moral of history, also to be deduced from other observations concerning agriculture, is that the capitalist system works against a rational agriculture, or that a rational agriculture is

* We find in Marx's Paris manuscripts of 1844:

> As for large landed property, its defenders have always, sophistically, identified the economic advantages offered by large-scale agriculture with large-scale landed property, as if it were not precisely as a result of the abolition of property that this advantage, for one thing, would receive its greatest possible extension, and, for another, only then would be of social benefit. In the same way, they have attacked the huckstering spirit of small landed property, as if large landed property did not contain huckstering latent within it . . .[9]

To indicate that Marx's refusal to champion large-scale production *per se* was well rooted, we may mention that he also formulated the question in this way in the course of a discussion in the General Council of the International, as cited below.[10]

incompatible with the capitalist system (although the latter promotes technical improvements in agriculture), and needs either the hand of the small peasant living by his own labor or the control of associated producers.[11]

To be sure, Marx's own choice is the second of the two alternatives--that is, socialized (including cooperative) agriculture "under the control of associated producers"—but here peasant ownership seems to be counterposed to large-scale *capitalist* ownership to the advantage of the former.

But it would be as disingenuous to invent a "Marx for the peasant" as it has been to fabricate a "Marx against the peasant." The issue is quite different: Is the actual trend of economic development under capitalism against the peasant or not?

2. THE HISTORICAL VIEW

The actual trend of economic development: this moot question concerns us here only in order to lay a basis for understanding Marx's political and programmatic views. Especially in moving from economic theory to politics, the meaning of *trend* has at least three aspects: the *direction* of change—trend proper; the *tempo* of change, including the problem of zigzags, interruptions, and so on; and the *forms* in which the change manifests itself.

The common fate of economic prognoses is that foreseen tendencies work out in a more complex way than expected. The question of tempo, too, has a long history in all fields, mostly because of the telescopic-lens effect. If you look down your nose at your feet, the range of view is rather limited but you may be able to make a very accurate estimate of distance in centimeters. If you look through a telescopic lens at unfamiliar terrain, you will be able to see far off and descry the winds of change, but everything is brought close up.

Marx's analysis of capitalism pointed to the tendency toward concentration and centralization, and hence the decline of the little man, not only in industry but also in agriculture.* In both fields, this

---

* Marx did not discover the tendency through his economic analysis; it was already a well-known observation when he started looking into political economy. We find in his 1844 manuscripts: "In general the relationship of large and small

tendency has worked itself out in various forms in different countries. The differences in form are bound to affect political policy to an important degree. A historical perspective on the tendency is necessary. For Marx, small-holding agriculture once played a progressive role:

> This form of free self-managing peasant proprietorship of land parcels as the prevailing normal form constitutes, on the one hand, the economic foundation of society during the best periods of classical antiquity, and on the other hand, it is found among modern nations as one of the forms arising from the dissolution of feudal landownership . . .
>
> The free ownership of the self-managing peasant is evidently the most normal form of landed property for small-scale operation . . . Ownership of the land is as necessary for full development of this mode of production as ownership of tools is for free development of handicraft production. Here is the basis for the development of personal independence. It is a necessary transitional stage for the development of agriculture itself.[14]

Marx had taken this broad historical view as far back as 1845.* Note that the small-peasant mode of production was important not only for the development of the economy but for the development of the modern human being ("for the development of personal independence"). He made the same point in the first volume of *Capital:*

---

landed property is like that of big and small capital. But in addition, there are special circumstances which lead inevitably to the accumulation of large landed property and to the absorption of small property by it."[12] The following year he noted in an unfinished manuscript that it is in the nature of modern factory industry, through the operation of laws like the Corn Laws, "to convert the peasants into the very poorest proletarians through high rents and factory methods of exploiting landed property."[13]

* In *The German Ideology* Marx flayed Stirner for judging the small peasant unhistorically:

About what kind of "small owners" does [Stirner] fancy that he is talking? About the propertyless peasants who only *became* "small owners" as a result of the parcelling out of large landed property, or about those who are being ruined nowadays as a result of concentration? . . . [Stirner] makes himself ridiculous even in Germany by his unreasonable demand that these peasants should have jumped the stage of parcellation, which did not yet exist and was at that time the only revolutionary form for them . . . [I]t was not possible for these peasants to organize themselves communistically, since they lacked all the means necessary for bringing about the first condition of communist association, namely collective husbandry, and since, on the contrary, parcellation was only one of the conditions which subsequently evoked the need for such an association. In general, a communist movement can never originate from the countryside, but only from the towns.[15]

> The private property of the laborer in his means of production is the foundation of petty industry, whether agricultural, manufacturing, or both; petty industry, again, is an essential condition for the development of social production and of the free individuality of the laborer himself.[16]

Contrariwise, there was a time when the degradation of the peasantry, after the Thirty Years War, could also mean the "lowest point of degradation" for the whole of Germany.[17]

The human values of rural life were once real ones; there are still shards and remnants about—idealized by (say) the New York executive who buys a Vermont farm in order to recapture them on weekends. But the road to further development of the free individuality no longer leads through Brattleboro any more than the sturdy virtues of the pioneers can be recaptured at the Frontier Hotel in Las Vegas. This is Marx's meaning in going right on from "It is a necessary transitional stage for the development of agriculture itself" to his longest exposition of the forces undermining the peasant economy. It begins as follows:

> The causes which bring about its downfall show its limitations. These are: Destruction of rural domestic industry, which forms its normal supplement as a result of the development of large-scale industry; a gradual impoverishment and exhaustion of the soil subjected to this cultivation; usurpation by big landowners of the common lands, which constitute the second supplement of the management of land parcels everywhere and which alone enable it to raise cattle; competition, either of the plantation system or large-scale capitalist agriculture. Improvements in agriculture, which on the one hand cause a fall in agricultural prices and, on the other, require greater outlays and more extensive material conditions of production, also contribute toward this, as in England during the first half of the eighteenth century.
>
> Proprietorship of land parcels by its very nature excludes the development of social productive forces of labor, social forms of labor, social concentration of capital, large-scale cattle-raising, and the progressive application of science.
>
> Usury and a taxation system must impoverish it everywhere. The expenditure of capital in the price of the land withdraws this capital from cultivation. An infinite fragmentation of means of production, and isolation of the producers themselves. Monstrous waste of human energy. Progressive deterioration of conditions of

production and increased prices of means of production—an inevitable law of proprietorship of parcels. Calamity of seasonal abundance for this mode of production.[18]

It is not our task here to consider which of these causes remained operative, which softened, which were counteracted by measures of state support, and so on. We are interested in the forms taken by the trend itself. Small agricultural production "is irretrievably lapsing into decline and ruin"[19]—such was the often-repeated opinion set down by Marx and Engels.* It is necessary to see concretely what this is supposed to mean.

3. DECLINE OF THE PEASANT: NOMINAL OWNERSHIP

The simplest form of the decline of the peasant economy is to be seen in terms of the concentration and centralization of landownership. Although this is sometimes taken to be synonymous with the decline thesis, we shall see that it is not even decisive for Marx's view of the matter.

In this form, the tendency of decline has been spotty, as a result of counteractive forces in different national situations,[23] and also slower than Marx expected, as usual. However, in the two "purest" capitalist countries, England and the United States, the result has been unmistakable. England, of course, was already in Marx's time the very model of a capitalist society based on uprooting the peasantry from the land. In the U.S., concentration of ownership worked itself out in a more zigzag course, but the evidence today is massive and indisput-

---

* Stronger terms appearing in English translations are sometimes misleading. Marx's *Wage-Labor and Capital* speaks of "the inevitable ruin of the intermediate classes of burghers and the peasant class under the present system," but a garbled English version introduces the word *destruction*.[20] In *Capital* Marx wrote that modern industry "annihilates that bulwark of the old society, the 'peasant,' and replaces him with the wage-laborer."[21] The context is evidently Britain and the United States, which also explains the quotation marks around "peasant." Elsewhere Marx and Engels generally used a term with the force of "ruin."[22]

able.* For many other parts of the world the facts are still controverted.

But the simple concentration and centralization of ownership is, for Marx, not the only and not necessarily the main criterion to determine the meaning of agrarian development.

Let us begin with a point Engels had to make against a book by Anton Menger. Menger had argued that in the Roman Empire the economic preconditions of socialism were even more highly developed than under capitalism, since in those days "half the province of Africa was held as the property of six people," and so on. This was surely a formidable case of centralization! But, Engels pointed out, the relation between concentration-centralization and socialism was not that kind of mechanical thing. Part of his reply went as follows, under the title "Lawyers' Socialism":

> Now, this [modern industrial production] gets compared with the conditions of imperial Rome, where it was not a question of large-scale machine production either in industry or in the agricultural economy. To be sure, we find a concentration in land *ownership,* but one must be a lawyer to consider this as equivalent to the development of socially organized labor in big enterprises. If we put before Herr Menger three examples of landownership: an Irish landlord who owns 50,000 acres, which are worked by 5000 tenants in small lots averaging ten acres each; a Scottish landlord who has turned 50,000 acres into hunting grounds; and an American giant farm of 10,000 acres in which wheat is cultivated as in a large-scale industry—he will say that in the first two cases the concentration of the means of production has gone five times as far as the last case.[25]

Menger's approach was unenlightening because it took the *form* (concentration) as decisive, disregarding the social relations of production

---

* It sounds like a rough summary of Marx when an agrarian historian summarizes the U.S. development as follows. The mass of people

> were suddenly and cruelly made aware of how that process of headlong economic expansion and concentration had left them, the common workers, without economic security. The former homesteaders and the artisans had become workers in factories and tenants and laborers on the land, dependent for their livelihood on the small number of people who controlled a great part of the country's wealth. No less than forty percent of the farmers were by now tenants, and of the other farms a great many were mortgaged.[24]

This was written by none other than D. Mitrany, five years before his *Marx Against the Peasant*. Three decades have passed since then, and the small American family farmer is even more out of the picture.

underlying the form. Concentration on the Roman African scale would become significant if occurring on the basis of modern society. And in fact, twenty-two years before, Marx had remarked in the Inaugural Address of the International that, as English landownership had concentrated 11 percent in ten years, "the land question will become singularly simplified, as it had become in the Roman empire, when Nero grinned at the discovery that half the Province of Africa was owned by six gentlemen."[26]

This sort of confusion between superficial forms and underlying social realities goes to the heart of the present problem. One aspect was heavily emphasized by Marx: the question of the peasant's landownership as "nominal ownership."

The impact of capitalist development on small-scale production, in agriculture as in industry, is reflected only partly by ownership statistics. In industry, the vassal relation of car dealers to Detroit or the satellite status of parts suppliers to prime contractors is well known; but the pattern holds also for agriculture. A peasant, holding juridical ownership over a parcel of land, who is completely at the mercy of the banker, moneylender, or mortgagee—how independent is such a peasant?

This way of looking behind the form of juridical ownership was not invented by Marx as an amendment to *Capital;* it was familiar to him when he had barely started his economic studies. Thus, in *The German Ideology:*

How deeply [Stirner] has penetrated into the concentration of landed property can already be deduced from the fact that he sees in it only the most obvious act of concentration, the mere "buying-up." Incidentally, from what [Stirner] says it is not possible to perceive to what extent small landowners cease to be owners by becoming day-laborers [in addition].[27]

To this day, it is typical of Marx's critics that they see "only the most obvious act of concentration." Writing the above in 1845, Marx points only to the fact that small peasants are so often forced to hire out their labor-power on the side because they cannot make ends meet as independent cultivators; insofar as they begin to rely on their income as day-laborers to tide them over, the peasant economy becomes an appendage of the larger economy that is engulfing it.

There are other minor respects in which the subordination of the peasant economy is symbolized. Later Marx was to comment that "the bookkeeping tenant-farmer was not produced until the rise of a capitalist agriculture" whereas the old peasants kept their accounts in their heads[28]—a symbol of the subordination of the former to the encircling economy.

In the course of the 1848 revolution, Marx begins to emphasize the most widespread form in which peasant landownership is hollowed out, made tenuous and ghostly, by the capitalist system that englobes it. This is through the channel of mortgages and the consequent "interest slavery," the debt burden in general, and the resulting clutch of usury, supplemented by the bloodletting peculiar to the state known as taxation, with the addition of court costs and legal costs of various kinds.

> Especially in France, as in countries generally where parcellization dominates, the rule of the feudal lords has turned into the rule of the capitalists, the feudal burdens of the peasants into bourgeois mortgage obligations.[28a]

In the spring of 1849 Marx thought the French peasantry might be radicalized by the tax burdens imposed by the bourgeois provisional government. The tax, he wrote, has shown "the difference between formal and real property ownership":

> it became clear . . . that the formal owner of the soil had become a vassal of the capitalists and that the tax hit only the debt-encumbered vassal. Now when in addition the real landowner [i.e., the capitalist] more than ever let the poor peasant feel his authority by withdrawing credit, by debt-seizures, etc., the revolution [actually the provisional government] became more and more odious to the peasant.[29]

Marx detailed the conception in his *Class Struggles in France* in reviewing the revolution: in one way or another "the French peasant cedes to the capitalist" the greater part of the income produced by his labor, and "therefore he has sunk to the level of the *Irish tenant farmer*—all under the pretense of being a *private proprietor.*" For the most part, the peasants' "enjoyment of property is limited to the fanatical assertion of their title to their fancied property" in the form of lawsuits.[30] This was echoed by Engels in his account of the 1848 revolution in Germany: the class of independent small freeholders "was a class of freeholders by name only" because the burden of mortgages and other debts was so heavy "that not the peasant, but the usurer who had advanced the money, was the real landowner."[31]

From the "mortgage servitude of the small peasants,"[32] Engels later went on to the analysis that "the actual higher ownership of landed property is transferred to the stock exchange" as the bank system expands, incorporates, and more and more takes over control of land from debtors' hands; if "the agricultural revolution of prairie cultivation" continues, then "the time can be foreseen when [not only Germany's but] England's and France's land will also be in the hands of the stock exchange"—that is, of finance capital.[33]

While Engels came back to this view of peasant ownership more than once,[34] it was Marx who started using *nominal proprietor* as a term. An article of his in 1858 made an approach:

> The fact is that the large majority of the French peasantry are owners in name only—the mortgagees and the Government being the real proprietors.[35]

In 1869, at a session of the International's General Council on the land collectivization resolution for the coming congress, Marx said:

> We see that both forms of private property in land [small-scale and large-scale] have led to bad results. The small man is only a nominal proprietor, but he is the more dangerous because he still fancies that he is a proprietor.[36]

So too in a draft for his essay on the Paris Commune in 1871:

> °°the peasant proprietorship itself has become nominal, leaving to the peasant the delusion of proprietorship and expropriating him from the fruits of his own labour.[37]

And in an argument for land nationalization the following year:

> °°[Although the French peasant is] bound to give away the greater part of his produce to the state, in the form of taxes, to the law tribe, in the form of judiciary costs [,] and to the usurer, in the form of interest . . . he still clings with frantic fondness to his spot of soil and his merely nominal proprietorship in the same.[38]

Obviously the question of nominal ownership will vary considerably from small peasants to bigger peasants, and statistics treating the peasantry as a homogeneous social class will hardly be illuminating.

4. DECLINE: RELATIVE FORMS

The full meaning of the decline of the peasant economy has yet another aspect, even after nominal ownership has been taken into account.

In referring to the palmy days of the peasant economy in *Capital,* Marx calls it a mode of production more than once. It used to be "the economic foundation of society," whereas "among modern nations" (that is, under capitalist conditions) it is left "as one of the forms arising from the dissolution of feudal landownership," as a form of property in the interstices of a social system to which it is alien.[39] The decline of the peasant economy has more than a quantitative side. Its qualitative side asks: What is the social meaning of the peasantry and the peasant economy with relation to the rest of the economy?

This is the most basic consideration. It was expressed by Marx in a passage immediately preceding one quoted above about the nominal proprietorship of the peasant:

> °°this peasant proprietorship has long since outgrown its normal phase, that is, the phase in which it was a reality, a mode of production and a form of property which responded to the economical wants of society and placed the rural producers themselves into normal conditions of life. It has entered its period of decay. On the one side a large *prolétariat foncier* (rural proletariat) has grown out of it whose interests are identical with those of the townish wages labourers. The mode of production itself has become superannuated by the modern progress of agronomy.[40]

What is decaying, in fact, is not only peasant ownership as a form of property but *all nonbourgeois relationships on the land.* To be sure, noncapitalist forms of big landownership went first, for obvious reasons; the peasant parcel is the most stubborn survivor—"the last conquest" of capital, as Marx put it.[41]

Here too there was considerable continuity in Marx's thinking. Marx had taken this approach in his very first study on economics, in the 1844 manuscripts. Here Marx had already written two or three pages of argumentation explaining the "special circumstances which lead inevitably to the accumulation of large landed property and to the absorption of small property by it." He envisaged the complete absorption of the agricultural sphere by capitalist relations, in a simplistic way: the bourgeoisification of the landowner into a capitalist "so that there remain altogether only two classes of the population—the working class and the class of capitalists." This will constitute "the final overthrow of the old [aristocracy] and the final establishment of the money aristocracy."[42] Here the thrust of the argument does not specially concern the decline of the smallholding peasants but rather the withering-away of *any* nonbourgeois class and social relationship on the land.

This approach, therefore, does not simply compare the peasantry today to the peasantry yesterday, quantitatively or otherwise, but rather stresses the relation of the peasantry *to the other classes of modern society*, then and now.

This is the approach Marx took in *The Eighteenth Brumaire* to explain how French society had changed between the first Napoleon and his nephew. "The economic development of smallholding property has radically changed the relation of the peasants to the other classes of society," he begins. At the turn of the century the peasantry, consolidated on the land of the ousted nobility, was a barrier "against the landed aristocracy which had just been overthrown," its boundary markers "formed the natural fortifications of the bourgeoisie" against feudal counterrevolution.

> But in the course of the nineteenth century the feudal lords were replaced by urban usurers; the feudal obligation that went with the land was replaced by the mortgage; aristocratic landed property was replaced by bourgeois capital. The small holding of the peasant is now only the pretext that allows the capitalist to draw profits, interest and rent from the soil, while leaving it to the tiller of the soil himself to see how he can extract his wages.[43]

Behind the form of peasant property lies the reality of "enslavement by capital," Marx adds. This is not simply an agitational flourish. If (as Marx explains in the third volume of *Capital*) the independent peasant can be regarded as a one-person combination of a landlord who has himself (and family) as his tenant, a capitalist who employs himself as a laborer, and a worker who draws a wage from himself as employer,[44] then the "profits, interest and rent" which he should be getting as landlord-capitalist are being siphoned off (through mortgagee, usurer, bank, state tax bureau, etc.) into the coffers of the dominant capitalist class, leaving him only the equivalent of his wage—and not always that much. Marx commented, of the sharecropper (métayer): "this poor fellow who merely combines in his own person the misfortune of the wage-worker with the misery of the small capitalist, might in fact consider himself lucky if he were put on fixed wages."[45] In terms of economic reality, he is working for his wage-equivalent, despite his self-image as a mini-landowner or farmer.*

Thus we have seen two different ways in which modern capitalism "annihilates the peasant" and "replaces him by the wage-laborer."[47] One is the obvious act of separating the peasants from their land altogether and forcing them to earn a living as laborers in agriculture or industry. The other is the above-described "enslavement by capital" while they still remain nominal proprietors of their land but are actually working for the equivalent of a wage. The independent peasant of the good old days and the pseudo-independent peasant inside the toils of a capitalist economy both hold the same *formal* relationship to their land, but behind the form is a different social (interclass) relation, a different mode of exploitation, a different economic reality.

To be sure, these two different ways in which the peasant is reduced to the equivalent of a wage-worker are not at all equivalent in social consequences, the biggest difference being their effect on political consciousness.

There is still another respect in which the meaning of the peasant's small holding has changed with the development of capitalism: in the amount of social independence possible for the peasant. In large part, independence concretely used to mean self-sufficiency.

> ... the peasant of today has lost half of his former productive activity. Formerly he and his family produced, from raw material he had made himself, the greater part of the industrial products that he needed; the rest of what he required was supplied by village neighbors who plied a trade in addition to farming and were paid mostly in articles of exchange or in reciprocal services. The family, and still more the village, was self-sufficient, produced almost everything it needed. ... Capitalist production put an end to this by its money economy and large-scale industry.[48]

The "free peasant" becomes less free than ever even if ownership of the land remains untouched. Engels sums up:

> Possession of the means of production by the individual pro-

---

* Cf. Marx on the French peasant, who "cedes to the capitalist, in the form of *interest* on the *mortgages* encumbering the soil and in the form of interest on the *advances made by the usurer without mortgages*, not only ground rent, not only the industrial profit, in a word, not only the *whole net profit*, but even a *part of the wages*"—hence "the pretense of being a *private proprietor.*"[46]

ducers nowadays no longer grants these producers real freedom. Handicraft has already been ruined in the cities ... The self-supporting small peasant is neither in the safe possession of his tiny patch of land nor is he free. He as well as his house, his farmstead and his few fields belong to the usurer; his livelihood is more uncertain than that of the proletarian, who at least does have tranquil days now and then, which is never the case with the eternally tortured debt slave.[49]

For all these reasons, the decline of the peasant economy must also be understood in terms of *social weight:* the decrease in the relative economic and social weight of the peasantry and its activities. If the peasant population becomes a smaller percentage of the total population as the latter figure rises with the development of industry; if the produce of the peasant sector of the economy becomes an ever smaller percentage either of agricultural production as a whole or (more important) of total national production, and therefore a less important factor in the economic life of the nation, then it follows that the socioeconomic weight of the peasantry has declined as capitalist economy has expanded. The same result obtains from the growing gap between the level of wealth and culture among the owning class in the city and the owning class on the land.

As mentioned, it should go without saying that the decline of the peasantry does not automatically produce *pari passu* a progressive change in the peasant's political consciousness. When, regarding the transformation from peasant to wage-laborer, Marx wrote that "Thus the desire for social changes and the class antagonisms are brought to the same level in the country as in the towns,"[50] he was taking the long historical view with the telescopic lens. He was identifying the transmission gears between the economics and the politics of the peasant question, though the transmission is rarely smooth.

The social conditions of existence on the land make for greater lags in consciousness than do urban conditions. This can be confirmed by comparing the radicalization of landless peasants who come to the city and become factory workers, as against those who remain on the land as day-laborers, rural proletarians in a peasant milieu. For example: on the land the day-laborer may be able to retain a morsel of land on the side, and even perhaps illusions about a future as a micro-landowner. This, plus community pressures and conditioning, may keep the day-laborer identifying with peasant concerns and sharing the peasant mentality long after personal reality has changed. On the other hand, in the city there are the obvious factors of greater concentration of proletarian numbers and the accompanying cultural impact of this fact.

5. SMALL AND BIG PEASANTS

The politics of the peasantry, perhaps even more than its economic life, is closely conditioned by its intraclass differentiation. There are important distinctions within the peasantry, in terms of real social relations of production as against mere forms of ownership, even though the boundaries are naturally not hard and fast.

All discussions of the peasantry speak of small peasants and big peasants, but for Marx the distinction is not at bottom a merely quantitative one, like the difference between small fleas and big fleas. For him, keeping this distinction in mind is fundamental to a revolutionary political solution of the peasant question. "Moreover people forget, besides the main point—big landed property—that there are various kinds of peasants," Engels remarked in a letter, apropros of the to-do in the International over the issue of land nationalization.[51] It eventually became clearer that people "forget" this, in the socialist movement, especially in order to adapt to the bigger peasants—and their votes.

What is a small peasant?

> By small peasant we mean here the owner or tenant—
> particularly the former—of a patch of land no bigger, as a rule,
> than he and his family can till, and no smaller than can sustain
> the family. This small peasant, just like the small handicraftsman,
> is therefore a toiler who differs from the modern proletarian in
> that he still possesses his instruments of labor; hence a survival of
> a past mode of production.[52]

To give this definition its negative form, the small peasant is one who does not employ hired labor, on a regular basis, and thus is not primarily an employer.

In contrast, a big peasant "cannot manage without wage-workers."[53] Marx writes that "the more prosperous peasants" have the possibility of

> exploiting agricultural wage-laborers for their own account, much
> as in feudal times, when the more well-to-do peasant serfs them-

selves also held serfs. In this way, they gradually acquire the possibility of accumulating a certain amount of wealth and themselves becoming transformed into future capitalists.[54]

This is similar to the possibility of the urban petty-bourgeois to grow into a small capitalist, as we saw in the preceding chapter.[55]

As always, there is a spectrum between the small and the big peasant; for the small peasant of the family farmstead may have to hire a day-laborer now and then, and a small peasant with (say) a team of horses is obviously bigger than the poor wight who not only lacks livestock but has to hire out part of the time; and so on. *Middle peasant* is a term of convenience for the in-between spectrum. Not only is this stratum defined by the others, but its politics is heavily conditioned by its milieu, as Engels observes:

> Where the middle peasant lives among small-holding peasants his interests and views will not differ greatly from theirs; he knows from his own experience how many of his kind have already sunk to the level of small peasants. But where middle and big peasants predominate and the operation of the farm requires, generally, the help of male and female servants it is quite a different matter.[56]

In his account of 1848–1849 in Germany, Engels expressly lumps the big and middle peasants together as "proprietors of more or less extensive farms, and each of them commanding the services of several agricultural laborers." For, as he goes on to relate, they lumped themselves together politically in the situation:

> This class [big and middle peasants taken together], placed between the large untaxed feudal landowners, and the smaller peasantry and farm laborers, for obvious reasons found in an alliance with the anti-feudal middle class of the towns its most natural political course.[57]

As late as 1869 Engels still wrote off the middle peasant, "who will also be reactionary and is not very numerous."[58] As we have seen, his expectations in this regard later became more flexible. But then, the middle peasantry itself is such a flexible classification that one can say little more about it in general than that, like intermediate strata in general, it consists of "iron filings" in a sense we have used before.

There is still another analog with our discussion of the petty-bourgeoisie. We saw that the splitting of the artisan into "two persons" also applies to the independent peasant.[59] In *Capital,* as already mentioned, Marx dissects the peasant more finely into three or four parts. When a small farmer

> works for himself and sells his own product, he is first considered as his own employer (capitalist), who makes use of himself as a laborer, and second as his own landlord, who makes use of himself as his own tenant. To himself as wage-worker he pays wages, to himself as capitalist he gives the profit, and to himself as landlord he pays rent.[60]

Politically speaking, one may ask about this multiple economic persona: Which side is uppermost or dominant in any particular case or type of case? What forces, events, or circumstances move an aggregate of peasants to think of themselves as workers rather than as landowners or employers? This formulates a question for a concrete case investigation.

To be sure, all this applies to some degree to the small peasant as well; but the middle peasant is doubly intermediate.

The owner-peasant and the tenant farmer can be treated together in some cases: obviously there may be big and small among both; but the tenant farmer has to be separated out in certain political connections especially. Leaving aside the evident possibility of specific demands relevant only to the tenant's situation, there is (thought Engels) likely to be a difference in their attitude to the bigger issue of land nationalization. Land nationalization means different things to the owner-peasant on the one hand, and, on the other, to "the tenant farmer, to whom it is a matter of indifference whether the land belongs to the state or to a large proprietor"[61]—at any rate, as long as there is the possibility of renting it.

Lastly, there are the rural workers who neither own nor rent land to till on their own, but hire out their labor to others: the day-laborers or farmhands, making up the agricultural proletariat. The rural proletariat may be understood to include craftsmen performing jobs auxiliary to agriculture, within the same milieu.*

---

* One sometimes finds the rural laborer subsumed under the peasantry, especially in passing or implicitly. This may be merely a terminological convenience: the farmhands are being regarded *socially* as part of a peasant population, particularly where the dividing lines are still tenuous; for example, the laborers may till small plots, they may be related to peasants on all sides, and not separately organized in any way, perhaps still hoping to save enough pennies to buy a patch of land. At one point Engels' *Condition of the Working Class in*

6. HOSTILITY AND CONCERN

One of the obstacles to understanding Marx's and Engels' political approach to the peasant question is an accompaniment of the "Marx against the peasant" myth, that is, the charge that they were irrationally biased and hostile to peasants, instead of being persuaded by a view of society derived from history and experience. There are few complaints so wide of the mark; it needs to be cleared up so that the substantive issues can be tackled fruitfully.

In the first place, a depreciatory and scornful attitude toward peasants is so pervasive and deep-rooted in modern Western culture that it is simply diversionary to point a finger to Marx when he touches on it. The English language itself (like other Western languages) testifies to the common equation of peasant or peasant-serf status with stupidity, vice and ill repute; perhaps the best-known example is the etymology of *villain; boor* is another.

There are two reasons for this tradition. One is a fact: the cultural backwardness attendant on peasant life (of which more later), especially as seen with urban or upper-class eyes that are incapable of a balanced historical view of the compensatory virtues of an alien culture. A second reason is the basic class antagonism toward the peasantry on the part of the two ruling classes that incubated the dominant ideas and pervasive conceptions of our epoch. For the landed aristocracy, the peasant was both a despicable object of exploitation, who could be squeezed all the more tranquilly by being demoted to a subhuman status, and also a continual danger that had to be brutally repressed. The bourgeoisie's attitude toward the peasant had to be more ambivalent, especially in its period of struggle against the feudal rulers; but it was counterposed to the peasantry as an urban class buying its products, as well as the representatives of a system that had to crowd out part of the rural population and subject the rest to its own economic power. Indeed, one agrarian historian has ideological peasant-baiting coming in with the rise of the bourgeoisie, in the sixteenth century and after the German peasant war.[64]

For Marx, "hostility" to the peasant, as to the capitalist class, is a

---

England shows this usage by others when he quotes a bourgeois Liberal source.[62] Another terminological point about some socialist literature, usually quite clear in context, is the use of *peasantry* to refer only to the small peasantry. Engels makes this usage explicit in an 1847 piece.[63]

social question. The problem is not hostility to certain people; the problem is a social formation which is a fossil representative of an old and reactionary social order, which as a class stands in the way of a progressive modernization and humanization of society. Marx had no doubt that the peasantry had to be superseded, just as he had no doubt that the capitalist class had to be abolished: how, when, and by whom was another matter. If this is a form of hostility, let us remember that Marx held the same opinion *mutatis mutandis* about other classes, including the proto-proletarian class of artisanal workers and (in a different form) even the moderate proletariat as it exists today.

The argument from psychological hostility is sterile. Marx's central question about a social stratum was: *What can be expected from it in terms of helping or hindering the revolutionary transformation of society?* When a class (or a system) is obsolete, the historical problem is not merely to abolish it, but to transcend it, which means to carry over its enduring contributions and values in a higher form.

More important is a related question: concern with and interest in the problems of the rural sector of society. It is generally true that the socialist movement at large has reflected and shared bourgeois society's depreciation of the peasant world, and has historically devoted a minimum of attention to the countryside except for vote-catching. That socialist movements have mainly been urban-centered explains this if it does not justify it.

But there are no socialist figures in the nineteenth century to whom this reproach applies less than to Marx and Engels.

Even in terms of personal background, Marx's upbringing in Trier should not be confused with that of socialists coming from urban jungles like London, New York, or Paris. Trier was a town dependent on a surrounding countryside; for example, it has been pointed out that many of the children with whom Marx went to school must have been from Moselle rural families.[65] We have seen that the first economic questions in which he got involved, as a democratic journalist in 1842, dealt not with the workers but with the economic oppression of the Rhenish peasantry and countrypeople, and that it was these issues that first oriented him toward socialism.[66] While these considerations are not in the least decisive, from my own standpoint, they are at least as relevant as the ingredients of the "Marx against the peasant" legend.

Engels, on the other hand, came from an industrial town and milieu; but Engels' personal interest in peasant questions, however derived, was very great. The following indubitable statement will come as a surprise to all mythologists: *Up to his time at least, there is no figure in the history of socialism who wrote more extensively on the history and problems of the peasantry and the countryside.*

We shall have occasion to mention some of his writings on the subject; and if many of them are little known and seldom quoted, that reflects not Engels but the socialist (urban) tradition of lack of interest in the question.*

It was not until the nineteenth century was nearing its end that the problem of catching rural votes for the growing Social-Democracies forced the peasantry into the consciousness of the parties, for opportunistic reasons. As Engels noted in 1894: "The bourgeois and reactionary parties greatly wonder why everywhere among Socialists the peasant question has now suddenly been placed upon the order of the day. What they should be wondering at, by rights, is that this has not been done long ago."[68]

A comparison is in order when the peasant historian D. Mitrany lauds Proudhon as "something unique in the history of Socialism" because of his "sympathy for the peasant."[69] It is true enough that Proudhon's was "a socialism for peasants"[70] in the sense that he wrote within the framework of the peasant and petty-bourgeois mentality; but an examination of some dozens of volumes of his collected works

* We remind the reader that Chapter 7 set forth Engels' role in 1847 in proposing the perspective of a proletarian alliance with the peasantry and petty-bourgeoisie, at a time when Marx showed no sign of thinking along these lines. (Where did Engels get this complex of ideas? Certainly not from his new associates of the Communist League; this is clear from the contents of the trial issue of the *Kommunistische Zeitung* in September 1847—it did not contain a single mention of the peasantry.) Next, during the revolution of 1848–1849 the N.R.Z. group innovated a whole body of revolutionary peasant politics, as will be seen in the next chapter. Following the revolution, Engels' first historical work was *The Peasant War in Germany*. This inaugurated a whole series of historical investigations, many remaining in manuscript. Such an essay as "The Mark" was written explicitly as socialist education for peasants; note its first and last paragraphs. An index to marxological interest in the peasantry is the fact that most of these writings of Engels' are virtually never mentioned or cited, in acres and acres of Marxist and anti-Marxist literature. —Engels' interest in the question characteristically extended down to details. A tiny one: in 1865 he translated a Danish folk song from the period of the medieval peasant war in Jutland, for publication in the party press, along with the following comment: "In a country like Germany, where the owning class comprises feudal aristocracy as much as bourgeoisie, and the proletariat comprises agricultural proletarians as much as or more than industrial workers, this vigorous old peasants' song is right to the point." The point of the song was peasant resistance to oppressive taxation.[67]

shows no special writing of note *about* the peasantry and its problems or history.[71] In this respect Engels stands in first place. On the other hand, his writings were not guaranteed to make peasants happy.

7. HIKER'S VIEW

Engels' concern with and interest in the peasantry in human terms can be seen most clearly in a little-known manuscript in which he also developed most fully a social-psychological portrait of the mind of the peasant, associated with the political role played by the class.

The context is very important. Threatened with arrest by the Prussian government in Cologne in the autumn of 1848, Engels left the city for a while. Then, deported from Belgium, and after a short stay in a dark and dismal Paris, he started on foot through France on his way to Geneva and Bern. In an unfinished manuscript, he recorded his *Reisebilder*—travel sketches—of the French countryside through which he walked, in a sort of holiday from revolution.

The mood is usually gay, and the writer records a love affair with France: not the France of the capital city but the France of the countrypeople. He is enchanted by the glories of the wine, women, scenery, and food characteristic of peasant France; he is delighted with the bonhomie of its people, whom he keeps praising as against the Germans. "These peasants are a goodhumored, hospitable, cheerful people . . . bearers of many time-honored virtues . . ." and so on. He likes them as human beings. And it is in the midst of this eulogy of peasant France that he digresses to the one dark note that intrudes on his warm feeling for the people: the social mentality of the peasant.

He begins by striking a note to which we will return in the next section:

> But a peasant remains a peasant, and the conditions of existence of the peasants never cease making their influence felt. In spite of all the personal virtues of the French peasants, in spite of the fact that his living conditions are better developed than those of the peasants on the east bank of the Rhine, still in France as in Germany the peasant is the barbarian in the midst of civilization.[72]

The modern reader must understand that *barbarian* here is not a cuss-word but a historical reference to (then accepted) stages of civilization. The context has already made clear that the epithet is not a personal one. The reasons are the social conditions of life:

> The isolation of the peasant in a secluded village with a small population that changes only with the generations, the arduous and monotonous work that binds him to the soil more than any serfdom and that always stays the same from father unto son, the fixity and sameness of all conditions of existence, the limited horizon in which the family becomes the most important and decisive relationship for him—all this reduces the peasant's range of vision to the narrowest limits possible in modern society generally. The great movements of history pass over his head, from time to time carrying him away but without his having any idea of the nature of the motive force or its origin or end.[73]

The walker reviews the highlights of peasant movements from the Middle Ages to the revolution of 1830. In the French Revolution "the peasants were revolutionary . . . just until their property rights were made secure on the soil . . . Once these ends were attained, they turned with all the rage of their blindly grasping nature against the movement in the big cities which they could not understand, especially against the movement in Paris." The peasant became a worshiper of Napoleon and a fanatical nationalist: *"la France* has had a lofty significance for him ever since he got hereditary possession of a piece of France." He hates the foreigner fanatically because *l'étranger* means a ravaging invader. The Bourbon restoration threatened his land title; the July 1830 revolution consolidated it.[74]

Yet inevitably the peasant was bilked by the very developments he welcomed:

> But as always they enjoyed little of the fruits of victory. The bourgeoisie immediately began to exploit their rural allies with all the strength at their disposal. The fact that the soil could be parcelled out and divided up bore fruit—in the form of the impoverishment of the peasants and the mortgaging of their pieces of land—which had already begun ripening under the Restoration. After 1830 these results appeared in more and more generalized and threatening forms. But the pressure that big capital exerted on the peasant remained for him simply a personal relationship between him and his creditor; he did not and could not see that this more and more generalized and regularized

relationship was gradually developing into a class relationship between the class of big capitalists and the class of small land-holders.

The old feudal burdens are forgotten; the new enserfment to mortgage and usury is not understood.

> . . . the interest he has to pay and even the ever-renewing and oppressive collateral fees for the usurer are modern bourgeois financial charges which hit all debtors in a similar way; the oppression is exercised in a wholly modern and up-to-date form, and the peasant is sucked dry and ruined in accordance with exactly the same legal principles that alone made his property secure for him.

But he cannot see beyond this:

> The peasant cannot see any class relationship in mortgage profiteering; he cannot call for its suppression without putting his own property in jeopardy at the same time. The pressing burden of usury throws him into a state of complete bewilderment instead of into motion. The only relief he can see is in reduction of taxes. [75]

If he cannot understand what is squeezing him immediately, still less can he understand what industrial depression means for the far-off city people. Those never-satisfied Parisians are simply troublemakers, and the bourgeois press tells him they are nothing but *partageurs*, dividers-up; the peasants' exasperation knows no bounds.

> I have talked with hundreds of peasants in the most various sections of France, and among all of them reigned this fanaticism against Paris and especially against the Paris workers. "I wish that there goddamned Paris got blown up first thing tomorrow": this was the mildest of the good wishes expressed. It stands to reason that for the peasants the old feelings of scorn for city people were increased and confirmed by this year's events. [76]

We peasants have to save France, they decide; and that means supporting Bonaparte. Enthusiasm for Bonaparte and hatred of Paris are their passions. "The whole politics of the French peasantry was restricted to these two passions and to the most unthinking, animal-like amazement at the whole European convulsion." The republican Provisional Government made sure of the result by adding to the taxation on the peasant, for it "had no understanding of how to tie up the interests of the peasants with the revolution."

Here Engels' notes miss the point that the bourgeois government's interests required soaking the peasant rather than "understanding." His immediate conclusion is interestingly one-sided, especially when compared with Marx's superior analysis in 1850 or his own in other writings:

> The present attitude of the peasants toward the revolution of 1848 is not a result of any mistakes and fortuitous blunders; it is a natural thing, it is based on the life-situation and social position of the small property-owners. Before the French proletariat puts through its demands, it would first have to suppress a general peasant war, a war that even the abolition of all mortgage debts would only postpone for a short time.[77]

What this shows is how strongly Engels was impressed with the reactionary mental sets he was encountering among the peasantry. Taken literally, this pessimistic statement excluded the possibility of an alliance with the peasantry for all time.* It was a swing induced by a state of mind that is made explicit in the next paragraph:

> One must spend two weeks consorting with almost no one but peasants, peasants from the most various sections, one must have had the occasion to see again and again the same obtuse narrow-mindedness everywhere, the same total ignorance of all urban, industrial and commercial conditions, the same blindness in politics, the same aimless guesswork about everything beyond the village boundary, the same pattern of applying peasant conditions as the measuring-rod for the most prodigious circumstances of history—in a word, one must have gotten to know the French peasants in precisely the year 1848 to feel the disheartening impression produced by this obstinate thickheadedness.[79]

A few pages away is an enlightening counterpoint to this. At one village through which Engels passed, a force of three to four hundred

---

* However, it should be clear that the pessimism was justified for the moment, as an estimate of the situation in October 1848 in France. By the same token it meant that a proletarian revolution had become impossible. Engels' pessimism about the current prospect did not depend only on his acquaintance with the peasantry. His travel sketches begin with a hail-and-farewell to Paris: after bloody class struggles "the workers, breadless and weaponless, ground their teeth in suppressed anger . . . But Paris was dead; it was Paris no more."[78]

Paris workers were engaged in building a dam, as part of a National Workshops project. They were well paid and in good spirits—

> But otherwise they were completely demoralized by their isolation in a little village. Not a sign of any concern with the interests of their class, with the issues of the day that so closely affect the workers. They seemed not to read newspapers any more. All of politics in their ranks was limited to handing out nicknames [after leading politicians] ... The arduous labor, the relatively good living conditions, and especially the separation from Paris and displacement to a quiet isolated corner of France had markedly restricted their range of vision. They were already becoming peasantized, though they had been there only two months.[80]

This strikingly showed the relation between the peasants' conditions of life and the peasant mentality but it also showed how little the phenomenon had in common with the eternal.

8. THE PEASANT MENTALITY

The Greeks had a word for the kind of social mentality that Engels was describing in his travel sketches: the privatized person, withdrawn from public concerns, *apolitical* in the original sense of isolation from the sociopolitical community of the larger whole. The word was *idiotes.*

In English the word *idiot* lost its Greek meaning many centuries ago. In German the etymological meaning was retained until well into the nineteenth century. What then did the classical scholar Marx mean when, just before the midpoint of the century, he wrote into the *Communist Manifesto* a remark about *dem Idiotismus des Landlebens,* that is, about the privatized apartness of rural life? It is highly doubtful that his meaning is adequately summed up by "the idiocy of rural life"—the phrase that translated it forty years later.*

---

* The testimony in German philological sources on the meaning of *Idiotismus* seems to be as unanimous as its disregard by marxologists.[81] It should be understood that, after the modern meaning of *Idiotismus* began to enter German in the nineteenth century as a dubious neologism, the old Greek-rooted meaning was gradually displaced; as usual there was an overlap, with both meanings in use for a while. However, it is difficult to believe that in 1847–1848 this word would be used with no consciousness of its correct Greek meaning by a university-

The Manifesto had a different point to make—one that might be equally unpalatable to idealizers of the peasantry, but that requires to be understood. The peasant population stood outside modern civilization within a nation, just as industrially retarded nations stand outside the current of modern civilization in the world. Civilization here means, in social and class terms, nothing else than the most advanced society then in existence, the developed bourgeois civilization of the West. For, says the Manifesto, through its massive urbanization the bourgeoisie

> has thus rescued a considerable part of the population from the *Idiotismus* of rural life. Just as it has made the country dependent on the towns, so it has made barbarian and semibarbarian countries dependent on the civilized ones, nations of peasants on nations of bourgeois, the East on the West.[84]

Not accidentally, we must mention that *barbarian* retained its classical flavor also: *standing outside the bounds of high civilization.* (To be sure, to the Greeks this meant Greek civilization; to Marx, it refers to the advanced bourgeois civilization celebrated in the Manifesto.) It was a turn of phrase when in 1850 Marx described the peasantry as "the class that represents barbarism within civilization"[85]—a combination that made the same point as the Manifesto, the comparison of the peasantry within the nation to the classical barbarians without. Similar comparisons occur elsewhere,[86] not as insults but as comments on a class social pattern.*

Another part of the context to keep in mind is that the cultural

---

educated scholar who had just written his doctoral dissertation on Greek philosophy and liked to read Greek drama in the original. Furthermore, even today in German *Idiotismus* does not primarily mean idiocy (which is *Idiotie*); it usually means idiom, like its cognate in French *idiotisme*. —The 1850 translation of the Manifesto by Macfarlane in the *Red Republican* reads: "the idiotism of country life," with uncertain import.[82] The translation by the Pauls is knowledgeable: "the seclusion and ignorance of rural life."[83]

* Since Marx's alleged insult to the peasantry has so often aroused a show of indignation, we suggest attention to a famous description of the eternal peasant: "The emptiness of ages in his face . . . dead to rapture and despair . . . Stolid . . . a brother to the ox . . . [with] loosened . . . brutal jaw . . . Whose breath blew out the light within his brain? . . . This monstrous thing distorted and soul-quenched . . . this dumb terror . . ." This rhapsody is from Edwin Markham's renowned poem "The Man with the Hoe," based on Millet's painting; it is commonly included in anthologies of "Songs of Freedom" and such. I suggest that this expresses the typical bourgeois-liberal, not revolutionary, attitude toward this class; for there can be no revolutionary expectations from the zombies here portrayed.

deformation of an isolated rural population is one aspect of the separation of town and country which has been brought to a high pitch by capitalism (as we shall discuss in Volume 3). But this separation of town and country does not leave the urban population undeformed:

> The contradiction between town and country ... is the most crass expression of the subjection of the individual under the division of labor ... a subjection which makes one man into a restricted town-animal, another into a restricted country-animal, and daily creates anew the conflict between their interests.[87]

Part of the deformation suffered by the industrial worker, observed Marx in *Capital,* is that he loses the need to exercise the "knowledge, the judgment, and the will, which, though in ever so small a degree, are practised by the independent peasant or handicraftsman, in the same way as the savage makes the whole art of war consist in the exercise of his personal cunning." As a result, "intelligence in production" tends to be more concentrated in the employing capital than in the worker.[88] (This is not an insult to the proletariat.) For such reasons, wrote Engels in 1873, the socialist abolition of the separation between town and country is necessary for the health of both industry and agriculture. On the basis of the abolition of capitalism, it "will be able to deliver the rural population from the isolation and stupor in which it has vegetated almost unchanged for thousands of years."[89]

"Rural population" includes more than the peasantry. The mentality of the precapitalist countryside was by no means applicable only to peasants; it went along with certain conditions of existence, and therefore often characterized not only rural producers but also the beginnings of small-town life.

Young Engels learned much of this during his first sojourn in England, not from Marxist theory but from his investigation of English life and history. An early article discussed the England of the sixteenth and seventeenth centuries in relation to contemporary France and Germany:

> The peasants at that time used to lead a quiet, peaceful life of honest piety harassed by few worries, but on the other hand inert, not united by common interests and lacking any education or any mental activity; they were still at a prehistoric stage of development. The situation in the towns was not very different. [Details follow.] ... In short, England was then in a position in which unfortunately the majority of the French and in particular

the Germans still find themselves, in a position of antediluvian apathy with regard to anything of general or spiritual interest, in social infancy, when there is as yet no society, no life, no consciousness and no activity. This position is a *de facto* continuation of feudalism and medieval mental apathy, which will only be surmounted with the emergence of modern feudalism [i.e., capitalism], the division of society into property owners and the propertyless. We on the Continent, I repeat, still find ourselves entrenched in this position.[90]

He set it down again, a few months later, in his book on *The Condition of the Working Class*, particularly describing the life of the rural weavers—"the English industrial workers of those days" though "no proletarians"—and the social description is similar. It closes with an Edwin Markhamish (that is, bourgeois liberal) sentiment: "In truth, they were not human beings; they were merely toiling machines in the service of the few aristocrats . . ."[91]

For Marx too, this social analysis preceded Marxism.[92] A little later, in *The German Ideology*, the causative factor stressed is the isolation and dispersal of the peasantry, in addition to its common interest (as property-holders) with the large landowners.[93] The dispersion factor was heavily emphasized in Engels' later writings as well.[94]

But it is the total pattern of a sluggish social form that is most important. In an article for American readers explaining why Switzerland was playing a reactionary role, Engels made a comparison with the American West:

> The [Swiss] agricultural population is quite as stationary as the pastoral; they have nothing in common with the agricultural population of the American Far West, whose very aliment is change, and who clear every twelvemonth an amount of land far larger than all Switzerland.

The trouble with the Swiss peasant—and for that matter with rural life in general—is immobility, societal torpor, *stasis*.

> The Swiss peasant tills the patch of ground his father and grandfather tilled before him; he tills it in the same slovenly way as they did; . . . he lives about as they did, and consequently he thinks very nearly in the same way as they did.

The old petty manufactures, combined with agricultural pursuits, without the use of steam, still marked the Swiss system.

If, then, Switzerland carries on her manufacturing production almost exclusively upon the system in practice all over Europe *before* the invention of steam, how can we expect to find other than corresponding ideas in the minds of the producers; if steam has not revolutionized Swiss production and intercommunication, how could it overthrow the hereditary ways of thinking?[95]

9. ATOMIZATION AND INITIATIVE

In *The Eighteenth Brumaire* Marx emphasized still another aspect that cannot be summed up under dispersion; it is atomization.

The small-holding peasants form a vast mass, the members of which live in similar conditions but without entering into manifold relations with one another. Their mode of production isolates them from one another instead of bringing them into mutual intercourse. The isolation is increased by France's bad means of communication and by the poverty of the peasants. Their field of production, the small holding, admits of no division of labor in its cultivation, no application of science and, therefore, no diversity of development, no variety of talent, no wealth of social relationships. Each individual peasant family is almost self-sufficient; it itself directly produces the major part of its consumption and thus acquires its means of life more through exchange with nature than in intercourse with society. A small holding, a peasant and his family; alongside them another small holding, another peasant and another family. A few score of these make up a village; and a few score of villages make up a Department. In this way, the great mass of the French nation is formed by simple addition of homologous magnitudes, much as potatoes in a sack form a sack of potatoes.[96]

A sack of potatoes goes nowhere unless it is carried. The atomization of the peasantry as a class has political consequences basic to Marx's view of the dynamics of revolution.

One of the basic political characteristics of the peasantry is its relative lack of social initiative, and its necessary dependence on the initiative and leadership of one of the urban classes in any revolutionary movement. (To be sure, the peasantry has also accepted the domination and leadership of the landowning class, but in this case it is hardly revolutionary.[97])

The key passage from *The Eighteenth Brumaire*, begun above, says further:

> Insofar as there is merely a local interconnection among these small-holding peasants, and the identity of their interests begets no community, no national bond and no political organization among them, they do not form a class [subjectively].[98]

That is, they do not act as a class.* But the peasantry is incapable of acting in a vanguard role in society. This is not due to immaturity, as was once true of, say, the early bourgeoisie; it is not an adolescent class, like the proletariat, but a senescent one.

> They are consequently incapable of enforcing their class interests in their own name, whether through a parliament or through a Convention. They cannot represent themselves, they must be represented.[101]

Marx wrote this while the peasants were being wielded as a semi-conscious battering ram in the hands of Bonaparte to destroy the Third Republic. Bonapartism was not a peasant movement, though it utilized the movement of the peasants; and Bonaparte was not a peasant leader, though he led the peasants by the nose. The peasantry, as usual, was a tool.

This view of the political role of the peasantry was seen clearly by Engels even before 1848 and its experiences; and he expressed it even as he was proposing the idea of a proletarian bloc with the peasantry and petty-bourgeoisie (as explained in Chapter 7). The idea of an alliance was not based on illusions. The small peasants, wrote Engels in 1847,

* This is Marx's last echo of the Hegelianized distinction between a "class in itself" and a "class for itself," noted earlier.[99] Fortunately, it was subsequently dropped, for it is not an enlightening way to make the valid distinction. —About the same time, Engels made a related point, with a very dubious qualification: the peasantry "will never assert its interests and assume its position as an independent class, except in countries where universal suffrage is established."[100] The thought here, no doubt, is that the peasantry is drawn into political life at least when it is given the vote; and of course this is true. To that extent the peasant becomes conscious of itself politically. The difficulty with Engels' formulation is the word *independent:* even when the peasantry acts as a class at the ballot box, to what extent does it act independently, rather than as a tail to another's kite? *The Eighteenth Brumaire* explained that Bonaparte established his plebiscitary universal suffrage in order to use the peasantry as voting cattle for his own purposes.

can be counted on for greater courage than the petty-bourgeoisie, but like the petty-bourgeoisie

> they are also thoroughly incapable of all historical initiative. Even their emancipation from the chains of serfdom comes about only under the protection of the bourgeoisie. Where the absence of both nobility and bourgeoisie permits it to rule, as in the mountain cantons of Switzerland and in Norway, there also rule prefeudal barbarism, local narrowmindedness, stuffy fanatical bigotry and faithful rectitude. Where, as in Germany, the nobility still remains in existence along with the peasantry, the latter are squeezed in between nobility and bourgeoisie just like the petty-bourgeoisie. In order to protect the interests of agriculture against the growing power of trade and industry, they must ally themselves with the nobility. In order to safeguard themselves from the overweening competition of the nobility and especially of bourgeois land-owners, they must ally themselves with the bourgeoisie. Which side they finally join depends on the nature of their property. The big peasants of eastern Germany, who themselves exercise a certain amount of feudal authority over their farm-hands, are too closely connected in all their interests with the nobility to think seriously of cutting loose from them. The small landholders in the west who arose out of the splitting-up of the nobility's estates, and the small peasants in the east who are subject to corvée labor service, are too directly oppressed by, or stand too directly in opposition to, the nobility not to join the side of the bourgeoisie.[102]

For Engels this analysis was taught by history, not simply by a deduction from the two-headedness of the peasants' social status: so he emphasized later the same year. The bourgeois liberal Heinzen, he asks, directs his revolutionary moral homilies to what class?

> Above all to the small peasants, to that class which in our times is the least capable of all of seizing the revolutionary initiative. For 600 years, all progressive movements have come from the towns ... The industrial proletariat of the towns has become the copestone of all modern democracy; the small bourgeois and still more the peasants are completely dependent on its initiative. This is proved by the French Revolution of 1789 and the most recent history of England, France and the eastern states of America.[103]

At this point, on the eve of the revolution, it seemed to Engels that the most favorable revolutionary prospect was that the peasants would help the bourgeoisie in the latter's struggle:

> What else can they do? Since they are owners like the bourgeoisie, almost all their interests are held in common with the bourgeoisie for the time being. All the political measures they are strong enough to put through profit the bourgeoisie not much more than themselves.[104] But they are weak compared with the bourgeoisie, since the latter are wealthy and have their hands on the main lever of all political power in our century: industry. Together with the bourgeoisie they can do much; against the bourgeoisie, nothing.[105]

After the revolutionary experience of 1848–1849, nothing had to be changed. Engels' account of the revolution in Germany drives the lesson home again. The small peasants and rural workers would benefit from the victory of the revolution and could be expected to join in—

> But at the same time it is quite as evident, and equally borne out by the history of all modern countries, that the agricultural population, in consequence of its dispersion over a great space, and of the difficulty of bringing about an agreement among any considerable portion of it, never can attempt a successful independent movement; they require the initiatory impulse of the more concentrated, more enlightened, more easily moved people of the towns.[106]

Marx likewise, writing on the events in France, summed up that "The history of the last three years [1848–1850] has, however, provided proof that this class of the population is absolutely incapable of any revolutionary initiative."[107] In later writings on the history of the peasantry, Engels traced the course of its capacity for "self-help" as against "deliverance only from without."[108]

10. BASE FOR DESPOTISM

A class with the characteristics described in this chapter could, to be sure, become a revolutionary force of a certain type, and it could become part of a revolutionary bloc, but history showed that even in its best times its revolutionary activity was spasmodic. Usually it was politically passive. At worst, and not infrequently, it went into action as the tool of reaction.

Given its normal apathy, the peasantry was *par excellence* the class on which thoroughgoing despotisms based themselves. Generalizing on the pattern by which Bonaparte rode into power on the backs of the peasantry, Marx wrote, continuing a passage which we have already quoted:

> They [the peasants] cannot represent themselves, they must be represented. Their representative must at the same time appear as their master, as an authority over them, as an unlimited governmental power that protects them against the other classes and sends them rain and sunshine from above. The political influence of the small-holding peasants, therefore, finds its final expression in the executive power subordinating society to itself.[109]

A peasant infrastructure tends to produce a bureaucratic superstructure. Marx explains the seeming paradox:

> By its very nature, small-holding property forms a suitable basis for an all-powerful and innumerable bureaucracy. It creates a uniform level of relationships and persons over the whole surface of the land. Hence it also permits of uniform action from a supreme center on all points of this uniform mass. It annihilates the aristocratic intermediate grades between the mass of the people and the state power. On all sides, therefore, it calls forth the direct interference of this state power and the interposition of its immediate organs. Finally, it produces an unemployed surplus population for which there is no place either on the land or in the towns, and which accordingly reaches out for state offices as a sort of respectable alms, and provokes the creation of state posts.[110]

It is, then, the "decentralization" of peasant society (its dispersion and atomization) that nourishes the monstrous overcentralization of this state. It is the "equality" of the underlying population (the "uniform level" of a uniform mass) that forms the basis of the tremendous hierarchization of the "unlimited governmental power." It is the "independence" of the small cultivators—from each other as well as from the rest of society—that renders them helplessly dependent on a savior-master. These pairs of opposites, which abstractly seem so flatly incompatible, are united in the concrete context, like the two sides of a medal.*

From French Bonapartism to Oriental despotism: Marx made the connection in the few years following the publication of *The Eighteenth Brumaire*. This connection—specifically the connection between the peasants' conditions of existence and certain types of highly bureaucratized despotism—was spelled out in the course of his investigations into Indian and Chinese society and the Russian czarist state, and has been set forth in considerable detail in our Volume 1.**

Oriental despotism—the political structure resting on the localized, atomized peasant communities of what Marx called the "archaic formation" of society, or the "Asiatic" mode of production—is the best exemplification of the unity of opposites that Marx first analyzed in the quite different society of the Second Empire. Here, in a different mode of production, was the little world of the peasant *idiotes*. A working definition of *Idiotismus* can virtually be derived from some key points in Marx's descriptions of the conditions from which despotism arose. Let us recall some typical elements, at the expense of some repetition.

The empire, united by the central power, might be huge, but "the whole empire, not counting the few larger towns, was divided into *villages*, each of which possessed a completely separate organization and formed a little world in itself."[112] The people were "dispersed . . . over the surface of the country, and agglomerated in small centers by the domestic union of agricultural and manufacturing pursuits."[113] Hence they were easy prey for conquest by successive invaders "who founded their empires on the passive basis of the unresisting and unchanging society," whose "worst feature" was "the dissolution of society into stereotype [i.e., uniform] and disconnected atoms."[114] The village

---

* "This transformation into its opposite, this final landing at a point diametrically opposed to the starting point, is the strictly necessary fate of all historical movements which are unclear about their causes and conditions of existence and hence are directed toward merely illusory goals." —So Engels, on the transformation of the humanism of the Enlightenment into admiration of "the Semiramis of the North . . . called Catherine II of Russia."[111]

** In Volume 1, almost all of the last three chapters (on Oriental despotism and Russian czarism) is pertinent generally, but most relevant is the material in Chapter 21, sections 5-8, and Chapter 22, section 4.

communities seemed to be "idyllic republics" but, Marx added, "I believe that no one could think of any more solid foundation for Asiatic despotism and stagnation."[115] This remark in a letter was expanded in an article:

> ... we must not forget that these idyllic village communities, inoffensive though they may appear, had always been the solid foundation of Oriental despotism, that they restrained the human mind within the smallest possible compass, making it the unresisting tool of superstition, enslaving it beneath traditional rules, depriving it of all grandeur and historical energies. We must not forget the barbarian egotism [cf. *Idiotismus*] which, concentrating on some miserable patch of land, had quietly witnessed the ruin of empires, the perpetration of unspeakable cruelties [and so on] ...[116]

Both Marx and Engels, we also saw, applied this approach liberally to the Russian state. Marx emphasized the isolation of the Russian peasant commune: "its isolation, the lack of liaison between the life of one commune and the others'—this *localized microcosm* ... which, wherever it is found, has given rise to a more or less central despotism over the communes."[117] Engels made the point repeatedly, as in this 1875 passage:

> Such a complete isolation of the individual [village] communities from one another, which creates throughout the country similar, but the very opposite of common, interests, is the natural basis for *Oriental despotism*, and from India to Russia this form of society, wherever it prevailed, has always produced it and always found its complement in it.

Czarist despotism, he added, was "the necessary and logical product of Russian social conditions" of this sort.[118]

In his 1894 thesis on the peasant question, Engels emphasized the peasants' apathy for the same purpose: it "is the strongest pillar not only of the parliamentary corruption in Paris and Rome but also of Russian despotism."[119]

11. RIDING THE PEASANT

And so, historically, the question has been posed: *Who will ride the peasantry to power?* And in whose interests?

In periods of apathy, the peasantry provided a passive base for rule. But the peasants could also be ridden in the name of revolution—someone else's revolution. For example, Engels explained that Russian czarism had carried this maneuver out in order to annex Poland—"in the name of the right of revolution, arming the [Polish] serfs against their masters." He continued:

°°Talk about a war of class against class as something extremely revolutionary;—why, Russia set such a war on foot in Poland nearly 100 years ago, and a fine specimen of a class-war it was, when Russian soldiers and Little Russian serfs went in company to burn down the castles of Polish lords, merely to prepare Russian annexation, which being once accomplished the same Russian soldiers put the serfs back again under the yoke of their lords.[120]

The peasantry was an easy class to convince that "the enemy of your enemy is your friend."

Riding the peasantry has another side. It has often been accompanied by a "cult of the peasant"—an idealization and glorification of peasant and rural virtues—usually by urban intellectuals. This propagandistic idealization is the reverse side of the real exploitation of the peasantry, especially when it is useful to hold their virtues up as a model for a rebellious working class. This combination of cultism and exploitation has been seen from ancient Greece to Mussolini's Italy and more modern dictatorships in peasant countries.* A close analog is the Western tradition of idealization and "worship" of Woman on a pedestal, combined with the practical subjection and oppression of women—a combination which Marx and Engels attacked, as we shall see.[123]

* On ancient Greece, compare M. I. Finkelstein's discussion of the historical pattern: on the one hand, "the urban masses became restive," and on the other, the peasant was "still the pliant victim of the authoritarian obscurantism of the earlier age, the true bulwark of society in the eyes of the aristocratic ideologues, and an object of contempt at the same time." There is also an interesting comparison with the nineteenth-century cult of the yeomanry of Old England.[121] As for Mussolini, the British fascist Drennan praised him on just this point, giving suitable quotations.[122]

In Marx's time, it was Bakunin who was the most prominent representative of this combination. This feature of the anarchist founder was duly noticed and highlighted when Marx, Engels, and Paul Lafargue worked on a pamphlet in 1873 to expose the way in which the Bakuninist faction had bored from within to rule or ruin the International. They aimed a shaft at a notorious article Bakunin had published in 1862 as an appeal to the Russian czar to make the social revolution at the head of the People. "We would prefer to follow Romanoff, if Romanoff could and would transform himself from a Petersburg [that is, urban and Westernized] emperor into a peasant czar," Bakunin had written.*

Bakunin's peasant cultism was calculated. What he glorified in the peasantry was precisely its "barbarism," he often said, and his view of that class was very similar to Marx's—except standing on its head. All of the characteristics which for Marx made the peasantry unsuitable as a class revolutionary vanguard were, for Bakunin, precisely the reasons for adopting it as his chosen instrument of pandestruction (along with the lumpen-class). It could be used in the fashion traditional to would-be despots.[126]

The Engels-Lafargue-Marx pamphlet then makes the connection between Russian despotism and Bonapartism in its last words: "After this piece of brainwork by the master prostrating himself before his peasant czar, it was surely in order for his disciples and friends Albert Richard and Gaspard Blanc to yell: Long live Napoleon III, emperor of the peasants!"[127]

However, the Bakunin counterpart of Bonapartist socialism was not so much czarist socialism (whatever that might be imagined to be) but rather *peasant socialism*. For Marx, this belonged in the same category as the "reactionary socialism" and "petty-bourgeois socialism" analyzed in the *Communist Manifesto*. He had occasion to emphasize this in marginal notes on Bakunin's book *Statism and Anarchy*. These notes were somewhat telegraphic jottings set down for his own eyes only, hence not well developed, but in one such passage Marx suggested why

---

* So quoted in the pamphlet.[124] The translation "peasant czar" (probably provided by N. Utin of the Geneva branch of the International) was a loose one; the original Russian phrase, *zemsky Tzar*, had been duly given a few pages before.[125] Literally it means *czar of the (national) soil*. But in counterposition to "Petersburg emperor," the translation is close to the mark. In any case, my present point is that the exposé pamphlet chose to highlight this side of Bakunin's politics.

the conception of a progressive social revolution based on the peasantry was a mirage:

> A radical social revolution is bound up with certain historical conditions of economic development; the latter are its prerequisite. It is therefore possible only where, along with capitalist production, the industrial proletariat at least occupies an important position among the mass of the people. . . . [But Bakunin] understands absolutely nothing about social revolution—only its political phrases; its economic conditions do not exist for him. Now since all hitherto existing economic forms, developed or undeveloped, involve the subjection of workers (be it in the form of wage-workers, peasants, etc.), he believes that in all of them a *radical revolution* is equally possible. But even more! He wants the European social revolution which is founded on the economic basis of capitalist production to be carried out on the level of the Russian or Slavic agricultural and pastoral peoples and not go beyond this level . . .[128]

Marx concludes: "The will, not the economic conditions, is the foundation of his social revolution."* In the case of peasant-revolution theorists, the will has to be imposed not only on history but also on the peasantry. The Bakunin concept of anarchist revolution was a modern variant of the old pattern of riding the peasantry to political power.

The realistic question was not whether the peasantry could make a peasant revolution or reasonable facsimile thereof, but rather whether this class would ally itself with progress or reaction, and under what circumstances.

---

* Compare Marx's similar summing-up of another type of instant revolutionist, exemplified by the Schapper-Willich faction, a quarter-century previously: "Instead of the actual conditions, *pure will* becomes the drive-wheel of the revolution for them."[129]

13 | THE PEASANT QUESTION: TOWARD A REVOLUTIONARY ALLIANCE

The preceding chapter has sufficiently emphasized the negative features of the peasantry, from the standpoint of Marx's hopes for revolution. But none of this gainsays a proposition that Marx and Engels developed more and more as time went on, and which is the subject of this chapter: *It is essential for the revolutionary proletarian movement to do everything possible to win over (at least a part of) the peasantry to its own side; and it is possible to make at least considerable gains in this direction, given suitable policies.*

They argued that great success could be attained without in the least going outside the framework of socialist principles. There was a special problem of principle we must deal with first.

1. A QUESTION OF PRIORITIES

The special problem was the relation of the peasantry to the rural proletariat.

"Which of these [several] subdivisions of the rural population can be won over by the Social-Democratic Party?" asks Engels in his main essay on the peasant question.[1] He answers: first and foremost, the rural proletariat. From a basic standpoint, the farm worker is the class kin of the industrial proletarian, and more likely than a peasant to understand the socialist solution.

> Of course a workers' party has to fight, in the first place, on behalf of the wage-workers, that is, for the male and female servantry and the day-laborers. It is unquestionably forbidden to make any promises to the peasants [in the party program] which include the continuance of the wage-slavery of the workers.[2]

Later we will discuss the program of immediate and socialist demands directed to the rural proletariat, to win them over to the social-revolutionary forces.

For Germany particularly, Engels—writing toward the end of his life and near the end of the century—emphasized the basic importance of radicalization among the rural workers as the key to overthrowing the political power of East German Junkerdom and expropriating their big landed estates: "Here we are confronted by rural proletarians in masses and our task is clear." The prospect is good: "it can be only a question of time, and of only a very short time, before we win over to our side the rural workers of Prussia east of the Elbe. But once we have the East-Elbe rural workers a different wind will blow at once all over Germany." The power of Prussian Junkerdom is based on these exploited rural proletarian masses; and this power in turn provides the basis for Prussia's overlordship in Germany, and for "the specifically Prussian character" of the bureaucracy and the army officer corps. This Prussian stronghold is based not only on farm labor proper, but on labor in the two characteristic rural industries, beet-sugar refining and liquor distilling.[3]

> Sow the seed of Social-Democracy among these workers, give them courage and cohesion to insist upon their rights, and the glory of the Junkers will be at an end. The great reactionary power, which to Germany represents the same barbarous, predatory element as Russian czardom does to the whole of Europe, will collapse like a pricked bubble. The "picked regiments" of the Prussian army will become Social-Democratic, which will result in a shift in power that is pregnant with an entire upheaval. But for this reason it is of vastly greater importance to win the rural proletariat east of the Elbe than the small peasants of Western Germany or yet the middle peasants of Southern Germany. It is here, in East-Elbe Prussia, that the decisive battle of our cause will have to be fought . . .[4]

This introduces a consideration which we will elaborate in Volume 3, in connection with the road to political power; we stress, in anticipation, that its importance was not only enormous for the future of Germany and of Europe but, for present purposes, highlights the concreteness of the problem. The rural proletariat was not a Chosen Class in some abstract philosophical way but it was in fact one of the main keys to the coming social revolution. "Wherever medium-sized and large estates prevail," as in northern and eastern Germany, farm laborers become a numerous class, "and it is *there* that the industrial workers of the towns find their *most numerous and most natural allies.*"[5]

This was also the easiest case for socialist policy. But this fact does not mean that the rural proletariat is as easily radicalized as urban workers. Even apart from the cultural conditions under which they live, agricultural workers tend to be more dependent on their employers than industrial workers, hence harder to organize. Engels had noted such difficulties already in his *Condition of the Working Class in England,* together with some forces making for change.[6] More than once Marx or Engels took occasion to signalize the outbreak of strikes among farm workers, as class struggles of special significance. In a *New York Tribune* article of 1853 Marx called special attention to "a fact which deserves more notice," namely "a regular strike amongst agricultural laborers [in England] , a thing that has never taken place before."[7] In 1869 he stressed that one of the important factors in the Irish movement was "the coming out of the °agricultural labouring class° against the °farming class°"—the latter class comprising mainly big landowners.[8] When in 1872 Engels started contributing "Letters from London" to the Italian socialist press, his first article hailed the strike movement of English farm workers and their advancing organization: "The farm workers' union became for the terrified landowners and tenant farmers what the International is for the reactionary governments of Europe—a bogy the very name of which sets them quaking." Since the movement had successes, Engels became characteristically enthusiastic: "This first great victory marks the beginning of a new era in the intellectual and social life of the rural proletariat, which has joined *en masse* the movement of the town proletarians against the tyranny of capital."[9] In Germany the prospects were naturally less good:

> The agricultural proletariat [wrote Engels in 1865] is that section of the working class which is clarified as to its own interests and its own social situation with the most difficulty and last of all; in other words, that section which longest remains an instrument, without consciousness of itself, in the hands of the privileged class that exploits it [the landed aristocracy].... The fight against the feudal and bureaucratic reaction—for both are now inseparable in our country—is in Germany equivalent to the

struggle for the mental and political emancipation of the rural proletariat; and as long as the rural proletariat has not been drawn into the movement, the urban proletariat in Germany cannot and will not accomplish the least bit . . .[10]

We see that the crucial importance of the rural proletariat was not an opinion that Engels came to only late in life. Marx too had understood the role of this sector even before writing the Manifesto. In an 1847 article, he had made the point in a contrast between the Galician peasant (taken as an example) and the English agricultural day-laborer: the former sees the "property question" only as "the transformation of feudal landed property into small bourgeois landed property," just like the pre-1789 French peasant; but the latter has to deal with the English farmer, that is, with an "industrial capitalist who carries on agriculture like a factory." As a result, he thought, "The abolition of capital . . . is the property question as understood by the English agricultural day-laborer just as well as by the English factory worker."[11]

Among the peasantry itself, of course, socialist hopes and expectations center on the small peasant.

Not only is he, of all peasants, the most important for Western Europe in general, but he is also the critical case that decides the entire question. Once we have clarified in our minds our attitude to the small peasant we have all the data needed to determine our stand relative to the other constituent parts of the rural population.[12]

We will see below how this is to be implemented.

If we consider the following list of social strata on the land, in which the categories *big, middle, small* also include tenant farmers:

1. Landowning class
2. Big peasantry
3. Middle peasantry
4. Small peasantry
5. Rural proletariat

Marx and Engels would draw the main line of social struggle between 3 and 4, expecting it to float up through 3 according to concrete circumstances. Below the line there was a strict rule of priority: the interests of the rural proletariat take precedence.

Socialists must keep in mind, remarked Engels in a letter to Marx, that there are various kinds of peasant property-owners in Germany:

in the first place the big peasant, against whose reactionary nature the day-laborer and farm-hand must be incited; in the second place, the middle peasant, who will also be reactionary and is not very numerous; and in the third place, the debt-laden small peasant, who can be interested by tackling the mortgage problem.[13]

In answer to an inquiry from Italy, Engels formulated the idea on behalf of the General Council of the International:

Our policy with regard to the agricultural population has naturally been in general as follows: Where there are extensive estates, there the tenant farmer is the capitalist with respect to the [farm] laborer, and there we must side with the laborer. Next, where there are small farms, although the tenant farmer may nominally be a small capitalist or landowner (as in France and part of Germany), yet in reality he is generally reduced to the same state of poverty as the proletarian, and so we must work for him. No doubt it is the same in Italy.[14]

Above all, it would be "a direct violation . . . of the fundamental principle of socialism in general" to support the interests of peasant employers *as against their day-laborers.*[15]

This principle set boundaries within which the peasant question could be considered.

2. NO AUTOMATIC FORMULAS

Engels had no inkling of the marxological future when he wrote in 1873, in the course of a controversy on the housing question: "I need hardly defend myself against Mülberger's suggestion that I fail to appreciate the necessity of drawing the peasants into the movement."[16] The present chapter shows the extent to which he and Marx were concerned to bring this about. But we may make some general observations in advance.

For one thing, we will not find Marx or Engels changing their tune about the negative features of the peasantry and its limited potentialities; their concern with the positive side did not mean fostering illusions or tickling peasant champions under the chin. Anything that might happen was likely to develop slowly; for, as Engels observed, "a peasant people has to be swindled for a century-long before it learns by experience."[17] Even in his very positive 1894 thesis, Engels' claims were moderate. "The peasant has so far largely manifested himself as a factor of political power only by his apathy, which has its roots in the isolation of rustic life," he summed up; but he was looking forward: this apathy "is by no means insuperable."[18]

Secondly: much of their attention concentrated on the French and German peasantry, but we shall see that they had no iron formulas for political policy automatically applying to any peasantry in the world. Their conclusions had to vary considerably depending on the actual socioeconomic and political position of a given peasantry under concrete circumstances. Taken on an international scale, the peasantry lived under different social systems: at least three—capitalism, feudalism, and the "Asiatic" mode of production. Put somewhat more precisely, they lived under socioeconomic conditions in which features of one or more of these systems were unevenly combined to various degrees.

Therefore, different countries—different cases. A major difference was the stage or degree of bourgeoisification. Even within Western Europe there was a wide spectrum confronting Marx. At one end was Britain, where "big landed estates and large-scale agriculture have totally displaced the self-supporting peasant." There was virtually no peasant question (although there were agricultural problems). The next country, France, already showed a different visage; for known historical reasons, it combined a relatively advanced bourgeoisification with the overriding weight of a peasant population, without a large noncapitalist ruling class on the land. This last element did exist in Germany, particularly in the Prussian east, together with a weaker bourgeoisie. Still, these countries were already pell-mell on the road to capitalist development. Italy was far behind; and then there were retarded countries like Ireland and Spain, which could not be forgotten. "From Ireland to Sicily, from Andalusia to Russia and Bulgaria, the peasant is a very essential factor of the population, production and political power."[19] And besides there were great variations inside most of these countries.

Then the case of semi-Asiatic Russia begins to move out of the European framework, as does Turkey. Beyond are the cases of India and China, and nothing less than the rest of the world, some countries nearly untouched by internal capitalist development and many still without even a weak proletariat. At the other end of the spectrum, even the capitalistically developed United States was a special case because of the availability of new land for small farmsteads and rural enterprises.

In his 1894 article, which dealt with France and Germany, Engels called attention to the internal variations for Germany alone. He begins, "The rural population to which we can address ourselves consists of quite different parts, which vary greatly with the various regions," and he ends with a qualification: "We, of course, investigate this question only in broad outline; we single out only clear-cut forms. We lack space to give consideration to intermediate stages and mixed rural populations."[20] This reminder applies also to this chapter.

3. PRELUDE TO REVOLUTION

Marx and Engels developed their programmatic views on the peasant question in response mainly to experience, especially the experience of revolution in 1848–1849.

In the case of Marx there is no indication of a particular interest in the question from 1843 to 1848, that is, between his departure from Germany and the outbreak of the revolution. Engels (as described in Chapter 7) began at least by 1847 to advocate a revolutionary bloc of the proletariat with the peasantry and petty-bourgeoisie in anticipation of the coming upsurge. Let us recall too, without going over this ground again, that the *Communist Manifesto,* in the final form given by Marx, took a very negative view of the peasantry, as of the petty-bourgeoisie. The existence of a specific peasant question was not even mentioned. To be sure, the Manifesto's ten-point program does have four points on agriculture (1, 7, 8, 9) but only from the standpoint of the aims and needs of a workers' government. In addition, points 3 and 5 would be of special interest to peasants; but 3 would dismay them, and 5 is stated without relevance to the peasants' problem of usury. In fact, in the telescopic lens of the Manifesto the continuing existence of the peasantry is barely recognized. It is viewed in passing mentions as a thing of the past or rapidly getting there, or of no evident interest if still vegetating in the present. About the only passage in which it is not part of a list or mentioned in association with the petty-bourgeoisie is the one about "the *Idiotismus* of rural life," which alludes to peasants only by implication. In Part IV, on current politics, the peasantry is not mentioned at all, even when the Polish party of agrarian revolution is listed.[21]

On the eve of the revolution, Engels, in Paris, was talking about collaboration to Flocon, Ledru-Rollin's partner in the radical movement around *La Réforme,* for which Engels had written articles from London. It was January 1848; the Manifesto was not yet off the press. Engels informed Flocon that "we had now decided in London to come out publicly as Communists." Flocon's response to communism, reported Engels in a letter, was: "you tend to despotism, you will kill the revolution in France, we have eleven million small peasants who are likewise the fiercest property-owners," and so on. Then he cursed the peasants for their political backwardness, and agreed to political cooperation.[22]

It was precisely Flocon's group in power, tied to the petty-bourgeois Democracy, that a few months later found itself supporting open despotism in the shape of the Cavaignac dictatorship—and this because it *subordinated* itself to the backwardness of the eleven million peasants who were the fiercest property-owners. There was a different course available for revolutionists: reaching out to the peasantry for support of communist demands.

This was the course taken in March when, with the revolution under way, Marx and Engels drew up "The Demands of the Communist Party in Germany." This document contained the first program of immediate demands on behalf of the peasantry that they put forward, comprising points 6 through 9. The demands were: (6) all feudal exactions on the rural population to be abolished without compensation; (7) state ownership of all feudal domains and properties; (8) mortgages on peasant lands taken over by the state, with interest paid to the state; (9) land rent to be paid to the state as a tax. The program also stated:

> All the measures mentioned under 6, 7, 8 and 9 have been formulated to reduce the public and other burdens on peasants and small tenant-farmers, without diminishing the means required to defray state expenses and without imperiling production itself.
> The actual landowner who is neither a peasant nor tenant-farmer has no share in production. Consumption by him is therefore nothing but an abuse.

At the end the program directly appealed for the revolutionary alliance:

"It is in the interests of the German proletariat and of the petty-bourgeoisie and small peasantry to work with all their energy to carry through the above measures."[23]

This was a beginning, though evidently these demands by themselves were not likely to get the small peasantry flocking to the Communist banner; for example, nothing was said about rent or interest reduction. On the other hand, neither was anything said about land nationalization, and obviously the program assumed the continued existence of a peasantry. Point 7 said of the "royal and other feudal domains" that they "shall be cultivated on a large scale and with the most up-to-date scientific devices in the interests of the whole of society," but this did not preclude the existence of small-scale farming outside of those domains.

These Demands, however, were drawn up while Marx and Engels were still in Paris, though they looked to Germany. Actual experience with the problem was still to come.

In France itself, the heavy pressure of the peasantry on the revolution was already clear. While the Demands were being written, a letter by Engels summed up his expectation of the antirevolutionary role of the French peasants, pessimistically but accurately:

> In the National Assembly there now enters a new element: peasants, who make up five-sevenths of the French nation and are for the party of *Le National*, the petty-bourgeoisie [actually, the republican bourgeoisie]. It is very probable that this party will win out, and that the people from *La Réforme* will fall, and then there will be another revolution.[24]

But in eastern Germany, where Napoleon's antifeudal influence had not penetrated, the peasants broke out in revolutionary action to take over the land. In a historical article written several decades later, Engels still emphasized it was a revolutionary portent:

> Especially in Silesia, where the system of latifundia and the accompanying depression of the population to the level of day-laboring cottagers was most strongly developed, the peasants stormed the castles, burned the already settled redemption deeds, and forced the gracious lords to sign written renunciations of all further [feudal] services. These excesses—wicked even in the eyes of the then ruling bourgeoisie—were indeed suppressed with military force and severely punished; but now even the emptiest-

headed Junker saw that serf-labor had become impossible: Better none than rebellious peasants like these![25]

Then in April Marx and Engels arrived in Cologne, less than a month after the first shots had been fired in Berlin.

4. THE PEASANT POLICY OF THE *N.R.Z.*

When Marx launched the *Neue Rheinische Zeitung* at the beginning of June, the immediate audience was of course urban. Besides, the peasantry of the Rhineland was still far from the revolutionary energy of the Silesians. But from the first month the *N.R.Z.* took up the cudgels for the embattled peasants.

On June 10, Minister Patow published a memorandum purporting to provide for the elimination of feudal rights in the countryside, but also revealing how heavy the feudal burden was. This brought the first big blast in the *N.R.Z.* on the issue:

> Reading this memorandum, it is incomprehensible why a peasants' war has not long since broken out in the provinces of old Prussia. . . .
>
> The Berlin revolution [of March] has made all these feudal conditions impossible for the whole future. The peasants had immediately abolished them in practice, as was entirely natural. The government had nothing further to do than to give legal form *to the abolition of all feudal burdens already actually carried out by the will of the people.*
>
> But before the aristocracy decides on an August 4th [1789 in France: first abolition of feudal rights], their castles must first go up in flames.

Through Patow's memo, the bourgeois conciliationists of the National Assembly

> are now likewise invited to betray the peasant revolution, which broke out all over Germany in March, to the aristocracy. The government is responsible for the consequences which the application of the Patow principles will have on the countryside.[26]

After a stinging analysis of the government proposals, the conclusion was: "The government *is provoking a peasants' war,*" especially in

Silesia. This was no doubt a hope and an aim rather than a confident prediction.

The main peasant issue, then, as adumbrated by point 6 of the Demands, was the compensation or indemnification of the landowning aristocracy for the "redemption" of their land by the peasants. Marx and Engels followed this up vigorously, emphasizing that feudal rights had already been abolished from below by the revolutionary action of the peasants themselves, and these claims should not be restored even partially, under the guise of a law to abolish feudal burdens which actually restored part of what the peasants had swept away. So went a major article by Marx at the end of July. The government understands that: "It is impossible to bring back the whole of the old status quo; the peasants would slaughter their feudal barons without further ado." Therefore the government hopes to quiet the peasants with small concessions, and even thereby gain their votes. It is willing to forbid plucking the peasants' geese but not plucking the peasants themselves.[27]

This article raised the issue from the agitational level to an insight into the class relations of the bourgeoisie with the old rulers. The bourgeois minister is willing to encroach on feudal property rights—hence the partial concessions—but not on bourgeois property rights, specifically the bourgeois property rights erected on the ruins of feudal property by the redemption procedure, which transmutes feudal claims into cash payments:

> And it is simply for this reason that he will not revise the redemption agreements, because by these agreements the feudal property relations have been transformed into *bourgeois* property relations, because he therefore cannot revise them without formally violating bourgeois property at the same time. And bourgeois property is naturally just as sacred and inviolable as feudal property is open to attack and, depending on the minister's need and courage, even violation.[28]

Marx makes the contrast with the way in which the French Revolution consolidated itself on the peasantry by sweeping away feudal rights.

> The French bourgeoisie of 1789 did not for a moment leave its allies, the peasants, in the lurch. It knew that the basis of its rule was the smashing of feudalism in the countryside, the establishment of a free, landowning peasant class.*

* In December Marx returned to this comparison, in his article on "The Bourgeoisie and the Counterrevolution," in which he reviewed the role of the Patow bill—"the sorriest piece of bungling of the impotent bourgeois desire to

The German bourgeoisie of 1848 without any hesitation betrays these peasants, who are its *most natural allies*, flesh of its flesh, without whom it is powerless against the nobility.[32]

The next major article on this issue came from Engels in early August. First he demonstrates that, according to principles inadvertently laid down by the government itself, it is the landowners who legally owe money to the peasants, not vice versa—wages for unpaid labor service. But just as in all other countries

the transformation of feudal property into bourgeois property and of feudal power into [the power of] capital is always a new and crude defraudment of the bondsman for the benefit of the feudal lords. The bondsman must always *buy* his freedom, buy it dearly. The bourgeois state proceeds according to the principle: The only thing you get free is death.[33]

Moreover, the redemption system will have a lasting economic effect of great importance. On the government's basis, it is mainly the bigger peasants who can buy themselves off, by giving up a parcel of their land. But the small peasant, who cannot do this, must borrow:

The necessary consequence of these enormous exactions from the peasants is . . . that they fall into the hands of the usurers. Usury is the necessary companion of a *free* small-peasant class, as France, the Palatinate and the Rhineland show. The Prussian science of redemption has made it possible for the small peasants of the old province [of Prussia] to enjoy the burden of usury even before they are free. The Prussian government has in general understood from way back how to subject the oppressed classes simultaneously to the burden of feudal as well as modern bourgeois conditions, and thus make their yoke doubly heavy.[34]

We may add, briefly, that the *N.R.Z.* raised other peasant issues as they came up. For example, on July 26 an article by Engels exposed the way in which the regional estates-assembly setup kept control in the hands of the landowners, giving little representation even to the bigger

abolish the feudal privileges." The contrast with France has been quoted in Chapter 9.[29] Again, in his defense speech before the Cologne jury on February 8, 1849: "If the Assembly didn't know how to crush the enemy in the army, then it was a question above all of gaining a friend in the peasantry. Even that it renounced."[30] A few years later Marx had occasion to make the point that even the French bourgeoisie of the eighteenth century had held back from an alliance with the peasantry: "nothing did more to retard the French bourgeoisie in its victory than the fact that it did not decide until 1789 to make common cause with the peasants."[31]

peasants.[35] On August 6 he highlighted the way peasants were treated by the agricultural commissioners, whose "dictatorial powers must be abolished."[36]

5. THE *N.R.Z.* GOES TO THE PEASANTS

The group around the *N.R.Z.* was not only a revolutionary political center but also an organizing center when possible. Since the Communist League had been put on the shelf, the *N.R.Z.* group was a loose operation, organizationally speaking. Its political leader was, of course, Marx, both publicly as editor of the paper and as the left-wing leader inside the Democratic Association movement. The leading activist of the "Marx party" (as its enemies called it) in the Workers Association was Karl Schapper.

Indication that a crossroads had been reached came by September with the growing crisis of the government and the rise of discontent among the people. The *N.R.Z.* group swung into a new initiative: at a mass meeting in Cologne under its leadership, a "Committee of Public Safety" was set up as an embryonic dual power, the name recalling the French Revolution.[37] But Cologne was also a Prussian fortress and a troop concentration point; in a decisive confrontation the town would not be a sufficient base. The movement had to be extended to the countryside not merely journalistically but organizationally.

The turn toward practical work on the agrarian question began in August, with the Workers Association as the main lever, and with the "Demands of the Communist Party of Germany" as the program.[38] The Democratic Association would not do; the strain of real revolutionary activity was bound to be more than its petty-bourgeois leftists could take.*

The Democratic Association was useful in a preparatory role. A

---

* Hammen writes:

This matter of going to the land, of using agrarian discontent, of organizing societies and holding meetings in the country was pressed by Marx, Engels and their faithful supporters. . . . It was the Worker-Society [Workers Association], however, directed and inspired by Moll and Schapper, that did the most to carry out this agrarian approach. The regular Democratic Society was less active.[39]

But when the September crisis became sticky, the Democratic leftists became active in pulling out.

Rhineland regional conference on August 13-14 was persuaded to recommend that antigovernment propaganda be started in the rural areas, by sending organizers, holding meetings, and founding groups, because (said the conference) the peasantry had been radicalized by the issues of taxation, the feudal burdens, and bureaucratic harassment. "The major proposal of the Congress calling for the exploitation of agrarian and peasant unrest," says Hammen, "certainly was Marxian-inspired."[40] There certainly was no one else to inspire it.

The decisions on this point were stressed when Moll reported on the conference at the Cologne Workers Association on September 3. All the associations, he said, were to "undertake the obligation of making the rounds of the countryside in the vicinity, working on the peasants and factory workers, setting up associations in the villages, and remaining in regular contact with them."[41] The Workers Association had already started work before this. On August 21 its leadership had taken up the question, "How is the proletariat on the land to be helped?"[42]

On August 27 a delegation from the Cologne association visited the first target, the town of Worringen ten miles down-river. It was a center of more than one type of rural producer: peasants, farm laborers, and also industrial workers who lived in the neighboring villages.[43] After a discussion with the peasants on political and social conditions, a local association of forty members was established. The Cologne organizers returned two weeks later to consolidate the branch and prepare for a demonstration. That Sunday, September 10, two Cologne organizers also appeared in the village of Wesslingen (or Wesseling) for a meeting with the peasants, who set up a branch organization after the burgo-master broke up the meeting by jailing the organizers overnight.[44]

The membership of the Workers Association was actively prepared for the new activities, by educational courses utilizing the "Demands" program. A big printing of leaflets bearing this program was widely distributed through the rural area and also in Cologne. The members went over the Demands point by point, in order to be armed with arguments, information, and ideas. (Engels was among those who gave the educational talks.)

Another aim of the internal education of the Association was stress on the importance of peasant work. Its journal told the readers, for example: "The revolutionary force of Germany lies in the peasantry and the working class; this has been shown since March in most of our fatherland . . . If the peasants and workers unite, if they stick together energetically, then they will soon be liberated from feudal burdens, usury, and the pressing weight of capital."[45] Educational work on the agrarian question continued through the rest of the year.[46] Also continuing were systematic reports in the association's press on peasant ferment, demonstrations, and battles elsewhere in Germany[47]—publicity that served a twofold purpose.*

Of great potential importance was the fact that the "Marx party" established a new paper on September 10, alongside the *N.R.Z.* and the Workers Association organ. This was called the *Neue Kölnische Zeitung*, subtitled "For citizens, peasants and soldiers." It was, it announced, for the Social and Democratic Republic ("Social-Democratic" or "Socialist-Democratic" in the current nomenclature) and was published in the interests of "all classes of working people."[49]

6. ORGANIZING A PEASANT MOVEMENT

In this practical program for a worker-peasant revolutionary alliance, the first big gun was fired on September 17 with a Sunday mass demonstration at Worringen. The political ground had been tilled for only a short while, but the results were already considerable.**

---

* Hammen: "The Communists were counting heavily on agrarian unrest. Both the *Neue Rheinische Zeitung* and the Worker-Society paper carried numerous reports of peasant disturbances, large protest meetings and scattered acts of violence throughout Germany. Such accounts encouraged the workers and Democrats in the cities to look to the peasants for help, and conversely, local agrarian ferment was more likely to crystallize if the peasants saw that their grievances were part of a nationwide pattern."[48]

** Hammen relates:

Optimistic reports from Worringen indicated that almost all the people, townsmen and peasants, in that area had adopted the "new view." The mayor, on the other hand, sent alarming reports to the Prussian authorities in Cologne, speaking of dangerous "rebels" from Cologne spreading atheistic, communistic and treasonable ideas among the peasants. The "Demands of the Communist Party" were being distributed. He even reported that Marx and Schapper had been there spreading Communist ideas.... Sunday, September 17, 1848, stands out as a red-letter day for the Communists. The organizational éclat and the unanimity of sentiment made it a testimonial to the success of the Communist-led Worker-Society in recruiting a following among the peasants and villages.[50]

Despite the mayor's report, it is not likely that Marx went to Worringen himself. In these activities Marx functioned as public political leader and spokesman, overburdened editor, and officer in one or another association, but he did not speak at the demonstrations. He was technically an alien, having abandoned Prussian citizenship a few years before. Besides, he was a poor public speaker.

Arrangements were made to transport Cologne supporters by wagons and coal barges, in addition to those who would walk. The police used harassment to prevent transportation from Cologne. The army commandant, Colonel Engels (no relation), placed the forts on alert, trained cannon on the city, and made preparations to shut down the city gates. But despite hindrance and provocation, the demonstration took place as planned. In a meadow along the Rhine, a big speakers' platform was set up, red flag above, flanked by black-red-gold republican banners. About eight to ten thousand attended, in near-unanimous support of the speeches for revolution and socialism. The whole affair went through under the open leadership of the *N.R.Z.* group, with Schapper elected chairman and Engels secretary. Delegates from other towns and rural areas had also been invited, and attended; Lassalle, for example, spoke for the Düsseldorf movement. Several police informers were spotted and dumped in the Rhine by the crowd.[51]

The Worringen demonstration did indeed demonstrate that something new had appeared on the scene. The report in the *Deutsche Zeitung* noted: "This is the first big example in our province of the fact that the subversive party is also trying to get control of the masses in the countryside."[52] This episode was probably the most brilliant example of socialists' organizing an alliance with revolutionary peasants to be seen until well into the twentieth century.

Correspondingly, the Cologne workers were encouraged to try to win over support among the peasants. The peasants, Moll told the Workers Association, wanted to hear the "humanist doctrines of democracy and socialism."[53]

On the same day as the Worringen event, a giant rally of many thousands also demonstrated in Frankfurt, the home of the Assembly itself, against the timidity and capitulation of the Assembly majority. Treating it as a popular uprising, the Imperial Ministry, having no armed force of its own, called in Prussian, Austrian, and Hessian troops to "restore order."

Engels' two articles on the Frankfurt movement are important for the emphasis laid on the role of the nearby peasantry. The fighting was carried on "by the workers of Frankfurt, Offenbach and Hanau, and by the peasants of the surrounding region . . ." While the Frankfurt middle classes did not lift a finger, powerful aid came from "the peasants from countless localities round about." Of September 19 Engels writes:

> The influx of peasants during the night must have been very great . . . The revolutionary attitude of the Odenwald, Nassau and

Hesse-Cassel peasants [prevented the sending of more troops] . . . If only the uprising holds on today, then all of Odenwald, Nassau, Hesse-Cassel and Rheinhessen, and the whole population in and around Fulda, Coblenz, Mannheim and Aschaffenburg will be under arms, and the troops will be unable to suppress the uprising.[54]

But, he wrote, he did not expect the revolutionists to win. His second article gave the specific reasons: the effectiveness of artillery in the broad streets, and the opposition of the middle classes; and

The superior forces of the troops, who were rapidly brought in by railway as against the slow influx of peasants coming in on foot, did the rest.

But

The raging peasants will not just lay down their arms without further ado. If they cannot break up the National Assembly, still they have enough to do to clean house at home . . . The peasants' war of this spring will not have attained its goal—until it has brought about its outcome, the liberation of the peasants from feudalism.[55]

The Frankfurt events provided additional reason for the authorities in Cologne to go into a panic over the peasant work of the "Marx party," which announced that the next rural mass demonstration would be held on October 1 in Wesslingen (the town where the first organizers had been arrested). In Cologne itself, a popular mass meeting on September 20, addressed by Engels among others, supported the Frankfurt barricade fighters against the "traitors" of the Frankfurt assembly. The *N.R.Z.* announced that its resolutions would be placarded around the city. The second regional conference of the Democratic Associations was scheduled to open in Cologne on Monday, the 25th. Early that morning, concerted police raids planned over the weekend attempted to arrest the whole *N.R.Z.* cadre who had spoken at the Worringen rally, on the charge of "conspiracy for subversion."[56]

The formal, and probably the largest part of the actual, motivation for the government's September attack on the Cologne movement was the peasant work of the "Marx party." This makes good sense from the standpoint of the Rhenish authorities: if only the urban workers moved, the result would be a putsch; if the rural areas also rose, it would be a first-class rebellion; if the Berlin region ignited in the wake of Frankfurt and the Rhineland, it could mean the German revolution.*

In spite of all, the October 1 demonstration was held at Wesslingen. Two weeks later, another big rally at Worringen again: this time the government banned the meeting and assembled troops to stop it, but gave up this patently illegal stand when the Workers Association went ahead anyway.

> Throughout the fall [relates Hammen] new societies were formed in the small towns and among the peasants. The distribution of the "Demands of the Communist Party" continued. When revolutionary tension was high in November, the Committee urged the members of the Cologne Worker-Society to organize and participate in regular Sunday rallies in the country. The Society's paper reported that their emissaries were everywhere received with "joy and enthusiasm."[57]

But, as we know, the liberal bourgeoisie in Frankfurt and Berlin moved steadily rightward. By December came Marx's series of articles on the bourgeoisie's commitment to the counterrevolution. Concomitantly the peasant agitation in the *N.R.Z.* was stepped up. In effect, in the course of abandoning the illusion that the bourgeoisie could be the main revolutionary ally, Marx turned more and more to the peasantry to play this role.[58]

7. THE *N.R.Z.* LINE IN PERMANENCE

December was a turning-point because the new and more right-wing Manteuffel cabinet openly struck at the peasantry.

> On December 20, 1848 [related Engels in a later historical article], it issued a provisional ordinance, whereby feudal services

---

* The events in Cologne in September 1848 will come up again in Volume 3, in connection with problems of revolutionary strategy. —The arrest orders, including Engels', remained in force for a while afterward, though the events of September 25 produced a standoff. It was at this point that Engels left Cologne, eventually taking his October hike through France (described in the preceding chapter) and staying in Switzerland till mid-January, when he returned to Cologne. By a martial-law decree in Cologne, the *N.R.Z.* and other periodicals were suspended; the *N.R.Z.* did not appear between September 27 and October 12. Marx had not been named in the original arrest orders, since he had not spoken at Worringen, but the authorities soon devised other charges against him and he stood trial in February.

were, with only a few exceptions, reinstituted on the old footing, pending further adjustments. It was this ordinance that prompted [Wilhelm] Wolff to deal with the situation of the Silesian peasants in the *Neue Rheinische Zeitung.*[59]

Wilhelm Wolff was one of the key members of Marx's team, the editorial board of the *N.R.Z.* And he was a rare bird indeed: a peasant boy who had achieved an education by enormous effort and had become a consistent revolutionary. In a later biographical article, Engels recounted why the Manteuffel ordinance spurred Wolff to write:

> The hopes of the enserfed peasants of Old [East] Prussia were thereby destroyed; the peasants' situation had to be made clear to them in order to move them to action. And for this Wolff was the man. Not only because he himself was by origin an enserfed son of the peasantry and as a child had had to do labor-service on the manor; not only because he still fully felt the hatred of the feudal oppressor that such a childhood generated in his breast: no one was so well acquainted with the feudal mode of serfdom in all its details as he, and precisely in that province which offered a complete catalogue of all its varied forms—Silesia.[60]

Wolff began writing a number of articles in the *N.R.Z.* dealing with and directed to the peasantry. The main theme was the enormous wealth which the landowning aristocracy had sweated out of the peasants since their enserfment. An initial article by Marx had brought up the demand being raised by the French peasantry for the "return of the billion [francs]"—that is, the recovery of the enormous compensation paid to the old landowners after the Bourbon Restoration. Marx then hoped that this issue would radicalize the French countryside; it "is the first revolutionary measure," he wrote optimistically, "that hurls the peasants into the revolution."[61]

It was this theme, adapted to Germany, that was developed by Wolff in a series of popular articles entitled "The Silesian Billion." According to Hammen, Wolff "wrote most of them, though they unquestionably were prompted by Marx who always kept the revolutionary potential of the peasants in mind."[62] In response to demand, a reprint of the series in ten thousand copies was published and distributed around Silesia itself, necessarily illegally in that region.[63] Wolff's articles were still being read by German peasants some forty years later.*

---

* In 1851 Marx planned to publish a collection of *N.R.Z.* articles, including Wolff's series on the Silesian peasantry, but the project never materialized.[64] In 1876 Engels published a biography of Wolff in a series of articles, in which well

Wolff's close collaboration with Marx and Engels, which had begun in 1846 in Brussels, continued till his death in 1864. (He is "Lupus" in the Marx-Engels correspondence.) It was to him that Marx dedicated the first volume of *Capital.* After 1849 Wolff settled in Manchester. "For several years," wrote Engels, "Wolff was the sole political co-thinker I had in Manchester; no wonder that we saw each other almost daily, and that I often had occasion enough to marvel at his almost instinctively correct judgment on the events of the day."[66] The daily influence of this peasant-born revolutionary was no doubt one reason Engels devoted so much attention to the peasant question in politics and history.

The peasant work of the *N.R.Z.* group in 1848–1849 represented only a beginning. It had no sequel since the situation that produced it came to an end with the advance of the counterrevolution in Germany. It stands, however, as an acting out of Marx's and Engels' first approach to the peasant question as a political actuality.

Almost a half century later—forty-five years, to be exact—Engels was to write his fullest thesis on the peasant question, "The Peasant Question in France and Germany," from which we have already quoted several times. The viewpoint spelled out there is an embodiment of the *N.R.Z.* line: the proletarian socialist movement must look to the peasantry for a revolutionary alliance against capitalism, but without illusions in the peasantry. This viewpoint is to be distinguished from two other conceptions that were already rife and are still dominant today: (1) the conception of the peasantry as the main social force for revolution and the primary revolutionary class; and (2) the reformist tendency to neglect the peasantry as any kind of revolutionary force.

It is true that the difficulty was not merely the antipeasant views of the urban movements, but also the anti–working-class prejudices of the peasants, "prejudices arising out of their entire economic position, their upbringing and their isolated mode of life, prejudices nurtured by the bourgeois press and the big landowners."[67]

Since the rise of the working-class movement in Western Europe, particularly in those parts where small peasant holdings predomi-

---

over half of the total bulk was devoted to an anthology of Wolff's writings on the peasant question.[65] In 1866 Wolff's "Silesian Billion" series was republished in Zurich for distribution in Germany during the period of the Anti-Socialist Law. Engels' introduction included an essay "On the History of the Prussian Peasants," which traced the origin and development of the "infamous conditions, unequaled even in Russia" of the peasants of eastern Germany, through the sham-emancipation period of 1806–1807 and up through 1849.

nate, it has not been particularly difficult for the bourgeoisie to
render the socialist workers suspicious and odious in the minds of
the peasants as *partageux,* as people who want to "divide up," as
lazy greedy city dwellers who have an eye on the property of the
peasants.[68]

Engels does not deny that the peasant is prevented from giving ear to
socialist propaganda "for the time being by his deep-rooted sense of
property."

> The more difficult it is for him to defend his endangered patch of
> land the more desperately he clings to it, the more he regards the
> Social-Democrats, who speak of transferring landed property to
> the whole of society, as just as dangerous a foe as the usurer and
> the lawyer.[69]

Yet the socialists must strive to win over the peasantry in spite of all,
since their party aims at the conquest of political power:

> But in order to conquer political power this party must first go
> from the towns to the country, must become a power in the
> countryside. This party [which understands that the big land-
> owners are enemies of the peasant] —may this party calmly leave
> the doomed peasant in the hands of his false protectors until he
> has been transformed from a passive into an active opponent of
> the industrial workers? This brings us right into the thick of the
> peasant question.[70]

More than once Engels stressed that even in the developed countries
of Western Europe, socialism could not succeed against the opposition
of the peasantry. "No lasting transformation is possible in France
against the will of the small peasant," he wrote.[71] A year before,
similarly: "even in France the Socialists are realizing more and more
that no lasting victory is possible for them, unless they first win the
great mass of the people, that is, in this case, the peasants."[72] With this
Engels is saying two things: if we cannot actually gain the active
support of one or another section of the peasantry, it is still basically
important to neutralize them at least; and even if political power can be
conquered against the will of the small peasant, it cannot be maintained
and a socialist transformation of society will not be carried through.

In the period of explosive change between 1849 and 1894, what
necessarily changed in Marx's and Engels' writings on the peasant
question was their estimation of what to expect at a given time, in a

given country, and under given circumstances, just as their expectations of other revolutionary developments changed. In the rest of this chapter, we consider their views on different national cases, as they sought to estimate the current revolutionary potential of the peasantry within the framework of the possibilities for social revolution. How nearly correct their estimate was at any time or place is secondary here; the main point is what their approach implied for their conception of the role of a class in revolution.

8. GERMANY: TO 1850

After the suppression of the *Neue Rheinische Zeitung* and the end of the "Marx party" in Cologne as a political center, there was a last futile aftermath of the German revolution, the armed "campaign for the Reich constitution" which saw some fighting in South Germany and the Rhineland in 1849. Marx and Engels continued their peasant policy. In Baden they tried—in vain—to get the allegedly revolutionary provisional government to win over "the big agricultural majority of the population" by immediately abolishing all feudal burdens on the peasantry, by doing what the Frankfurt liberals had refused to do.[73] Though the Baden leftists funked, Engels' account of that armed campaign reported that "a large part" of the peasantry supported the revolutionary struggle.[74] In his *Revolution and Counterrevolution in Germany* written in 1852, his summary gave them less credit, unless he was including the rural laborers with the peasantry:

°°A portion of the poorer country population, laborers and petty farmers [read: small peasants], generally joined them [the working classes of the towns] after the actual outbreak of the conflict. . . .

As to country people that joined the insurrection, they were principally thrown into the arms of the revolutionary party by the relatively enormous load of taxation, and partly of feudal burdens, pressing upon them. Without any initiative of their own, they formed the tail of the other classes engaged in the insurrection, wavering between the working men on one side, and the petty trading class [read: petty-bourgeoisie] on the other. Their own private social position, in almost every case, decided which way they turned; the agricultural laborer generally supported the city artisan, the small farmer was apt to go hand in hand with the small shopkeeper.[75]

It was after the failure of this armed campaign that Marx and Engels settled in London. In Chapter 10 we have explained the evolution of their views during 1850, particularly the period in which they wrote the "Address to the Communist League," which still assumed that the revolution was around the corner, though in a brief lull. Let us now relate the peasant question to this period.

As we saw, Marx and Engels emerged from the experience of 1848–1849 with the conviction that the petty-bourgeois Democracy would, once in power, become the most dangerous enemy of the real revolution. The revolutionary period ahead would unfold in two continuous phases. In phase 1, the revolutionary proletarian party would march against the existing ruling classes in alliance with the Democracy; but the joint victory would put the latter in power, and it would inevitably betray the aims of the movement and its working-class ally. The working classes must be prepared for phase 2, which would pit the consistent revolutionaries against the vacillating and compromising Democrats, to make the revolution "permanent."

What lay immediately ahead—as the Address saw it in March 1850—was the period of alliance. The Address is very clear that at this point the petty-bourgeois Democracy has the support of both the peasants and the rural proletariat—of the rural proletariat "insofar as the latter has not yet found a support in the independent urban proletariat." The peasants, it says, are the allies of the Democracy—allies in the coming revolutionary struggle against the government. To be sure, the proletariat is also an ally of the Democracy at this point, but the picture has the peasantry under the influence of the urban petty-bourgeois Democratic leaders, not of the proletarian left.[76] The great emphasis in the Address is the question of priorities set forth in the first section of this chapter: the primacy of the rural proletariat in the agrarian policy of the workers' party. The Address expects that the rural proletariat can be won over even before phase 2 opens. Therefore the Communists should direct the main appeal of their demands toward the rural proletariat rather than the peasantry, *and make no concessions to the peasants at the expense of the rural laborers.*

As in the first French Revolution, the petty-bourgeois [once in power] will give the feudal lands to the peasants as free property, that is to say, try to leave the rural proletariat in existence and form a petty-bourgeois peasant class which will go through the same cycle of impoverishment and indebtedness which the French peasant is now still going through.

The workers must oppose this plan in the interest of the rural proletariat and in their own interest. They must demand that the confiscated feudal property remain state property and be converted into workers' colonies [cooperatives] cultivated by the associated rural proletariat with all the advantages of large-scale agriculture, through which the principle of common property immediately obtains a firm basis in the midst of the tottering bourgeois relations. Just as the Democrats combine with the peasants, so must the workers combine with the rural proletariat.[77]

The alliance in phase 1 is clearly seen as follows: the petty-bourgeois Democrats *followed by the peasantry* in alliance with the proletarian movement *which is followed by the rural proletariat.*

It is crucial to understand that the problem raised here is how to dispose of the "confiscated feudal property," the lands of the expropriated aristocracy. There is no question raised about the land presently held by the peasantry. The tension that is foreseen is with a peasantry that will want to expand its holdings by taking over the domains newly acquired by the revolution. If this happens, then (in addition to certain economic consequences) the rural laborers will remain in their present exploited state, still day-laborers working for newly enriched peasants. The revolution will have served only to benefit the peasants at the expense of the land proletariat. It is against the threat of such an outcome that the Address proposes a different solution: turning the new domains over to cooperative associations of the laborers, to be worked as "common property."

It goes without saying that it would be easier to win over the peasantry by promising to give them the feudal lands as private property, that is, by vying with the Democrats in selling out the interests of the rural proletariat. The principle of class priorities means that, where a choice has to be made, Marx chooses the interests of the class exploited by peasant employers; and no doubt this choice will be resented especially by peasants big enough to be employers of agricultural labor.

The line of the Address did not mean giving up the effort to win over the peasantry too; for the revolution had something else to offer to the peasants. Only the Communist insistence on carrying the revolution through to the end ("in permanence") would assure them free ownership of their *present* holdings, without indemnification to the nobility and without crushing burdens imposed by the government and by the pressure of capital. Those peasants who would support the Democracy against the revolution, because of the promise of the feudal lands, would lose all, because the Democrats were incapable of carrying through the revolution. Those peasants who supported the Permanent Revolution would do so once they realized what the real stakes were. This process of realization and education would be the task of phase 2. In the end the revolution could triumph only if decisive sections of the Democracy's followers could be detached. That meant the small peasants above all.

This summary lays out Marx's "plan of war," but of course it was not put to the test, since the expected revolutionary resurgence did not materialize. But before Marx came to that conclusion in September, he gave added evidence of the importance of the small peasantry to the plan. In June, Marx and Engels wrote a second Address to the membership, which indicated some organizational details in addition to the plan outline. In it is a fairly specific account of what the Communists had done in carrying on peasant work and what they should do:

> Where peasants' and day-laborers' associations exist, as in Schleswig-Holstein and Mecklenburg, League members have succeeded in winning direct influence over them, and in part in getting them directly under their control. The Saxon, Franconian, Hessian and Nassau associations of workers and day-laborers are likewise in large part under the leadership of the League. . . . The Central Council alerts all local groups and members that such influence over associations of workers, sport groups, peasants and day-laborers, etc. is of the highest importance and must be gained everywhere. It calls on the district leaderships and on all local groups in direct correspondence with it to send a special report in their next letter on what is going on in this regard.[78]

9. GERMANY: ON THE PEASANT WAR

During the same summer, Engels was writing his history *The Peasant War in Germany*. Although the subject matter went back to the sixteenth century, the work was put into the political framework of the present, beginning with an invocation of the recent revolution: "the, Peasant War is not entirely far removed from our present-day struggle, and the opponents who have to be fought remain essentially the same." And it ended on a similar note: "The bulk of the nation—petty burghers, owners of workshops (artisans), and the peasants—were left in the lurch by its currently natural allies, the bourgeoisie, because it was too revolutionary, and partly by the proletariat, because it was not sufficiently advanced."[79] The lesson was clear: today the peasants must not leave the proletariat in the lurch, or vice versa, for they were natural allies; another Peasant War was needed.*

Marx put this thought into the modern context in 1856, in a letter to Engels, after a discussion of revolutionary possibilities:

°The whole thing in Germany° will depend on the possibility °to back the Proletarian revolution by some second edition of the Peasants' war.° Then the thing will be first-rate.[82]

The relevance of the Peasant War to the revolution of 1848, and more generally to the modern revolution, came up again when Lassalle published his verse drama *Franz von Sickingen* in 1859. Where Engels' hero had been Thomas Münzer, Lassalle's was the leader of the knightly class of the time—the class that was hostile to the regime but incapable of making common cause with the revolting peasants, whose labor they lived on too. In separate letters to Lassalle, Marx and Engels gave their criticism as requested. Both pointed out the political meaning of leaving the peasants' struggle and Münzer's plebeian revolt out of the picture, especially since Sickingen's dilemma (as Marx wrote) represented "really the tragic collision that spelled the doom, and properly so, of

---

* Of course, invocations of the Peasant War in German radical circles were neither new nor few. Already in 1844 Marx had quoted Münzer's communistic views, and had called the Peasant War "the most radical fact of German history."[80] Engels had given a short précis of the period in an 1843 article, which flaunted Münzer's communism and stated that after the suppression, "the peasants [were] reduced to their former servitude."[81] All these mentions had been stimulated by the publication in the 1830s and 1840s of a number of historical works on the Peasant War, especially one by Wilhelm Zimmerman in 1841-1843, which provided the factual basis for Engels' 1850 history.

the revolutionary party of 1848-1849"[83]—that is, of the bourgeois Democracy which could not make common cause with the oppressed classes in those years. Lassalle's omission misses "the *really* tragic element in Sickingen's fate," wrote Engels:

> As I see it, the mass of the nobility directly subject at that time to the emperor had no intention of concluding an alliance with the peasantry. The dependence of their income on the oppressing of the latter did not permit this. An alliance with the cities would have been more feasible. But no such alliance was effected, or was effected only to a very limited extent. But a national revolution of the nobility could have been accomplished only by means of an alliance with the townsmen and the peasants, particularly the latter. . . . Here, I dare say, lay the tragic collision between the historically necessary postulate and the practically impossible execution.[84]

It is no exaggeration to say, though it would be digressive to show, that most of Lassalleanism is dramatized in the obvious elitism of *Franz von Sickingen.* It certainly embodies the reformist pattern of viewing the peasantry as a negligible quantity (except as voting cattle); and it goes along with the Lassallean "one reactionary mass" theory which Marx attacked.[85] Because of Lassalle's orientation toward an alliance with the aristocracy against the bourgeoisie, he also closed off the possibility of alliance with the peasantry, for reasons more modern than motivated the disaffected knights of the sixteenth century. Engels remarked acidly: "in a predominantly agricultural country like Prussia it is a vile thing to jump on the bourgeoisie exclusively, in the name of the industrial proletariat, but at the same time not mention with so much as a word the patriarchal exploitation of the rural proletariat under the whip of the big feudal aristocracy."[86] The same applied to the exploitation of the peasantry.

10. GERMANY: TOWARD A PEASANT ALLIANCE

In *The Peasant War in Germany,* Engels extended the perspective of a revolutionary alliance with the peasantry back into the past. From the 1850s on, he and Marx returned frequently to the problem of working it out in the present and future.

The revolution of 1848-1849 had not been able to complete the emancipation of the peasants from feudal burdens, let alone from capitalist exploitation: this, "although in a changed form, remains a question still to be settled in a revolution to come," wrote Marx in 1858.[87] Germany therefore showed a pattern in which the newer evils of capitalism were growing apace while the old evils of feudalism still hung over the heads of many peasants. Here was an uneven and combined development that gave a double dynamism to the peasant element in the coming social revolution.

The Prussian government was still harassing the peasantry in the interests of the old reaction. "At this very moment," Marx informed his *New York Tribune* readers in 1853,

> the Prussian Government is hatching two very dangerous projects, the one of limiting the free sub-division of real property, the other subjecting public instruction to the Church. They could not have selected two objects more appropriate to alienate the peasantry of Rhenish Prussia and the middle classes throughout the monarchy.[88]

But at the very same time capitalist development was in full swing. The combination spelled an important contrast between the situation of the German peasantry and that of England or France. In Germany

> The industrial revolution is still going on, even under the most unfavorable conditions. Domestic-industry [cottage industry] based on small, free or tenant-run landownership is still constantly struggling against machinery and steam; the foundering small peasant grabs onto domestic-industry as his final sheet-anchor; but he hardly gets industrialized before he is again crushed by steam and machinery. His extra earnings from agriculture, the potatoes he grows himself, become the strongest force depressing his wages for the capitalists, who can now bestow the whole of the normal surplus-value on the foreign customer as their sole means of maintaining a competitive position on the world market, and whose entire profit is made through the deduction from the normal wage.[89]

And similarly, in a letter the following month:

> Our great advantage is that with us the industrial revolution is only in full swing, while in France and England it is in the main consummated. . . . With us, on the other hand, everything is still in full flow. Remnants of the old peasant industrial production for the satisfaction of the producer's personal needs are being supplanted by capitalist domestic-industry, while in other places

capitalist domestic-industry is already succumbing in its turn to machinery. And the very nature of our industry, limping behind at the very end, makes the social upheaval all the more fundamental.[90]

The peasant gets the worst of both worlds. A couple of years later Engels stressed the effects of the continuing dominance in German capitalism of "rural domestic-industry and manufacture" (such as beet-sugar manufacture and spirit-distilling on the estates) instead of urban-concentrated big industry. As domestic-industry spreads in the rural areas, the industrial revolution is spread over a wider territory than in France or England, even if still on a lower level. This explains why the German revolutionary movement "has spread so tremendously over the greater part of the country instead of being confined exclusively to urban centers."[91]

It is perfectly clear that in Germany a victorious rising in the capital and in the other big cities will be possible only when the majority of the smaller towns and a great part of the rural districts have become ripe for the revolutionary change.

The expansion of this rural domestic-industry "thus revolutionizes the German peasantry more and more." The destruction of this kind of industry by machinery and factory production would mean the destruction of livelihood for rural millions.

Should it be Germany's fate to undergo also this transformation while still under the old social conditions it will unquestionably be the turning-point. If the working class of no other country has taken the initiative by that time, Germany will certainly strike first, and the peasant sons of the "glorious army" will bravely lend assistance.[92]

This passage, and this essay, end with a strong expectation of peasant radicalization. Besides the transformation of peasants into industrial workers, one may expect

the destruction of the old isolation and with it the destruction of the political nullity of the small peasants who are dragged into the "social whirlpool"; the extension of the industrial revolution over the rural areas and thus the transformation of the most stable and conservative class of the population into a revolutionary hotbed; and, as the culmination of it all, the expropriation of the peasants engaged in home-industry by machinery, which drives them forcibly into insurrection.[93]

This would be the "second edition of the Peasants' war" that Marx looked to as backing for proletarian revolution.

When Engels' *Peasant War in Germany* was first published in book form in 1870, his preface returned to the question of the proletarian-peasant alliance. He was relatively optimistic about the "feudal peasant" who still owed labor-service to the lord: "Now that the bourgeoisie has failed in its duty of freeing these people from serfdom, it will not be difficult to convince them that they can expect salvation only from the working class."[94] The tenant farmers likewise: "The bourgeoisie never does anything for these people, unless it is compelled to. From whom then should they expect salvation if not from the workers?" The free small-holding peasant is a harder case, even though he can expect nothing from the bourgeoisie and its usurers; for most of them cling to their property, their little patch of ground:

> It will have to be brought home to them all the same that they can be freed from the usurer only when a government dependent on the people has transformed all mortgages into debts to the state, and thereby lowered the interest rates. And this can be brought about only by the working class.[95]

Engels ended his 1882 essay on "The Mark" with the same appeal to the peasant. Since times are hard in agriculture,

> the restoration of a free peasant class, starved and stunted as it is, had this value—that it has put the peasant in a position, with the aid of his natural comrade, the worker, to help himself, as soon as he once understands *how*.[96]

In his last year, Engels was quite confident that the appeal would be heard: "If it continues in this fashion, by the end of the century we [the German party] shall conquer the greater part of the middle strata of society, petty-bourgeois and small peasants, and grow into the decisive power in the land ..."[97] For the socialists could *not* be the decisive power in the land merely with the support of the working class; power meant winning over "the greater part of the middle strata" as well.

11. FRANCE: TOWARD THE ALLIANCE

As we know from Marx's analysis of Bonapartism, the peasantry was the decisive class force that ensured reaction after the turmoil of 1848. From the long perspective of nearly a half century later, Engels could summarize the post-revolution role of the peasants negatively:

> The hazy socialistic aspirations of the Revolution of February 1848 were rapidly disposed of by the reactionary ballots of the French peasantry; the peasant, who wanted peace of mind, dug up from his treasured memories the legend of Napoleon, the emperor of the peasants, and created the Second Empire. We all know what this one feat of the peasants cost the people of France; it is still suffering from its aftermath.[98]

True in historical hindsight. But at the time Marx and Engels never considered this outcome a foregone conclusion: everything depended on whether the peasantry could be won by alternatives to reaction. Indeed, in view of the "Marx against the peasant" legend, it is worth stressing that for the next two decades Marx was most often mistaken in his expectations because his hopes for peasant radicalization were excessive. Certainly neither he nor Engels forgot that

> °°there was another mighty class in France, mighty, not by the large individual properties of its members, but by its numbers and its very wants. . . . slow to act, and slow to be acted upon, as all rural populations; it stuck to its old traditions, distrusted the wisdom of the apostles of all parties from the towns . . .[99]

Their expectations were highest, of course, up to September 1850, while they believed that a revolutionary situation still existed. An interesting feature of the second part of Marx's *Class Struggles in France* (written mostly in February 1850) is its way of looking at the two-sided character of the support given by the peasants to the Bonapartist reaction. Marx does not see it simply as negative; he sees it as the peasants' distorted, ignorant, "barbarous" form of revolt to smash an unbearable status quo.

> December 10, 1848 [Bonaparte's election as president through peasant votes] was the day of the *peasant insurrection*. Only from this day does the February [i.e., the revolution] of the French peasants date. The symbol that expressed their entry into the revolutionary movement [was Bonaparte] . . . Napoleon was

to the peasants not a person but a program. With banners, with beat of drums and blare of trumpets, they marched to the polling booths shouting: ... No more taxes, down with the rich, down with the republic, long live the emperor! Behind the emperor was hidden the peasant war. The republic that they voted down was the *republic of the rich.*

December 10 was the coup d'état of the peasants, which overthrew the existing government. ... For a moment active heroes of the revolutionary drama, they could no longer be forced back into the inactive and spineless role of the chorus.[100]

It goes without saying that this skewed-revolutionary motivation did not make their choice, Bonaparte, a representative of revolution; for the peasants were being duped and used, as usual. What it testified to was a revolutionary élan which was being harnessed by reaction but which could also serve other ends under other leaders; it reflected a revolutionary potential, hence something quite different from the peasantry's usual apathy.

Around early 1850 Marx thought he saw the peasants already getting disillusioned with their peasant emperor, and published a remarkably optimistic view of the degree of radicalization among them:

The great mass of the rural population, ruined by the results of land parcellization, by the tax burden and the purely fiscal and (even from the bourgeois standpoint) deleterious character of most of the taxes, disillusioned about Louis Napoleon's promises and the reactionary deputies—the mass of the rural population has thrown itself into the arms of the revolutionary party and embraces a socialism which, to be sure, is still mostly very crude and bourgeois.

... a class which was politically dead up to now, that of the peasants, has been swept into the movement and won for the revolution.[101]

As a result, "the Napoleon of the peasant insurrection dissolved like an apparition," thought Marx at this point.[102] In the third installment of *The Class Struggles in France,* he wrote of "the gradual revolutionizing of the peasants," of "this revolutionizing of the most stationary class," which in turn necessitated repressive governmental measures that "inoculated every village with revolution; they *localized and peasantized the revolution."* He set the overthrow of capitalism and the establishment of a socialist government as the program for the peasant too:

The *constitutional republic* is the dictatorship of his united exploiters; *the social-democratic, the red* republic, is the dictatorship of his allies.[103]

We need hardly point out that the rosy glow of confidence in the peasantry was unjustified, but this error was only part of the larger misestimation, which was corrected in September when Marx recognized that the revolutionary situation had passed. The important point for us is what Marx expected from a peasantry caught up in social revolution.

In this sense, Marx's expectations continued even after September, for we have seen that all through the 1850s he expected thoroughgoing disillusionment with Bonaparte among both the bourgeoisie and the peasantry,[104] and therefore an upturn in the radicalization of the countryside. This was true even after December 1851, Bonaparte's coup d'état. Of course, immediate hopes in the discontent of the peasants were dashed; it was clear that Bonaparte had successfully utilized their relapse into normal conservatism and apathy. But writing in 1852, Marx still saw the peasantry, or a considerable part of it, as a potentially revolutionary force. In *The Eighteenth Brumaire*, far from giving up the peasantry as a bad job after this "feat" of theirs, Marx highlights the fact that the "emperor of the peasants" is already using military and police force to quell peasant discontent. There had been "no similar persecution of the peasants" since Louis XIV.*

In this complex situation Marx dwells on the two souls in the breast of the peasantry:

> But let there be no misunderstanding. The Bonaparte dynasty represents not the revolutionary, but the conservative peasant; not the peasant that strikes out beyond the condition of his social existence, the small holding, but rather the peasant who wants to consolidate this holding; not the country folk who, linked up with the towns, want to overthrow the old order through their own energies, but on the contrary those who, in stupefied seclusion within this old order, want to see themselves and their small holdings saved and favored by the ghost of the empire. It repre-

* Years later, in Eugène Ténot's study *La Province en Décembre 1851*, Marx found "a great many new details" on peasant attitudes at the time of Bonaparte's coup. "If the Parisians had held out one or two days longer," he wrote Engels, "the empire would have been *foutu* [done for]. The movement (republican) among the country people was much bigger than we knew."[105]

sents not the enlightenment, but the superstition of the peasant; not his judgment, but his prejudice; not his future, but his past . . .[106]

"Under the parliamentary republic" of 1848–1850, adds Marx, "the modern and the traditional consciousness of the French peasant contended for mastery." This was the conflict between his future and his past, again. In the present, capitalist development was draining thè peasant. And—"With the progressive undermining of small-holding property, the state structure erected upon it collapses."[107]

When he is disappointed in the Napoleonic Restoration, the French peasant will part with his belief in his small holding, the entire state edifice erected on this small holding will fall to the ground and *the proletarian revolution will obtain that chorus without which its solo song becomes a swan song in all peasant countries.*[108]

The emphasis is Marx's; and there are few stronger statements of the impossibility of proletarian revolution "in peasant countries" (even France) without the support of the peasantry. The statement is embedded in a prediction about developments in France which was, once again, grossly overoptimistic about the peasantry—so overoptimistic that, when Marx republished this essay in 1869, with Bonaparte still in the saddle, he cut this passage out. The prediction had to go, since in 1869 it read as a disappointed hope; but our attention should be fixed on the italicized statement, as a general conception.

Since the peasants' interests are in opposition to those of the bourgeoisie, Marx concludes: "Hence the peasants find their natural ally and leader in the *urban proletariat,* whose task is the overthrow of the bourgeois order."[109]

He kept looking for revolutionary stirrings among the French peasants through the 1850s. Twice in 1853 he reported, in articles for the *New York Tribune,* that Bonaparte was losing peasant support.[110] Three years later, he was again reporting "disaffection," "agricultural misery," and "the present revolutionary disposition of this class" imperiling the dynasty; and so on.[111] If he sinned in estimating the revolutionary potential of the French peasantry, it was in inflating it, not in depreciating it.

12. FRANCE: THE COMMUNE AND AFTER

From early on, Engels linked the peasant question closely to the problem of revolutionary defense against the armed forces of the state; for these armed forces were dependent, everywhere on the Continent, on the sons of the peasantry to make up their ranks. We will take up the most prominent such problem in Volume 3, in connection with Germany. Suffice it to say here that this fact is another indication of how superficial the "Marx against the peasant" approach is; for the peasant question was vital to the revolution in ways that had nothing to do with one's opinion of the peasant way of life.

In 1851 Engels wrote a memorandum, not for publication, on the military problem that would be faced by a revolutionary France if, the following year, it threw off Bonaparte's yoke and was attacked by the armies of the Holy Alliance. Since he concludes that a new-baked workers' state "will have to carry on war with the means and according to the method of the general contemporary military operation"—not being in a position to transform the military sphere in twenty-four hours on the day after the revolution—he likewise concludes that the main source of regular soldiers will remain the same: "the °mob° and the peasants."[112] In addition, he sees a peasant militia operating in the countryside as a guard against counterrevolution, as well as a proletarian militia in the cities, and the two cooperating to garrison the fortresses and "to disarm the rebel [counterrevolutionary] departments and classes," while the regular troops defend the borders.[113] It is made quite clear that, even apart from other political and social considerations, a proletarian revolution in France could not survive *militarily* without support from at least a decisive section of the peasantry.

A revolution came not one year but twenty years after Engels' memo, and the problem was not that which was expected. It could be better described in terms of Marx's statement in *The Eighteenth Brumaire:* the Paris Commune sang a solo song, which became a swan song when it failed to obtain the chorus from the countryside. The Versailles government succeeded in isolating the Parisians from the provinces, thus preventing an alliance of the working people of the city with the working people on the land.

It is instructive to note that Marx's analysis in *The Civil War in France,* written while the Commune was still struggling to survive and without the benefit of historical hindsight, lays far more emphasis on the peasant question than the Commune itself did or than is even to be found in knowledgeable books written long afterwards, such as Jellinek's history. Furthermore, this analysis was condensed by Marx from a considerably more extensive discussion of the peasant question in his first draft. In both versions, most of the space was devoted to developing a specific program of peasant demands for the Commune. We will return to this program in the next chapter. Here we stress that this was a program for cementing a proletarian-peasant alliance behind the spreading of a Commune revolution to all France.

"The Commune was perfectly right in telling the peasants that 'its victory was their only hope!' " So begins this passage in *The Civil War*. It explains that the pro-Bonapartist leaning of the peasantry was already undermined: "this prejudice of the past, how could it have withstood the appeal of the Commune to the living interests and urgent wants of the peasantry?"

> The Rurals [landowners behind the Versailles government] — this was, in fact, their chief apprehension—knew that three months' free communication of Communal Paris with the provinces would bring about a general rising of the peasants, and hence their anxiety to establish a police blockade around Paris . . .[114]

In the first draft, this passage reads as follows:

> °°The "rurals" know that three months rule of the Republican Empire in France, would be the signal of the rising of the peasantry and the agricultural Proletariat against them. Hence their ferocious hatred of the Commune! What they fear even more than the emancipation of the townish [urban] proletariat is the emancipation of the peasants. The peasants would soon acclaim the townish proletariat as their own leaders and seniors.

On the basis of considerable exposition, the draft concludes (similarly to the final version) that "What separates the peasant from the proletarian is, therefore, no longer his real interest, but his delusive prejudice." The Commune is "the only form of government" that can rescue the peasant from an economic blind-alley, "without annihilating his position as a really independent producer." It ends: "Being immediately benefited by the Communal Republic, he [the peasant] would soon confide in it [trust it]."[115]

The Commune told the peasants that "its victory was their only hope" in a manifesto which was not only much delayed but which had to be distributed to the rural areas by scatter-drops from balloons: such was the effect of the blockade. The Parisians were unable to send organizers and agitators into the country districts to carry their message, which was summarized in the manifesto as "The land to the peasant, the tool to the worker, work for all."*

When the London conference of the International met four months after the fall of the Commune, Marx pressed vigorously for the movement to make a turn on peasant work. The skimpy minutes show him opening this discussion with a statement which is summarized as follows:

> *Marx*, on propaganda in the countryside, says that it is indispensable, but not only from the point of view of counteracting militarism.[118]

That is, much of the concern awakened on the peasant question stemmed from the recognized need to counteract the military power of the government—a consideration that the urban radical mind could grasp easily enough, and that was already well known and beyond dispute in the movement. But Marx had not even mentioned this point in his *Civil War in France*, which was addressed to the public; there he had been concerned with the broader issue, the forging of a general social-revolutionary alliance with the peasantry.

The minutes show Marx objecting to taking a purely organizational approach to the problem; this is "too narrow: the big question is how one can reconcile the interests of the cities and of the countryside." This had been done in general and in brief in *The Civil War in France*,

---

* Although Marx praised the intent and main point of the manifesto "To the Workers of the Countryside" in *The Civil War in France*, it appears from his notebook of press excerpts that he thought it a poor job on the whole—"dismal" is his one-word evaluation. He had just copied out some sentences from a Paris paper's report about the manifesto:

"The provinces bestir themselves more weakly in favor of Paris than we want to believe. They are indeed not so much in favor of Paris as against Versailles . . . Socialism has to conquer the peasant as it has conquered the worker . . . The peasant is as much calumniated in Paris as the Paris worker is in the provinces." [From *La Social*, May 3, 1871]

To this Marx added a brief remark indicating he doubted that the manifesto would help much "to make the peasant socialist."[116] The text of the manifesto suggests more than one possible reason for Marx's dissatisfaction: above all, it is richer in elocutionary sympathy for the peasant's plight than in spelling out a concrete peasant program.[117]

but he wanted a more detailed and locally specific approach; therefore the various Federal Councils should prepare reports on this question for the next congress. Both proposals were incorporated into a resolution which was adopted unanimously.[119] It was entitled "Agricultural Producers"—a term inclusive of peasants and farm laborers. Section 1 provided for reports to the next congress "on the means of securing the adhesion of the agricultural producers to the movement of the industrial proletariat." Section 2 asked the Federal Councils to send "agitators" (delegates, organizers) to the rural districts, to hold meetings, spread principles, and found rural branches.[120]

After this, the minutes summarize a statement by Marx as follows: "There has been too much preoccupation with urban workers; we will always fail."[121] That is, we will always fail as long as we preoccupy ourselves only with urban workers.

In the ensuing years, as we have indicated elsewhere, it was Engels who in fact paid most attention to the revolutionary need for a proletarian-peasant alliance. As concerned France, we may set down the following two statements as representative.

In a survey of the European labor movement of 1877, Engels' section on France saw the republicanization of the peasants as "a change of the highest importance": "It means also the approaching alliance between the workingmen of the towns and the peasantry of the country." The peasants "must soon find out that their only real remedy lies in an alliance with the only class that has no interest in their present miserable conditions, the working class of the town." The fate of the Commune is reflected in Engels' expectation that the dominance of republicanism will pave the way for the organization of an independent political party of the workers and also furnish "the ground, too, upon which they can unite with the hitherto hostile mass of the peasantry and thus render future victories not, as heretofore, shortlived triumphs of Paris over France, but final triumphs of all the oppressed classes of France, led by the workmen of Paris and the large provincial towns."[122]

The peasantry would have to realize, he thought, "that they are being robbed" by capital. The socialists must persist even if there are no apparent results for a long time: "It is a long and wearisome task to enlighten peasants on political matters, but they will not be so stupid as not to realize at this juncture that they are being robbed. But once they have spotted that, there is nothing for them but to turn to the Socialists, the only party which is not involved in the thefts . . ."[123]

By the time these last words were written, the nature of the problem in the movement had changed: it had swung from ignoring the peasantry to vote-catching by opportunist appeals to peasant prejudices. This was the target of Engels' major work, "The Peasant Question in France and Germany."

13. ITALY, DENMARK, SPAIN

Outside of the more industrialized countries of Western Europe, which we have been considering, the importance of a proletarian-peasant alliance was even greater and clearer. In these countries, the problems to be taken up in the next chapter were more difficult. However, there were complications where the national question intervened and where prebourgeois social systems were especially prominent.

Italy's situation was not complicated in this way. A didactic letter by Engels to an Italian comrade spelled out the ABC of the matter in an intentionally elementary way, keeping in mind that the main problem of alliance under consideration was not with the peasantry (who were not organized politically as a class) but with the petty-bourgeois republican movement of the Mazzini type.

In the background of this problem is the need for a political bloc of "the working people—peasants, handicraftsmen, agricultural and industrial workers." (The order is tailored to Italy.) The socialist movement is young and weak. "Throughout the country the agricultural population far outweighs the urban." Even in the towns, industry is undeveloped, "hence *typical* proletarians are scarce." The town population is still largely "the petty and middle bourgeoisie of the Middle Ages in decay and disintegration, for the most part proletarians of the future but not yet proletarians of the present." These class elements, made desperate by the prospect of economic ruin, will furnish the ranks and leaders of a revolutionary movement. "On this road it will be followed by the peasants, who are prevented from displaying any effective initiative by their lands being too scattered and by their illiteracy, but who in any event will be powerful and indispensable allies."[124]

Denmark was a country that consisted mainly of a capital city plus a rural hinterland. Toward the end of 1871 Engels gave the General Council of the International an interesting report on the political situation there. The Danish branch was based on the small town proletariat, emphasized agitation among the agricultural laborers, and wanted to reach out to the small peasants to win them away from the "Peasants Friends party" of the landed nobility and big peasants.

> The International [in Denmark] aims at freeing the small peasants and agricultural laborers from this submission to the men who grow rich out of their labour [the two upper-class parties], and is endeavouring to form them into an independent party—distinct from the so-called *"Peasants Friends,"* but in intimate union with the working men of the towns.[125]

Engels followed the Danish situation for years, with great appreciation of the peasant work of the Danish socialists. In 1872 he congratulated their leader:

> °°Altogether with regard to the all-important question of enlisting the small peasantry and *Husmaendene* [cotters] in the proletarian movement the Danes, owing to their local circumstances and to their great political intelligence, are now in advance of all other nations.[126]

A few years later, his account of the Danish socialists' alliance with the peasant party had to be more critical of their tactics.[127] But the crux is that the Danes captured his attention and admiration by the energy with which they strove for a three-way alliance of the city proletariat, the farm laborers, and the small peasantry, as the key to revolution.

In Spain, theory was confirmed negatively—as has too often been true. One had to point to the disabling characteristics of the peasantry, as Marx did often enough, but in the last analysis it was the task of revolutionists to find a solution; and a failure was *their* failure. In 1854 Marx wrote, looking backward:

> The defeat of the revolution of 1820-1823 can be easily ex⁻ plained. It was a bourgeois revolution, more accurately an urban revolution, while the countryside—ignorant, inert, devoted to the church's ceremonial pomp—remained passive spectators of the conflict of factions, which it hardly understood. In the few provinces in which exceptionally it actively participated in the struggle, this took place rather on the side of the counterrevolution—a fact which need not surprise one in Spain, "that storehouse of old customs, that repository of everything that is elsewhere gone and forgotten" . . . The fact that the revolutionary

party did not know how to unite the interests of the peasantry with the urban movement was confirmed by two men both of whom played a substantial role in the revolution, Generals Morillo and San Miguel. [Marx then quotes them.]

The revolutionists' punishment was that they were "forced to rely entirely on the army and its leaders."[128]

It is such situations that give rise to endless and pointless controversies over whether the failure was due to the torpor of the peasants, the betrayal of the army leaders, *or* the incapacity of the revolutionary leadership.

14. IRELAND: THE NATIONAL COMPLICATION

Ireland was the most prominent case before Marx of an interpenetration of peasant question and national question. Colonial oppression by England was combined with a socioeconomic and cultural association of the two peoples that was much closer than, say, between England and India. Industrialized Irish peasants became proletarians *in England;* an Irish liberation movement—like the Fenians of the 1860s, whom Marx and Engels supported against English imperialism—was perhaps as active in England (and the United States) as in Ireland itself; and so on. The enormous interest in Ireland and the Irish movement taken by Marx and Engels was fed from several directions,* but at bottom was the very close and immediate connection they saw between the revolutionary potential of the Irish peasantry and the fate of the proletarian revolution in England.

They were keenly aware of the weaknesses and self-defeating tactics of the Fenian leadership (an important subject outside the purview of this chapter), but there could be no question of counterposing a nonexistent Irish working-class movement. The Irish revolution that Marx supported and hoped for was going to be a peasant revolution primarily. "What the Irish need," wrote Marx to Engels, "is: (1) Self-government and independence from England. (2) An agrarian revolu-

---

* Besides the basic political motivation, plus the role of the Irish in English trade unions and the International, we should not overlook two others: Engels' Irish wife Mary Burns was a militant revolutionary nationalist; and Marx's daughters were all fanatically pro-Fenian.

tion."[129] The overthrow of English rule would doom landlordism both in Ireland and in England:

> But I was long ago convinced that the social revolution must begin *seriously* from the ground up, that is, from land ownership.[130]

What Marx worked out as he went along was the interweaving of three problems: the struggle of the Irish workers in England; the land question and peasant exploitation in Ireland; and the question of Irish national liberation. He did not start with the preconception that Irish national freedom depended on agrarian revolution; this became clear to him as he wrestled with the concrete problem. In 1867 he gave an hour-and-a-half lecture on the historical roots of the Irish question, concluding: "The Irish question is therefore not simply a nationality question, but a question of land and existence. Ruin or revolution is the watchword . . ."[131] In a letter of 1869 he stressed that in Ireland the peasant struggle against landlordism "is not merely a simple economic question but at the same time a *national* question" since the landlords are "mortally hated oppressors" from another country, England.[132] There was a reciprocal effect: the same day, as it happened, Engels wrote Marx a letter chortling over the electoral victory of the Fenians: "if the English workers cannot take an example from the peasants of Tipperary, they are in a bad way."[133]

About a month later Marx wrote a statement for the International on the Irish question, giving the Irish peasant struggle a key spot on the world stage: England is the bulwark of European landlordism and capitalism; its most vulnerable point is its hold on Ireland; if landlordism fell in Ireland it would fall in England.

> In Ireland this is a hundred times easier since *the economic struggle there is concentrated exclusively on landed property,* since this struggle is at the same time national, and since the people there are more revolutionary and exasperated than in England.[134]

And again:

> Ireland is the bulwark of the *English landed aristocracy.* . . . Ireland is therefore the great means by which the English aristocracy maintains *its domination in England itself.*
> If . . . the English army and police were to withdraw from Ireland tomorrow, you would at once have an agrarian revolution

there. . . . The destruction of the English landed aristocracy in Ireland is an infinitely easier operation than in England itself, because in Ireland *the land question* has hitherto been the *exclusive form* of the social question . . . This quite apart from the Irish being more passionate and revolutionary in character than the English.[135]

Therefore:

I have come to the conclusion that the decisive blow against the English ruling classes . . . *cannot* be delivered *in England* but *only in Ireland.*[136]

Marx had already informed Engels that this represented a newly thought-out conclusion for him.[137]

This line of thought played a very important role in the practical work of the International in England. Under Marx's guidance, the International became a considerable force for cementing an alliance between the Irish peasant revolution and the English working-class struggle. And because of England's international role, the consequences would be seen also on the Continent: such was the prospect.

The breakdown of England's landownership system in Ireland, Marx thought, would also lead to an alliance in the English countryside (without peasants). Arrayed against the English landowning power at home would be "the British farmers, wincing under high rents and . . . low prices; the British agricultural labourers, at last impatient of their traditional position of ill-used beasts of burden," plus the dubious support of the bourgeois party that labeled itself "Radical."[138] Needless to say, such an alliance on the English countryside would be of vital concern to the proletarian movement.

In Ireland itself, the bourgeois liberal-nationalist leadership which based itself on peasant support* was as hostile to an alliance with the English working class as their English counterparts. For "to these gentry," wrote Engels, "the whole labor movement is pure heresy and the Irish peasant must not on any account be allowed to know that the socialist workers are his sole allies in Europe."[142]

---

* The case in point at this juncture was the Dublin *Irishman,* which systematically refused to inform its readership of the International's support to Irish freedom. "Stupidity and wretchedness," Marx called it.[139] Engels thought it was also "a calculated policy of the leaders in order to maintain their domination over the peasant. Added to this, a nation of peasants always has to take its literary

15. RUSSIA: HOPE IN THE PEASANT

When we come to Russia and Poland, Marx's and Engels' expectations from the revolutionary potential of the peasantry are so abundantly expressed that we need give only illustrative cases. The reason was not only the overwhelming peasant composition of the producing population, though this fact was basic. Since they regarded czarism as the kingpin of all European reaction, a revolution in Russia was most important from the standpoint of its international consequences: it was a way to blow up European reaction from within its main center. As long as no socialist movement or proletarian alternative was in sight, it virtually made no difference to Marx who, or what class, launched the revolutionary struggle, so long as it at least weakened the Muscovite colossus. It was only toward the end of his life that a proletarian socialist movement of some sort took its first shaky steps in Russia; until then, therefore, hope for revolution in Russia meant hope in the revolutionary potential of its peasantry above all, even if this potential were to be realized under the leadership of disaffected upper-class elements. Marx's and Engels' estimations more often show wishful thinking about activity by the Russian peasantry than any other European class.

Of course, incidental remarks in personal letters between the two men were less weightily considered than published articles; but still they indicate lines of thought. As early as 1851, Engels mused, in a letter to Marx, about the dangers to Germany of a European "brawl," and remarked: "Outside of Hungary, Germany would have only one possible ally, Russia—provided that a peasant revolution was carried out there."[143] A few years later Marx told the readers of the *New York Tribune,* regarding the czar's plans for the coming emancipation of the serfs:

> If we recollect that since 1842 the insurrections of serfs against their landlords and stewards have become epidemic; that

---

representatives from the bourgeoisie of the towns and their ideologists . . ."[140]
Again, some years later:

> Soon after Union (1800) began the *liberal nationalist* opposition of the *townsmen,* which, as in every peasant country whose townlets are shrinking (e.g., Denmark) finds its natural-born leaders in the *lawyers.* The latter also need the peasants; they therefore had to find slogans that attracted the peasants.[141]

something like sixty nobles . . . have been annually murdered by the peasants; that during the late [Crimean] war the insurrections increased enormously, and in the western provinces were directed chiefly against the Government . . . there can be little doubt that, even if the nobility does not resist the emancipation, the attempt to realize the committee's proposals [for a Parliament of Nobles] must be the signal for a tremendous conflagration among the rural population of Russia. . . . [The serfs] are surer than ever to rise. And if they do, the Russian 1793 will be at hand; the reign of terror of these half-Asiatic serfs will be something unequaled in history; but it will be the second turning point in Russian history, and finally place real and general civilization in the place of that sham and show introduced by Peter the Great.[144]

With an insurrectionary movement going on in Poland and Lithuania in 1863,* Engels wrote to Marx: "What surprises me most is that no peasant movement is breaking out in Great Russia."[147] Twelve years later there was still no peasant insurrection in Russia, but, to Engels, the peasant movement "will irresistibly be pushed farther along" because of the oppressive conditions of the peasant masses.[148] He expressed this sentiment in a context that deserves some attention.

The context was his polemic against one Tkachov, an old-style Russian revolutionary influenced by Blanquism and Bakunin.[149] Tkachov had attacked Engels' views from the standpoint of "peasant socialism": the Russian peasant was an "instinctive revolutionist," who, because of his village-communal institutions, was closer to socialism than was the Western socialist movement. Engels' reply raked this conception of building a revolutionary socialist movement on peasant-style revolutionism and the conception of peasant socialism in general. But within this framework, he went on to give credit to the revolutionary potential of the peasant in his own way.

It is clear that the condition of the Russian peasants since the emancipation from serfdom has become intolerable and cannot

---

* An uprising had broken out in Russian Poland in January, with the demand *inter alia* to free the peasants from feudal burdens. In a letter to Marx, Engels observed that the movement was doing better in Lithuania than in Poland, for one thing "because here [in Lithuania] the peasants participate in it more and the business directly becomes agrarian in character . . ."[145] Similarly Marx later wrote that the restoration of partitioned Poland "is *impossible* without a peasant uprising."[146]

be maintained much longer, and that for this reason alone if for no other a revolution is in the offing in Russia. . . .

Russia undoubtedly is on the eve of a revolution. . . . Here all the conditions of a revolution are combined, of a revolution which, started by the upper classes of the capital, perhaps even by the government itself, must be rapidly carried further, beyond the first constitutional phase, by the peasants; of a revolution which will be of the greatest importance for the whole of Europe if only because it will destroy at one blow the last, so far intact, reserve of the entire European reaction. This revolution is surely approaching.[150]

At this time Engels expected the *initiative* in the revolution to come from the urban upper classes (as was indeed the case in March 1917); of the proletariat there were only beginnings. The revolutionary push of the peasant masses would provide the gigantic groundswell that would carry the revolution "beyond the first constitutional phase."[151] How far beyond it? The crystal ball did not always give the same answer; nor was a definite prognostication necessary. Marx had long before spoken of the coming "1793" in Russia. In a letter to a correspondent in 1885, Engels opined that "Russia faces its 1789," after vigorously asserting that "The so-called emancipation of the peasants has created a thoroughly revolutionary situation, by moving the peasants into a situation in which they can neither live nor die," a situation sharpened by the rapid development of large industry.[152]

But as industrial development changed Russia, especially by producing a new working class and its concomitant socialist movement, Engels' emphasis shifted accordingly. In an 1894 postscript to the polemic against Tkachov, Engels referred back to the possibility "after the Crimean War" of "direct parliamentary rule by the nobility and the bureaucracy" as a consequence of the overthrow of the czarist autocracy; but by 1894 the bourgeoisification of Russian society had gone on apace. What Engels now stressed was the perspective of a Russian revolution "in combination with a revolution in Western Europe." In any case, a revolution in Russia would "lead the peasants out into the large arena" of the outside world, and it would "also give a fresh impulse to the labor movement in the West," for only the victory of the modern industrial proletariat would permit Russia to achieve its own socialist transformation.[153]

The problem of the Russian revolution, then, changed rapidly in the last part of the century, and this must be borne in mind also in connection with the problems discussed in the next chapter. What did not change for Marx or Engels, however, was the international motivation for spurring revolution in Russia. This added greatly to the importance of peasant movements elsewhere in the Slavic world and on the periphery of the Russian empire, such as those in Poland and Turkey.*

---

* This is no doubt one reason why both Marx and Engels heaped high praise on the Turkish peasantry. The connection is especially visible in a letter of Marx's in 1878, giving two grounds for taking Turkey's side against Russia. One is that defeat of Russia would have hastened revolution in Russia and hence all over Europe. But his first ground is this: "because we have studied the *Turkish peasant*—hence the mass of the Turkish people—and thus have come to know him as being unqualifiedly one of the *ablest and worthiest representatives of the peasantry in Europe.*"[154] Engels had similarly praised the Turkish peasant in a letter the previous year, and was to do so again in an article in 1890, in both cases in the context of Turkey's role as a threat to Russian power.[155] Marx particularly counterposed the social health of the Turkish peasantry to the reactionary role of the Turkish government.

14 | THE PEASANT QUESTION: PROGRAMMATIC PROBLEMS

For Marx there was never any question about the end-goal of the agrarian revolution: it was the socialization of agriculture on the basis of social ownership of the land. But this left open a number of political problems about the road by which the goal was to be attained, before and after a proletarian conquest of power. There were associated problems of tempo and form—how fast to move, what forms to use for reorganization. In this programmatic area, a great deal of flexibility was in order.

Marx and Engels have not often been given credit for the considerable flexibility which in fact they demonstrated as they adapted their practical programmatic proposals to time, place, and circumstance within a framework comporting with the goal. The main problem that shadowed all considerations was, of course, that of bringing the peasantry along, particularly the small peasants.

In this chapter, by exception, we anticipate in part a question to be treated at large in a later volume, namely, the socialist reorganization of society after a proletarian conquest of power. Here we deal with some issues bearing on the peasant question, but without the general context that will be set forth. While this entails leaving some loose ends now, there is no good alternative; for on no other question is there a closer connection between immediate policy and future (post-revolution) program. That connection exists first and foremost in the minds of the peasants themselves.

1. SOCIALIZATION OF LAND

The goal of land socialization and the abolition of private property in the soil was already strongly stated in Marx's Paris manuscripts of

1844. There his argument is directed first against the parcellization of large landed estates as a solution of the problem of monopoly—because of its economic disadvantages and because it will only lead back to "accumulation" once again, just as small-unit competition does in industry. The only real solution is to negate monopoly in a different form:

> To do that, however, is not to return to feudal ownership, but to abolish private property in the soil altogether. . . . Association [socialism], applied to land, shares the economic advantage of large-scale landed property, and first brings to realization the original tendency inherent in [land] division, namely, equality. In the same way association also re-establishes, now on a rational basis, no longer mediated by serfdom, overlordship and the silly mysticism of property, the intimate ties of man with the earth, since the earth ceases to be an object of huckstering, and through free labor and free enjoyment becomes once more a true personal property of man.[1]

The ten-point program in the *Communist Manifesto*—by and large a compilation of demands popular among the revolutionary left—included this goal as point no. 1: "Expropriation of landed property and application of ground rent for state expenditures."*

The case for land socialization was conveniently summarized by Marx many years later in a memorandum which was specifically concerned with England. This summary argument, which was intended as a guide to a popularized presentation, stresses that land nationalization is a "social necessity" because it makes possible the vast increase in production needed to satisfy "the ever-growing wants of the people," by fully utilizing the scientific knowledge and technical means which are applicable only in large-scale operations; because "a few individuals" (owners) cannot be allowed to regulate agricultural production "according to their whims and private interests or to ignorantly exhaust the powers of the soil"; and because capitalist cultivation leads to "the ever-increasing price of agricultural produce" for the masses of people while it "degrades the producer [land-tiller] himself to a mere beast of burden."[3]

---

* So in the German original. The standard (Moore-Engels) translation of 1888 reads: "Abolition of property in land and application of all rents of land to public purposes."[2] The softening of the first phrase (expropriation) no doubt reflects greater sensitivity to peasant fears of outright expropriation.

The basic importance of the question struck Marx forcibly in the middle of a letter to Engels in 1851, and we get a strong statement in a passing remark:

> But the more I go into the crap, the more I become convinced that the reform of agriculture, hence also of the property shit based on it, is the alpha and omega of the coming revolutionary transformation. Without that, Father Malthus would prove to be right.[3a]

But land socialization was by no means a closed question in the socialist movement. It was opposed by a number of petty-bourgeois radical currents: in England, Feargus O'Connor's wing of Chartism; in France and Belgium, the Proudhonists; in Germany, such allies of the socialists as the South German People's Party. The two viewpoints locked horns inside the International. At the Brussels congress in 1868, land socialization was passed by a small and uncertain majority; but at the Basel Congress the following year, it was adopted overwhelmingly, against only a handful of Proudhonist votes.

This decision fluttered the International's opponents on all sides. The reformist leaders in Switzerland, Austria, and Germany "are yelling blue murder," Marx wrote in a letter.[4] In South Germany, the People's Party denounced it; and so Wilhelm Liebknecht—opportunist as usual—wanted to maintain socialist neutrality toward the International decision, but a majority of the party executive overruled him.

It had taken three congresses before the International was able to get to this point, for the social pressure of the peasant mass outside the movement was felt inside it through a variety of transmission belts. When the General Council was discussing the issue prior to the Basel Congress, a visitor from Paris, the future anarchist Elisée Reclus, assured the Council members they need not be concerned with the peasantry, for "The peasants know very little what is going [on in] the world, they do not come to your Congresses, they do not even know that they are held; we have very little care about them. The men in the towns are for collective property." To this blinkered urban-radical view, Marx replied (as summarized in the minutes): "The small peasantry is not at the Congresses, but their idealistic [i.e., ideological] representatives are there. The Proudhonists are very strong upon the point and they were at Brussels . . ."[5]

Immediately upon the adoption of the Basel resolution, International activists in England were instrumental in establishing the Land

and Labour League, whose first plank was the nationalization of the land.[6] Marx thought this enormously important:

> The formation of the *Land and Labour League* (which was directly brought about by the General Council, by the bye) is to be considered an outcome of the Basel Congress; thereby the workers' party completely cuts loose from the bourgeoisie, nationalization of land being the starting point.[7]

But the adoption of the principle did not foreclose programmatic questions of implementation. It was clear in the International debates that, although land collectivization would vest *ownership* in a workers' state—that is, the power to determine how the land would be worked and by whom—it did not mean that the state must necessarily take over agriculture directly. At the Basel Congress, for example, one common idea was that small-holding peasants might continue in cultivation of their land without rent, at least for their own lifetime; cooperatives were another popular form, as we shall see.

Nor did the adoption of the principle mean that, regardless of national circumstances, a workers' state should nationalize the land by decree in one blow. This was a matter of tempo. Marx already indicated this before Basel, in the General Council's pre-congress discussion:

> In England the land could be transformed into common property by act of Parliament in the course of a fortnight. In France it must be accomplished by means of the proprietors' indebtedness and liability to taxation.[8]

And by implication less developed countries might see even slower tempos. This element of flexibility applied not only to use, then, but also to ownership of the land.

On this point particularly there would naturally be a great difference in ways and means applied to big peasants and small peasants. Writing to Marx about the brouhaha over the Basel "resolution on landed property," Engels remarked that "people forget . . . that there are various kinds of peasants," and that "for the present the proletariat has no interest in calling in question *small* landownership."[9] The following year he utilized a new preface to his *Peasant War in Germany* to make the point publicly. The context is the plan to turn large landed estates into cooperative agricultural associations.

> And here we come to the famous decision of the International Working Men's Congress in Basel: that it is in the interest of

society to transform landed property into common, national property. This resolution was adopted mainly for the countries where there is big landed property, and where, in connection with that, these big estates are being operated with one master and many laborers. This state of affairs, however, is still as a whole predominant in Germany, and therefore, next to England, the decision was *most timely precisely for Germany*.[10]

A similar view appears in the rough notes that Marx jotted down for himself in 1874-1875 on reading one of Bakunin's polemics. Apropos of a passage in which Bakunin jibed that the peasantry does not enjoy "the good will of the Marxists," who want the urban proletariat to dominate it, Marx scribbled this comment:

> ... where the peasant exists in mass numbers as a private-property owner, where he even forms a more or less considerable majority, as in all the states of the western European continent where he has not disappeared and been replaced by agricultural day-laborers as in England, the following cases come up: Either he obstructs, wrecks every workers' revolution, as he has done in France up to now; or else the proletariat ...* must, as the government, take measures whereby the peasant sees his situation immediately improved and which therefore win him over to the revolution—measures, however, which in embryo facilitate the transition from private property in land to collective property, so that the peasant comes to it by himself, for economic reasons.

This establishes the general approach; the note continues with a specific rejection of the idea of taking away the small peasant's land:

> But the peasant should not be antagonized, for example by proclaiming the abolition of the right to inheritance** or the abolition of his property. The latter is possible only where the capital-

---

* I have here removed an explanatory parenthesis, which goes as follows: "(for the property-owning peasant does not belong to the proletariat, and even where he does belong to it on the basis of his situation he does not believe he belongs to it)." When does the "property-owning peasant" belong to the proletariat "on the basis of his situation"? Marx may have two cases in mind: the peasants who actually maintain themselves by part-time day-labor for others (see above, Chapter 13, sec. 5), and those who are really working for a wage-equivalent, with themselves as employers (same chapter, sec. 4). In both situations peasants may fondly continue to think of themselves as little landowners.

** Abolition of the right of inheritance was a favorite nostrum of Bakunin's, often attacked by Marx. For example, in a letter of 1870 Marx concluded: °°"the proclamation of the *abolition of inheritance* would not be a serious act, but a

istic tenant-farmer has ousted the peasant and the actual cultivator of the soil is just as much a proletarian, a wage-worker, as is the urban worker, and therefore *directly*, not indirectly, has exactly the same interests as he does.

The warning could hardly be spelled out more clearly. But if Marx was opposed to expropriating the land tilled by the small peasant, he was equally opposed to breaking up the large estates already owned and worked capitalistically in order to turn this land over to small-holders.[13] And this bisymmetric side of the perspective was set down in the last sentence of the note on Bakunin:

> Still less should parcellized property be strengthened by enlarging the parcels simply by the peasants' annexation of the large estates, as in the Bakuninist revolutionary plan of campaign.[14]

Marx never believed that, even in a Western European country like France, a revolutionary government was somehow duty-bound by principle to decree the immediate nationalization of all land, including that of the mass of small peasantry, regardless of other considerations. The complete process might take a generation, as envisaged at Basel; meanwhile there was plenty for a revolutionary government to do in order to move in that direction, as its goal. Marx came back to this in the aforementioned memorandum on land nationalization in England, in 1872, contrasting the application of the program in England as against France:

> °°France has often been alluded to, but with its *peasantry proprietorship* it is farther off the nationalisation of land than England with its landlordism. . . . Peasantry proprietorship being thus the greatest obstacle to the "nationalisation of land," France, in its present state, is certainly not the place where we must look for a solution of this great problem.[15]

England was the country where the socialist solution was most immediately applicable. Here, where the ruling class intertwined both the industrial capitalist class and the big landowners, where the aristocratic wing operated the land capitalistically and the bourgeois wing aspired

---

foolish menace, rallying the whole peasantry and the whole small middle-class round the reaction."[11] To be sure, this plank was not Bakunin's invention; it was older than socialism itself, and was one of the popular leftist demands included in the ten-point program of the *Communist Manifesto*,[12] before Marx learned its political significance.

to landed estates, the same act would shake both parts of the ruling class to the foundations. Marx's memorandum begins: "The property in the soil—that original source of all wealth, has become the great problem upon the solution of which depends the future of the working class." And toward the end: "The nationalisation of land will work a complete change in the relations between labour and capital and finally do away altogether with capitalist production."[16] This applied specifically to England, and depended upon a political, not merely an economic, analysis—as was true also of Marx's view that the overthrow of British landownership in Ireland would strike a fatal blow at British capitalism at home. (As far as economic considerations alone are concerned, nationalization of land is by no means incompatible with capitalism: Marx made this clear more than once.[17])

Some radicals wanted land nationalization as a means of establishing (or re-establishing) a class of small-holding farmers; the case of the Chartist wing under Feargus O'Connor will be discussed in section 5 below. Marx's memorandum of 1872 once again opposes this economic nostrum:

> °°To nationalise the land and let it out in small plots to individuals or workingmen's societies, would, under a middle-class [i.e., bourgeois] government, only bring about a reckless competition amongst them, and cause a certain increase of "Rent," and thus lend new facilities to the appropriators for feeding upon the producers.[18]

Whichever way a workers' state might decide to organize the operation of the land, it had to own the land, in the name of society as a whole, so that it could carry out its goals. Marx's memorandum quotes the Belgian socialist leader César de Paepe at the Brussels Congress of 1868: "The soil must become the property of rural associations, or the property of the whole nation. The future will decide the question." Marx disagrees with leaving the question open:

> °°I say on the contrary: "The future will decide that the land cannot be owned but nationally. To give up the soil to the hands of associated rural labourers, would be to surrender all society to one exclusive class of producers. . . ."[19]

This is the basic ground for rejecting any sort of syndicalist setup as flagrantly undemocratic. The earth could not be handed over to ownership-control by narrow groups of workers, independent of control by working people as a whole, any more than the Food Workers Union had a right to decide who would be fed.

But cooperative associations of rural laborers do have a key role in Marx's program for socialist agriculture: this brings us to Marx's and Engels' views on the operation of socialized land.

2. SOCIALIST AGRICULTURE: COOPERATIVES

The first step in socialist agriculture, then, would be to organize the operation of the big landed estates taken over from their semifeudal or capitalistic owners, including state domains—even if the rest of the land still remained for a period in the hands of the small-holders who already tilled it themselves. Engels (who got most concrete about all this) thought this first step would be "perfectly simple." There is no record that the possibility of direct state operation of this land occurred to him; on the other hand there is no reason to suppose he, or any other socialist, would have rejected it if it seemed indicated by circumstances. The fact is that while Engels repeatedly outlined the socialist solution, he did so always in terms of cooperative associations.

Here is how Engels explained it in his last work on the peasant question, after a good deal of discussion of peasant policy:

> Only the big landed estates present a perfectly simple case. Here we are dealing with undisguised capitalist production and no scruples of any sort need restrain us. Here we are confronted by rural proletarians in masses and our task is clear. As soon as our party is in possession of political power it has simply to expropriate the big landed proprietors just like the manufacturers in industry.... The big estates thus restored to the community are to be turned over to be organized into cooperatives. They are to be assigned to them for their use and benefit under the control of the community.* Nothing can as yet be stated as to the terms of

---

* Earlier in this essay, Engels had listed the demands in the French party's agrarian program of 1892; on this issue the French demand was for "the leasing of public domain land to communities which are to rent all this land, whether owned by them or rented, to associations of propertyless families of farm laborers for common cultivation, on condition that the employment of wage-workers be prohibited and that the communities exercise control." Engels does not comment on this plank as such, since he goes on to discuss the peasant demands.[20]

their tenure. At any rate the transformation of the capitalist enterprise into a socialist enterprise is here fully prepared for and
can be carried into execution overnight, precisely as in Mr.
Krupp's or Mr. von Stumm's factory. And the example of these
agricultural cooperatives would convince also the last of the still
resistant small-holding peasants, and surely also many big
peasants, of the advantages of cooperative, large-scale production.[21]

Socialist thinking had followed these general lines, with differing
details, for a half century and more. As we saw, this perspective for
socialist agriculture had been included in the "Address to the Communist League" of March 1850.[22] The Basel Congress of 1869 showed
how popular it was. In Engels' already-mentioned comment on the
Basel Congress, in his preface to an 1870 edition of *The Peasant War in
Germany*, he made the same analogy as above between socialization of
the factories and of the big landed estates; hence the land should be

> withdrawn from the private ownership of the big peasants and the
> still bigger feudal lords, transformed into public property and
> cultivated by cooperative associations of agricultural workers on
> their common account.[23]

Just as socialization could be carried out most easily both in the big
factory and the big landed estate, so also the problem of the small
peasant holding on the land was similar to that of the little artisan
workshop in the town: it is the bigger enterprises which "are a better
handle for us to take hold of," wrote Engels to a German correspondent.

> And this is politically reflected in the fact that the rural prole-
> tarians on the big estates become Social-Democrats, just like the
> urban proletarians, as soon as the latter can work on them, where-
> as the bankrupt peasant and the urban artisan come to the Social-
> Democracy only by the detour of anti-Semitism.*[24]

---

* That is, via the movement of political anti-Semitism in Germany. This was
an important point often made by the Socialists: the petty property-holders in
both town and country tended to be first attracted by, and to have to pass
through, a movement like the Christian Social party, which appealed in terms of
demagogic agitation against banks as well as of anti-Semitism (hence "the socialism of fools," in Bebel's famous phrase). Engels makes the link-up several times in
his 1894 essay on the peasant question,[25] and likewise in his letter on anti-
Semitism of April 19, 1890.[26]

Engels urged that the proposal to turn big estates into rural coopera-tive associations should be brought up formally in the Reichstag by the socialist deputies, even though it had no chance of being adopted by the existing state. It would be a powerful propaganda weapon, he told Bebel:

> When you bring up proposals in the Reichstag, there is one that should not be forgotten. The state lands are mostly leased out to big farmers; to the very smallest extent they are sold to peasants, whose lots are so small, however, that the new peasants have to resort to day-labor on the big farms. The demand to make would be: *leasing of the big undivided lands to cooperative societies of agricultural workers for collective cultivation.* . . . I believe that this firebrand must be thrown among the agricultural day-laborers, and this can indeed be done in one of the many debates on state-socialism. This and this alone is the way to win the agricultural workers; this is the best method of pointing out to them that they are later ordained to cultivate the big estates of the present fine gentlemen, for the common account.[27]

The idea is that it should be used as a transitional demand, that is, a demand bridging the gap between minimum demands (for immediate reforms) and maximum demands (involving the realization of social-ism).

The proposal for large-scale operation of the land through agricul-tural cooperatives was by no means limited to rural laborers, however. It was also a possibility for peasants, insofar as the latter were weaned away from their historical obsession with "This is my own patch of dirt." The laborers' cooperatives could offer an example and a demon-stration of the advantages. As the peasants flounder more and more in economic straits, we cannot vie with "the anti-Semites, peasant-leaguers and similar parties who derive pleasure from promising everything and keeping nothing"—so Engels argued in his essay on the peasant ques-tion, referring specifically in this case to the big and middle peasants. We can, he wrote, only

> recommend here too the pooling of farms to form cooperative enterprises, in which the exploitation of wage labor will be elimi-nated more and more, and their gradual transformation into branches of the great national producers' cooperative with each branch enjoying equal rights and duties can be instituted.[28]

Engels gets most specific not in presenting some scheme of his own but in summarizing the agrarian plan proposed in the 1870s by the Danish socialists (and perhaps embroidering on it). The following passage is one of the most detailed pictures of some facet of economic policy in a socialist society ever written down by Marx or Engels; and it is ironic that it treats the allegedly ignored peasant question rather than industry. In Denmark—

> The peasants of a village or parish . . . were to pool their land to form a single big farm in order to cultivate it for common account and distribute the yield in proportion to the land, money and labor contributed. . . . [I]f we apply this idea to a region of small holdings we shall find that if these are pooled and the aggregate area cultivated on a large scale, part of the labor power employed hitherto is rendered superfluous. It is precisely this saving of labor that represents one of the main advantages of large-scale farming. Employment can be found for this labor power in two ways. Either additional land taken from big estates in the neighborhood is placed at the disposal of the peasant cooperative or the peasants in question are provided with the means and the opportunity of engaging in industry as an accessory calling, primarily and as far as possible for their own use. In either case their economic position is improved and simultaneously the general social directing agency is assured the necessary influence to transform the peasant cooperative to a higher form, and to equalize the rights and duties of the cooperative as a whole as well as of its individual members with those of the other departments of the entire community. How this is to be carried out in practice in each particular case will depend upon the circumstances of the case and the conditions under which we take possession of political power. We may thus possibly be in a position to offer these cooperatives yet further advantages: assumption of their entire mortgage indebtedness by the national bank with a simultaneous sharp reduction of the interest rate; advances from public funds for the establishment of large-scale production (to be made not necessarily or primarily in money but in the form of required products: machinery, artificial fertilizer, etc.), and other advantages.
>
> The main point is and will be to make the peasants understand that we can save, preserve their houses and fields for them only by transforming them into cooperative property operated cooperatively. . . . Should it really be impossible to make the

peasants understand that this is in their own interest, that it is the sole means of their salvation?[29]

Engels made this proposal more briefly on other occasions, as in a series of popular articles for English workers in which it was concisely summarized as "the nationalisation of the land and its cultivation by co-operative societies under national control."[30] He also made it as a means of "rejuvenating common landownership" such as had once existed in the Mark community of early Germany.[31] Marx made the same connection with the still existing remnant of the old type of Russian village commune. It suffers, he wrote, from the isolation of the individual communes, among other things, but—

> Today this is an obstacle which can be very easily overcome. All that need to be done is to replace the *volost*, a government institution, by an assembly of peasants elected by the communes themselves, which would serve as an economic and administrative organ to protect their interests.[32]

And he discussed the possibility that, given a Russian revolution, it might develop into part of a socialist system. Earlier, in his first draft for *The Civil War in France*, he had counterposed some form of "associated labor" to the continuation of small-holding peasant cultivation.[33]

3. FLEXIBILITY AND VARIATION

So far this chapter has dealt with questions on which Marx held relatively fixed views, for the first involved the basic goal of socialism in agriculture, and the second involved the basic pattern of class priorities on socialized land. We now come to a number of questions involving the spectrum of *transitional measures* between capitalism and socialism.

This is the area in which Marx and Engels not only allowed for but insisted on a wide-ranging flexibility. Flexibility was required by the general principle of "different countries—different cases," as explained in the preceding chapter; it was also required because such historical circumstances as the way in which power was achieved could strongly condition the first measures taken by a workers' state. Thus, while the goal of socialized agriculture on socially owned land was beyond question, the measures to be taken looking to the collectivization of land cultivation were a quite different matter. Let us cite two cases, one quite unequivocal in its answer, the other quite problematical.

At the unequivocal end of the spectrum was a policy question of great political importance: the tenure of the small peasant. We have already seen more than one occasion on which Marx or Engels assumed or indicated in passing that the small peasants' cultivation of their own patch of ground was not to be forcibly disrupted. In an 1869 letter to Marx, Engels had remarked in the midst of another discussion: "Besides, it may of course be added that meanwhile the proletariat has no interest in raising the question of *small* landownership."[34] In his final essay on the peasant question, Engels came to dot the *i*'s: compulsory collectivization of the small peasants' land was completely excluded:

> What, then, is our attitude towards the small peasantry? How shall we have to deal with it on the day of our accession to power?
>
> To begin with, the French [party] program is absolutely correct in stating: that we foresee the inevitable doom of the small peasant but that it is not our mission to hasten it by any interference on our part.
>
> Secondly, it is just as evident that when we are in possession of state power we shall not even think of forcibly expropriating the small peasants (regardless of whether with or without compensation), as we shall have to do in the case of the big landowners. Our task relative to the small peasant consists, in the first place, in effecting a transition of his private enterprise and private possession to cooperative ones, not forcibly but by dint of example and the proffer of social assistance for this purpose. And then of course we shall have ample means of showing to the small peasant prospective advantages that must be obvious to him even today.[35]

The Danish example[36] is cited in this connection.

Socialists, Engels stressed, cannot promise the small peasants to *preserve* their property against capitalist encroachments, that is, against the inroads of economic forces they had been warned about. "We can only promise them," writes Engels, "that we shall not interfere in their property relations by force, against their will."[37] When Kautsky made a similar statement in the party press, he was criticized for favoring peasant enterprise; and Engels was disgusted by this "wiseacreism." He wrote to Kautsky: "To deduce, from the fact that we tell the small peasants we will not drive them forcibly from house and home, that we also want to provide them with the economic requisites for continued private enterprise—this is a bit thick after all. It is quite clear that, as things stand today, you would pose these two [propositions] differently."[38]

The case of the big and middle peasants was, of course, different, not simply because they were bigger but because their operations depended on the use of wage-labor; in the case of big peasants or tenant-farmers, the actual producers were the laborers. If these peasant-growers draw the necessary conclusions, writes Engels, "it will be incumbent upon us to facilitate to the best of our ability also their transition to the changed mode of production. . . . Most likely we shall be able to abstain here as well from resorting to forcible expropriation, and as for the rest to count on future economic developments making also these harder pates amenable to reason."[39] We might add some obvious considerations, such as the fact that big peasants might have some difficulty in obtaining wage-labor if socialized agriculture offered a more attractive alternative to farmhands.

Toward the other end of the spectrum are the questions subsumed under the later catchword, "Land to the peasants"—questions which we will sort out below. Here policy had to depend very much on the socioeconomic position and historical circumstances of the country and time; here national differences were often augmented by systemic differences.

In one of his passages deprecating speculation about the details of the society of the future, Engels remarks that

> Even the transitional measures will everywhere have to be in accordance with the relations existing at the moment. In countries of small landed property they will be substantially different from those in countries where big landed property prevails, etc.[40]

In his 1894 essay he discusses the special agrarian program adopted by the French party at Nantes, in supplementation of the general party program. He reminds the French that the generalities in its preamble do not apply to the whole world:

> Once we cite the program in support of our contention we must cite the entire program, which considerably modifies the proposition quoted in Nantes; for it makes the general historical truth expressed in it dependent upon the conditions under which alone

it can remain a truth today in Western Europe and North America.[41]

So generalities will not do; in the next sections we shall have to tie the issues down to countries and periods. When we do so, we shall see that even a slogan like "Land to the peasants"—which, in the myths of marxology, is often supposed to be fundamentally incompatible with Marx's views—was in fact an open question, depending on time and place.

4. FLEXIBILITY: IN AMERICA

England and the United States are the most extreme cases, for here there was no class of peasantry overshadowing the land question as there was in most of the Continent. In both countries the question raised inside the proletarian movement was not that of sparing or preserving a small peasantry but of *creating* one where none existed. It should go without saying that Marx could not support such a plan for a moment; but it is all the more interesting to see his political approach to genuine mass movements that did propose this retrogressive step.

This case occurred in the United States in 1846, while Marx and Engels were engaged in building their Communist Correspondence Committee in Brussels. A self-styled Communist named Hermann Kriege, a disciple of Wilhelm Weitling, had emigrated to America the year before. As editor of the *Volks-Tribun* and (at first) in the name of "Communism," Kriege adopted whole the agrarian program of the American National Reformers for the salvation of the proletariat and of society: 160 acres of free land (no more) for everyone, establishing a population of small-holding cultivators and solving the problem of poverty forevermore.*

* This was the practical side of Kriege's "communism"; for the rest, he depended on effusions about "love," self-sacrifice, communion with the Infinite, and similar profundities. Kriege himself was no peasant but a university-educated intellectual, even though he echoed Weitling's slogan "Down with reason." In America he gave himself out as a representative of German Communism; hence he was a fatal discreditment to the real German Communists, especially when, after substituting Free Soil agitation for a revolutionary social program, he also allied himself with Tammany Hall, appealed to the rich for support, and opposed the abolition of slavery (since it would increase competition among workers). After

In a circular on behalf of the Communist Correspondence Committee, Marx and Engels had no difficulty explaining why the 160-acre utopia was no economic solution for the ills of society, and demolishing Kriege's Communist pretensions. But we must pay special attention to the political attitude they recommended toward the National Reformers and the Free Soil movement that put forward this very un-Communist program. First this:

> We fully recognize the historical justification of the movement of the American National Reformers. We know that this movement aims at a state of affairs that right now would, to be sure, promote the industrialization of modern bourgeois society, but must drive onward to communism through its own consequences, as a result of a proletarian movement, as an attack on property in general, and in particular under the conditions presently existing in America.[43]

This was "the positive content of the movement"—of the American agrarian movement, not Kriege's—and Marx was for taking full account of this positive side:

> If Kriege had conceived of the Free Soil movement as an initial form of the proletarian movement which was necessary under specific conditions, as a movement which must necessarily develop into a communist movement because of the conditions of life of the class from which it stems; if he had shown how the communist tendencies in America had to make their appearance at the beginning in this agrarian form which is apparently in contradiction with all communism, then there would have been nothing to say against it.[44]

But, continue Marx and Engels, Kriege did not take this flexible political attitude toward the mass movement while criticizing the formal programmatic aim it set; instead of considering it as an elementary and subordinate form of a proletarian movement, "he presents it as the highest, the ultimate goal of any movement in general, and thereby transforms the actual aim of the movement into sheer extravagant

---

returning to Germany in 1848, where he played the role of an anti-working-class bourgeois liberal in the Democratic movement, he came back to the United States, went insane before dying on the last day of 1850, and was buried wrapped in an American flag in accordance with his wish. By 1849 even Weitling had repudiated his former disciple.[42]

nonsense." Indeed, Kriege adopted the peasant mentality, hailing the 160-acre homestead as the fulfillment at long last of the "old dreams of Europeans."

> Which Europeans are these, then [replied Marx and Engels], whose "dreams" are here fulfilled? Not the communist workers, but rather the bankrupt shopkeepers and artisans or ruined cotters who aspire to the good fortune of again becoming petty-bourgeois and peasants. And what kind of "desire" is this that is to be attained by means of the 1400 million acres? None other than transforming *everybody into private-property owners*—a desire which is just as feasible and just as communist as transforming everybody into emperors, kings and popes.[45]

We observe, then, that without supporting the program of the land reform movement, Marx counseled a sympathetic approach to collaboration with it or in it, rather than simple negation—critical participation designed not to reinforce the illusions of the movement but to lead it in another direction as soon as it could be weaned away from those illusions.* Later on, of course, the illusions became even less tenable: in the *Grundrisse* notebooks Marx remarked that in the United States the possibility of a worker's accumulating enough to become, say, a tenant-farmer "is already now coming to an end."[47] But even in peasantless America, Marx looked to the land-tillers as allies; in 1877, for example, he was expecting that, under President Hayes, "the great expropriations of land (exactly of the fertile land) will turn the farmers of the West, who are already grumbling very loudly, into allied troops of the workers."[48] However, farmer-labor alliances in America were going to be a special problem for a long time.

---

* Less than two years later, the *Communist Manifesto* had a very general reference to this movement: "In accordance with Section II, the relations of the Communists to the existing working-class parties are self-evident, hence their relations to the Chartists in England and the Agrarian Reformers in North America."[46] Presumably this refers to the first sentences of Section II, which state that "The Communists do not form a separate party opposed to other working-class parties," and so on.

5. FLEXIBILITY: IN ENGLAND

In England, a problem similar to that of the American agrarian reformers was raised by the "Land Plan" advocated by the Chartist leader Feargus O'Connor, who openly said that "Peasant proprietorship is the best basis of society."[49] Engels first mentioned the issue as follows:

> About two years ago [1845] the Chartist workers founded an association whose aim is to buy up landed property and distribute it among its members in small farms. The hope is in this way to lessen the excessive competition among the factory workers by removing a part of the workers from the labor market, to form a class of small peasants, wholly new and essentially democratic.[50]

That put the best face on it. The left Chartists, such as Harney and Ernest Jonès (who were also closest to Marx and Engels), naturally took a dim view of the plan. Its sponsor, O'Connor, was not only the most prestigious leader of the movement but had also involved most of the Chartist executive in his National Land Company operation; therefore open opposition to the scheme was a delicate matter, capable of splitting the movement. Moreover, O'Connor himself was just then being made the butt of virulent attack and slander by the bourgeois world. Even Karl Schapper, then Marx's and Engels' associate in the Communist League, may have been caught up in the agrarian plan. (According to Schoyen: "the *Deutsche Londoner Zeitung,* in which Schapper's influence was dominant, was unrestrained in its praise of the scheme."[51])

The above-quoted article on the land plan, which Engels wrote for the French press in 1847, was tactful, postponing a direct critique for "a more detailed account later," but it clearly took the same line as in the Kriege case of the preceding year. The Chartist land society, wrote Engels,

> has assumed such dimensions that it is already beginning to disturb the landed aristocracy; for it is clear that this movement, if it continues to grow in the same proportion as it has up to now, will end by being transformed into national agitation for the people's taking possession of the national soil.

This is the programmatic crux of the article, making clear that the movement had a future only insofar as it adopted land nationalization as its goal, rather than the chimerical aim for which O'Connor had founded it. Meanwhile, Engels wrote, it was of significance as a class-struggle movement:

> The bourgeoisie does not like this society; it sees it as a lever in the hands of the people that will let them emancipate themselves without needing the help of the middle class. It is particularly the more or less liberal petty-bourgeoisie which glowers balefully at the land society, because it already finds the Chartists much more independent of its support than before the founding of the association.[52]

The rest of the article is devoted to a defense of O'Connor against the campaign of personal attack and slander that was rife in the bourgeois press.*

A couple of weeks later, writing to Marx from Paris, Engels referred less diplomatically to O'Connor's "nonsense."[54] In the single issue of the *Kommunistische Zeitschrift* of the Communist League, which came out in September, a note (probably written by Wilhelm Wolff, not Engels) gave the land scheme a brief treatment similar to Engels', being a combination of pat and slap: "the sympathy it [the plan] meets with shows that the people earnestly want the liberation of the soil. Unfortunately O'Connor's plan is based on the division of goods and not the community of goods."[55] Here, too, more is promised on the subject later. In any case, the Land Plan collapsed the following July. But O'Connor continued to push the aim, and in 1850 Marx and Engels published a last comment for its obituary:

> The main point of conflict between the two Chartist wings is the land question. O'Connor and his tendency would like to use the Charter to dispose part of the workers on small pieces of land and in the end make land parcellization the general pattern in England. We know how he tried and failed to establish such parcellization on a small scale through a joint-stock company. The tendency of every bourgeois revolution to break up large-scale landownership could make this parcellization look for a while like something revolutionary in the eyes of the English

---

* A few days before writing this article, Engels had written Marx in admiration of O'Connor's command of vituperative language in replying to press attacks: "a masterpiece of brilliant vituperation, often better than Cobbett and approaching Shakespeare."[53] There could be no higher literary praise. But this letter did not discuss the land plan.

workers, although it is followed up as a rule by the unfailing tendency of the small property to get concentrated and be ruined in the face of big-scale agriculture. The revolutionary wing of the Chartists is against this demand for parcellization, counterposing the demand for the confiscation of all landed property, and demands that it not be divided but remain national property.[56]

In these two cases—Kriege in America and O'Connor in England—there were different circumstances, but the main approach was common: the decisive criterion for Marx and Engels was that there was a real mass movement of class struggle going on behind the chimerical banner of Every Man a Peasant, and therefore it was the duty of the Communists to help this movement find its real program, not turn their backs on it.[57]

Another aspect of this problem was raised in Germany by the line of the *Neue Rheinische Zeitung* group during the 1848-1849 revolution; this is already suggested by the account given in the preceding chapter. There we saw that the *N.R.Z.*'s main thrust on the peasant question was the campaign against any indemnification of the landowners and for the complete liberation of the peasantry from all feudal obligations without any payments whatever. This meant making it as easy as possible for the peasant to get ownership and control of the land worked, even in a small parcel, and thus to become a completely free small-holder.*

---

* This was all that was left of a view that both Marx and Engels had held *before* becoming socialists, namely, the then-general liberal view that the peasantry should be entirely free of controls in selling and acquiring parcels of land. The issue came up because the Prussian government, eager to preserve a strong peasantry as a base for itself against bourgeois influence, wanted to set a legal limit on parcellization of land, and the liberal bourgeoisie energetically opposed this in the name of economic liberty. As editor of the *Rheinische Zeitung* Marx planned to discuss this question in an article, which was never written; but his opinion was indicated briefly in his 1843 study of the Moselle peasants' plight.[58] The related question of primogeniture was discussed the following summer in Marx's manuscript critique of Hegel's philosophy of right, on the same liberal basis.[59] The young Engels' opinion was given in 1841 in an article criticizing E. M. Arndt, who was "opposed to the unlimited freedom and divisibility of the land; he sees as its inevitable result the parcellization of land into pieces too small to provide a living." Engels here upheld complete "freedom of the soil" as a guard against the two extremes of concentration and splintering, even though it might mean constant fluctuation, for "I prefer the surging ocean with its grand freedom to the narrow inland lake with its peaceful surface whose tiny ripples are broken every three yards by a spit of land, tree root, or rock."[60] He was to discover that there were phenomena other than oceans and lakes.

This would have meant strengthening the small peasantry—as against the landowners' regime. Marx had no inhibitions against such a strengthening of the peasantry. The distinctive feature of his policy was that it permitted the following combinations: (1) complete support to and stimulation of the revolutionary potential of the peasantry as against the old ruling class, represented by the absolutist government and the aristocracy; and (2) *no* commitment to the peasantry to preserve their small-holding economy against the erosive pressures of modern society, that is, of industrializing capitalism. Thus Marx steered a course between the ever-present Scylla and Charybdis on the question of indemnification: he rejected, on the one hand, a negative attitude based on the principle one must do nothing to strengthen the class of small-holding peasants, that is, on sectarian grounds; and on the other hand he avoided the attractive course of currying peasant favor by identifying with the small-property aspirations of the peasants, that is, the opportunist course.

6. LAND TO THE PEASANTS: ITALY

If we leave the more highly industrialized or industrializing countries of Western Europe and America, and go only as far as Italy, we find Marx's approach making a thoroughgoing adaptation. The watchword of "Land to the peasants" enters the realm of revolutionary socialist policy.

Italy was still overwhelmingly peasant in population, with next to nothing of a modern proletariat: this has already been emphasized with respect to the problem of revolutionary alliances.[61] By the same token,

> The emancipation of the Italian peasant will not take place in the same form as that of the English factory worker; but the more both of them understand the form proper to their situation the more they will come to an understanding in substance.[62]

This was clear enough in 1872, when Engels wrote it. What were appropriate forms for Italy?

Already two decades before, Marx was advocating a peasant-centered land program for Italy. The question came up in the Italian republican emigration in London, as it split over Mazzini's policy of orienting toward the support of the upper classes rather than of the peasant masses. Marx strongly aligned himself with the opponents of Mazzini.[63]

> I consider Mazzini's policy fundamentally wrong. . . . [H]e fails to appeal to the part of Italy oppressed for centuries, the peasants, and thus he prepares new resources for the counter-revolution. Mr. Mazzini knows only the cities with their liberal aristocracy and their *citoyens éclairés* [enlightened citizens]. The material needs of the Italian country people—who are bled as white and are as systematically enervated and stultified as the Irish—are of course beneath notice for the pie-in-the-sky phrases of his cosmopolitan–neo-Catholic–idealist manifestoes. But, to be sure, it would have taken courage to tell the bourgeoisie and the aristocracy that the first step toward making Italy independent is the complete emancipation of the peasants and the transformation of their sharecropping system into free bourgeois property.[64]

Land to the peasants as their "free bourgeois property" was, for Marx, the precondition for mobilizing these peasants on behalf of revolution from below; and this was the crucial goal.* Two days later, he repeated the same view in a letter to Engels, supporting Mazzini's opponents.

> . . . they insist on a direct appeal to the material interests of the Italian peasants, which cannot be made without attacking on the other side the material interests of the bourgeoisie and liberal nobility, who form the great Mazzinist phalanx. This last point is exceedingly important. If Mazzini or anyone else who puts himself at the head of the Italian agitation does not this time openly and immediately transform the peasants from *métayers* [sharecroppers] into free landowners (the position of the Italian peasants is appalling; I have now waded right through the filthy story) the Austrian government will, in case of revolution, take refuge in Galician methods.[66]

Engels replied that "It is fortunate that a country which instead of proletarians has almost nothing but *lazzaroni* [lumpen-elements] does

---

* As indicated also by the continuation of this passage: "Mazzini seems to regard a loan of ten million francs as more revolutionary than winning over ten million people. I am very much afraid that if worse comes to worst, the Austrian government *itself* will change the property system in Italy and reform it in the 'Galician' way."[65] The "Galician" reference is to Austria's manipulation, in 1846 and 1848, of Galician peasant hostility to landlordism as a stick to beat the Polish nationalist movement, thus playing class and national antagonisms against each other—after which the peasants themselves were suppressed or swindled in reward for their services to reaction.

at least possess *métayers.*"[67] In a *New York Tribune* article, Marx, criticizing the Mazzinians for failing "to seriously occupy themselves with the material condition of the Italian country population, if they expect to find an echo" to their slogans, promised to write a special article on the question: "I intend to dwell on the material circumstances in which by far the greater portion of the rural inhabitants of that country are placed, and which have made them till now, if not reactionary, at least indifferent to the national struggle of Italy."[68] He did not get around to writing this article, which evidently would have demonstrated that a serious orientation toward appealing to peasant interests was necessary to the success of the national liberation struggle which Mazzini was botching.

It was, then, no new departure when, about four decades later, Engels repeated the same advice to an Italian comrade. Antonio Labriola had written an article advocating the distribution of untilled land (*terra libera*) in Eritrea to Italian peasants. Engels agreed:

> As far as his *terra libera* is concerned, it is indeed the highest demand that one could make of the present Italian government, that it distribute the landed property to small peasants for cultivation by themselves, and not to the monopolists, individuals or companies, in the colonies. The small-peasant economy is the natural and best condition for the colonies established today by the bourgeois governments—on this, cf. Marx's *Capital*, Vol. 1, last chapter, "The Modern Theory of Colonization."* We socialists can therefore in good conscience support the introduction of the small-peasant economy in already established colonies. But whether this will be carried out is another matter. All present-day governments are sold to and under the yoke of the financiers and stock-exchange to too great an extent to expect that the financial speculators will refrain from seizing the colonies for their own exploitation. But one can fight against this, even in the form of demanding that the government guarantee the same advantages to the Italian peasants emigrating there that they seek and largely find in Buenos Aires.[70]

* There are two different senses of *colony* involved in this passage. In the mentioned chapter of *Capital*, Marx deals with "real Colonies, virgin soils, colonized by free immigrants," and in this sense "The United States are, speaking economically, still only a Colony of Europe."[69] In this sense *colony* means an offshoot settlement, as in "utopian socialist colony." But Eritrea had just been established as a political colony of Italy's. The proposal, then, was about establishing one kind of colony inside another: colonies of Italian peasants (settlements) inside the colonial territory of Eritrea.

The proposal, then, Engels felt, would collide with the opposition of finance capital. This meant that, on the basis of a socialist demand for the distribution of available land for small peasant cultivation, the peasantry could be set into motion against the centers of capitalist power in Italy.

Ireland, too, was geographically part of Western Europe, but, in terms of social development, leagues behind the capitalistically advanced countries. As we saw in the preceding chapter, what was on the order of the day was an agrarian revolution with an aim "concentrated exclusively on landed property," [71] but with an international impact that would be massively anticapitalist. This combination was decisive for Marx. There was no question but that at home the drive-wheel of the Irish revolution was the peasants' aspiration to own the land they tilled. Marx energetically supported this Irish movement and its basic land demands as well as the fight for national independence, even while he was critical of its methods, such as conspiratorial terrorism; and under his guidance the International agitated in this spirit.

This attitude was spelled out by Engels in response to an interviewer's question, when he landed in New York on a visit to America in 1888. The interviewer was an old comrade, Theodor Cuno, representing the *New Yorker Volkszeitung.* Because of Americans' intense interest in the Irish struggle, Engels was asked about the position of socialism in Ireland, and he answered:

> A purely socialist movement should not be expected from Ireland for some time. The people first want to become small landowning peasants, and when they do, the mortgages will come along and ruin them once again. In the meantime there is no reason why we should not help them to liberate themselves from the landlords, that is, to change over from a semifeudal to a capitalistic condition. [72]

This struck the two complementary notes: we support these peasants with *their* programmatic demand, but we openly warn them that they will find this program untenable after their victory.

7. LAND TO THE PEASANTS:
EASTERN EUROPE

When we come to Eastern Europe, Marx's advocacy of the program-matic demand summarized by the later slogan "Land to the peasants" becomes heavily stressed. We find this true most often with reference to Poland, because of his frequent involvement with support of Polish national-revolutionary movements. But the position applied far more widely to the peasant countries of the Slavic east.

Marx and Engels first gave public utterance to this programmatic view on Poland at a London meeting commemorating the Cracow uprising of 1846, held (as it happened) on the same day that the February revolution of 1848 was exploding on the other side of the Channel. The *Communist Manifesto* was coming off the press that same week, with its statement of support to the Polish revolutionary tendency "that insists on an agrarian revolution as the prime condition for national emancipation."[73] What would an agrarian revolution mean in Poland?

At the commemoration meeting, Marx's speech stressed that it was a question of a social revolution in Poland, not merely a political one. But was the Cracow revolution "communist," as has been claimed, asked Marx, just "because it tried to break the chains of feudalism, to liberate tributary property and transform it into free property, into modern property?" No, it was not communist, but nevertheless it aimed at a great social overturn.

> The men who were at the head of the Cracow revolutionary movement had the deep conviction that only a democratic Poland could be independent, and a Polish democracy was impossible without the abolition of feudal rights, without the agrarian move-ment which would transform the tribute-paying peasants into free property-owners, into modern property-owners. Put Polish aristo-crats in the place of the Russian autocrat and you will have conferred naturalization papers on despotism.[74]

This transformation of the peasants into owners of the land they tilled was the economic content of the social overturn to come, and it was intertwined with the democratic and liberatory character of the Cracow movement: "The Cracow revolution has given a glorious example to all of Europe by identifying the cause of the nation with the cause of democracy and the liberation of the oppressed class." Marx pointed to the close analogy with Ireland. This revolution, he said, "finds the confirmation of its principles in Ireland, where the narrowly national [i.e., nationalist] party has been buried with O'Connell and the new national party is above all reformatory and democratic." [75]

Reformatory and democratic: for land reform (land to the peasants) and the overthrow of the autocracy—this was the social-revolutionary side of the national revolution.

Engels' speech at the meeting stressed that the 1846 Cracow uprising was fundamentally different from the Warsaw revolt of 1830. In 1830 the Polish aristocracy had excluded three-quarters of the nation from the revolution: "They left intact the brutalizing servitude of the peasants and the infamous condition of the Jews." They rejected Lelewel's effort to unite the national cause with the cause of liberty "by emancipating the Jews and peasants, by having the peasants participate in the ownership of the soil, by reconstructing Poland on the basis of democracy and equality." In contrast, in the Cracow uprising the revolutionists "attacked three powers at the same time; they proclaimed the freedom of the peasants, agrarian reform, the emancipation of the Jews, without for a moment worrying whether that might offend this or that aristocratic interest." [76]

The following characteristic of Marx's and Engels' approach cannot be overemphasized: the land issue (land to the peasants, to begin with) was weighed not simply as an element in a certain agrarian program, but as an inextricable part of an international struggle for the overthrow of autocracy in Eastern Europe and the democratization of the social system.

Less than two months later, Marx and Engels were in Cologne. Throughout the revolution, the question of Poland was alive in Germany, for Prussia held a part of Poland alongside its partition partners, Russia and Austria. The Frankfurt assembly kept debating policy, and the *Neue Rheinische Zeitung* kept denouncing it for holding on to Polish territory. Most important was a series of articles by Engels published in August and September of 1848, in which he dotted a number of *i*'s.

The Poles, wrote Engels, understand that their national independence is inseparable "from the overthrow of the aristocracy and agrarian reform internally." He spelled this out for all of East Europe:

> The big agricultural lands between the Baltic and the Black Sea can escape from patriarchal-feudal barbarism only through an

agrarian revolution which transforms the enserfed or corvée-burdened peasants into free landowners, a revolution which is altogether the same as the French Revolution in the countryside. The Polish nation has the merit of being the first to proclaim this, among all the neighboring agricultural peoples. . . . And especially since the Cracow uprising of 1846, the struggle for the independence of Poland has at the same time been the struggle for *agrarian democracy*—the only one possible in East Europe—against patriarchal-feudal absolutism.[77]

The social content of "agrarian democracy" was the free ownership of his land by the peasant. "Wherein," asked Engels, "lies the inexorable and iron necessity for Poland to regain its freedom?" In the fact that aristocratic rule is obsolete, and also

in the fact that the establishment of agrarian democracy for Poland has become a vital question not only politically but also socially; in the fact that the Polish people's source of existence, agriculture, is headed for ruin if the peasant who is enserfed or liable for labor-service does not become a free landowner . . .

Therefore the Poland of the aristocracy must be replaced by "the Poland of the *peasant* democracy."[78]

The position applies to all Slavdom: Engels repeats this with marked emphasis. "The merit of the Poles," he reiterates toward the end of the series, "lies in the fact that they were the first to recognize and popularize agrarian democracy as the sole possible form of liberation for all Slavic nations . . ."[79]

A quarter century later, there was another occasion when Engels spelled out the agrarian content of the Polish revolution. A group of Polish revolutionary émigrés in London had issued an "Address to the English People," on the occasion of the czar's visit to England in 1874; Engels wrote it up for the German party press. He begins with extensive and approving quotations from the Polish address; one of the passages recalled that the Cracow manifesto proclaimed "the proposition that *the peasants should become owners of the soil* which they have cultivated for centuries." Further on, Engels emphasizes that the great merit of the Polish revolutionary movements of 1846 and 1863 was this:

These movements were not only national[ist]; they were simultaneously aimed directly toward the liberation of the peasants and the transference of landed property to the latter. In 1871 the great mass of the Polish emigration in France entered the service of the Commune . . . Doesn't this prove that these Poles stand altogether abreast of the modern movement?[80]

Once again, then, a double emphasis, especially for an audience that looked on the Polish movement as a matter of nationalism only: national liberation meant social revolution at home (land to the peasants) and stimulation of revolution on the international scale. It follows that the simple peasant demand must be assessed in terms larger than the agrarian question itself.

The national-liberation element was not a necessity for this complex of agrarian revolution and international social revolution; it was an added source of dynamism in Poland. It was not present, of course, in the Russian case. Just as Marx and Engels discussed this programmatic demand only in connection with live revolutionary movements in Poland, so also they did *not* discuss it specifically for Russia, where there was as yet no movement to raise it.

As far as its application to Russia was concerned, the only element of dubiety for a while was the Populist claim that the Russian peasant had a special affinity for communistic organization because of the village-commune (artel) tradition. Marx was usually willing to leave open the question whether the Russian peasantry might go directly from the artel to socialized agriculture, in the context of a general social revolution. Even so, in 1881, as he tried to draft a letter to Zasulich on the possibility of the direct transition, we can see the "Land to the peasants" idea in his line of thought.*

---

* The passage in question takes off from the thought that the commune can become "the *direct starting point* of the economic system toward which modern society is tending," because the peasant's familiarity with it would facilitate the transition. Then Marx adds: "An altogether archaic peculiarity . . . likewise works in the same direction."[81] This archaic peculiarity is the fact that land areas of different fertility were each divided into individual holdings in order to equalize the yield for everyone. In the passage that follows, the bracketed italics show strike-outs in the manuscript:

> This arrangement, maintained by the Russian commune to the present day, is contrary to agronomic requirements [*both in collective cultivation and in individual private cultivation*]. Aside from other disadvantages, it necessarily causes a dissipation of energy and time. [*But as starting point of collective cultivation, there are great advantages. Round out the working area of the peasant and he will reign in it as master.*] Nevertheless, it favors [*as a starting point*] the transition to collective cultivation, to which at first blush it seems so contrary. The parcel [Here the manuscript breaks off].[82]

But by the 1890s Engels, like the nascent group of Russian Marxists, cast the Populist claim aside entirely, as outlived. More than ever, the "struggle for agrarian democracy, against patriarchal-feudal absolutism" was "the only one possible in East Europe."[83]

8. IMMEDIATE PROGRAMS

Let us now turn back from peasant countries (countries with a peasant majority) to Western Europe, particularly France and Germany, above all because here Engels, near the end of his life, had to deal with the peasant question in a context that was vital to the future of the socialist movement.

This peasant question asked: *How do we socialists get the support of the peasantry now*—right now, this minute? In 1848 and 1871 Marx and Engels had to deal with this question in the midst of a revolutionary situation; in 1894 Engels had to deal with it for quite different reasons.

The first special peasant program drawn up by Marx and Engels figured as part of the "Demands of the Communist Party of Germany" in March 1848; it was described in Chapter 13. Put together on the basis of little previous experience right after the outbreak of the revolution, it was directed to an existing revolutionary situation—unlike most peasant programs. As we saw, one of its points (no indemnification for the abolition of feudal burdens) turned out to be the mainspring of peasant activity in 1848–1849.

The second time Marx worked out something like a detailed program of peasant demands was also designed for a revolutionary situation, this time *ex post facto*. In *The Civil War in France* Marx devoted a section to discussing what the Paris Commune should have done, or might have done, to gain peasant support, and what this would have meant for the revolution; it is an informal programmatic presentation, derived in part

---

At this point Marx either had to explain a complicated idea or else give up the whole exposition, and he chose the latter. The key difficulty was that making the peasant "master" of a "rounded out" plot of his own pointed away from the *direct* transition to collective cultivation; it pointed to an indirect transition that was contrary to the Populist hope and to the very assumption Marx had started with in this letter. It pointed in the direction of *Land to the peasants.*

from his reading of the Commune press and in part from his own judgment and experience. This section is longer in Marx's first draft of the Address than in the very much condensed version that was published in the name of the International.

Following this draft, here is a summary of the way in which, Marx argues, the peasant will benefit from the victory of the Commune, why the Commune "represents above all the interest of the *French peasantry.*"

1. The Commune will save the peasant from the burden of paying for the cost of the war, particularly the heavy indemnity to be paid the Prussians; it will make "the authors of the war"—the bourgeois, the rich landowners, and their state agents—do the paying.

2. The Commune will abolish conscription, the "blood-tax on the peasant"; for peasant sons were the main source of cannon-fodder.

3. It will provide cheaper government, rather than heavier taxes "for the payment of a parasitical and costly state-machinery."

4. It "will free him of the incubus of the mortgages," whereas the bourgeoisie will continue to "grind down" the peasant through the usurer.

5. It will abolish the bureaucratic legal apparatus ("the parasitical judiciary body") which gets rich from milking the peasant—"the notary, the huissier [bailiff], etc." Since Commune officials will get only "workmen's salaries," "it will break down this whole judiciary cobweb which entangles the French peasant." (The published Address summed it up this way: The Commune "would have ... transformed his present blood-suckers, the notary, advocate [lawyer], executor, and other judicial vampires, into salaried communal agents, elected by, and responsible to, himself.")

6. The bourgeoisie will keep the peasant "under the rule of the gendarme, the Commune will restore him to independent, social and political life."

7. The Commune would confer enlightenment by the schoolteacher; the bourgeoisie, "stultification by the rule of the priest." Priests would be paid by voluntary contributions only, not by state taxes.[84]

At this point there is a noteworthy difference between the draft and the published Address. In the draft there follows a section presenting a socialist solution, looking to replace small-scale production with "associated" (socialized) production. This section is omitted in the Address (which, of course, was to be signed by the General Council). The program as it stands consists only of immediate benefits. It is only in a separate, preceding passage that Marx explains that the Commune "intended" to abolish capitalist property, and it is in this passage on the ultimate aims that he includes "transforming the means of production, land and capital" into instruments of "associated labor," that is, social ownership.[85]

As a result, the emphasis in the published Address is overwhelmingly on the immediate advantages the peasants would gain from the Commune. On the other hand, the draft is even more explicit in pledging no expropriation of the peasant. Here is the summary in the draft:

> °°If the Commune, as we have shown, is the only power that can give him [the peasant] immediate great loans [boons?] [86] even in its present economical conditions, it is the only form of government that can secure to him the transformation of his present economical conditions, rescue him from expropriation by the landlord on the one hand, save him from grinding, [d]rudging and misery on the pretext of proprietorship on the other, that can convert his nominal proprietorship of the land into real proprietorship of the fruits of his labour, that can combine for him the profits of modern agronomy, dictated by social wants and every day now encroaching upon him as a hostile agency, without annihilating his position as a really independent producer. Being immediately benefited by Communal Republic, he would soon confide in it [trust it] .[87]

This discussion of the possibilities of an appeal to the peasants by the Commune was, however, too much *ad hoc*—situation-linked and conjunctural—to be of general value as a guide. In this field as in many others, Marx and Engels preferred to address themselves to systematic analysis of a question only when a real political situation demanded it. This did not come about until the 1890s. But in 1874–1875 Marx at least had occasion to note the nature of the need, in the course of marginal comments on a polemic published by Bakunin. The latter, with his usual gay abandon to slander and his delightful disregard of the authoritarian demands of evidence, had charged that the "Marxists" want the proletariat to dominate the "common peasant folk," and therefore want the Germans to dominate the Slavs. The social revolution—Marx scribbled on the side—is "possible only where, along with capitalist production, the industrial proletariat occupies at least an important position among the mass of people." But if the proletariat itself is not yet a majority of the people, it must gain the support of allies:

> And in order for it to have any chance of victory at all, it must at least be able to do immediately as much for the peasants, *mutatis mutandis,* as the French bourgeoisie did in its own revolution for the French peasants of that time. What a nice idea, that labor rule involves oppression of rural labor![88]

The word *immediately,* here again, means: immediately on gaining power. More often, of course, *immediate demands* suggests demands raised for adoption by the present regime. The difference is by no means absolute: on the one hand, a revolutionary party would presumably carry out in power the demands it raises in opposition; on the other, peasants are afraid to trust socialists in the present because of their fear of future expropriation. In his 1894 essay on "The Peasant Question in France and Germany," Engels discussed the whole complex of immediate policy under these several questions:

> How is Social-Democracy to overcome this [peasant] prejudice? What can it offer to the doomed small peasant without becoming untrue to itself? . . .

> How was the peasant to be helped, not the peasant as a future proletarian but as a present propertied peasant, without violating the basic principles of the general socialist program? . . .

> What, then, is our attitude toward the small peasantry? How shall we have to deal with it on the day of our accession to power?[89]

In the 1890s these issues were raised sharply as a concrete *party* problem.

9. "THE PEASANT QUESTION IN FRANCE AND GERMANY"

The impulsion that led Engels to write "The Peasant Question" was the development especially in the French and German parties of what he considered an opportunist (reformist) tendency that was seriously compromising socialist principles in order to "catch the peasant."*

In France, the Marxist group, called the French Workers Party, was one of seven socialist groups at this time. Led by Jules Guesde and Paul Lafargue, it was making progress slowly. Lafargue and his wife Laura (Marx's daughter) kept in regular correspondence with Engels. In 1891 Lafargue won election to the Chamber of Deputies from the Lille area, making a first for the party. Given the majority mass of the rural population, further party progress meant extending socialist propaganda and organization to the countryside. In 1892 the party's first agrarian program was adopted at its Marseilles congress; this program dealt mainly with the interests of the agricultural laborers, tenants, and sharecroppers, and seemed to be effective in gaining rural support.

Then in 1893 Lafargue was defeated for reelection. He wrote Engels: "I had a majority in the town of Lille, it was the votes of the sixteen rural areas which gave my opponent the majority."[92] In October he reported to Engels that "The winning of the rural areas is the Socialists' main objective, even though the towns are far from being won," and that additions to the party's agrarian program were being prepared for

> the next congress, which will be specially devoted to the agrarian question and will be held at Nantes, in the heart of the Chouan country [center of peasant counterrevolution in 1793], where the Republic is still not accepted, but where rural socialism is making headway ... The Nantes Socialists, who have a rich ship-owner, Brunellière, at their head, have organized the peasants in unions which centralize and coordinate their efforts; so far they have succeeded in deferring the expropriation of the peasants.[93]

It was the big landowners who were trying to get the small peasants off the land. The peasant "unions" were peasant organizations formed to preserve the small holdings.

---

* The summary of the party situation given in this section is based mainly on Engels' letters, the letters of the Lafargues to Engels, and a number of special studies published in recent years.[90] —*Opportunist* and *reformist* are, of course, not synonymous. An adequate definition of *opportunist* is implied by Engels' reproof to Lafargue on the peasant question: "you allowed yourself to lean a bit too much towards the opportunist tendency. At Nantes [the party congress] you came near to sacrificing the future of the party to a momentary triumph."[91] *Opportunist* is defined by this relationship between momentary gains and future (continuing, permanent) interests; *reformist* describes a political position or ideology.

In September 1894 the party congress at Nantes did adopt an expanded agrarian program which was obviously designed to make a new type of appeal to the small-holding peasantry and even to bigger landholders employing farm laborers. This is the Nantes program discussed below.

There was no doubt in Engels' mind that the decisive motivation was simply "vote-catching" for electoral success. The party "did such good business" among peasants with the Marseilles planks that, "since appetite comes with eating," it was moved to increase its wares.[94] After talking to a leading party writer and Guesde adviser,[95] Engels wrote to Laura: "He really believed that it was not only possible but necessary to gain over the mass of the French peasants to socialism between now and the next general .elections."[96] The ensuing years, especially up to 1898, were to show that this was not simply an aberration on the peasant question but rather the first big manifestation of the devolution of the party toward parliamentary reformism.[97]

A similar development was taking place in the German party, with a difference. While in France the entire party leadership was moving in this direction with some circumspection, in Germany a cruder form of opportunist peasant-catching had been adopted by one wing, which however constituted the leadership of the party in South Germany, especially Bavaria. The leader of this tendency, Georg von Vollmar, whose bailiwick was Upper Bavaria, was the real founder of the reformist movement in the German Social-Democracy. (Eduard Bernstein came along a little later to provide a theoretical rationale for the process.)

Thus in Germany, too, the process of parliamentary degeneration in the party broke out first on the peasant question, and for essentially the same reason: the need to win a mass source of votes for immediate electoral success. Unlike the French, however, Vollmar very quickly extended his theoretical views from the special question of the agrarian program to advocating the general transformation of socialism into a movement of gradualist social reform.

The German leader, Bebel,

> complains with reason [wrote Engels] that the party is going bourgeois. That is the misfortune of all extreme parties when the time approaches for them to become "possible." But our party cannot go beyond a certain limit in this respect without betraying itself, and it seems to me that in France as in Germany we have

now reached that point. Fortunately there is still time to call a halt.[98]

Calling a halt became even more imperative when the German party congress met at Frankfurt in October 1894, a month after Nantes. Vollmar not only came out more boldly for a reformist peasant policy but also publicly stated—falsely—that Engels himself had expressly approved the French decisions at Nantes. This news was repeated in the bourgeois press. Engels then felt compelled to come out with a public criticism of the new peasant-catching opportunism on both sides of the Rhine—reluctantly, because of the burden of working on his own and Marx's writings. (He also had less than a year to live, as it turned out.)

First he published a letter in the party organ repudiating Vollmar's false statement. Since this letter offers a brief preview of two of the issues, we quote it here. Engels related that he had sent only two comments on the Nantes program to French comrades. There was one before the congress, which he summarizes as follows:

The development of capitalism irretrievably destroys small-peasant landownership. Our party is entirely clear on that, but it has absolutely no reason to hasten this process still more by its own intervention. In principle one can take no exception to correctly selected measures which would make the inevitable ruin of the small peasants less painful; if you go further than that, if you want to sustain the small peasant permanently, then in my opinion you are trying to do what is economically impossible, sacrificing principle, and becoming reactionary.

The second [communication], *after* the congress, limited itself to expressing my surmise that our French friends would remain alone in the socialist world in their attempt to perpetuate not only the small-peasant property-owners but also the small farmers who exploit others' labor.[99]

Before the month was up, Engels had written "The Peasant Question in France and Germany," and it was published in the party theoretical journal. We have already quoted extensively from this essay on a number of questions discussed up to this point. It was the last word on the view of the peasant question which Marx and Engels had been developing over a span of a half century.

10. PROGRAMMATIC ISSUES:
PRINCIPLE AND PRACTICALITY

Engels wholeheartedly accepts the immediacy of the peasant problem. He rejects the approach that sees the political problem solved by the predicted decline of the small peasantry and its proletarianization:

> The greater the number of peasants whom we can save from being actually hurled down into the proletariat, whom we can win to our side while they are still peasants, the more quickly and easily the social transformation will be accomplished.

For then the party will have the support of at least a cadre of peasant revolutionists who will facilitate the social revolution on the land. And—

> It will serve us nought to wait with this transformation until capitalist production has developed everywhere to its utmost consequences, until the last small handicraftsman and the last small peasant have fallen victim to capitalist large-scale production.[100]

Rather, whatever expenditure of effort is devoted to easing the peasants' lot, and easing them into a relationship of confidence, is "an excellent investment because it will effect a perhaps tenfold saving in the cost of the social reorganization in general. In this sense we can, therefore, afford to deal very liberally with the peasants."

This rejects, also, two other approaches that were known to the socialist movement: the crudely sectarian approach ("The business of revolutionists is to advocate revolution and nothing else") and *ouvriérisme* or proletarianism ("the business of a proletarian movement is to be concerned only with proletarians"). But outside of such infantile-leftist tendencies, the mainstream of the socialist movement was certainly in favor of winning the rural population. *Winning whom to what, how, at what cost?*

The political differences involved will be exhibited through a discussion of eight questions, taken within the framework of the peasant question. But we must keep in mind that this problem complex arose at this time as proxy for a general trend to parliamentary reformism. In more than one area, the increasingly conscious reformist wing was overlaying questions of principle with its own favorite problem-posing approach: (1) How can our party be practical, realistic, and above all successful in winning elections, instead of visionary, utopian, romantic, and above all small? (2) In line with this high aspiration, what really attractive measures can we propose to the peasants that will achieve the aims *they* want to vote for? The latter measures were termed *practical.* In reading Engels' "Peasant Question," one must understand that there is often an undercurrent of polemic on the meaning of practical politics, that is, opportunist adaptation to short-term gains. If the reformists plumed themselves on their sober practicality, Engels was often intent on stressing that the reformist planks, while practically giving up socialist principles, had no really practical and lasting solution for the rescue of a peasantry struggling to stay afloat in a sea of capitalism and mortgages.

Here then are critical issues raised in "The Peasant Question."

1. *What exactly do you wish to convince the peasant to do?*

One or another peasant might be persuaded to (a) join the socialist party; (b) vote for its candidates; (c) at least carry on a militant fight against the government, preferably in alliance with the working-class movement; (d) move close enough to socialism so that, in a revolutionary situation, the upsurge would carry him over to the socialist side; (e) lose enough anti-socialist prejudice so that, in a revolutionary situation, he would at least be neutralized.

These different levels of achievement are basic to understanding the difference between Engels' approach and that of the reformists. For the reformists, the first two (a, b) are everything, the crux being the acquisition of peasant votes; the last two (d, e) are nothing; and there would be a sliding scale of interest in (c). For Engels, the decisive achievement is represented by the last two (d, e) in the sense that all efforts are fully justified even if these are the sole results. When peasant struggle (c) is stimulated in addition, the cup runneth over. The value of a cadre of supporters among the peasantry (a, b) could be great as a means of achieving the other goals. And finally: whereas the reformists regarded the amassment of peasant votes as requiring peasant party members to herd them to the polls, Engels regarded peasant membership in the party as a good only in a limited quantity—like starch in the diet. (We will come back to this.)

2. *To which peasants are you directing your appeal? Which sections of the rural population are you most interested in winning over?*

We saw Marx's and Engels' answer in Chapter 13.[101] First comes the rural proletariat—the wage-workers on the land—and then the small peasantry. But organizing the agricultural laborers means organizing them against their employers, who are often big and even middle peasants, not only big landowners. Therefore there is a basic question of priorities: the rural proletariat is most important to the socialist movement, most easily won, and so on. And there is the basic question of the class line of exploitation: productive labor versus exploiters of labor. Aside from unusual individuals as always, it is not possible for a revolutionary party to englobe both the classes that live by productive labor and also the classes that live by exploiting the latter. This combination literally injects the class struggle into the ranks of the party itself, and the difficulty cannot be conjured away by denying the existence of the class struggle philosophically.

At the Marseilles congress two years before Nantes, the French had adopted a program not only for small peasants but also for "property-less rural *workers*," Engels' article reminds. The demands started with "minimum wages fixed by trade unions and community councils," and went on.[102] Experience shows that it is often easier to win such demands from big capitalist interests than from little micro-employers who are scratching for sustenance themselves. In any case, such demands can be realized only in struggle against small employers as well as big landowners. Whom would the party take under its wing?

The problem was brought up not so much by the demands in the Nantes program as by the "theoretical preamble" to the program, and it is against the ideas in the preamble that Engels directs his primary attack. The role of the preamble was permissive; the French did not—as yet—overtly draw the logical conclusions from their generalities, but the South German reformists did.

The Nantes preamble came out for protecting not only the small peasants but also tenant farmers "who, if they exploit day-laborers, are to a certain extent compelled to do so because of the exploitation to which they themselves are subjected."[103] It is the typical viewpoint of the petty-bourgeois small producer or shopkeeper: "Please don't object if I have to exploit you, because look at all the troubles *I* have!" If harassed employers are "compelled" to exploit their hands, they touch the fellow-feelings of reformists who are so eager to give employers protection against the vicissitudes of a society dominated by big capital; and if their laborers organized to better their conditions at the employers' expense, they would surely be showing a lamentable lack of practicality.

The Nantes preamble also proclaimed a principle which, if applied to the rest of society, would have scrapped socialism completely: the party's aim was "to bring together all the elements of rural production, all occupations which by virtue of various rights and titles utilize the national soil, to wage an identical struggle against the common foe: the feudality of landownership."[104] The principle is the solidarity of all rural classes, exploiters and exploited, against a common foe, and the common foe is not even capitalism on the land but rather the enemy of capitalism, the obsolescent remains of the precapitalist ruling class. A party that carried out such principles consistently could expect not only to catch a few peasants but also a few more rich ship-owners. As yet, the theoretical content of the preamble did not show up in the program—except for one plank.*

But in South Germany the Social-Democrats were acting it out in practical politics. They gave priority to winning over the bigger peasants, not the small working peasants and not the farm laborers. As Engels reported to a friend:

> . . . Vollmar comes along in Frankfurt [party congress of 1894] and wants to bribe the *peasantry as a whole,* though the peasant he has to deal with in Upper Bavaria is not the debt-ridden small peasant of the Rhineland, but the middle and even the big peasant, who exploits male and female farm-hands and sells cattle and grain in quantity. And that cannot be done without giving up the whole principle. We can win over the Alpine peasants and the Lower Saxon and Schleswig-Holstein big peasants only if we sacrifice the field-hands and day-laborers to them, and in doing that we lose more politically than we gain.[106]

And a little later:

> The Bavarians, who have become very, very opportunist, *and almost* are an ordinary People's Party (that is, most of the leaders and many of the new party recruits), had voted for the [govern-

---

* Engels points out that the program calls for tax relief not only for "all peasants living by their own labor" but also for others (hence employers of labor) if they are burdened by mortgages. This begins to act out the supraclass principles of the preamble, depending on the differentiation made.[105]

ment] budget as a whole in the Bavarian Diet; and in particular Vollmar had organized a peasant campaign to rope in the Upper Bavarian big-peasant crowd who own 25 to 80 acres of land (10 to 30 hectares) and who therefore *cannot get along at all without wage-laborers—but not their farm-hands.*[107]

The appellation "People's Party" is intended to recall the typical petty-bourgeois democratic party—the South German People's Party—which the socialists (especially Wilhelm Liebknecht) had clung to for so long before they were pushed to establish an independent socialist party in a break with it. It specialized in keeping a working-class wing in suspension under the domination of bourgeois reformers. Now the Bavarian reformists were repackaging the same combination under the label of a socialist party.

From Engels' standpoint, the dispute was not over practical ways of winning the peasant to socialism but over the class character and basic aim of the revolutionary party.

3. *Do you tell the peasants the truth (as you see it) about their position under capitalism, or do you entice them with the illusion that their small holding can really achieve prosperity under this system?*

Engels came down hardest not on the Nantes planks as such but on the deceptive claim with which they were offered.* If colored aspirin is sold as a cancer cure, it is no attack on aspirin to impeach the fraud; and if the patient is simultaneously informed that the illness is incurable, still another question arises. This is what the Nantes theoretical preamble did. In one sentence it stated flatly that "small-holding ownership is irretrievably doomed"—adding, with Engels' lively agreement, that "still it is not for socialism to hasten this doom" which is the work of capitalist forces. Yet in the next paragraph, after a confused *whereas*, it proclaims that it is the socialists' "imperative duty to maintain the peasants themselves tilling their patches of land in possession of the same as against the fisk, the usurer, and the encroachments of the newly arisen big landowners"—and this is even followed by the extension of the same protection to labor exploiters, as we have seen.[109]

---

* After reading Lafargue's report to the Nantes congress, which put the best theoretical face on the business, Engels wrote him that "although I do not agree with what the Nantes resolution said, I think I agree with what it tried to say."[108] This was a diplomatic approach. There was good reason for Engels to diplomatize, but we have the advantage of hindsight.

Engels' comment cuts to the heart of the attempt to give lip service to principles that are being gutted: "The preamble thus imposes upon socialism the imperative duty to carry out something which it had declared to be impossible in the preceding paragraph."[110] The contradiction was indubitable, but it could not remain a mere matter of muddle-headedness. Either the peasants' cancer cure was being advocated as cynical social demagogy (hence Engels' repeated statements in this article that this sort of thing should be left to the political anti-Semitic movement which specialized in it),[111] or else the theory would eventually be dropped as "outlived dogma" as soon as it had performed its function of soothing the party into accepting the opportunist practice.

While socialists have no interest in *hastening* the demise of the small peasant, argues Engels, they also cannot accept "the mission . . . to convert the present sham property of the small peasant in his fields into real property, that is to say, to convert the small tenant into an owner and the indebted owner into a debtless owner." This is not the way to gain "real freedom" for the peasant; it protects "only the particular form of his servitude; it prolongs a situation in which he can neither live nor die." Such planks may gain peasants' support with the desired speed but "only if we make them a promise which we ourselves know we shall not be able to keep," and "only to lose him again on the morrow if we cannot keep our promise." As bad as this would be in relation to the small peasant, "it would border on treason were we to promise the same to the big and middle peasants."[112]

At best the immediate demands offered on behalf of the small peasants in the Marseilles and Nantes agrarian programs could only be presented as palliatives, as measures to ease the suffering of the small producers as long as capitalism remained to oppress them—not as *solutions* leading to a permanently prosperous existence in the status quo. It was important for the socialists to put forward palliatives, for peasants as for proletarians; but insofar as the peasants insisted on a status-quo solution, they became the easy prey of reactionary social demagogues.

11. PROGRAMMATIC ISSUES:
SOME BOUNDARIES

The next group of issues concerns the context in which even the good demands were to be understood.

4. *Of the immediate reforms proposed, which ones are special peasant demands, and which are general socialist demands that also help the peasant, among others?*

The question serves to qualify the claim that the reformists (insofar as they do not abandon socialist principles) have unearthed some hitherto undiscovered practical ways to help the peasant. The application of certain *general* socialist demands to the plight of the peasant was already one of the positive features of the "Demands of the Communist Party of Germany" in 1848.

Tax reform is a typical example. The Nantes program proposed the substitution of a progressive income tax for direct and indirect taxes. Engels commented that almost every party's program had included this plank for years; but he argued that it could provide no solution to the peasants' problem.[113] Likewise with demands for free health services, and other proposals good in themselves.[114]

5. *Which of the "immediate" demands are really achievable under capitalism and which are not?*

This question, too, undercuts the claim that the reformist approach provides practical solutions for the peasant right now. The income tax plank applies here as well. Engels argues that if it is a question of raising the entire state budget by the income tax and abolishing all other taxes, "no government except a socialist one can undertake any such thing." The same argument is directed against the plank proposing tough laws against excessive interest (usury), "a police measure that has always failed everywhere for the last two thousand years."[115] For as long as the peasant has no alternative to the usurer, the law will be somehow circumvented, and insofar as it is not, then private capital ceases to be interested in giving peasants credit when they need it.

Unattainability under capitalism is, of course, not itself a reason for refraining from raising a demand. (It is possible that Engels' emphasis in this article might tend to give his readers a contrary impression.) Both Engels and Marx had often enough raised proposals that were "transitional" demands, the fight for them showing that capitalism could not satisfy the people's needs but that socialism could. The difference from the reformists' approach was not in the legitimacy of the demand but in the political context of the struggle for them; and this was precisely what was beclouded by the Nantes preamble.

6. *Which of the demands are of little consequence even as palliatives?*

This is the main sense of Engels' point against the Nantes plank on hunting and fishing rights for peasants. Practically speaking, the proceeds could not result in more than one day's catch.[116] Here again, this is not an argument against supporting such a peasant demand, but only against inflating it as a salvation of the peasantry, that is, not telling the truth.

Small-scale palliatives could have small-scale advantages that were by no means contemptible; concrete situations required investigation. In a quite different context, Engels once had occasion to write a Russian economist about such palliative measures for peasants:

> The petty palliative measures which, in Germany (as you have become convinced) and also elsewhere, have done precious little good might perhaps help the people get over the political crisis here and there in Russia and keep their [cottage domestic] industry going for a while until they themselves get to have a say in things.[117]

7. *Which demands, while helping the small peasant a little, mainly redound to the interests of the big landowner?*

This, of course, is a classic device: a measure is passed with fanfare on the plea of helping the poor while actually it chiefly benefits the ruling class. There is certainly no reason for socialists to lend their own name and cover to such a swindle, as they scratch around for peasant-catching planks. Engels points the finger at two points in the Nantes platform. One, which advocates lowering certain transportation charges for farm produce, "is on the whole in effect in Germany, and mainly in the interests—of the big landowners." Another, advocating government aid to soil improvement and technical progress in agriculture, "is also above all in the interest of the big landed estates."[118]

Naturally, the socialists should favor technological progress, but particular measures had to be examined to see how they were financed and for whose benefit; in any case it was a deception to treat such planks as an answer to the small peasants' plight.

With the eighth and last issue, we return to the area of basic principle in a very specific way.

8. *Which demands, insofar as they help peasants at all, do so only at the cost of socialist principles?*

An important case is alluded to only in passing in Engels' 1894 article; he had taken it up bluntly in a letter to Lafargue the previous March. The socialist deputy Jean Jaurès—casting about as usual for a means of saving the peasant from an admittedly inevitable doom—came up with a proposal to give the state a monopoly of grain importing, to keep prices up and prevent speculation. Other socialist deputies, including Guesde, supported this. Engels was appalled.

In the first place, Engels showed, the scheme in part had the effect of a protective tariff, "purely to the advantage of the big landowners into the bargain, since the small ones *have no grain to sell,* their produce not even sufficing for their own consumption." The Zurich social-reformists had been advocating this measure for years.[119] Even more revealing: a similar proposal for a state monopoly of grain importation was made in the Reichstag by the Prussian Junker, Count Kanitz: "This motion, made in the interest of the landed aristocracy of Eastern Germany, *is almost literally the proposition Jaurès* which was to show the way to the Socialist world how to use their parliamentary position in the interest of the working class and the peasantry."[120]

In the second place, the proposal was a gross example of *"State-socialism* which represents one of the *infantile diseases* of proletarian socialism," for application by a state dominated by the very speculators to be controlled.* This means that the same elements who enriched themselves from the Panama swindle would be given another means of fleecing the people: "you want to present them with several thousand millions and the national credit, so that they can clean out other people's pockets more thoroughly by means of *State-socialism!"*[121]

As for the tariff-like effect of the proposal: even the peasant advocate Jaurès agreed theoretically that socialists should not support the protective-tariff solution: while this might give some immediate benefit to the peasant (in the course of enriching the big landowners) the small gain would be at the expense of a substantial blow at the conditions of the urban workers. Jaurès—whom an admirer has praised as a "peasant

---

* This passage is of great interest for the analysis of state-socialism, and we will return to it in Volume 3.

of genius calibre"[122]—characteristically shilly-shallied on the tariff issue as on other basic class questions. Thus the opportunist peasant-catching campaign progressed, from protecting big-peasant exploiters of labor at the expense of the farm workers to pumping vitality into the peasant economy at the expense of the urban workers.

The history of socialism records a constant pattern: deviations from principle are first justified by opportunists on practical immediate grounds (along with scorn of dogmatists who cling to principle "rigidly"), and in a second phase the deviation itself is turned into the principle. This was the case in the later working-out of the peasant question by German reformism. In France, Jaurès was pressed by bourgeois attacks on his alleged hypocrisy (really his two-headedness on the peasant question) to explain how he could be for socialization in industry but not on the land; and so he wound up with the lapidary formula that "Socialism has no systematic preference for one or another way of organizing labor."[123] That is, socialism has no preference for a socialist way of organizing industry . . .

Thus the French socialists launched their peasant program with a contradiction: "the imperative duty to carry out something which it had declared to be impossible." But, in real politics, such a contradiction never remains within the sphere of logic and is not settled by debaters. It had to be acted out in political life, where it was gradually revealed that at stake was the difference between a class party of proletarian revolution and a parliamentary "people's party" of bourgeois reform.

12. PEASANTS AND THE PARTY

All this leaves a number of programmatic planks for immediate reforms on behalf of the small peasant and rural laborer, for integration into a socialist program with the proper theoretical context.

Among them are eight planks from the Marseilles program which Engels summarizes without criticism or objection. The point he makes about them is, again, directed to the opportunists' claim of a new practicality:

> As we see, the demands made in the interests of the peasants . . . are not very far-reaching. Part of them has already been

realized elsewhere. . . . The other points, too, could be carried
into effect without any substantial impairment of the existing
capitalist order. So much simply in characterization of the program. No reproach is intended; quite the contrary.[124]

Other specific demands come up in the course of the article.

Of great interest also is this passage of general import, following
Engels' rejection of the use of force in changing peasant property
relations:

> Moreover, we can advocate that the struggle of the capitalists and
> big landlords against the small peasants should be waged from
> now on with a minimum of unfair means and that direct robbery
> and cheating, which are practised only too often, be as far as
> possible prevented. In this we shall succeed only in exceptional
> cases. Under the developed capitalist mode of production nobody
> can tell where honesty ends and cheating begins. But always it
> will make a considerable difference whether public authority is
> on the side of the cheater or the cheated. We of course are
> decidedly on the side of the small peasant; we shall do everything
> at all permissible to make his lot more bearable, to facilitate his
> transition to the cooperative should he decide to do so, and even
> to make it possible for him to remain on his small holding for a
> protracted length of time to think the matter over, should he still
> be unable to bring himself to this decision. We do this not only
> because we consider the small peasant living by his own labor as
> virtually belonging to us, but also in the direct interest of the
> party.[125]

Within the boundaries thus marked out by Engels, the elaboration of
a program of demands for peasants need not be a difficulty for the
party. It was different with a stickier question: the local "peasantizing"
of party membership.

This problem concerned not individual memberships but rather the
ingestion and integration of recognizable social strata. It depended on
the basis on which party membership was expanded. A peasant—even
more, a rural worker—who really did become a socialist and revolutionary and who accordingly joined the party was a valuable acquisition. But peasants who were encouraged to join a rural party branch
with their peasant mentalities essentially unchanged, in expectation of
immediate boons—these tended to be alien elements.

It was the latter pattern that was showing up especially in South

Germany: as we saw, Engels noted that preference was being given by the regional party leadership to the bigger and more influential peasants (who could furnish voters) and not to the farm workers. Engels challenged this conception of building the party:

> I flatly deny that the socialist workers' party of any country is charged with the task of taking into its fold, in addition to the rural proletarians and the small peasants, also the middle and big peasants and perhaps even the tenants of big estates, the capitalist cattle breeders, and the other capitalist exploiters of the national soil. To all of them the feudality of landownership may appear to be a common foe. On certain questions we may make common cause with them and be able to fight side by side with them for definite aims. We can use in our party individuals from every class of society, but have no use whatever for any groups representing capitalist, middle-bourgeois or middle-peasant interests.[126]

"We have no more use for the peasant as a party member if he expects us to perpetuate his property in his small holding than for the small handicraftsman who would fain be perpetuated as a master. These people belong to the anti-Semites," wrote Engels rather bitterly.[127] For in his opinion the South German section of the party was already becoming a political Frankenstein's monster, as a result of Vollmar's social grafting of transplanted classes on the body of the proletarian party. In the month that saw the publication of Engels' article, the press had carried an open exchange of polemics between Vollmar and Bebel. Engels wrote to a correspondent:

> The row in the party did not get me stirred up very much; it is much better if something comes up from time to time and gets chewed over regularly than if people go to sleep. It is exactly the ever-increasing and irresistible expansion of the party that entails the fact that the new elements are harder to digest than the earlier recruits. We already have the workers of the big cities, therefore the most intelligent and alert people; those who come along now are either workers in small towns or rural districts, or students, salesmen, etc., or petty-bourgeois who are struggling against ruin, and rural domestic-industry people who still have a patch of land of their own or on rental; and now, into the bargain, regular small peasants too. And since in fact our party is the only really progressive party, and besides the only one that is strong enough to force through progressive things, there is ever-

present temptation to do a little socialist work also on the debt-ridden middle and big peasants who are becoming rebellious, especially in the rural areas where these people are predominant. That way, next, things go beyond the bounds of what is permissible in principle in our party; next, there are rows, but our party has so healthy a constitution that all of that hurts nothing.[128]

Engels died a few months after writing this valiant attempt to stress the positive side of the conflict in the party. But, as we know in hindsight, the Social-Democratic Party was suffering from a fatal disease. That belongs to another story, but it should be borne in mind in connection with the chapters to follow.

15 | THE LUMPEN-CLASS VERSUS THE PROLETARIAT

There is another class or class stratum that plays a significant part in the politics of revolution and requires special discussion: a class with no name. At any rate, it has no established name except one devised by Marx half-fortuitously and before he had himself begun to understand its nature; and this name has given rise to endless misunderstanding and mistranslation. This is the so-called *lumpenproletariat.*⁎

1. GENESIS OF THE LUMPENPROLETARIAT

The first problem about this class is: *what is it?*

Marx did not work this out until 1852, by which time he made this much clear: the label did *not* mean any sector of the modern proletariat; it did not mean unemployed workers, or pauperized workers, or indeed any kind of genuine workers at all. The initial confusion, however, was not due to unfortunate terminology. There was a tangled and blurred historical period that needed to be understood first: the period in which the elements of the modern proletariat came into existence and took shape.

We saw in Volume 1 that the term *proletariat* itself arose trailing clouds of confusion, and for the same reason.[1] It took on its modern meaning (wage-workers) in the couple of decades before the *Communist Manifesto,* but did not lose its old meaning immediately. This coexisting older meaning was, for centuries, the "rabble" that lived in poverty from hand to mouth, the lowest stratum of propertyless

⁎ For the origin of the term and its first use by Marx and Engels, see Special Note G.

freemen, the depressed plebeian mass; the name did not necessarily imply a working status of any kind. In this long-established usage, the "proletariat" comprised not only workers of various sorts but also an amorphous mass of adventitious, unsettled, irregular, and disreputable elements, including itinerant workers and vagrants shading into malefactors—like the Roman *proletarii*. There was a basic distinction between this gray mass and the modern working class, which Marx later put into these words: "The Roman proletariat lived at the expense of society, while modern society lives at the expense of the proletariat."[2]

It is this Roman precedent that is the subject when the word *lumpenproletariat* occurs in *The German Ideology* some time in 1845: "The [Roman] plebeians, midway between freemen and slaves, never succeeded in becoming more than a lumpenproletariat."[3] But in the same work Marx shows that he is already quite aware of the historical importance of the *Lumpen* "who have existed in every epoch and whose existence *on a mass scale* after the decline of the Middle Ages preceded the mass formation of the ordinary proletariat . . ."[4] And in the next paragraph, this social formation is called a lumpenproletariat. This word, evidently coined for the nonce, is written down as a description, not as a sociological term.

This proto-class, this lumpen-plebs, was a big constituent of the lowest stratum of urban society during the transitional centuries, without any clear line between producing elements and nonproducing or purely parasitic elements. A lumpen-class of some kind has accompanied different social systems; it reached new proportions out of the decay of European feudalism.* Of the plebeian opposition in the towns at the time of the German Peasant War in the sixteenth century, Engels wrote that it consisted of "ruined burghers," journeymen and day-laborers and other townspeople without civic rights, and also:

* Compare the following from the *Encyclopedia of the Social Sciences:*

> The destruction of the precapitalist mediaeval order of society was accompanied by the rise of an increasingly large army of outlawed individuals, belonging nowhere and having no secure place in society; these, as beggars, vagabonds, tramps, mercenaries and adventurers, infested the highways, pillaging and killing. This gray army of decayed and degenerate individuals, of socially shipwrecked and homeless elements, composed the beginnings of the proletariat; but they represented a potential not an actual proletariat.[5]

This army of the rootless was *one* of the sources from which the modern proletariat developed. Marx describes the process in *Capital,* particularly Chapters 26-28 of the first volume (in the German edition, Chapter 24, sections 1-3); Chapter 28 should be read in the present connection. The breaking up of the

the numerous precursors of the lumpenproletariat, who may be found even in the lowest stages of urban development. The lumpenproletariat is, generally speaking, a phenomenon evident in a more or less developed form in all the phases of society to date. The number of people without a definite occupation and a stable domicile increased greatly at that particular time, due to the decay of feudalism in a society in which every occupation, every sphere of life, was still fenced off by countless privileges. The number of vagabonds in all the developed countries was never so great as in the first half of the sixteenth century. In wartime some of these tramps joined the armies, others begged their way across the countryside, and others still eked out a meager living in the towns as day-laborers or whatever else was not under guild jurisdiction. All three groups played a part in the Peasant War; the first in the armies of princes, which overpowered the peasants; the second in the peasant conspiracies and peasant troops, where its demoralizing influence was evident at all times; and the third in the clashes of the urban parties. It must be recalled, however, that a great many of them, namely those living in the towns, still had a substantial element of sound peasant nature, and had not as yet been possessed by the venality and depravity of the present-day civilized lumpenproletariat.

Plainly, the plebeian opposition in the towns of that day was of a mixed nature. It combined the depraved elements of the old feudal and guild society with the undeveloped, budding proletarian elements of the dawning, modern bourgeois society.[7]

Considerably later, Engels painted much the same picture in a criticism of Kautsky's book *Communism in Central Germany in the Time of the Reformation*. One deficiency, he wrote the author, was:

> Very defective inquiry into the development and role of the declassed, almost pariah-like elements standing almost wholly outside the feudal structure which inevitably had to spring up

bands of feudal retainers and the clearing of people off the soil created a plebeian mass that no longer had a legal mode of existence, and could not suddenly adapt itself to the new capitalist discipline. Marx calls it the *vogelfrei* proletariat—"outlaw," that is, "free" and footloose because placed outside the legal society.

> They were turned *en masse* into beggars, robbers, vagabonds, partly from inclination, in most cases from stress of circumstances. Hence at the end of the 15th and during the whole of the 16th century, throughout Western Europe a bloody legislation against vagabondage. The fathers of the present working class were chastised for their enforced transformation into vagabonds and paupers.[6]

Thus capitalism created a mass lumpenproletariat as its by-product.

every time a town was formed, and which constituted the lowest stratum of every town population in the Middle Ages, without any rights, detached from the *Markgenossenschaft* [village community], from feudal dependency and from the guild corporation. This is difficult, but it is the *main basis;* for gradually, with the dissolution of feudal ties, this [stratum] becomes the *pre*-proletariat, which in 1789 makes the revolution in the Paris faubourgs and absorbs all outcasts of feudal and guild society. You speak of proletarians—the expression squints—and include the weavers, whose importance you depict quite correctly—but only *after* declassed and nonguild journeymen weavers came into existence, and only *insofar as* this happened, can you count them among your "proletariat."[8]

The expression *proletariat* was ambiguous when applied to the plebeian mixture making up what Engels here calls the preproletariat (and which in *The German Ideology* had been called "the latent proletariat").[9] The expression "squints," he writes, meaning that it looks both ways.

But even up to the 1830s and 1840s the term *proletariat* in its centuries-old inclusive meaning was freely being used for *all* of the elements we have been discussing. In 1838 a prominent book by A. G. de Cassagnac made this explicit as a result of growing consciousness that wage-workers were no longer *precisely* the same as the rest of this old-proletariat. In a spirit of classification he distinguished among four groups making up the "proletariat," of which the "workers" were only one. The other three were the beggars, the thieves, and the prostitutes.[10] The French historian-statesman Guizot adopted the same classification.[11]

Note that in Cassagnac's "proletariat" three out of four groups constitute exactly the type of elements that Marx called the lumpenproletariat. But in the world of the 1840s the packaging of these four groups under the single label of *proletariat,* while still the dominant approach by inertia, was intolerable for anyone trying to make sense of the new developments. It was doubly intolerable if it is true (as I have suggested)[12] that the modern meaning of *proletariat* arose especially in the milieu of the new socialist-communist movement of the 1830s as a special designation for the newly prominent class of wage-workers. Some other term would have to be found for the other three groups in Cassagnac's "proletariat," and this was the function assumed (for Marx) by *lumpenproletariat.*

Thus a natural confusion was engendered by overlapping movements in language in the junction between an old and a new social era. The word *lumpenproletariat* came in to designate a part of the old-proletariat but not of the modern proletariat.

Still, there was a remaining element of ambiguity insofar as the social distinction between old-proletariat and modern proletariat was not yet complete and was even less completely grasped by contemporaries.

2. FROM 1847 THROUGH THE REVOLUTION

In *The German Ideology* both uses of *lumpenproletariat* referred mainly to the past, to obsolete social elements. The next usage brought it to the present, and was also the first time the word appeared in print (as far as I know).

In a minor article written around the year-end 1846–1847, Engels used the term in passing in the course of criticizing a poem by the "True Socialist" Karl Beck, whom we have mentioned before.[13] Engels found one praiseworthy passage in Beck's poem, a passage which he calls a "portrayal of the lumpenproletariat." A beggar warns his daughter that if she bears a bastard the child is doomed to grow up into a thing that goes about begging, foraging in the gutters, huckstering on odd jobs, and the like—a derelict (says the summary couplet)

That scrambles to steal and pimp and pray,
And boozes the dregs of conscience away.[14]

It is implied that there is an existing social stratum to be called the lumpenproletariat. Engels spells out the implication a few months later in an unpublished manuscript, in a passage explaining why the proletariat cannot be expected to take the leadership of the coming revolution, because it is too weak and too badly split up and scattered:[15]

And the propertyless classes, in common parlance the working classes? . . . This division [of the propertyless or working classes] into farm-hands, day-laborers, artisan journeymen, factory workers, and lumpenproletariat . . . already makes it impossible for them to mutually clarify themselves about their unity of interests, to come to an understanding, to constitute themselves into a *single* class.

Engels then sketches the backward consciousness of each section. For the last-mentioned, he writes: "The *Lump*[16] lends his fists for a few *talers* to fight out the spats among bourgeoisie, nobility and police."[17]

There is a throwback here to the earlier sprawling conception of the "propertyless classes" as a unitary social formation, indicated by the apologetic reference to common parlance (*vulgo*); and in this framework the lumpenproletariat is quite clearly viewed as a constituent sector.

The well-known passage in the *Communist Manifesto* emphasizes the shady social role of the lumpenproletariat even more strongly. We must go back to the original text.*

> The lumpenproletariat, this passive putrefaction of the lowest strata of the old society, is here and there swept into the movement by a proletarian revolution, [but] in accordance with all its conditions of life it is more apt to sell itself to reactionary intrigues.[19]

This rotting mass is a "dangerous class," to be sure, but what the Manifesto emphasizes is that it is a danger to the revolution. This statement was partly a summary of some past history and partly a prediction. The prediction was realized all too well in the course of the revolution of 1848–1849.

The first case in point came, appropriately, when the revolutionary tide reached the city which—then and now—has a claim to the title of World Capital of the Lumpenproletariat: Naples, with its *lazzaroni*.**

---

* The standard (Moore-Engels) translation of 1888 avoided using the unfamiliar German word *Lumpenproletariat*, and came up with the following:

> The "dangerous class," the social scum, that passively rotting mass thrown off by the lowest layers of old society, may, here and there, be swept into the movement by a proletarian revolution, its conditions of life, however, prepare it far more for the part of a bribed tool of reactionary intrigue.[18]

The rendering "dangerous class" is discussed in Special Note G. In addition, there are two small differences to be noted. This translation elaborates "of" into "thrown off by," thereby intensifying the implication of an element that *separates itself* from the working class; and the statement about the possible role of the lumpenproletariat in revolution is weakened by "may." Both changes reflect the later evolution of Marx's and Engels' views.

**Contemporary Naples is outstanding in the modern world as the home of an active movement for monarchism. Hobsbawm refers to Naples historically as "the fortress of pauper Bourbonism." He writes, "The *lazzaroni* of Naples, the quintessential 'mob,' were passionate defenders of Church and King, and even more savage anti-Jacobins in 1799." Hobsbawm, however, does not focus on the lumpenproletariat as such but on the usually broader phenomenon of the "mob," which, while it may include a high proportion of lumpen-elements, is more like

Engels related the fate of the revolution in Naples in the first number of the *Neue Rheinische Zeitung*. The Bourbon king, Ferdinand II, mobilized his troops to overthrow the Chamber of Deputies, which was supported by the National Guard. At first "the 20,000 lazzaroni of Naples" were on the fence. The National Guard fought heroically against superior forces, and might even have won; but the failure of the French fleet offshore to intervene on the side of the bourgeois revolution pushed the lazzaroni over to the king's camp. "By this step of the Neapolitan lumpenproletariat the defeat of the revolution was determined." With the help of the lazzaroni, who were "the most greedy" of the king's myrmidons, the National Guard was butchered. Engels also mentions that, years back, the lazzaroni formed the bulk of the *Sanfedisti*, papal storm-troops formed after 1815 to combat the revolutionary republicans.[22]

Next: Paris. In one of the articles relating the events of the "June days," Engels dwells on the savage role played by the Mobile Guard, which had been formed by the Provisional Government soon after the February seizure of power:

> The Mobile Guard, which is recruited mostly out of the Paris lumpenproletariat, has, in its short period of existence, already been considerably transformed by means of good pay into a praetorian guard for the existing rulers. The organized lumpenproletariat gave battle to the unorganized working proletariat. As was to be expected, it put itself at the disposal of the bourgeoisie just as the lazzaroni in Naples had put themselves at the disposal of Ferdinand. Only those sections of the Mobile Guard that consisted of *real* workers went over to the other side.
>
> But how despicable does this whole present business in Paris show up, when one sees these elements—yesterday beggars, vagabonds, rogues, street gamins and petty thieves—of the Mobile Guard, whom in March and April every bourgeois called a rascally band of brigands fit for any infamy and not to be tolerated any longer; when this band of brigands is now petted, praised, re-

the older plebs in degenerate form. But his chapter on "The City Mob" is very useful supplementary reading for our present subject: particularly for insights like the symbiotic relation between "the rulers and the parasitic poor," the situation of "the unskilled dole-drawing proletariat who lived on ducal bounties" in Parma, or "the intermittent and short riot" as the classic pattern of the "mob."[20] It was natural for Bakunin, the lumpen-Prince, to have his greatest drawing power in Naples: "The worst Bakuninists in the whole of Italy are in Naples," remarked Engels.[21] We should make clear that Marx used *lazzaroni* (Neapolitan beggars, vagabonds and the like) as a synonym for the lumpen-elements, *faute de mieux*.

warded and decorated because these "young heroes," these "children of Paris" of incomparable valor who scaled the barricades with the grandest courage, etc.—because these mindless barricade-fighters of Februāry now shoot just as mindlessly at the working proletariat as they did before at the soldiers, because they let themselves be bought out with thirty sous a day to massacre their brothers! Honor to these bought-out vagabonds because they shot down the best and most revolutionary section of the Paris workers for thirty sous a day![23]

Next: Belgium. There had been no uprising, but the government had panicked and cracked down in all directions. Eighteen republican leaders and militants of the Democratic movement were condemned to death after a sham trial. Engels quotes the *Journal d'Anvers* on the lack of interest in the affair on the part of the Antwerp population. "Only in the working classes,"claimed the paper, was there much feeling, and this was a feeling of hostility against the republicans. After "working classes," Engels inserted parenthetically: "read: lumpenproletariat."[24]

Then came the counterrevolution in Vienna in November, and the exploits of Baron Jellachich in smashing the Democrats with his "Croatian" troops. An article by Marx connected the pattern with Paris:

> In Paris the Mobile Guard, in Vienna the "Croatians"—in both places lazzaroni, an armed and bought-out lumpenproletariat versus the working and thinking proletariat. In *Berlin* we will soon see the third act.[25]

That expectation was fulfilled in a matter of days. In an article on "The Counterrevolution in Berlin," Marx summarized the pattern of counterrevolution in Europe as (like the revolution itself) it traveled from Italy to Paris to Vienna and Berlin. On Naples and Paris, his summary paragraphs are these:

> In *Naples* the lazzaronidom [*Lazzaronitum*], in alliance with the monarchy, against the bourgeoisie.
> In *Paris* the greatest historical struggle that has ever taken place. The bourgeoisie, in alliance with the lazzaronidom, against the working class.[26]

Finally, as for the "German campaign for the Reich constitution" in 1849, Engels summed up the role of the lumpen-elements crisply:

> ... the lumpenproletariat was, as everywhere, up for sale from the second day of the movement on; they demanded that the

Committee of Safety give them arms and a stipend in the morning, and let themselves be bought up by the big bourgeoisie in the afternoon, to guard the latter's buildings or tear down the barricades in the evening. On the whole they stood on the side with the bourgeoisie, which paid them best, and with this money they had a merry old time while the movement lasted.[27]

There certainly was no doubt in Marx's and Engels' minds about the dangerous role of the lumpenproletariat as an antirevolutionary tool, on the basis of the experience of the revolution as well as of history.

3. THE "REFUSE OF ALL CLASSES"

In a number of passages so far cited for the term *lumpenproletariat* we may note a certain ambivalence on whether this social stratum is to be regarded as a part of the proletariat or not. When it is contrasted to the "working proletariat" there is an implication that the lumpen-elements may be regarded as a part of the "non-working proletariat" in some way—if only by other people, as no doubt was the case. This confusing implication gets spelled out in Marx's 1850 work on *The Class Struggles in France*, for the last time.

The case in point is the composition of the Mobile Guard in France, which Engels had discussed on the heels of the June days. Marx explains that, after the February revolution, the Provisional Government felt the lack of a reliable armed force to use against the proletariat. He writes: "There consequently remained but one way out: *to play off one part of the proletariat against the other.*" He describes two ways in which this was done; the second way was by rallying "an army of industrial workers" through the so-called National Workshops. The first way was by playing off the lumpen-elements of the Mobile Guard against the proletariat:

> For this purpose the Provisional Government formed 24 battalions of *Mobile Guards*, each a thousand strong, composed of young men from 15 to 20 years. They belonged for the most part to the *lumpenproletariat*, which in all big towns forms a mass sharply differentiated from the industrial proletariat, a recruiting ground for thieves and criminals of all kinds, living on the crumbs of society, people without a definite trade, vagabonds, *gens sans*

feu et sans aveu [homeless, rootless people], varying according to the degree of civilization of the nation to which they belong, but never renouncing their lazzaroni character; at the youthful age at which the Provisional Government recruited them, thoroughly malleable, as capable of the most heroic deeds and the most exalted sacrifices as of the basest banditry and the foulest corruption. The Provisional Government paid them one franc 50 centimes a day, that is, it bought them. It gave them their own uniform, that is, it differentiated them outwardly from the blue-collars [*Bluse*, overall-wearing workers]. In part it had assigned them officers from the standing army as leaders; in part they themselves elected young sons of the bourgeoisie whose rodomontades about death for the fatherland and devotion to the republic captivated them.

And so the Paris proletariat was confronted with an army, drawn from its own midst, of 24,000 young, strong, foolhardy men. . . . It [the proletariat] regarded it [the Mobile Guard] as the *proletarian* guard in contradistinction to the bourgeois National Guard. Its error was pardonable.[28]

The ambivalence here is plain: on the one hand, the lumpen-elements are drawn "from its own midst," that is, generated out of the ranks of the proletariat, and on the other hand "sharply differentiated from the industrial proletariat." Differentiated as one part is differentiated from another part? The language reflects the confusion of the French workers and their "pardonable" error; indeed it sounds as if it harks back to the terminology of the old-proletariat.

Viewed historically, the solution of the terminological confusion was also plain. For historically the lumpenproletariat *was* drawn from the midst of the working masses in the sense of being *precipitated out of them* (to use a chemical term) by the processes of developing bourgeois society. Engels' later term "social scum" also suggests a process of separation. But scum separates by floating upward; these waste-products of society fall to the bottom, like the detritus that accumulates at the bottom of a canyon by disintegration and decay from all the strata above, making the streams muddy and turbid as it is carried off.

About the same time Marx and Engels published a book review with an interesting passage on certain dubious circles on the periphery of society, with only an incidental mention of the lumpenproletariat. It serves to throw light on the subject from a quite different angle. The starting point is a couple of books on the Paris conspiratorial societies, which the reviewers use to explain the banefulness and futility of the Blanquist type of sect. A sharp distinction is made between the rank-and-file workers who follow these conspiratorial sects and the "professional conspirators" who work at it full-time and live off the proceeds. (The latter elements are here called a class, but the term must be taken loosely.)

> This class's position in life conditions its whole character from the outset. The proletarian conspiracy naturally offers them only very limited and uncertain means of livelihood. They are therefore continually forced to dip their fingers into the conspiracy's treasury. Many of them also come into direct collision with bourgeois society in general and cut a more or less graceful figure before the police courts. They are impelled into the circles which Paris calls *la bohême*, by their precarious existence, which in regard to particulars is more dependent on chance than on their own actions; by their irregular life, whose only fixed stops are the wineshops—the conspirators' meeting-places; by their inevitable association with all kinds of dubious people. These democratic bohemians of proletarian origin (there is also a democratic *bohême* of bourgeois origin, the democratic loafers and bar-flies) are therefore either workers who have given up working and as a result have become dissolute, or elements that stem from the lumpenproletariat and carry over all the dissolute habits of this class into their new life. It can be understood how under these circumstances a couple of jailbirds are to be found involved in almost every conspiracy trial.
>
> The whole life of these professional conspirators bears the character of the *bohême* most markedly.[29]

We will meet this *bohême* again, for a closer look. Let us note that in this passage it is treated as being more inclusive than the lumpenproletariat. The difference narrows in the next passage to be discussed, but we should not think that we are dealing with hard-edged social strata susceptible of exact definition.[29a]

The basic breakthrough on the meaning of the lumpenproletariat was made two years later, in Marx's portrait of that class in *The Eighteenth Brumaire of Louis Bonaparte*. The scene is still—or again—France, especially Paris.

As we saw, Engels pointed the finger at the Mobile Guard at the first opportunity in 1848. In his *Class Struggles in France* Marx continued the discussion of the Mobile Guard, and already referred to "the Society of December 10, that organization of the Paris lumpenproletariat."[30] This society, whose name commemorated Bonaparte's election to the presidency on December 10, 1848, was a sort of storm-troop organization established and paid by Bonaparte to further his plans. It played an important part in his coup d'état. Now Marx devotes a special analysis to this new embodiment of the lumpen-counterrevolution:

> On the pretext of founding a benevolent society, the lumpen-proletariat of Paris had been organized into secret sections, each section being led by Bonapartist agents, with a Bonapartist general at the head of the whole. Alongside decayed roués with dubious means of subsistence and of dubious origin, alongside ruined and adventurous offshoots of the bourgeoisie, were vaga-bonds, discharged soldiers, discharged jailbirds, escaped galley slaves, swindlers, mountebanks, lazzaroni, pickpockets, tricksters, gamblers, pimps, brothel keepers, porters, littérateurs, organ-grinders, rag-pickers, knife-grinders,* tinkers, beggars—in short, the whole indefinite, disintegrated mass, thrown hither and thither, which the French term *la bohème;* from this kindred element Bonaparte formed the core of the Society of December 10. A "benevolent society"—insofar as, like Bonaparte, all its members felt the need of benefiting themselves at the expense of the laboring nation. This Bonaparte, who constitutes himself *chief of the lumpenproletariat,* who here alone rediscovers in mass form the interests which he personally pursues, who recog-nizes in this scum, offal, refuse of all classes the only class upon which he can base himself unconditionally, is the real Bona-parte . . .[31]

To Bonaparte the state is a masquerade "to mask the pettiest knavery [*Lumperei*] ":

> In this Society of December 10, he assembles ten thousand rascally fellows [*Lumpenkerls*] who are to play the part of the people as Nick Bottom that of the lion [in Shakespeare] . . . [It is] the society of disorder, prostitution and theft . . .[32]

---

* Note that knife-grinders also appeared in the portrayal of the lumpenprole-tariat by Karl Beck's beggar. As in the case of other occupations mentioned here and elsewhere, it is a question of certain itinerant occupations then associated with vagabondry (like tinkers in Britain).

The French bourgeoisie balked at the domination of the working proletariat; it has brought the lumpenproletariat to domination, with the chief of the Society of December 10 at the head.[33]

The view that is now made clear, and will be consistently repeated, is that this class formed out of social detritus and offscourings is generated as the waste-product *of all classes*. This "refuse of all classes" is the general sewer of society. It is not only the lowest strata that produce this sediment, and, of the working masses, it is not only the proletariat. It is contrasted to the "laboring nation" as a whole, in analysis, even though in the third citation above the literary form of the sentence seems to contrast it to the "working proletariat" once again.

4. THE TOOLS OF REACTION

Marx and Engels never used the German word *Lumpenproletariat* when writing in English or French; they sought a native substitute that would suggest the social element, as when they impressed *lazzaroni* for the purpose. In English they occasionally used *mob*.*

Both *lazzaroni* and *mob* occur in Marx's explanation in the *New York Tribune* of the events of the Spanish revolution in 1813–1814, when the city lumpenproletariat aided the counterrevolutionary reaction. The "mob" (what Hobsbawm calls the "Church and King Mob") gave the king a triumphant welcome to Madrid; the "rabble" hurried to remove the word Liberty over the entrance to the Cortes; and one of the factors in the victory of the reaction was "these shameless demonstrations of the town mob, partly paid for their performances, and like the Lazzaroni of Naples, preferring the wanton rule of kings and monks to the sober regime of the middle classes."[34]

Marx even uses *mob* in a letter to Engels, in German, dealing with the American Civil War. Of the Southern slaveholding oligarchy:

In a part of the °"poor whites"° they found the °mob,° who acted for them as substitutes of the Zouaves.[35]

And in a letter to Marx, Engels uses still another combination, referring to the French revolutionary terror of 1793: one of the elements was

---

* For their first use of *mob* in this way, and the background of the word in English and German, see Special Note G, page 633.

the *"Lumpenmob"* which took advantage of the terror to line its own pockets.[36]

All in all, one of the most consistent notes struck about the *Lumpenmob* is its aptness for use as a tool of reaction. For example, describing a demonstration in Hyde Park assaulted by the police, with many arrests, Marx notes that the prisoners are guarded by shady figures "pressed into the service of the London police out of the Irish lumpenproletariat."[37]

Marx's and Engels' views on the role of the lumpen-class only hardened as time went on. By 1870 there was a special reason for the vehemence of Engels' language in a new preface to *The Peasant War in Germany.* He is stressing that the proletariat, still far from a majority in Germany, is compelled to seek allies. "These are to be found only among the petty-bourgeoisie, the lumpenproletariat of the cities, the small peasants and the agricultural laborers." He proceeds to evaluate these. On the second category:

> The *lumpenproletariat,* this scum of depraved elements from all classes, with headquarters in the big cities, is the worst of all the possible allies. This rabble is absolutely venal and absolutely brazen. If the French workers, in every revolution, inscribed on the houses: *Mort aux voleurs!* Death to thieves! and even shot some, they did it not out of reverence for property, but because they rightly considered it necessary above all to get rid of that gang. Every leader of the workers who uses these scoundrels as guards or relies on them for support proves himself by this action alone a traitor to the movement.[38]

For around this time they were beginning to discover the peculiarities of Bakunin's ideology, especially those aspects emphasized in his Russian-language writings. They set forth these elements of the Bakuninist plan of revolution in the exposé which they published in 1873 on behalf of the International.*

Bakunin (going beyond suggestions in Weitling) was the first figure

---

* The political nature of Bakuninism that is expounded in this pamphlet—written by Engels and Lafargue with contributions by Marx, and published as *L'Alliance de la Démocratie Socialiste et l'Association Internationale des Travailleurs*—is fully confirmed by modern studies of Bakunin's ideology, like Pyziur's, in spite of the marxological custom of depreciating its exposé of the founder of the anarchist movement. This custom owes a great deal to the disgraceful treatment of Bakuninism (as of Lassalleanism) in Mehring's overrated biography of Marx.[39] We will return to this subject in Volume 3.

to systematically proclaim the lumpen-elements as the class motor of his revolution, or an important gear in it. Indeed, "the very type of the revolutionary" for Bakunin (explained Marx, Engels, et al., in the International pamphlet) was the brigand, the only true revolutionary in Russia.[40] More generally, his revolutionary vanguard was to be systematically based on the *déclassés*, the socially declassed—those who have lost their place in society and lead a marginal existence. The International pamphlet quoted the text of a letter by Bakunin to a follower, explaining why Italy and Spain are the most revolutionary countries, including this:

> There exists in Italy [Bakunin wrote] what is lacking in other countries: a youth which is ardent, energetic, *completely displaced, without a career, without a way out,* and which, despite its bourgeois origin, is not morally and intellectually exhausted like the bourgeois youth of the other countries.[41]

In Bakunin's ideology, the proletariat in the Marxian sense—that is, wage-workers who work more or less stably and, worse still, get paid more or less regularly—are "bourgeois" (an all-purpose imprecation with little content). The Bakuninist stand-in for the proletariat is the lumpen-world, which is to play the role as Nick Bottom did that of the lion.[42] These are the urban déclassés of the lower classes. Then, as we have already seen, there is the peasantry (because they represent "barbarism"), plus the déclassé offscourings or refuse of the upper classes, to which the Russian aristocracy makes its rich contribution. All these make up the "marginal class," "restless and fierce," which is to make the revolution.[43] That is, these are the class elements which Bakunin believes can be "ridden" by a conspiratorial vanguard in order to seize power.

All in all, here was a theory of the revolutionary class that was destined to go far—but it is the negation of Marx's.

Utilization of this "restless and fierce" (that is, unstable and vicious) class was not confined to adventurers like Bakunin, though it was not always acknowledged or theorized. For this class is available and it is volatile. These two attractive features are specially tempting to ambitious leaders who have neither the hope nor the desire to move real social forces into motion through a protracted process. A case in point was portrayed by Engels, as he described the operation of the self-styled "Marxist" group in England, the Social Democratic Federation under H. M. Hyndman, of whom Marx and Engels took the dimmest of views.

The occasion was a trough of depression and mounting unemployment in 1886. A reformist workers' group which proposed to cure the crisis by "fair trade" (retaliatory tariffs) called a demonstration in Trafalgar Square; the S.D.F. called its own meeting for the same place. Engels reports:

> So two meetings took place . . . Kautsky was there and went away before the rumpus started; he told me that the mass of the real workers had been among the pro-tariff people, whereas Hyndman & Co. had a mixed audience of people looking to go on a spree, part of them already a little high. If Kautsky who has been here hardly a year could see this, the gentlemen of the Federation must have seen it even better. Nevertheless, when it already all seemed to be petering out, they put an old favorite idea of Hyndman's into operation, namely, a parade of "unemployed" through Pall Mall . . . The unemployed who followed them in order to hold a renewed meeting in Hyde Park were mostly the sort who don't want any kind of work at all, peddlers, street bums, police spies, spivs. . . . During the parade, during this small second meeting, and afterwards, the masses of the lumpenproletariat whom Hyndman had taken for the unemployed surged through some adjoining elegant streets, looted jewelry shops and others, used the breadloaves and mutton joints they had [previously] looted solely to break in windows, and then scattered, without meeting resistance.[44]

In another letter about the same event Engels describes the crowd as: "masses of the poor devils of the East End who vegetate in the borderland between working class and Lumpenproletariat, and a sufficient admixture of roughs and 'Arrys . . ."[44a] This sort of thing was the antithesis of Marx's and Engels' idea of effective revolutionary activity. In any case, it was typical of the lumpen-class that the target was jewelry shops, not No. 10 Downing Street.*

---

* Engels must have written along these lines to his old friend Harney, the former left Chartist, now very old and retired but still a champion of working-class emancipation. We have only Harney's reply, showing a keen understanding of the difference between proletarian circles and a lumpen-brawl, as well as a dim view of "Hyndman and Co."

"Violent language" excited by the sight of misery [wrote Harney] *I* certainly could and would excuse—as long as addressed to *bona fide working men* (mechanics, labourers, &c.)—but any encouragement ad-

5. ECONOMIC MEANING:
THE ANALYSIS IN *CAPITAL*

A finishing touch to Marx's view of the relation between the lumpen-class and the proletariat is given in the first volume of *Capital*. The "disintegrated mass" of social excreta is clearly and definitively distinguished not only from any part of the proletariat but even from the *nonworking* elements of the producing classes.

The rife confusion on this point would be hard to account for, therefore, except that translations (into English and other languages) have helped to obscure the meaning of the passage. We shall see that Marx refers here to "the lumpenproletariat proper," a phrase which signals a careful distinction; but it is replaced, in the Moore-Aveling translation edited by Engels, by the phrase "the 'dangerous' classes," which we discuss elsewhere.[46]

The context is Marx's analysis of the "industrial reserve army" as a basic phenomenon of the capitalist system. The brief reference to the lumpenproletariat will be clear only if we start a little way back.

Developed capitalism, in Marx's analysis, needs "a surplus laboring population"—surplus in relation to capitalism's ability to utilize this population productively. "It forms a disposable industrial reserve army . . . a mass of human material always ready for exploitation." As capitalism's cyclical needs for labor go up and down, this reserve army can be employed or discarded as necessary. When on "reserve," it is unemployed or partially employed. "The whole form of the movement of modern industry depends, therefore, upon the constant transformation of a part of the laboring population into unemployed or half-employed hands." The movements of wages are determined "by the varying proportions in which the working class is divided into active and reserve army . . . by the extent to which it is now absorbed, now set free [discarded]."[47]

This pool of "surplus" workers, or "reserve army" of labor, "exists in every possible form. Every laborer belongs to it during the time when he is only partially employed or wholly unemployed." Its forms are three: "the floating, the latent, the stagnant."[48] It is with the last form that we come to the lowest stratum of the working proletariat:

The third category of the relative surplus-production, the stagnant, forms a part of the active labor army but with extremely irregular employment. Hence it furnishes to capital an inexhaustible reservoir of disposable labor-power. Its conditions of life sink below the average normal level of the working class . . . But it forms at the same time a self-reproducing and self-perpetuating element of the working class . . .[49]

This is still a sector of the proletariat. It is not a question of how many days a year this stagnant sector works, and still less of pinning a proletarian label as an honorific decoration. The point is objectively economic: this sector has a function to play in the processes of capitalism, whether employed or not at any given time. And the same is true of the next stratum:

The lowest sediment of the relative surplus-production, finally, dwells in the sphere of pauperism. Exclusive of vagabonds, criminals, prostitutes, in a word the lumpenproletariat proper,* this layer of society consists of three categories.[50]

It is clear that "vagabonds, criminals, prostitutes" are illustrative examples of "the lumpenproletariat proper," which is being sharply separated from even the lowest sedimentary layers of the proletariat, even from those unable to work at all. For the three categories in this lowest layer are: those able to work; orphans and pauper children; and

Third, the demoralized and ragged [*Verlumpte*], and those unable to work, chiefly people who succumb to their incapacity for adaptation, due to the division of labor . . . [Marx then gives examples.]

A key question: why is this lowest, rock-bottom category of the "lowest sediment" of the relative surplus-population *still considered a sector of the proletariat at all,* on strictly objective economic grounds? The answer is given in the same passage:

Pauperism is the hospital of the active labor-army and the dead weight of the industrial reserve army. Its production is included in that of the relative surplus-population, its necessity in theirs; along with the surplus-population, pauperism forms a condition of capitalist production, and of the capitalist development of wealth.[51]

This segment Marx then calls "the lazarus-layers of the working class,"

* At this point the standard translation reads: "the 'dangerous' classes."

whose extent denotes the size of "official pauperism."[52] In turn, he makes clear that "official pauperism" denotes "that part of the working class which has forfeited its condition of existence (the sale of labor-power), and vegetates upon public alms."[53]

The "lazarus-layers" or pauperized segments of the working class constitute "a condition of capitalist production," not merely a consequence of capitalist conditions. But the lumpenproletariat falls outside this relationship: it does not constitute an economic condition for the existence of capitalism; it is produced as a *consequence* of developed capitalism, as a waste product—just as certain contemporary forms of crime are a consequence of the social order but not a prerequisite for it.

Marx's analysis in the *Grundrisse* manuscripts emphasizes even more strongly that pauperism is an integral and indispensable feature of the socioeconomic system. "Free labor = latent pauperism," he writes aphoristically; that is, the worker always remains free to be relegated to the lazarus-layers of the reserve army. Previous societies had surplus people but they were surplus nonworkers. "The invention of surplus workers, that is, of propertyless people who work, belongs to the period of capital."[54]

While the lumpenproletariat, then, is sharply distinguished from the pauperized layers of the surplus population, still it may be recruited from the lazarus-layers: that is a different matter. Continuous unemployment and consequent demoralization may push individuals out of the working classes altogether and into the underworld or the skid rows. This is also a form of declassment, a precipitation out of the proletariat.

6. THE UPPER-CLASS "LUMPENPROLETARIAT"

We now come to Marx's use of *lumpenproletariat* with what seems to be an extended meaning, but upon which examination throws a new light on the base meaning.

To begin with, let us return to Marx's impressment in 1850 and 1852 of the French term *la bohème* (or *la bohème*) as an approximation of *lumpenproletariat*.[55] It connoted certain shady circles on the margin of society.* At the other end of Bonaparte's career, Marx re-

* A caution: nowadays bohemianism is likely to connote an unconventional style of literary-artistic life involving garrets, cheap cafés, pleasing disorder, *carpe*

turns to *la bohème* in *The Civil War in France;* but this time it has an extended meaning, similar to that given currency by Charles Hugo's popular novel of 1859, *La Bohème Dorée.* Marx refers to "the exodus from Paris [to Versailles] of the high Bonapartist and capitalist bohême," and later remarks that Versaillese Paris after the fall of the Commune is

> the Paris of the Boulevards, male and female—the rich, the capitalist, the gilded, the idle Paris, now thronging with its lackeys, its blacklegs, its literary *bohême,* and its cocottes . . .[56]

These are upper-class elements: not detritus from the poor lower strata of society, but hangers-on of the rich and powerful. What they have in common with the poor lumpen-class is that they are *functionally outside the social structure.* To be sure, they also have in common a purely parasitic role, but this is not distinctive, for there are also functional elements in bourgeois society that are parasitic in a definable sense from Marx's standpoint.[57] What is distinctive about this gilded rabble is that its personnel is socially functionless even in bourgeois terms.

In a draft for *The Civil War in France* Marx linked the two kinds of bohemians as complementary: the reactionary party fleeing Communard Paris, he writes, was followed by its hangers-on, including "the whole band of low *bohème* (the common criminals) that form the complement of that *bohème of quality.*"[58]

Lumpenproletariat was also given a similarly extended meaning by Marx. This should be distinguished from a merely metaphorical usage, as when Marx in 1848 called the writing staff of the bourgeois *Kölnische Zeitung* a "literary lumpenproletariat"[59] (read: knavish hacks); or when he denounced a certain journalist as a "notorious literary lumpenproletarian."[60] When Gottfried Kinkel established a German

---

diem, Puccini's opera, unrecognized genius, New York's Greenwich Village in the 1920s and so on. Both meanings branch off from the original signification of *bohemian*—the gypsy, presumed to come from Bohemia; the two represent different sides of the popular conception of gypsy life. The bohemian as *malefactor* was stridently portrayed, as it happens, in a noted play that was on the boards in Paris when Marx first arrived in that city in 1843: *Les Bohémiens de Paris* by Dennery and Grange. It was only a few years later, however, that Henri Murger's novel, on which Puccini's *La Bohème* is based, started appearing in print. Thus both sides of the meaning coexisted for a period. There was an overlapping both in literature and in living space: one common denominator of the petty underworld, the struggling artists' world, and the workers' world is—cheap lodgings.

émigré organ in London, Marx opined that its "editors are recruited wholly out of the literary lumpenproletariat," and raked "the lumpen-proletarian gang of rogues that has gathered round Gottfried Kinkel."[61] There may be an implicit connection here with life style, that is, with the literary bohemia of the Parisian garret; for in the case of another German émigré littérateur, E. Biskamp, a letter by Marx mentioned his wretched circumstances and how he managed to eke out a miserable existence as a *bohémien.* The French form of the term was probably suggested by the French background of the lumpen-bohemian world.[62] But these casual expressions are not to be taken literally any more than Marx's calling rural schoolteachers "the proletarians of the learned class."[63]

Something more than metaphor is evident in the following case. Marx is describing the dominance of the "finance aristocracy" under the king of the bourgeoisie, Louis Philippe:

> ... the same prostitution, the same shameless cheating, the same mania to get rich was repeated in every sphere, from the Court to the Café Borgne [disreputable saloon], to get rich not by produc-tion, but by pocketing the already available wealth of others. Clashing every moment with the bourgeois laws themselves, an unbridled assertion of unhealthy and dissolute appetites mani-fested itself, particularly at the top of bourgeois society—lusts wherein wealth derived from gambling naturally seeks its satisfac-tion, where pleasure becomes debauched, where money, filth and blood commingle. The finance aristocracy, in its mode of acquisi-tion as well as in its pleasures, is nothing but the *rebirth of the lumpenproletariat on the heights of bourgeois society.*[64]

This "finance aristocracy" is not the finance capital that plays an integral role in bourgeois economy; it is the vultures and raiders (Kreugers and Insulls) who swing from speculation to swindling; who do not gain their wealth "by production" *even from the bourgeois standpoint;* who are near-criminal or extralegal excrescences from the body social of the rich as the other lumpen-elements are from the poor; who are indeed as dangerous to the long-range interests of the real capitalist class as the others are to the real proletariat. As excrescences not functionally integral to the social system, they are economic demimondaines, outsiders in a special sense, just as the lower-class lumpen-elements are dropouts from society in a special sense. They are lumpen-bourgeois.

References to such an upper-class lumpen-stratum are most plentiful in *The Eighteenth Brumaire,* because Marx considered them to be most plentiful in the parasitic superstructure that Bonaparte raised on top of the already existing superstructure of society. Moreover, Marx regarded Bonaparte's utilization of the state apparatus as parasitically oriented; that is, for Bonaparte the state was to be used as a "protection racket" to skim off a fat "take" for the benefit of himself and his lumpen-entourage.*

Marx does not believe this phenomenon is a requisite of Bonapart-*ism,* though the latter opens the door to it wide—for example, it is not a feature of the Bonapartist pattern set by Bismarck; rather, it flows from the personal character of Louis Napoleon Bonaparte himself, a character that plays a prominent part in all of Marx's detailed analyses of this period of French history. Still less is it a requisite of capitalism; on the contrary, it is inimical to capitalism and to the short-range and long-range interests of the bourgeoisie. (All through the 1850s Marx's surprise is that the French bourgeoisie continues to tolerate Bona-parte.)[66] While capitalism does not require this type of parasitism, it leaves society not only open to this cancer but even especially susceptible to it.

Bonaparte was not only the "emperor of the lumpenproletarians,"[67] that is, the leader of this class reservoir of reaction, but he himself "was a bohemian, a princely lumpenproletarian"[68]—Bonaparte himself was the source of this phenomenon at this particular time and place. The same applies to his personally selected tools, his "mob":

> But, above all, Bonaparte looks on himself as the chief of the Society of December 10, as the representative of the lumpen-proletariat to which he himself, his entourage, his government and his army belong, and whose prime consideration is to benefit itself . . .

The bourgeoisie has to prosper, to be sure, but above all "the Bona-partist lumpenproletariat is to enrich itself."[69] The regime's financial measures are similarly motivated: "Handing out presents or going into hock—that is all there is to the financial science of the lumpen-proletariat, the upper-class kind [of lumpenproletariat] or the common kind."[70]

---

* Note Marx's analogous use of the phrase *respectable paupers:*

A pauper, like a capitalist (*rentier*), lives on the revenue of the country. He does not enter into the production costs of the product . . . Ditto, for a criminal who is fed in prison. A large part of the "unproductive laborers," holders of State sinecures, etc., are simply respectable paupers.[65]

Writing for the Chartist press, Engels as always avoided using *lumpenproletariat* in English; and, just as in other cases he used *mob* for the lower-class kind, so here he resorted to the Briticism *swell mob* (stylishly dressed pickpockets) to describe the upper-class scum around Bonaparte:

> Besides the mass of the peasantry, Louis Napoleon, himself a species of lofty swell-mob's-man, and surrounded by the élite of the fashionable swell mob, found support in the most degraded and dissolute portion of the population of the towns. [71]

Bonaparte, added Engels, relied upon the peasantry for votes, "upon the mob for noisy demonstrations," and upon the army for coercion.

The variegated lumpen-elements around Bonaparte were truly the "scum, offal, refuse of all classes," not simply recruited from the lower strata. That went for the peasantry too:

> The army itself is no longer the flower of the peasant youth; it is the swamp-flower of the peasant lumpenproletariat. It consists in large measure of *remplaçants*, of substitutes, just as the second Bonaparte is himself only a *remplaçant*, the substitute for Napoleon. [72]

These peasant draft-substitutes—why are they lumpen-elements? Certainly not because of underworld activity. The label here derives from the central idea of the classification: they are elements that are being squeezed out of the peasant economy and hence out of a place in society; they are being exuded, extruded, excreted from the class structure and onto the scrapheap.

This is the conception to be borne in mind when next we hear of lumpen-aristocrats. Dealing with a period in Polish history when big peasants developed into "a sort of *peasant middle class*, the *Equestrian Order*" which eventually collapsed, Marx writes that

> this Equestrian Order, incapable of playing the role of a real middle class, is transformed into the lumpenproletariat of the aristocracy. [73]

Writing much later, Engels is describing the formation of the Prussian Junkerdom. There is the "petty landowning gentry"; there are the younger sons in the army or civil service who make up the "less wealthy petty nobility"; and

On the lower fringes of all this clique of nobles, there naturally emerges a numerous parasitic nobility, a noble lumpenproletariat, which lives on debts, dubious gambling, importunate begging and political espionage.[74]

It emerges "naturally" because every class and social formation throws off its *disjecta.*

These waste-product elements may find a new social berth on a lower class level (declassment), as when the indigent scion of aristocracy becomes a schoolteacher, the parson's son "goes into trade," or the bankrupt shopkeeper goes to work in a factory. But the déclassé who succeeds in relocating socially thereby avoids falling into the lumpen-class.

7. THE CLASS CLOACA

With some additional illustrations from the writings of Marx and Engels, let us emphasize a point that has already been made in the preceding section: the lumpen-class is not only a social formation outside the proletariat, it is best defined as the class cloaca that is functionally outside the ongoing social structure.

It is interesting to see how this relationship is confusedly expressed in Marx's first notes on political economy, the Paris manuscripts of 1844—that is, before he had got very far in his analysis of the social structure, and before the concept of the lumpenproletariat had even achieved expression. The context is his charge that capital is interested in the worker not as a human being but only as a source of capital, as a commodity, and otherwise lets him starve in unemployment. He complains:

> Political economy therefore does not recognize the unemployed worker, the working human being, insofar as he is outside this labor relationship. The rascal, swindler, beggar, the unemployed or starving or down-and-out or criminal worker/human-being, are *figures* that do not exist *for political economy* . . .[75]

Since the unemployed and pauperized workers are here put in the same bag with criminals and beggars, he does not yet understand that the latter (typifying the lumpen-class proper) *are* outside the purview of political economy, that is, outside the social system of which a political economy is the theoretical expression. This is an objective feature of the society, not a defect of the political economists.

It may seem callous to group criminals and beggars together, but the criterion is not a moral or juridical one, which may have force in some other connection. For that matter, it is important to understand that there are *working* lumpen-elements too, even though Marx began by contrasting the lumpenproletariat to the "working proletariat." We have seen working lumpenproletarians listed as examples more than once, from peddlers and knife-grinders to prostitutes and brothel keepers (the latter approximating lumpen-bourgeois). This category is specifically noted in the *Grundrisse* notebooks, as Marx explains the distinction between productive and unproductive labor:

> From the whore to the pope, there is a mass of such riffraff [doing unproductive labor]. But the honest and "working" lumpenproletariat falls under this head too; e.g., big gang of hangers-on offering service etc. in port cities etc.[76]

The example, as often, is that of casual and irregular labor, like that of a tramp who offers to cut wood for a meal. Another reference to the lumpen-class in the *Grundrisse*, a dozen pages away, speaks however only of the dishonest lumpenproletariat. It is merely a passing mention as Marx argues that the worker cannot advance by heaping up savings as good bourgeois urge, for he would achieve only a brutalizing asceticism "if he saved money in good ascetic style and so piled up prizes for the lumpenproletariat, swindlers, etc., who would increase in proportion to the demand."[77]

The casual laborer without ties or roots is also the subject of a reference in a chatty tourist note from Marx, visiting Cannes. The town

> is "monumental," since it consists only of hotels; here [there are] no plebeian "masses," outside of the *garçons d'hôtels, de café,* etc. and *domestiques* belonging to the lumpenproletariat.

The whole town is a "den of idlers or adventurers ... a dreary hangout."[78] Marx sees Cannes as a concentration of parasitic excrescences, where even the serving personnel are adventitious hangers-on.

What all these elements, honest or dishonest, have in common is that they are functionless outsiders, as discards of the system or self-discards. To be sure, a nonworking status may be the indicator, as when the Roman plebs degenerated into lumpen-elements. When the free peasants of ancient Rome were stripped of land and livelihood, says

Marx, "The Roman proletarians became not wage-laborers but a *mob fainéant* [mob of do-nothings] more abject than the former 'poor whites' in the South of the United States . . .."[79]

Individuals who are torn from their social roots and left treading air are natural candidates for the lumpen-class, and therefore we have seen Marx use the term more than once about émigrés. Lest it be thought that its use is always derogatory, let us note that it occurs in a bleak comment about a sympathetic figure, an émigré Pole on whose fate Marx reported sadly in a letter to Engels. Having fallen into the deepest poverty, he "had sunk down to being a lumpenproletarian in Whitechapel," and was finally burned to death in a slum fire. "First to go to the dogs [*verlumpen*], then to starve, and finally get burned to death, is all one can ask for in this 'best of worlds,' " grumbles Marx at a time when his own affairs were grim.[80] To be sure, Whitechapel itself—more generally, the East End of London of which Whitechapel is a part— brought the lumpen-class to mind, for this was its stamping-ground, as well as the home of the most depressed sectors of the London working class at this time. We saw, in Chapter 4, that when the "New Unionism" revolutionized the East End, Engels cheered particularly because this meant that the lumpenproletariat would be pushed into the background and the real workers of the district would come to the fore.[81]

To repeat and to sum up: the lumpen-class is the catch-all for those who fall out, or drop out, of the existing social structure so that they are no longer functionally an integral part of the society. To survive at all, in the interstices of the society, they may have to adopt a parasitic mode of existence. The tendency toward illegality, criminality, and so on simply arises from the scarcity of other choices.

Experience demonstrated to Marx and Engels that, on the whole, the elements of the lumpen-class tend to be inhospitable to social ideals socially implemented—for what is society to them, or they to society?— and that they are typically moved by cynical self-interest on the most vulgar level, however rationalized; hence they tend to be venal, available to the highest bidder; attracted to the bandwagon of the winner, or distracted by circuses with or without bread; unlikely to become serious about any social cause or motivated by any political vision; untrustworthy even when bought up, and dangerous even as tools: "the worst of all possible allies." As Engels said, "Every leader of the workers who . . . relies on them for support proves himself by this action alone a traitor to the movement."

III | MIXED-CLASS ELEMENTS

16 | INTELLECTUAL LABOR AND LABORERS

There is a considerable marxological literature devoted to the subject of Marx's views on "intellectuals," for the *soi-disant* intellectuals are endlessly fascinated by the subject. But Marx did not address himself to the question, which did not become a prominent preoccupation until after his time; and it is difficult to say what an intellectual is—there are scores of definitions and two rarely agree. It is more fruitful to begin with something more definite.

Most discussions about intellectuals actually operate by pointing a finger rather than defining. They may point to certain occupations (like writers or professors), or to certain occupational groups (like professionals or white-collar workers), or to certain sociopsychological categories (like scholars or "thinkers"). These elements are all found in the general area dominated by brain work or intellectual (mental) labor as distinguished more or less clearly from manual and physical labor.

1. MARX'S AREA OF CONCERN

We begin by examining Marx's views on the role of elements typical of this general area, without being concerned with whether we are really discussing "intellectuals," whatever they are. The way in which Marx posed the question to himself was more concrete: it concerned the role of *educated people* (the so-called "educated classes") and of education as a class attribute.

Marx naturally recognized that the proletarian movement needs people with a variety of advanced skills, abilities, talents, training, and knowledge. In many or most cases these attributes are furthered by a more or less high degree of education. Moreover, some occupations which socialists want to affect, or which they need for the new social order, depend heavily on a high level of formal training: scientists and technologists, professionals of many sorts, teachers on several levels, academics in general, students in particular, writers and artists, and others who are primarily engaged in the production and dissemination of ideas.

Especially in Marx's time, this type of ability was usually to be sought among the so-called "educated classes"—which meant the social strata that could afford long schooling for their scions.* The working classes tend to suffer from relatively poor access to formal education, both because of deliberate discrimination and because of biases built into the system (for example, workers' families cannot so easily afford long abstinence from paid work even if education is free). Hence the above-listed occupations, especially because of the educational prerequisites, tended to be filled by the progeny of the upper classes, from the more affluent reaches of the petty-bourgeoisie through the bourgeoisie on to the aristocracy or its remnants.

The consequence was a serious disadvantage for the proletarian movement for many practical purposes. The class background of the proletariat prepared it well for many movement needs—organizational efficiency and militancy, for instance—but poorly for the struggle in the arena of national opinion using the available instruments of publicism.

Therefore the acquirement of educated recruits took on a special importance. But these tended to be bourgeois elements, however sympathetic to the working class. A potentiality was created; an extra class tension was introduced into the proletarian movement, reflecting class antagonisms outside the movement. This was the nature of the problem. This problem concerns *educated* recruits, not necessarily people called intellectuals. Unless, of course, an intellectual is defined as an educated person, as has been done; but this empties the word of any special meaning.

The focus of Marx's interest, then, was not on the disjunction Intellectuals versus Workers—whatever that may be defined to mean.

---

* In practice, the term *educated classes* was usually used for the new and old ruling classes, that is, the aristocracy and the bourgeoisie, in countries where both were powerful. Marx used it this way regarding Germany, in an 1873 Afterword to *Capital.*[1] Regarding Russia, Engels wrote in 1890: "alongside the nobility there now stood the beginnings of a second educated class, the bourgeoisie." He used *enlightened classes* similarly.[2]

That view of the problem was invented later by intellectuals. Marx's concern was directed to the class background, hence the class-biased training and predispositions, of the educated elements who could be useful to the proletarian movement if they could be assimilated. This is the main subject of the next three chapters.

In this chapter we consider Marx's views on the role of intellectual (mental) labor in general. There is going to be a constant problem with the ambiguity of the English word *intellectual,* which leads to ambiguous English translations from the German. For example, *geistige Arbeit* means intellectual or mental labor or "brain work" as distinct from manual or physical labor; but it does not mean the work specifically performed by an "intellectual" (which as a noun in English acquires a specially portentous meaning). *Geistig* has a scope not easily duplicated by any single English word: mental, spiritual, moral, intellectual, psychological, all in the sense of pertaining to the mind rather than the body. (But in English one no longer says *spiritual labor* when one means intellectual or mental labor, as is done in the extant translation of Marx's *Theories of Surplus Value.*)[3] When *intellectual* becomes a noun, the German equivalent is not a derivative of *Geist* but rather *Intellektuelle, Intelligenz.* In the following pages, *intellectual* as an adjective (as in *intellectual labor*) never means *pertaining to intellectuals;* it is used much as Marx uses the German *geistig.*

2. INTEGRAL HUMAN LABOR

The distinction between intellectual and physical labor, between the labor of head and hand, is a real one, even if not absolute. It is their *separation* which, to Marx, is a distortion of humanity. The labor of the whole person involves both.

Marx takes this as a fundamental proposition in *Capital.* In fact, he defines human labor, as distinct from the sometimes similar labor of animals, on the basis of this criterion. What marks labor as human is its intellectual (mental) component. "We presuppose labor in a form that stamps it as exclusively human," he writes. It is true that a spider does weaving and a bee does the work of an architect—

> But what distinguishes the worst architect from the best of bees is this, that the architect raises his structure in imagination before

he erects it in reality. At the end of every labor-process, we get a result that already existed in the imagination of the laborer at its commencement, hence already existed in idea-form [*ideel*].* He not only effects a change of form in the material on which he works, but he also realizes a purpose of his own that gives the law to his modus operandi, and to which he must subordinate his will.[4]

The alteration of the material in the labor process was "designed from the commencement," he adds. The material is adapted to "the wants of man."[5]

In his essay on "The Part Played by Labor in the Transition from Ape to Man," Engels later emphasized the evolutionary task performed by labor, but it must be added: by *human* labor. While stressing the decisive role of the hand, he writes: "Thus the hand is not only the organ of labor, *it is also the product of labor.*" The mental component of labor was itself an attribute of a physical advance, the human brain. Engels writes that only through a long and complex evolution in which physical change (of the hand, for instance) interacted with mental-physical change in the brain and senses—only through this process of change "has the human hand attained the high degree of perfection that has enabled it to conjure into being the pictures of Raphael, the statues of Thorwaldsen, the music of Paganini."[6] Just as, for Marx, the labor process is not merely an exertion of muscle, so also the process of artistic creation is not merely an activity of little gray cells. The whole person is involved in both cases; and to the extent that this is not true, the person is being crippled.

The combination of intellectual and physical labor is natural when one is working purely individually; but the combination of laborers permits separation:

> So far as the labor-process is purely individual, one and the same laborer unites in himself all the functions that later on become separated. . . . As in the natural body head and hand wait upon each other, so the labor-process unites the labor of the hand with that of the head. Later on they part company and even become deadly foes. The product ceases to be the direct product of the individual, and becomes a social product, produced in common by a collective laborer, i.e., by a combination of workmen . . .[7]

* This last phrase ("hence . . .") is omitted from the standard English translation; one wonders why.

Such separation reaches a high point in capitalism, and its most extreme forms are characteristic of capitalism. Physical and intellectual labor remain associated in the labor process only in the "collective laborer," the aggregate of workers producing a particular commodity; but for the individual worker, intellectual labor is increasingly divorced from physical.

This separation has nothing to do with the distinction between laborers who are directly engaged in working on material and those who are not. For instance (following an example given by Marx), janitors or floor-sweepers have nothing directly to do with working up the raw material, yet are just as much a part of the "living production machine" (the collective laborer) as are the others. So too "the works engineer has yet another relation and in the main works only with his brain, and so on," but is also a part of the collective laborer.[8]

> It is indeed the characteristic feature of the capitalist mode of production that it separates the various kinds of labor from each other, therefore also mental and manual labor—or kinds of labor in which one or the other predominates—and distributes them among different people. This however does not prevent the material product from being the *common product* of these persons . . .[9]

Brain workers or manual workers, touching the material or not, they are all producing the commodity, in the same economic relation to it and to the capitalist; they are all producing surplus-value and hence producing capital (their embodied labor); they are all parts of the collective laborer, all proletarians—intellectual and manual laborers alike.

In short, included in the labor that goes to enhance the value of a commodity are

> all intellectual labors which are directly consumed in material production. Not only the laborer working directly with his hands or a machine, but overlooker, engineer, manager, clerk, etc.—in a word, the labor of the whole personnel required in a particular sphere of material production to produce a particular commodity, whose joint labor (cooperation) is required for commodity production.[10]

And for the same reason intellectual labor may be embodied also in immaterial commodities, such as services, from operating an elevator to opera-singing for a profit-making enterprise.

3. CAPITALISM AND INTELLECTUALS

Intellectual labor, or brain work, is, then, a necessary and integral part of the process of production, as much an attribute of the "collective laborer" as manual labor is. But in popular parlance, including that of many sociologists, intellectual activity is often viewed as something typically outside of the process of production—something external to the workaday world (for example, the work of sociologists in discussing the definition of intellectual). More generally, it is often considered something distinctive when it is detached not only from manual labor but from any practice.

From Marx's standpoint the important line of demarcation runs not between manual and intellectual labor but through two other pairs. There is an important line between work in the process of production and work outside of production; there is another between socially useful and necessary work as against work that is socially useless or harmful. It is class society that separates out the category of intellectual labor so sharply and that gives a special honorific weight to intellectual activity detached from practice. This is one aspect of the tendency of class society to intensify the division of labor in socially deleterious forms.

Marx wrote in *The German Ideology,* expounding his new thesis that the ruling ideas are the ideas of the ruling class:

> The division of labor, which we already saw above . . . as one of the chief forces of history up to now, manifests itself also in the ruling class as the division of mental and material labor, so that inside this class one part appears as the thinkers of this class (its active, conceptive ideologues, who make their main livelihood out of cultivating the class's illusion about itself) while the others' relation to these ideas and illusions is more one of passive receptivity, since they are the active members of this class in reality and have less time to make up illusions and ideas about themselves. Within this class, this cleavage can even develop into a certain opposition and hostility between the two parts, but given any practical collision endangering the class itself, this passes away of itself, whereupon there also vanishes the appearance that the ruling ideas were not the ideas of the ruling class and had a power distinct from the power of this class.[11]

It is widely recognized that the intellectual as a social type seems to come into historical prominence with the beginnings of the bourgeois era. Yet previous classes had their ideologues and thinkers, who made "their main livelihood out of cultivating the class's illusion about itself" or imposing this set of illusions on all of society. Thus, in the Middle Ages the intellectual specialists of the ruling class were usually provided by the Church; and from early on, religion, the intellectualization of people's relation to nature, also provided the ideologies and ideologists for handling illusions about the relation of person to person. "The first form of ideologists, *priests,*" Marx noted, were coincident with the appearance of a division between material and intellectual labor. And "the *division of labor* implies the possibility, nay the fact, that intellectual and material activity, that enjoyment and labor, production and consumption, devolve on different individuals . . ."[11a]

What, then, makes this kind of intellectual specialist a prominent outgrowth of the bourgeois era? What must have changed was the division of labor between the establishment's thinkers and doers, a division so visibly deepened in modern times that a new label was required for a newly important social element. In the Middle Ages the Church, main source of intellectual operatives, was itself the biggest landowner and lord in the ongoing system. The case is different with capitalism in this respect as in others. The same reasons that produce the political inaptitude of the capitalist class[12] also make it less likely than other ruling classes to provide its own intellectual rationalizers from its own ranks: capitalists *qua* capitalists are interested in profits, not philosophy, and in cotton-spinning as against theory-spinning. It leaves far more room than ever before for the assignment of ancillary duties to professional specialists: in the one case, professional politicians; in the other, professional ideology-fabricators.[13] Thus, on the highest level of the system it introduces a division of labor between those who stuff moneybags and those who stuff heads. This appears as the difference between doing and thinking.

Consequently, the rise of a newly prominent social stratum produces *intellectual* as a noun. As an adjective, *intellectual* has naturally pointed in different directions depending on what it is counterposed to. If counterposed to *physical,* it means pertaining to the mind; if counterposed to *emotional* (as in a "purely intellectual response to music"), it emphasizes reason or logic (and by extension may also be counterposed to *moral*). But it is also commonly counterposed to *practical:* for example, a "merely intellectual revolutionary" is charged with failing to put ideas into practice or action, with divorcing thinking from doing. It is this usage that generally gives rise to the noun *intellectual,* as actually used by most people, other than intellectuals trying to fabricate an acceptable definition. The label *an intellectual* tends to connote the onesidedness of a specialist in the manipulation of ideas and abstract rationalization divorced from the responsibility of performance. Counterposing "Men of Ideas" (the title of a well-known sociological work on the subject) to "men of action," it is the obverse of the Practical Man or Woman who scorns ideas and dismisses theory. Which explains why intellectualism and anti-intellectualism are Siamese twins.

The growth of a stratum of intellectuals is connected with the deepening of class differentiations in society. Marx quotes Necker on the "contrast between wealth that does not labor and poverty that labors in order to live," and then comments that this contrast

> also gives rise to a contrast of knowledge. Knowledge and labor become separated. The former confronts the latter as capital, or as a luxury article for the rich.[14]

Marx then quotes an interesting passage from Necker which ends as follows: "is it not certain that this inequality of knowledge has become necessary for the maintenance of all the social inequalities *which gave rise to it?"* Certainly Marx did not conceive of the analysis of capitalist production as the province only of something narrowly called economics:

> Man himself is the basis of his material production, as of any other production that he carries on. All circumstances, therefore, which affect man, the *subject* of production, more or less modify all his functions and activities, and therefore too his functions and activities as the creator of material wealth, of commodities. In this respect it can in fact be shown that *all* human relations and functions, however and in whatever form they may appear, influence material production and have a more or less decisive influence on it.[15]

The widened split between intellectual and physical labor has far-reaching cultural as well as socioeconomic effects, and so presents a basic challenge to the socialist reorganization of society. From this viewpoint it will be taken up again in Volume 3 of this work. Suffice to say now that, for Marx, this disjunction is an offense to the humanness of labor and destructive of the wholeness of the human being, and must therefore be overcome. Confinement to purely intellectual labor—

intellectual labor detached from practice—means a distorting onesided-ness in the conditions of life as well as of labor. Insofar as the intellectual emerges as a distinctive social type, this is a pathological symptom. Just as modern class society called it into being on such a scale, Marx points in the direction of abolishing it. We will see that the abolition—more accurately, the transcendence—of the intellectuals as a pathological social element is one of the goals of the good society, along with the elimination of criminals, racists, feeble-minded, and other undesirables.

However, nothing in these pages depends on a special definition of the noun form of *intellectual*. Where it is used, especially in the next two chapters with reference to the problems of the socialist movement in Marx's time, it refers in a general way to educated recruits of bourgeois background who aspire to specialize in the manipulation of ideas, or conceive this to be their special contribution.

4. PRODUCTIVE AND UNPRODUCTIVE LABOR

Marx's discussion of the forms and role of intellectual labor is largely found under the head of his analyses of productive and unproductive labor. Of course, there is no question of a separate economics of intellectual labor in any sense; we are mainly concerned with removing misconceptions about the relationship of some types of nonmanual labor to the productive process. Let us first summarize Marx's basic views on the subject.

1. What is a "productive laborer"? Not simply one who produces something. We are talking about productive laborers *under capitalism* and from the standpoint of the capitalist system, not from the stand-point of justice, humanity, abstract society, or some other social order.

2. In terms of capitalism, only those laborers are productive who produce capital, by producing surplus-value.

> Capitalist production is not merely the production of com-modities, it is essentially the production of surplus-value. . . . That laborer alone is productive who produces surplus-value for the capitalist, and thus works for the self-expansion of capital.[16]

Working out the proposition in his notebook, Marx enlarged on the

statement that *"Productive labor* is simply labor that produces *capital."*
The piano maker is a productive worker, but not the piano player, even
though the latter does produce something, namely music; but this
playing "is not for this reason *productive labor* in the *economic sense;*
no more than the labor of a fool who produces phantasmagoria." Labor
that does not produce capital may be useful or harmful: no matter; it is
unproductive labor in either case (in the aforesaid economic sense).[17]

Spelled out more formally: productive labor is wage-labor which
produces a vendible commodity whose sale can replace the value of the
labor embodied in it, thereby producing a surplus-value and hence new
capital.[18]

3. The label *productive laborer*, rather than unproductive, is not in
the least honorific, under capitalism. One can produce goods or services
of the greatest importance to humanity, and even necessary for capitalism itself, without being "productive"; and contrariwise one can produce commodities that are socially worthless or harmful and still be
productive, since these attributes are irrelevant to capitalism's view of
the matter.[19]

Thus Marx takes up the argument of the economist Storch that
professors and writers are necessarily productive because they produce
enlightenment. Marx retorts that they may also produce obscurantism.
Poets and painters may "produce" good taste, but also bad taste;
physicians may be said to "produce" health, but also illness. Besides:

> it can just as well be said that illness produces physicians, stupid-
> ity produces professors and writers, lack of taste poets and
> painters, immorality moralists, superstition preachers, and general
> insecurity produces the sovereign.[20]

All of these activities or services "produce a real or imagined use-value,"
but they do not produce commodities. Indeed, some of these activities
may be quite necessary for capitalism, still without being commodities,
hence not productive. A capitalist's cook performs labor that has a
use-value for the capitalist, without producing any commodity with
exchange-value.[21]

Marx illustrates further with many examples of intellectual labor,
productive and unproductive.

> If we may take an example from outside the sphere of production
> of material objects, a schoolmaster is a productive laborer when,
> in addition to belaboring the heads of his scholars, he works like a

horse to enrich the school proprietor. That the latter had laid out his capital in a teaching factory, instead of in a sausage factory, does not alter the relation. . . . to be a productive laborer is, therefore, not a piece of luck but a misfortune.[22]

Note that this schoolmaster labors for a private school, not for a government board of education. At this point in *Capital*, Marx says he will explain further in "Book IV," which we know as his *Theories of Surplus Value*; hence the absence of further discussion in this area in *Capital*. He had already given similar examples in his notebook. "Actors are productive workers not insofar as they produce a play but [insofar as they] increase their employer's wealth."[23] (Again a privately owned theater company is assumed.) He scouts the confused ideas of political economists who assume that "a thief is also a productive worker, in that he indirectly produces books on criminal law," and so on. On the other hand, workers on meretricious luxury goods "are indeed productive °as far as they increase the capital of their master; unproductive as to the material result of their labour.° In fact this 'productive' worker is just as little interested in the crap he has to make as the capitalist himself who employs him . . ."[24]

The promised explication in *Theories of Surplus Value* is quite voluminous. While the content repeats what we have already explained, the examples of intellectual labor that are given are especially useful.

A music performer is not *per se* a productive laborer, even though it is argued that the musician produces fine memories; just as (Marx adds) drinking champagne may produce a hangover without being economically productive. But there is nothing derogatory to music in this:

> If the music is good and if the listener understands music, the consumption of music is more sublime than the consumption of champagne, although the production of the latter is a "productive labor" and the production of the former is not.[25]

But an artist may also be a productive laborer, depending on the economic relationship: "A writer is a productive laborer not insofar as he produces ideas, but insofar as he enriches the publisher who publishes his works, or if he is a wage-laborer for a capitalist."[26]

> *The same* kind of labor may be *productive* or *unproductive*. For example Milton, who wrote *Paradise Lost* for five pounds, was an *unproductive laborer*. On the other hand, the writer who turns out stuff for his publisher in factory style is a *productive laborer*.

Milton produced *Paradise Lost* for the same reason that a silk-worm produces silk. It was an activity of *his nature.* Later he sold the product for £5. But the literary proletarian of Leipzig who fabricates books (for example, Compendia of Economics) under the direction of his publisher is a *productive laborer;* for his product is from the outset subsumed under capital, and comes into being only for the purpose of increasing that capital. A singer who sells her song for her own account is an *unproductive laborer.* But the same singer commissioned by an entrepreneur to sing in order to make money for him is a *productive laborer;* for she produces capital.[27]

Economically there is a distinction between two types of non-material production. One generates the kind of vendible commodity that exists independently of the producer, such as books and paintings. These being commodities, what about the labor put in by the writer or painter? Here Marx refines his example of the encyclopedia hack.*

Here capitalist production is applicable only to a very restricted extent: as for example when a writer of a joint work—say an encyclopedia—exploits a number of others as hacks. In this sphere for the most part a *transitional form to capitalist production* remains in existence, in which the various scientific or artistic producers, handicraftsmen or experts work for the collective trading capital of the book-trade—a relation that has nothing to do with the capitalist mode of production proper and even formally has not yet been brought under its sway. The fact that the exploitation of labor is at its highest precisely in these transitional forms in no way alters the case.

Then there is the other type of nonmaterial production, where—

2. The production cannot be separated from the act of producing, as is the case with all performing artists, orators, actors, teachers, physicians, priests, etc. Here too the capitalist mode of production is met with only to a small extent, and from the nature of the case can only be applied in a few spheres. For example, teachers in educational establishments may be mere wage-laborers for the entrepreneur of the establishment; many such educational factories exist in England. Although in relation

* *De se fabulatur:* Marx is no doubt thinking of the dozens of articles that he and Engels carpentered for the *New American Cyclopaedia,* articles he considered to be hack-work.[28]

to the pupils these teachers are not *productive laborers*, they are productive laborers in relation to their employer. He exchanges his capital for their labor-power, and enriches himself through this process. It is the same with enterprises such as theaters, places of entertainment, etc. In such cases the actor's relation to the public is that of an artist, but in relation to his employer he is a *productive laborer*. All these manifestations of capitalist production in this sphere are so insignificant compared with the totality of production that they can be left entirely out of account.[29]

These types of intellectual labor are indeed "insignificant" in effect on the total economy, but of course not insignificant from the standpoint of the status of arts, letters, science and other intellectual pursuits within capitalist society. How is this intellectual sphere affected by its *economic* relations, as distinct from other (social and political) channels by which the ruling social powers subordinate the intellectual world to their own interests?

5. BOURGEOIS ATTITUDES AND REWARDS

Ever since Adam Smith made the economic distinction between productive and unproductive laborers—a distinction that Marx merely refined—bourgeois thought has taken offense at the implications. If *productive laborer* is not an honorific term within the framework of capitalism but a badge of misfortune, this reflects something damaging about capitalism. The English economist Senior resented the idea that Moses would have to be classed as an unproductive laborer, and Marx took the occasion to discredit unhistorical economics:

These people are so dominated by their fixed bourgeois ideas that they would think they were insulting Aristotle or Julius Caesar if they called them "unproductive laborers." Aristotle and Caesar would have regarded even the title "laborers" as an insult.[30]

Marx explained the source of the resentment:

The great mass of so-called "higher grade" workers—such as state officials, military people, artists, doctors, priests, judges, lawyers, etc.—some of whom are not only not productive but in essence destructive, but who know how to appropriate to themselves a very great part of the "material" wealth partly through the sale of their "immaterial" commodities and partly by forcibly imposing the latter on other people—found it not at all pleasant to be relegated *economically* to the same class as clowns and menial servants and to appear merely as people partaking in the consumption, parasites on the actual producers (or rather agents of production). This was a peculiar profanation precisely of those functions which had hitherto been surrounded with a halo and had enjoyed superstitious veneration.

Since Adam Smith thought that the expenses for these "unproductive laborers" should be cut down to the indispensable minimum—

> In the first place therefore it becomes a principal task for the sycophants of this society, and especially of the upper classes, to restore in theoretical terms even the purely parasitic section of these '"unproductive laborers," or to justify the exaggerated claims of the section which is indispensable. The *dependence* of the ideological, etc., classes* on the *capitalists* was in fact proclaimed.[32]

But why did Adam Smith put forward this offensive view? Why was he, unlike his successors, able to write that "The labor of some of the most respectable orders in the society is, like that of menial servants, unproductive of any value," that kings and generals and such are unproductive, hence maintained out of the product of other people's industry, that "In the same class must be ranked ... churchmen, lawyers, physicians, men of letters of all kinds; players, buffoons, musicians, opera-singers, opera-dancers, etc."?

"This is the language of the still revolutionary bourgeoisie, which has not yet subjected to itself the whole of society, the state, etc.," explained Marx. But—

> When on the other hand the bourgeoisie has conquered the field, partly itself taking over the state, partly making a compromise with its former possessors, and has likewise given recognition to the ideological orders as flesh of its flesh and everywhere transformed them into its functionaries, of like nature to itself; when it itself no longer confronts these as the representative of

---

* Ideological "classes": that is, class sectors or elements; for this loose use of *class*, see the remarks in my Foreword to Volume 1.[31] In the next passages to be cited, Marx uses the term *ideological orders* (*Stände,* ranks or professions).

productive labor, but when the real productive laborers rise against it and moreover tell it that it lives on other people's industry; when it is educated enough not to be entirely absorbed in production, but to want also to consume "in a cultured way"; when the intellectual labors themselves are more and more performed in its *service* and enter into the service of capitalist production—then things take a new turn, and the bourgeoisie tries to justify "economically," from its own standpoint, what it had previously criticized and fought against. . . . In addition to this, these economists, who themselves are priests, professors, etc., are eager to prove their "productive" usefulness, to justify their wages "economically."[33]

The bourgeoisie comes to accept the necessity of "a superstructure of ideological orders" functioning in its behalf.[34] But this does not mean that all types of intellectual production share equally in the rewards. Different social systems favor different types of intellectual production.

Thus for example different kinds of intellectual production correspond to the capitalist mode of production and to the mode of production of the Middle Ages. If material production itself is not conceived in its *specific historical* form, it is impossible to understand what is specific in the intellectual production corresponding to it and the reciprocal influence of one on the other. Otherwise one cannot get beyond inanities. . . .

Further: from the specific form of material production arises in the first place a specific structure of society, in the second place a specific relation of men to nature. Their state system and their intellectual outlook are determined by both. Therefore also the kind of their intellectual production.[35]

The relation between material and intellectual production is not a simple one, but some things can be said about capitalism:

For instance, capitalist production is hostile to certain branches of intellectual production, for example art and poetry. If this is left out of account, it opens the way to the illusions of the French in the eighteenth century . . .

This refers to the illusion that "Because we are further ahead than the ancients in mechanics, etc., why shouldn't we be able to make an epic too?"—along with the conclusion that a dull poetic epic of Voltaire's (Marx mentions the *Henriade*) must be greater than the *Iliad!*[36] In other words, Marx is denying that socioeconomic progress entails intellectual advance in some automatic way. But if "capitalist production is hostile to certain branches of intellectual production," it is on the other hand usually thought to favor other branches—for example, science.

6. THE PLACE OF SCIENTIFIC LABOR

No one doubts that a would-be epic writer in modern Los Angeles, Liverpool, Lyons or Leipzig has a "specific historical" disadvantage compared with a bard in an ancient preliterate society. Modern society is hostile to this form of intellectual production. But isn't the case different for those intellectual laborers of today who produce an immaterial good (knowledge) far more important to capitalist interests, namely, scientists?

The case is indeed different for certain scientists and for certain fields of knowledge, specifically those that affect the forms and level of production. In fact, so basic is this difference that Marx's *Capital* makes this type of intellectual labor into an economic category of its own, called "general labor," differentiated from "collective labor."* General labor is "all scientific labor, all discovery and all invention." It utilizes the labor of previous workers (scientists, inventors, and so on) in addition to the cooperative labors of existing scientific workers; whereas the other and more usual category of labor comprises only the direct labor exerted by (existing) individuals.[37] If this category of labor is "general," it is because of its general application: not merely to a particular commodity or labor-process but to all subsequent applications of labor in a given labor-process. Through this means, the productive power of (ordinary, collective) labor is increased by "progress in the field of intellectual production, notably natural science and its practical application."[38]

Marx points to other cases where society develops powers that cost the capitalist nothing, yet increase the power of production—for example, development of the division of labor, or the growth of population. "Another force of production which costs it [capital] nothing is °scientific power.° . . . In short, all the social powers that develop with

---

* The extant English versions of *Capital* translate these terms differently: universal labor (for *allgemeine Arbeit*) and cooperative labor (for *gemeinschaftliche*).

the growth of population and the historical development of society cost it nothing."[39] Like the collective power of labor, indeed like all the social powers of production, science (or "scientific power") appears as the collective power of capital. Scientific power is just another, though very important, case "where the combination and, as it were, the communal spirit of labor is transferred into the machine etc."[40] It must not be thought that this applies only to science of some high-level sort; on the contrary, the economic principle equally involves the crystalliza-tion of various sorts of *skill* into the embodiment of machinery.

> Capital, in its real development, combines mass labor with skill, but in such a way that the former loses its physical power and the skill exists not in the laborer but in the machine and the factory operating as a whole through [a] scientific combination with the machine. The social spirit of labor achieves an objective existence apart from the individual laborers.[41]

In fact, in this whole discussion *science* is best given its broad German sense of *Wissenschaft*—accumulated knowledge and know-how. The body of discovered knowledge which is objectified in a machine of advanced design, or in a set of factory procedures leading to greater productivity, is not basically different from the body of technical knowledge which permitted a master worker in a medieval guild to outproduce the novice who had not yet learned the trade. Marx discusses this situation as follows:

> ... in the guild system it must also become clear that the particular kind of property which labor creates is not based simply on labor or exchange of labor but on an objective connec-tion of the worker with a community and conditions he finds given, on the basis of which he proceeds. These too are products of a [certain] labor, of the labor of world history; of the labor of the community—of its historical development, which does not proceed from the labor of individuals nor the exchange of their labors.[42]

The contribution to capital made by this type of intellectual labor is, then, immense and beyond question; but to an equally immense degree it "costs capital nothing." Marx generalizes on the tendency of capital-ism toward undervaluing this type of intellectual labor:

> The product of mental labor—science—always stands far below its value, because the labor-time needed to reproduce it has no relation at all to the labor-time required for its original produc-

tion. For example, a schoolboy can learn the binomial theorem in an hour.[43]

For another example, the intellectual labor-time needed to develop the transistor has no relation at all to the labor-time required to produce it once the knowledge has been communicated. Everyone knows the slight reward to an inventor as compared with the harvest reaped by the entrepreneur who exploits the invention; but in addition Marx points out that even an initial entrepreneur often goes bankrupt; it is typically not the trail blazer who makes money out of a contribution by intellectual labor, but rather a later entrepreneur who benefits from a cheap buy-up:

> It is, therefore, generally the most worthless and miserable sort of money-capitalists who draw the greatest profit out of all new developments of the general labor of the human intellect and their social application through combined labor.[44]

Of course, the intellectual laborer may be compensated for a lack of monetary reward by honors, prizes, and luxuriously inscribed scrolls.

7. INTELLECTUAL LABOR
AND SOCIALISM

But in scientists, inventors and such technological innovators we have been discussing the cream of the cream of intellectual laborers, from the standpoint of capitalism. The case is quite different with those laborers in the intellectual fields who are only an overhead expense or drain on the wealth produced by others: poets, for example, whose "production" of poems has exactly the same economic meaning for capital as a lunatic's production of hallucinations. These intellectual producers have essentially the same economic relation to the capitalist as the latter's valet, mistress, or bodyguard.

The same goes for intellectual operatives who may be of far more value to the bourgeoisie than poets: for example, economics professors, ecclesiastical prelates, or eclectic philosophers. But these are valuable in the same way that the statesman or soldier is valuable. Marx takes up an economist's challenge: the soldier who protects the harvest—is he not as "productive" as the farmer who reaps it? Marx's answer (omitting the argumentation) is that the soldier certainly does produce something—he produces "defense"—but he does not produce surplus-value, that is, wealth in the capitalist form. Hence, in the framework of capitalism, he is not a productive worker

> in the same way as a large part of the unproductive laborers who produce nothing themselves, either intellectual or material, but who are useful and necessary only because of the faulty social relations—they owe their existence to social evils.[45]

But then there are also other intellectual laborers who owe their existence not to social evils or to the bourgeoisie's special needs, but to general social needs. That does not necessarily help them a bit, as far as their economic relation to capital is concerned. They are equally part of the band of retainers that have to be fed out of the production of wealth by others.

Differences among these various types of unproductive intellectual laborers do come into play, however, from another side.

In time of business depression and industrial crisis, even productive workers in essential industries may be thrown on the scrapheap; the havoc in the field of luxury goods is even greater. The consumption of luxuries decreases; productive laborers engaged in the creation of luxury commodities are thrown out of work. What happens to unproductive laborers?

It goes without saying that the services of unproductive laborers will be less in demand on the whole (even if we allow for an increase in intellectual laborers skilled in explaining why the breakdown must not sap confidence in the system). Marx points out that they "receive for their services a portion of the capitalists' luxury expense fund" which is now hard-hit. And besides, these unproductive intellectual laborers are not even luxury workers: "these laborers are themselves *pro tanto* luxuries."[46] Contributions to the symphony orchestra, university, church, or opera association come out of the same fund as expenditures for butlers, yachts, private chefs or fashionable paintings, and also, on a system-wide scale, out of the same fund as expenditures for prison wardens, generals, politicians, lawyers, judges, Boy Scout leaders, or asylum-keepers. The question then is posed materially of the order or priority enjoyed by various types of intellectual laborers in their claims on the "capitalists' luxury expense fund."

The case of an economic crisis underlines the problem of choice, but the question of priorities which is highlighted applies also to more constant situations. Other things being equal, what conditions maximize the amount of "living space" in the economy for the unproductive intellectual laborers? Under what conditions can a relatively high proportion of unproductive laborers live on available revenue—high in comparison with the proportion of productive workers?

Marx points out that the answer to this question is quite different in the society of the medieval barons and that of the modern bourgeoisie. A baron could keep a relatively large band of retainers on the basis of a small total wealth, for reasons which do not obtain under capitalism. Today the proportion of unproductive laborers maintained can be kept large only

> because the productivity of the productive laborers is large, and therefore their surplus produce upon which the retainers feed. In this case the labor of the productive laborers is not productive because there are so many retainers, but on the contrary—there are so many retainers because the labor of the productive laborers is so productive.[47]

We may well conclude that this proportion—the size of society's band of unproductive laborers—may change again when socialist society succeeds the capitalist. Change how? If, as Marx and other socialists confidently expect, socialist society would lead to a great leap forward in the forces of production, the living space for intellectual labor would be vastly increased. This would be proposed as long-range effect. But in the short run, that is, for a period of transition, the picture may be more mixed.

Let us (following another passage in Marx) assume a considerable initial increase in productivity, so great that the proportion of the population "directly engaged in material production" is reduced from two-thirds to one-third. If this gain were to be more or less evenly distributed (as in a socialist democracy), everybody "would have two-thirds more time for unproductive labor and leisure. But in capitalist production everything seems and in fact is contradictory." What would in this case happen under capitalism? Of course, "the owners of profit and rent" would increase their revenue, as well as their retinue of unproductive laborers who provide them with services, including "the horde of flunkeys, the soldiers, sailors, police, lower officials, and so on, mistresses, grooms, clowns and jugglers." These latter are examples of unproductive laborers of lower culture. But in addition there will also be an increase in "ill-paid artists, musicians, lawyers, physicians, scholars, schoolmasters, inventors, etc." who "on the whole have a higher level of culture than the unproductive workers had previously."[48]

Thus this last-named stratum of intellectual laborers may be directly benefited by the conditions of capitalist prosperity, and perhaps directly harmed by the immediate consequences of an equalitarian reorganization of society, along with noxious excrescences of capitalist society lopped off at the same time. In the short run, the efforts of a socialist society to catch up on the social deficit accumulated over centuries may mean that there will be less available for unproductive laborers in general and for the intellectual strata in particular. This refers only to tangible material rewards, of course: there are other goods and rewards, which can be read about at length in many socialist propaganda tracts arguing that intellectual elements will be happier on the whole in a socialist democracy than in an exploitive society. Such considerations may influence the happy few; but Marx might not be persuaded that rosy visions, even true ones, can be expected to move masses into struggle, even masses of intellectuals who themselves produce visions as their immaterial commodity. There is reason to believe that most vendors of the immaterial are hardly less determined than others to be paid in cash.

In this respect the intellectual-labor segment of the capitalist retinue is not qualitatively different from others. They are far from homogeneous and far from singleminded in their service, but it is no common material interest as intellectuals (in any sense) that alienates them from it.

A very minor conclusion from Marx's analysis of intellectual labor is the pointlessness of the frequently posed question *Are the intellectuals a class?* If *class* is used in a popular nontechnical sense (meaning classification), as we have seen Marx or Engels do more than once, and if some meaningful definition of *intellectual* is fixed on, then an affirmative answer is as irrefutable as it is immaterial to our present subject.* But if a socioeconomic class in the Marxist sense is meant, the answer is plainly no.

---

* For a piquant example of the confusion involved in posing the question *Are the intellectuals a class?* there is Karl Kautsky's major article on "Die Intelligenz und die Sozialdemokratie" in the *Neue Zeit,* published shortly before Engels' death. Here Kautsky argues that there are *no* class interests that bind intellectuals together as a social group—and in the very course of making this argument he more than once refers to them as a "class."[49] What this illustrates is the insouciance with which this common noun was formerly used, before the aspiration for scientific terminology in sociology became an obsession.

17 | THE SOCIAL ROLE OF INTELLECTUAL ELEMENTS

Now let us focus not on intellectual laborers in general but more narrowly on the particular intellectual stratum that became prominent with the rise of the bourgeoisie, as identified in the previous chapter.[1] If, as Marx thought, the ruling ideas of an epoch tend to be the ideas of the ruling class, here we have the human agents of this process. They provide a service to "society," that is, to the class whose interests are usually identified with the interests of society; and this service primarily consists in providing and manipulating ideas. Such a service, to be eligible for reward, must be necessary or congenial to the continued well-being of the dominant powers in society.

1. THE "SERVANTS OF POWER"

The foregoing simply restates Marx's basic view of class society and historical change ("historical materialism"). But principles of social dynamics are implemented not by theories but by human beings, hence by social strata. The sway of bourgeois ideology is exerted in the last analysis through people, not through ethereal forces. And this is the social sense in which the intellectuals who perform this service are properly regarded as *bourgeois intellectuals*, regardless of personal origin: "the *ideological* representatives and spokesmen of the [given] classes, their learned men, lawyers, physicians, etc., in short: their so-called *capacités* [men of talent]."[2] One must not imagine, warned Marx (in a context discussing the French petty-bourgeoisie but in words applying broadly), that the political or ideological representatives of this class "are indeed all shopkeepers or enthusiastic champions of shopkeepers."

> According to their education and their individual position they may be as far apart as heaven from earth. What makes them representatives of the petty-bourgeoisie is the fact that in their minds they do not get beyond the limits which the latter do not get beyond in life, that they are consequently driven, theoretically, to the same problems and solutions to which material interest and social position drive the latter practically. This is, in general, the relationship between the *political* and *literary representatives* of a class and the class they represent.[3]

And it is in this spirit that Marx refers, in the same work, to *"capital, with its retinue of lawyers, professors and smooth-tongued orators."*[4] As early as *The German Ideology*, Marx had pointed to the intellectual strata whose social function it was to foster suitable fantasies. Kant's philosophy, he wrote, reflected the need, in the German society of the time, to convert French bourgeois liberalism into purely ideological concepts and moral postulates, at a time when both bourgeoisie and aristocracy were swathed in illusions about Germany's role in the Napoleonic era.

> Given these universal illusions, it was quite in order that the professions [*Stände*] privileged in illusions, the ideologists, the schoolmasters, the students, the Tugendbund [patriotic society] members, should talk big and give a suitable highflown expression to the universal fantasy-spinning and indifference.[5]

They were the illusion-makers.

Thus Marx directs attention to the social role of these ideological servicemen, not their individual motivation or psychology; it is best to assume that all upstanding intellectuals are motivated by the search for Truth and Light just as all bureaucrats desire Justice. However, those seekers for Truth and Light whose search leads them counter to the interests of the dominant class are less likely to be heard from; and so the objective result for society is scarcely determined by good intentions. If a particular intellectual activity is more or less socially neutral by nature—say, chess-playing—its practitioners will be expected at least not to use their activities and prestige to contravene the dominant social interests. In any case, for Marx the interests of the ruling class establish the decisive conditioning influences, boundaries of behavior, place in the social structure, and lines of activity leading to rewards.

In the most general sense, this describes the role of intellectual elements in relation to the larger social forces. Marx mentioned the generality in the course of an 1847 article:

> The abolition of feudal property relations and the establishment of modern bourgeois society was therefore not at all the result of a certain doctrine which stemmed from a particular theoretical principle as its *kernel* and deduced further conclusions from it. Rather, the principles and theories that the writers of the bourgeoisie put forward during its struggle with feudalism were nothing but the theoretical expression of the practical movement . . .[6]

In spite of the intensive "nothing but" in the last sentence, Marx also recognized that there was a "reciprocal influence" of material and intellectual production, not a simple one-way effect, and in the 1890s Engels had occasion to emphasize the semi-autonomous role of ideological factors (including ideological laborers) within the boundaries of a system.[7]

During the 1848 revolution, the Frankfurt parliament was crammed with professorial and literary representatives of the bourgeoisie who lived out the problem of how the intellectual represents the class. After discussing one example, the ex-radical Ruge, Engels commented:

> He, like all of the more or less ideological Left, sees his most cherished pet enthusiasms, his greatest efforts of thought, wrecked by the class whose representative he is. His philanthropic-cosmopolitan scheme is wrecked by mean huckster minds, and he himself, without knowing it or wanting to, must represent these huckster minds in a more or less ideologically distorted fashion. The ideologue proposes, the huckster disposes. Tragic irony of world history![7a]

However, Marx devoted no general theoretical work to this question any more than to dozens of others, and in practice we find that his ad hoc references to this sort of ideological labor were more often provoked by the offenses of particularly objectionable apologists of the status quo than by broad historical considerations. The provocations were plentiful.

Thus he wrote about the Franco-Prussian War: "It has given our professors the best opportunity of discrediting themselves in the eyes of the whole world for being servile pedants."[8] Then, in his Second

Address on the war, he noted that when the Prussian king abandoned his promise of defensive war only, the "stage managers" arranged for the appearance of public pressure on him. "They at once gave the cue to the liberal German middle class [bourgeoisie], with its professors, its capitalists, its aldermen, and its penmen."[9] In his notebook on the economist Adolph Wagner, he waxed sarcastic about the academic mind: German society, he wrote, has emerged out of feudal into capitalist economy, "but the professors still stand with one foot in the old crap, as is natural. From being serfs of the landowners they have changed over to being serfs of the state, *vulgo* [in popular parlance] the government."[10] In the 1850s Marx saw Bonaparte's regime losing the support not only of the bourgeoisie but of virtually every stratum of civil society—and therefore, at long last, of the intellectuals:

> °°Liberty, not only in its bodily forms, but in its very soul, its intellectual life, has shriveled at the coarse touch of these resurrectionists of a bygone epoch [the Bonapartists]. Consequently, the representatives of intellectual France, by no means distinguished by too nice a delicacy of political conscience, never failing to gather around every regime, from the Regent to Robespierre—from Louis XIV to Louis Philippe—from the first Empire to the second Republic—have, for the first time in French history, seceded in mass from an established government.[11]

Among the more violent imprecations is Engels' treatment, in an unpublished 1847 manuscript, of the whole tribe of penpushers, the *Herren Literaten*, as "this lowest of all venal classes."[12]

To be sure, it was probably Marx's opinion that the mass of the intellectual hacks who made their living as camp-followers of the established social powers constituted the large majority of the trade; therefore this type is of more significance in establishing the character of an intelligentsia as a social stratum than is, for example, a discussion of Goethe's relationship to the society of his time. Two remarks are necessary for perspective. Firstly: there is obviously an element of emotional and even intestinal revulsion in Marx's and Engels' reaction to the role of the intellectual laborers who provide a system's rulers with their ideological cover; and while the reasons for and justification of this revulsion need no explanation, it must be separated from a comprehension of the socioeconomic place of intellectual laborers of this sort. Secondly: the present subject merges into another one which is not in our purview, namely, how the needs and pressures of the status quo and its establishment are reflected not in the services performed by the hacks but in the intellectual products of the most highminded of philosophers, writers, artists, and ideologists—a subject on which there is a considerable literature. For some purposes it is enlightening to examine the relation to social issues of Balzac, Byron, Beethoven, or Bacon; but geniuses do not constitute a social stratum.

Is the offense of ideological laborers the fact that they act as intellectual sycophants of a bad system and society? Would their souls be saved if they did the same job for a good system, say, socialism; that is, transferred their apologetic role from the overthrown capitalists to the ascendant proletariat? Not in Marx's view: the great significance of social emancipation is that it also emancipates the thinker from a fate as a class instrument into a "free agent of thought." In the following passage Marx is discussing the stake of middle-class elements (of various sorts) in the victory of the Paris Commune, that is, in the coming of a socialist society. Although written in rough English, it uses *science* with the wider meaning of *Wissenschaft*—knowledge and learning as well as science in the usual sense.

> °°They feel that only the working class can emancipate them from priest rule, convert science from an instrument of class rule into a popular force, convert the men of science themselves from the panderers to class prejudice, place hunting state parasites, and allies of capital into free agents of thought! Science can only play its genuine part in the Republic of Labour.[13]

Clearly, intellectuals are not "free agents of thought" today. Tomorrow they can hope to be independent vis-à-vis the new state and social powers.

None of this implies that intellectual operatives necessarily play their roles consciously. Systematic hypocrisy of a conscious sort is exceptional; and it is undesirable, since sincerity and a projection of personal righteousness is a great aid to persuasiveness. No hypocrite can be a first-rate apologist; lack of conviction makes advocates ineffective even if it does not make them alcoholics. It is therefore an occupational necessity for intellectuals to reject Marx's view of their social role and class dependency. One of the ideas they cannot entertain is the idea that they are "The Servants of Power."*

---

* This is the title of an interesting book by Loren Baritz on the utilization of social scientists by American industry; its preface treats the subject as an example of the role of intellectuals.

If the indentured "men of ideas" must cling to the feeling of independence from class power, they must also ascribe the same independence to the realm of ideas itself. The notion that social ideas are not autonomous creations of the intellect but intimately related to class domination—this notion is seen to be as abhorrent as the attendant idea that they themselves are servitors of a power outside their skulls. Marx's method of interpreting social change and its ideologies, a class analysis of history, comes to look like a personal insult. To prove it wrong they need only look into their own souls, with its consciousness of integrity. Ironically, therefore, it is the "men of ideas" who need no ideas to refute Marxism; they can do it by intuition and introspection. Thus, their maintenance of a false consciousness does not depend altogether on ideological and other pressures as it usually does in the case of the working class; it is built into their life-condition. The intellectuals become carriers of the ideological malady because they are also its deepest-diseased victims.

2. THE EXCEPTIONAL CASES

No social stratum acts in unison like a regiment on parade; and few social strata are naturally as variegated as the intellectual category we are examining. As in every other case without exception, the social tendency we have described has exceptions.

Recognition of this fact was a platitude before Marx, and already in *The German Ideology* he mentioned it as a matter of course. Bourgeois development produces a class, the proletariat, from which arises the communist consciousness, "which can, of course, also arise among the other classes by dint of looking at the situation of this class."[14] But only with particular individuals, not as a class phenomenon. He first made this point polemically in a refutation of Heinzen's nonclass radicalism, which counterposed "humanity" to class society:

> It is very "possible" that particular individuals are not "always" determined by the class to which they belong—a fact that is as little decisive for the class struggle as was the defection of a few nobles to the Third Estates for the French Revolution. And at that time these nobles at least went over to *one* class, the revolutionary class, the bourgeoisie. But Mr. Heinzen lets all classes melt away before the ceremonial idea of "humanity."[15]

It is true (Marx goes on to say) that particular individuals are not determined, but it is not true "that *whole classes* which are based on *economic* conditions independent of their will and are set by these conditions in the most antagonistic opposition to each other, can break out of their real relationships by virtue of the quality of 'humanity' inherent in all men."[16]

Clearly there is even more room for special cases in a group which, while conditioned by economic pressures, does not itself form an independent class, and does not have the degree of homogeneity characteristic of a class. "Looking at the situation of this class [the proletariat]" with close familiarity and some empathy can lead particular individuals to a degree of independence from bourgeois apologetics even apart from full-fledged communism. Marx's admiration for the corps of British factory inspectors is well known, and he wrote it down very strongly:

> ... I willingly embrace the opportunity of paying my respects to those British factory-inspectors, who, in the teeth of all powerful class-interests, have taken up the protection of the down-trodden multitude with a moral courage, a steadfast energy, and an intellectual superiority of which there are not to be found many parallels in these times of mammon-worship.[17]

Yet, without detracting an iota from one's proper admiration for their moral courage, we know that the attitude adopted by these intellectually superior men was in the long run beneficial and necessary for the continued health of capitalism, and that the "powerful class interests" that hated them were typical of the myopic profit-grubbers whose unchecked excesses would have buried capitalism long ago. Without following this thought further, we only note that a distinction must be observed between admirable bourgeois friends of labor, who do not make a basic break with their own class, and social revolutionaries of bourgeois origin, who do.*

---

* What such a basic break means seems to be a mystery to some bourgeois intellectuals. Henderson and Chaloner, who have specialized in research on Engels, wrote as follows: "Although Engels' own livelihood—and the future of Karl Marx—depended upon the continued prosperity of the cotton trade Engels' venomous hatred of the capitalist system was so uncontrolled that he rejoiced at any misfortune that befell the industry."[18] This should be treasured as a definition-by-example of what Marx liked to call the *Spiessbürger* mentality (philistine mind).

The *Communist Manifesto* is concerned with the latter type, and specifically with the recruitment of trained personnel. There are three paragraphs on the question: *How does the proletarian movement acquire educated elements?* It sees three ways in which such elements are gained from the bourgeoisie.

Firstly, in its struggle against the aristocracy, the bourgeoisie seeks help from the proletariat and thus drags it into the political arena:

> The bourgeoisie itself, therefore, supplies the proletariat with its own elements of education, i.e., with weapons against itself.

Secondly:

> Further, as we have already seen, entire sections of the ruling classes are, by the advance of industry, precipitated into the proletariat, or are at least threatened in their conditions of existence. These also supply the proletariat with a mass of elements of education.*

This has to do with the proletarianization of middle-class elements, discussed elsewhere.[20] Here there is yet no question of bourgeois ideologists or intellectuals. That comes in the next paragraph only:

> Finally, in times when the class struggle nears the decisive hour, the process of dissolution going on within the ruling class, in fact within the whole range of old society, assumes such a violent, glaring character, that a small section of the ruling class cuts itself adrift, and joins the revolutionary class, the class that holds the future in its hands. Just as, therefore, at an earlier period, a section of the nobility went over to the bourgeoisie, so now a portion of the bourgeoisie goes over to the proletariat, and in particular, a portion of the bourgeois ideologists, who have raised themselves to the level of comprehending theoretically the historical movement as a whole.[21]

Let us remark on two things.

---

* These first two paragraphs are quoted here from the original (1848) text, not the Moore-Engels translation of 1888 which sought to make the Manifesto more accessible to an English public forty years afterward. In the first paragraph, the 1888 translation makes it "elements of *political and general* education" (adding the italicized words). In the second paragraph, it changes "mass of elements of education" to: "fresh elements of enlightenment and progress." In both cases, the changes obscure the original emphasis on *education,* that is, the acquisition of elements from the "educated classes" whether politically educated or not.[19]

1. Marx's concern is not how the proletarian movement gains "intellectuals," though this is how it seems to read to many intellectuals who write books on Marx. The subject is much broader: how the movement may be reinforced by *educated* individuals breaking with the bourgeoisie. The "bourgeois ideologists" among these are given special attention only at the end of the third passage.

2. The coming over of "a small section" of the bourgeoisie is seen as occurring only shortly before the revolutionary victory. Before that, special individuals might be expected, examples being well known at the time. The prominent cases were more than exceptional: they were rare and extraordinary men and even rarer women, including not only geniuses (Saint-Simon, for example) but others who were at least prodigies. To equate a Robert Owen or a Fourier with the case of some littérateur or academic who finally joined the socialist party in the 1890s is simply pointless. And no section or portion of the bourgeoisie, however small, came over with Owen or any other one of these exceptional individuals, even if the noun *intellectual* is defined in some way to cover the practical businessman Owen, the traveling salesman Fourier, and the rest.

In short, the Manifesto's treatment of these special individuals does not have in view the later problem of socialist recruitment from a stratum of bourgeois intellectuals. However, it offered some guidance in the treatment of similar problems. These problems multiplied in the German party in the ensuing decades as reform-minded intellectuals found no progressive bourgeois party with enough courage, integrity, and consistency to attract them, and found only the Social-Democratic Party at hand as a surrogate—especially after the removal of the Anti-Socialist Law in 1890.

The problem then became the very opposite of that discussed in the Manifesto: what to do about "bourgeois ideologists" who come over to the proletarian party not as a result of cutting themselves loose from their own class but in order to cut the proletarian party loose from its "antiquated" class-struggle foundations, that is, in order to convert it into the bourgeois reform party they lacked. This is how Marx and Engels saw the main problem to the end.

3. SOME GUIDELINES

But of course there is no rule of thumb for distinguishing the exceptional individuals of one type from the bourgeois intellectuals of the other; nothing for it but the individual tryout. A full treatment of this problem would at this point require a short history of the German movement and its relation to Marx and Engels, but in this and the next chapter we summarize the highlights of their conclusions and developing attitudes. Here are some general conclusions to begin with.

1. From the start Marx's dominant attitude toward bourgeois elements, whether intellectuals of some sort or not, who approach the proletarian movement may be summed up as mistrust tempered by hope, or apprehension sweetened by expectation. The hope was, however, considerably greater than Jesus' view of rich men and the needle's eye, after which "they that heard it said, Who then can be saved?" Marx was by no means so pessimistic about the chances of an intellectual's squeezing through to aid the revolutionary party with his educated talents.

Engels made an important distinction in a letter to the party's newspaper editor, then E. Bernstein, mentioning that he had liked some articles of his: "also your treatment of the 'intellectuals' as people who fall into our lap of themselves insofar as they are worth anything, but who, insofar as they had to be wooed, can only become harmful to us . . ."[22] No doubt one reason for Engels' lively approval of Bernstein's articles was the standoffishness—almost studied condescension—with which he treated this source of recruitment; he most certainly did not woo them.*

---

* The title and target of Bernstein's two-article series was the statement "We [the party] are lacking in intellectuals," which quoted claim he proceeded to deny. "If we had to wait till we have converted men of learning, etc., to socialism in considerable numbers," he wrote, "then our opponents could relax in good cheer: that way we will *never* get anywhere." This is so, he explained, because they stem from the bourgeoisie and remain bound up with it in their interests and way of life. "There are an insignificant number of exceptional cases when a man of learning dares to come out against the social conceptions dominant in society," and even then mostly behind closed doors.

And of the "educated people" who have dared to break with the prejudices of their class, once again the overwhelming majority have been brought to do so only through the steady growth of the workers' movement. It is on the latter, on the movement of the working class, that it alone depends; and the more intensively and compellingly the movement makes its way, the sooner will it encourage the more intelligent forces coming from the

2. In any case the number of real exceptions to the rule was expected to remain small—at least until "the class struggle nears the decisive hour" (in the words of the Manifesto). Up to 1848's decisive hour, the exceptional cases had become prominent among the leaders and publicists. For decades after the defeat and the ensuing reaction, the "men of ideas" found that they had other ideas after all. Engels remarked in a letter to Marx:

> The supply of *heads* that since '48 were brought over to the proletariat from other classes seems to have totally dried up since then, and in all countries. It seems the workers must do it *themselves* more and more.[24]

This was a plain statement of fact. Even later, not long before there was indeed an influx of intellectuals into the German party in the aftermath of an electoral victory, Engels wrote wryly that Kautsky "claims he has found one very good Ph.D. If he *really* is good, he would be very welcome."[25]

3. Among the least welcome recruits were the *failed intellectuals:* those who, unable to meet the competition, sought greener fields in which to exercise meager talents. At hand are a couple of examples that happen to relate to students. In a letter of 1883 Engels noted that

> the philistine elements, which were drawn into the party shortly before the Anti-Socialist Law [1878] and prevail particularly among college graduates and undergraduates who did not get as far as the examinations, are still there and will bear close watching . . .[26]

The same thrust occurs in an 1891 letter referring to "the students who were being driven into the Social-Democracy out of fear of the examinations."[27] Students show up here because the type is objectively verifiable in their case, but they are by no means the main problem. However, this type should not be confused with a very different one:

---

educated classes to join with it. . . . Of the danger for the Social-Democracy that may be tied up with this growth this is not the place to speak; it is a question only of making clear that the accession of these intellectuals depends on the size of the workers' movement, not the other way round. These accessions can at the most serve us as a measure of our strength; their influx will always be only a secondary matter. In the most favorable case they supply valuable fellow-fighters on the political field; in the economic class struggle its influence is just about nil.[23]

As against concern with this stratum of bourgeois intellectuals, he counterposed the recruitment of the "educated proletariat," of which more later in this chapter.

the *frustrated intellectuals* who cannot realize their intellectual aspirations under bourgeois conditions and turn to the alternative world for noncareerist reasons.

4. Another positive element is constituted by the underpaid-overexploited intellectual laborers, who are kept at a near-proletarian level of subsistence because their type of contribution is low-valued by bourgeois society. In this connection we get the term "intellectual proletarian" or "literary proletarian" and the like—quite common in socialist literature and sometimes used by Marx or Engels too. This literature often failed to distinguish between two different meanings of the term. In Marx's terms, the only scientifically precise use of *intellectual proletarian* would refer to the intellectual laborers (analyzed in the preceding chapter) who actually produce surplus-value for a capitalist entrepreneur—by, say, the fabrication of "Compendia of Economics" for a publisher "in factory style," to take an example already given.[28] But no less legitimate was a metaphorical usage, in which certain underpaid intellectual laborers were called "proletarian" to emphasize that they remained poor and propertyless regardless of talent, that is, shared these aspects of the proletarian life-condition. In this way Marx referred to rural schoolteachers as "the proletarians of the learned class."[29] This kind of reference to the "intellectual proletariat" became even more plentiful in the period of the Second International, especially where the scientific distinction was not important for publicist purposes.

In either case Marx's receptivity to these more or less intellectual elements, who merged with the proletarian movement as fellow-exploited, would obviously be far greater than to bourgeois intellectuals who came from other directions.

5. One of the most objectionable types was the fellow-traveler who wished to keep a foot in both camps, without cutting ties with the bourgeois establishment. Engels saw the very model of this variety in a Dr. Max Quarck (who later did join the party):

°°This Quarck is one of half a dozen young literati who hover about the boundary land between our Party and the Katheder-Sozialismus [academic state-socialism], take jolly good care to keep clear of all the risks involved in being connected with our Party, and yet expect to reap all the benefits that may accrue from such connection. They make a lively propaganda for *das soziale Kaisertum der Hohenzollern* [the social monarchy of the

Hohenzollerns] (which Quarck has dithyrambically celebrated),
for Rodbertus against Marx . . . and especially for each other.[30]

For such elements their privileged status as Thinkers in the workers'
movement could be parlayed into a form of prestige back in the
intellectual establishment. Engels warned against the characterless types
who are driven by "the need to come forward, not in the eyes of the
workers but of the philistines, as a Very Important worthy, who
doesn't long remain the terrible man-eater for which he passes."[31]

6. An intellectual's motivation for coming over to the proletarian
movement was, then, always important for the prognosis; but *why*
often translated into *when*. When the party had an electoral success,
career opportunities opened for ideologues; when the trade-union
movement became respectable, the penpusher and the *porte-parole*
could enjoy safe jobs; when the party became legal, progressive politicians could give free rein to their good intentions without being
inconvenienced by the police, and moreover be sure of a good press
when they denounced narrow class-struggle dogmas which would harm
the party by depriving it of such splendid recruits as themselves. We
shall see examples of the conjunctures at which this occurred.

4. TENDENCIES AMONG
RADICAL INTELLECTUALS

The German party began making its first impressive gains after
Marx's death, and so the problem of radical intellectuals in its most
acute forms fell mostly to Engels. However, the first big episode
pointing to the coming problem came in 1879 (the "manifesto of the
three Zurichers," or Höchberg tendency), and we shall see Marx's
violent reaction in several connections.

A good introduction to the overall patterns is provided by an open
letter Engels published in 1890. It was evoked by a faction of young
intellectuals in the German party self-styled the *Jungen* (Youth), whose
positive side was that it attacked the beginnings of opportunist degeneration among the Social-Democratic parliamentarians; but the standpoint it counterposed was elitist and sectarian. (The group's leaders
mostly wound up eventually as authoritarian rightists)[32] Engels stayed

out of the melee until the group's paper made public use of his name as if he were a supporter, in a ploy common to literary clique wars. He was then forced to state his opinion equally publicly. We are interested here in his analysis of the group as a coterie of radical intellectuals.

Engels' open letter mapped a good deal of the terrain:

> As for theory, I find in it [the group's paper] . . . a strenuously distorted "Marxism": characterized, in the first place, by a big misunderstanding of the viewpoint they claim to represent; in the second place, by gross ignorance of the always decisive historical facts; in the third place, by the consciousness of their own immeasurable superiority which is so profitably evident to German littérateurs. . . .
>
> As for practice, I found in it a reckless disregard of all the actual circumstances of the party struggle, a death-defying "overcoming of obstacles" in fantasy, which indeed does all honor to the unflagging youthful ardor of the authors but which, in the course of being translated from idea into reality, would be capable of burying even the strongest party of millions under the well-deserved laughter of the whole enemy world. And that even a little sect cannot allow itself such acrobatic politics without paying a penalty—on this the gentlemen have since had their own experiences. . . .

Above all, in summary:

> Let them understand that their "academic education"—which in any case needs a basic, critical self-review—gives them no officer's commission with a claim to a corresponding post in the party; that in our party everyone must serve in the ranks; that posts of responsibility in the party will be won not simply by literary talent and theoretical knowledge, even if both of these are present beyond a doubt, but that in addition what is required is thorough familiarity with the conditions of the party struggle and seasoning in its forms, tested personnel reliability and sound character, and, finally, willing enlistment in the ranks of the fighters;—in short, that they, the "academically educated people," have far more to learn from the workers, all in all, than the latter have to learn from them.[33]

This touches on or suggests some of the major tendencies arising out of the entrance of these "academically educated people" into a movement dominated by a working-class membership and built by working-class activists. Let us enlarge on five such tendencies, beginning with one not directly exemplified by the *Jungen.*

1. *Reformism and bourgeoisification.*

While the *Jungen* had begun with an appearance of leftism, the main tendency of intellectual recruits to the German party was to the right, that is, toward accommodation with the bourgeois world from which they were not breaking.

In 1879, in response to the imposition of the Anti-Socialist Law by Bismarck the previous year, a trio of leading party "literati" (to use Marx's favorite designation) came out with a programmatic article making the first open proposal to turn the party into a bourgeoisified social-reform party of parliamentarism. The matter was quite serious since it was likely that the trio's leader, Karl Höchberg, rich scion of a banking family, was going to be entrusted with launching the party's organ in emigration, since he could provide the money to do it. In this article, wrote Engels to a friend, they

> come out as wholly ordinary bourgeois, peaceful philanthropists; they accuse the party of having been too exclusively a *"workers' party,"* of having provoked the hatred of the bourgeoisie, and they lay claim to the leadership of the movement for "educated" bourgeois of their own stamp.[34]

In mid-September Marx and Engels sent a Circular Letter on this crisis to the party leadership; it is one of the three or four most important political statements ever drawn up by them, and we shall have several occasions to come back to it. To a friend Marx wrote that the party needed editorial talent of a quite different sort, an editor who would keep at arm's length "the pack of Ph. D.'s and students, etc. and the professorial-socialism [*Kathedersozialismus*] crew that strut about in the *Zukunft* [Höchberg's bimonthly] . . ." The Höchberg trio, on the contrary, fostered parliamentary cretinism.

> These fellows—ciphers in theory, good-for-nothing in practice— want to draw the teeth of socialism (which they have hashed together after some university recipes) and especially of the Social-Democratic *party,* to enlighten the workers, or, as they put it, to provide them with "elements of education" through their own confused half-knowledge, and above all to make the party respectable in the eyes of the philistines. They are wretched *counterrevolutionary* windbags.

Höchberg had come to London to enlighten Engels, and "was stunned when Engels gave it to him straight: he is a 'peaceful' evolutionary and expects proletarian emancipation actually only from 'educated bourgeois,' i.e., people like himself."[35]

Three years later Engels, writing to the same friend, referred back to this unsuccessful attempt by the "Messrs. Literati" of the party "to carry out a turn toward a reactionary, bourgeois, tame and educated tendency." The Höchberg program had "demanded that the party's behavior be more eddicated* and respectable, more presentable in the drawingroom." They "would like to beg off the Anti-Socialist Law at any price through mildness and softness, cringing and tameness, because it makes short work of their literary livelihood." He expected that when the Anti-Socialist Law was abolished, they "will form a separate right wing, in which case we can then treat with them from case to case, until they finally and definitively fall on their asses."[36]

But the problem became worse as the party showed electoral strength, and thus became "possible" for left-wing intellectuals who retained prudent regard for their standing in the bourgeois world. By 1884 Engels was expressing the following view, as he opined that the possible demise of a party magazine was no misfortune:

> It is becoming more and more apparent that the great majority of the *literary* party people** in Germany belong to the opportunists and pussyfooters, who feel in quite the right atmosphere from the *literary* standpoint—however disagreeable the Anti-Socialist Law may be to them from the pecuniary standpoint; they can express themselves without let or hindrance—we are hindered from giving them a whack. Hence, merely filling up such a magazine every month requires an enormous amount of patient forbearance, and gradually gets it overrunning with philanthropism, humanitarianism, sentimentalism, and whatever all the antirevolutionary vices of the Freiwalds, Quarcks, Schippels, Rosuses, etc. are called.[37]

A year later came one of the many attempts by the party parliamentarians to steer the movement toward the peaceful haven of reform

---

* *Eddicated* [*jebildet*] , as the ironically plebeian form of *educated*, was much used in Engels' letters to mock the intellectual pretensions of college-trained recruits who deigned to bestow their talents on the movement. It will be seen several times in the following pages.

** *Literary* refers to writing for the movement, not writing general or belletristic literature. *Party literature* means writings published by or for the party. (Hence Marx's characteristic use of *literati* in the same sense.)

politics. Engels as usual linked this to the top layer of bourgeois-educated elements that was encrusting the party, while the party remained overwhelmingly proletarian in its ranks:

> The row in the German party did not surprise me. In a land of petty-bourgeois philistines [*Spiessbürger*] like Germany the party is also bound to have a philistine "educated" right wing, which it shakes off at the decisive moment. Philistine-socialism dates from 1844 in Germany and was already criticized in the *Communist Manifesto*. It is as immortal as the German philistine himself.[38]

These people, he added, are "suppressing the proletarian character of the party and trying to replace it with a crass-esthetic-sentimental philanthropism without force or life."

2. Abstractionism and sentimental socialism.

The substitution of abstractions for realities, the disembodying of ideas, is one of the characteristic afflictions of intellectuals that Marx was specially sensitive to. It was nowhere more rife than among German intellectuals, for historical reasons that Marx explained more than once. Even in the course of the rough-and-tumble of the 1848 revolutionary upsurge, he took occasion to comment on this aspect of the bourgeois-liberal savants who pullulated in the Frankfurt National Assembly—the "assembly of professors," as he called it.

> Messrs. Professors, who "make history" for their private delectations, must let such things happen as the bombardment of Vienna, the murder of Robert Blum, the barbarism of Windischgrätz! These gentlemen, who have Germany's cultural history so close to their hearts, leave the practical exercise of this culture to a Jellachich and his Croats! While the professors make the theory of history, history is taking its own stormy course, and concerns itself very little with the history of these gentlemen the professors.[39]

One of the characteristic forms of intellectual abstractionism which cropped up in the movement was the subordination of social struggle to some purely ideological *ism* which is given primacy—for example, atheism as a social movement. There were such types among the few intellectuals attracted to the First International, including Peter Fox, with whom Marx collaborated well. But Fox's weak side was that his previous contacts with workers had been only as a propagandist for atheism. Marx commented: "But it is so easy to get rationalism [anti-supernaturalism] across among the English workers that one must watch out very much as soon as literati, bourgeois or semi-literati take part in the movement."[40] The trouble was the tendency to *substitute* this sort of ideological preoccupation for the concerns of a class movement. There were going to be innumerable other examples in the next hundred years.

Similarly, for Marx "sentimentalism" is a question of the *substitution* of a sentimental emphasis for a class-struggle approach to social and political issues. Nor did he have any greater use for the daydreaming type of propaganda exercise in the press: "You will have noticed [Marx wrote a friend] that semi-erudite philistine fantasies show up in the *Volksstaat* from time to time. This stuff comes from schoolmasters, Ph.D.'s and students."[41]

Following the 1875 fusion with the Lassalleans, Marx began to sense a certain effluvium in the winds that blew from some of the new "educated elements" in the united party:

A rotten spirit is making itself felt in our party in Germany, not so much among the masses as among the leaders (upper-class and "workers"). The compromise with the Lassalleans has led to a compromise with other halfway elements too: in Berlin (via [*Johann*] *Most*) with Dühring and his "admirers," but also with a whole gang of half-mature students and superwise Ph.D.'s who want to give socialism a "higher, idealistic" orientation, that is, to replace its materialist basis (which demands serious objective study from anyone who tries to use it) by modern mythology with its goddesses of Justice, Liberty, Equality and *Fraternité*. Dr. Höchberg, who publishes the *Zukunft*, is a representative of this tendency and has "bought his way" into the party—with the "noblest" intentions, I assume, but I don't give a damn for "intentions." Anything more miserable than his *Zukunft* program has seldom seen the light of day with more "modest presumption."[42]

This was two years before Höchberg's "rotten spirit" emerged fullblown as open reformism, in the aforementioned 1879 eruption.

3. Instability and ultraism.

Because the bourgeois intellectual is more detached from social realities, or tries to be, and may in some cases be less inhibited by money considerations, he or she can be more volatile, erratic, and unstable than most workers—at least in terms of ideas, if not action. This pattern may reach a peak with students, who after all are apprentice intellectuals, and who are still relatively untrammeled by responsibility. In the socialist movement, an outsize proportion of intellectuals have been generally found both in the right wing and in the more exotic ultraradical sects—in the latter often as a stopover to the former, as the case of the *Jungen* illustrated. Oscillatory motion is a characteristic feature. Marx even commented along these lines on the fact that his own writings sold so well in Russia—to the educated classes, of course, not the masses.

> But too much should not be made of all this. The Russian aristocracy is, in its youth, educated at German universities and in Paris. They always run after the most extreme that the West can offer.
>
> It is pure gourmandise, such as a part of the French aristocracy practised during the eighteenth century. *Ce n'est pas pour les tailleurs et les bottiers* [It's not for the tailors and shoemakers], said Voltaire in those days of his own Enlightenment. This does not prevent the same Russians, once they enter state service, from becoming rascals.[43]

These same types were to be found among the intellectuals attracted by Bakuninist rhetoric about abstention from politics, "social liquidation," and other grandiose phrases.

> All this sounds extremely radical and is so simple that it can be learnt by heart in five minutes; that is why the Bakuninist theory has speedily found favor also in Italy and Spain among young lawyers, doctors [Ph.D.s] and other doctrinaires.[44]

These types lack seriousness; dilettantism goes along with the pattern. One of Engels' last letters noted the problem of

> a country like Italy, where the socialist party, like all the other parties, suffers from the invasion, as of locusts, by that "declassed bourgeois youth" of which Bakunin was so proud. Result: pullulation of literary dilettantism, only too often turning into sensationalism, and necessarily followed by a coterie spirit which dominates the press.[45]

It is not the merely personal characteristics of individuals that form this pattern; on the contrary, these characteristics crop up widely and regularly because they flow from a social molding force. These types are in a hurry, they are impatient—not necessarily out of vulgar career ism but because there are so many other life-alternatives pulling at them. They are scornful of a course that demands a long investment in plugging away and waiting—unlike workers who plug away and wait most of their lives. It was to H. M. Hyndman, the most thorough bourgeois who ever led a self-styled Marxist group, that Engels applied the biting Gallic saying: *"Cet homme n'ira pas loin, il ne sait pas attendre"*—This man won't go far, he doesn't know how to wait.[46] The get-rich-quick pattern, in politics as elsewhere, betrays the bourgeois mentality.

4. Elitism and authoritarianism.

Perhaps the most prominent tendency among intellectuals—built in by their onesidedness—is to assume the natural superiority of the educated talents and their prerogative to become shepherds leading the flock of the unenlightened.

This does not necessarily mean that the elitist intellectuals themselves aspire to the role of authoritarian leader, which role is usually outside their taste or competence. It does mean their tendency to support, justify or accept the necessity of some sort of control from above over the inferior masses, especially if the Leader is enlightened enough to recognize the intellectual's claim to special status as first lieutenant. Hence this tendency operates just as forcibly in a parliamentary setup as in a dictatorial one, and the context of this discussion is in no way peculiar to totalitarianisms. However, extreme authoritarianisms exhibit all tendencies in an extreme way, hence most visibly. In 1852 Marx, writing for the *New York Tribune*, attacked the self-styled Democrats who connived with Bonaparte's regime, some of them even looking up to that protofascist despot as the hope of revolution.[47] To the inevitable objections Marx replied roundly:

°°To the gentlemen of the Democratic press, and especially of the German Democratic press, who, as usual, have yelled the loudest, I say they are all bigoted Crypto-Royalists. These gentlemen can not do without kings, gods and popes. Scarcely got out of the leading strings of their old rulers, they manufacture new ones for themselves, and grow indignant at those infidels and rebels who render themselves obnoxious by publishing unpleasant truths, revealing compromising facts and thus committing *lèse*-majesty and sacrilege against the newly-elevated Democratic gods and kings.[48]

Marx's target was the tendency of the bourgeois literati to grab the coattails of Power and to look for salvation to a savior-ruler (a suitably enlightened one), but in any case not to the ignorant masses, who might be so barbaric as even to rebel against their intellectual superiors. This was a pervasive issue in Marx's and Engels' explosive denunciation of the Höchberg tendency in 1879. In their aforementioned Circular Letter, they drew a bead on the following passage in what they called the "manifesto of the Three Zurichers":

> "The movement [wrote the trio], which Lassalle regarded as an eminently political one, to which he summoned not only the workers but all honest democrats, *at the head of which* were to march the independent representatives of science and *all men imbued with true love of humanity,* was lowered ... to a *one-sided struggle of the industrial workers in their own interests."* [The emphasis is by Marx as he quotes this.] [49]

This openly stated an appeal to eradicate the class-struggle character of the movement and replace proletarian socialism with an allegedly non-class socialism officered by bourgeois intellectuals of the educated classes. Marx and Engels underlined this:

> In the opinion of these gentlemen, then, the Social-Democratic Party should *not* be a onesided workers' party but an all-sided party of "all men imbued with true love of humanity." It must prove this above all by laying aside coarse proletarian passions and placing itself under the guidance of educated, philanthropic bourgeois "in order to cultivate good taste" and "learn good form" ... Then, too, *"numerous adherents* from the circles of the *educated* and *propertied* classes will make their appearance ..."

The Höchberg article indicated further that such elements "among the so-called upper strata of society" are needed especially because "the Party still lacks men fit to represent it in the Reichstag." Only in rare cases can "the simple worker" be entrusted with the deputy's mandate. In this way the Höchberg group specifically linked party leadership by educated bourgeois to the development of reformist parliamentarism. In short, concluded Marx and Engels in the Circular Letter, the trio's viewpoint amounts to this: "the working class of itself is incapable of its own emancipation. For this purpose it must place itself under the leadership of 'educated and propertied' bourgeois who alone possess the 'time and opportunity' to acquaint themselves with what is good for the workers ..." [50]

The de facto domination of the party's Reichstag group by educated bourgeois opportunists was precisely what Marx—and especially Engels after Marx's death—continued to attack, as the immediate manifestation of the "rotten spirit" that permeated the party leadership and created the need for a split. All during the decade before his death, Engels inveighed against "the schoolmarmish supercilious snobbery of our so-called educated people"[51] as the great danger to the party, reiterating the warning that this destroyed the principle of self-emancipation:

> It's always these people who consider their bit of an education as absolutely indispensable, thanks to which the workers are not to emancipate themselves but rather gain salvation through it; the emancipation of the working class is, to them, possible only by the eddicated bourgeois philistine; how are the poor, helpless, uneddicated workers to take care of it themselves![52]

In 1890 the worsening of the situation was exemplified by the *Jungen* faction:

> There has been a students' revolt in the German party. For the past 2-3 years, a crowd of students, littérateurs and other young declassed bourgeois has rushed into the party, arriving just in time to occupy most of the editorial positions on the new journals which pullulate, and, as usual, they regard the bourgeois university as a socialist Saint-Cyr which gives them the right to enter the party's ranks with an officer's commission if not a general's. . . .
> These fine fellows, whose impotence is equaled only by their arrogance, have found support in the new recruits of the party in Berlin—typical Berlinism, comprising cheek, cowardice, bluster and *gift of the gab* all rolled into one, seems to have come to the surface again for a moment; it formed the chorus for the student gentry.[53]

The party is afflicted in Germany, Engels wrote to an American comrade, "with the arrogant Germans who want to play schoolmaster and commander in one, and make the natives disgusted with learning even the best things from them."[54] With this ironical use of "natives" for the workers, the bourgeois-educated "commanders" are implicitly compared in attitude with colonialists who see themselves as the benevolent masters of inferiors.

This intellectualist syndrome was by no means peculiar to the educated snobs of Germany. In Britain they had formed an organization, the Fabian Society, which Engels observed over a number of years.

> You [Kautsky] see something unfinished in the Fabian Society. On the contrary, this crowd is only *too* finished: a clique of bourgeois "socialists" of diverse calibers, from careerists to sentimental socialists and philanthropists, united only by their fear of the threatening rule of the workers and doing all in their power to spike this danger by making *their own* leadership secure, the leadership exercised by the "eddicated."[55]

The Fabians were

> these stuck-up bourgeois, who would graciously condescend to emancipate the proletariat from above if it will only be sensible enough to realize that such a raw and uneducated mass cannot free itself and can achieve nothing except by the grace of these smart lawyers, literati and sentimental females.[56]

Their American similars were the class-consciously bourgeois radicals of the Bellamy movement, who called socialism "Nationalism":

> They are the counterparts of the Fabians in this country. Superficial and shallow as the Dismal Swamp, but conceited about the glorious magnanimity with which they, as eddicated bourgeois, condescend to emancipate the workers; in return for which, however, the latter must behave themselves and obediently carry out the orders of the eddicated °cranks° and their isms.[57]

But these were observations from outside. Engels' concern kept coming back to the German party, whose internal evolution he could follow more closely. It was not only a question of the bourgeois recruits: there were the party leaders who fawned on the "eddicated" and truckled to them. On top the worst case was Wilhelm Liebknecht, who "not only has himself welcomed every halfway social-democratic 'eddicated' man with open arms and without looking him over closely, but besides, his son-in-law, the fat dullard Bruno Geiser, is one of the biggest howlers."[58] Later, when socialist workers' hostility to the opportunism of the party parliamentarians involved Geiser especially, Engels wrote: "We owe all this garbage mostly to Liebknecht with his predilection for educated wiseacres and people in bourgeois positions who can be shown off before the philistines. He can't resist a littérateur and a businessman who are flirting with socialism."[59] From time to time Engels had occasion to make similar comments on Liebknecht's role,[60] and no doubt had him particularly in mind in the following:

> ... our lads in Germany are really splendid fellows, now that the Anti-Socialist Law has freed them from the "eddicated" gentlemen who had made the attempt before 1878 to schoolmaster the workers from above, with their ignorant university-type confusion—an attempt to which only too many of the "leaders" unfortunately lent a hand. This rotten stuff has not yet been entirely eliminated, but still the movement has again entered a definitely revolutionary channel.[61]

But in fact it was the elitist intellectuals and bourgeois careerists who eventually won out in the party—in alliance with the trade-unionist bureaucracy which the intellectuals joined in fostering. That, however, is another and longer story.

5. *Sectarianism and sectism.*

Here we can only touch on this problem, since the general subject of party organization, including socialist sects, will be taken up in Volume 3. Anticipating some conclusions, it must be emphasized that sectism involves the tendency to *counterpose* socialism as a Good Idea to the class movement as a defective reality.

Since the crux of Marx's politics is the central place he gives to the militant movement of the class as such, regardless of its temporary program,[62] there is no kind of socialism more antithetical than Marx's to the typical intellectual mentality. We will see why Marx and Engels fulminated against a series of socialist sects, some of them set up by more or less Marxistical intellectuals; but it will suffice to stress now that the general reason was always the sect's conception of the relation between the intellectual idea (bodied forth in the sect) and the class-in-movement.

This, along with preceding point 4, indicates the source of the close association in socialist history between intellectuals and sectism: firstly, predilection for the primacy of ideas over material interests; and secondly, elitist fear of a mass movement which is not under the control of Superior Minds. This intellectualist fear of self-moving masses is transmuted into programmatic terms by the ultimatistic requirement that a class movement must measure up to intellectually established political standards before it can be accepted without contamination.

This is also why the test case has often been the attitude of revolutionaries or would-be revolutionaries to the reality of a reformist trade-union movement which reflects the working class as it is at a particular stage. As explained in Chapter 4 above, only Marx's theory established an integral link between social revolution and reformist trade unions as class organizations; only his theory saw trade unions as a revolutionary fact even if and when they are antirevolutionary in politics; only it saw the social struggle as one in which the basic division was not along idea lines but along class lines.

To put it still another way: sectists saw socialism primarily as a *concept to convince people of;* that is, they looked at socialism in the same way that intellectuals habitually look at the world. Marx saw socialism as the necessary outcome of the proletariat's struggle; his theory argued that it was this class whose own struggle, even under nonsocialist leadership and on a relatively low level, shakes the foundations of capitalist society. Marx and Engels reiterated that "Every step of real movement is more important than a dozen programs."[63] Radical intellectuals often hear this as expressing contempt for ideas and glorification of pragmatic shortsightedness; that is, they have no idea what it means.

This is not to say that the only source of sectism in the history of socialism is the influence of intellectuals. While the phenomenon is by no means limited to intellectuals, the following can be stated: *the sect is a form of organization characteristically congenial to the intellectual as a radical elitist.* (In nonradical and mass-party contexts, the analogous form is often the clique or academic coterie.) The sect provides an organizational package to express the predilection of intellectuals for elitist modes of influence—for their strength lies in their heads rather than in numbers, money or brawn; to express their insistence on the primacy of the idea over material interests—for they have only the former to offer; to express their propensity to seek insulation against the masses, the Dark Masses who impinge on their consciousness mainly as a dangerously uncontrollable beast-organism.

5. INTELLECTUAL ELITISM:
THE CASE OF LASSALLE

Conflicts with intellectual-elitist tendencies peppered Marx's career. We have already discussed Marx's earliest attack on a tendency embodying a fullblown intellectual elitism: his polemic against the

Bauer group in *The Holy Family.*[64] By this time, the latter part of 1844, young Engels too was becoming conscious of the patronizing arrogance of the intellectual circles with which he and Marx were beginning to break. In a letter to Marx (only his second) he satirically predicted that the Bauer group was due to discover a new messiah who would erect a New Jerusalem, complete with well-planned privies, after which it would "declare that it is all in all, that it unites capital, talent and labor in its own head, that everything produced is produced by *it* and not by the impotent masses—and commandeer everything for itself."[65]

But, as Marx's friend Heine was singing around this same time: *"Other times, and other birds! / Other birds, and other songs!"*[66] When the German social-democratic movement was founded in the 1860s under the leadership of Ferdinand Lassalle, this clever man was not singing the rather simple-minded songs of the Bauerite elitists, who were so naive as to denounce the Stupid Masses openly.

Lassalle is one of the outstanding exceptions to the rule that intellectuals themselves do not aspire to be Maximum Leader. Here we are concerned not with the main line of Lassalle's politics (state-socialism),[67] nor primarily with his aspiration to become literally the dictator of the workers' movement, but rather with his self-image as a Captain of Intellect in politics* and with Marx's reaction to this aspect of Lassalle.

Marx first became aware of Lassalle's "longing for dictatorship" in 1856, without quite believing the initial reports that came to him.[68] But by 1862–1863 the pattern was plain.[69] In 1863 Lassalle sent Marx a pamphlet of his in which he made his bid for leadership of the German workers' movement. Marx commented in a letter to Engels:

> He behaves—with an air of great importance bandying about phrases borrowed from us—altogether as if he were the future workers' dictator. The problem of wage-labor versus capital he solves like "child's play" (literally). To wit, the workers must agitate for *universal suffrage* and then send people like him "armed with the unsheathed sword of science [*Wissenschaft*]" into the Chamber of Deputies.[70]

Here is how Lassalle had put it in the pamphlet, addressing himself to the workers:

* It is in this sense that Lasalle can be called an intellectual, if one insists. For our purposes the essential thing is his role as the Educated Bourgeois who condescends to put himself at the head of the workers' movement.

When that [universal suffrage] comes, you can depend upon it, there will be at your side men who understand your position and are devoted to your cause—men, armed with the shining sword of science, who know how to defend your interests. And then you, the unpropertied classes, will only have yourselves and your bad voting to blame if the representatives of your cause remain in a minority . . .[71]

This is a frank statement of the attitude later assumed by most of the Social-Democratic deputies blessed with a bourgeois education, who thought in terms of *we* and *they*—the latter being the ignorant workers who sometimes made trouble by presuming to dictate to their representatives.

In one respect Lassalle did carry out the pattern of the elitist intellectual clambering up to the ear of power. The mantle of "workers' dictator" was only his preliminary to a higher aim: steering the kaiser himself toward the Social Monarchy, that is, an allegedly anticapitalist welfare regime carried out by the royal power, based not on the bourgeoisie but on a working class organized as Lassalle's instrument. Marx understood this completely by 1865, though the secret documents that spelled out Lassalle's aims were not revealed till over half a century later. Marx summed it up in terms of the characters in Schiller's drama *Don Carlos:* "Lassalle wanted to play the Marquis Posa of the proletariat with Philip II of the Uckermark, Bismarck acting as procurer between him and the Prussian kingdom."[72] The Marquis Posa figure was the standard model of the Good Royal Advisor whispering progressive aspirations into the monarch's left ear.[73]

Also instructive is the discussion held by Marx and Engels with Lassalle on the latter's poetic drama *Franz von Sickingen.* It was typical that the hero of the period chosen by Lassalle was not any leader of the Peasant War (such as Thomas Münzer) but the head of the knights' opposition, Sickingen—an opposition which, while rebellious against the princes, lived by its own exploitation of the peasantry. Both Marx and Engels pointed this out in separate letters. Marx added that Sickingen and his co-leader Ulrich von Hutten "just like the *educated* Polish nobility of 1830, on the one hand, made themselves exponents of modern ideas, while on the other they actually represented the interests of a reactionary class."[74] Not for the first time Marx underlines that the interests of a reactionary class can be clothed in modernizing ideas as well as in reactionary ones.

Sickingen was not portrayed as an intellectual (any more than Rudolph of Gerolstein in Sue's *Mysteries of Paris*). But, while in a letter to Marx Lassalle disparaged Ulrich von Hutten precisely because he *was* an intellectual type rather than a statesmanly man of action like Sickingen, we know now that in fact Lassalle identified himself personally with Hutten, not Sickingen.[75] Thus we are pointed back again to the relationship of Sue to Rudolph: the intellectual glorifies the Leader on horseback, who in turn proves his worth by listening to the former's wisdom; the philosopher-king is tutored by the king's philosopher, who is the wisest servitor in the entourage of power; the schoolmaster wields his rod at the side of the Master.

6. "THE ALTITUDE OF ITS GREAT INTELLECTS"

Another element, not to be neglected, in Marx's attitude on the relation of intellectuals to the workers' movement is sure to offend intellectuals. This was his generally low opinion of the intellectual caliber of the intellectuals, that is, of bourgeois thinkers who, whatever their politics, were unable to break out of the constricting and deforming frame imposed by the dominant ideas of their class society. This view was given acid epigrammatic form in *Capital*:

> On the level plain, simple mounds look like hills; and the imbecile flatness of the present bourgeoisie is to be measured by the altitude of its great intellects.[76]

The target here was John Stuart Mill as an economist, but among the post-Ricardian economists Marx played few favorites—except perhaps for his special attention to Malthus as an intellectual charlatan. Marx thought Mill was dreadfully "shallow," as he says in his Afterword to *Capital*. Here he explains why this situation obtains; the discussion is in terms of economics but applies more generally. There is little point in explaining this view of Marx's as a case of "jealousy" or cantankerousness, or utilizing some other all-purpose psychiatric device, which will fail to account for his treatment of Ricardo as a giant.

Marx thinks that "the great capacity for theory, which used to be considered a hereditary German possession, had almost completely disappeared among the so-called educated classes in Germany" because the later crop of thinkers could not think their way through the *social* conditions that faced them; they were up against "the limits beyond which [they] could not pass."[77] That is, they could not arrive at real explanations that did not point outside the bounds of the system. Then, in addition, the rising prominence of the class struggle sounded the knell of scientific social inquiry:

> It was thenceforth no longer a question whether this theorem or that was true, but whether it was useful to capital or harmful, expedient or inexpedient, politically dangerous or not. In place of disinterested inquirers, there were hired prizefighters; in place of genuine scientific research, the bad conscience and the evil intent of apologetic.[78]

That is, bourgeois intellectuals could no longer be "free agents of thought."[79] At best, some who tried to avoid becoming sycophants of the ruling class sought a harmonious middle ground for the interests of capital and labor—"Hence a shallow syncretism, of which John Stuart Mill is the best representative."[80]

In France, Guizot had begun as a pioneer in the class interpretation of history, but he could not maintain this level, Marx points out. A scientific approach went by the board as he had to write a whitewash account of the Louis Philippe regime and his own role in it; and history was reduced to good and bad leaders. Marx concludes: "Indeed, not only *les rois s'en vont,* but also *les capacités de la bourgeoisie s'en vont"*—Not only do kings pass, but also the talented among the bourgeoisie.[81]

Not only the talented: Marx liked also to pillory the representative ranks of the bourgeoisie and the ruling circles for their ignorance of, unconcern with, and cynicism about the cultural heritage of society which the "better elements" were supposed to treasure. The division of labor "has, to a certain extent, emasculated the general intellect of the middle-class men by the circumspection of all their energies and mental faculties within the narrow spheres of their mercantile, industrial and professional concerns."[82] He wrote a cutting portrait of the bourgeois mind and its intellectual narrowness for the *New York Tribune:*

Although the middle class do not aim at the learning of the old school, they do not for that cultivate either modern science or literature. The ledger, the desk, business, that is education sufficient. Their daughters, when expensively educated, are superficially endowed with a few "accomplishments"; but the real education of the mind and the storing it with knowledge is not even dreamed of. . . .

The cramped and narrow sphere in which they move is to a certain degree due to the social system of which they form a part. As the Russian nobility live uneasily betwixt the oppression of the Czar above them and the dread of the enslaved masses below them, so the English middle class are hemmed in by the aristocracy on the one hand and the working class on the other.[83]

All the more reason, then, to give close inspection to the educated bourgeois elements who knocked on the door of the workers' party. For a considerable period of time, in Germany, this was no arduous task: the number of salutary intellectuals who entered the German party's ranks—say, up to Marx's death—was small, though a few exceptions were prominent. In the following years, Engels' appreciation of the exceptions was often flavored with his mordant opinion of the others. In praise of Eduard Bernstein (then still writing as a staunch revolutionist) Engels remarked to Bebel: "In theoretical matters, Ede has a very receptive mind, clever and quick-witted, but he still lacks self-confidence—truly a rare thing nowadays and, compared with the general swelled head of even the pettiest educated jackass, it is really a good thing relatively speaking." Bernstein and Kautsky are listed as "real pearls" in comparison with "the ghastly second-growth of literati that have latched on to the party," and Engels' approval of the second is expressed thus: "Kautsky learned a fearful mass of nonsense from the universities, but he has taken all possible pains to unlearn it again." Outside these two pearls, *all* the other posts in the party press are held by "the Messrs. Philistines" who (Engels hopes) can be gotten rid of in the inevitable split that is coming. This in 1885.[84] Engels' opinion of Kautsky had gone up somewhat from four years before, when he had characterized him as "an extremely fine fellow but a born pedant and hairsplitter, in whose hands complicated questions do not become simple but rather simple questions become complicated." He judged him unfit to edit a newspaper, where "such a doctrinaire is a real misfortune . . ."[85] Both men eventually did some good work before they collapsed; this made them exceptions.

Given their general opinion of the pickings, it is clear why Marx and Engels were made especially apprehensive by the tendency of the bourgeois-educated recruits to come into the movement as *teachers*. Teaching what? Their still bourgeois or half-bourgeois ideas, now taking on a pink tinge. Otherwise they would have to adopt the role of learners, apprentices, and novices—learning from the socialist workers how to think like revolutionists, like enemies of the class in whose matrix their own minds had been formed and their consciousness educated. In Marx's and Engels' eyes, these people came into the party ignorant—ignorant of socialist thought and action, and only half-learned in "the fearful mass of nonsense from the universities."

> Another big mistake in Germany [wrote Engels in 1878] is that the students and other ignorant "men of learning" are allowed to send the greatest nonsense into the world on a mass scale, as scientific representatives of the party. This is, however, a children's disease that they will get over, and it was indeed to shorten it that I made an example of Dühring in such detail [in *Anti-Dühring*].[86]

That was an optimistic view; meanwhile it was precisely these bourgeois-educated ignoramuses who made a row over Engels' exposure of the learned Dr. Dühring and even threatened to get its publication in the party press stopped.

A similar point is also made in the Circular Letter of 1879 against the Höchberg trio: besides attacking this tendency as politically degenerative, it argued that these self-important "educated elements" were incompetent even to make an *educational* contribution to the movement:

> . . . in order to be of use to the proletarian movement these people must bring real educative elements into it. But with the great majority of the German bourgeois converts that is not the case. Neither the *Zukunft* nor the *Neue Gesellschaft* has contributed anything which could advance the movement one step further. Here there is an absolute lack of real educational material, whether factual or theoretical. In its place there are attempts to bring superficially mastered socialist ideas into harmony with the exceedingly varied theoretical standpoints which these gentlemen have brought with them from the universities or elsewhere and of which, owing to the process of decomposition which the

remnants of German philosophy are at present undergoing, one was more confused than the other. Instead of thoroughly studying the new science themselves to begin with, each of them preferred to trim it to fit the point of view he had brought along, made himself forthwith a private science of his own and at once came forward with the pretension of wanting to teach it.[87]

Thus they produce only "desperate confusion": "Educative elements whose first principle is to teach what they have not learned can very well be dispensed with by the party." Engels makes a similar remark in a letter attacking opportunist trends in the party on the issue of bimetallism. "But that's our gentlemen the literati all over," he adds. "Just like the bourgeois literati, they think they have the privilege of learning nothing and arguing about everything." And he denounces their "economic ignorance, new-baked utopianism, and arrogance."[88]

Another overall charge made, especially by Engels, is that these bourgeois ideologues think they can manufacture intellectual productions simply out of *ideas,* rather than solid facts, information and concrete research leavened by theory.

The people who do not want to learn anything on principle and only make literature about literature and, incidentally, out of literature (nine-tenths of present-day German scribbling is scribbling about other scribbling) naturally achieve more printed pages per year than those who grind away and are willing to write about other books only (1) if they have mastered these other books, and (2) if there is something in them worth the trouble.[89]

Engels' admonition was: Do some real work, gentlemen, instead of merely sucking ideas out of your thumb! He wrote the following to a young intellectual who, he thought, was one of the exceptions:

You, who have really done something, must have noticed yourself how few of the young literary men who fasten themselves on to the party give themselves the trouble to study economics, the history of economics, the history of trade, of industry, of agriculture, of the formations of society. . . . The self-sufficiency of the journalist must serve for everything here and the result looks like it. It often seems as if these gentlemen think anything is good enough for the workers. If these gentlemen only knew that Marx thought his best things were still not good enough for the workers, how he regarded it as a crime to offer the workers anything but the very best![90]

Marx had given the same advice to the bourgeois ideologists in his preface to the French edition of *Capital:* "There is no royal road to science, and only those who do not dread the fatiguing climb of its steep paths have a chance of gaining its luminous summits."[91] The case is the same with the royal road to Marxism.

A correspondent's letter to Engels once informed him that socialism could not be put into practice until there was a uniform level of education and reasoning ability, plainly implying that the mass of people were lacking in these qualities necessary for the leadership of society. Engels reacted sharply as usual to this sort of "supercilious snobbery" from intellectuals who, in his opinion, were still less fit to lead society, on both counts. The biggest obstacle, he replied, leaving aside the peasantry, is "the pushy, superclever educated people, who know how to do everything so much the better the less they understand it."

> You speak of the absence of uniform reasoning ability. This exists—but on the part of the educated people stemming from aristocratic and bourgeois circles, who have no idea how much they still have to learn from the workers.[92]

7. THE STUDENTS

There was no socialist student movement during most of Marx's lifetime; the beginnings appeared by the end of the 1870s, but the movement did not become significant until two decades later. Up to the 1860s student movements had played significant sociopolitical roles more than once, as in the case of the national-democratic Burschenschaften of Germany in the first half of the century; but university students came overwhelmingly from bourgeois and aristocratic families and made little contact with socialist ideas.

Therefore there is little comment to be found in Marx or Engels on students as a distinctive group or factor in social or political life. Where students are mentioned at all it is simply as a type of educated bourgeois element in most cases. Indeed, more than once Marx uses the word *students* not for current university enrollees but as a generic term for educated elements who have long been out of school.[93] His *Studiosus* and *Ex-Studiosus*, which formally meant *student* and *ex-student*, is virtually such a generic term for an academic or intellectual. (For example, he often tagged one of these labels onto Carl Schurz, whom he regarded as an especially contemptible type.)[94]

The main exception, both in social reality and in Marx's and Engels' writings, concerns the period of the revolution of 1848–1849, when a distinctive student presence cropped up in some places. This presence was observed in Engels' main work on the revolution in Germany, in passages that are more descriptive than analytical. Engels notes both the strong and weak sides of student revolutionism.

In Vienna, recounts Engels, bourgeois supremacy was based on the National Guard it had established and on a "Committee of Public Safety."

> But at the same time, the working classes were partially armed too; they and the students had borne the brunt of the fight, as far as fight there had been; and the students, about 4,000 strong, well armed and far better disciplined than the National Guard, formed the nucleus, the real strength of the revolutionary force, and were noways willing to act as a mere instrument in the hands of the Committee of Safety. Though they recognized it and even were its most enthusiastic supporters, they yet formed a sort of independent and rather turbulent body, deliberating for themselves in the "Aula," keeping an intermediate position between the bourgeoisie and the working classes, preventing, by constant agitation, things to settle down to the old everyday tranquillity, and very often forcing their resolutions upon the Committee of Safety.[95]

The workers also constituted a nuisance as far as the bourgeoisie was concerned, since keeping them employed at public works was expensive:

> ... trade was at a standstill, and the continuous agitation and excitement kept up by the students and working people was certainly not the means to "restore confidence," as the phrase went. Thus, a certain coolness very soon sprung up between the middle classes on the one side, and the turbulent students and working people on the other ...

But the alliance of the bourgeoisie with the students and workers was recemented by the counterattacks of the old regime's forces.[96]

The picture at this point, then, is of a student-worker alliance as the left wing of the revolution. But in the next stage, as the victorious bourgeoisie drew away from the workers in fear and the latter demanded military organization for themselves in distrust, "confusion and helplessness" reigned.

> The Academic Legion, full of zeal for the struggle against imperial despotism, were entirely incapable of understanding the nature of the estrangement of the two classes, or of otherwise comprehending the necessities of the situation. . . . The council of the Academic Legion passed heroic resolutions, but was noways able to take the lead.[97]

The bourgeoisie backed off; but the working class could not take over; and the student forces were immobilized by incomprehension.

On the other hand, in Germany, when armed struggle broke out in May 1849, the student elements took an active part at first but lacked stick-to-it-iveness, unlike the core forces formed by the urban workers and the rural poor.

> The greater part of the young men of all classes, below the capitalist class, was to be found, for a time at least, in the ranks of the insurgent armies, but this rather indiscriminate aggregate of young men very soon thinned as soon as the aspect of affairs took a somewhat serious turn. The students particularly, those "representatives of the intellect," as they liked to call themselves, were the first to quit their standards, unless they were retained by the bestowal of officer's rank, for which they, of course, had very seldom any qualification.[98]

The contrast between these German student forces and the Viennese was also made by Engels in his special account of this 1849 campaign, in which he served. In the Palatinate he noted the students' penchant for adorning themselves, for lack of guns, with the dangling cavalry sabers that made a furious clatter in the streets as they were grandly dragged about by the "self-commissioned officers."[99] Later we get another vignette:

> In Bretten a delegation of students came to us with the declaration that this eternal marching-about in face of the enemy was not to their liking, and they requested release from service. The answer they got, of course, was that no one was released in face of the enemy, but if they wanted to desert they were free to do so. Thereupon about half the company marched off; the rest soon melted away through individual desertions till only the

riflemen were left. In general, during the whole campaign the students showed themselves to be malcontent, nervous young gentlemen who always wanted to be let in on the operation plans but complained of wounded feet and grumbled if the campaign did not offer all the amenities of a vacation trip. Among these "representatives of intellect" there were only a few who constituted exceptions by virtue of their truly revolutionary character and splendid courage.[100]

So much for the revolution. As with other social strata, the question mark over the students was not only their revolutionary consistency and stamina, but in particular their potentiality as an ally of the proletarian movement. We find this question coming up in the correspondence of Marx and Engels in the mid-1860s, not as a theorization but as an immediate practical problem. In France they saw anti-Bonaparte unrest gathering strength in both military and student ranks,* and both developments seemed to point to bourgeois disaffection from the regime. Marx commented that "The student business is a symptom of the worse marks of antagonisms in the army itself,"[101] and Engels agreed, adding: "It is very important that the Paris students fight on the side of the proletariat, no matter how confused this may be in their own minds. The Ecole Polytechnique will follow soon enough."[102]

But the issue of the student alliance did not loom very large until a mass socialist student movement began forming toward the end of the century, in the wake of the growing numbers and power of the parties of the Second International. Only a year before his death, Engels sent a message of cordial greetings to the first International Congress of Socialist Students held in Geneva. Its content is quite striking in terms of what it implies about the role he envisioned for the intellectual laborers in the productive process who are here called the "intellectual proletariat":

> May your efforts to awaken consciousness among the students succeed, so that out of their ranks will come the intellectual

---

* In October 1865 three regiments of the army mutinied over shipment to Mexico, then under the rule of Maximilian. In that month too, French participants in the International Student Congress at Liège had made a protest against the Bonaparte regime, and were subsequently expelled from school. Among the protesters were both Paul Lafargue and Jean Longuet, who had helped to organize the congress.

proletariat, who are called on to play an important role in the coming revolution, at the side of and in the midst of their brothers, the manual workers.

The bourgeois revolutions of the past required from the universities merely lawyers as the best raw material for politicians; the emancipation of the working class needs, besides, physicians, engineers, chemists, agronomists and other specialists; for it is a question not only of leading in the political machinery but also of taking the entire production of society in hand; and here, in place of high-sounding phrases, solid knowledge is needed.[103]

What this says diplomatically—by pitching it in positive terms—is that students in general should *not* expect to become the political leaders of the proletariat but rather specialists and technicians of the sort needed by the revolutionary society, contributing not "high-sounding phrases" but "solid knowledge." It points to a limited role for them as a social type, as we might expect in view of Engels' opinions on and experience with intellectuals.

18 | INTELLECTUALS AND THE PROLETARIAN MOVEMENT

The preceding chapter has already paid considerable attention to the role of intellectuals not merely in society at large but also inside the socialist and working-class movement. Now we turn to some specific problems under the latter head, and to some specific cases.

One important overall feature of the attitude taken by Marx and Engels is that it requires a "fight on two fronts" at almost every point, that is, the rejection of bisymmetrical mistakes. If, on the one hand, some in the movement welcomed intellectuals uncritically and without a sifting scrutiny, there was the opposite error of others who proposed an exclusionary policy with or without a theory of "proletarianism" (*ouvriérisme*). There was a constant tendency for vivid appreciation of the dangers of one course to bring about sympathy for the opposite mistake, in a familiar pattern.

Marx recognized that there was a positive role for intellectuals in the movement, but that it had to be a limited one.* Both sides of this view are to be traced through the following sections.

1. THE POSITIVE ROLE

If Marx's mistrust of intellectuals who approached the movement made it clear that he was not inclined to exaggerate their virtues, he was

---

* The "fight on two fronts" feature of Marx's view is a favorite recourse of marxologists who want to demonstrate that Marx looked to an intellectual elite rather than to the working class and who suffer from the difficulty that there is not a scintilla of evidence. Thus one eminent marxologist uses the bare fact of Marx's opposition to *excluding* nonworkers from the movement as an important

nevertheless far from blind to the needs they could fill. We have seen this in connection with "exceptional cases" in general.

The positive role of intellectuals for the socialist movement may be conveniently divided into three aspects: one distinctive of the earliest days of the movement, a second becoming prominent as the movement grew, and a third that looked toward the socialist future. Though there is the usual overlap, these three roles did not necessarily involve the same people or the same kind of people.

1. *Ideological innovators and initiators.* This was the frequent role of the most important figures in the early days of the movement, but, as we have already discussed, this involved extraordinary individuals for the most part, not class strata. Where socialism began as an ideological innovation, whether by an educated bourgeois or an educated worker, the next historical problem was always the *fusion* of the socialist idea with a real working-class movement that was groping its way to consciousness. This, and not the mode of innovation, was the crucial pass: what happened at this point was more important than whether the idea originally came from a bourgeois or a proletarian cranium.

Young Engels grasped this problem before his association with Marx, in fact immediately after coming to England, and he set it forth in his early work on *The Condition of the Working Class in England.* At this point "socialism" meant Owenism, a mixed-class group around a bourgeois innovator; but alongside it was a class movement of the proletariat organized in the Chartist movement (which, to be sure, also had its middle-class reform wing).

> In its present form, Socialism [Owenism] can never become the common possession of the working class; it must even condescend to return for a moment to the Chartist standpoint. But true proletarian socialism, having passed through Chartism and been purified of its bourgeois elements—as is true of how it has already developed in the case of many socialists and many Chartists, who are nearly all socialists—will indeed assume, within a short time, an important role in the history of the development of the English people. . . .
>
> We see, therefore, that the workers' movement is divided into two sections, the Chartists and the Socialists. The Chartists are

---

part of his case: see Special Note H. —As previously explained,[1] *intellectuals* is used here as a short form for the educated bourgeois recruits about whom Marx was concerned, whether or not individual cases conform to one or another definition of the term.

the most backward, the least developed, but in exchange they are genuine proletarians in the flesh, the representatives of the proletariat. The Socialists are more far-seeing, proposing practical measures against distress, but they come originally from the bourgeoisie and for this reason are incapable of amalgamating with the working class. The fusion of Socialism with Chartism, the reproduction of French Communism in an English manner, will be the next step, and has partly already begun. Only when this has been brought about will the working class really be the ruler of England . . .[2]

Quite complete here is the general conception of the fusion of socialist ideas (with or without the ideologists) and the proletarian movement. When he looked back to this period from the vantage point of 1871, Engels' picture was naturally a bit different. He told an Italian comrade that his situation in Naples was much like that of the early German movement twenty-five years before:

> At that time we had only a few men among the proletariat in Switzerland, France and England [as well as Germany] who were imbued with socialist and communist ideas, we had few means of working among the masses, and like you we had to find supporters among the schoolmasters, journalists and students. Fortunately, in this period of the movement such men, who did not exactly belong to the working class, were easily found; later, when the workingpeople dominated the movement as a mass, they certainly became rare.[3]

This was written soon after the fall of the Paris Commune, and for a whole dark period socialism was not exactly swamped by an influx of educated, or uneducated, bourgeois recruits.

When the movement got going again, there was a great deal of variation from country to country. One of the contrasts was between the largely proletarian character of the German movement and the relatively nonproletarian makeup of the socialist revival in England in the 1880s which began with Hyndman's Democratic (later Social Democratic) Federation. In 1883 Engels wrote to Bebel:

> . . . in the last period there emerged out of the bourgeoisie a large number of young heads who—to the shame of the English workers it must be said—grasp things better and take them up more ardently than do the workers. For even in the Democratic Federation the workers mostly accept the new program only

reluctantly and outwardly. . . . Don't for anything in the world be taken in by the claim there is a really proletarian movement going on here. I know Liebknecht would like to make himself and everyone else believe this, but it is not the case. The elements now active can become important, now that they have accepted our theoretical program and thus acquired a basis; but only in case a spontaneous movement breaks out here among the workers and they succeed in getting control of it. Till then they will remain individual heads, behind whom there is only a hodgepodge of confused sects, remnants of the great movement of the '40s, and nothing more.[4]

The root of the difference lay in the favored economic position of England, of its working class as well as its bourgeoisie, as Engels explained more than once. He thought the turn of industrial depression was reducing this difference, and indeed by the end of the decade it did. In 1884 Engels wrote Bebel that this was "the secret of . . . the present sudden emergence of a socialist movement here" in England:

> Till now the organized workers—trade unions—have still remained quite remote from it; the movement is going on among "educated" elements derived from the bourgeoisie, who here and there seek contact with the masses and in places find it. These elements are of very varying value morally and intellectually, and it will take some time before they sort themselves out and things become clarified. But it will hardly go altogether back to sleep again.[5]

2. *Ideological services to an ongoing movement.* This was the main problem, and as such we have kept it in the forefront up to now; it need not be further discussed at this point. However, it must be understood that the recruitment of intellectuals was only one type of solution; the other was the training and outfitting of workers to take over these posts and responsibilities, the most important of which were not the literary ones, such as editing, but party leadership and parliamentary representation.

The talents of educated recruits were in sore demand especially as the movement grew. Socialist periodicals multiplied, but could a competent editor be made on the spot out of a worker without experience? On the other hand, how readily could a revolutionary proletarian propagandist and publicist be made out of an *Ex-Studiosus?*

3. *Intellectual labor for a socialist society.* We have already seen this

need emphasized, especially in connection with students:[6] specialists, technicians, and scientific talents in the productive work of society.

Far from seeing socialist society as overrun with intellectuals, Engels thought the big problem at the beginning would be the lack of intellectual laborers capable of shucking their bourgeois training and working loyally for a workers' state. In the letter already quoted to a correspondent who implied that the mass of people were too lacking in reasoning ability to lead society,[7] Engels asserted his belief that the organized workers had already shown they were more competent to carry on their own affairs than bourgeois elements. But what if the educated bourgeois refuse to lend their talents to build a socialist society, or even try to stab it in the back?

> To be sure, we still lack technicians, agronomists, engineers, chemists, architects, etc., but if worse comes to worst we can buy these just as well as the capitalists do; and if a stern example is made of a few traitors—which are sure to crop up among this lot—then they will find it in their own interest to stop robbing us. But outside of such specialists, among whom I also count the schoolteachers, we can get along very well without the rest of the "educated people" . . .[8]

Note that the intellectual laborers with whom Engels is concerned here are not the ideological manipulators but those whose work is closely related to the production of material wealth, for he is thinking especially of the first struggles of socialist society to win the economic battle for survival. The same concern is evident in two letters to Bebel, which say much the same thing in somewhat different ways. The first takes off from an apparently unrelated question, his hope that there will be no war for the following reason:

> In order to take over the ownership and operation of the means of production, we need people who have been technically trained, and in mass numbers at that. These we don't have; till now we have even been rather glad that we have been largely spared the "educated" people.

This is an interesting statement; it is followed by Engels' typical optimism about the self-healing powers of the movement:

> Now it's different. Now we are strong enough to be able to stand any quantity of educated Quarcks and digest them; and I foresee that in the next 8-10 years we will recruit enough young technical

people, physicians, lawyers and schoolmasters to have the factories and big estates administered for the nation by party comrades. Then, therefore, our entry into power will be quite natural and will come off smoothly—relatively speaking. On the other hand, if we come to the helm prematurely, the technical people will be our main enemies, and they will deceive and betray us wherever they can; we will have to use terror against them, and still get done in anyway. That is what *constantly* happened on a small scale to the French revolutionaries: even in routine administration they had to leave the subordinate posts where the real work was done in the hands of the old reactionaries, and the latter obstructed and crippled everything. That is why I hope and desire that our splendid and sure development which is advancing with the calm and inescapability of a natural process will remain on its natural lines.[9]

And a couple of weeks later, after Bebel's encouraging reply:

I am glad to hear that there is so much of a trend in our direction already in force among the technically educated circles at present. However, in 1848 and 1870–71 I had too many nice experiences with the French republicans—who indeed were even bourgeois, showing how far one gets with such followers and sympathizers who keep quiet in time of danger, and how horribly one can compromise oneself—not to wish that, for such an important business as the socialization of big industry and big agriculture, we should still have a few years' more time to give the gentlemen a closer inspection in advance as to their ability and character. That would not only avoid friction; in a critical moment it might also avert an otherwise inevitable decisive defeat. Otherwise there will be colossal blunders en masse; that is indeed inevitable. In fact you yourself say that among the bids enough are from people who have more things they want from us than they have talent or knowledge; and I haven't forgotten what Singer told me the nun said of the students who were being driven into the Social Democracy out of fear of the examinations. Yet the fact is, *they are coming*, a token of what is in the offing.[10]

Confidence that "they are coming"—that socialist society would get an adequate supply of "brain workers" or "educated proletariat"—was expressed in the party press by an article of E. Bernstein's to which Engels gave considerable praise. This article saw them coming from two sources, eventually if not immediately: a technically trained stratum of government employees formed especially by Bismarck's statification measures; and the "overproduction" of brain workers ("chemists, architects, engineers of all kinds, accountants, etc.") who were being spewed out of the educational institutions into unsuitable jobs at low salary—"in short, an educated proletariat, an army of starveling 'intellectuals,' is in existence and grows from day to day, people whose lot is in no wise more enviable than that of the 'ordinary' wage-worker." These elements are seen as playing a necessary but auxiliary role; above all, it is clear that a leadership role in politics or in the party is not reserved for such an "educated proletariat," let alone for the bourgeois *Intelligenzen.*[11]

2. ANTI-INTELLECTUALISM AND EXCLUSIONISM

A critical attitude toward, or political mistrust of, bourgeois intellectual elements is not "anti-intellectualism," just as intellectual integrity is not defined as the integrity of intellectuals. Anti-intellectualism is another sprawling term that it would be unprofitable to pin down, but for practical purposes we mean hostility to theory and theoretical work, to education as such, to the cultural heritage of the past, to the need for serious study, and similar backward hostilities.

Such anti-intellectualist tendencies were far from rare in the early socialist movement, and not unknown later; they cropped up often enough to draw Marx's denunciation and scorn. It is hardly necessary to document Marx's insistence on the need for theoretical development, education (especially inside the movement), and the absorption of the best of society's learning and culture as the legacy to be taken over by socialist society.* But a look at some of the concrete issues leads to a more important problem: the exclusionary tendency.

---

* However, as a service to marxologists who wish to prove that Marx was "anti-intellectual," we offer the following material. Visiting Algeria a year before his death, Marx wrote a chatty letter to his daughter Laura, ending with a moral fable from the Arabs, who remember "they once produced great philosophers, scholars, etc., but Europeans sneer at them for their ignorance today." Here is the fable:

A ferryman keeps a small boat for crossing a turbulent river. A philosopher, headed for the opposite bank, gets in, and the following dialogue

Marx had to go through no developmental change on the question of "proletarian" anti-intellectualism. We have seen that from the beginning, as a new-fledged socialist, he was struck with admiration for the spirit he encountered in the Paris workers' clubs of the 1840s: "the studiousness, the craving for knowledge," and their "unceasing urge for development" and thirst for education, all of which testified to the "nobility" of the movement.[13] It is indeed an important fact, too often overlooked in historical accounts, that the organized socialist movement had a far-ranging cultural-educational impact on the workers who joined it, culminating in the production of what later came to be called "worker-intellectuals," meaning workers who developed their literary and other intellectual skills to the point where they could carry out tasks thought peculiar to bourgeois educated elements. We have noted the pride with which Marx in 1850 introduced an article written for his magazine by a working tailor (who was later to become secretary of the International): before the proletariat wins on the barricades, he wrote, "it announces the coming of its rule by a series of intellectual victories."[14]

In sharp contrast was another type not uncommon in the Paris of 1850. That year, discussing the Blanquist-type conspiratorialists who infested the movement, Marx noted that they

> look with deepest disdain on a more theoretical clarification of the workers as to their class interests. Hence their irritation—which is not proletarian but plebeian—at the *habits noirs* [frock coats], the more or less educated people who represent this side of the movement, people from whom, as the official representatives of the party, they can never make themselves entirely independent.[15]

These left-Jacobin types scorned theory—that is, the development of the workers' movement on the basis of ideas as well as struggle—because they viewed "action" (in practice, putsches) as a substitute for theory. A resolute band needed only a minimum of primitive ideas in order to carry out futile gestures; but a movement of the class could mature

---

takes place:—*Philosopher:* Ferryman, do you know *history?* *Ferryman:* No! *Philosopher:* Then you have lost half your life!—And again: *Philosopher:* Have you studied mathematics? *Ferryman:* No! *Philosopher:* Then you have lost more than half your life.—Hardly had the philosopher said this when the wind upset the boat and threw both philosopher and ferryman into the water. Now the *ferryman* yells: Can you swim? *Philosopher:* No! *Ferryman:* Then you have lost your *whole* life.[12]

only on the basis of an overall view of social change, that is, of theory.

Among the German artisan-communist elements Marx more often encountered a different kind of anti-intellectual primitivism: a know-nothing denunciation of educated people or intellectual laborers as such, accompanied by self-preening as "professional proletarians." This type of narrow mentality Marx and Engels associated with the *Straubinger* and the *Knote*—two words that occur very often in their correspondence in this connection.* They are shorthand labels, as in this typical remark of Marx's, writing about a Chartist meeting held in 1856 on the anniversary of the 1848 revolution:

> ... the German bumpkin *Scherzer* (°old boy°) came forward and in truly awful *Straubinger* style denounced the German "men of learning" [*Gelehrten*], the "intellectual workers" who had left them (the bumpkins) in the lurch and thus forced them to make fools of themselves in front of the other nations.[17]

Marx had only scorn for the kind of "professional proletarian" (real or alleged) who exhibited horny hands (real or alleged) as proof of political superiority and moral purity. This tactic, incidentally, was mainly directed to naive intellectuals engaged in Going to the People or in slumming; it was not calculated to impress other workers.

The same pattern, elevated from an individual's ploy to a sect's theory, became the *ouvriérisme* characteristic especially of parts of the later syndicalist movement. This "proletarianism," a basically mystical doctrine ascribing virtue only to certified proletarians, was the other side of the medal to intellectualism, if the latter is taken to mean a one-sided glorification of idea-manipulation talents.

In some cases, both sides of this picture can be seen fading into each other, like a lap-dissolve in the movies. Since the crux of intellectualism is its one-sidedness, Marx was mistrustful not only of bourgeois intellectuals but of the sort of ex-worker who emulated their vices. A case in point was Johann Most, who had a much-publicized career first as a

---

* *Straubinger:* in general, a traveling journeyman; by extension, an artisanal worker still filled with the narrow guild outlook and its petty-bourgeois prejudices. Marx and Engels in correspondence used this term freely as an all-purpose cuss-word for the mentality of the backward artisan types then found frequently in working-class circles.[16] —*Knote:* originally, a guild journeyman; later defined in dictionaries as *lout, clodhopper, boor*. Marx and Engels used it frequently with the contemptuous force of the second meaning, but especially with reference to elements suggesting the first, hence a somewhat more pejorative version of *Straubinger*. I have translated it, in the next citation, as *bumpkin*.

muddlehead in the German movement and later as an anarchist in America. A bookbinder turned writer and editor,* Most was in 1877 the most vociferous Social-Democratic supporter of Professor Eugen Dühring, an academic who aspired to become the leading theoretician both of socialism and anti-Semitism. It was Most who organized the effort to have the party press stop publishing Engels' articles against Dühring, later collected into a book.[19] Engels' demolition of Dühringism was especially resented by the party's Berlin intelligentsia, then a small factor; Most carried more weight. A month before Most's interdiction attempt, Marx had commented on Most's attitude: "if Herr Most has not understood that much can be learned from Engels' positive elucidations not only by ordinary workers, but even by ex-workers like himself who imagine they can get to know and pass judgment on everything in a twinkling, but also by people who are really scientifically educated, then I feel sorry for his powers of judgment."[20] The campaign by Most and the Berlin intellectuals to gag Engels' articles on Dühring failed, but not without causing some turmoil in the party. In the autumn of that year Marx wrote a friend (in the same letter that dealt with the "superwise doctors" of the Höchberg group):

> Workers themselves, when they give up working, like Herr Most & Co., and become *literati by profession*, are continually doing "theoretical" mischief and are continually ready to take up with muddleheads from the allegedly "learned" caste.[21]

Cases naturally had to be judged on their merits, not on the class credentials of an individual.

A more important case in point, the most talented *Straubinger* of all, was Wilhelm Weitling. As we have seen, the maturity of the young Marx can almost be measured by the advance in his understanding of what Weitling represented, from his initial enthusiasm of 1844 to his confrontation with him in 1846. It was one day in 1846 that Weitling's scorn of theoretical analysis caused Marx to strike the table and cry: "Ignorance has never yet helped anybody." The target of this anger was

---

* Most, son of a lawyer's clerk and a governess, "decided on the honorable craft of a bookbinder" (as his anarchist biographer tells us) and became in turn an apprentice, journeyman, and independent tradesman (the guild route) up to the age of 23, at which advanced age he became an ex-worker in permanence.[18]

not merely Weitling but the *Straubinger* type of artisan-radicalism in general.*

The German artisan-communists who were organized in London as the League of the Just also faced a confrontation between the old *Straubinger* radicalism of Weitling and the new proletarian communism being developed by Marx. By 1847, not only had Weitling himself departed but the decisive leadership—Karl Schapper at its head—had opted for Marx. Still, when the newly named Communist League held its first congress in the summer of that year, there was still a rearguard seeking to hang on to the old narrow ideas.

A typical pattern resulted. Here were two bourgeois-educated new-comers of high intellectual attainment, Marx and Engels, who were proposing a new orientation; and although the League's own leaders were sponsoring them, they were vulnerable to *Straubinger* prejudices. One of the members, Friedrich Lessner, who had himself been orig-inally radicalized by reading Weitling, later recalled that "the opponents of Marx raised the cry of 'down with the "intellectuals," ' not only at the first congress, but all through the intervening period to November," and even at the second congress of November-December where Marx and Engels were assigned to write the Manifesto.[22] This cry did not get very far here, where it rang as an echo of the past; but it still had a flourishing future in every nook and cranny of the working-class move-ment that was still in process of clarification and maturation.

Some significant cases affecting Marx are considered in the following sections; but another typical case may be mentioned here, as seen through Engels' eyes. In 1881 Engels characterized as follows the French socialist group represented by the paper *Le Prolétaire*, which was in process of forming the social-reformist movement ("Possi-bilists") opposed to the Marxist party:

> *Le Prolétaire* was the paper put out by the very narrowest-minded clique among all the Paris workers who liked to write. It had a rule that only real manual workers could collaborate with advice or by writing for it. The most thickheaded Weitlingite kind of hatred against "men of learning" [*Gelehrten*, i.e., university-educated people] was on the order of the day. Therefore this paper was also absolutely empty of content, but it claimed to be the purest expression of the Paris proletariat.[23]

* Since the case of Weitling is illustrative in several respects, and since it keeps cropping up in marxological writings, it is the subject of Special Note I.

In this case, as in many others, a form of "proletarianism" was institutionalized by an exclusionary policy: in the best cases, as a way of keeping workers uncontaminated by bourgeois influences—a quite futile way; in the worst cases, as a means of keeping control of a group or movement in the hands of a "proletarian" coterie, which then utilized its control of this little section of the class to become its broker in accommodations with the bourgeois state and society. This is one reason why a façade of "proletarianism" often constituted a store front for merchandising quite ordinary social-reformism.

3. THE CASE OF THE WILLICH-SCHAPPER GROUP

The pattern exemplified by the "Down with the intellectuals" sentiment at the first congress of the Communist League in 1847 was repeated in that organization following the 1848–1849 defeat of the revolution; but whereas it was unsuccessful when the movement was on the upswing, it flowered as part of the process of disintegration. The new impulsion was similar to the old, and recurred in the socialist movement hundreds of times in the next hundred years: in an internal fight over policy and ideas, one faction claims that its own proletarian composition (real or alleged) guarantees its political correctness or purity, and denounces the nonproletarian composition of its opponent faction (real or alleged) all the more enthusiastically in proportion to its inability to refute its arguments.

In the Communist League, of course, since Marx and Engels were the outstanding nonproletarians, anyone who disliked their ideas had this brittle weapon to hand. In 1850 in the backwash of defeat and disappointment, Schapper—the key figure in the old leadership who had been instrumental in aligning it with Marx in 1847—reverted to the "old crap" (to use a favorite nontechnical term of Marx's). This veteran of the movement, six years older than Marx, had been an active radical since his student days seventeen years before; son of a poor rural parson, he had gone through high school to the University of Gießen, studying forestry. After helping to organize a conspiratorial putsch by the nationalist-democratic movement, after a jail sentence, and after involvement in bourgeois-republican revolutionism, he became a traveling professional revolutionary. As such, he worked at odd jobs to earn a living till he became a skilled typesetter. This ex-student, turned peripatetic organizer, advanced from the ideology of Young Germany and Mazzini to the artisan-communism of Weitling, the socialist utopianism of Cabet, and the left-Jacobinism of the Babouvist-Blanquist type of conspiratorial sects that arose between the revolutions of 1830 and 1848.[24]

Except for Schapper's beginnings as a university student, this course of development was typical of the artisan membership of the groups that he was active in organizing, particularly the League of the Just, which changed its name to Communist League in June 1847 under Marx's influence. Of this type, Schapper was one of the best. When young Engels met him and his comrades Joseph Moll and Heinrich Bauer, they were already experienced revolutionists. Four decades later, old Engels paid them homage in an essay on the history of the Communist League: "They were the first revolutionary proletarians whom I met ... I shall never forget the deep impression that these three real men made upon me, who was then still only wanting to become a man."[25] Further on in this essay Engels puts the matter of the League's social composition less lyrically and more precisely: the members of the League, he explained, were "almost exclusively artisans."[26]

> The greatest honor is due to them, in that they, who were themselves not yet full proletarians but only an appendage of the petty-bourgeoisie, an appendage which was passing into the modern proletariat but which did not yet stand in direct opposition to the bourgeoisie, that is, to big capital—in that these artisans were capable of instinctively anticipating their future development and of constituting themselves, even if not yet with full consciousness, the party of the proletariat.[27]

This is what had separated them from an unreconstructed *Straubinger* like Weitling, whose personal background was very similar to theirs but who had evolved in a different direction.

"But," Engels continued, "it was also inevitable that their old handicraft prejudices should be a stumbling-block to them at every moment ..." Although, unlike Weitling, they sought to identify themselves with the modern proletariat, their notion of what this meant was as vague as the term was amorphous. When Schapper wrote the leading article for the League's *Kommunistische Zeitschrift* in September 1847 (having already met Engels but not Marx), he defined the proletariat in the old sense of the propertyless, and specified: "Proletarians in present-day society are all who cannot live on their capital: the worker as well as the man of learning, the artist as well as the small bourgeois . . ."[28]

The past to which Schapper reverted in 1850 was that of the putschist Jacobinism of the old bourgeois-republican movement, and indeed for the next few years he allied himself with the pink Democracy. This collapse to the right was initially presented with a brave roar which sounds to our modern ears as ultraleftist: as the Communist League split in September 1850 Schapper supported the group that insisted the revolution was still around the corner and that an insurrection must be hothouse-forced. As we have seen, Marx vigorously opposed this course.[29]

In this situation Schapper picked up the blunt instrument of "proletarianism" as a handy argument-substitute. At the meeting of the Central Committee on September 15, the ex-student strove to paint the dispute as one between the "proletariat" (meaning his own supporters among the worker-artisans of the group) and "the people who represent the party on the theoretical side"; or between "those who work with the pen" and "those who work in other ways."[30] We will see in a moment the reason for this strange dichotomy: writers and nonwriters, of all things. The extant minutes do not record that Schapper at this meeting explicitly advocated limiting membership to workers. Shortly thereafter, the Cologne committee of the League (which had now become the Central Committee following the split) criticized the documents it had received from Schapper's group:

> . . . the attempt to expel the Majority [Marx's supporters] of the central committee was based . . . partly on the general principle that the League should expel all writers. It was argued that the League was exclusively intended for factory workers and artisans and that if these groups only had the will they would be able to seize the reins of power as soon as revolution should break out again and so would be able to carry out the communist reorganization of society without further ado.[31]

This emphasis on getting rid of *writers* rather than nonworkers in general had a reason. We have not yet mentioned the inspiritor of the Willich-Schapper group: August von Willich, who had kept silent during the September 15 debate and let Schapper do the talking. Schapper, at least, had long made his livelihood as a journeyman and was quite at home in the workers' milieu. Willich was quite another matter—though no one could accuse him of being a writer or having any proclivities "on the theoretical side." This new recruit to communism was a military martinet who had fought with the rebels in the 1849 uprising and had then moved left. Sprung from an old aristocratic family, he had been a Prussian career officer before his recent radicalization, after which he had converted to an artisanal occupation (carpenter) like his predecessors.* It would have been difficult for him to pass himself off as a proletarian or reasonable facsimile thereof.

The Willich-Schapper group, therefore, could make only gingerly use of its appeal to *Straubinger* prejudices; but it could be more scornful of the people "on the theoretical side" who appealed to theory as well as practical sense to oppose the idea of instant-revolutionism. The Cologne committee's statement included also a contrast between the Willich-Schapper form of anti-intellectualism and Marx's viewpoint:

> According to the Manifesto and the Address [to the Communist League, of March], the course of development of the proletarian movement goes as follows: the proletariat, once having come to consciousness of its own class situation, absorbs into this situation all the educational elements of the old society, and thus attains an understanding in theoretical terms of the lines of development of a communist revolution [and then proceeds to practice] ... In contrast, this new-old standpoint [of Willich-Schapper] declares all theoretical work to be settled, sets itself in hostile contradiction to all writing activity, and thinks it can realize the end-goal of the movement on the basis of the present-day development, in particular, of a new German revolution. So it is consequently quite natural that these same people, who apparently represent the interests of the "pure proletariat" so exclusively, trumpet forth the bare phrase *revolution* in their latest proclamation sent out into the world in the name of a "democratic-socialist committee" in partnership with Frenchmen, Poles and Hungarians and present themselves as the champions of the

---

* Willich emigrated to America three years later; in the Civil War he rose to brigadier-general, became an active Republican politician, and in 1870 offered (in vain) to fight for Prussia against France.[32] Whereas Schapper returned to Marx's side by 1856 and sharply regretted his break, Willich's contribution from America consisted of the continued invention of slanders against Marx.

petty-bourgeois social-democratic republic. In this way, then, the proletariat . . . is once again summoned into battle in the interests of another class . . .[33]

The group's scorn of theoretical work was useful in its subsequent career: these self-proclaimed champions of the proletariat against writers and theoreticians shortly entered into close collaboration with the petty-bourgeois Democracy in emigration, the same elements who had been denounced in Marx's and Engels' "Address to the Communist League" in March 1850—but not until they had written various fire-breathing putschist-conspiratorial documents which were a godsend to the Prussian government's prosecution of the Communists in Cologne and provided much of the ammunition for it in the show-trial of 1852.[34]

By this time it was clear in practice that this group's seemingly ultraleftist stance, with its demand for instant revolution, was only the other side of the coin of simple opportunism, with its usual get-rich-quick calculations, and that the former had transformed itself into the latter without difficulty. Marx—fulfilling his function on the theoretical side—had already pointed this very pattern out in so many words in the September 15, 1850, debate. There he showed in advance that the actual politics of the revolution-mongers was, in fact, opportunistic: German-patriotic rather than internationalist, and "social-democratic" rather than proletarian-communist. They were using the term *proletariat* merely ritualistically. "To make this phrase effective," Marx said, "it was necessary to describe the petty-bourgeois as proletarians so that in practice it was the petty-bourgeois and not the proletarians who were represented. The actual revolutionary process had to be replaced by revolutionary catchwords."[35] (This same substitution had been made by Schapper in his leading article in the *Kommunistische Zeitschrift*.)

In practice it turned out that the *Straubinger* who wanted to use "proletarianism" as an exclusionary principle became a wing of the petty-bourgeois Democracy, where they functioned as brokers between their own "proletarian" clientele and the middle-class Democrats. The connection was not fortuitous: an independent proletarian movement can afford to admit a leavening of educated recruits breaking from the bourgeois world, but "proletarian" brokers, approaching an alien class movement for a deal, like to have pure merchandise to sell.

4. EXCLUSIONISM IN THE
   FIRST INTERNATIONAL

A proposal for the exclusion of nonworkers from membership or leadership of the movement came up later in the International, with several similarities to the Willich-Schapper case. It came from the Proudhonists, who dominated the French section of the International. Since they had been, with the British trade-unionists, the initiatory force in 1864, this was a very serious problem which could not simply be voted out of existence by the General Council.

Here was the pattern: the advocacy of exclusionism came from that national current in the International which most systematically represented the old petty-bourgeois radicalism of the artisan stratum, the French *Straubinger;* while the staunchest opposition to exclusionism came from the representatives of the British trade unions, which constituted by far the most proletarian part of the movement.

From the beginning Marx was naturally aware of the danger that the new organization might be swamped by intellectual radicals without any class commitment. As we have seen, for him the absolute test was not the social origin of an individual but rather the overall social composition of the organization. There was consensus in the International on the test for nonworker individuals: personal life-commitment to the working-class movement without careerist motivation. With this approach, a sprinkling of recruits from the educated classes could be a help, although the flooding of the organization with intellectual elements would be a disaster calling in question the class character of the movement. It was a question of a qualitative change due to an overdose, like the amount of pepper in soup or the proportion of arsenic in a medical compound.

In the General Council, the first question along these lines concerned the "honorable member" category for notables, a custom that saddled the rolls of workers' organizations with bourgeois radicals who were willing to accept homage but not responsibility and to give their names but no loyalty. Louis Blanc had made a bid to become such an Hon. Member of the new International. Marx wrote to Engels: "Surmising that an attempt of this sort would be made, I had however already put through the by-law, fortunately, that no one (outside of workers' *societies*) was to be *invited,* and that no person could be an *honorary member.*"[36] At the same time, as he discusses in the same letter, he worked closely with people of bourgeois origin (like Fox and Lefort[37]) who were scarcely as socialistic as Louis Blanc but who had entered into the work of the International as responsible and loyal members and committed activists. On this issue, too, the test was not simply individual ideology but personal commitment to the class movement.

Hence the pattern of the fight on two fronts. If Louis Blanc had to be kept at arm's length, people like Lefort had to be allowed to contribute their loyal service. Lefort was a radical-republican reformer oriented to parliamentary democracy, no revolutionary, but he had played a useful part in founding the International and was sincerely devoted to building it. However, the working-class membership of the French section followed the Proudhonist leadership of Tolain; and the Proudhonists decided there was room in France only for their own tendency. They could not Proudhonize the whole International but they could make it a Proudhonist sect in their own country. To this end they presented the General Council with an ultimatum: Lefort, who was the International's press agent in Paris, had to be dismissed.[38] Thus the Proudhonists adopted the policy of exclusionism, at least from posts, in order to ensure their own monopoly of ideas and control in the organization.

This presented Marx and the General Council with a dilemma. Marx had been initially impressed quite favorably with Tolain in spite of his ideology, especially because he had recently run as an independent working-class candidate.[39] On their part the Proudhonists had no criticism of Marx's functioning in the affairs of the International.*

---

* Perhaps if Marx had insisted on Lefort's right to fill a post, these same Proudhonists would have eventually discovered that he was a dictator, if not an agent of the kaiser. But in point of fact it was Marx who was instrumental in persuading the General Council to yield to their ultimatum, since the British members trusted Marx's judgment in these matters. So completely satisfactory did the Proudhonists find Marx's organizational conduct and policies that even later they voiced no criticism. Even in the "history" of the International by Tolain's lieutenant Fribourg, written after both Tolain and Fribourg were reviling the Paris Communards as "sanguinary maniacs" and with other such pleasantries, not once did Fribourg charge Marx with any antidemocratic or objectionable action: an amazing fact in those days, when political conflicts were accompanied by charges of bureaucratic crimes and embezzlement as automatically as saying hello. This casts a backlight on the common marxological assertion that Marx "suppressed" Bakunin's faction because of political disagreement, rather than because the Bakuninists were systematically wrecking the organization from within in order to replace it with their own group. Politically the Proudhonists were in deeper disagreement with Marx than Bakunin seemed to be; but organizationally speaking, the Proudhonists did not engage in the wrecking tactics throughout the International that were the Bakuninists' stock in trade.

There was no tension in this area. The conflict was over the presence of the French republicans in the International, with Lefort the crux. The Proudhonists' ultimatum was: *him or us*. Reluctantly Marx had to conclude that the Proudhonist sectists could not be persuaded to utilize Lefort's talents rather than demand his head, and that the General Council had no practical alternative to sacrificing Lefort in order to appease them and preserve the movement. When the French row started, Marx summed it up for Engels as follows:

> ... it seems to me that this time both sides do each other an injustice ... There is the following added circumstance: The workers [of the French section] seem to be set on *excluding* every °literary man,° which however is nonsense, since they need them in the press, but it is excusable in view of the continual betrayal by °literary men.° On the other side, the latter are suspicious of *every workers' movement* which behaves in a way contrary to them. . . .
>
> So then: in Paris too there are, on the one side, *Lefort* (a literary man, well-to-do in addition, therefore "a bourgeois," but a man of purest reputation and, as far as La Belle France is concerned, the real founder of our society) and, on the other, *Tolain, Fribourg, Limousin,* etc., who are workers. Well, I will let you know the outcome.[40]

In a memorandum Marx jotted down the two motivations for the choice that had to be made: *"International character of the Society is endangered"* (if the Proudhonists pulled out), since the lack of a French section at this point would mean there was no large Continental contingent to balance the British presence; and *"The class character of the movement."*[41] True, the class character of the Proudhonist group was similar to that of the old Communist League, that is, based largely on artisanal workers (though without the proletarian-communist orientation of people like Schapper, Moll and H. Bauer); Tolain and Fribourg were engravers; but the International's hope was that through these workers it could reach other strata.

The outcome came quickly as, in the following two weeks, the General Council was subjected to a round of quarrels between Tolain and Fribourg (who had come over from Paris to press their case) and Lefort.[42] While the General Council, following Marx's lead, agreed to remove Lefort from the Paris post, it rejected the Proudhonist concept involved, stating "that it does not sanction the principle that none but an ouvrier [worker] is admissible as an official in our Society."[43]

When the first congress of the International took place in Geneva in 1866, Tolain went to bat for his exclusionist principle, this time formulated as a motion to restrict congress delegates to manual workers. He argued that the class struggle made it "useful, even indispensable, that all men who have the duty of representing working-class groups should be workers."[44] In classic fashion, he struck an ultraleftist pose as he argued that "under present conditions, we have to consider as opponents all members of the privileged classes, privileged either by virtue of capital or a diploma." Then he appealed to the principle of self-emancipation: the working class "wants to achieve its own salvation itself, without anyone's protection. It is therefore necessary that its delegates belong neither to the liberal professions nor to the caste of capitalists."[45] The point of this leftist phraseology is that it came from a reformist whom even the Bonapartist government considered fairly respectable, and whose rapid rightward development in the next few years provided a special commentary on the rhetoric.

Two leading British trade-union delegates answered him, apparently stirred especially by his statement that anyone with a degree was an enemy. In refutation both pointed to the man whose role in the International had not been impugned by anyone, least of all by the Proudhonists: namely, Dr. Karl Marx.* Cremer, of the carpenters and joiners, began by stating that the nonmanual workers on the General Council were above suspicion: "far from it, it is likely that without their devotion, the Association would not have been able to establish itself in England so thoroughly. Among those members I will mention one only, Citizen Marx, who has devoted all his life to the triumph of the working classes."[46]

James Carter, of the perfumers, made two points important in this connection:

> Citizen Karl Marx has just been mentioned; he has perfectly understood the importance of this first congress, where there

---

* It is because of a misunderstanding of the context of these speeches that the marxological myth has grown up, repeated from one book to another, that the Proudhonists' exclusionary proposal was aimed at Marx in the first place, or that Tolain was "gunning" for Marx. Just the contrary: Cremer and Carter brought Marx's name into the debate because his role in the International would be regarded as the best refutation of Tolain's blanket proposal, not in order to defend Marx himself. Tolain's motion would not have made sense as an attack on Marx for the simple reason that Marx was not a delegate at the congress. And, we can add on top of all this, Tolain even tried to claim in the debate that Marx agreed with him!

should be only working-class delegates; therefore he refused the delegateship he was offered in the General Council. But this is not the reason to prevent him or anyone else from coming into our midst; on the contrary, men who devote themselves completely to the proletarian cause are too rare for us to push them aside. The middle class only triumphed when, rich and powerful as it was in numbers, it allied itself with men of science . . .[47]

Tolain then utilized Carter's argument to co-opt Marx for his own side of the debate: "As a worker, I thank Citizen Marx for not accepting the delegateship offered him. In doing that, Citizen Marx showed that workers' congresses should be made up only of manual workers."[48]

Of course, Citizen Marx had no such position, nor had Carter said so. Marx had several reasons for not wishing to go to Geneva as a delegate—mainly his work on *Capital,* and, very likely, his distaste for sterile debates like those forced on the congress by the Proudhonists—but he may also have told the General Council that he preferred them to send trade-unionist delegates to this first congress; we do not know.[49]

The congress defeated Tolain's motion, but it gained twenty votes against twenty-five.

Later Marx learned about another aspect of Tolain's motivation, one which seems to have been confirmed by events. He told Engels that the General Council's secretary for France

> has given me the key to Tolain's and Fribourg's operation. They want to come out in 1869 as *workers'* candidates to the Corps Législatif, on the "principle" that *only workers* can represent workers. It was therefore extremely important for the gentlemen to have this principle proclaimed by the congress [of the International].[50]

Tolain did succeed in getting himself elected as the candidate of the Paris workers; and it was as deputy that he voted in the Versailles assembly to support the massacre of the Paris Commune, that is, of his constituents. Like other advocates of exclusionism, he used an artificial "proletarianism" as a device to establish himself as broker for the working class, broker to the bourgeoisie.

The counterposition of views can be put this way. Tolain and his similars utilized "proletarianism" as a touchstone for individuals, since their aim was to substitute a particular individual as the plenipotentiary for the class—an individual who, holding the proxy power given him by his clientele, could thereby become influential in the really important circles, that is, the circles that really ruled in society. Thus Tolain was quite sincere in primping himself as the "representative of the workers" in the Versailles assembly of the counterrevolution, that is, as the assembly's proletarian broker, while the real leaders of the workers were fighting with the Commune. In this view, "self-emancipation" meant that the workers relied for "protection" (as Tolain had put it) not on the bourgeoisie and not on the state but on an honest-to-goodness worker like himself, who "protected" his clientele by pleading with the bourgeoisie and the state to do them justice.

In contrast, for Marx the crux was the predominantly proletarian nature of the *movement* in practice, that is, in composition, leadership, etc.; and if this were ensured, then it could safely use the services of committed intellectual laborers, in limited numbers.

5. THE ISSUE OF
CLASS COMPOSITION

In the letter last quoted, Marx discussed another point that arose in the General Council right after the Geneva congress:

> As a demonstration against the Messrs' Frenchmen—who wanted to exclude everybody except "manual workers," first from membership in the International, then at least from eligibility to be elected delegate to the congress—the Englishmen yesterday proposed *me* as president of the General Council. I declared I could not undertake the thing under *any* circumstances, and for my part proposed *Odger*, who was thereupon re-elected, although some voted for me in spite of my declaration.[51]

Marx did not refuse because of some general principle that a "brain worker" should be debarred from filling the post. He did, however, feel that there was a question of symbolizing or signaling what the International aspired to be, by the selection of a workers' leader to what was going to be a largely symbolic position anyway. (A year later the presidency was abolished unanimously, on Marx's initiative.)[52] The Council minutes reported more ambiguously: "He, Marx, thought himself incapacitated [not debarred] because he was a head worker and not a hand worker."[53] Behind Marx's refusal were also a couple of other considerations. Perhaps dominant was his desire to devote himself as much as possible to finishing *Capital;* and his election to the presidency would have set him up as the target and whipping-boy for all the ambitious champions of "proletarianism" inside and outside the International.*

There could be only one president; but since there were many members on the General Council, their election posed a question similar to the admission of members: the question of proportion, or overdose. Marx stated this explicitly when a physician named Sexton was proposed. One of the Council members wondered "whether it was desirable to add professional men to the Council . . ." The minutes record Marx's opinion, not on Sexton but on the principle raised: "Citizen *Marx* did not think there was anything to fear from the admission of professional men while the great majority of the Council was composed of workers . . ."[57]

The problem of balance in social composition—proportion of

---

* We should mention three other issues in this area that are only superficially relevant. (1) At the same Council meeting, the journalist Peter Fox was elected general secretary over the trade-unionist Cremer; but there was a special reason. Cremer had recently abandoned that post in rather reprehensible fashion and plainly could not be relied on; Fox was the only immediate alternative, but in spite of all, Cremer was later given back the post for a while.[54] (2) The year before, Marx had been urged to take over the editorship of the *Bee-Hive.* He was very wary of the responsibility: "I shall consider the thing from all its 24 sides before I take a step one way or the other," he wrote Engels.[55] He did not accept; we have no record of his motivation, though it is not hard to reconstruct. (3) When Engels joined the General Council in 1870, he was proposed for financial secretary. The minutes report: "Cit. Engels objected that none but working men ought to be appointed to have anything to do [with] the finances." But "Cit. Marx did not consider the objection tenable; an ex-commercial man was the best for the office."[56] Engels persisted in refusing—justifiably, in my opinion, for a reason previously touched on. Handling money was the touchiest job in the workers' movement, riskier to reputation than anything else; for charges of financial irregularity were routine as soon as a conflict started, the absence of evidence being only proof of the cleverness of the embezzler. Also, there was among the Council members an undercurrent of resentment against Engels, at least for a while. He, unknown to them until he moved to London in 1870 and had been co-opted onto the Council, thereafter plainly became Marx's right-hand man and confidant. Of course, the fact of old friendship was well known and explanatory, but to envious elements it looked like this: a Johnny-come-lately who has had no previous part in building the International suddenly arrives and takes on status as Marx's close colleague, overshadowing older members. This is my own reconstruction of the situation—there were only grumblings and so there is little to go on—and it is not clear how many Council members were thus affected.

workers to nonworkers or brain workers—was naturally more important for membership in general and the makeup of the branches in particular. The question was not a hard one as far as the major European countries were concerned, since from the outset the branches and sections were overwhelmingly working-class in England, France, Belgium, Switzerland and Germany. It was the United States that precipitated the issue in 1872, with the antics of the notorious Section 12, dominated by Victoria Woodhull, who was then going through her short-lived radical and feminist phase.

The problem was not only that Section 12 was the hearth of every exotic ism and crackpot fad then popular—with its socialism, as well as its feminism, figuring uneasily in this company—and not only that its membership was overwhelmingly if not exclusively middle-class, professional and intellectual; but, into the bargain, it also publicly repudiated even lip-service to the International's program of proletarian socialism.* It was not a borderline case but a provocation. Working-class elements in the American sections, especially Section 1, considered Section 12 a discreditment and an embarrassment to the organization. For the first time, issue was taken over whether the International should be working-class in character, and over what exactly this meant in terms of concrete regulations.

As a result of the Section 12 problem, the General Council adopted guidelines written by Marx, establishing a maximum percentage for nonworkers:

> Considering, that the I.W.A. . . . is to consist exclusively of "working men's societies" . . .
>
> that, consequently . . . [the rule that] "Everybody who acknowledges and defends the principles of the I.W.A. is eligible

---

* Marx spotlighted such public declarations by Section 12 as that it must "remonstrate against the vain assumption . . . that the International . . . is an organization of the working classes." Section 12, like Tolain, did not reject the principle of working-class self-emancipation; it merely redefined it into its opposite: "The statement that the emancipation of the working classes can only be conquered by themselves, cannot be denied, yet it is true so far as it describes the fact that the working classes cannot be emancipated against their will."[58] An article by Engels ironically explained that, whereas in Europe the bourgeois press has made the International such a bogeyman "that no one need be afraid that the International will ever be led astray from its original aims by a mass influx of bourgeois elements," the United States was so much more advanced that "while the men of the European bourgeoisie trembled before the International, two bourgeois American women . . . conceived the plan of exploiting this fear-inspiring society . . ."[59]

to become a member," although it confers upon the active adherents of the International who are no working men the right either of individual membership or of admission to working men's sections, does in no way legitimate the foundation of sections exclusively or principally composed of members not belonging to the working class;

that for this very reason the General Council was some months ago precluded from recognising a Slavonian section exclusively composed of students;

that . . . the General Rules and Regulations are to be adapted "to local circumstances of each country";

that the social conditions of the United States, though in many respects most favourable to the success of the working-class movement, peculiarly facilitate the intrusion into the International of bogus reformers, middle-class quacks and trading politicians;

For these reasons the General Council recommends that in future there be admitted no new American section of which two-thirds at least do not consist of wages-labourers.[60]

The choice of the fraction two-thirds was, of course, arbitrary; the intent was to maintain the proletarian proportion above a mere majority and definitely less than 100 percent (which would mean exclusionism). The one-third allowance for non–wage-workers left plenty of room for exceptional cases—the exceptional cases of bourgeois adherents who had genuinely come over to the standpoint of the proletarian movement, as distinct from the Woodhull types. A motivation that Marx stressed at two Council meetings was that the International must not be used locally, or anywhere, as a steppingstone to parliamentary careers by ambitious individuals.[61]

The guidelines written for the American problem applied to any "new American section." Four months later, July 1872, in preparation for the Hague Congress, the by-laws were amended to make the two-thirds rule applicable to all sections. Marx added: "for special conditions, such as they exist in Poland and in other countries, special clauses may be made."[62]

Thus, under the pressure of dealing with the American faddists, institutional form was given to Marx's view that, in a genuinely working-class movement, special provisions of scrutiny were necessary to regulate the influx of elements of other class origin.

6. THE CASE OF BAKUNIN

The pattern which we have now seen in the cases of Weitling, Willich-Schapper and Tolain was acted out for another, but not the last, time by Michael Bakunin, the founder of the anarchist movement.

In 1873, in his book *Statism and Anarchy*, Bakunin made a then-routine charge which has become a marxological favorite. Anyone who reads the socialist polemics of the time in any bulk soon discovers that virtually everyone gets around to accusing virtually everyone else of seeking to exploit the workers, establish a dictatorship or despotism, embezzling, and other peccadillos; and the charges are often true all around in one particular or another. Even so, few rivaled Bakunin in the insouciance with which he scattered smears or in the disdain with which he regarded the little matter of evidence.

In the case of Bakunin's 1873 book, Marx made a notebook summary (apparently with a view to writing an attack on it); he occasionally interpolated marginal comments of his own—very laconic, indeed telegraphic jottings. Here is a relevant passage.*

> "But those who are elected will be fervently convinced people and, furthermore, learned socialists. The phrase *'learned socialism'* "—
>
>> [MARX] has been used only in opposition to utopian socialism, which would like to saddle the people with new chimerical fancies, instead of reserving its science for the comprehension of the social movement created by the people themselves; see my book against Proudhon—,
>
> "which are constantly encountered in the works and speeches of Lassalleans and Marxists, show by themselves alone that the so-called people's state will be nothing but the very despotic government of the masses of people by a new and numerically very small aristocracy of real or alleged learned men. The people are not learned, which means they will be entirely comprised within the governed herd. A fine emancipation!" (p. 279, 280.)
>
> "The Marxists feel this" (!) "contradiction and, recognizing that the government of learned men,"
>
>> [MARX] quelle rêverie! [what a fantasy!]

---

* For clarity, Bakunin's words are given in quotation marks (as in Marx's notebook); Marx's interpolated comments are preceded by his name in brackets and are deep-indented. As always, brackets enclose my own explanatory insertions. The exclamation point in parentheses is Marx's.

"the most oppressive, odious and despicable in the world, will be an actual dictatorship despite all democratic forms, they console themselves with the thought that this dictatorship will be only transitory and short-lived."[63]

Here Bakunin amalgamates the "Lassalleans and Marxists" into one, although it is hard to believe that he was unaware of the antagonism in the German movement between Marx's friends and the Lassalleans. He brings Lassalle in to smear Marx because, as we saw earlier,[64] Lassalle did speak publicly of the special role of "men of science" and think privately in terms of a dictatorship by such deserving thinkers over the voting cattle whom they herded. Likewise, the term *people's state* was specifically Lassallean. Bakunin is, then, echoing a widespread charge against *Lassalle*.[65] His special contribution is this: he uses it to smear Marx, without purporting to adduce any more evidence on this than on the racist smears that pepper his book.*

Now it may be supposed that a man who gets so indignant at the alleged aim of the "Marxists" to establish a Dictatorship of the Intelligentsia is himself free of this detestable ambition. On the contrary; such a dictatorship was the crux of Bakunin's political perspective. We have

* It was Bakunin's regular pattern to accuse Marx in public of exactly what he, Bakunin, was planning in secret—the difference being that *his* ends were admirable whereas Marx's were always "oppressive, odious and despicable." Bakunin's admiring biographer, E. H. Carr, explains his subject in the following way:

> This contrast between the roles assigned [by Bakunin] to the International as a whole and to the [Bakuninist] Alliance explains the inconsistency with which Bakunin has frequently been reproached. In the International he demanded complete freedom for the individual. He denounced the despotism of Marx and the General Council, who wanted to "turn the International into a sort of monstrously colossal State, subject to a single official opinion represented by a strong central authority." ... But these principles did not in the least apply to the select and secret Alliance, whose members were to be "like unseen pilots in the tempest of popular passion." The revolution was to be directed "not by any visible power, but by the collective dictatorship of all the members of the Alliance." For this purpose, members of the Alliance must be willing to submit their personal freedom to discipline as rigid as that of the Jesuits (Bakunin returns more than once to this comparison), whose strength lay in the "obliteration of the individual before the collective will, organization and activity." Bakunin could see nothing incompatible in demanding the loosest form of organization for the International and the strictest possible discipline in the ranks of the Alliance.[66]

There is nothing incompatible in these two proposals, if Bakunin is understood; for his objective was to destroy the International in effect and replace it with his own secret band of collective dictators, through a boring-from-within operation. The incompatibility lies only in Carr's (and others') myth that Bakunin was a champion of something called libertarianism.

seen that he expected much from his beloved lumpen-class, brigands and peasant "barbarians,"[67] but it was not this barricade-fodder that was to lead the troops. While the revolutionary masses were to be warned of the bureaucratic dangers of organization and kept free of such sins, the leaders were to be organized in secret societies of relatively small membership:

> These societies [wrote Bakunin] were to be limited to a small number of persons, but would include, as far as possible, all men of talent, knowledge, intelligence and influence, who, while obeying a central authority [that is, Bakunin himself as Secret Chief], would in turn exert a sort of invisible sway over the masses.[68]

The leadership of the lumpen-troops, Bakunin expected, would be mainly in the hands of elements of the intelligentsia.* This intelligentsia, in his eyes, "is composed of innumerable persons of all strata: gentry, civil servants, clergy, merchants, townspeople and peasants . . . [I]n its very way of life it is in contradiction to the existing reality of Russia . . . It creates, we might say, a homeless wandering church of freedom."[70] That is, Bakunin is thinking particularly of disaffiliated individuals, déclassé bourgeois youth, extruded from the old classes—in short, a stratum of lumpen-intellectuals.

This lumpen-intellectual stratum is to constitute the general staff of the revolution:

> a sort of revolutionary general staff composed of devoted, energetic, intelligent individuals who are above all sincere friends of the people, not ambitious or vainglorious—capable of serving as intermediaries between the revolutionary idea and the popular instincts.[71]

So Bakunin was quoted in the Engels-Lafargue-Marx pamphlet pub-

---

* Pyziur explains that

Bakunin laid all his hopes of revolutionizing the country [Russia] on the intelligentsia. In his time, the formation of this new stratum of Russian society was proceeding rapidly . . . The Russian term for it, *raznochintzy* (people of various positions), is a clear indication of its social origin. This class was formed from various splinters of Russian society, united by the possession of education . . .[69]

We need not here broach the question of defining this "class" of splinters. This much is clear: in this backward Russian society, education brought awareness of how inferior the society was *even from the standpoint of the ruling class*; hence corrective dissent tended to appear as revolutionary unrest. In general, this applies

lished by the International. In line with this, the pamphlet also pointed to the social composition of the Bakuninist operation, especially in Italy:

> All the alleged sections of the Italian International are led by lawyers without cases, doctors without patients and without scientific knowledge, students of billiards, traveling salesmen and other commercial employees, and, mainly, small-paper journalists with a more or less dubious reputation.[72]

Not long before, Engels had written in a letter:

> In Italy the journalists, lawyers and doctors have pushed themselves so much to the fore that up to now we have never been able to come in direct contact with the workers; this is now beginning to change and we find that the workers, as everywhere, are quite different from their spokesmen.[73]

In 1870 a published piece by Bakunin drew one of his imaginary pictures of the intellectual hordes following him. Engels commented in a letter to Marx:

> Bakunin's letter [to the editor] is really very naive. What a misfortune for the world it would be—if it were not an awful lie—that there were 40,000 revolutionary students in Russia without a proletariat or even merely a revolutionary peasant behind them, and without any career ahead of them other than the dilemma of Siberia or emigration to Western Europe. If anything could ruin the Western European movement, it would be the importation of these 40,000 ± [more or less] educated, ambitious, hungry Russian nihilists; nothing but officer-cadets without an army, which we are to supply for them; a nice prospect—that to bring unity to the European proletariat it must be put under Russian command! Nevertheless, however much B[akunin] may be exaggerating, it still is crystal-clear that the danger is there. "Holy Russia" will spew out a certain number of these Russians "without careers" every year, and under the pretext of *principe international*, they will everywhere insinuate themselves into positions as leaders, bring into the sections [of the International]

---

more or less to national situations where the overriding issue is *modernization,* an issue which by definition arises only after a decisive section of the world has been bourgeoisified. Therefore an intelligentsia of this sort is characteristic of retarded situations, not of advanced countries.

their private intrigues which are inevitable among Russians, and then the General Council will have its work cut out for it.[74]

Seven years later, this "nice prospect" seemed to be looming in one place, Italy, as the conspiratorial sect of Bakuninists—not forty thousand, but "a band of young lawyers, doctors [academics], literati, clerks, etc., under Bakunin's personal command"—seized control wherever revolutionary workers started to become active. So Engels reported in an article. But when the movement reached the industrial north, the more advanced workers did not "let themselves be long held in tutelage by those broken-down young bourgeois, who had thrown themselves into socialism because (in Bakunin's words) they found themselves in a 'blind-alley career.'" The proletariat would not stay under the control of "people who derive their vocation as leaders of the workers' movement from their situation as seedy bourgeois."[75]

This picture of the social composition of the Bakuninist movement, although phrased pejoratively, corresponded to the aims of Bakunin himself.

At the same time that Bakunin looked to the dictatorship of his band of lumpen-intellectuals, he matched the Weitling pattern[76] in another way—in a similar type of anti-intellectualism. These were two sides of the same coin. The troops (barricade-fodder) were not to be contaminated by exposure to confusing ideas, if they were to remain pristinely fierce enough to hack the old society to pieces in accordance with the call to Pandestruction; nor were they to be overeducated to the point where they might question the General Staff, those "unseen pilots" who were wielding the lumpen-army in order to remold the world closer to their heart's desire.

As early as 1847, when Marx was busy giving lectures to the German workers' club in Brussels, Bakunin wrote that Marx was "ruining the workers by making theorists of them."[77] While Bakunin often represented himself as a theoretician, he also urged: "Let us leave to others the task of developing the theoretical principles of social revolution and content ourselves with applying them, with incorporating them into acts."[78] There was no real contradiction: the development of theoretical principles was his own province, and the henchmen should content themselves with applying them in action.

The International pamphlet by Engels, Lafargue and Marx took care to bring out this aspect of Bakuninism. It exhibited one of Bakunin's joint productions with Nechayev where they

> preach the cult of ignorance to the Russian youth under the pretext that present-day science is only an official science (can one imagine an official mathematics, physics, chemistry?), and that such is the opinion of the best people in the West.[79]

As against this view, Marx preached the necessity for revolutionaries to absorb the best of the attainments of bourgeois and past societies and integrate it into the education of the proletarian movement. The International pamphlet contemptuously quoted the principle laid down by the anarchist duo:

> A revolutionary [wrote Bakunin and Nechayev] scorns all doctrinairism and renounces the science of this world, leaving it for future generations. He knows only a single science: destruction. For that and nothing but that, he studies mechanics, physics, chemistry and perhaps medicine.[80]

The pamphlet also denounced Bakunin's collaboration with his cousin, the governor of Siberia, in quashing the project for the founding of a university there as "an intellectual center in their country." The pamphlet added: "Bakunin's hatred of science dates from far back."[81]

Dictatorial domination—for the intelligentsia; anti-intellectualism—for the masses: this was the outlook written down and spelled out by the Great Libertarian whose undocumented invented smears against Marx are repeated in quantity in the pages of modern marxology.

7. "THE MOST DANGEROUS PEOPLE"

Let us summarize the views that Marx and Engels left in legacy on this problem, in terms of their characteristic fight on two fronts against bisymmetric mistakes. On the one hand: rejection of "proletarianism" and its exclusionary practice—a tendency that was to gain new life especially in the French syndicalist movement. On the other hand: no truckling to intellectuals in the movement.

We have seen that Marx's and Engels' views emerged as the problem flared up in the German party in waves. One of the first signs was the accession of some intellectuals after the 1875 unification, and one of the first flareups was signalized by the Höchberg "manifesto" of 1879. Already, even though there were as yet few Höchberg-type elements in the party, Marx and Engels were filled with apprehension:

> In general [wrote Engels], it's about time we came out against the philanthropic big bourgeois and petty-bourgeois, students and doctors [academics] who are pushing their way into the party and want to water down the class struggle of the proletariat against its oppressor into a general Institute for Human Brotherhood . . .[82]

The still-small intellectualist wing in the party had reacted to Bismarck's Anti-Socialist Law by calling for a retreat to the right. But Bismarck's persecution drove the working-class ranks to the left. The danger seemed to diminish; yet in early 1883 Engels still lamented: "Oh this damned German flabbiness of thought and will, which was brought with so much effort into the party along with the 'eddicated,' if only we were rid of it again!"[83] The following year the problem became more serious as the result of an electoral victory by the Social-Democracy. (Typically, the "men of ideas" are attracted by a display of political muscle.) Between the first and second ballots of the election, Engels kept his fingers crossed about the quality of the Social-Democratic candidates being elected: "The worst ones (the eddicated ones) have already been elected; those yet to come [in the second balloting] are mostly workers, and they can only improve the company."[84]

In this first decade after Marx's death, Engels redoubled his private warnings to the Bebel leadership of the party. As we saw, he regarded Liebknecht as next to hopeless, "with his predilection for educated wiseacres and people in bourgeois positions."

> But precisely in Germany [he wrote to Bebel] these are the most dangerous people, and Marx and I have fought them without a letup since 1845. Once they have been allowed into the party, where they push themselves forward everywhere, they have to be kept down without a letup, since their petty-bourgeois standpoint is every moment in conflict with, or tries to distort, that of the proletarian masses.

"As sure as anything, the split is coming" with these elements, he predicted, not for the first time. "My confidence in our proletariat is just as unqualified as my mistrust of the wholly rotten German philistinedom is unbounded."[85]

When in 1890 the government bowed to increased socialist strength and scrapped its Anti-Socialist Law, the problem naturally deepened as another bar to careerists was removed. Engels had new cause to warn that "the present strong rush of literati and students to join the party involves harm for it in various ways as long as these gentlemen are not kept within proper limits."[86] To be sure, he expressed optimism as ever:

> We are now strong enough in Germany to stand a great deal. One of the greatest services that the Anti-Socialist Law did for us was to free us from the importunities of the socialistically tinged German intellectual [*Studiosus*]. We are now strong enough even to digest the German intellectual, who is again making himself very evident.[87]

His optimism was based on confidence in the working-class composition of the German party:

> Since the brilliant test which they passed from 1878 on [under the Anti-Socialist Law], I have had unqualified confidence in our workers, and only in them. Like every great party they will make mistakes in detail in the course of their development, perhaps big mistakes. The masses learn indeed only through the consequences of their own mistakes, through experiments on their own bodies. But all that will be overcome . . .[88]

When Engels died five years later, the influence of intellectuals in the upper circles of the party was still mounting. Soon after his death, one of those he had considered an exception, Eduard Bernstein, came out with his relapse to the Höchberg-reformism of his early days, giving it the new brand-name of Revisionism. The fresh young *Studiosen* and university-certified *Doktoren* were encouraged to stream into the party and take it over in alliance with the trade-union bureaucracy—to "eddicate" the working-class membership, as Engels would have put it.

The rest of this story involves the whole subsequent history of the Social-Democracy, which is not our subject. Suffice to note in conclusion that when the problem of the role of intellectuals in the party reached a crisis point in discussion at the Dresden party congress of 1903, the repeated letters of Marx and Engels to the German party leaders were still potent. At the 1903 congress, it was Bebel and

Kautsky in particular[89] who tried to articulate Marx's approach, an approach that had been energetically drummed into them. Bebel told the delegates:

> After the developments of the last few years, I have, alas, come around to the following opinion in my old age: Scrutinize every party comrade, but in the case of an academic or an intellectual, scrutinize him two or three times. (*Stormy applause.*)

He went on to give the fight-on-two-fronts approach:

> We need the intelligence of the academics and intellectuals. Their fortunate circumstances and social position have allowed them to bring to bear scientific capacities which permit them to be active for our party in outstanding fashion, if they behave honorably and uprightly in accord with the party. But there is where the danger also lies, on the other hand. . . . precisely as academics, as men and women with greater knowledge and, in a certain sense, also with greater intellect and deeper insight, they damn-well have the obligation in everything they do to make doubly and triply sure they are on the correct road, and to find out from the proletarians how the masses of people think, how they feel, and what they want—masses who know better than academics what the struggle of the proletariat is all about.[90]

It should not be thought that the intellectuals were the villains of the piece, in the process of deradicalization and bourgeoisification that led the Social-Democracy down the road to its political breakdown in 1914. The decisive motive forces came rather from the hardening bureaucracies of the trade unions and party institutions and their interaction with the bourgeois state. This combination was a mighty power. But the intellectuals typically represented the servants of power, not the power of intellect.

APPENDICES

MARX ON THE ABOLITION
OF THE PROLETARIAT
BY AUTOMATION
A note to Chapter 2, page 47

One way of dismissing the problem of proletarian revolution, or at least of proletarian class struggle, has traditionally been to do away with the proletariat—to "vanish" it, as magicians say. This prestidigitation has been going on since the early nineteenth century, that is, virtually since the rise of the modern proletariat. It reached the status of a movement ideology with the vogue of Technocracy several decades ago. In 1933 Stuart Chase announced portentously:

> The automatic process continually displaces the manual worker. . . . What becomes of the class struggle theory? Where are the toiling masses, without a worker in the plant? . . . The official labor movement, it is significant to note, has not progressed in the new mass production industries, and in the next phase, the automatic industry, there will be nobody to organize. When this development proceeds to a certain point, which we may or may not have reached, the whole Marxian thesis stands in need of substantial revision.[1]

This was published not long before the explosive rise of the CIO, centered in the mass-production industries, transformed the American labor movement and initiated a period of intensified class struggle. Since then, the news that the proletariat has virtually ceased to exist has come regularly from other prophets, the latest wave following hard on the escalation of the term *automation* into *cybernation*.

This note is not the place to take up the twentieth-century form of the myth about the disappearance of the proletariat, especially since this myth has been given its just deserts in excellent studies of the question.[2] What faced Marx was not any claim that the process was taking place but merely the prediction that it would eventually take place *under capitalism*.

The issue was already well known before Marx read his first book on economics; he noted it in his first manuscript on political economy, and he gave the essential answer in his first lecture on the subject.

In one of the early works of modern political economy, in 1819, Sismondi had remarked of English manufactures that "In fact, nothing remains to be desired but that the King, living quite alone on the island, should by continuously turning a crank cause automatons [*des automates*] to do all the work of England." Marx quoted this in his Paris manuscripts of 1844, without direct comment.[3] The idea appeared also in the main work by Andrew Ure, the apologist for the factory system, and was quoted therefrom by Marx in his 1847 work against Proudhon: "on the automatic plan," wrote Ure, "skilled labour gets progressively superseded, and will, eventually, be replaced by mere onlookers of machines."[4] The same year, in lectures later published as *Wage-Labor and Capital*, Marx answered:

> If the whole class of wage-workers were to be abolished owing to machinery, how dreadful that would be for capital which, without wage-labor, ceases to be capital![5]

For one thing, while there is no doubt that automatic machinery can produce commodities with a minimum of human labor, the machines are not programmed to buy their own products and consume them. In short, while this tendency appears early in capitalism, it cannot work itself out to the predicted end without bursting the bounds of that system.

Marx grapples with the issue in his *Grundrisse* notebooks of 1857–1858,* where another passage from Ure is taken as text. Ure was defining the factory: "This term, in its strictest sense, involves the idea of a vast automaton, composed of numerous *mechanical and intellectual organs* operating together and without interruption to produce one and the same object, all of these organs being subordinated to a motive force which moves by itself."[6] Marx accepts, and even emphasizes, that it is indeed the tendency of capital to move toward the minimization and eventual virtual elimination of human labor. From its start capital devaluates the old craftsman's concern for skill and quality, and substitutes production for quantity, mass production, because it is interested only in exchange value and surplus value.

> The developed principle of capital is indeed to make special skill superfluous, and to make manual labor, directly physical labor in

---

* In reading passages from the *Grundrisse*, one must always bear in mind that these notebooks were scribbled by Marx for his own use or as possible rough drafts for future publication; their form often reflects carbuncles and insomnia as well as a train of thought.

general, superfluous, as skilled labor as well as muscular exertion; instead, to put the skill into the dead forces of nature.[7]

This is a *tendency* under capitalism; how far it develops into realization is another matter. In any case, the tendency toward automation is built into capitalism:

> Once involved in the production process of capital, however, the means of labor goes through various metamorphoses, of which the last is the *machine*, or better, an *automatic system of machinery* (system of machinery: the *automatic* system is only its most complete and adequate form and for the first time changes machinery into a system)—set into motion by an automaton, a moving force which sets itself into motion; this automaton consisting of numerous mechanical and intellectual organs, so that the workers themselves are made into mere conscious appendages of it.[8]

Here Marx is taking up Ure's own formulation.* The crux of his answer is that, in proportion as scientific technology replaces "direct labor" in production, it presses outside the bounds of the capitalist system.

> ... to that same extent, direct labor together with its quantity disappears as the determining principle of production—the creation of use-values—and is not only reduced quantitatively to a slight proportion, but also qualitatively to a subordinate though still indispensable aspect, as compared to the general scientific labor, the technological application of the natural sciences on the one hand, as well as [compared to] the general force of production arising from the social structuring of the whole of production—[a force of production] which appears as a natural endowment of social labor (although it is a historical product). Thus capital works to its own dissolution as the form dominating production.[12]

A little further on, he remarks also that as "capital—entirely unintentionally—reduces human labor, the expenditure of energy, to a min-

---

* Marx quotes part of this passage from Ure also in *Capital*,[9] but there it leads to discussing the alienation of the worker as an appendage of the machine, not the abolition of labor. On the side, it may be of interest to compare a passage in Marx's *Theories of Surplus Value* where he discusses how "science realized *in the machine* appears as *capital* in relation to the laborers."[10] This involves Marx's conception of the relation between use-value and exchange-value, which is covered in the first volume of *Capital* only in abstract form. For an indication that this is enough only "for the time being," see his remarks in a letter to Engels of April 2, 1858.[11]

imum," the consequence is that "This will redound to the advantage of emancipated labor, and is the condition for its emancipation." [13]

The whole process is looked at again, some pages later, from an interesting side. As large industry develops, Marx explains, the tendency is for the creation of real wealth to depend less on the amount of labor used and more on the power of the technological agencies used, which in turn depends on advances in science and technology. An enormous disproportion develops between the more and more abstract labor applied and the power of the production process it takes care of. [14]

> It is no longer true so much that labor figures as [something] comprised in the production process, but rather the human being has the relation of caretaker and regulator to the production process itself. . . . He steps alongside the production process, instead of being its main agent. . . . As soon as labor in its direct form has ceased to be the great source of wealth, labor time ceases and must cease to be its measure, and hence exchange value [ceases and must cease to be the measure] of use-value. The *surplus labor of the mass of people* has ceased to be the condition for the development of general wealth, just as the *non-labor* of the few [ceases to be the condition] for the development of the general powers of the human head.

This leads right to the basic conclusion:

> Thereupon production based on exchange value breaks down, and the direct material production process gets stripped of the forms of poverty and contradictoriness. The free development of individualities [is the result], and therefore not the reduction in necessary labor time in order to constitute surplus value, but rather the reduction in general of the necessary labor of society to a minimum, [an outcome] which then corresponds to the artistic, scientific, etc., cultivation of individuals, by virtue of the free time and means made available to all of them. [15]

Thus, under socialism, the unleashed power of technology can bring about the liberation of the individual from the contradictions inherent in capitalism, but under capitalism it only sharpens contradictions. For all this, continues Marx, bears on a contradiction of capital: capital strives to reduce labor time to a minimum while at the same time labor time is its measure and source of wealth (that is, of commodity values). To do the first, it calls on the power of science, technology, and social organization in order to make the creation of wealth relatively independent of the labor time used to create it. At the same time it still has to use labor time to measure the giant social forces unleashed and to confine the latter within the limits so set.

Productive forces and social relationships—two different sides of the development of the social individual—appear to capital only as means, and are only means for it, to carry on production on its own narrowly limited foundation. In fact, however, they are the material conditions for blowing up this foundation.[16]

This states, from another angle, what is contained in the more famous lines from *Capital:* "Centralization of the means of production and socialization of labor at last reach a point where they become incompatible with their capitalist integument. This integument is burst asunder. The knell of capitalist private property sounds."[17]

Marx argues that technology can, and will, replace direct human labor in the production of *use-values,* but it does not produce exchange-values. As labor is reduced toward the minimum, then by the same token capital "without wage-labor, ceases to be capital." The tendency toward the abolition of labor which was rightly heralded by Ure as the very perfection of capital is also the tendency which negates capital as it works itself out. The long-heralded abolition of the proletariat is a reality of the future, but only over the dead body of capitalism. Given the replacement of capitalism, this abolition not only becomes possible but is a necessary consequence of technological trends. It is also the necessary basis for the flowering of the human individuality freed from the blind coercion of material scarcity.

Short of those happy days, however—namely, today—the main effect of far-extended automation is in shaking the wage and profit system, not in shaking "the whole Marxian thesis" of proletarian revolution. The classes involved in direct labor are undergoing internal changes as always, but they are not likely to be merely predicted out of existence.

SPECIAL	MARX'S CONVERSATION
NOTE	WITH HAMANN
B	A note to Chapter 5, page 145

There is an alleged statement by Marx on trade-union/party relations that has cropped up regularly for the last fifty years or so, often in efforts to prove that Marx held syndicalist or reformist views of some sort on the matter.* According to this story, Marx confided these opinions for the first and only time to a total stranger during a trip abroad—a stranger who had arranged this meeting for his own purposes and who then proceeded to publish his own account of the conversation in the course of a faction fight.

To separate the kernels of truth from the chaff, it is enough to bring the facts together. In the course of this inquiry we will also get a look at the German trade-union movement of the 1860s, on which we have cited Marx elsewhere, and we will have done an exercise in the evaluation of Marx-quotations.

1. A CHAT WITH STRANGERS

In late 1869 Marx took a month off for a restorative trip to Germany with his ailing daughter Jenny, mainly for a stay with his friend Dr. Kugelmann in Hanover, where he stopped from September 18 to October 7. There a Hanover unionist named J. Hamann requested a discussion, which took place on September 30. Writing to Engels with some miscellaneous news, Marx included the following item:

* For example, this Hamann conversation has been used for semi-syndicalist purposes by Daniel De Leon and by a wing of the early German Communist Party; with reformist overtones, by the French Kautskyan, Lucien Laurat. Most recently it has turned up in a two-volume compilation of *Gespräche [Conversations] mit Marx und Engels*, where it is shoveled in without the least explanation.[1]

I have *just* chatted away an hour with a delegation of 4 Lassalleans who were sent to me by the local branch of the General German Workers Association. Naturally I behaved in a very reserved and diplomatizing manner, but *sub rosa* I told the people what they had to be told. We parted good friends. Their invitation in the name of the Association, to deliver a lecture for them, I naturally declined.[2]

This is the conversation in which Marx is supposed to have enunciated unique opinions. On the contrary, we see, Marx was "reserved" about his views and "diplomatized" in expressing them. That is, he was afraid that too strong an exposition of his criticisms of the Lassallean GGWA would disturb the delegation of "Lassalleans," and so he tactfully limited himself to his essential critique of the organization.* He was even gratified when, despite this critique, they "parted good friends." All this means that he had not the least idea of what Hamann's group stood for or what they were doing—and that Hamann did not tell him, merely posing questions for answer. It means that Marx did not even know that his visitors belonged to an active opposition to the GGWA leadership that was soon going to split away.

This should not be surprising, for the ignorance was mutual. At this point Marx was apprised only of the public facts about the conflict in the Schweitzer movement. (It was only days later, on October 3, that Marx finally met with some leaders of the opposition who had joined up with Bebel and Liebknecht; Liebknecht himself was unable to come to Hanover.) On his part, a man like Hamann could have no idea of how Marx really felt about the Schweitzer leadership in the movement. This was at the tail end of a period when Schweitzer had been making overtures to the International and to Marx, and when publicly Marx was maintaining an attitude of neutrality between the Schweitzer organization and the Bebel-Liebknecht group.[3] The result: Hamann had no reason to know that Marx was hostile to Schweitzer's views, and Marx obviously assumed his visitors were Schweitzer men from the local Lassallean branch.

This was not exactly the ideal situation for Marx to decide to reveal an opinion he had never expressed before! On the contrary, if we want to know in general what Marx told the Hanover delegation about trade-union/party relations, we need only look to the exposition (also

---

* The General German Workers Association (*Allgemeine Deutsche Arbeiterverein*, ADAV) had been founded by Lassalle in May 1863, and is usually regarded as the pioneer socialist party of Germany. When Lassalle died in August 1864, the presidency eventually passed to the movement's editor, J. B. von Schweitzer, who assumed public leadership in mid-1867.

"diplomatizing") in Marx's letter to Schweitzer himself of October 13, 1868.[4]

But if we want to know what Marx's exposition meant to Hamann—and how Hamann might tend to represent Marx's views to his fellow unionists who were getting ready for a crucial vote on Schweitzer's dictatorship—we have to summarize the situation that faced these unionists at that very moment.

2. THE TRADE-UNIONISTS' REVOLT OF 1869

Following is a brief summary for our present limited purposes.[5]

The middle 1860s in Germany saw a sharp rise in strike struggles and workers' organization. By 1868 there was a strike wave, and trade unions started developing rapidly. The GGWA, the only socialist organization that existed as yet on a national scale, was hostile to this development. Lassalleanism saw the working class essentially as shock troops to be mobilized by a political leadership vis-à-vis the state power. Its organizational form was a presidential dictatorship by statute, first under Lassalle and then under Schweitzer. In the Lassallean concept, any workers' organization other than the Lassallean political party was an irrelevancy, and an organization independent of party control was a threat to Humanity.

But the reality of the class struggle outside the GGWA impelled dissidents to raise their voices inside the organization, especially by the time of its Hamburg congress in September 1868. The congress went so far as to come out in favor of strikes, but recoiled at the un-Lassallean proposal that socialists should actually help to found trade unions; a majority voted this counterrevolutionary idea down. But Schweitzer himself was willing to be more flexible than the sect members whom he had helped to fossilize with "infallible" Lassallean concepts. He wanted to tack and veer before the storm of strikes in order to bring these unruly forces under proper control, instead of flatly confronting them as an enemy. He therefore set about—with the help of the cigarworkers' leader, F. W. Fritzsche—to establish trade-union organizations, trade unions that would be integral cogs in his party empire and completely subject to his presidential dictatorship.

Meanwhile, outside of Prussia, August Bebel and Wilhelm Liebknecht were slowly breaking with their stultifying course of subordinating the workers' circles in which they had influence to the bourgeois-liberal People's Party. Under continual pressure from Marx and from the intense upsurge in working-class struggles, Bebel and Liebknecht finally started moving toward independent class organization. Their movement began helping to form trade unions, but on the basis of model statutes drawn up by Bebel which established a pattern of organizational autonomy for the unions. These unions usually had the word "International" in their titles, in order to imply a link with *the* International even though a statutory link was illegal.

When the GGWA met at Elberfeld in March 1869, the anti-Schweitzer opposition had managed to get Bebel and Liebknecht on the platform to present their case. To be sure, the majority upheld Schweitzer, but a third of the delegates abstained from voting: a bad moral defeat for him. "With this," Engels wrote Marx with his usual bounce, "the disintegration process of specific Lassalleanism has begun and must proceed swiftly."[6] The congress even amended the statutes so as to reduce the presidential powers.

After the congress the pressure on Schweitzer continued, and the "dictator" (as Engels' letter had called him) panicked. On June 18 he decreed a merger with a splinter group of true-Lassalleans that the Countess Hatzfeldt (Lassalle's ex-patron) had whittled off a couple of years before. This merger, uncomplicated by a membership vote, also restored the old presidential powers in full dictatorial splendor. The dissidents had had enough; led by Wilhelm Bracke, they denounced this "coup d'état" and headed toward a split. By August 7 they held a joint congress with the Bebel-Liebknecht forces at Eisenach and formed the Social-Democratic Workers Party ("Eisenachers").

But even before this, the trade-unionists imprisoned in the Schweitzerian barracks had begun to revolt too. Fritzsche led the revolt in the cigarworkers' union, which he had founded in 1865. Schweitzer promptly issued a decree removing him from office. On July 14 the GGWA Executive gave the president power to expel oppositionists at will. Then the racking struggle against the dictatorship spread to the metalworkers' union.

And this brings us to J. Hamann, the chief treasurer of the metalworkers' union in Hanover. Not because of his prominence in these events—on the contrary, I cannot even verify his first name from the sources*—but because, as this storm was coming to a head, he got the

---

* The Eisenach party organ *Volksstaat*, which published many metalworkers' union notices in this period, could not decide whether Hamann's initial was J. or H., the latter appearing quite often. The abovementioned *Gespräche mit Marx und Engels* gives his first name as Joseph, for unstated reasons. His name was Johannes Hamann, according to a letter to me from Dieter Schneider of the

idea of asking the visiting leader of the International for an opinion on some of the issues.

3. BACKGROUND OF THE CONVERSATION

The "Lassallean" metalworkers' union (*Allgemeine Deutsche Metall-arbeiterschaft*) had been founded only a year before under the leadership of Louis Schulze of Hanover, who was now the union president. Around the end of August 1869, Schulze went to Berlin to protest the July 14 decree, unsuccessfully, and sent a circular to the membership attacking the dictatorship. A Schweitzer lieutenant returned the favor with a foray into Hanover, the seat of the Union Executive. There was an exchange of claims about who had what majority; then Schulze resigned his post, with a blast against Schweitzer, thereby precipitating a new election to take the issue to the membership. The vote was indecisive, however, for the anti-Schweitzer vote was divided between two candidates. (It was about this point in the fast-breaking events that Hamann's conversation with Marx took place; but let us finish this chapter of the story before returning to it.)

On October 9, Schweitzer called on his dictatorial powers to settle the opposition's hash. In a long statement defending the central party's control over its unions, and attacking the metalworkers' Executive for not expelling Schulze as a supporter of Bebel-Liebknecht, the Lassallean pope decreed that the Executive was dissolved, installed his own man as president of the union, and announced a second election from which Schulze would be excluded. The encyclical then lambasted the followers of Bebel-Liebknecht as splitters and infiltrators, and called on all good members to report on other members who helped these "tools or supporters of the bourgeoisie." Schweitzer ended with a paean to "unity and strength": "Long live party unity!"

As Schweitzer's man launched the inevitable witch-hunt against Schulze's supporters, the latter looked around for an alternative. There was one. In mid-August another metalworkers' union had been founded at a congress in Nuremberg, of the "International" type, that is, based on Bebel's model statutes. A fusion was soon arranged between the dissident group of the GGWA union and the new "International" union. On November 28-30, at a congress in Brunswick, the two met

German metalworkers' union, who has co-authored a union history.[7] I am also indebted to this letter by Schneider for some other details to be mentioned and other aid, but he is in no way associated with interpretations expressed here.

together and established a new and autonomous organization, the Internationale Metallarbeiterschaft. The GGWA union's treasury was brought over to the new union by J. Hamann, who remained chief treasurer.

On the eve of this unity congress, in the November 27 issue of the Eisenach party's weekly—now called the *Volksstaat* and still edited by Liebknecht—there is an interesting group of three items, on an inside page largely devoted to trade-union news, notices and other accounts. The first is a final Call to the members of the ex-Lassallean metalworkers' union to attend the Brunswick congress, signed by Carl Bomm as business manager. The third is a report on a visit to Hanover by Schweitzer himself on the previous Sunday, relating how his meeting had been energetically upset by metalworkers led by Bomm, Schulze, and Hamann, who attacked Schweitzer from the floor and then staged a walkout.

Sandwiched in between these two items of factional interest is— Hamann's report on his conversation with Marx on issues involved (unbeknown to Marx) in this turmoil. More accurately, it is the *Volksstaat*'s reprint of Hamann's report; as the first sentence shows, Hamann's account had originally appeared in the union's monthly bulletin, as part of a Call (*Aufruf*)—that is, as a direct contribution to the split, not simply as a report of general political interest.*

Following is the complete text of the item, as it was published in the *Volksstaat.*[9]

MARX ON TRADE UNIONS

The following appears in a Call by J. Hamann, the chief treasurer of the Allgemeine Deutsche Metallarbeiterschaft (see No. 4 of the trade-union organ published in Hanover): The trade unions can never and must never be made dependent on a political organization—this is proved to us only too clearly by the present decline of our union. This is also the opinion of the greatest political economist and writer now living, Dr. Karl Marx, Lassalle's teacher, who stopped over in Hanover for a short time. I too could not refrain from getting personally acquainted with the man of science, and requested a discussion with him in order to hear the advice of this great inquirer into social questions and his opinions on trade unions. This was kindly vouchsafed to me; and the next day I visited him along with four friends, and held a

---

* The bulletin, whose title is the name of the union, is no longer extant, the last file having been destroyed during the Nazi period (according to Dieter Schneider). Therefore Hamann's original article is not available. Since we know that the bulletin's first number was dated July 1, No. 4 must have been dated October 1.[8]

discussion for one and a half hours. Here I bring out only the main points and adhere strictly to the truth.

My first question to Dr. Karl Marx was this: Must the trade unions predominantly be dependent on a political organization, if they are to be viable? The answer was: "The trade unions should never be connected up with a political organization nor be made dependent on one, if they are to fulfill their task; should this happen, it means a deathblow to them. The trade unions are the schools for socialism. In the trade unions the workers are trained to be socialists, for there the struggle with capital is carried on before their eyes day-in day-out. All political parties, no matter which, without exception, inspire the masses of workers for only a temporary period of time, whereas the trade unions have a lasting hold on the mass of workers, only they are in a position to constitute a real workers' party and set up a bulwark against the power of capital. The greater mass of the workers have arrived at the understanding that their material condition must be improved, no matter which party they want to belong to. But if the material condition of the worker is improved, then he can devote himself more to the upbringing of his children; his wife and children will not have to go into the factories; he himself can improve his mind and take better care of his body; and he then becomes a socialist without being aware of it."

The second question I raised was this: Is it proper for a trade union to possess its own organ? I then explained that, since a while back, we had been publishing our accounts monthly in circulars, and special circumstances affecting the union's interests had brought the question up for discussion, but the reproach had been hurled at us from various quarters that it was presumptuous and overweening, an offence against the organization, and more of the same. The answer was as follows: "I am not surprised to hear that; but you should not pay attention to such phrases; indeed, a union's organ is the binding link; in its pages the various opinions for-and-against should come up for discussion, the wage conditions in the various trades should be made known, but never should it be the property of an individual person—rather, if it is to fulfill its purpose it must be the property of the collectivity. The grounds for this I need not enlarge on further, for they are so obvious that everyone must understand that this is one of the prime basic conditions for the trade unions to reach full flowering."

Such is the opinion of this man, who is generally known to be the greatest authority in the science of political economy. If anyone doubts this statement, he can address himself directly to Dr. Karl Marx, 1, Modena Villas, Maitland Park, London, for the latter has stated he will be glad to confirm this statement of his.

Finally, he also offers us this advice: never to attach ourselves to a person, but always keep one's eyes on the issue and form our opinion on the basis of it. "It's not Liebknecht, or Dr. Schweitzer, or myself that matters to you, only the issue—this is the truth."

And with this statement I can only concur fully.

J. Hamann

4. THE BLURRED IMAGE

Were it not for the latter-day use made of this minor polemical contribution to the 1869 fight, it would be a sterile business to try to deduce from its words just what Marx might have told his visitors as they sat around Dr. Kugelmann's living room. This implies no accusation against Hamann's bona fides. More knowledgeable people have spent more time on more of Marx's words than Hamann was able to do, and have reported less accurately what they absorbed. To try to discern the original through this blurred echo of it is something like making out the details of an unfocused form photographed in the dusk, through a warped window, on film that already bears an underlay of images.

For one thing, Hamann's fulsome praise of Marx does not imply acquaintance with Marx's writings or ideas. He knew Marx was the "greatest political economist" etc. because both sides in the socialist struggle had recently said so. Both Schweitzer's and Liebknecht's organs had published flattering notices on *Capital* and its author; the Basel Congress of the International, then at its zenith, had just taken place and had officially recommended Marx's *Capital* to the world.

As for the image underlay: what we have of Hamann's ideas (brief passages of argumentation in the course of Calls published in the *Volksstaat*) suggests nothing more than an elementary reformist emphasis on the material aims of good trade-unionism as against excessive politicalization. In another context there would be little reason to stress this. Hamann was in a violently polarizing situation, where the Schweitzerites swung to overwhelming emphasis on the primacy of politics over immediate interests—interpreted as the primacy of the party leadership over the unionists—while the opposition swung to a heavy and healthy emphasis on the necessary autonomy of the "economic" organization and the role of the immediate struggle as an organizer of troops in the class struggle. Both polarizations, as they flew apart, headed in disastrous directions, as we know from the eventual tendencies taken on in the movement. But we can hardly expect a

Hamann to figure out in advance solutions to the basic problems of the movement, when even the "theoretician" of the anti-Schweitzerians, namely Liebknecht, fell on his face continually, as the Marx-Engels correspondence records.

This comment would be supererogatory except that this bedeviled Hanover metalworker, caught in the midst of a tumultuous split, is supposed—after a chat with Marx—to have become a reliable authority on Marx's views, even if they had not been communicated in a "reserved and diplomatizing manner." This reflects not on Hamann himself but only on the authorities who quote his squib with the same gravity as they quote from the *Communist Manifesto.*

Hamann's use of quotation marks should not be understood as a claim that he had transcribed Marx's exact words. It is a fact—a deplorable fact—that it was common practice to use quote marks for paraphrased summaries, not only in popular journalism but even in more serious places.* Hamann is honestly giving his own summary of what he had gathered from Marx's conversation. As he said, he was bringing out "only the main points."

The main point dealt with the subordination of the trade unions to the organizational discipline of the political party, as against the trade union's need for organizational autonomy. Schweitzer stood for the first, the opposition for the second; and on this main issue, Marx's position was strongly and unequivocally on the side of the opposition. This was what Hamann discovered during the conversation; and on this he was quite right. But as soon as we get beyond this, things get blurry.

The primitiveness of Hamann's grasp of the other issues is shown by the first sentence he ascribes to Marx: "The trade unions should never be connected up [*in Zusammenhang gebracht*] with a political organization nor be made dependent on one . . ." Here two different thoughts are treated as interchangeable. The International was precisely a format for bringing trade unions into a *connection* with the political movement, a type of connection alien to Lassalleanism. Marx was then at the height of accomplishing, very publicly, precisely what Hamann's report has him warning against, if the words are taken seriously. It is this obviously garbled paraphrase which later was taken to be evidence that Marx favored what came to be called the "neutrality" of trade unions

---

* Even Jean Jaurès, a scholar by training and a professor by vocation, was caught one day on this practice; his defense was in effect that his summary quote was accurate. Henderson and Chaloner have made a brouhaha over this feature of Engels' quotes from the sources in *The Condition of the Working Class in England*, as originally published.[10] (In the new Marx-Engels *Collected Works*, these quotes are revised back to the original sources.) The commonness of the custom is not a defense but an explanation, and in any case it should be a caution against unjustified assumptions.

in politics—a conception which is the mirror image of Schweitzer's political barracks-control.

The other element in the Hamann report that is most clearly garbled is the sentence in which Marx is supposed to say that *only* the trade unions "are in a position to institute a real workers party."* Marx could not possibly have made any such generalization. A bare five weeks before this conversation, Marx's friends along with Hamann's had just constituted a real workers' party, at Eisenach—and not at all on the organizational basis of trade unions. It is possible to speculate what Hamann heard that came off his pen in this form (perhaps the idea that a trade-union basis was one way for a workers' party to come into existence), but such speculation is only a mental exercise.

On the other hand, there are shards of Marxiana in this report of Hamann's which sound quite authentic, as one might expect: "The trade unions are the schools of socialism," and so on. Marx's warning against the cult of personality was directed against the cult of Lassalle as much as of Schweitzer; he had said as much elsewhere. But there is nothing new to be learned.

The "authenticity" of the Hamann report is sometimes taken as proved by the fact that Marx sent in no correction, although he probably saw it in the paper.** But if the circumstances are understood,

---

* This was the sole sentence quoted by De Leon (see the footnote on page 580). In general, it is the "syndicalist" ingredient in the stew, although the British Labor Party could agree with it without difficulty; actually, it occupies the common ground between syndicalism and reformism.

** Marx certainly received the *Volksstaat:* although there is no direct evidence that he saw the item or that he read every page carefully (the Hamann report was far from prominent on an inside page with a small heading), still we can assume that it would be called to his attention even if he missed it. The more important point is that Marx made a practice of *not* writing in corrections to editors who printed misstatements about him, whether in bourgeois or socialist papers. There were important exceptions, but they were exceptions to a rule: "if I denied everything that has been said and written of me, I would require a score of secretaries," he told one interviewer at the end of 1878 (following the flood of pseudo-Marxiana unleashed after the Paris Commune).[11] He made a longer and stronger statement to the same effect in a letter in 1881.[12] There are many cases in point; we may note especially a biographical article which was full of incorrect facts but which Marx praised as a good one because of its good general tendency.[13] We come closer to the Hamann case in time and space when we note that in 1865 Marx and Engels exchanged letters about what Schweitzer's paper had done in its account of a speech by Marx. The speech was made into "colossal muck"; it had Marx "talking pure Schweitzerism," wrote Engels. Marx then informed his friend that he had written Liebknecht that the quotes were the exact opposite of what he had really said.[14] But he sent no correction to Schweitzer for publication. Finally we should note that Marx and Engels frequently expressed their chagrin and disgust at the stuff Liebknecht put into the *Volksstaat*, without

it is clear that there was nothing much for him to correct that would have seemed important at the time. It is not reasonable to credit Marx with sufficient ESP to anticipate the future triumphs of marxology in the interpretation of Marx-quotes. It was enough for Marx that readers of Hamann's report in the difficult situation of 1869 would have been moved a step in the right direction by its concrete meaning for the ongoing struggle.

---

ever making a public demonstration. The sharpest statement came later, when Engels wrote that "The *Volksstaat* under William [Liebknecht] is becoming worse and worse and more and more boring . . . Something readable only here and there."[15]

PERMANENT REVOLUTION:
ON THE ORIGIN OF THE TERM

A note to Chapter 8, page 204

The standard marxological practice has long been to treat the term and concept of permanent revolution as "Blanquist," as has been true also of the term *dictatorship of the proletariat.* In one case as in the other, the claim is nothing but a myth. No one has even tried to adduce any evidence that Blanqui or his followers ever used the phrase before Marx. The myth has fed only on itself, by dint of being endlessly repeated by eminent authorities.

1. THE "BLANQUIST" MYTH

The leading authorities on Blanqui have never found it in his writings or in his movement. Maurice Dommanget is the best case in point: although he habitually seeks reasons to make a proto-Marxist out of Blanqui, he does not endow Blanqui with paternity for permanent revolution.[1] Spitzer makes mention only of "the idea of the 'permanent revolution' which is sometimes attributed to Blanqui."[2] This means that neither turned up any Blanquist source for the term. Spitzer's reference for the "sometimes attributed" is to Andler, who makes the standard claim with the standard lack of evidence, in a context which shows he does not know how Marx used the term and the concept.[3] Spitzer also thinks he sees the idea—not the term—in Proudhon, but the passage to which he refers explicitly advocates the idea of gradualism in social change *without* revolution, that is, uninterrupted change by reform.[4]

We have also shown in Chapter 8 that the idea of permanent revolution itself is alien to and incompatible with Blanqui's views on revolution.[5]

The irrelevance of Blanqui in this connection is further borne out by an ironical fact: the only contemporary passage that used the term *permanent revolution* in proximity to the name of Blanqui was by Marx himself. This is the passage in Marx's *Class Struggles in France,* quoted in Chapter 10 above,[6] which refers to "revolutionary socialism . . . *Communism,* for which the bourgeoisie has itself invented the name of *Blanqui,"* and which then associates this socialism or communism with "the declaration of the permanence of the revolution." Marx is here saying that it is the bourgeoisie that has invented the system of calling revolutionary socialism by Blanqui's name—which was true. (The system was reinvented a half century later by Eduard Bernstein.) As a matter of fact, at the time Marx was writing about, Blanqui was in jail and there was virtually no movement led by him. What follows after Marx's mention of Blanqui is *Marx's* own formulation of the content of this revolutionary socialism or communism, which has thus been sufficiently distinguished from the bogeyman invented by the bourgeoisie.[7]

As a supplement to the modern marxological effort to fob *permanent revolution* off on Blanqui, there is also a sporadic effort to blur the fact that Marx made it his own. Perhaps the most influential source of this kind of scholarship was Boris Nicolaievsky. In a much-quoted article on another subject, Nicolaievsky was carried away by his enthusiasm for claiming that Marx must be divorced from the authorship of the "Address to the Communist League" of March 1850 (discussed in Special Note E). He incautiously asserts that this Address included "the slogan of 'permanent revolution' which he [Marx] never mentions anywhere else in his writings." He then adds a footnote to inform the reader that what he has just asserted is untrue:

> If we leave out his early *Judenfrage* ["On the Jewish Question"] , Marx speaks of "permanent revolution" only in *The Class Struggles in France,* using the term to describe Blanqui's position. We know that this work was written at the same time as the "Appeal" [the March address] . On the other hand "permanent revolution" kept popping up again and again in the publications of the leftist opposition to Marx in Cologne in 1848-1849 [meaning Gottschalk] .[8]

The last sentence was discussed in Chapter 8.[9] So to footnote the assertion that Marx *never* mentions permanent revolution *anywhere* other than the Address, Nicolaievsky adds in small type the queasy admission that he knows of Marx's use of the term in *three* places. Of course, we have discussed several other passages, which Nicolaievsky ignores.

2. THE FRENCH
REVOLUTIONARY CONNECTION

If not Blanqui, who did originate the term? As far as I know, no pre-Marx use of the term has ever been documented—although Marx's first uses of it do not sound as if he is coining a new expression, as we shall see. But there is widespread confidence that it must have originated in the writings of the French Revolution (perhaps newspapers or pamphlets). Thus a dissertation by F. W. Seidler on the history of the word *revolution* states that the idea of permanent revolution stems from the French Revolution, but it mentions no actual use of the term.[10] Guérin's well-researched work on the left wing of the Revolution pays much attention to permanent revolution as a pattern, but likewise mentions no actual use of the term; one assumes his research found none.[11] But the belief cannot be dismissed, since the problem of permanent revolution—the perspective of continuing on to a vaguely adumbrated social phase of the revolutionary process—was so important at the time. We must leave open the possibility that the term did appear, though no one has pointed to it.

That the revolutionaries of the 1840s would have looked back to the French Revolution for such terms was characteristic of the period. Engels later wrote:

> When the February Revolution broke out, all of us, as far as our conceptions of the conditions and the course of revolutionary movements were concerned, were under the spell of previous historical experience, particularly that of France. . . . It was, therefore, natural and unavoidable that our conceptions of the nature and the course of the "social" revolution proclaimed in Paris in February 1848, of the revolution of the proletariat, should be strongly colored by memories of the prototypes of 1789 and 1830.[12]

Also Marx: "the Revolution of 1848 knew nothing better to do than to parody, now 1789, now the revolutionary traditions of 1793 to 1795."[13]

In Chapter 8 we quoted Engels' 1884 reference to the French revolutionary period, Marat, and permanent revolution.[14] His context referred directly to Alfred Bougeart's biography *Marat,* but in that book one finds no mention of permanent revolution, term or concept. The connection was made in Engels' mind, not by Bougeart; for Marat's politics certainly evoked the pattern of permanent revolution.

3. FIRST USES

Marx's first uses of the term are typical in that they make clear that the context is the French Revolution. The first known use by Marx—or anyone else—occurs in his 1843 essay "On the Jewish Question," written after heavy reading on the French Revolution.*

At times of heightened self-confidence, political life seeks to suppress its own presumption, [namely] the civil society and its elements, and to set itself up as the real species-life of man without any contradictions. But it can do this only in *violent* contradiction with its own conditions of existence, only by declaring the revolution to be *permanent* and hence the political drama ends with the restoration of religion, private property and all the elements of the civil society just as inevitably as war ends with peace.[16]

De-Hegelianized and stripped down, this passage might read: "Sometimes a political movement gets too cocky and tries to abolish the social order on which its political institutions are based, in order to achieve a human and harmonious existence. Hence it must get into violent conflict with its own social foundations; it must try to drive the revolution forward without a letup," and so on.

This, of course, has in mind a particular case, the left Jacobin attempt to drive the revolution beyond its bourgeois boundaries at a time when social conditions were not yet developed enough to make this possible; hence the inevitable failure.

The following year, in *The Holy Family*, Marx comes back to this experience:

. . . the French Revolution gave rise to ideas which led beyond the *ideas* of the entire old world order [that is, of both the Old Regime and the new bourgeois order]. The revolutionary movement which began in 1789 in the *Cercle Sociale* [of Fauchet], which in its mid-course had *Leclerc* and *Roux* [Enragé leaders] as its main representatives, and which finally with *Babeuf's* conspiracy was defeated for the moment, had given rise to the *communist* idea . . .[17]

Under Robespierre, Marx explains, the political movement "had wanted to *overreach* itself and had been *extravagant,*" but once "the feudal structure had been smashed by the hammer of revolution," the Jacobin

---

* The largest body of extant notes by Marx on his French Revolution studies is on a book by Levasseur, but the notes contain no evocation of permanent revolution.[15]

regime gave way to the Directorate, under which bourgeois society "began to develop *prosaically*" and powerfully. However, with Napoleon's coup d'état the state once again set out to subordinate civil life to autonomous political power (as we have discussed elsewhere [18]), by means of another form of "terror" (that is, force), but for Napoleon the motive was not revolution but war (national aggrandizement). It is in this context that Marx writes: Napoleon *"executed the Terror by substituting permanent war for permanent revolution."* [19]

In this passage *permanent revolution* describes the whole of the French Revolution, not a special theory or pattern. The balancing of the two *permanents* is a grace note. A year later Engels said much the same thing without using the special term: "Napoleon applied the *reign of terror*, which had done its work in France, *to other countries, in the shape of war,*" [20] and so on.

In both of Marx's first uses of the term, there is as yet no necessary implication that any special concept about revolution is involved in the term. The full significance of the French Revolutionary pattern was understood only when it was taught by the events of the revolution in 1848–1849.

HAIR!
OR, MARXISM AND PILOSITY
A note to Chapter 8, page 222

If the radical Hegelian D. F. Strauss preferred the old police state to a proliferation of beards, somé trivialogists may suspect that Engels preserved his beard in order to encourage the overthrow of the state. When his beard had achieved the sage gray color we know from photographs, Engels liked to regale his London friends (so we are told by the English socialist E. B. Bax) with the hairy tale

> of how he, wearing a beard, at that time regarded as a great eccentricity, being worn by few Englishmen, when he went out for a stroll on Sunday morning would meet occasionally a fellow bearded man, who would greet him with something like religious fervour.[1]

On the other hand, in 1852 Marx and Engels had written in their most forgettable joint work that a certain German liberal retired for a while "in order to grow a beard, without which no prophet can succeed."[2] This was a hoary as well as hirsute quip.

The truth is that Engels' pogonophilia had begun well before the revolution, in a year that saw the first stirrings of German bourgeois liberalism, 1840. Not yet twenty years old, working as a commercial apprentice with a Bremen firm, young Friedrich wrote home to his sister about the latest revolt of youth:

> Last Sunday we had a mustache-evening . . . I sent out a circular to all young people able to raise a mustache, saying it was high time to challenge all the philistines and the best way to do it was to wear mustaches. Whoever had courage enough to defy the philistines and wear a mustache was to sign up. Right away I got together a dozen mustaches; and October 25, when our mustaches became a month old, was set for a collective mustache-jubilee.

In the course of this mustache orgy, young Engels stood to propose the following toast:

Mustaches were worn in each age and time
By all brave men in every clime;
Our paladins, whose swords and slashes
Once saved the land, bore dark mustaches.
So, in these warlike times, decide
To sport mustaches, all, with pride.
The philistines may scorn and scoff
And even shave mustaches off,
But we're no philistines, we can stick it,
So let yours grow as thick as a thicket.
Long live good Christians all unbowed
Who with mustaches are endowed
And down with all the philistine hounds
Who rule mustaches out of bounds.

At ten o'clock, some of the insurrectionists had to leave because they did not have a house key and would be locked out; but Engels and others of the hard core stayed at the Rathskeller where the uprising was taking place. Engels defiantly ate eight oysters even though he didn't like them.[3]

How the counterrevolution took place is not known, but three and a half months later Engels eliminated the face-fleece. Then there was a sharp revulsion and the pendulum swung back to rebellion. He wrote his sister:

> Today I shaved off my mustache and buried its youthful corpse amidst grievous lamentations. . . . Now I'm going to let it grow back again, for I certainly can't let myself be seen anywhere. At the singing-school I was the only one with a mustache and I always made fun of the philistines who never got over their astonishment that I could have the effrontery to go into respectable society so unshaven. However, the ladies found it very pleasing, and my old man too.[4]

Two and a half weeks later he reported that the mustache "is now once again in full bloom, flourishing," and that he would not shave it off "even to please a king."[5] Alas, even by May it had not regained its pristine splendor; and we also learn of a factor he had not previously mentioned: "I would look interesting perhaps," he wrote his sister, "if, instead of my presently young mustache, I still had my old Bremen mustache and my growth of long hair."[6]

So ends the shaggy story of Engels' first rebellion.

The following year, young Marx, writing his first article for the *Rheinische Zeitung* against the censorship of the press, let his hair down in an attempt to touch the hearts of his readers. "You consider it despotic to cut a free man's hair against his will," he wrote, "but the censorship daily carves the flesh of thinking people . . ." [7] We do not know why this anguished comparison was on his mind, or how much hair was on his head, at this time. About six years before, while he was a student at Bonn, a group portrait of the Trier Students Association on the campus had shown that he was probably the hairiest of the lot.[8] We may never know whether any despot wanted to cut his hair against his will. But then, nobody even knows whether Adam was created with a full-grown beard.

THE ADDRESS
TO THE COMMUNIST LEAGUE
OF MARCH 1850
A note to Chapter 10, page 259

More than any other writing by Marx and Engels, this circular letter sent to the membership of the Communist League in the spring of 1850 has been the target of remarkable exercises in exegesis by ingenious marxologists. These efforts roughly divide into two types. Many—for example, George Lichtheim—assert that the Address represented a temporary "Blanquist aberration" for Marx, from which he recovered at some later date.[1] This serves to declare it null and void as an expression of Marx's Marxism. A smaller contingent presses beyond this myth and into fantasyland with the assertion that Marx never really held with the infamous document even when it was written.

The general reason for these special operations on the Address is the uncompromising revolutionary spirit of the document. It breathes this spirit from every paragraph, and therefore offends people who can think kindly of Marx only as a bearded gentleman browsing through statistical abstracts in the British Museum.

In this volume the March Address is considered in connection with the permanent revolution problem, the relation between bourgeois revolution and proletarian revolution. In Volume 3 it will play an important role with respect to Marx's views on the road to power, and in this connection Marx's relationship to Blanqui and Blanquism will be considered at large; it will be important also for yet another question, that of party organization. In this note we are interested only in establishing Marx's continuing responsibility for the contents and ideas of the March Address.

Insofar as it is merely claimed that Marx later silently abandoned the ideas of the March Address, refutation must come from the main body of this work. This note, however, indicates at least that neither Marx nor Engels was aware of his alleged transmogrification. It is mainly in transports of enthusiasm that marxologists claim otherwise. Thus, an eminent authority wrote in passing of the March Address that it was "recalled and condemned by its author [meaning Marx] that same summer," but it should not be supposed that this marxologist meant what he wrote. It was only a Pickwickian way of expressing the mistaken opinion that Marx implicitly contradicted the content of the Address by his speech at the split meeting of the Communist League executive on September 15, 1850, which we have set forth in Chapter 3.[2]

1. MARX'S OFFICIAL DOCUMENTS

One of the handles found by some enterprising marxologists is the fact that the March Address was issued in the name of the Central Committee of the League, and therefore not actually signed by Marx and Engels. This is as good a place as any to take up Marx's attitude toward such documents of his. There are four such documents of great importance; indeed, these four have a claim to be considered the four most important pieces Marx ever wrote as specific presentations of political policy. (They are rivaled only by the circular letter to the German party leadership written by Marx and Engels in September 1879, including "The Manifesto of the Three Zurichers.")[3]

In chronological order these four were: the *Communist Manifesto,* the March Address, the Inaugural Address of the International, and *The Civil War in France.* Although all of these were issued as organization statements without a personal signature, it is only the March Address that has ever been impugned for this reason.

There was a reason why so many basic documents were written as movement statements rather than personal remarks: it usually required some such need before Marx undertook the chore of marshaling his political views into a formal presentation. But there were disadvantages —and not only because some future marxologist would seize on the organizational sponsorship to claim that Marx somehow didn't really mean what he wrote. The disadvantage that Marx was painfully aware of has already been brought out in connection with the Manifesto. As Engels told Marx about his own draft: ". . . I mean to get it through [the League] in a form in which there will at least be nothing contrary to our views."[4]

The last two of the four documents were written for the General Council of the International, to be signed by all Council members; and we know a good deal more about the conditions under which they were drafted. The one that was written under the greatest political constraint was the Inaugural Address; it was a very ticklish business to find formulations that would not bring objections from the very disparate elements brought together at the inception of the International, and yet would also express the basic principles that Marx felt were rock-bottom conditions for the political program of the movement.* It is a supreme understatement to say that Marx did not pour all his views into the Inaugural Address!—and yet not even marxologists have claimed he wrote anything in that brilliant essay with which he disagreed. Marx explained to Engels privately:

> It was very difficult to frame the thing so that our view should appear in a form acceptable from the present standpoint of the workers' movement. . . . It will take time before the reawakened movement allows the old boldness of speech. It will be necessary to be *fortiter in re, suaviter in modo* [strong in content, gentle in manner].[6]

The Civil War in France had been preceded by two Addresses on the War, likewise written by Marx. When he sent copies of the Second Address on the War to Engels, he reminded his friend: "You must not forget that the General Council °has to deal with susceptibilities° from all sides and hence cannot write the same way we two can in our own name."[7] This caution applies to *The Civil War in France* as well. Although this work is sometimes discussed as if Marx had set it down as a definitive thesis on various problems of revolution, the fact is that it was primarily an educational-propagandist undertaking of the hour. Marx had to consider what fit into this aim, as well as what might make it difficult to get a quick, unanimous approval by the General Council under pressure.[8] When Marx's daughter Jenny wrote to friends that "The French translation of the *Civil War* has made a very good impression on the [Communard] refugees, for it has equally satisfied all parties—Blanquists, Proudhonists, and Communists,"[9] the remarkable difficulty of this accomplishment must be appreciated.

In short, these group-sponsored documents, written but not signed by Marx or by Marx and Engels, expressed the authors' views but did not necessarily include everything they might have written on the subject under other circumstances. Which is exactly what we should have known in advance.

It is worth noting another aspect of these documents. Since they were written to be signed by a group or its executive, they were

* A good overview of Marx's problem is given by Collins and Abramsky, in a chapter beginning: "Marx's task was to reconcile the irreconcilable." Yet even these excellent writers unaccountably complain that Marx left out trade-unionism—"a strange omission"—despite the well-known hostility of the French Proudhonist founders of the International to trade unions and strikes.[5]

presumably drafted more or less on the basis of previous discussions or exchanges of opinion. This has to be qualified where we know the facts. We saw that the writing of the Manifesto was preceded by lively discussion and controversy in the group; but it was apparently agreed that Marx's final draft—the one that went to the printer—need not be reviewed by the League executive, let alone subjected to amendment. Thus, Marx's final formulations were no doubt conditioned by the previous discussions, but were not dependent on formal approval in the last stage. In the case of the Inaugural Address, there was indeed a meeting of the General Council at which a couple of inconsequential amendments were made before the document was approved.[10] In the case of *The Civil War in France,* the address was "carried unanimously without discussion" upon being read to the Council, but of course the members had been discussing the Commune revolution from the start.[11] In all three of these cases, where we know something of the background, it is clear that Marx drafted the document with the signing group in mind but that in fact the signing group itself made no changes, or no significant changes, in the draft.

In the case of the March Address, we know least of all about the organizational circumstances of its adoption, because of the paucity of extant documents on this period of the Communist League.[12] Just as gods always live in the darkness just beyond the circle of light thrown by our knowledge, so also marxological myths. In this sense, Nicolaievsky's treatment of the March Address is divine. In the same note in which, as we saw,[13] he informed us that Marx mentioned permanent revolution *only* in the March Address, he also asserted that

> we have at our disposal the final text of the document as it was approved by the London Central Committee of the re-established League—of course, after Willich and the followers of Schapper had made their corrections.[14]

"Of course," Nicolaievsky knows nothing whatever about how the "final text" (which implies a preliminary text) was approved, and still less about "corrections" made by anyone. In fact, not to put a fine point on it, his statement about these unknown corrections and approvals is pure fiction. To this fiction he adds the footnoted statement that

> there is no doubt that this document did not express the private opinion of Marx and Engels but rather the compromise accepted by the various factions of the League.

This utter absence of doubt about this fantasy is based on a single remarkable argument which we will see. But we now discern the claim:

the March Address "did not express the private opinion of Marx and Engels" but rather an opinion which they simply wrote down as amanuenses for "various factions," with which they presumably disagreed. Nicolaievsky is trying to say that the views of the March Address are to be assigned to Willich and Schapper, and were not held by Marx and Engels even when the document was sent out.

This would be a breathtaking scenario to support even if there were a bit of evidence. It will be seen as impressively divine when we find out that there is no evidence at all. To be sure, Nicolaievsky's fantasy is the *ne plus ultra* of marxology on this problem; but the facts also expose the milder myth that Marx and Engels subsequently repudiated the views they held in 1850.

2. THE LINEUP IN
THE SEPTEMBER 1850 SPLIT

Since the myth about the "Blanquist aberration" in the March Address was not invented until after the authors' death,* they had no occasion to confront it directly. But their several back-references to the 1850 document are sufficient to demolish the myth.

We can begin with the same Communist League split discussion of September 15, 1850, which is supposed to show Marx repudiating the March Address. If this were so (leaving aside a content analysis of the claim) we should hardly expect to find Marx explicitly flaunting the Address, along with the Manifesto, as his programmatic banner. Furthermore, the myth has it, and must have it, that the Address really represented the program of the Willich-Schapper faction against Marx. We should then hardly expect that, at this meeting, it is Marx who is

---

* The inventor was Eduard Bernstein, of course; it was set forth in a chapter of Bernstein's first "Revisionist" book, which was published in English as *Evolutionary Socialism;* but this English version omitted the entire section of the book in which this was done. However, Bernstein did not limit the myth to the March Address. His thesis was that *all* of Marx's writings of the period around the 1848 revolution were permeated with "Blanquism," and that the March Address merely expressed this Blanquism to the greatest degree. For him, the *Communist Manifesto* was full of "Blanquism" also.[15] With Bernstein, therefore, the issue is plain: anything whatsoever smacking of revolution is "Blanquist" to him. He raises no doubt about the authorship of the March Address by Marx and Engels; and for him their "Blanquist aberration" lasted long beyond 1850. He is not responsible, therefore, for the advanced form that this Blanquist myth has taken with Nicolaievsky, Lichtheim, Wolfe and others.

defending the Address *against Willich-Schapper*. But even the sketchy extant minutes show this very clearly.

The very passage from Marx's speech which is supposed to contradict the Address is introduced by Marx with these words:

> In just the last debate over the question of "the position of the German proletariat in the next revolution," views were expressed by members of the [Willich-Schapper] Minority of the C.C. that directly contradict the next-to-the-last circular [the March Address], and even the Manifesto.[16]

It is the Willich-Schapper faction, Marx argues, that is repudiating the March Address. It is this that leads him to explain that "Instead of the actual conditions, *pure will* becomes the drive-wheel of the revolution for them," and so on.[17] This speech is the opposite of a repudiation: it is explicitly presented by Marx as a defense of the Address as well as of the Manifesto.

The debate, Marx went on to say, shows what "principled differences" are at stake, for although the Willich-Schapper people still consider themselves communists, "the views they are now expressing are anti-communist and could at most be called social-democratic."[18] Schapper then took the floor, and showed that he repudiated the concept of permanent revolution in favor of the Blanquist type of direct seizure of power by the "proletariat" (alias the Communist League) without any intervening phase of any kind.[19]

> The question at issue [said Schapper] is whether at the outset we chop off heads or get our own heads chopped off. In France the workers will have their turn and thereupon so will *we* in Germany. If this were not the case, then it is true I would lay me down to sleep ... Comes our turn, then we can take such measures as to ensure power for the proletariat. I am fanatical about this view. The Central Committee, however, has resolved on the opposite. ... I do not hold the opinion that the bourgeois will come to power in Germany, and I am a fanatical enthusiast in this respect; were I not, I wouldn't give a farthing for the whole business.[20]

This is the viewpoint that demands an immediate proletarian revolution with no first stage.

To this, Marx, in rebuttal, counterposed his view of the permanent revolution in its last version as embodied in the March Address. The petty-bourgeois Democracy will take power next time, and the Communists will go into opposition to the new regime, in order to press the revolution on to proletarian power. Schapper is looking forward to

being the government, Marx is aiming to *oppose* the government.*
Schapper's perspective of forming a "proletarian" government at the
outset will be self-defeating, argued Marx:

> If the proletariat came to power, it would not take directly
> proletarian measures but petty-bourgeois ones. Our party can
> become the government only when conditions allow it to put *its
> own* outlook into effect. Louis Blanc offers the best example of
> how you fare when you come to power too early. Anyway, in
> France it is not the proletarians alone that will come to power
> but along with them the peasants and petty-bourgeois, and it is
> not their own measures but the *latter's* that they will have to put
> into effect. The Commune of Paris [1792-1794] shows that you
> don't need to be in the government in order to put something
> into effect. Anyway, why don't any of the other members of the
> Minority express their views, especially Citizen Willich, since at
> the time they all unanimously approved the [March] circular?[22]

So goes the summary of Marx's argument in the minutes. The last
sentence shows Marx for the second time flaunting the March Address
as his own programmatic position *against* Willich-Schapper. And incidentally the passing reference in this sentence to the unanimous approval of the March Address when it was adopted should be matched
against the Nicolaievskian invention of a fictional controversy in which
Willich-Schapper made "corrections."

3. THE ADDRESS AND
THE COLOGNE TRIAL

Following this split, Marx and his followers transferred the League's
Central Committee out of London to Cologne. In December, the
Cologne committee sent out a circular (an Address) which gives us more
information about the authorship of the March Address and its relation
to the Willich-Schapper group. The Cologne people denounced the
Willich-Schapper position as "based on principles that are diametrically
opposed to the principles of the League" and to the policies followed.[23]

---

* In a letter to a friend a few months later, Engels remarked: "It's incomprehensible how, after the experiences they have gone through, there can still be
asses whose supreme ambition is, the very day after the first victorious insurrection—what they call the revolution—to enter into some government or other, and
in four weeks get crushed, or get discredited and thrown aside, like Blanc and
Flocon in 1848!"[21]

The Willich-Schapper attack, they told the members, was not directed against some kind of "bourgeois socialism"; on the contrary—

> it damned the authors of the party Manifesto of 1848 and of the first "Address of the Central Committee" of this year [the March Address], in which the policies of the party are expounded in detail; indeed, it also condemned the *Manifesto and the policies of the party itself.*[24]

The Cologne leaders assume everyone knows that the "authors" of the March Address as well as of the Manifesto were Marx and Engels, and furthermore that the Willich-Schapper group condemned these political statements as well as their authors.

The Cologne circular then goes on to expound the programmatic difference between the two sides, and it introduces Marx's standpoint with these words: "the Manifesto and the [March] Address set out the course of development of the proletarian movement as follows ..." Once again these two documents are coupled as expressing Marx's position counterposed to Willich-Schapper's. It is true that Marx thought· the Cologne circular, which had been drafted by Heinrich Bürgers, was not a competent political exposition, but there is no question about the clarity with which it reports the relation of the Address to the ongoing fight.

While the factions were arguing, reaction had consolidated itself in Germany and cast about for a "Communist conspiracy" to expose in order to send the German public scurrying to the Crown for protection from the Red Menace. In May 1851 a police raid started preparations for a conspiracy trial; documents were seized; the trial itself was to get under way in October 1852. Thus, for the first time the March Address was published in the German bourgeois press, in June 1851. The immediate problem raised by its publication was the effect it might have on the coming trial of Communist League members, as well as its general political meaning for the public. Marx wrote to Engels to tell him about the publication of the document:

> This was the "Address to the League" written by the two of us*—at bottom nothing but a plan of war against the Democracy. From one standpoint its publication was good, in contrast with Bürgers' document [the Cologne committee's circular] which is more or less absurd in form and not very cheering in content. On the other hand, a few passages will aggravate the situation of the present prisoners.[26]

* There is another passage in this letter in which Marx incidentally makes clear the authorship of the Address: "the silly *Augsburger Allgemeine Zeitung* makes the document that we wrote a child of Messrs. Mazzini and Ruge ..."[25]

The "True Socialist" Karl Grün had utilized the publication of the Address for a roundhouse attack on the Marx group, anticipating marxologists by several decades. In his letter to Engels, Marx ruefully summarized Grün's absurdities:

> There is naturally no lack of Friends of Light phrases and most extremely "anarchistic" phrases.[27] Doing everything from above! Police state! Formally excommunicate and exclude dissenters. *Mon Dieu!* That beats everything.[28]

But while Marx was outraged by the slanderous invention of views that resembled nothing in the Address, his correspondence with Engels shows them both to be unquestioningly in accord with what *is* in the document. Engels' reply referred to "our old document" just as casually as Marx's letter.[29] He too was concerned in the first place with its possible impact on the defendants in Cologne; otherwise he praises the Address as an educational document:

> . . . in every respect it is of enormous advantage that the thing has been made public and has gone about through all the papers. The individual quiet bands of budding Communists, who are not known at all and who must be meeting in all parts of Germany judging by past experience, will get an excellent point of support in it . . .

The *Augsburger Allgemeine Zeitung* (Marx had reported) had editorially denounced the Address as "madness! madness!" but Engels comments wryly that the paper's account of its content "shows it understood this 'madness' only too well—in fact there was no way to misunderstand it."[30]

Johannes Miquel—still presumably a Communist sympathizer and not yet the kaiser's minister—had expressed the fear to Marx that the publication of the Address would have an unfavorable effect on the Democracy. Engels discusses this fear, minimizing the difference between the newly published document and the attacks on the Democracy that they had published in bulk in the *N.R.Z.*

> Miquel should however consider that we continuously and uninterruptedly prosecuted these gentlemen [the Democracy] in writings that were more or less party manifestos after all.

Engels is thus clearly unimpressed by the fact that the Address differs from the *N.R.Z.* articles in being an official document of the League. He continues:

> So now, why the outcry over a program that simply summarizes, in a very calm and especially quite impersonal way, what we

printed long ago? . . . Any halfway intelligent Democrat must have known in advance what he had to expect from our party—the document [March Address] could not have told him much that was new. If they made an alliance pro tempore with the Communists, they were fully informed of the conditions and duration of the alliance, and it could occur to nobody but Hanoverian middle peasants and lawyers to believe that since 1850 the Communists had been converted from the principles and policies of the *Neue Rheinische Zeitung.*[31]

What Engels thought would never occur to a dolt has in fact become a fixture of many marxological productions.*

4. THE ADDRESS FROM 1852 TO 1885

Marx spent the last months of 1852 working on his pamphlet *Revelations on the Communist Trial in Cologne,* which is mainly an exposé of the evidence used by the prosecution against the Communist League defendants. It is a defense pamphlet, not a political manifesto, and treats the documents accordingly. Published in January, the pamphlet has only a passing reference to the "confiscated Addresses of the Central Committee" along a line foreshadowed in the Marx-Engels correspondence: the addresses, it argues, "were concerned exclusively with the relations of the Communists to the future government of the Democracy, hence not to the government of Friedrich Wilhelm IV."[33]

Most significant for our purposes is what is not in the *Revelations.* The government had seized many documents of the Willich-Schapper league, filled with enough inflammatory pseudorevolutionary rhetoric to delight a police prosecutor's heart; and, since none of the defendants belonged to this group, the prosecution systematically sought to argue that Willich-Schapper documents applied just as much to the Marx group, the differences being merely due to a clash of personalities. Naturally, the defendants, as well as Marx in the *Revelations,* repu-

---

* Let us note, for the sake of completeness before leaving 1851, that a month after this correspondence with Engels, Marx included an intentionally vague reference to the authorship of the March Address in a long communication to a journalist named Ebner, whose articles he was trying to influence. This communication gave Marx's views on the activities of the émigré radicals, and mentioned that their hatred of Marx had been increased with the publication of the Address, "since he [Marx] was supposed to be its author." Marx's caution in this formulation turned out to be justified: Ebner was later discovered to be an Austrian government agent.[32]

diated not only the documents of the Willich-Schapper league but also separated themselves vigorously from its conceptions, on a carefully political basis. If there was anything to the marxological myth that the March Address represented the politics of Willich-Schapper and not of Marx, then the *Revelations* was the place to reveal it, as a means of helping to clear the defendants. But of course there was no question of this.

Toward the end of 1853, Marx again had to deal with Willich, who had been publishing slanderous attacks on Marx in his American exile. Marx's polemic against Willich, *The Knight of the Noble Consciousness,* was published at the beginning of 1854, and is now as justly forgotten as the writings of its target. But it has a definitive reference to the authorship of the March Address. More than that, just as he did on September 15, 1850, Marx here presents the Address as his own *as against Willich.*

In the *Revelations* Marx had remarked of the Willich-Schapper group that they "have never laid claim to the honor of possessing their own ideas. What is true of them is their peculiar misunderstanding of other people's ideas . . ."[34]

In the new pamphlet Marx reported that Willich had tried to show the public he did have a stock of his own ideas: he had presented an exposition of the measures that the petty-bourgeois Democracy would undertake in power. This exposition, Marx then explained, though it was an attempt to write something original, was really cribbed—from the March Address by Marx and Engels.

> In a circular written by Engels and myself, which the Saxon police seized at Bürgers' house, which was published in the most widely read German papers and formed the basis for the Cologne bill of indictment, there is a longer exposition on the pious aspirations of the German petty-bourgeoisie. This is the text on which Willich preaches his sermon. Let the reader compare the original and the copy.[35]

If that does not settle it, there is more.

A couple of decades later, the German party republished Marx's *Revelations on the Cologne Communist Trial,* as a note on a historical episode. To this 1875 edition Marx added a Postscript; since he had decided not to omit anything from the text, he pointed to whatever he thought needed special comment in the old pamphlet. Some of the corrections are of minutiae.[36] This was an opportunity also to correct the references to the March Address—if there were anything to correct. There is no correction.

Ten years later a third edition of the *Revelations* was published. Marx dead, Engels wrote a considerable introduction, "On the History of the Communist League," which duly mentions the authorship of the March Address. *And in addition, in the appendix to this 1885 edition, Engels reprinted the whole text of the March Address for the edification of the new generation of socialists.* In fact, it is from this reprint by Engels that the text of the Address is usually republished today.

In the body of the essay Engels introduces the reprint as follows:

> So the League was organized anew, the Address of March 1850—printed in the appendix, IX, no. 1—was issued, and Heinrich Bauer was sent to Germany as emissary. The Address drawn up [*redigierte*] by Marx and myself is still of interest today, because even now the petty-bourgeois Democracy in Germany is still the party that must certainly come to the helm to begin with, as the savior of society from the communist workers on the occasion of the next European upheaval, which is now due soon . . . Much of what is said in it therefore holds good today.[37]

It would appear that this settles the question for good and all, or rather adds the final capstone to the peculiar controversy—not only as to the authorship of the Address but also as to the continuing regard in which Marx and Engels held it, with due qualification for the fact that it was written for a specific historical conjuncture. For a third of a century, in *every* reference to the Address, public or private, Marx and Engels had claimed authorship and continuing responsibility. Nowhere and by no one had this even been called into question.

5. ADVENTURE IN LEXICOGRAPHY

But what is plain to ordinary minds is only a challenge to the ingenious. So what if Marx and Engels had set down more than a half dozen times that they had *written* the March Address? Now, forty-five years afterward, in the very act of reprinting the document, Engels says that the Address was *redigierte* by Marx and himself. If you look up *redigieren* in a German, or German-English, dictionary, you will find that it means *edit, revise*. The truth is finally out: Marx and Engels only *edited* the address, but were not its authors! Armed with what they think is the dictionary meaning of *redigieren*, valiant writers have found it possible to ignore all other evidence.

We can now present the whole of Nicolaievsky's statement on the issue, of which we previously quoted a sentence:

> I am not raising here the question of the authorship of this "Appeal" [the March Address] but I must point out that it can

be attributed to Marx and Engels only with important reservations. True, in his letter to Engels of July 13, 1851, Marx refers to it as "drafted by both of us."* However, in his article, *A contribution to the history of the Communist League,* Engels is much more circumspect, speaking only of the *editing* of this document by himself and Marx. However this may be, there is no doubt that this document did not express the private opinion of Marx and Engels but rather the compromise accepted by the various factions of the League.[38]

Thus, after explaining that he is "not raising" the question of authorship, he marshals the evidence for his doubt-free conclusion that the document written down by Marx and Engels did not express their "private opinion." This evidence can be found in any desk dictionary: the dictionary meaning of *redigieren,* which Nicolaievsky thinks means only *edit.*

Before we dispose of this evidence, we may mention two reasons why a doubt should have crept in anyway, even aside from all the preceding statements by Marx and Engels. In the first place, he might have wondered why Engels in 1885 reprinted a document which he and Marx had merely edited, without agreeing with it. In the second place, he might have wondered whether Engels was using *redigieren* according to his desk dictionary.

The German *redigieren* is a foreign loan-word related to the French *rédiger.* (As a matter of fact, it probably entered the language in the sixteenth century from the Italian *redigere,* but by the nineteenth its French cognate would have more force for a writer.) In French, *rédiger* had—and still has—a range of meaning extending from *edit* (a paper), *draw up* (a document), *draft* (an article), to *write, write out.* True, our doubts would remind us that Engels was not writing French, but the objection is not as relevant as it may seem. Especially in the nineteenth century, much writing by literary Germans was peppered with Gallicisms which did not necessarily show up in the dictionary. Marx's predilection for foreignisms in German was notoriously even greater than Engels' and much deplored by his German editors. Heinrich Heine was an even more prominent case, having spent the last quarter century of his life in French exile; but then, Engels had lived abroad much longer than that. In any case, at the time there would have been nothing unusual about Engels' use of *redigieren* in the sense of the French *rédiger* even if the Gallicized usage were not sanctioned by a

---

* The word that Nicolaievsky translates as *drafted* is *verfasst,* which unequivocally means *written, composed, authored (by someone).* The passage in question is given above on page 606, ref. note 26.

dictionary. All this should raise doubts even without further research. But as a matter of fact *redigieren* is not one of the unsanctioned cases. To extend research a little beyond the nearest desk dictionary, Nicolaievsky should have checked at least the nineteenth century *Fremdwörterbücher,* German dictionaries of foreignisms. At the time Engels reprinted the March Address, many such works were authoritatively defining *redigieren* as *draft* and *write* in addition to *edit, revise.* I counted nine such authorities before I quit looking.[39] In point of fact, Engels' statement that the Address was *redigierte* by Marx and himself does not even offer lexicographical difficulties.

So there is no doubt (as Nicolaievsky would say) that the Address is just what it purports to be and what Marx and Engels always said it was—an expression of the views of Marx and Engels, which *mutatis mutandum* continued to reflect their political thought right up to the end: no probable, possible shadow of doubt, no possible doubt whatever.

THE ALLEGED THEORY
OF THE DISAPPEARANCE
OF THE MIDDLE CLASSES
A note to Chapter 11, page 291

Among the theories invented in Marx's name—by obliging critics who then handily refute their own creations—few are hardier than the myth that Marx had a theory according to which the "middle classes" were doomed to "disappear." We have given an example elsewhere[1] of the marxological propensity to concoct a "theory" out of passing statements by Marx or Engels; and a similar caution applies here. Diligent exegesis of some remark by Marx about the middle class does not immediately constitute proof that Marx was propounding a scientific theory in making the remark. If this principle of common sense is to be disregarded, I suggest that the next discovery heralded by marxology should be the Theory of Revolution by Stupidity, propounded by Marx in 1863.*

1. WHAT MIDDLE CLASS?

Marx presented no theory about disappearing middle classes. This was one of the theories conferred on Marx by Eduard Bernstein, seeking to replace Marx's proletarian socialism with a middle-class socialism similar to English Fabianism.[3] For Bernsteinian purposes it was not necessary to be clear about the amorphous term *middle class* or its fuzzier plural form, since the positive aim was to dislodge socialism from its proletarian base. In fact, the protean meaning of *middle class*, which we have discussed,[4] was a distinct advantage, since, being a blur already, it could be hocused out of or into existence with a minimum of effort. This is not to object in general to any use of class terms with ill-defined boundaries; such terms may be as useful as a sweep of the

---

* The total evidence for this proposed theory is Marx's remark in a letter to Engels, reminiscing about changes since 1848: "Besides, we now know what a role is played in revolutions by stupidity, and how it is exploited by scoundrels."[2]

arm to a speaker; but a sweep of the arm does not help much with the statement of a scientific theory.

Stricter definition is called for when it is alleged that Marx had a theory about the disappearance of a blur. What middle class or classes was Marx supposed to have predicted the disappearance of? We have explained that in English Marx usually used *middle class* to denote the bourgeoisie proper; but obviously the bourgeoisie is not the victim of the alleged theory. There are two other possibilities.

One is the petty-bourgeoisie proper, as defined in Chapter 11. Without question, Marx was confident it was declining, and without question this has come to pass, but we shall see he did not predict it would "disappear." In any case, what he stated was a *tendency*. Scientifically speaking, all statements about social "laws" deal with tendencies, implicitly or explicitly, and a great deal of nonsense about Marx's alleged predictions would be avoided if this were kept in mind. The following passage from Marx's *Theories of Surplus Value* is pitched in terms of two prominent petty-bourgeois elements:

> ... the handicraftsman or peasant who produces with his own means of production will either gradually be transformed into a small capitalist who also exploits the labor of others, or he will suffer the loss of his means of production (in the first instance the latter may happen although he remains their *nominal* owner, as in the case of mortgages)* and be transformed into a wage-laborer. This is the tendency in the form of society in which the capitalist mode of production predominates.[5]

The foregoing statement by Marx was an evaluation in the course of a scientific analysis. It may be compared with one of Marx's journalistic surveys of the contemporary scene, written in 1859:

> °°The ruin of the small middle class during the last eight years is a general fact to be observed all over Europe, but nowhere so strikingly as in Germany. Does this phenomenon need any explanation? I answer in one word: Look at the millionaires of to-day who were the poor devils of yesterday. For one man of nothing to become a millionaire over-night, a thousand $1,000-men must have been turned into beggars during the day. The magic of the Stock Exchange will do this sort of thing in the twinkling of an eye, quite apart from the slower methods by which modern industry centralizes fortunes.[6]

Here the "small middle class" in ruin is clearly the petty-bourgeoisie, shading into the small bourgeoisie.

---

* For the significance of nominal ownership, see above, Chapter 12, section 3.

However, the decline of the petty-bourgeoisie is generally conceded nowadays. The concocted theory of the "disappearance of the middle classes" usually depends on using *middle classes* to refer holus-bolus to all intermediate class elements in society without other distinction. Marx is then reproached with failing to allow for the *replacement* of the old and declining intermediate class, the petty-bourgeoisie, with newer intermediate elements, which are labeled the "new middle class(es)." While there is no question that the old petty-bourgeoisie functioned as a distinct social class, the assumption is made that the aggregation of etceteras called the "new middle class" also constitutes such an integral class. Still another assumption to be kept in view is the identification of *disappearing* with *declining*.

2. HOW TO READ
THE *COMMUNIST MANIFESTO*

The myth about the "disappearance of the middle classes" is usually based on selected phrases from the *Communist Manifesto*. This is enough to give pause, since it is precisely in matters of basic economic theory that the Manifesto is most obviously an immature work of Marx's. However brilliantly the Manifesto fulfilled its task of simplifying many complex ideas and telescoping history into a compendium of lapidary formulations, for the sake of a sweeping view of social evolution and political perspectives and a maximum impact as a party programmatic statement—all in a few pages—it is not fair to expect it also to take the place of *Capital*.

Still, let us see what is, and what is not, in the Manifesto on this question.

It is well known that the Manifesto, striving to spotlight the struggle of the polar classes, enthusiastically depicted something like a duel situation: "Society as a whole is more and more splitting up into two great hostile camps, into two great classes directly facing each other: bourgeoisie and proletariat."[7] This clearly puts it as a tendency, a direction of development. So also the glowing description of the triumph of the bourgeoisie as it "pushed into the background every class handed down from the Middle Ages."[8] When a class is pushed into the background, it does not disappear.

The Manifesto's glorification of bourgeois achievement becomes a little stickier when it proclaims that the bourgeoisie "has converted the physician, the lawyer, the priest, the poet, the man of science, into its paid wage-laborers."[9] *Has* converted, mind you!—this is not a prediction. This either proves that Marx thought his father (a lawyer), his poet friend Heine, Alexander Humboldt, Adam Smith, et al., were all working for proletarian wages—or else it proves we have to read the language of the Manifesto with some common sense. This swingeing statement has a point to make, but it hardly intends to proclaim a grandiose theory about the Disappearance of the Professional Classes. In fact, the Manifesto is crammed with global statements, beginning with "all . . . ," which no one would support under oath—like the good news for obese burghers that "All that is solid melts into air . . ."

But the passage that refers specifically to the petty-bourgeoisie is not as far-reaching as the announcement about the converted lawyers, priests, poets, et al. Nor is it as expansive as it is sometimes made out to be, *if the original text is read, as published in 1848:*

> The previously existing small intermediate strata [*Mittel-stände*] —the small industrials, merchants and rentiers, the artisans and peasants—all these classes sink down into the proletariat, partly because their small capital does not suffice for the carrying on of large-scale industry and succumbs in competition with the larger capitalists, partly because their skill is rendered worthless by new methods of production. Thus the proletariat is recruited from all classes of the population.*

* So goes the original text.[10] Moore's standard translation of 1888, edited by Engels, sought to modernize the language, with the result that it is an uncertain guide to unanticipated controversies. It goes as follows, with some points of difference italicized:

> The *lower strata of the middle class*—the small *tradespeople*, shop-keepers, and *retired tradesmen* generally, the handicraftsmen and peasants —all these sink *gradually* into the proletariat, partly because their diminutive capital does not suffice for the scale on which Modern Industry is carried on, and is swamped in the competition with the *large* capitalists, partly because their *specialized* skill is rendered worthless by new methods of production. Thus the proletariat is recruited from all classes of the population.[11]

The key change is in the first phrase, which states what the passage is about: the small intermediate strata *that have existed up to now*. The italicized qualification is completely omitted, perhaps because the time reference was considered superannuated in 1888. Whatever the reason was in 1888, it is quite clear that the passage was concerned with the old intermediate strata, and was not a statement about middle classes in general or for the future. Moreover, the 1848 text clearly included both the old petty-bourgeoisie and small bourgeois employers and manufacturers; two phrases pointing to the latter were dropped in 1888. Thus, insofar as the subject was broader than the old petty-bourgeoisie, it extended not to other types of intermediate elements but to the lower ranks of the bourgeoisie itself.

Thus, through a qualifier, "previously existing"—*which was omitted from the English version*—this statement makes clear it is referring to the *old* class structure. And this is exactly what one would expect from the context, which has to do with what has been happening up to the present and not with predictions about the future.

But isn't there another passage, a couple of pages later, which explicitly predicts that "other classes" will "finally disappear"? No, there is not—*not in the original text of the Manifesto as published in 1848*. The "disappearance" is again shadowed forth by a translation which was worded in 1888 without clairvoyant anticipation of what clever exegetes can do. This passage uses much the same language as the one just discussed. A translation of the original shows that it too was concerned with tendencies going on in the present, and not with predictions of the class structure of the future:

> Of all the classes that stand face to face with the bourgeoisie nowadays, the proletariat alone is a really revolutionary class. The other classes are decaying and being ruined in the face of large-scale industry; the proletariat is its most characteristic product.
>
> The intermediate strata, the small industrial, the small merchant, the artisan, the peasant, all these fight against the bourgeoisie, to safeguard their existence from ruin as intermediate strata. They are therefore not revolutionary, but conservative.*

---

* The English version goes as follows, with some points of difference italicized:

> Of all the classes that stand face to face with the bourgeoisie today, the proletariat alone is a really revolutionary class. The other classes *decay and finally disappear* in the face of Modern Industry: the proletariat is its special and essential product.
>
> *The lower middle class*, the small manufacturer, the shopkeeper, the artisan, the peasant, all these fight against the bourgeoisie, *to save from extinction their existence as fractions of the middle class.* They are therefore not revolutionary, but conservative.[12]

Alas, Moore used *disappear* for *gehen unter* (go under), which is not what a rabbit does in the hands of a magician. Interpreting the present tense as future, he gratuitously inserted *finally*, even though the passage is tied to the present with the strong word *heutzutage* (nowadays, in the present day). And so the meaning of the English version is distorted by the two words *finally disappear*—and neither of these two words exists in the original! The new language about *fractions of the middle class* is an added flourish, which Moore perhaps thought very contemporary-sounding. The word *extinction* is of a piece with *disappear:* the German is *Untergang*, a going-under (noun equivalent of *gehen unter*). All these little modernizing changes would have seemed harmless in 1888—until the myth of the disappearing middle class was invented.

Once we remove the changes introduced by the 1888 English version, the meaning is perfectly plain: it is a statement about present tendencies. And it is about the same intermediate strata as the previous passage.

But if the intermediate strata are"being ruined," doesn't this mean they will eventually "disappear"? This would require a separate demonstration; but fortunately a passage in the Manifesto finally does get explicit about the coming fate of the petty-bourgeois intermediates and does look into the future. Even the word *disappear* occurs. But the mythical theory does not.

> In the countries where modern civilization developed, a new petty-bourgeoisie was formed, which hovers between the proletariat and the bourgeoisie and continually renews itself as a supplementary part of bourgeois society. The members of this class, however, are being constantly hurled down into the proletariat by the action of competition; indeed, with the development of large-scale industry they even see a time approaching when they will completely disappear as an independent part of modern society and will be replaced, in commerce, manufacturing and agriculture, by labor overseers and stewards [*Domestiken*].*

Here we learn that not even the traditional petty-bourgeoisie is actually disappearing. Just the reverse: it "continually renews itself." True, individual members of this class are "constantly" being proletarianized, but the class limps on, in a more and more ruined state. Furthermore, some day this class will completely disappear *as an independent part of society*—which is not identical with simply disappearing like the rabbit in a magician's hat. But while these petty-bourgeois elements (small-property-holding producers) move into the background of society as more and more dependent hangers-on of the real bourgeois powers, the Manifesto immediately indicates that their places in the foreground are taken by new elements arising out of the needs of the bourgeoisie itself. They tend to be replaced, as capital develops, by another kind of intermediate element, the various employees of capital hired to super-

---

* Again, this is the original text.[13] The important difference from the standard English version comes in the last phrase, where *durch Arbeitsaufseher und Domestiken* is blurred into: "by overlookers, bailiffs and shopmen."[14] The import of *Domestiken* is thus lost. This word cannot here mean domestics in the sense of household servants, since it refers to people "in commerce, manufacturing and agriculture." I translate it *stewards* (as did the first English version of the Manifesto in 1850), instead of *servitors*, since *stewards* has a broader connotation; in fact, many elements of new clerical, white-collar, salaried, managerial or bureaucratic sectors of the so-called "new middle classes" function as stewards of the capitalist controllers on a high or low level.

intend the labor process and to serve the new needs of the owners of commerce, factory and farm—"labor overseers and stewards." These elements are certainly new in the mass, and they are certainly in the middle of something, and so they are "new middle class" elements of a sort.

If, then, one looks for Marx's theory of the disappearing middle classes in the *Communist Manifesto,* which is supposed to be its natural habitat, it hardly meets the eye. But even if it were much clearer in the Manifesto, the conclusion to follow would not be essentially affected.

3. STEWARDS AND SALESPEOPLE IN *CAPITAL*

Does the alleged theory, predicting the disappearance of all social strata except genuine proletarians and vouched-for capitalists, appear in *Capital* or in Marx's unpublished economic studies (*Theories of Surplus Value,* or the *Grundrisse* notebooks, etc.)? This is where it has to be found, if it ever existed. The answer is no. On the contrary, we find *Capital* taking note, where necessary, of the new elements whom the Manifesto had called overseers of labor and stewards of capital.

Whereas some latter-day analysts think such components of the productive force are ticketed *middle-class* as soon as they are called "salaried employees," Marx sees them usually as "a special kind of wage-laborer." The capitalist, relieved of actual labor,

hands over the work of direct and constant supervision of the individual workmen, and groups of workmen, to a special kind of wage-laborer. An industrial army of workmen, under the command of a capitalist, requires, like a real army, officers (managers), and sergeants (foremen, overlookers), who, while the work is being done, command in the name of the capitalist. The work of supervision becomes their established and exclusive function.[15]

Marx points out that even industrial capitalists get a wage for their labor of superintendence insofar as they perform this function. This fact ceases to be a bit of curiosa when this function is separated from the person of the capitalist and embodied in hired managers and other stewards of capital. Their wages "assume the form of wages for skilled labor" in sufficiently large-scale enterprises. "The capitalist mode of production has brought matters to a point where the work of supervision, entirely divorced from the ownership of capital, is always readily obtainable. It has, therefore, come to be useless for the capitalist to perform it himself." Cooperative factories prove that the capitalist is redundant, insofar as his function has to do only with the social necessities of production. It is the capitalist corporation, the joint-stock company form developed out of the credit system, that has "an increasing tendency to separate this work of management as a function from the ownership of capital." Since the stewards perform the real functions, "the capitalist disappears as superfluous from the production process."[16]

The capitalist disappears! But this disappearance is like the other one we encountered, when the petty-bourgeoisie disappeared "as an independent part of modern society." Marx has not magicked the capitalist class out of existence; it is advisable to keep an eye on the whole statement.

For those who see the "new middle class" as especially prominent in commerce and selling, Marx has a few explanations about the role of employees of merchant capital. In general, the salesclerk is "the industrial capitalist's wage-laborer,"[17] but if the whole commercial operation is removed from the industrial capitalist's sphere and turned over to a commercial capitalist, the salesclerk's position in the economy is not basically changed. The changes, which Marx sets forth in their complexity, do not concern us here. Suffice to say that in many respects "a commercial employee is a wage-worker like any other" even though not directly creating surplus-value for the employer. "The unpaid labor of these clerks, while it does not create surplus-value, enables him [the employer] to appropriate surplus-value, which, in effect, amounts to the same thing with respect to his capital."[18]

Since commercial capital is simply a part of industrial capital that has been separated out in order to engage autonomously in the process of circulation (rather than production), Marx advises us to eliminate this complication-- for the purpose of seeing the basic relationships—by looking at the office of an industrial capitalist who still operates his own circulation process (markets his own goods, etc.). As the scale of production increases, commercial operations multiply ("calculation of prices, bookkeeping, managing funds, correspondence," and so on).

> The more developed the scale of production, the greater, if not proportionately greater, the commercial operations of the industrial capital, and consequently the labor and other costs of circulation involved in realizing value and surplus-value. This necessitates the employment of commercial wage-workers who make up the actual office staff.[19]

Thus, along with the large scale of production and the expansion of the credit system, the ranks of commercial wage-workers tend to increase.

Marx repeatedly makes clear that they produce no surplus-value directly, that is, they are not directly employed as proletarians (as we have explained elsewhere[20]), but this is precisely one of the cases where the technical line between proletarians and other wage-workers becomes minor. Marx emphasizes what unites these two sectors of wageworkers even in economic theory:

> The commercial worker produces no surplus-value directly. But the price of his labor is determined by the value of his labor-power . . . The commercial worker, in the strict sense of the term, belongs to the better-paid class of wage-workers—to those whose labor is classed as skilled and stands above average labor. Yet the wage tends to fall [like that of the others] . . .[21]

Today, when clerical workers and commercial employees are often miserably underpaid as compared with industrial labor, the similarities take over even more decisively. Incidentally, Marx's manuscript at this point left an extra two pages for further elaboration on the subject, which he never got back to.[22]

In the second volume of *Capital* there is some additional discussion, along the same lines, of the "buying and selling agent" of capital: "We shall assume that he is a mere wage-laborer, even one of the better-paid, for all the difference it makes." Functions like bookkeeping also form a necessary "appendage" to production, converted "into an independent function of special agents exclusively entrusted with it."[23]

4. ON "THE COURSE OF BOURGEOIS SOCIETY"

So it is clear that Marx had no problem in seeing the expansion of the new working force required by the development of large-scale production, the credit system, and the joint-stock company. Most of this new force consisted of new wage-workers, when viewed from the standpoint of basic relations, workers who were moreover necessary to the productive process in one way or another. But Marx also had occasion to refer to the growth of other intermediate elements. And in the fourth volume of *Capital* he even referred to these as the "middle classes."

Ironically, this occurs as he reproaches Ricardo for forgetting about them:

> What he forgets to bring out in relief is the continual growth of the middle classes which stand in the middle between workmen

on one side and the capitalist and landlord on the other and which to an ever-increasing extent are largely °fed° directly out of revenue; which weigh as a burden on the °working° base and increase the social security and power of the °upper ten thousand.°[24]

These middle-class (intermediate) elements are maintained out of the capitalists' revenue, rather than out of their own small production like the old petty-bourgeoisie. It is Marx who insists here on noting their "continual growth," for he is arguing that the development of machinery and labor productivity does not release the working class from "wage-slavery" but reinforces the wage system and the power of the economic rulers. But even so he does not claim that he is discovering this as a novelty, as do the present-day discoverers of the "new middle classes"; he reproaches Ricardo for "forgetting" them, for failing to put this phenomenon in the foreground.

Marx makes a similar point a few pages before this passage, also in connection with the consequences of an increased accumulation of capital:

> The quantity of articles entering into consumption, or—to use Ricardo's expression—the quantity of articles entering into the gross revenue, can be increased without thereby increasing the portion of this quantity which is transformed into variable capital [wages]. It [the latter portion] can even decrease. In this case more is consumed as revenue by the capitalists, landlords, their °retainers,° the unproductive classes, the state, the intermediate classes (people engaged in trade), etc.[25]

These "retainers," "intermediate classes" (*Zwischenklassen*), and so on, are not necessarily the same type of elements discussed before, that is, wage-workers necessary to production. So one must gather from Marx's discussion. He continues: Ricardo had wrongly assumed that every accumulation of capital means a proportional increase in the demand for labor and in the variable capital (wage bill), because he did not understand that "the constant part of the capital grows at a faster rate than the variable."

> However, this does not prevent revenue from continually growing, in value and in quantity. But it is not true that consequently a larger part of the total product is laid out in wages in the same proportion. The classes and subclasses that do not live directly from labor increase and live better than before, and the number of unproductive workers increases as well.[26]

Perhaps the most direct contradiction of the myth that Marx predicted the endless increase of the proletariat and the disappearance of middle classes is a passage directed against Malthus, in which Marx flatly states that what takes place under capitalism is the very opposite of the mythical theory:

> His highest hope—which he himself calls more or less utopian—is that the mass of the middle class may grow and that the proletariat (the working proletariat) may form a relatively smaller and smaller part of the total population (even though it grows absolutely). This is in fact the *course* of bourgeois society.[27]

The actual course of capitalism, says Marx, is that the "mass of the middle class" grows and the *relative* proportion of the proletariat to the total population decreases. Note that here, as elsewhere, Marx's preference is not for statements predicting the future but for statements about the *tendency* of the present. The two are not the same thing, of course. Thus, there is not a single future tense in the following statement from Marx's letter to the Labor Parliament that met in Manchester in 1854:

> °°Of all countries Great Britain has seen developed on the grandest scale the despotism of capital and the slavery of labor. In no other country have the intermediate degrees between the millionaire, commanding whole industrial armies, and the wage-slave living only from hand to mouth, so radically been swept away from the soil. There exist no longer, as in continental countries, large classes of peasants and artizans almost equally dependent on their own property and their own labor. A complete divorce of property from labor has been effected in Great Britain. In no other country, therefore, has the war between the two classes that constitute modern society, assumed so colossal dimensions and features so distinct and palpable.*

One should not conclude from the sweeping language—*"complete divorce of property from labor"*—that Marx thought there were no more shopkeepers in England than snakes in Ireland; he knew the statistics in detail. The preceding sentence had stressed that there no longer existed *large* classes of rural and urban petty-bourgeois elements of the old small-property-holding type ("almost equally dependent on their own property and their own labor"). The most important point to be grasped is this: for Marx, the basic characteristic of English bour-

---

* This passage is actually quoted from the *New York Tribune* article[28] into which Marx incorporated part of his "Letter to the Labour Parliament." The latter was published as such in *The People's Paper* and may have embodied some minor errors, such as the substitution of *gradually* for *radically* in the second sentence of the above-quoted passage.[29]

geois society that differentiated it from the Continent was that the petty-bourgeoisie had disappeared as a class with social weight. Hence his conclusion—without niggling qualifications of little concern to the Labor Parliament people—about "the war between the two classes that constitute [*in the sense of* create] modern society."

The thought is stated more strictly in a passage, written about a decade later, that went into the third volume of *Capital.* It is in the unfinished chapter on "Classes," which no doubt would have had more to say on the general subject. Even in the few paragraphs extant, there is a reference which could scarcely have been written by one who thought the "middle classes" were disappearing. The class pattern, writes Marx, does not appear in pure form even in England, where the economic structure is most highly developed. "Middle and transitional stages [of classes, *Übergangsstufen*] even here obliterate lines of demarcation everywhere," especially in urban economy.[30]

The propensity to quote out of context is worsened when one "knows" in advance that Marx had a theory (about the disappearing middle class, for example) and thus merely looks for handy illustrations. The eye may fall on a statement like this: "all possessing classes gradually change into capitalists, all oppressed classes into proletarians, and thereby the reactionary party fades away by itself."[31] Behold, a new marxological theory, the Theory of the Disappearance of Reaction. But the context wipes this newborn theory away. It is from Engels' pamphlet *The Prussian Military Question and the German Workers Party,* which was directed against a recrudescence of feudal socialism in its Lassallean form. The preceding paragraph had specified that the Reaction here in question was "the feudal-bureaucratic party," the *pre*bourgeois ruling classes that were indeed fading away; and it was the "possessing classes" of this obsolescent society that were being bourgeoisified. In context, the statement was not a generalization about society but a very limited statement about the processes actually going on at the time in Germany's class structure.

5. PROLETARIANIZATION

In his letter to the Labor Parliament, Marx followed the passage quoted above with a conclusion: "it is precisely from these facts that the working classes of Britain, before all others, are competent and called upon to act as leaders in the great movement that must finally result in the absolute emancipation of labor."[32] If the working classes are leaders, they must be leading *other* social strata.

One reason why the alleged "disappearance of the middle classes" was supposed to be so vital to Marx was a related myth, according to which the Marxian revolution was to be made by a proletariat that is by itself the overwhelming majority of society. But in fact we have already seen in other chapters that for Marx the proletarian revolution means a proletarian-led movement, a movement in which the proletariat wins the hegemony of the disaffected classes and social strata. Marx's theory of revolution depends in no way and to no degree on the actual disappearance of intermediate elements, but on the fading out of their social weight in the real struggles of society, on their subordination as independent class entities.

Thus the revolution certainly does not depend on the conversion of every last petty-bourgeois or other middle-class element into a proletarian; still, it may be facilitated to an important extent by the proletarianization of intermediate strata. Proletarianization is therefore no negligible question. But it has a related series of meanings, by virtue of the realities of modern society.

If we think of proletarianization in concentric circles (like the schematic social circles of Chapter 2), then the core is formed by those elements that are proletarianized in the narrow, technical-economic sense, that is, hurled out of petty-bourgeois or other middle-class ways of making a living and into proletarian jobs, as when a tailor, teacher, or tavernkeeper ends up on a Ford assembly line. Or the tailor, teacher, or tavernkeeper may be forced out of an independent livelihood as a self-employed worker and compelled to do tailoring, etc., in a wage-paid job in private enterprise, thus becoming a proletarian who uses the same skills as before. Or the conditions of bookkeepers, salespersons, other white-collar or commercial employees, and so on—whom Marx once mentioned as typically enjoying a better-paid position—may be reduced to that of lower-paid industrial workers, or below; and so their status, relationship to the employer, modes of thought, forms of organization, and the like, may tend to assimilate to the proletariat's more and more. This last case obviously uses proletarianization in a much looser sense than the first.

There are forces operative under latter-day capitalism that tend to homogenize the situation of all wage-workers, whether technically proletarians or not; and these homogenizing forces can be examined and evaluated without prior determination of what classes are disappearing or fading. After all, sections of the proletariat may take on a middle-class mentality for a longer or shorter time without disappearing as a class or tending to do so.

Proletarianization as a tendency, in a loose sense, is visible even outside the ranks of wage-earners and small-property-holders. To take an extreme example: when the ranks of the medical profession begin to consist in the majority not of fee-for-service practitioners (the largest mass of traditional petty-bourgeois enterprisers still in existence in many countries and hence a focus of reaction) but of salaried medicos working either for a private or a governmental institution, they do not necessarily become proletarians and they certainly do not adopt the mentality of factory workers; but they surely start moving in a visible direction, as is evidenced by the phenomenon of doctor unionization.

Indeed, in many fields, unionization—the adoption of the specifically proletarian form of organization—may be viewed as a rough index to proletarianization in the broadest sense, as long as this does not enforce hard-and-fast assumptions. In political terms, another concentric circle may perhaps be added on the outer periphery if we consider those social strata and elements which are induced by experience to look to the organized working class for social leadership, especially in crisis situations.

While proletarianization can be given concrete meanings, ranging from socioeconomic to sociopolitical terms, the concept of the "new middle class," in contrast, remains a wraith even for many who claim that this concept alone makes Marx obsolete. It is one thing to recognize the existence of increasing numbers of new intermediate elements of various sorts, as Marx did; it is another thing to construct out of these elements an organic class that is meaningful enough to seriously affect social and political life. This requires a cohesiveness, a fund of common interests, an objective basis for solidarity and social unity, such as do not exist among the disparate elements of this ectoplasmic class-construct. C. Wright Mills called it an "occupational salad,"[33] but this may be too complimentary, since a good salad needs considerable togetherness; the "new middle class" is more like a dish of herring and strawberries.

Dahrendorf admits that "there is no word in any modern language to describe this group"—and he suggests no word in Latin, Sanskrit, or Old Franconian—"this group that is no group, class that is no class, and stratum that is no stratum."[34] In short, it is a concept that is no concept. Even Marx failed to predict that it would be dreamed up. Somebody should invent a theory about its disappearance.

The "new middle classes," or rather the variety of intermediate elements thrown up by latter-day capitalism, may, in part or for a time, share some of the same sociopolitical characteristics as the old petty-bourgeoisie. The expression "petty-bourgeois characteristics (mentality, etc.)" becomes a historical or metaphorical description of the new in-betweeners, just as the expression "aristocratic airs" may be applied to elements that succeeded the aristocracy as ruling class. It would be interesting, to be sure, to make a catalogue of similarities and differences, though that is not our task. However, the differences are on a larger scale than the similarities. Above all, the new in-betweeners are not bunched together in one life-situation like the old petty-bourgeoisie, but are more scattered along an extensive continuum, shading off at one end into the working classes proper and at the other into the social penumbra around the bourgeoisie.

At the working-class end of this spectrum there is hetereogeneity and fragmentation to be found as in all other strata. Clerical workers in large office forces are increasingly amenable to union organization; on the other hand, workers in some luxury trades "are strongly attached, without knowing it, to the old rubbish," as Marx mentioned.[35] The working life-situation has to be examined concretely: for example, luxury production is socially dependent on the bourgeoisie through its economic dependence on the amount of surplus-value being extracted from the rest of the working class; the reactionary tendencies of a "servant class" are well known; and not altogether dissimilar is the position of upper secretarial employees working discretely; and so on.

One social characteristic of these intermediate elements is atomization. This is what conditions the meaning of class polarization in modern society, not the disappearance of all intermediates. As the polar classes tense apart, there no longer is a compact class like the old petty-bourgeoisie in the living space between them.

SPECIAL NOTE G	ON THE ORIGIN OF THE TERM LUMPENPROLETARIAT

A note to Chapter 15, page 453

Unfortunately, as far as I know there is no inquiry into the origin of the German term *Lumpenproletariat*. Pending research by someone competent in German philology, the following remarks must be tentative; but they may help to erase certain common misconceptions, which in turn have favored common mistranslations whenever an attempt has been made to find a vernacular equivalent. It is only in recent times that English translations or citations have begun to naturalize the word (not capitalized) with any frequency.

Was Marx, in *The German Ideology*, the first to use the term? Certainly no prior use has been recorded. Yet this first use by Marx does not sound consciously innovative, arising rather fortuitously out of a dialogue with Max Stirner's *The Ego and His Own*, which had been published less than a year before the writing of *The German Ideology* began.[1] As far as I can make out, it happened in the following way.

The word *Lumpen* (plural: same) means *rag*. By extension it began to mean *person in rags*, and, by a common twist Marxists will understand, its meaning darkened from *ragamuffin* to *bad person, riffraff, knave*.[2] But in this latter usage, by the eighteenth century or earlier, it mutated to *Lump* (plural: *Lumpen*, formerly also *Lumpe* as in Stirner). This form gave rise to a large number of pejorative and invective terms, beginning with *Lumpen-* as the combining form. But these *Lumpen-* words were formed from *Lump*, not from *Lumpen* (which had its own combinations, such as *Lumpensammler*, rag-picker).

The important conclusion that follows is that the governing meaning of the pejorative prefix to *Lumpenproletariat* is related not to rags but to *bad people*.[3] Yet the common assumption has been that it means *rags, tatters*, and the result has been the widespread and misleading translation "tatterdemalion proletariat," "proletariat in rags," "*prolétariat en haillons*," and the like, all of which stress extreme poverty; hence also "slum proletariat," which is equally misleading. But, as Chapter 15 shows, it is not poverty that defines the lumpenproletariat

628

and accounts for Marx's and Engels' usages. One of the unfortunate consequences of such translations is that they reinforce the erroneous conception of the lumpenproletariat as a part of the proletariat, the most depressed part.

In the century before Marx, large numbers of *Lumpen-* combinations were already in use for a variety of depreciatory and vituperative purposes. There is a longer list of such words in a 1716 lexicon and in the 1820 Heinsius dictionary than in most modern works,[4] and the list makes clear that *Lumpen-* could be freely tacked on to almost any word ad hoc: *Lumpenfrau, Lumpenkönig, Lumpenbuch, Lumpenfranzösisch,* and so on. There were undoubtedly scores of such combinations that no dictionary felt obliged to record; that is, the door was wide open to the ad hoc formation of *Lumpen-* words. This is why Marx, in 1845, did not have to feel he was inventing a new technical term when he prefixed this common pejorative to a less common word, *proletariat.**

1. A LUMPEN-LEXICON

Marx's first use of the combined term is in *The German Ideology*, in two distinct passages: in Part 1, called "Feuerbach," and in Part II, Chapter 3, called "Saint Max" (on Max Stirner). Although Part 1 was started first, we know that "the order of the text that appears in the published form does not at all correspond to the chronological writing of the manuscript."[8] There is a distinct possibility—only a possibility in the absence of definite information one way or the other—that the passage on Stirner was written before the other. Even if this is not so, there can be little doubt that the Stirner material involved here was already in Marx's mind when he began writing. Over three-quarters of

---

* Hence it is not surprising there is no record of anyone else hitting on this combination; doubtless some German peasant called his nag a *Lumpenpferd* or some critic called a rhymester a *Lumpendichter* without thereby going down in the annals of philology. Even the encyclopedic *Trübners Deutsches Wörterbuch* makes no mention of the term in its historical essay on *Lump* and *Lumpen* combinations; and to this day *Lumpenproletariat* does not usually appear even in large German dictionaries.[5] When listed in German encyclopedias, it is treated as a term peculiar to Marx, not as a German word.[6] Indeed, a modern dictionary of *Fremdenwörter* published by the Leipzig Bibliographic Institute of the D.D.R. lists it as a foreign loan word![7]—although it is only the second component that is non-German.

the long first volume of *The German Ideology* is on Stirner (omitted from most English editions of the work).

This is important, and may be decisive, since Stirner's book makes frequent use of *Lump* and its compounds, especially *Lumperei,* for the purpose of labeling social phenomena. On the one hand, he uses these words in senses that are close to meaning *Lumpenproletariat;* on the other hand, he more than once uses *Proletariat* with the same import. To be sure, he does not happen to prefix *Lumpen-* to the word *Proletariat,* but his failure to do so is almost accidental, so often do the two elements flirt with each other on the wings of Stirner's rhetoric.* The flirtation becomes hottest on one page of Stirner's section on "Political Liberalism," *and Marx's use of the term* Lumpenproletariat *occurs as he is discussing the content of this page.*

The context amply explains how the term comes off Marx's pen. Stirner's passage begins with an invocation of precisely those social elements who would be called lumpenproletarian. The bourgeois, he writes, grow morally indignant at shady elements:

> the sharper, the demirep, the thief, robber, and murderer, the gambler, the penniless man without an established situation, the frivolous man . . . All these lack settlement . . . in short, they belong, because their existence does not rest on a *secure basis,* to the dangerous "individuals or isolated persons," to the dangerous *proletariat;* they . . . have "nothing to lose," and so nothing to risk. . . . They form the class of the unstable, restless, changeable, i.e., of the proletarians, and, if they give voice to their unsettled nature, are called "unruly fellows."
>
> This is the broad sense of the so-called proletariat or pauperism.[10]

Marx cites parts of this passage and proceeds to attack Stirner's identification of the proletariat with these elements, and especially with pauperism as such. He explains that "pauperism is the position only of the ruined proletariat, the lowest level to which the proletarian sinks . . ." For Stirner, the *entire* proletariat consists of ruined individuals, "of a collection of *ragamuffins* [*Lumpen*] , who have existed in every epoch and whose existence *on a mass scale* after the decline of the Middle Ages preceded the mass formation of the ordinary proletariat, as Saint Max [Stirner] can ascertain by a perusal of English and French

---

* When McLellan paraphrases a key passage of Stirner's (one that we discuss immediately below), he even inserts the word *Lumpenproletariat* as if Stirner himself had used it, so strong is the connection.[9] But in fact Stirner wrote *Lumpe* at that point. If McLellan is justified—and I think he is—it is because the context makes the two interchangeable in hindsight.

legislation and literature."[11] Note that later this historical precedent is given by Marx and Engels as the origin of the lumpenproletariat; at this point, this social element is simply called the *Lumpen*. Here we have a confirmation of the fact that the *Lumpe(n)* so freely described by Stirner are to be equated with the lumpenproletariat as later understood by Marx. *And indeed in the very next paragraph, when these elements are referred to again, Marx's pen writes* Lumpenproletariat *instead of* Lumpe(n).*

This occurs as Marx makes the point that Stirner changes his use of *Proletariat* from the previously described *Lumpe* to the real proletariat, the real workers. "This," writes Marx, "occurs on pages 151 and 152,[14] where the lumpenproletariat becomes transformed into 'workers,' into ordinary proletarians . . ."[15]

There it is: the formation *Lumpenproletariat* slips out almost unawares, as simply another one of the several combinations with *Lumpen-* that are before Marx's eyes at this moment, *Lumperei, Lumpengesindel, Lumpengesellschaft*, all frequently used by Stirner. Where Stirner had used *Lumpe* to signify his idea of the proletariat, Marx simply spelled out Stirner's thought, which makes this connection time and again.[16] It must be understood that when Marx writes *Lumpenproletariat* at this point, he is still referring to Stirner's line of thought, not his own.

But—as Marx mentioned in this same passage—Stirner's rhetoric did not invent this social element; it only played with it. This social element *had* played a mass historical role, precisely in the formation of the real proletariat, during the transition from the Middle Ages to the present bourgeois era. Going even further back, it could also be discerned in mass in Roman society. This is the connection in which it is mentioned in the first chapter of *The German Ideology*, which may or may not have been written before the Stirner passage:

> The [Roman] plebeians, midway between freemen and slaves, never succeeded in becoming more than a lumpenproletariat.[17]

And with this statement, already quoted in Chapter 15, the term started its career as the label of a class or class element.

We may mention in this connection that forty years later Engels still

---

* Compare the 1847 passage, cited in Chapter 15, where Engels first writes *Lumpenproletariat* and then *Lump*, both with the same reference.[12] In an 1860 pamphlet Engels uses *Lumpentum* (riffraff) for the Bonapartist storm-troop elements elsewhere stamped lumpenproletarian.[13] Both examples show that he saw no critical difference between *Lumpenproletariat* and some other *Lumpen-* combinations.

identified the so-called proletariat of the latter-day Roman empire as a lumpenproletariat:

> In contrast [with the slaves of the plantation economy] were the free proletarians—however, not *working* but *lumpen*proletariat. Today in ever-increasing extent society is based on the labor of the proletarians . . . ; the Roman lumpenproletarians were parasites, not only useless but even detrimental to the society and hence without any decisive power.[17a]

2. THE TRANSLATION PROBLEM

The career of mistranslations, or misleading translations, of the German word *Lumpenproletariat* started with the passage in the *Communist Manifesto*. The difficulty was that the word was as untranslatable as could be, since no word existed in English (or French or any other language) for this hitherto unlabeled social formation. Translators were understandably reluctant to adopt one of the two satisfactory solutions: naturalization (as is becoming common today), or invention of a brand-new term. But an old word or term could not fail to be misleading.

The first attempt was made in the first English translation of the Manifesto, by Helen Macfarlane, published in 1850 in Harney's *Red Republican*—that is, under circumstances suggesting that the authors of the Manifesto may have helped the enterprise.* The Macfarlane transla-

---

* This first translation has been neglected as a political document. After all, Harney was at the time a political friend of Marx and Engels, especially the latter; both had had writings published in Harney's *Democratic Review* earlier in 1850. The translator, Helen Macfarlane, was "the admired acquaintance of Marx and Engels" (Schoyen).[18] The admiration was clearly mutual. When Macfarlane, the best socialist woman writer of the time, sat down to translate a German document with unfamiliar ideas, would she have hesitated to check difficult points with the authors, who were readily available and no doubt eager to ensure an accurate rendering? This line of thought does not make Marx and Engels responsible for the Macfarlane version, but it warrants treating this translation with special attention. Incidentally, the editorial note introducing the translation was the first public announcement of the Manifesto's authorship, and must have been published by agreement with Marx and Engels. Some months later, Engels was planning to use the Macfarlane translation as the basis of a discussion circle in Manchester with some of Harney's friends; later in 1851 Marx tried to get his American friends to reprint it as a pamphlet, and perhaps even wanted to publish it in the *New York Tribune*.[19] Engels had worked on an English translation of his own in April 1848, but we do not know what he did with his draft.[20]

tion dealt with *Lumpenproletariat* in the same way that Marx and Engels did more than once later: it made it *mob*.

> The Mob,—this product of the decomposition of the lowest substrata of the old Social system,—is partly forced into the revolutionary Proletarian movement. The social position of this portion of the people makes it, however, in general a ready and venal tool for Reactionist intrigues.[21]

We should keep in mind that at the time *mob* was still often used to mean not merely a tumultuous crowd but also a class or social stratum in a loose sense,[22] very like the old usage of *proletariat* or, later, *the masses*. It was for its day a better translation than any subsequently devised, even if not entirely adequate.* We should also note that the phrase "this portion of the people"—added by the translator, probably to avoid a pronoun with indefinite antecedent—does not represent this mob-element to be a portion of the proletariat.

When Samuel Moore did the now standard English translation of 1888, with Engels editing the product, the result was much less happy. However, the Moore-Engels version did *not* use a phrase implying a part of the proletariat—the error that proliferated later; it used nothing like "tatterdemalion proletariat," "slum proletariat," and such. It turned *Lumpenproletariat* into two terms: "The 'dangerous class,' the social scum . . ."[26]

"Social scum" is to the point, and is dealt with in Chapter 15. But it is quite another matter with "dangerous class"—and still worse with the plural "the 'dangerous' classes" which is used in the Moore-Aveling-Engels translation of the first volume of *Capital*.[27] The Manifesto translation even puts it in quote marks, thus pointing to its past use. But its use had usually been to impeach the working class, or the lower

---

* As it happens, at just about the same time Macfarlane was drafting her translation, Marx and Engels published an article (in German) in which *Lumpenproletariat* and *mob* were explicitly presented as synonyms. I believe it is their first use of *mob* in this way. The context is a discussion of the Roman Catholic Church as a center of reaction in England and its use of lumpen-Irish for its own purposes:

> Catholicism has its sole support in England in the two extremes of society, the aristocracy and the lumpenproletariat. The lumpenproletariat, the °mob° that is Irish or of Irish descent, is Catholic by extraction.[23]

One need not, however, jump to the conclusion that this use was related to Macfarlane's. *Mob* had started entering Germany by the 1840s; ten years before the above-cited use, Heine had reported to a German paper that in England "the gentry as well as the high nobility, and the mob like the latter, are very aristocratically inclined."[24] By the 1860s, says Ladendorf, *der Mob* was freely naturalized.[25]

classes in general, as a "danger" to society because of susceptibility to revolution, anarchy, and other iniquities. "Dangerous classes" was used to blur the difference between workers and the "criminal classes," between the proletariat and the "social scum."[28] It was perhaps Lorenz von Stein's influential 1842 book on French socialism that had started the theme; the modern proletariat, he wrote, "has to be called dangerous: dangerous by virtue of its numbers and the bold mettle it has often shown, dangerous by virtue of its consciousness of unity, finally, dangerous by virtue of its feeling that only through revolution can it achieve the realization of its designs."[29] Stirner's book, as we saw, also referred to the "dangerous proletariat," perhaps echoing Stein, but not clearly referring to the modern working class as Stein had done.[30] The "dangerous" tag became a well-known phrase, expressing the horror of ruling-class respectability at the menacing miasma exhaling from the dark underworld of society.

No doubt the phrase was also extensively used for the dubious lumpen-elements; in fact, Marx himself used it this way in his second draft of *The Civil War in France*.* To be sure, "dangerous class" certainly reflected Marx's opinion of these elements. But the public career of this phrase made it ambiguous and misleading as a rendering of *Lumpenproletariat*.

---

* When the pro-Versailles reactionaries finally decided to leave Paris, "they at last purged Paris from their presence by an unmolested Exodus, dragging along with them the cocottes, the lazzaroni and the other dangerous class of the capital." So wrote Marx in rough English.[31] Perhaps he intended the plural, "dangerous classes," meaning simply dangerous social elements.

TWO ADVENTURES IN
SOPHISTICATED MARXOLOGY

A note to Chapter 18, page 540,
with a glance at Chapter 3, page 50

This Special Note began as a modest footnote in Chapter 3 on Marx's use of *asses*, in rejoinder to Professor Shlomo Avineri. But quoting Avineri on *asses* opened a Pandora's box; the subject ramified, as we shall see, from a thesis about *asses* to a thesis about intellectuals. Following the ramifications is not an idle enterprise: it will offer us an insight into the methods of marxology, a subject that we slight in this work in our emphasis on positive presentation.

Avineri has expressed umbrage more than once at Marx's offense in calling certified proletarians *asses*. His context is a thesis about Marx and "the intellectuals" that is quite popular among marxologists. This thesis claims that Marx looked to the rule of the intellectuals, not the proletariat, and it was first invented by Bakunin.[1] Avineri is unusual in that he purports to present "documentation" for this thesis or something like it. Since we want to be sure we have before us· all possible documentation from Marx not only on this matter but also on the question of *asses*, we must examine Avineri's proffered documentation with interest.

Professor Avineri is unusual in another respect, the sophistication of his writings on Marx; for he has an advantage over many writers in the field in that he has actually read Marx's works. His book *The Social and Political Thought of Karl Marx* is one of the more knowledgeable productions on the subject. Naturally he has his own notion of what needs discussing, and we and Voltaire will fight to the death for his right to his opinion, since this may appear odd at first blush. His chapter section on Marx's theory of the proletariat (pages 52-64) is almost entirely devoted to Marx's early years up to the Manifesto, that is, to the beginnings of Marx's thinking on the subject. The rest of Marx's life—the theory of the mature Marx—is covered in a laconic half page.

1. DOCUMENTATION: ON ASSES, INTELLECTUALS,
AND CERTIFIED PROLETARIANS

> Hood an ass with rev'rend purple,
> So you can hide his too ambitious ears,
> And he shall pass for a cathedral doctor.
>
> (*Ben Jonson*)

Let us take up this pithy précis. I pass over its first sentence, since I do not understand it: "Nevertheless, because Marx's relation to the proletariat is not immediate but is reached through speculative considerations, he does not reveal much empathy [for] or spiritual attachment to the members of the working class." I think this says that since he was not himself a proletarian he could have no empathy for or "spiritual attachment" to proletarians, but I hesitate to impute such a blatant non sequitur to a sophisticated marxologist; and since Marx's passionate evocations of workers' conditions of life in *Capital* and elsewhere are notorious, I hesitate to believe this means what it says. But never mind—no matter.

The rest of Avineri's terse treatment goes as follows, in toto, including two footnotes:

> Marx's sceptical view of the proletariat's ability to conceive its own goals and realize them without outside intellectual help has often been documented. It suits his remark that revolutions never start with the "masses" but originate in elite groups.[1] Much as Marx always opposed those socialists who tried explicitly to dissociate themselves from the proletariat, a chief reason for the split in the League of Communists in 1850 was Marx's uncertainty about what would happen to the League if it were to be exclusively proletarian in membership. Marx's opponents within the League even went so far as to accuse him of trying to impose intellectual discipline on the proletarian movement; and Weitling was sometimes snubbed by Marx as the Tailors' King.[2]

[1] See Marx's article "The Indian Revolt" (*New York Daily Tribune*, 16 September 1857): "The first blow dealt to the French Monarchy proceeded from the nobility, not from the peasants. The Indian Revolt does not commence with the *ryots*, tortured, dishonoured and stripped naked by the British, but with the sepoys, clad, fed, petted and pampered by them."

[2] *Cf. Werke*, VIII, 598-600. In a letter to Engels (20 August 1852) Marx says: "Asses more stupid than these German workers do not exist" (*MEGA* III, 1, p. 382). No wonder that the new East German edition of the Marx/ Engels correspondence carefully omits this letter!

So Avineri,[2] on Marx's "sceptical view of the proletariat's ability to conceive its own goals and realize them without outside intellectual help." Most readers will assume that *intellectual help* means *help from intellectuals* (and we will see that Avineri really does mean this). Now, to be sure, we have emphasized at some length that in Marx's view the proletariat needed a great deal of help, for it could win only at the head of an alliance with other class elements. But why Avineri's single insistence on the help of the intellectuals only, unless some other concept is being insinuated? We see that Avineri is so sophisticated that he refrains from rushing in where others have trodden, namely, putting down in so many words the common thesis that Marx looked to a revolution led by an intellectual elite and not by the working class. Avineri does not *say* this; but his laudable restraint makes the subsequent presentation look odd.

Proceeding to documentation, he remarks that this skeptical view of Marx's has "often been documented": this seems to imply that a considerable documentation exists somewhere, and if he offers a few examples these must be particularly cogent since they are selected from such a mass.

1. First documentation: he adduces Marx's "remark that revolutions never start with the 'masses' but originate in elite groups." This statement is explained by a footnote, where we learn that Marx made no such remark, that the "remark"—not to put a fine point on it—is a fabrication. But it is not a dishonest fabrication, for anyone who bothers to look down to the bottom of the page can discover that the remark is Avineri's concoction, not Marx's. The chasm between the provocative statement in the text and the irrelevancy in the small-type footnote is not uncommon in the methods of marxology; what is commendable is that Avineri honorably offers his own refutation.

We discover in the footnote that the "intellectual help" came in the first case not from "intellectuals" but from French nobles, and in the second from Indian sepoys—not groups that come readily to mind as representatives of intellectuality. We discover that this help was given not to proletarians but to peasants (French peasants or Indian ryots). In short, the help was given by nonintellectuals to nonproletarians; and this somehow documents a thesis about intellectuals and proletarians. In neither of the two historical cases is there a proletariat even in presence, for Marx to be skeptical about.

We discover that the flat counterposition of masses to elite is a sort of pun by Avineri: the sepoys were native Indian soldiers who came right out of the Indian masses. By tagging them *elite* Avineri is word-playing on the notion of a social or class elite, whereas the sepoys' favored position was that of troops given extra privileges in order to buy them off.

We discover that another manipulation is exercised with the word *start*. It was well known before Marx that the initial crack in a regime or system often comes on top (reacting to pressure from below, to be sure), after which the masses pour through the crack so opened up.* Marx's mere mention of this well-known historical pattern becomes documentation of a *theory* that the proletariat (who do not figure in the picture) can never realize a revolution without intellectuals, whoever they are.

In Marx's article, unquoted by Avineri's documentation, the two historical cases are offered as examples of a preceding generalization. This generalization is not the one invented by our marxologist. Marx's goes as follows: "There is something in human history like retribution; and it is a rule of historical retribution that its instrument be forged not by the offended, but by the offender himself."[4] Incidentally, the content of Marx's article is a denunciation of British atrocities in India, brimming with "empathy or sympathetic attachment" to the oppressed people under attack.

2. The second item of documentation concerns the split in the Communist League of September 15, 1850, which we have already covered from several aspects.

There is an introductory clause: "Much as Marx always opposed . . ." It sounds as if it is giving Marx due credit for something. One sees that Marx opposed socialists who tried to "dissociate" themselves from the proletariat—the farthest he went in "spiritual attachment"—and it appears he opposed only those who did so "explicitly." There is no documentation.

The nub of this item is Avineri's flat assertion that "a chief reason for the split . . . was Marx's uncertainty about what would happen to the League if it were to be exclusively proletarian in membership." There is no documentation for this statement. We have stressed, of course, that Marx always opposed proletarian exclusionism; what we need is enlightenment about this unexplained "uncertainty," and some

---

* A very strong statement of this pattern was written by Marx in a *New York Tribune* article: "To hold out any chances of success, revolutionary movements must, in modern society, borrow their colors, at the beginning, from those elements of the people which, although opposed to the existing government, are quite in harmony with existing society. In one word, revolutions must receive their tickets of admission to the official stage from the ruling classes themselves."[3] The context of this statement is Bonapartist France. We will return to it in Volume 3.

evidence that this undocumented uncertainty was "a" chief reason for the split, or had anything to do with it.

While Avineri offers no documentation, the reliable documents about this episode are known and not voluminous.[5] There is nothing in them that has any more resemblance to Avineri's assertion than the footnote about French nobles and Indian sepoys has to the fabricated "remark." There is no record that Marx worried about "what would happen to the League if it were to be exclusively proletarian in membership"—though any responsible leader should have done so—and so we have no more idea than Avineri about the nonexistent content of this fabricated remark. The second fiction is that Marx was "uncertain" about this unraised question—though it is hard to imagine that anyone could be "certain" about it. The third fiction is that this invented uncertainty was any reason for the split, whose reasons we know fairly well.*

3. The next piece of evidence refers to what Marx's opponents "went so far as to accuse" Marx of, namely, "trying to impose intellectual discipline on the proletarian movement." Avineri, as a responsible scholar, now provides us with a footnote, which refers to certain pages containing part of the minutes of the September 15 meeting. Unfortunately there is nothing whatever in these pages about this accusation or anything similar.[9]

Still, there must have been accusations flying around in all directions, like the dishes heaved by the Duchess' cook, since no split

---

*There were aspects of the Communist League split discussion that are more material here than Avineri's nondocuments; some are discussed under other headings. Two passages from Marx's talks at the meeting, referring to the proletariat, are of present interest. (1) Marx openly attacked the demagogic use of *proletariat* as a catch-phrase with a nonproletarian content:

> Just as the [bourgeois] Democrats abused the word *people* so now the word *proletariat* has been degraded to a mere phrase. To make this phrase effective it was necessary to describe the petty-bourgeois as proletarians so that in practice it was the petty-bourgeois and not the proletarians who were represented.[6]

This hits Schapper, who had explicitly included the petty-bourgeoisie as a part of his "proletariat," in the *Kommunistische Zeitschrift.*[7] (2) In a second speech at this meeting, Marx spoke strongly against the idea of a proletarian party taking control of government in a situation when it could not introduce measures "appropriate to the proletariat" but only put into effect the program of the petty-bourgeoisie. This polemic against an adventuristic, premature seizure of power (or dreams about it) will be important for our examination of other subjects. In the course of it Marx stated: "I have always gainsaid the momentary opinions of the proletariat."[8] This, in fact, was one of the sources of Marx's strength; it is the other side of advocating proletarian revolution to a class that has not yet risen to revolutionary consciousness.

discussion is complete without them. Instead of speculating about what Avineri might have had in mind (like subsequent spates of slander) we must ask what this has to do with "documenting" Marx's alleged views about intellectuals. The interesting thing is not what gossip the sectarians-in-a-frenzy "went so far" as to spread, if any, but what factual basis Avineri has for bringing up this trash. Plainly, if he is going to devote a total of fifteen lines (plus footnotes) to Marx's lifetime views on the proletariat, it is odd to devote twenty percent of this space to unspecified gossip by unidentified factionalists about unmentioned crimes.

But still, the question is somehow raised about "intellectual discipline on the proletarian movement." It is not a question of Marx's views, which are not adduced by Avineri, but of charges made by his opponents. If this injection of the question has any relevance, it must be because the Schapper-Willich group *opposed* such discipline. Did they? While we do not know what "intellectual" discipline means here exactly, we can be sure that the Schapper-Willich group was strongly in favor of a superdisciplined organization, for they were (theoretically) getting ready to sally forth into Tooley Street at any moment in order to overthrow every European government in sight. Willich's plan was essentially to pounce on Germany with an elite brigade of five thousand well-organized bravos chosen from "the People of the Lord"—so Engels described it in a letter to Marx without much exaggeration.[10] Willich was a military martinet by training and nature, and leaned to barracks discipline, not simply "intellectual discipline."

Avineri's unexplained phrase suggests *discipline by intellectuals* over hapless proletarians writhing in their sinister grip; but this well-known scenario was not played out in the split. It was the Schapper-Willich sect that, following the separation, adopted formal statutes abandoning the democratic setup Marx had insisted on for the Communist League, and establishing a *dictatorship of the Central Committee* in so many words, that is, the dictatorship of the ex-student Schapper and the ex–military martinet Willich.[11]

4. Avineri's second footnote, which we have seen is mistaken about the first part of the sentence it is hung on, is also attached to the final revelation: that Marx sometimes "snubbed" Wilhelm Weitling as "the Tailors' King." Before we ask what this climactic offense means, let us note that the reader need not look into the footnoted pages of the Marx-Engels *Werke* for Avineri's reference: there is no more to be found there on this point than on the other. Weitling was not even mentioned in the split discussion, nor was he involved in the situation; he had lost all influence in the League over three years previously.

The historic snub can be explored only as an adventure in irrelevance. The reader may assume that "Tailors' King" was a simple insult. The tag "King of the Tailors" referred historically to John of Leyden, the leader of the Anabaptist rebels in the Reformation, one of the primitive communists in the pantheon of the movement. When Weitling's critics applied the label to him, it was a sarcastic thrust at his pretensions to be a Great Man, a notorious failing of his. (See Engels' remarks on this in his history of the Communist League,[12] and Marx's application of the label to Schweitzer.) Since Avineri inserts this tidbit without explanation, it is hard to say whether he thinks the "snub" consisted in calling Weitling a tailor; but of course, on the contrary, Weitling flaunted his (former) trade as a political banner—it made him a Certified Worker. The John of Leyden title was a rather mild jibe at overpretentions in a movement which, after 1847, had come to see Weitling as an obsolete figure, increasingly pathetic. But even this jibe had nothing special to do with Marx; it appears to have been common coin. Weitling's American biographer and admirer, Wittke, refers to him in this way in passing; or perhaps Wittke is quoting Weydemeyer (or Marx).[13] Marx certainly used this catch-phrase about Weitling on at least one occasion: in a letter to Engels in 1853, commenting on the slanders printed in Weitling's U.S. paper on the victims of the then recent Cologne Communist trial, Marx mentioned "the poison spread by this King of the Tailors and dictator of the Communia [utopian] colony."[14] For Weitling did indeed blossom out as a full-fledged dictator as soon as he got something to dictate to, in line with his firm principles in favor of a messianic dictatorship[15]—just as John of Leyden became dictator over the Anabaptist community in Münster. One wonders whether Avineri got the point of Marx's analogy between the two Tailor Kings.

Whatever all this means, where or how Marx "snubbed" Weitling with this derisive label is a portentous event that research reveals not. Yet, without this information, how do we know whether this historic snubbery does or does not prove that Marx held the "sceptical view of the proletariat's ability [etc.]" which Avineri's documentation has not yet documented?

Finally, there is the implication that Marx's snubbing of Weitling was a blow against the proletariat because Weitling was an honest-to-goodness proletarian. Leaving the non sequitur aside, our Special Note I gives information on Weitling's actual class role and pretensions to intellectual dictatorship.

5. And now to the *asses*. In his second footnote, hard on the mistaken reference to the *Werke*, Avineri introduces a new indictment,

citing a letter by Marx. This new reference contains as many mistakes as it has lines.

First: the quotation ascribed to Marx ("Asses more stupid than these German workers . . .") was not written by Marx. It appeared in the middle of a report *to* Marx on the increasingly tense situation in Cologne, where the witchhunt trial was going to take place, by a Communist League member named A. Bermbach. Marx then sent the report on to Engels, in the letter which Avineri cites.

Second: this letter—which Avineri thinks was "carefully" omitted from the *Werke* because of this dreadful statement about asinine workers—appears in the *Werke* in all its glory, but under a corrected date.[16]

Third: although Avineri unfortunately seized on a remark about *asses* which was by somebody else, there is little difficulty in finding real invective by Marx about certified proletarians as "asses" and worse—and also about members of every other class, nation, party, race, creed, and color.

> By outward show let's not be cheated;
> An ass should like an ass be treated. (*John Gay*)

The case is similar to that of Mr. Deeds's treatment of pixillation.[17]

As a service to marxology, I suggest that Avineri's gaffe about Bermbach's report should be replaced with, say, this exhibit:

> As everywhere, there naturally exists also among the London workers °a knot of asses, fools and rogues, rallying° around a scoundrel. The scoundrel in this case is George Potter, °a rat of a man° . . .[18]

So Marx in a letter to Engels. Marx did not reserve the all-purpose *Esel* for such people, but bestowed it freely, even on Ernest Jones by 1857, likewise in a letter to Engels.[19] A doctoral dissertation listing and classifying all of Marx's scoldings against *asses* would be as voluminous as the dissertation on Shakespeare's use of semicolons in the First Folio. For

> He who does not know an ass when he sees one is himself an ass. (*Baltasar Gracián*)

We remind the reader that all this trivia is supposed to document Marx's alleged view that the proletariat cannot make a revolution without "outside intellectual help" . . .

We now return to Avineri's assurance that Marx's "sceptical view" about the proletariat "has often been documented." In response to my query asking where this documentation might be found,[20] Professor

Avineri kindly referred me to his article on "Marx and the Intellectuals," published shortly before his book. This disabused me of the notion that he had meant documentation by other marxologists; for the article offers only "documentation" by Marx, for a thesis involving "intellectual help" by intellectuals.[21] If we limit ourselves to documentation in a literal sense (not argumentation), then what in Marx constitutes Avineri's documentation?

With one exception—the case of Eccarius which is the subject of the next section—we have already taken up all of his documentation elsewhere:

1. Marx's recorded opposition to the *exclusion* of nonworkers from the International and the proletarian movement. This proves the workers need "help."

2. Marx's expressions of "disdain, if not outright contempt, for those leaders of the movement who were themselves of working-class origin . . . a certain intellectual *hauteur* is clearly visible in his comments." No comments are specified, except the "Tailors' King" snub to Weitling. (Eccarius is mentioned in this connection.) Ignored are Marx's expressions of admiration for some leaders of working-class origin, like Bebel, and of disdain (or even *hauteur*) for a vast array of leaders of nonworker origin.

3. The 1870 letter by Engels which we quoted elsewhere,[22] about the supply of intellectuals in the socialist movement. Avineri does not explain why he finds this letter offensive.

4. And finally, we are back with the *asses*. The Marx-Engels correspondence, says Avineri, is full of "allusions to the workers' intellectual limitations, stupidity, and narrowmindedness," sometimes even using such derogatory terms as " 'asses,' '*Knoten*,' '*Straubinger*.' " If he had added that it is full of such derogation (and worse) about all other kinds of people, he would at last have made a completely accurate statement. Then, with the Clown in *Twelfth Night*, we could give its definitive justification:

> Marry, sir, they praise me and make an ass of me; now my foes tell me plainly I am an ass; so that by my foes, sir, I profit in the knowledge of myself.

2. POOR ECCARIUS AND THE MARX-MONSTER

Thy friendship oft has made my heart to ache:
Do be my enemy—for friendship's sake.
                                        (*William Blake*)

The new item of alleged documentation to be considered is Avineri's second case of disdain and *hauteur:*

> . . . even one of his most loyal followers, George Eccarius, also a tailor by trade, came in for a generous measure of unearned contempt from his master and teacher.

There is no documentation, not a footnote; no further explanation; just a magisterial sentence, summing up a quarter century of Marx-Eccarius relations. Eccarius is declared a totally innocent victim of Marx's galloping disdain for workers, or perhaps for tailors. Let the reader now find out what is behind this scholarly judgment.

We would hesitate to devote a few pages to this story, except that there are two other objectives to be gained, as bonuses. A number of marxologists (not Avineri) have repeated the myth that Marx broke with all of his friends, being something of an inhuman monster. We will, in passing, see how this inhuman monster treated his loyal follower. And in the course, we will see Marx in an unaccustomed light, I think.

The facts demonstrate the exact opposite of Avineri's thesis. And we will document the facts.*

Johann Georg (in England, John George) Eccarius was born in Thuringia in 1818, became a tailor, and emigrated to London as a young man. He became a member of the League of the Just, which reorganized itself as the Communist League; a member of the League's executive; a leader of its front organization, the German Workers Educational Society; and an active trade-unionist, elected a member of the London Trades Council. In the course, though laboring under difficult financial conditions, often poor and sick, he educated himself, and became a talented writer in two languages. His real talent and thinking ability encouraged his burning ambition to get ahead as a writer; but it was Marx who encouraged him most of all.

Marx gave him his first chance to publish: Eccarius' article on "Tailoring in London or The Struggle Between Large and Small Capital" appeared in his London magazine *NRZ Revue* in 1850. Marx helped him write the article, edited it, and probably formulated some

---

* While usually our reference notes simply document the text, in this section they often lead to additional information, of which the text has been pruned.

of the passages; and then presented it to the public with a special blare of trumpets, which we have already partly quoted elsewhere:

> The author of this article is himself a *worker* in one of the London tailor shops. We ask the German bourgeoisie how many writers they have who are capable of comprehending the actual development in similar fashion.
>
> Before the proletariat wins its victory on the barricades and battle lines, it announces the coming of its rule by a series of intellectual victories.
>
> The reader will note how, instead of the sentimental-moral and psychological critique such as *Weitling* and other worker-writers bring out against existing conditions, here a purely materialist and free conception, undistorted by emotional grumbling, confronts bourgeois society and its development.[23]

The pride displayed here is a political statement. Eccarius became a collaborator on the magazine, and Marx planned to have him write other articles.[24]

When the split in the Communist League came in September, Eccarius ranged himself with Marx. After the split he worked to counteract the Schapper-Willich group's influence in the League and to help the Communists prosecuted in the Cologne witchhunt trial.[25] In the dark days of the 1850s he became part of the very small circle of coworkers and cothinkers around Marx, especially as a writer.[26] More: he became a family friend.[27] When he fell ill, Marx wrote to Engels: "poor Eccarius has come down with consumption. This is the most tragic thing I've lived to see here in London"[28]—this when Marx's own personal affairs were often as grim. In other letters Marx stressed that "poor Eccarius" was breaking down under the conditions of his "tailor shop hell."[29] So that Eccarius could quit tailoring under doctor's orders, Marx at his own expense (of course with Engels' assistance) rented lodgings for him near his own home so that he could eat with the Marx family. Thus Eccarius was set up to devoting his full time to taking care of his health, and writing articles for the German-American press at three dollars an article. When his health improved, Marx and Engels tried unsuccessfully to get him a tailoring job in Manchester, instead of his going back to the "stink tank" in London where he had broken down. When his children died of scarlet fever, they collected a fund for him.[30]

At the same time, Marx was helping to train Eccarius as a writer, revising and correcting his articles.[31] To an American comrade Marx explained why Eccarius' production was limited: "Eccarius has to tailor from five in the morning till eight in the evening and is in a serious condition." Therefore, urged Marx (whose own family was living from hand to mouth), Eccarius had first priority on payment: "If they will pay *money*, I am for Eccarius' getting something first, so that he doesn't need to tailor all day. In accordance with an arrangement with me, he is now to send regular correspondence. Do what you can to see he gets *something.*"[32] Poor Eccarius came first.

A curious incident supervened during these years, prefiguring Avineri. In his 1852–1853 pamphlet *Revelations on the Communist Trial in Cologne* Marx had given a detailed account of complex goings-on which included the following incidental sentence: "Not long before the Cologne court proceedings, Kinkel and Willich sent a journeyman tailor as emissary to Germany."[33] *Aha!* thundered Willich from America in the course of slander-filled articles: "Why does Herr Marx emphasize *journeyman tailor?*" There had been no emphasis. Marx actually had to explain that it was the simplest way to identify the man without giving his name publicly. And he added:

> [Willich] thus charges me with high treason to journeymen tailors collectively, and seeks to assure himself of their votes by a Pindaric ode on journeymen tailors. Out of consideration for the good name of journeymen tailors, he is generously silent about the fact that Eccarius, whom he had labeled one of the pariahs, is a journeyman tailor, which has not so far prevented Eccarius from becoming one of the greatest thinkers of the German proletariat and gaining a position of authority among the Chartists by his English articles in the *Red Republican,* in *Notes to the People,* and in the *People's Paper.*[34]

We note the same pride, with the same political content. In fact Marx, as he pushed Eccarius' reputation, habitually identified him as a worker, to make clear he was not just another littérateur.[35]

When the dark years ended, Marx had a right to think that his investment of friendship and time in Eccarius was going to pay off for the movement. And for a while it did. The big break came with the founding meeting of the International in St. Martin's Hall, in 1864. One of the French émigrés came to Marx to ask him to speak and also to "supply a German worker" as a speaker. "I supplied them with Eccarius, who made an excellent showing," Marx wrote Engels; Marx stayed mute on the platform.[36] Both Eccarius and Marx were elected to the General Council. From here on, Eccarius worked closely with Marx in the International and, after his mentor, was the most important German in its leadership.

It seems clear that without Marx to back him up Eccarius would not have lasted long in the General Council. Collins and Abramsky, in their valuable work *Karl Marx and the British Labour Movement,* think that his "tactless," "clumsy and over-sensitive" personality was a big negative factor. "It is certain that throughout his entire career in the International Eccarius was a controversial figure, disliked by the English members of the General Council against whom Marx had frequently to defend him . . ." Only part of this hostility was veiled hostility to Marx by certain members; Collins-Abramsky add: "A man gifted with subtlety and finesse might have negotiated such difficulties; Eccarius who was humorless and gauche in the extreme probably exacerbated them."[37] For that matter, as time went on Eccarius also increasingly alienated his German coworkers, like Lochner, Lessner, Pfänder and Jung.

Marx alone, as far as the record shows, saw no flaws in Eccarius.* Engels agreed that Eccarius was the man to take over the leadership of the German movement if only he would leave London.[39] When the International, crowning Marx's efforts, was successful in helping to establish the Reform League (for universal suffrage), Eccarius was made one of its officers,[40] pushed by Marx. Marx wrote admiringly of his protégé's ability as an election campaigner.[41]

Then the English kicked back, as Eccarius' ambitions outran discretion. The editorship of the *Workman's Advocate,* renamed *Commonwealth,* opened up in 1866, and three influential trade-union leaders wanted the job; so did Eccarius. So great was the respect for Marx in International circles that his influence was enough to get the lowly German tailor appointed over the others. Resentment against Eccarius boiled over.[42] Marx had second thoughts about his headlong support to Eccarius' ambitions, and for the first time voiced an inkling (to Engels) about his friend's "egoism":

> On my part it was a "political" mistake to yield to his pressure and propose him for the post . . . I knew in advance that the thing would fall on my back. Avoidance of any appearance of personal aims or misuse of personal influence for secret ends, and good collaboration with the English, must of course be more important for us than the satisfaction of Eccarius' more or less justified ambition.

* This was so even when an untoward episode took place in 1865, significant in hindsight. Marx had made a speech in which *inter alia* he had criticized the Lassalleans' pet state-help program. Eccarius wrote up a report for the Lassallean *Social-Demokrat,* and instead of including Marx's critique he put Lassalleanized views into Marx's mouth! Engels and Marx both thought the Lassalleans must have rewritten the article, but Eccarius admitted this was not so. Marx was amazed but, in a letter to Engels, hastens to make excuses for his friend's "incomprehensible blunder." He writes: "I have told Eccarius privately not to bother himself over the crap . . . Eccarius was very ill, and this is indeed to blame for the nonsense."[38] It is clear in hindsight that Eccarius had inaugurated his pattern of writing (especially for pay) whatever the recipients of his articles liked to hear or at least nothing that displeased them.

"Dry natures like Eccarius'," he wrote, "possess a certain dry egoism also, which easily leads them astray." And then, rather meditatively, he described a previous occasion when, against Marx's warning, Eccarius had pushed himself too fast, and come a cropper.

> The poor fellow has, of course, had a life of disappointments, and the honorary posts that the English spontaneously granted him, like vice-president of the International, etc., misled him so much that he now thought he could have revenge all at once for his whole past life. If he had heeded me, operated slowly, maintained a modest attitude, everything would have gone best. If, despite his lack of [self-] discipline and his headstrong pushing, I myself even went into the muck on his behalf, I was particularly induced to do so out of the consideration that he had always worked with us and never reaped any fruits. But one always makes blunders if one lets oneself be influenced by such considerations.[43]

But this brought about no change in Marx's relations with Eccarius; Marx blamed himself as much as Eccarius for this episode. Soon afterwards Marx helped Eccarius produce his most important work to date, a series of articles on the political economy of John Stuart Mill, first published in *Commonwealth*, and then as a brochure in Germany.[44] The study "was written with mighty assistance and coaching by Marx," related Engels later, with "whole pages" at the end being written by Marx himself, especially in more theoretical passages.[45] Marx's help was secret; Eccarius reaped considerable prestige, of course.[46]

In the General Council, Marx's continued support of Eccarius paid off for the latter. In July 1867 Eccarius was named general secretary. His literary ambitions also flowered: the *Times* itself took him on as correspondent to report on the Lausanne congress of the International. Marx approved mightily, for he expected that Eccarius' dispatches, carefully formulated, would be good publicity for the International (as they were indeed).[47]

What Eccarius' dispatches to the *Times* did besides was to scandalize International circles by their crude ridicule of the French (Proudhonist) delegation particularly. To Marx Eccarius claimed that the *Times* had rewritten his copy, and Marx swallowed this claim whole. "The *Times* shamefully blue-pencils Eccarius' articles," Marx informed Engels indignantly. He (Eccarius) should have realized that the "bourgeois editors" would exploit his "humorous" references to the French in order to ridicule the International; but (Marx enjoined Engels) we must keep Eccarius' authorship secret, because "The way they edited his stories could do him enormous damage." The trouble with this worker-writer,

Marx lamented, was lack of "diplomatic skill."[48] But it was not possible to keep Eccarius' authorship secret (I suspect Eccarius did not). On the General Council, Peter Fox launched an assault on Eccarius' dispatches, and only because of Marx's vigorous defense and counterattack did Eccarius get off.[49] As Collins and Abramsky summarize it, "Marx, by no means for the last time, defended Eccarius against his English critics and the affair subsided." Writing to Engels about his energetic battle to save Eccarius' hide, Marx nevertheless added: "Still, during the debate Eccarius got hauled over the coals good and proper."[50] He hoped it would be a lesson.

Even while Marx did this, he knew that, just before this, Eccarius had shafted Marx himself in a somewhat similar way; it was in a report Eccarius had written for the *Bee-Hive* on a General Council discussion about the Geneva Peace Congress. Marx had made an important speech for a half hour; yet Eccarius' report dismissed it with "a couple of phrases" (so Marx wrote to Engels).[51] We will see what this signified about Eccarius, but at the time it seemed to be just another incomprehensible blunder.

A year later, Eccarius' congress reports for the *Times* stirred a violent storm, because of a self-serving crudity so transparent as to lay his character bare to most. While the denunciations flew, Marx sent Engels a cool summary of the charges against Eccarius (all true):

> He [Eccarius] took almost *no part* in the Congress and afterwards presented himself in the *Times* as the °leading mind.° There he appropriated the *General Council proposals* as his private property, and ditto the applause bestowed on them as if it were directed to him. He suppressed the speeches *of the others* as much as possible and, in order to flatter the *Times, falsified* Dupont's concluding speech. Lessner, furthermore, has the grievance that when he (Lessner) read passages from my book [*Capital*] Eccarius suppressed this fact in the *Times;* ditto, his dispatches included the resolution on the book [recommending *Capital* to workers] only under °high pressure°; finally, he falsified the German resolution on war. . . .[52]

The only question was what to do about him, or to him; fury was general. Marx informed Engels: "I shall try to protect Eccarius against 'positive' measures, but this time I cannot come out for him so partisanly as I did last year . . ."[53] When the storm broke over Eccarius' head at the General Council, the minutes (which Eccarius as general secretary tried to suppress) inform us that his only defense was that "it was by mistake because he was so much confused." Lafargue answered flatly that he did not believe it. But one notes in the minutes that Marx then moved to pass on, and the meeting dropped the subject.[54] As he had indicated, Marx was trying to run interference for poor Eccarius without defending what he had done.

Marx did not fail to understand how Eccarius had tried to shaft him (Marx) personally and what he was up to; he was hoping that poor Eccarius could be reformed and his talents saved. To a mutual friend he let his hair down and explained why Eccarius had suppressed mention of *Capital* more than once:

> Eccarius, who is otherwise very sound, but at the same time very ambitious, has, in *Commonwealth* and on other occasions, *purposely refrained* from mentioning it. He likes to appropriate my theoretical work for *himself.* * At the Brussels congress Lessner in his speech on the machinery question spoke of *my book.* The correspondent of the *Daily News* reported it. Eccarius, reporting the congress sessions for the *Times, suppressed* it. His goings-on are so much the sillier since he not only owes his knowledge to me but also his post as general secretary in the General Council. I alone supported him (in the *Commonwealth* too) against the attacks from the English and French sides. He is relying on the experiences he has gone through to see to it that I keep my eye only on the cause and shut my eyes to personal stupidities![56]

Marx added elsewhere: "His egoism needs a °puff [blow] to set him right again.°"[57] One might think that by this time Marx would have given up on poor Eccarius; on the contrary, we will see him continue to push Eccarius into new posts!

In any case, over two decades of this relationship have passed, and our inhuman monster (Marx) has not yet brought himself to see the truth about Eccarius, let alone offend him with expressions of disdain and *hauteur.*

We get a glimpse of Eccarius' way with Marx in another letter by Marx around this time, again to a mutual friend. Someone (quite possibly Eccarius himself) was spreading the word of a break between him and Marx. This is a misunderstanding, wrote Marx:

> ... on the contrary, *to date* I have upheld him against the attacks of the English, etc. But *he*—his overweening and often narrow egoism perhaps developed as a result of his circumstances—commits unpleasant stupidities from time to time. For the most

---

* Collins and Abramsky propose the explanation that "Eccarius, while regarding Marx as his intellectual leader, was jealous of him."[55] Perhaps they mean *envious.* There is a less psychological factor involved: the concrete value to Eccarius of blurring public knowledge of *Capital* was that Eccarius could use its theoretical content in his own articles without credit, as he did.

part I take no notice of them. By exception my patience gives way. Then I give him a dressing-down, and °all is right again° till the next time. The poor devil is now very sick, and he always uses such times to say his *pater peccavi* [Father, I have sinned].[58]

In fact Marx was still absurdly soft on the poor devil. Writing to his friend Dr. Kugelmann about the worker-philosopher Dietzgen, Marx seized the occasion to vaunt about—Eccarius. "I always had an inkling that he [Dietzgen] was 'not a worker like Eccarius,' " he wrote.[59] In the course of 1869 we learn incidentally that he is still helping Eccarius out financially from his own pocket.[60]

Although Eccarius was still working for the *Times* (which, we learn, "gave him great praise and made him lucrative offers"[61]), his dispatches on the Basel Congress of 1869 launched no new scandal; Marx's dressing-downs had apparently had effect. But we must pause at a new vignette of Eccarius' vaulting egoism at work: at the congress (reported Lessner to Marx) he went around asking every foreigner whether he had heard of Eccarius![62] The ambitious man's egoism was so gigantic and so unconcealed that in another milieu it might have been accounted a mere quirk.

No new storm having broken out over Eccarius for a while, Marx reverted to his previous course of collaboration with and help to him. When another International project, the Land and Labor League (for land nationalization) was established in October 1869, Eccarius was appointed one of the joint secretaries—a paid job,[63] hence a plum that only Marx could have got for him. It is plain from the Marx-Engels correspondence that Marx was collaborating with him as closely as ever.[64] *And this went on for another two years.* As late as November 1871, when Eccarius was already almost visibly going over to the hate-Marx faction as the International bogged down in the mire of factional warfare, Marx still persuaded the General Council to appoint Eccarius as secretary for the United States—a post he promptly proceeded to use to knife both Marx and the Council.

But by this time the subjects we have set ourselves—Avineri's thesis or the Marx-monster fairy tale—are no longer relevant. In the course of a few months, as the International disintegrated politically, Eccarius formally and consciously went over to the camp of the English trade-union bureaucracy that was getting into bourgeois politics as the lib-lab wing of the Liberal Party. In this course his rites of passage included inciting its enemies against the General Council and bedding down with the anarchists for a short period in a rump International united only by common opposition to independent labor politics. It is not disdain and *hauteur* that Marx could now possibly express about this poor devil turned renegade, but rather furious denunciation of him as a simple turncoat, scamp, and traitor.

Only one key incident needs to be exhumed from oblivion: the point where Eccarius broke with Marx. Yes, it was Eccarius who decided to kick Marx demonstratively in the face, by sending a curt business note addressing him as "Dear Sir," and written in English, that is, as a stranger. It was already May 1872, and Eccarius was far gone; but Marx had not given up hope for him. On receiving this billet-doux from Eccarius, the Marx-monster actually sent an immediate letter pleading with him not to be a fool and forget about it all!

> You seem to have become foolish [Marx wrote], and since for the present I still consider this seizure of yours as transitory, you will allow me for the present to address you neither as Sir, nor Herr, nor Domine, and to write you in German instead of English.

Our monster then reminded Eccarius how he had defended him for years, stating quite accurately that "all the squabbles I ever had with the English [on the General Council] from the founding of the International up to the last Conference have sprung simply from my always taking your part . . ." He reviewed some of the cases. "You seem, however, to imagine that when you make blunders, people have to give you compliments, instead of telling you the truth like everybody else." Marvelous to relate, this letter ended as follows:

> Finally, I give you a piece of good advice. Don't think that your old personal and party friends are and remain any the less fond of you if they consider it their duty to face up to your °freaks° [freakish moods]. Contrariwise, don't imagine that the small clique of Englishmen who are using you for certain purposes are your friends. I could if I wished prove the contrary.
>
> And with this, *salut.* Since my birthday is day after tomorrow, I would not like to reach it with the unpleasant conviction that I have lost one of my oldest friends and cothinkers.—*Salut fraternel!*[65]

Eccarius apparently did not even reply to this appeal.[66] He did noise abroad his break with his mentor; we know he wrote to Wilhelm Liebknecht in Germany. Liebknecht concluded from his letter that Eccarius had gone out of his head, and wrote to Jenny Marx for information. Jenny replied she had asked Engels to write in her stead about "the dirty doings and infamies, which I can't think about without disgust and couldn't relate coldly and calmly enough." Engels' long letter summarized mainly the events of the last period, the gory details of which we have spared the reader. It is a very factual presentation, ending with the opinion that Eccarius' trouble was that he tried to turn the International into a "milch cow for himself, riding roughshod over all [other] considerations." If (he said) Liebknecht wrote to the other Continental coworkers of the General Council—Lochner, Lessner, Pfänder, Frankel—"you will hardly get so cool and unimpassioned an answer as from me."[67] But, then, Engels had not nursed Eccarius back to health for years, as Jenny had, nor had he seen Eccarius at work close up, as had Eccarius' colleagues in the Council.

Alas, Eccarius did not have what it took to capitalize on his break with everything that had ever made his life significant. By 1877 he was dismissed by the *Times,* having nothing more it wanted.[68] He was now a squeezed lemon. He died in 1889. Posthumously, this poor devil who had yearned to be recognized as a leader and theoretician of international socialism suffered a cruel blow: when the archives of the Austrian government were opened after the fall of the Hapsburgs in 1918, it was announced in the Austrian socialist press that Eccarius had been a spy who provided the Austrian government with confidential information about the International. Collins and Abramsky, who report this, explain that the accusation was possibly a misunderstanding, that it may have been due to Eccarius' writing reports for and getting paid by an Austrian editor who was indeed a police spy, and that the charge must be considered not proved, pending an examination of the Austrian police archives.[69] This is a sound caution.

* * *

Let us now remind ourselves that this is how sophisticated marxology has proved—by "documentation"—that Marx held a skeptical view of the proletariat. For the definition of *sophisticated,* the reader is referred exclusively to the Oxford English Dictionary.

In point of fact, the story of Marx's hopes for Eccarius illustrates a quite different point, one of some importance. Marx invested so much supportive effort in Eccarius because the tailor could, and did, become a first-class *worker-intellectual* (to use a later term). The importance to Marx of such a proletarian cadre has been stated elsewhere in these pages: it could eliminate or reduce the need for bourgeois intellectuals in the movement. Eccarius, like Wilhelm Wolff, was prized because his successes showed that proletarian elements could eventually do the jobs that tended to be monopolized by the "eddicated" bourgeois whose corruptive role Marx and Engels so often denounced. In short, the facts about the Marx-Eccarius story show precisely the reverse of the undocumented insinuations that are so popular with marxologists.

THE WEITLING MYTH:
HORNY-HANDED PROLETARIAN
VS. INTELLECTUAL
A note to Chapter 18, page 549

The marxological tradition that portrays Marx as an authoritarian has a subtradition, according to which he represented the intellectuals' aspiration for domination over the workers. For it cannot be denied that he was an intellectual himself (according to sundry definitions of that term) and of notoriously bourgeois origin at that; and it has been proved that he had no inhibition against treating even certified proletarians with disrespect. In this connection his definitive offense is sometimes taken to be his confrontation with Wilhelm Weitling in Brussels in 1846.*

The scenario goes as follows. On the one hand there is Weitling, then the best-known figure in the fledgling circles of German communism or socialism—ceremoniously referred to in some marxological works as a "born proletarian." On the other hand, there is the bourgeois intellectual Marx, seconded by the Manchester capitalist Engels, both of whom in 1846 are engaged in plotting to take over the communist movement. This is a very bold plot, since there is no such movement as yet. At a portentous meeting on March 30, 1846, the Intellectual argues the hapless Proletarian down, and seizes control—of something—thus dramatizing the Dictatorship of the Intellectuals over the proletariat.

This is a stirring tale, but the facts are even more interesting. To get at them, some irrelevancies must first be cleared away.

1. There was no decision-making meeting involved. There was a discussion gathering of members of the Communist Correspondence Committee, which was Marx's creation. Weitling had been living in London, where he was losing influence; on his way back to the Continent he stopped in Brussels, where he was invited to discuss his

* For example, see L. S. Feuer's *Marx and the Intellectuals* on the "worker-intellectual" Weitling: "at first enthusiastic about him, Marx later ousted him with his dialectical weapons from the communist movement; the hegemony of the political intellectual over the workers was established."[1] Just like that. (Weitling was "ousted" from nothing, with or without dialectical weapons.)

views at Marx's house. There was no question of a vote on anything—just talk—and there were only a handful present besides the principals. The main reason this soirée is well known is that a Russian visitor named P. V. Annenkov happened to be present, and in 1880 published an account of it in a book of memoirs. To be sure, it is dubious whether Annenkov altogether understood all that went on, or that his memory was fresh a third of a century later, but fortunately nothing hinges on this uncertainty.

2. There was no problem about combating Weitling's influence in the movement, though of course this would otherwise have had to be done. By this time Weitling had *already* lost the support of the main circle of German communists abroad, the League of the Just in London (soon to become the Communist League), and he enjoyed no credit with the Brussels people around Marx. During the preceding two years, while Weitling had been in England, with no Marx around to argue him down, he had succeeded singlehandedly in convincing the London group that he was passé.[2]

3. By this time, as we are told in some detail by his sympathetic biographer Wittke, Weitling had become "increasingly psychopathic." His mentally disturbed condition, or its manifestations at any rate, had begun in 1843–1844 in jail.[3]

4. For what it is worth (little), let us record that Weitling was no proletarian, born or otherwise, but had begun as a typical guild artisan of the time. Illegitimate son of a French officer and a German maidservant, he was apprenticed to a tailor and went through the guild route to become a journeyman and eventually a high-paid high-fashion ladies' tailor, later an independent small tradesman, and, at the end, a small businessman nearing bankruptcy.[4] Much more important is this: unlike other artisans who became communists, Weitling remained utterly alien to the proletarian condition. Biographer Wittke, a staunch anti-Marxist who usually has no truck with class analysis, summarizes his outlook as follows: "Weitling wrote with the rage and fire of the craftsman, the artisan and the petit bourgeois who were beginning to disintegrate under the impact of large-scale industry and were struggling for deliverance from forces that were depressing them into the proletariat." That Weitling's mentality *feared* descent into the abyss of the "unskilled city proletariat" is repeated by his biographer in even more detail later.[5] In the March 30 discussion, Marx put it accurately when he attacked his "artisan-communism," thus differentiating Weitlingism in class terms.[6]

5. At the March 30 meeting it was Weitling who was the best-known intellectual star, not a hapless worker. Though now on the decline, he was still an internationally known author, editor, journalist, and lec-

turer in at least three languages, with almost a decade of fame behind him. Two years before, Marx, a brand-new convert to socialism, had praised him as a "proletarian" thinker, for this was indeed how he was widely regarded.[7] All the "intellectual" advantage was on Weitling's side—except that now he had nothing of interest to say to the movement.

It was because of the "proletarian" label that Annenkov was surprised at his appearance: "The tailor-agitator Weitling turned out to be a fair-haired, handsome young man [he was over 37], wearing an elegant style of surtout and a coquettishly close-cropped beard, looking more like a traveling salesman than the stern and wrathful zealot I had presumed I would meet."[8]

Engels writes of this meeting in his 1885 article on the history of the Communist League, after giving Weitling full marks for his early impulsion to the movement: "But he was no longer the naive young journeyman tailor who, astonished at his own talents, was trying to clarify in his own mind just what a communist society would look like. He was now the great man, persecuted by the envious on account of his superiority, who scented rivals, secret enemies and traps everywhere—the prophet . . ."[9] Evidently Engels did not suspect a mental disorder in the clinical sense, even later when he poked fun at Weitling's "great works (including a new grammar, in which the dative case was abolished as an invention of the aristocrats)."[10] Weitling's inventions included a theory of the earth as center of the solar system, and other eccentricities.[11]

The foregoing aspects of the marxological tale are, however, irrelevancies because they do not bear on the real point of the March 30 episode precisely from the standpoint of the much-feared Dictatorship of the Intellectuals. *Among the protagonists in that discussion there was indeed an advocate of a Dictatorship of the Intellectuals in communist society*—one who had openly set forth his plan in some detail. It was Weitling.

This is not controversial. It is not just a question of Weitling's completely candid advocacy of a messianic dictatorship and his consistently ferocious denunciation of democracy and democratic methods. In his writings he worked out a blueprint for a hierarchy of learned men, scientists and technicians ruling his communist society from the top down in the name of *Intelligenz.* "In the first place," he wrote, "I adopted the principle which is admitted as an axiom in the learned world that philosophy must bear rule . . . What steps should be taken . . . to hand over the direction of the social order to knowledge?" At the apex of public power, therefore, he placed a triumvirate of Great

Philosopher-Scientists; beneath them, in serried ranks, selected by competitive examination, were the lesser lights of learning constituting various assemblies of masters, and so on.[12] This is the framework of "his intellectual-socialistic state," as one historian has called it.[13]

Weitling was by no means alone in envisioning hierarchic communisms—virtually all the utopia-makers excelled in this department. But not since Plato dreamed of Philosopher-Kings had anyone focused so completely on a vision of the future under a Dictatorship of Intellectuals or something like it. This, then, is the champion of the proletariat chosen by myth-makers to counter the plot for a Dictatorship of the Intellectuals . . .

This artisan-intellectual was also the representative of a crude sort of anti-intellectualism. The combination is not as bizarre as may be supposed.

According to Annenkov's account, this was what the discussion blew up over.* In his first rambling presentation Weitling made a thrust against the idea that it was necessary to "think up new economic theories," implying that only practical propaganda work was in order. For all necessary theories and the content of the propaganda had already been settled by Weitling's works. Annenkov reports Marx's reply as follows:

> The gist of his sarcastic speech was that to arouse the population without giving it firm and thoroughly reasoned out bases for its actions meant simply to deceive it. The stimulation of fantastic hopes that had just been mentioned [by Weitling] —Marx observed further on—led only to the ultimate ruin, and not the salvation, of the oppressed. Especially in Germany, to appeal to the workers without a rigorous scientific idea and without a positive doctrine had the same value as an empty and dishonest game at playing preacher, with someone supposed to be an inspired prophet on the one side and only asses listening to him with mouths agape allowed on the other.

In Annenkov's Russia, added Marx, there might still be room for a role

---

* Marx's anger had been aroused earlier in the discussion in a way not mentioned in Annenkov's account. We know from Weitling's own letter to M. Hess that our genial messiah insisted before the little audience that the Marx tendency was mainly motivated not by political opinions but simply by a desire to lay hands on the sources of money for the movement (which sources existed only in Weitling's paranoid fancy).[14] A nice opponent to argue with. Hess later wrote Marx that although he agreed with Weitling's politics against Marx, "W[eitling] is, as I have long known, a dirty fellow with respect to money."[15]

like Weitling's which could unite "nonsensical prophets and nonsensical followers." But—

> In a civilized country like Germany, Marx continued, developing his idea, people could do nothing without a positive doctrine and, in fact, had done nothing up to now except to make noise, cause harmful outbreaks, and ruin the very cause they had espoused.[16]

"The color rose in Weitling's pale cheeks," and "in a voice quivering with emotion" he vaunted his achievements and boasted of the letters of gratitude he had received from all parts of Germany (the messiah touch), adding

> that his modest, preparatory work was, perhaps, more important for the general cause than criticism and closet analyses of doctrines in seclusion from the suffering world and the miseries of the people. On hearing these last words, Marx, at the height of fury, slammed his fist down on the table so hard that the lamp on the table reverberated and tottered, and jumping up from his place, said at the same time: "Ignorance has never yet helped anybody."[17*]

If the theoretician of the Dictatorship of Intelligence sneered at the work of theory (criticism and analysis), the paradox is not hard to explain. There had to be a division of labor: it was the Prophet's task to invent the theory, and the task of the others to propagandize for it amidst the suffering world. In the future society, the Triumvirate of Great Philosophers would not take kindly to unlicensed upstarts who trespassed on their prerogative. The Dictatorship of the Intellectuals would brook no intellectual competition.[**]

This same combination of a form of intellectual elitism with a form

---

* To be sure, this was not intended to be taken as an original aphorism: in his doctoral dissertation Marx had had occasion to quote Spinoza's "ignorance is no argument."[18]

** Another suggestion is made by Wittke, whom I quote on this because he is an admirer of Weitling: Weitling, as an autodidact, had a "hatred of the learned" and of "the 'professors and doctors' whom he thoroughly disliked and secretly envied."[19] Perhaps; if so, he had many years ahead of him in America (after his retreat from Brussels) hating and envying the professors who turned down his crackpot astronomical theories. We may add the information here that in America Weitling quickly became a peaceful reformer, Bonapartist, scurrilous journalist, pro-imperialist, unsuccessful dictator of a utopian colony, anti-Semite, advocate of a storm-troop-like organization of "blue shirts," supporter of the Democratic Party and Tammany Hall, opponent of the labor movement as well as of women's suffrage, apologist for bad factory conditions, and, of course, opponent of communism.[20]

of anti-intellectualism was noted by Engels in a late work, reminiscing about the early Weitlingian artisan-communists of the 1840s in French Switzerland. At a time when the true messiah himself was in jail, a "revolutionary" confidence-man named Kuhlmann worked the pockets of his supporters.

> They who were otherwise arch-democrats and extreme equalitarians to the extent of fostering ineradicable suspicion against any schoolmaster, journalist, and any man generally who was not a manual worker as being an "erudite" who was out to exploit them, let themselves be persuaded by the melodramatically arrayed Kuhlmann that in the "new world" it would be the wisest of all, i.e., Kuhlmann who would regulate the distribution of pleasures and that therefore, even then, in the old world, the disciples ought to bring pleasures by the bushel to that same wisest of all while they themselves had to be content with crumbs.[21]

In other words: class solidarity consists in letting yourself be exploited not by bourgeois intellectuals but by annointed worker-messiahs. This is an example of the "proletarianism" which long masqueraded as leftism, but it had nothing to do with Marx's proletarian socialism.

MARX'S COURSE
IN APRIL-MAY 1848
A note to Chapter 8, page 214

In the marxological package of myths about Marx's line in 1848, one of the items is the claim that Marx was not concerned with the building of workers' organizations at the beginning of the revolution and during its first months, but only made a turn in this direction in early 1849 when he resigned from the Democratic Association.* This claim is obviously related to the similar fiction which has it (following Nicolaievsky and others) that the *N.R.Z.* did not concern itself with working-class issues and interests until late 1848 or early 1849.[3]

On the contrary, we will now see that Marx's *first* concern, directly after the outbreak of the revolution in Berlin, was the expansion and link-up of workers' organizations throughout Germany.[4]

It is important to understand, as the mythologists do not, that Marx did not counterpose workers' organization against Democratic organization during this whole period: they complemented each other, in his view, and required a division of labor from his supporters. Indeed, this was essentially true for Marx already before the revolution. In Brussels, where Marx and Engels were working when the revolution broke out, Marx had already worked out a two-tiered organizational policy. He had been instrumental in founding, and was active in building, two movements: both a Democratic Association and a workers' movement, the latter being further divisible into a Communist core group and its front organization, a broad workers' educational society. In Brussels

---

* This myth, now entrenched, was early promoted by the misunderstanding of Marx's course not only in Bernsteinian historians but also in G. Mayer's biography of Engels and Mehring's biography of Marx.[1] In the latter case, it is only one example among many of Mehring's inability to grasp Marx's *political* thought. The historian Oscar Hammen is a recent exception—probably because he is a historian, not a marxologist. Precisely in connection with the period under discussion, Hammen states quite vigorously that "Marx and Engels recognized the importance of covering Germany with a network of worker-societies as the vital link in their strategy of a Democratic Front," and he has a summary of Marx's efforts in this field in 1849.[2]

Marx could be personally active in both because the pressure of revolutionary events did not yet exist. Later, in Cologne, he could not be equally active in both; but this does not affect the principle of the thing. His group *was* active in both.[5]

Both in prerevolutionary Brussels and in revolutionary Cologne, the Marx group as a political tendency carried out a division of labor in founding and building both a workers' association and a Democratic club. This course had been prefigured in the *Communist Manifesto*. However, the question of which-to-build-when does not depend only on policies or theories: it is also a practical question, a question of how much is feasible in one or the other field at a given moment.

Upon the outbreak of the revolution in Paris in February, and the subsequent expulsion of Marx from Belgium, the leading committee of the Communist League was transferred to Paris, as the center of the revolution; in this connection it decided to give Marx "full discretionary power" to direct the organization's work in the emergency.[6] From March 4 to the end of the month, then, Marx was in direct charge of the League's work. In the middle of the month the revolution spread to Austria and Germany. The preparatory stay in Paris—the most important center of the German emigration[7]—was necessary in order to mobilize the German émigrés influenced by the League for an organized return to Germany. The period was used by Marx both to organize the Germans in Paris, and also to send advance organizers into Germany.

First: about organization in Paris. The existing four Paris sections of the Communist League were consolidated. At a meeting of the leading committee on March 8, the main item of business was the immediate formation of a German Workers' Club, an open and public organization for a working-class membership broader than the League itself.* Marx was assigned to draft its statutes, and he submitted his draft to another meeting held the very next day: such was the urgency of this step.[9]

What about a Democratic Association of German émigrés? One had already been formed in Paris, and its influence was a pernicious one. Led by Bornstedt and Herwegh, it took a weak bourgeois-republican stance in politics, and, much worse, was mainly engaged in organizing an adventurist "German Legion" which was to invade the homeland bearing the revolution on its bayonets, financed by French gold.[10] To

---

* In 1884 Engels, writing his sketch of the Communist League's history, says: "We founded a German communist club ..." meaning the German Workers' Club.[8] But the point of the workers' club, founded by Communists, was that it was *not* to be another "communist club." This is not the only case in which Engels, looking back from a distance, forgets the nuances of a policy.

Marx and the Communist League, this was as false politically as it was farcical militarily. One of the reasons the German Workers' Club was needed in a hurry was to mobilize the Paris Germans for an entirely different course, opposed to that of the Democratic Association. In short, in this first (Paris) period of the revolution, Marx had to organize a workers' association *as against* the existing Democratic Association. There might have been a point to helping a German Democratic Association in Paris only if some elements were found there who were sympathetic but unwilling to organize in a workers' group; but this is an academic question since the Democratic slot was pre-empted by the Bornstedt-Herwegh types.

Under the existing circumstances, Marx went to considerable effort to advertise, through correspondence and in the German and French press, that the workers' club had nothing to do with the Democratic Association and its Legion scheme. The longest explanation, written for Marx by his wife, went to Weydemeyer in Germany, asking him to spread this information in his own paper and to as many other German papers as possible.[11] Marx and the League committee put out a statement in French for the Paris press, along the same lines.[12]

In contrast, Marx's aim was to mobilize German revolutionaries in Paris to go home without public fanfare but with links established among themselves (preferably through the Communist League) that would facilitate their organized activity once they got into the movement at home. In point of fact, the League got three or four hundred to return to Germany under its aegis.[13] In terms of this course, the organizational program was the establishment of workers' associations as widely as possible and their speedy link-up into a national organization. This was started by the Communist League in Paris under Marx's leadership. The political program for this effort was drafted around March 21-29 in the shape of the seventeen "Demands of the Communist Party in Germany," whose content has already been discussed in Chapter 7.[14] It was published as a leaflet by the end of the month, republished in a number of German papers, and widely used by Communist League organizers and by Marx's group in Cologne.* For present purposes we need only remind that its heavy emphasis was on demands

---

* Let us dispose here of the myth, which has come to be repeated from one marxological work to another, that Marx and Engels did not openly use the seventeen Demands. This tale is based on quoting a sentence from a letter by Engels from Barmen, without understanding what Engels is writing about. The sentence, out of context, goes as follows: "If a single copy of our 17 Points were distributed here, all would be lost for us here." The context was Engels' mid-April trip to his home town Barmen to raise money for the *Neue Rheinische Zeitung* by selling shares—hopefully, to his relatives, family, and old friends who had once been sympathetic to radical talk. Thus the mission was primarily financial, though

of interest to workers and peasants, and secondarily to the petty-bourgeois component of the Democratic alliance.

With these goals the Communist League under Marx sent a number of organizers into Germany as advance emissaries. Karl Wallau was sent back to his home town, Mainz, before the end of March. Wallau was a member of the League central committee who had already worked closely with Marx in Brussels, as president of the German workers' association in that city. For Marx he was an ideal emissary. In Mainz, working with Adolph Cluss and others, he promptly founded a workers' association. Wilhelm Wolff, Marx's close associate and friend,[20] came by on April 3 and helped the Mainz people draft an appeal to other cities. The Mainz Appeal, issued on April 5, called for the formation of workers' associations throughout Germany, with the Mainz group acting as temporary center for responses, preliminary to forming a real nationwide organization and central committee.

On April 8, Marx and Engels, on their way from Paris to Cologne, stopped at Mainz for a couple of days and went over these plans with Wallau and Mainz activists.[21] Among the plans discussed, no doubt, was the spreading of the Mainz Appeal for the formation of workers' associations. It was widely reprinted, mainly in papers in western and southern Germany. In leaflet form, it was sent to workers' organiza-

---

he also kept an eye out for recruits to the Communist League.[15] It is clear from his correspondence that this visit home was enormously depressing; and anyone who wants to psychologize about Engels' relations with his Pietist profiteering father is welcome to this material, on condition that it is understood that it has nothing to do with the course actually followed by Marx. Engels had actually hoped that his father might take some shares; this is also mentioned in a letter that Marx sent him in Barmen, urgently pressing him to put the squeeze on the old man and other acquaintances.[16] But Engels had only bad news to report: his father thought even the bourgeois press was subversive, and would rather fill his son's associates with bullets than dollars; all the former radical bourgeois he had known were now fearful and despairing, antilabor, averse to discussing social questions as "incitement." Engels wrote back to Cologne: "At bottom, the thing is that even these radical bourgeois here see in us their main enemies of the future . . ." The sentence we started with follows at this point; that is, what would be "lost" would be the possibility of getting money for the *N.R.Z.* out of these ex-progressive bourgeois of Barmen. The next sentence is: "The mood among the bourgeois is truly vile." (Then Engels reports that the workers are beginning to stir a little, having formed "coalitions," but adds: "This, however, precisely is in *our* way." This remark is unexplained.) In any case it is the financial mission that is at stake.[17] In fact, precious little was extracted from these ex-progressives' pockets.[18] At the end of one letter, Engels mentions that "a beginning has been made for a circle of the [Communist] League."[19] So he apparently did make some recruits (unidentified), though no doubt if his bourgeois friends knew about this, "all would be lost" twice over. None of this has anything to do with the wide use actually made of the seventeen Demands in the course of the Marx group's work in Cologne.

tions all over the country. As Communist League organizers passed through Mainz, they took away batches of copies which they spread wherever they went; Wolff distributed copies even on a Rhine steamer and a railway train.

Wolff had left Mainz on the 6th, before Marx arrived, and went on to Cologne. In Cologne, he gave the Mainz Appeal directly to Dr. Gottschalk, the philanthropic physician who was engaged in organizing a new association in the city. The Cologne workers' association was founded on the 13th; it adopted an "address" acknowledging the Mainz initiative and definitely stating that "we too . . . established ourselves as a workers' association after the example of our sister city Mainz." Gottschalk had *not* wanted the new group to be a workers' association; characteristically, as we have seen,[22] he wanted the Cologne group to call itself a "Democratic-Socialist Club" instead. He was defeated on this proposal, showing that his politics were implicitly repudiated by the membership even before his personal popularity started to fade. The reference to the example of Mainz—that is, of Marx's organizational line—had to do with the open class character of the organization established.

Wallau was only the first of the Communist League activists to go back into Germany, on the initiative of the Paris leadership under Marx, as advance field organizers with the perspective of building a nationwide workers' association movement, as well as of recruiting League members where possible. There were a number of others, from the end of March through April and partly into May. Karl Schapper covered Wiesbaden and Hesse-Nassau. Weydemeyer was active in Hamm; F. A. Bergmann in Regensburg. Stephen Born went to Berlin and stayed there, losing his Communist politics in the course of his individual work. Wilhelm Wolff went not only to Mainz and Cologne, but also to Coblenz, Hanover, Berlin, and Breslau, and then worked in Silesia for some months (without dissolving his revolutionary politics).[23]

Ernst Dronke, a young man only recently recruited to the League, who had accompanied Marx and Engels from Paris through Mainz to Cologne, went out on an organizational tour of some extent, sending back important reports to Marx in Cologne. Dronke covered Coblenz, Frankfurt, Mainz, and other cities. His reports on the immediate outlook for building workers' associations or recruiting to the League came to Marx well into May, that is, close to the launching of the *Neue Rheinische Zeitung* on June 1. These reports were quite pessimistic, and may have been instrumental in discouraging further efforts in this direction on the nationwide scale that Marx had originally envisaged.[24] The Mainz Appeal had attracted a very limited response. Besides, the publication of the *N.R.Z.* immediately threw the whole Cologne cadre around Marx into strenuous day-to-day work.

The big picture is this: throughout the country the rush of revolutionary events, breaking over a politically inexperienced and untrained working class, overwhelmed the fragile new cadres of the Communist League. In 1884 Engels retrospectively put it this way: "The few hundred separate League members vanished in the enormous mass that had been suddenly hurled into the movement. Thus, the German proletariat at first appeared on the political stage as the extreme Democratic party."[25] It was unable to take the stage as an independent proletarian movement, though Marx had tried to take this course. This was quite to be expected from the hindsight of 1884; but Marx, himself "suddenly hurled into the movement" like everyone else, had to spend at least April and May of 1848 finding it out for himself. Emigré organizers could not improvise an independent proletarian movement simply by appearing on the scene, when the makings for it did not yet exist. A whole course of revolutionary experience had to be gone through by the working class, and this education is what 1848 provided.

Marx had to readapt himself to this reality by the middle of May. The sequence of events makes clear that this was not caused by an orientation toward working in the Democratic Association; the relation was vice-versa: he had to reorient himself in this practical direction because he had ascertained the immediate infeasibility of building a workers' association movement on a national scale.*

For the next several months, therefore, the work of the Marx group focused on Cologne, where—as we have explained[26]—they followed a division of labor in building a workers' association and a sympathetic Democratic Association side by side, in close alliance for some time. Here Marx put the Communist League form of organization on the shelf in favor of the open, broad workers' association component in this strategy (to be discussed in Volume 3). In the last months of the revolution, in 1849, Marx gave up working in the Democratic Association and counterposed the perspective of building a national workers' association. In doing this, he was not adopting this perspective for the first time but merely returning it to the *top* of the agenda.

---

* An indication is provided by this contrast. The Mainz Appeal of April 5 had suggested Mainz as temporary center to receive responses. On April 20 Schapper met with the Mainz leadership as a representative of the League central committee, and after this meeting the Mainz association began calling itself the "provisional central committee of the German Workers' Association." But on May 17, when the Mainz association issued another appeal, it did *not* use this label nor even mention the idea of a central workers' organization. This suggests that by mid-May the perspective was considered temporarily shelved.

REFERENCE NOTES

Titles are given in abbreviated form; full titles and publication data are provided in the Bibliography. Book and article titles are not distinguished in form. Page numbers apply to the edition cited in the Bibliography. Volume and page are usually separated by a colon: for example, 3:148 means Volume 3, page 148.

Some frequently used abbreviations are:

E = Engels
Ltr = Letter
M = Marx
ME = Marx and Engels
M/E = Marx or Engels
MEGA = Marx and Engels, *Gesamtausgabe*
ME:SC = Marx and Engels, *Selected Correspondence* (2nd ed., 1965)
ME:SW = Marx and Engels, *Selected Works in Three Volumes* (1969-1970)
MEW = Marx and Engels, *Werke*
NRZ = *Neue Rheinische Zeitung*
NRZ Revue = *Neue Rheinische Zeitung, Politisch-Ökonomische Revue*
Rev. after = Revised after the original text
Rev. from = Revised from an extant translation
RZ = *Rheinische Zeitung*
Tr. = Translation, translated in

The first source cited is the actual source of the quotation or statement; it is sometimes followed by a [bracketed] reference that cites an extant translation if the first reference is to the original, or vice versa. This second reference is given for the reader's convenience only; when it is to "Tr." with no title, it refers to the translation cited in the Bibliography.

FOREWORD

1. Meek: *Studies in Lab. Theory of Val.*, 241.
2. Ltr, M to E, 22 June 1867, in ME:SC, 188.
3. Sabine: *Hist. Polit. Theory*, 798.
4. Ltr, E to Bernstein, 2-3 Nov. 1882, MEW 35:388. Bernstein later quoted this in his autobiographical *My Years of Exile*, 210.
5. This "Engels vs. Marx" myth was discussed in *KMTR* 1, Foreword, sec. 5.
6. See esp. ltr, E to M, 13 Feb. 1851, MEW 27:190; ltr, E to M, 1 May 1851, ibid., 240; and re certain individuals cf. also ltr, M to Kugelmann, 11 Oct. 1867, MEW 31:561 (re Borkheim), and M: Revelations Com. Trial, MEW 8:413 [ME: Cologne Com. Trial, 63].
7. Ltr, E to Schmidt, 5 Aug. 1890, MEW 37:436 [ME:SW 3:484 or ME:SC, 415].
8. Ltr, E to P. Lafargue, 27 Aug. 1890, in E & Lafargue: Corr. (Fr.), 2:407, rev. from English ed., 2:386.
9. E: Reply to Ed. Bd. Sächs. Arb.-Ztg., MEW 22:69.
10. Ltr, G. A. Lopatin to M. N. Oshanina, 20 Sept. 1883, MEW 21:489 (retranslated from this German version); Lopatin published his letter in a book in 1893, with Engels' permission.
11. This is quoted from the reprint of Longuet's preface, titled "Marx et la Commune," in *Le Mouvement Socialiste*, 15 Jan. 1901; also reprinted in later editions of M: Civ. War Fr., with "traduction de Charles Longuet."
12. This has been related in many places but I cite it from the Longuet preface used in the preceding note.
13. Marx probably read this anecdote in Ernest Jones's *Notes to the People*, 2:583 (Nov. 1851), where it was used as an amusing filler.
14. Ltr, Hess to M, 29 May 1846, in *Bund Kom.* 1:344f. However, I have not actually found the phrase *Partei Marx* in the 1846 literature.
15. Qu. in Silberner: *M. Hess*, 256 fn (for Kriege), 257 (for Hess). Cf. ME: Circular Ag. Kriege, MEW 4:3 [ME:CW 6:35].
16. I make this statement from memory, without being able to cite an actual source.
17. Cf. M: Revelations Com. Trial, MEW 8:412 [ME: Cologne Com. Trial, 62, but this tr. does not follow the original on quote-marks].
18. Ibid., 412-64 passim, for over twenty mentions of *"Partei Marx"*; the quote-marks drop off only in a passage on 425-26; for *Partei Willich-Schapper*, see e.g. 413, 415, 425, 431.
19. Ltr, Mrs. Jenny Marx to Cluss, 28 Oct. 1852 (with quote-marks), MEW 28:640; ltr, E to Weydemeyer, 12 Apr. 1853 (without quote-marks), ibid., 581 [mistranslated in ME:SC, 78, as "Marxian party"].
20. Ltr, E to M, 1 Apr. 1852, MEW 28:46, quoting the *Kölnische Zeitung*; also see M: Herr Vogt, MEW 14:470, quoting Vogt; see also one use in M: Revelations Com. Trial, MEW 8:449.
21. Bakunin's "Letter to the Internationals of the Romagna," 23 Jan. 1872, in A. Lehning, ed.: *Mikhail Bakounine et l'Italie*, 1/II, 200, 219, 217 sq.; quoted in Manale: *Aux Origines*, 1422-24.
22. Qu. in Freymond, ed.: *Prem. Intle.*, 2:301-03.
23. Ibid., 307, 311-15 passim.
24. Manale: *Constitution du "marxisme,"* 831.
25. This brochure is noted in Rubel: *Charte*, 5.
26. For a quoteless example, ltr, E to Bebel, 5 Jan. 1889, MEW 37:131; the

earliest I know (also to Bebel) is of 18 Aug. 1886, MEW 36:509.
27. Ltr, E to P. Lafargue, 11 May 1889, in E & Lafargue: Corr. 2:239f.
28. Ltr, E to L. Lafargue, 11 June 1889, ibid., 277.
29. Ltr, L. Lafargue to E, 2 Jan. 1893, in E & Lafargue: Corr. (Fr.) 3:244 (English ed., 3:255).

1. PATTERNS OF REVOLUTION

1. M: K.M. bef. Cologne Jury, MEW 6:245.
2. See *KMTR* 1, Ch. 8, p. 123.
3. E: On Soc. Rel. Russ., in ME:SW 2:390.
4. ME: Com. Manif., in ME:CW 6:507.
5. M: June Rev., in NRZ, 29 June 1848, MEW 5:135.
6. See *KMTR* 1, Ch. 4, 6 and 7; also cf. discussion of Bernays in Ch. 13, sec. 1.
7. ME: Ger. Ideol., in ME:CW 5:46-47, rev. after MEW 3:33-34.
8. Ibid., 60 [MEW 3:47].
9. Ibid., 87 [MEW 3:68].
10. Ibid., 88 [MEW 3:68].
11. Ibid., 89 [MEW 3:69].
12. E: Com. & K.H., MEW 4:317.
13. ME: Com. Manif., in ME:CW 6:505f; cf. also 498, 504.
14. Ltr, E. to Van Patten, 18 Apr. 1883, in ME:SC, 362.
15. E: On Soc. Rel. Russ., in ME:SW 2:387.
16. Hook: *Twd. Und. K.M.*, 270.
17. The case of the *Deutsche Führerbriefe*, regardless of actual author, for which see Dutt: *Fasc. and Soc. Rev.*, 170-74.
18. On Danielson and Lopatin, see Uroyeva: *For All Time*, 97-100.
19. Ltr, E. to Com. Corr. Comm. of Brussels, 23 Oct. 1846, in ME:SC, 32, rev. after MEW 27:61.
20. Cf. discussion in *KMTR* 1, Ch. 6, sec. 2.
21. ME: Com. Manif., in ME:CW 6:495.
22. See *KMTR* 1, Ch. 23, sec. 5.
23. For the original German see MEW 4:473.
24. ME: Com. Manif., in ME:CW 6:495.
25. Marx's views on cooperatives will be discussed in Vol. 4.
26. M: 18th Brum., in ME:SW 1:400.
27. Ibid., 401.
28. M: Cap. 1:763-74.

2. THE SPECIAL CLASS

1. See *KMTR* 1, Ch. 6, sec. 1.
2. See *KMTR* 1, Ch. 6, p. 147 fn.
3. See *KMTR* 1, Ch. 6, p. 131.
4. *Komm. Zeitschr.*, in *Bund Kom.* 1:504; this will be noted again below, Ch. 18, sec. 3.
5. See *KMTR* 1, Ch. 6, p. 131f.
6. M: Grundrisse, 428, 430-32.

7. ME: Holy Fam., in ME:CW 4:37.
8. E: Hous. Ques., in ME:SW 2:361.
9. ME: Ger. Ideol., in ME:CW 5:74 [MEW 3:61].
10. E: Peasant War Ger./Pref., in ME:SW 2:163.
11. E: Revol. & C.R. Ger., in ME:SW 1:307.
12. ME: Com. Manif., in ME:CW 6:485.
13. M: Conspectus of Bak., MEW 18:633; the passage and its context are given below, Ch. 14, sec. 8, p. 435f.
14. ME: Ger. Ideol., MEW 3:54 [ME:CW 5:77]; M: Pov. Phil., in ME:CW 6:211 [M: Misère de la Phil., 177f]; M: 18th Brum., in ME:SW 1:478f; and there is an echo in ME: Com. Manif. in ME:CW 6:493 [MEW 4:471].
15. E: Debate on Poster Law, in NRZ 22-27 Apr. 1849, MEW 6:440.
16. M: Cap. 1:506 [MEW 23:529].
17. E: Princ. Com., in ME:CW 6:346 [MEW 4:368f].
18. E: Soc. Bismarck, I.
19. M: Cap. 1:645 [MEW 23:674].
20. E: Revol. & C.R. Ger., in ME:SW 1:332.
21. M: Pov. Phil., in ME:CW 6:211 [M: Misère de la Phil., 178].
22. M: Ltr to Lab. Parl., in ME: Art. Brit., 216f; repeated in a N.Y. Tribune article, M: Labor Parl., 29 Mar. 1854.

3. ANATOMY OF THE PROLETARIAT

1. ME: Com. Manif., in ME:CW 6:515.
2. See *KMTR* 1, Ch. 6, sec. 4.
3. ME: Holy Fam., in ME:CW 4:36.
4. Ibid., 37; this passage leads into the one already quoted above, Ch. 2, p. 36.
5. Ltr., M. to E., 17 Nov. 1862, in ME: Civ. War U.S., 261-62.
6. Ltr, E. to M., 18 Mar. 1852, in ME:SC, 71.
7. Ltr, Johannes Miquel to Marx, second half of July 1851; Marx's "warning," presumably in a letter to Miquel, is not extant; cf. E. Bernstein: *Briefe J.M. an K.M.*, 2nd installment, 68.
8. Ltr, Laura (Marx) Lafargue to Engels, begin. of Nov. 1887, in E & Lafargue: Corr., 2:69.
9. Ltr, E. to Bebel, 22-24 June 1885, MEW 36:336.
10. E: Rev. & C.R. Ger., in ME:SW 1:305.
11. Ibid.
12. Ibid., 305-06.
13. Ltr, E. to Bernstein, 30 Nov. 1881, MEW 35:237-38.
14. Collins & Abramsky, 70.
15. Ltr, E. to Bernstein, 11 Nov. 1884, MEW 36:234.
16. E. to Laura Lafargue, 5 Dec. 1892, in E & Lafargue: Corr. 3:221.
17. E. to Bernstein, 27 Feb.-1 Mar. 1883, MEW 35:443.
18. E. to Bernstein, 25 Jan. 1882, MEW 35:265-66.
19. Ltr, E. to M., 15 Aug. 1870, in ME:SC, 242.
20. E. Cond. Wkg. Cl. Eng./Pref. '92 Ger., in ME:SW 3:452.
21. Ltr, E. to Sorge, 31 Dec. 1892, in ME:SC, 451-52.
22. Ltr, E. to Bebel, 11 Dec. 1884, MEW 36:251.
23. Ltr,,E. to Kautsky, 8 Nov. 1884, MEW 36:230.
24. Ltr, E. to M., 24 Sept. 1852, MEW 28:145.
25. Ltr, E. to Laura Lafargue, 12 Nov. 1887, in E & Lafargue: Corr. 2:71.

26. Ltr, E. to M., 5 Feb. 1851, MEW 27:180.
27. Ltr, E. to M., 18 Nov. 1868, MEW 32:207.
28. Ltr, E. to Plekhanov, 21 May 1894, MEW 39:248.
29. Ltr, E to Sorge, 14 Sept. 1891. MEW 38:155.
30. Ltr, E. to Weydemeyer, 7 Aug. 1851, in ME: Ltrs. Amer., 26.
31. Ltr, E. to M., 23 May 1856, in ME:SC, 93.
32. Ltr, E. to M., 7 Oct. 1858, in ME:SC, 110.
33. Two loci of interest not cited in this section are: ltr, E. to M., 11 Aug. 1881, MEW 35:20; and E: Pref. to English ed. of *Capital*, 1886, in M: Cap. 1:6 [MEW 23:39f].
34. E: Eng. Elections, in ME: Art. Brit., 368.
35. E: French Com. Treaty, in E: Art. Lab. Stand., 22f.
36. Ltr, E. to Bebel, 30 Aug. 1883, in ME:SC, 365.
37. Ltr, E. to Kautsky, 12 Sept. 1882, in ME:SC, 351.
38. Ltr, E. to Schlüter, 1 Jan. 1895, in ME:SC, 477.
39. Ltr, M. to Liebknecht, 11 Feb. 1878, in ME:SC, 314.
40. Ltr, M. to E., 5 Apr. 1869, MEW 32:293; the two were Odger and Applegarth.
41. E: Cond. Wkg. Cl. Eng./Pref. '92 Ger., in ME:SW 3:452.
42. Ltr, E. to Sorge, 7 Dec. 1889, in ME:SC, 408.
43. Ltr, E. to M., 1 Nov. 1869, MEW 32:383.
44. Ltr, E. to M., 30 July 1869, MEW 32:354.
45. Ltr, E. to M., 15 Nov. 1857, MEW 29:211f.
46. Ltr, M. to E., 9 Apr. 1863, in ME:SC, 140.
47. See *KMTR* 1, Ch. 14, sec. 5.
48. ME: Ger. Ideol. in ME:CW 5:75.
49. Ltr, M. to Meyer & Vogt, 9 Apr. 1870, in ME:SC, 236-37; this letter summarizes and elaborates on Marx's statement for the International, adopted 1 Jan. 1870, which see in *G.C.F.I.* 68-70 [3], 404.
50. Ibid., 237.
51. E: Irish Internationalists, in ME: Art. Brit., 364-65.
52. M: Cap. 1:301, rev. after MEW 23:318; for a similar statement, ltr, M. to F. Lafargue, 12 Nov. 1866, in M: Ltrs. et Doc., 163 [MEW 31:536].
53. M: Civ. War. in U.S., in ME: Civ. War U.S., 81.
54. Ltr, M. to E., 17 Nov. 1862, in ME: Civ. War U.S., 261.
55. M: Gen. Counc. to F.C. of Rom. Switz., in *G.C.F.I.* 68-70 [3], 404, or in ME:SW 2:176.
56. M: Elec. Results, MEW 15:565-66.
57. Ltr, E. to Schlüter, 30 Mar. 1892, in ME:SC, 444.
58. Ltr, E. to Sorge, 2 Dec. 1893, in ME: Ltrs Amer., 258.
59. See *KMTR* 1, Ch. 6, sec. 6.
60. M: Econ. Ph. Mss., in ME:CW 3:280.
61. ME: Holy Fam., MEW 2:38 [ME:CW 4:36].
62. Ibid., 138 [ME:CW 4:130-31].
63. ME: Ger. Ideol., MEW 3:75 [ME:CW 5:77].
64. Ibid., 47f [ME:CW 5:60].
65. ME: Com. Manif., MEW 4:479, rev. from ME:CW 6:503.
66. M: Class Str. Fr., in ME:SW 1:213.
67. For ex., in two of Engels' late prefaces to the Manifesto: German edition of 1883 (in ME:SW 1:101) and English edition of 1888 (in ME: Sel. Wks./55, 1:28). It was also written into the General Rules of the International by Marx (see M: Gen. Rules, in ME:SW 2:19).
68. This tendency is further discussed below, Ch. 18, sec. 2.

69. ME: Holy Fam., in ME:CW 4:36.
70. See *KMTR* 1, Ch. 1, sec. 8, and Ch. 10, p.160 fn.
71. ME: Holy Fam., MEW 2:37 [ME:CW 4:36].
72. Ibíd., 143 [ME:CW 4:135].
73. Same, in ME:CW 4:82, rev. after MEW 2:86f.
74. See above, p. 25, ref. n. 10.
75. ME: Ger. Ideol., in ME:CW 5:52f, rev. after MEW 3:70.
76. Ibid., 214, rev. after MEW 3:195.
77. E: Berlin Deb. Rev., I, in NRZ, 14 June 1848, in ME: Rev. 48/49, 35.
78. Same, II, in NRZ, 15 June 1848, MEW 5:69.
79. E: Zeitungs-Halle, in ME: Rev. 48/49, 106f.
80. M: Class Str. Fr., in ME:SW 1:272, rev. after MEW 7:79.
81. ME: Edit. Note Eccarius, MEW 7:416.
82. Schoyen: *Chart. Chall.*, 213; the source is not given, perhaps dubious.
83. E: Bakun. at Work, in ME: Rev. in Spain, 213f.
84. M: Class Str. Fr., in ME:SW 1:253f.
85. Ibid., 277.
86. Qu. at end of Ch. 2 above, p. 48, ref. n. 22.
87. ME: Addr. Com. Lg./Mar., in ME:SW 1:184f.
88. M: Revel. Com. Trial, MEW 8:412.
89. Communist League: C.C. Session 15 Sept. 1850, in MEW 8:251 [ME: Col. Com. Trial, 251].
90. M: 18th Brum., in ME:SW 1:403.
91. Ltr, E. to M., 11 Dec. 1851, in ME:SC, 64-65.
92. M: Civ. War Fr., in ME:SW 2:224.
93. M: Pruss. That Canaille, qu. in *Reactionary Pruss.*, 22.

4. TRADE UNIONS AND CLASS

1. Thompson: *Labor Rewarded*, 75 et seq.; Pankhurst: *W. Thompson*, Ch. 12 and p. 202f; also see *KMTR* 1:145 fn.
2. Proudhon's view was given in his *De la Capacité Polit.*, 324-46. Parts of this revealing argumentation are quoted by Marx in M: Indiff. to Polit., in ME: Anarch. & A.-S., 97-99.
3. M: Pov. Phil., in ME:CW 6:206-12.
4. E: Crit. Notes on Proudh., 13-14, 17. Marx had previously summarized Proudhon's section on "association," without specific reference to trade unions, in his ltr, M to E, 8 Aug. 1851, MEW 27:297f.
5. For Jones on trade-unionism, see his paper *Notes to the People*, for Nov. 1851, p. 521; his article "The Policy of Truth," Feb. 1852; and the issue of Apr. 1852, p. 976.
6. Ltr, M to Ludlow, 10 Apr. 1869, in ME: Sel. Corr. (55), 364 fn; the reference is to M: Pov. Phil., last section, in ME:CW 6:206-12.
7. E: Anti-Dühr. (59), 362 [MEW 20:245f]; E: Soc. Utop. Sci., in ME:SW 3:125 [MEW 19:200].
8. Cole: *Hist. Soc. Thought*, 1, Ch. 11; Beer: *Hist. Brit. Soc.*, 1:334 et seq.
9. Ltr, E to Bebel, 15 Oct. 1875, in ME:SC, 300.
10. Cf. *KMTR* 1:133f.
11. E: Cond. Wkg. Cl. Eng., in ME:CW 4:527.
12. Ryazanov's commentary in ME: Com. Manif. (Ryazanov), 113.

13. Cf. *KMTR* 1:183, 185f.
14. E: Eng. Turnout, in ME:CW 4:585.
15. M: Econ. Phil. Mss., in ME:CW 3:235.
16. ME: Holy Fam., in ME:CW 4:52f.
17. ME: Ger. Ideol., in ME:CW 5:204f.
18. Ibid., 360f.
19. M: Pov. Phil., in ME:CW 6:210.
20. Ibid., 210-11.
21. Ibid., 211.
22. See above, Ch. 2, p. 41.
23. ME: Com. Manif., in ME:CW 6:492f.
24. Ibid., 493.
25. E: Trades Unions, II, in E: Art. Lab. Standard, 15.
26. Ltr, M to E, 19 Sept. 1868, MEW 32:155; ltr, E to M, 21 Sept. 1868, MEW 32:158.
27. Ltr, E to Bebel, 18-28 Mar. 1875, ME:SC, 293.
28. M: Cap. 1:741, rev. after MEW 23:770.
29. Ltr, M to E, 30 Jan. 1865, MEW 31:48.
30. M: Affairs Contin., N.Y. Tribune, 5 Sept. 1853.
31. E: Cond. Wkg. Cl. Eng., in ME:CW 4:505.
32. M: Wages, MEW 6:554.
33. E: Cond. Wkg. Cl. Eng., in ME:CW 4:506f.
34. Ibid., 507.
35. Ibid.
36. Ibid., 512.
37. Qu. in Bernstein: *Soz. Einst & Jetzt,* 70. See also the passage from Lassalle cited by Sombart: *Socialism & the Soc. Movemt.,* 170.
38. M: untitled article, N.Y. Tribune, 17 Oct. 1853.
39. See ltr, M to E, 20 May 1865, in ME:SC, 174.
40. For the theory of wages, consult Kautsky: *Econ. Doctr.,* III, Ch. 1; Blake: *Amer. Looks at K.M.,* Ch. 22; Rosdolsky: *Zur Entstehungsgesch.,* 330-66; Mandel: *Formation Econ. Th. K.M.,* Ch. 9.
41. M: Wages, Pr. & Pr., in ME:SW 2:75.
42. M: Notes for Rep. on W. P. & P., in *G.C.F.I.* 64-66 [1], 272.
43. M: Cap. 1:640; there is an indirect reference, via a citation, on p. 558 (n. 3) [MEW 23:669f, 582 (n. 63)]; likewise M: Cap. 2:340 [MEW 24:341].
44. E: Wages System, in E: Art. Lab. Standard, 9f.
45. E: Trades Unions, I, in E: Art. Lab. Standard, 11; the rest of this article is to the point. Cf. also conclusion of E: Wages Theory, in ibid., 34.
46. M: Wages, MEW 6:55.
47. M: Russ. Policy Ag. Turkey, N.Y. Tribune, 14 July 1853; repr. in ME: Art. Brit., 191f.
48. M: War—Strikes &c., N.Y. Tribune, 15 Nov. 1853.
49. Ltr, E to Sorge, 8 Feb. 1890, MEW 37:353.
50. M: War Ques.—Brit. &c., N.Y. Tribune, 24 Aug. 1853.
51. M: War Ques.—Fin. Matters, N.Y. Tribune, 21 Oct. 1853.
52. M: Report of Gen. Counc. to 4th Cong., in *G.C.F.I.* 68-70 [3], 326.
53. E: Trades Unions, II, in E: Art. Lab. Standard, 16.
54. Ltr, M to Schweitzer, 13 Feb. 1865, as qu. in ltr, M to E, 18 Feb. 1865, MEW 31:76. For the statement breaking relations, a few days later, see ME:SC, 166f.
55. Ltr, M to Kugelmann, 23 Feb. 1865, in ME:SC, 170.

56. E: Crit. Erfurt Prog., MEW 22:237 [ME:SW 3:438, tr. inadequate] .
57. *G.C.F.I.* 68-70 [3] , 292.
58. This is the text of Marx's draft, in *G.C.F.I.* 64-66 [1] , 347-49; the Congress text, with some changes, in *G.C.F.I.* 68-70 [3] , 290-92.
59. M: Wages, Pr. & Pr., in ME:SW 2:75f.
60. Esp. in the first article, E: Fair Day's Wages, and in the two articles on Trades Unions, in E: Art. Lab. Standard, 5-7, 11-18.
61. E: In Matter of Brentano, MEW 22:95f.
62. See the last section of this chapter, below; also the ref. to "bourgeois labor party" above, Ch. 3, p. 61.
63. Ltr, E to Bernstein, 17 June 1879, in ME:SC, 320.
64. E: Peasant War Ger./Pref. ('75), in ME:SW 2:169.
65. See *KMTR* 1:322, 325.
66. E: Soc. Utop. Sci./Intro., in ME:SW 3:114.
67. Ltr, E to Sorge, 9-11 Aug. 1891, in ME: Ltrs Amer., 235.
68. Ltr, E to M, 12 Dec. 1855, MEW 28:465.
69. Ltr, E to Sorge, 19 Apr. 1890, in ME: Ltrs Amer., 230.
70. Ltr, E to Bebel, 28 Oct. 1885, in ME:SC, 387.
71. See above, Ch. 3, sec. 4.
72. For an early (1848) reference to an "aristocracy" of well-off artisans, see the citation from Kinkel in Noyes: *Org. & Rev.*, 26.
73. Jones, "The Policy of Truth," *Notes to the People*, Vol. 2, 1852, p. 862.
74. Freymond, ed.: *Prem. Intle.*, 1:126 et seq., and 201 et seq. (esp. 203f).
75. *Northern Star*, 2 Nov. 1850, qu. in Schoyen: *Chart. Chall.*, 220.
76. ME: Review/May to Oct., MEW 7:445.
77. M: Cap. 1 in MEW 23:697 [M: Cap. 1:667] .
78. See below, Ch. 5, sec. 8.
79. Freymond, ed.: *Prem. Intle.*, 2:184.
80. Ltr, E to Cafiero, 16 July 1871, in ME: Corr. con Ital., 30 [MEW 33:662] .
81. E: Eng. in 1845 & 1885, in ME: Art. Brit., 392.
82. E: Interview N.Y. Volksztg., MEW 21:511f.
83. E: Eng. in 1845 & 1885, in ME: Art. Brit., 390.
84. E: Cond. Wkg. Cl. Eng./Pref. '92, in ME:SW 3:442.
85. See the passage qu. above, p. 107, ref. n. 80.
86. Ltr, E to Sorge, 22 Feb. 1888, in ME: Ltrs Amer., 196.
87. Ltr, E to Kelley-Wischnewetzky, 22 Feb. 1888, in ME: Ltrs Amer., 197.
88. Qu. from Engels in Hutt: *Brit. Trade Unionism*, 37, source not given.
89. Ltr, E to Sorge, 19 Apr. 1890, in ME: Ltrs Amer., 231, rev. after MEW 37:394f.
90. Ltr, E to Sorge, 7 Dec. 1889, in ME:SC, 407.
91. Ltr, E to L. Lafargue, 17 Oct. 1889, in E & Lafargue: Corr. 2:330.
92. Ltr, E to L. Lafargue, 10 May 1890, in ibid., 377.
93. E: Soc. Utop. Sci./Intro., in ME:SW 3:114.
94. E: Cond. Wkg. Cl. Eng./Pref. '92, in ME:SW 3:454.
95. Ltr, E to Schlüter, 11 Jan. 1890, in ME: Ltrs Amer., 222, rev. after MEW 37:340f.
96. E: May 4 in London, in ME: Art. Brit., 403.
97. E: On London Dock Str., in ME: Art. Brit., 401; the suspension points are in this source.
98. Ltr, E to Bernstein, 22 Aug. 1889, MEW 37:260f.

5. TRADE UNIONS AND POLITICS

1. E: Trades Unions, II, in E: Art. Lab. Standard, 15.
2. Ltr, E to Kautsky, 30 Apr. 1891, MEW 38:87.
3. Ltr, E to Bebel, 1-2 May 1891, MEW 38:95.
4. Ltr, E to L. Lafargue, 23 Oct. 1886, MEW 36:552; retrans. from Ger. (this letter not in E & Lafargue: Corr.).
5. Ltr, M to E, 27 July 1866, in ME:SC, 183.
6. M: untitled article, N.Y. Tribune, 17 Oct. 1853.
7. Ltr, E to Sorge, 7 Dec. 1889, in ME:SC, 407.
8. Ltr, E to Sorge, 19 Apr. 1890, in ME:SC, 412.
9. E: Interview/Chronicle, in E & Lafargue: Corr. 3:397.
10. ME: Com. Manif., in ME:CW 6:497, 518.
11. See above, Ch. 3, sec. 7-8.
12. Ltr, M to Schweitzer, 13 Oct. 1868, in ME:SC, 215.
13. Ltr, M to Kugelmann, 15 Jan. 1866, in ME:SC, 176.
14. M: untitled article, N.Y. Tribune, 17 Oct. 1853; partly quoted and reiterated in his untitled article, N.Y. Tribune, 18 Nov. 1853.
15. M: Turk. War—Indus. Dist., in N.Y. Tribune, 16 Dec. 1853.
16. E: Working Men's Party, in E: Art. Lab. Stand., 36.
17. Ibid., 36f.
18. See above, Ch. 4, p. 87 (ref. n. 21) and 88 (ref. n. 23).
19. See *KMTR* 1:32 et seq.
20. Ltr, M to Bolte, 23 Nov. 1871, in ME:SW 2:423f [MEW 33:332f].
21. Ltr, M to P. & L. Lafargue, 19 Apr. 1870, in M: Lettres et Doc., 174.
22. E: Trades Unions, II, in E: Art. Lab. Stand., 15f.
23. *G.C.F.I.* 70-71 [4], 204.
24. Cf. the discussion in Collins & Abramsky: *K.M. & Brit. Lab. Movemt.,* Ch. 12.
25. Ltr, M. to P. & L. Lafargue, 28 July 1870, in M: Ltrs et Doc., 179 [MEW 33:126].
26. Ltr, E to Liebknecht, 27-28 May 1872, MEW 33:475.
27. MEW 18:685 (quoted from the unpublished text of these minutes).
28. *First Intl./Minutes, Hague 1872,* ed. by Gerth, 29 (for the Ger.), 186 (Eng.).
29. Ibid., 262.
30. Guillaume: *L 'Internationale,* 2:330.
31. Harrison: *Before the Soc.,* Ch. 4; previously pub. in *Intl. Rev. of Social Hist.,* 1960 (Pt. 3), 1961 (Pt. 1).
32. Ltr, E to Sorge, 21 Sept. 1872, and 5 Oct. 1872, MEW 33:524, 530.
33. Ltr, E to Hepner, 30 Dec. 1872, in ME: Ltrs Amer., 112.
34. Ltr, M to Kugelmann, 18 May 1874, MEW 33:628.
35. Ltr, M to Frankel, 13 Oct. 1876, MEW 34:213 (retrans.).
36. Ltr, E to Becker, 21 Dec. 1876, MEW 34:236.
37. Ltr, Jenny Marx to Sorge, 20 or 21 Jan. 1877, MEW 34:526.
38. Ltr, M to Liebknecht, 11 Feb. 1878, in ME:SC, 314.
39. Ltr, E to Mahon, 23 June 1887, MEW 36:678.
40. *G.C.F.I.* 70-71 [4], 445.
41. E: Trades Unions, II, in E: Art. Lab. Stand., 17.
42. Ltr, E to Schlüter, 29 Jan. 1891, in ME: Ltrs Amer., 233.
43. Ltr, M to E, 19 Sept. 1868, MEW 32:155.

44. Ltr, E to M, 21 Sept. 1868, MEW 32:158.
45. Ltr, E to M, 30 Sept. 1868, MEW 32:170.
46. Ltr, E to M, 24 Sept. 1868, MEW 32:161.
47. Ltr, M to E, 29 Sept. 1868, MEW 32:169.
48. Ltr, M to E, 10 Oct. 1868, MEW 32:179f.
49. See above, this chap., p. 112f, ref. n. 12.
50. Ltr, M to Schweitzer, 13 Oct. 1868, in ME:SC, 214f.
51. Ltr, E to M, 22 Oct. 1868, MEW 32:187.
52. See above, Ch. 4, p. 88, ref. n. 27.
53. Ltr, E to Bebel, 18-28 Mar. 1875, in ME:SC, 356 [MEW 34:128].
54. Ltr, E to Schlüter, 29 Jan. 1891, in ME:Ltrs Amer., 233.
55. Ltr, M to Speyer, 10 Nov. 1871, MEW 33:318.
56. E: Workingmen of Eur., I.
57. Schorske: *Ger. Soc. Dem.,* 11.
58. E: To the Span. Fed. Council, in *G.C.F.I.* 70-71 [4], 480.
59. Harrison: *Land and Lab. League,* 178.
60. E: Eng. Elec., in ME: Art. Brit., 369f.
61. Ibid., 371f.
62. Ltr, E to Liebknecht, 27 Jan. 1874, MEW 33:615.
63. Ltr, E to Becker, 15 June 1885, MEW 36:327f.
64. Ltr, E to Plekhanov, 21 May 1894, in ME: On Brit. (1st ed.), 537 [MEW 39:248].
65. H.: *Karl Marx/Interview,* 15.
66. *G.C.F.I.* 68-70 [3], 297.
67. Ltr, M to E, 16 Sept. 1868, MEW 32:150.
68. Freymond, ed.: *Prem. Intle.,* 1:260-64, 403f, 430.
69. Ltr, E to M, 30 July 1869, MEW 32:353.
69a. Ltr, M to P. Lafargue, 19 Apr. 1870, in ME: Anarch. & A.-S., 46. The rest of this interesting passage will be taken up under anarchism in Volume 3.
70. Freymond, ed.: *Prem. Intle.* 2:180.
71. See above, Ch. 4, sec. 8.
72. Freymond, ed.: *Prem. Intle.,* 2:185.
73. E: Anti-Dühr., 398f.

6. THE PRINCIPLE OF CLASS SELF-EMANCIPATION

1. I found this delightful family motto in J. K. Hoyt's *Cyclopedia of Practical Quotations,* 808, ascribed to a Lord Bellew.
2. *The Republican,* 1 May 1871, qu. in Harrison: *Land & Lab. League,* 177.
3. Wolff (prob. author): *Pruss. Diet,* in *Bund Komm.* 1:521.
4. M: Provisional Rules of the Assoc., in *G.C.F.I.* 64-66 [1], 288; this formulation remained the same in later revisions of the Rules, such as the 1871 version, in ME:SW 2:19.
5. Ltr, E to Schmuilow, 7 Feb. 1893, MEW 39:24.
6. Laveleye: *Soc. of Today,* 152.
7. Villetard: *Hist. of Intl.,* 65f.
8. The membership card statement is reproduced in Jaeckh: *Die Internat.,* 223 ("conquered" replaced by "accomplished").
9. *G.C.F.I.* 64-66 [1], 54.
10. Ltr, M to E, 2 Dec. 1864, in ME: Civil War U.S., 273.

11. Puech: *Proudhonisme dans l'A.I.T.,* 103 fn.
12. Gen. Council: *To Working Men of G.B. & Ire.,* in *G.C.F.I.* 64-66 [1], 299.
13. Harrison: *Land & Lab. League,* 174, 195.
14. E: Pref./Com. Manif./1888, in ME: Sel. Wks. (55), 28.
15. M: Crit. Gotha Prog., in ME:SW 3:20.
16. See *KMTR* 1, Ch. 10.
17. See 1 Peter 4:8; Deut. 15:11 (emphasis added).
18. M: Commun. of Rh. B., MEW 4:200 [ME:CW 6:231].
19. Ibid., 194 [ME:CW 6:225].
20. M: Peuchet, in ME:CW 4:597.
21. E: Cond. Wkg. Cl. Eng., in ME:CW 4:564.
22. E: Manif. Lamartine, MEGA I, 6:339f; ME:CW 6:365 puts the last qu. in quotation marks but notes that it is Engels' "free translation" (paraphrase) of a Louis Blanc article in *La Réforme.*
23. E: Ger. Socialism, MEW 4:207 [ME:CW 6:207].
24. M: Pov. Phil., in ME:CW 6:177.
25. ME: Com. Manif., in ME:CW 6:513.
26. Ibid., 516f, 515, 495.
27. Qu. in E: True Soc., in ME:CW 5:561.
28. ME: Circ. Ag. Kriege, MEW 4:14 [ME:CW 6:47].
29. E: Debate on Pol. in Fr., NRZ 9 Aug. 1848, MEW 5:319.
30. E: Prosecution of Mont., N.Y. Tribune, 24 Nov. 1858.
31. M: War Ques.–Brit. &c., N.Y. Tribune, 24 Aug. 1853.
32. Ltr, E to M, 21 Jan. 1848, MEW 27:114.
33. Ltr, E to M, 25-26 Oct. 1847, MEW 27:93.
34. Ltr, M to Schweitzer, 13 Oct. 1868, in ME:SC, 215; cited in Ch. 5 above, p. 122f, ref. n. 12.
35. Ltr, M to E, 26 Sept. 1868, MEW 32:168.
36. Ltr, M to E, 10 Aug. 1869, MEW 32:361; the novel was Defoe's *Memoirs of a Cavalier,* 1720.
37. M: Debates Freed. Press, MEW 1:68 [ME:CW 1:172]; the passage is qu. in *KMTR* 1:40.
38. M: Belgian Massacres, in *G.C.F.I.* 68-70 [3], 314f.
39. *G.C.F.I.* 68-70 [3], 182.
40. So Marx too in M: 18th Brum., in ME:SW 1:426; see Joshua 6:5, 20.
41. M: Meeting, MEW 11:138.
42. M: Commun. of Rh. B., MEW 4:202 [ME:CW 6:233].
43. E: Berlin Concil.-Debates, MEW 5:45.
44. M: Deeds of H. of Hohenzoll., MEW 6:480.
45. M: Class Strug. Fr., in ME:SW 1:211.
46. Ibid., 237.
47. M: Address N.L.U., in ME:SW 2:157.
48. M: Class Str. Fr., in ME:SW 1:213.
49. Ltr, E to Harkness, Apr. 1888, in ME:SC, 401f.
50. Lassalle: *F. von Sickingen,* 19 (Act I, sc. 3); for related passages, see also 28, 54, 59, 69, 123, 136.
51. For the last qu., ltr, M to Lassalle, 19 Apr. 1859, MEW 29:592; for the whole ltr, ME:SC, 116-18; Engels' ltr, E to Lassalle, 18 May 1859, in ME:SC, 118-20.
52. Ltr, M to Kugelmann, in ME:SC, 169.
53. Ltr, E to Bernstein, 17 Aug. 1881, MEW 35:215.
54. M: Second Addr. of G.C., in ME:SW 2:200.

55. M: Civil War Fr., in ME:SW 2:223.
56. M: Civil War Fr., 1st Draft, in ME: Writings Par. Com., 162.
57. Ibid., 161. Re Comtism, see also Marx's 1871 interview, Landor: *Curtain Raised,* 132; and ltr, E to Tönnies, 24 Jan. 1895, MEW 39:394f [ME:SC, 478f].
58. M: Civil War Fr., 1st Draft, in ME: Writings Par. Com., 163.
59. Ibid., 164.
60. E: L. Feuerbach, in ME:SW 3:376.
61. ME: Com. Manif., in ME:CW 6:495.
62. For example, in connection with Bismarck (*KMTR* 1:426f) and Russia (ibid., 575-77, 582, 586).
63. Ltr, E to M, 17 Mar. 1858, MEW 29:305.
64. M: Civil War Fr., 1st Draft, in ME: Writings Par. Com., 126.
65. Ladendorf: *Hist. Schlagwb.,* 231f; there is no adjectival form in German or English dictionaries—*octroyal* is coined.

7. THE BOURGEOISIE AND BOURGEOIS REVOLUTION

1. See below, Ch. 11, p. 290.
2. See *KMTR* 1, Ch. 7-9.
3. See *KMTR* 1, Ch. 6, esp. sec. 7.
4. M: Crit. Heg. Phil. Rt./Intro., in ME:CW 3:176f [MEW 1:379f].
5. Same, in MEW 1:382f [ME:CW 3:179].
6. Ibid., 382-83, 385 [ME:CW 3:179-80, 182].
7. Ibid., 383, 385 [ME:CW 3:180, 181].
8. M: Aff. in Prussia, N.Y. Tribune, 1 Feb. 1859.
9. M: Crit. Heg. Phil. Rt./Intro., MEW 1:385f [ME:CW 3:182f].
10. Ibid., 386f [ME:CW 3:183].
11. Ibid., 387 [ME:CW 3:183f].
12. Ibid., 387f [ME:CW 3:184].
13. Ibid., 389 [ME:CW 3:185].
14. Ibid., 389f [ME:CW 3:185f].
15. See *KMTR* 1:144-46.
16. M: Crit. Heg. Phil. Rt./Intro., MEW 1:390f [ME:CW 3:186f].
17. Engels emphasized this repeatedly: in E: State of Ger., III, in ME:CW 6:32; in E: Pruss. Const., in ME:CW 6:65f; in E: Revol. & C.R. Ger., in ME:SW 1:304, 306, 308, 310.
18. ME: Great Men, in ME: Cologne Com. Trial, 152.
19. ME: Review/May to Oct., MEW 7:421-27.
20. E: Rapid Prog. Com., III, in ME:CW 4:238f.
21. See *KMTR* 1:219.
22. E: Late Butchery, in ME:CW 4:647.
23. E: Festival of Nations, in MEW 2:613 [ME:CW 6:5].
24. See *KMTR* 1, Ch. 3, sec. 4.
25. M: untitled article, N.Y. Tribune, 25 Nov. 1852.
26. For "Democratic Revolution" in this connection, cf. ltr, E to Commun. Corr. Comm. in Brussels, 23 Oct. 1846, in ME:SC, 32.
27. E: State of Ger., III, in ME:CW 6:29.
28. See *KMTR* 1:181.
29. Ltr, Mrs. Jenny Marx to M, bef. 10 Aug. 1844, MEW Eb.1:651 [ME:CW 3:580].

30. Ltr, Weitling to Hess, 31 Mar. 1846, in *Bund Kom.* 1:307. On the Weitling-Marx debate, see Spec. Note I, p. 654-59.
31. Ltr, E to Bebel, 25 Oct. 1888, MEW 37:118.
32. Cf. ME: Address Ger. Dem. Com. to O'Connor, in ME:CW 6:58-60.
33. Somerhausen: *Humanisme Agiss.*, 75.
34. E: Pruss. Const., in ME:CW 6:69-71.
35. ME: Com. Manif., in ME:CW 6:492.
36. M: June Rev., MEW 5:134.
37. Ltr, E to M, 18 Mar. 1852, in ME:SC, 71.
38. Saville: *E. Jones*, 18.
39. E: Eng. Ten Hr. Bill, in ME: Art. Brit., 99.
40. E: Princ. Com., in ME:CW 6:355.
41. E: Status Quo in Ger., MEW 4:45 [ME:CW 6:79f].
42. Ibid., 49 [ME:CW 6:83-84].
43. E: Protect. Tariff, MEW 4:60 [ME:CW 6:94].
44. E: True Soc., in ME:CW 5:556f.
45. Wolff: *Pruss. Diet*, in *Bund Kom.*, 1:517f, 530.
46. ME: Holy Fam., in ME:CW 4:37 [MEW 2:38].
47. M: Commun. of Rh. B., MEW 4:193 [ME:CW 6:222].
48. Ibid., 194 [ME:CW 6:225].
49. Ibid., 197 [ME:CW 6:228].
50. See above, Ch. 6, p. 157f.
51. M: Moral. Crit., MEW 4:339, 342 [ME:CW 6:319, 323].
52. M: Speech on Qu. Free Trade, in M: Misère de la Phil., 203 [ME:CW 6:457].
53. M: Moral. Crit., MEW 4:352 [ME:CW 6:332f].
54. Ibid., 351 [ME:CW 6:331f].
55. Ibid., 352f [ME:CW 6:333]; the last paragraph was cited in *KMTR* 1:481f, in another connection.
56. E: Commun. & K.H., MEW 4:312 [ME:CW 6:294].
57. For Cabet, see his *Voyage en Icarie*, 346; Johnson: *Utop. Com.*, 59, 140 fn. For Heinzen, see ME: Great Men, in ME: Cologne Com. Trial, 186. Also cf. the passage by Schapper, below, p. 190 fn.
58. E: Commun. & K.H., MEW 4:313 [ME:CW 6:295].
59. Ibid., 314f [ME:CW 6:292f].
60. Ibid., 317 [ME:CW 6:299].
61. Cf. above, this chap., p. 176, ref. n. 23.
62. Schapper: *Intro./Komm. Zeitschr.* in *Bund Kom.* 1:504.
63. E: Swiss Civ. War, MEW 4:391-92 [ME:CW 6:367-68].
64. Schapper (?): *Cit. Cabet's Emig. Scheme*, in *Bund Kom.* 1:510.
65. See Somerhausen: *Humanisme Agiss.*, Ch. 11 and 15.
66. E: Satisfied Majority, in ME:CW 6:440.
67. Ibid., 443f.
68. Ltr, E to E. Blank, 28 Mar. 1848, MEW 27:477.
69. Ltr, E to M, 25-26 Oct. 1847, MEW 27:93; Engels' use of French to quote Blanc indicates this is a direct qu.
70. E: Movements of 1847, in MEW 4:496 [ME:CW 6:522].
71. Ibid., 502 [ME:CW 6:528].
72. Ibid., 503 [ME:CW 6:529]; the qu. is from Heine's poem "Ritter Olaf."
73. E: Princ. Com., in ME:CW 6:356f, 355.
74. Ibid., 350.
75. Ibid., 350f, rev. after MEW 4:372f.
76. Ibid., 352.
77. Ibid., 355f, slightly rev. in style.

78. ME: Com. Manif., in ME:CW 6:486.
79. For England, cf. M: Chartists, in ME: Art. Brit., 118. For France, cf. *inter alia* M: Class Str. Fr., in ME:SW 1:214. For summary, see E: Soc. Utop. Sci./Intro., in ME:SW 3:110-12.
80. Ltr, E to M, 23-24 Nov. 1847, in ME:SC, 45.
81. M: Herr Vogt, in MEW 14:438, 439.
82. E: Soc. in Ger., MEW 22:248.
83. ME: Com. Manif., in ME:CW 6:519.
84. Ibid., 518f.
85. Ibid., 504; cf. MEW 4:481.
86. The Laura Lafargue tr. is quoted in a footnote by the translator of Adler: *Démoc. et Conseils*, 71. For this version, see the information in Andréas: *Manif. Com.*, 121f, 125f.
87. *Red Republican*, 23 Nov. 1850 (Vol. 1, no. 23), p. 183.
88. ME: Com. Manif., in ME:CW 6:505.
89. Ibid., 512.
90. E: Status Quo in Ger., MEW 4:45 [ME:CW 6:80].
91. Ibid., 47-48 [ME:CW 6:82f].
92. ME: Com. Manif., in ME:CW 6:519.
93. Ibid., 492.
94. Cf. McLellan: *K. Marx*, 194.
95. E: On Hist. C. L., in ME:SW 3:183f.
96. ME: Demands C.P. Ger., in Struik, ed.: *Birth of C.M.*, 190-02.
97. Ibid., 192.
98. Ltr, M to E, 13 Feb. 1863, MEW 30:324.
99. ME: Ger. Ideol., in ME:CW 5:46f [MEW 3:33].

8. PERMANENT REVOLUTION IN 1848

1. See above, Ch. 7, last section.
2. M: 18th Brum., in ME:SW 1:441.
3. Ltr, M to E, 9 Dec. 1851, MEW 27:383. Similarly in ltr, E to M, ab. 10 Aug. 1851, ibid., 305.
4. M: 18th Brum., in ME:SW 1:417.
5. For example, see the citations from Engels in sec. 1 of this chapter (ref. n. 7, 11).
6. E: French Work. Cl., MEW 6:557.
7. E: Hungar. Strug., MEW 6:166.
8. Ltr, E to Mrs. Jenny Marx, 25 July 1849, MEW 27:502.
9. Cf. E: Princ. Com., in ME:CW 6:356.
10. See Marx on Fazy in M: Herr Vogt, MEW 14:544, 548, 584; this work contains long characterizations of Fazy, e.g., 583-92, 548-49. Also see ltr, M to Becker, 9 Apr. 1860, MEW 30:527. Also cf. Heinzen: *Erlebtes*, 2:120f esp.
11. E: M & NRZ, in ME:SW 3:169f.
12. M: Speech on Poland 22 Feb. 1848, MEGA I, 6:409 [ME:CW 6:545].
13. M: Class Strug. Fr., in ME:SW 1:256-62, 291 esp.; also M: 18th Brum., in ME:SW 1:423-28.
14. For the April resolution see *Bund Kom.* 1:931-33 or MEW 6:585-87; on Gottschalk in general, see Becker: *K.M. & F.E. in Köln*, esp. 32-39, 181-201; and also ltr, E to Liebknecht, 29 Oct. 1889, MEW 37:298.

15. Nicolaievsky: *Who is Distort. Hist.*, 220 fn.
16. Nicolaievsky & M.-H.: *K. Marx*, 188.
17. The passages are quoted in Noyes: *Org. & Rev.*, 286f.
18. E: Bakun. at Work, MEW 18:481f [ME: Revol. in Spain, 220].
19. Spitzer: *Revol. Theor. Blanqui*, 171; the qu. from Blanqui was written in 1853.
20. E: Late Trial Cologne, in ME:SW 1:389.
21. Lenin, "Against Boycott," in his *Coll. Wks.*, 13:37.
22. E: Three New Constit., MEW 4:514.
23. E: Revol. in Paris, MEW 4:530.
24. "Information on Orders . . .," in NRZ, 19 Dec. 1848 to 14 Jan. 1849, MEW 6:576 [ME:CW 8:509]. For previous discussion of "party," see *KMTR* 1:153 fn.
25. M: Dem. Party, MEW 5:24; see 22f for the preceding exposition.
26. E: Debate on Pol. in Fr., MEW 5:347.
27. M: 18th of March, MEW 6:362.
28. Ltr, E to F. Kelley Wischnewetzky, 27 Jan. 1887, in ME:SC, 400.
29. Brisbane: *Mental Biog.*, 273; the passage was qu. in *KMTR* 1:212.
30. For the activity of M and E in the Cologne movement, the best account is G. Becker: *K.M. & F.E. in Köln;* for an English source, see Hammen: *Red 48ers*, 211 to end.
31. Nicolaievsky & M.-H.: *K. Marx*, 167.
32. E: Karl Marx, in ME:SW 3:80.
33. E: M & NRZ, MEW 21:21, rev. from ME:SW 3:169.
34. Ibid., 18, rev. from ME:SW 3:166 (which is misleading).
35. E: Berlin Concil.-Debates, MEW 5:46. For another brief example, see E: Fall of Camph. Min., MEW 5:96f.
36. E: Berlin Deb. Rev., MEW 5:65.
37. M: 18th Brum., in ME:SW 1:404.
38. Becker: *K.M. & F.E. in Köln*, 80-84; E: M & NRZ, in ME:SW 3:170; for press reaction, see Hammen: *Red 48ers*, 249-51.
39. E: Details ab. June 23, MEW 5:112.
40. E: June 23, MEW 5:119, 121.
41. M: June Revol., MEW 5:133.
42. Ibid., 134.
43. E: M & NRZ, in ME:SW 3:170; E: Karl Marx, ibid., 80.
44. E: Köln. Ztg. on June Rev., MEW 5:140f; cf. ME: Com. Manif., beginning of Part I.
45. M: Militia Bill, MEW 5:247.
46. M: Proudhon's Speech, MEW 5:308.
47. M: Report on Sp. Ag. Weitling (see Bibliography).
48. For a sidelight on this, cf. M/E: Turin Concordia, MEW 5:260f.
49. Cf. above, Ch. 7, p. 182, ref. n. 47.
50. E: Pref./K.M. Bef. Cologne Jury, MEW 21:200.
51. E: Berlin Concil.-Debates, MEW 5:46.
52. E: Berlin Deb. Rev., MEW 5:65.
53. M: Camphausen Min., MEW 5:33.
54. E: Concil.-Ass. of 15 June, MEW 5:79.
55. See above, Ch. 7, sec. 8, p. 193.
56. M: Debates Freed. Press, MEW 1:76 [ME:CW 1:180] ; cf. *KMTR* 1:41.
57. Ltr, E to W. Graeber, 13-20 Nov. 1839, MEW Eb.2:435 [ME:CW 2:486] ; ltr, E to F. Graeber, Dec.-Feb. 1840, ibid., 438 [ME:CW 2:489].

58. Qu. in Robertson: *Revs. of 1848*, 135.
59. E: Revol. & C.R. Ger., in ME:SW 1:349.
60. E: Debate on Pol. in Fr., MEW 5:334.
61. M: Bourg. & Counterrev., MEW 6:121, 115-16, 118.
62. Ltr, M to E, 11 Feb. 1865, MEW 31:68.
63. E: Ger. Camp. Const., MEW 7:113.
64. M: Aff. in Prussia, in N.Y. Tribune, 3 Dec. 1858.
65. M: King of Prussia's Insan., N.Y. Tribune, 27 Oct. 1858.
66. Cf. E: Revol. & C.R. Ger., in ME:SW 1:329; for some pre-1848 tremulation, see Hammen: *Spectre of Com.*, 418.
67. Ltr, E to M, 25 Apr. 1848, MEW 27:125.
68. E: Karl Marx, in ME:SW 3:80.
69. M: June Revol., MEW 5:135.
70. M: Victory Counterrev. Vienna, MEW 5:456.
71. See above, Ch. 7, sec. 7, p. 192.
72. M: Bourg. & Counterrev., MEW 6:109.
73. See above, Ch. 6, p. 157f.
74. M: Bourg. & Counterrev., MEW 6:110f.
75. Hammen: *Red 48ers*, 395f.
76. E: Peasant War Ger., 37; its last pages, 155-57, return to the analogy with 1848-49.
77. Ibid., 157, for 1850; the later view is in E: Peasant War Ger./Pref., in ME:SW 2:159.
78. E: Peasant War Ger./Pref., in ME:SW 2:160.
79. Ibid., 161f.
80. See my Foreword in *KMTR* 1:25.
81. See *KMTR* 1:321-24.
82. E: Peasant War Ger./Pref., in ME:SW 2:162. Cf. also summary passage in E: Role of Force, in ME:SW 3:391f.
83. M: Class Str. Fr., in ME:SW 1:227.

9. PERMANENT REVOLUTION: FINAL VERSION

1. M: Militia Bill, MEW 5:249.
2. M: June Revol., MEW 5:136.
3. E: Uprising in Frankf., MEW 5:410, 413.
3a. Newspaper Reports of Marx's Speech . . ., MEW 5:490 [ME:CW 7:570].
4. M: Bourg. & Counterrev., MEW 6:108f [ME:SW 1:140f].
5. Ibid., 121.
6. Ibid., 124.
7. See above, Ch. 8, p. 204f.
8. E: Mediation & Int., MEW 5:377.
9. M: Class Str. Fr., in ME:SW 1:223; cf. also M: 18th Brum., in ME:SW 1:403.
10. Ltr, E to Mehring, 14 July 1893, in ME:SC, 461.
11. M: Civil War Fr., in ME:SW 2:219f; cf. the drafts for this work, in ME: Writings Par. Com., 160, 210f. Also note discussion in *G.C.F.I.* 70-71 [4], 164f; and ltr, E to P. Lafargue, 27 June 1893, in E & Lafargue: Corr., 3:272.
12. M: Bourg. & Counterrev., MEW 6:124.
13. M: Speech at Work. Assoc. 15 Jan. 1849, MEW 6:579; cf. also statement by the Work. Assoc., MEW 6:585.

14. For more details on the electoral question, see *Bund Kom.* 1:903f; Becker: *K.M. & F.E. in Köln*, 183-95; Hammen: *Red 48ers*, 359-61.
15. M: Montesquieu LVI, MEW 6:190f.
16. Ibid., 191.
17. Ibid., 193.
18. For this statement, see above, Ch. 7, p. 182, ref. n. 47.
19. M: Montesquieu LVI, MEW 6:195.
20. Ibid., 195f.
21. M: March Assoc., MEW 6:335.
22. ME: Stein, MEW 6:298.
23. M *et al.*: Declaration, NRZ, 15 Apr. 1849, MEW 6:426; see also resolution of Work. Assoc., ibid., 584; and Becker: *K.M. & F.E. in Köln*, 246-50.
24. See above, Ch. 7, p. 169f.
25. Trotsky: *Perm. Rev.*, 19, 22f.
26. E: Concil.-Ass. of 15 June, MEW 5:79; for context, see above, Ch. 8, p. 221. Cf. also M/E: Downfall of Camph. Government, in MEW:CW 7:106.
27. M: K.M. Bef. Cologne Jury, MEW 6:257.
28. M: Köln. Ztg. on Elec., MEW 6:217.
29. M: To Workers of Col., MEW 6:519.
30. E: Ger. Camp. Const., MEW 7:111f.
31. Ibid., 113.
32. M: Crit. Heg. Ph. Rt./Intro., MEW 1:391 [ME:CW 3:187].
33. E: Revol. Uprising, MEW 6:525f.
34. M: Revol. Movemt., MEW 6:148.
35. E: Revol. & C.R. Ger., in ME:SW 1:339.
36. M: Revol. Movemt., MEW 6:149f.
37. Ltr, E to E. Blank, 15 Apr. 1848, MEW 27:481.
38. M: Class Str. Fr., in ME:SW 1:213.
39. Ibid., 227.
40. MEW 7:579f, ed. note 51; see also ME:SW 1:535, ed. note 13.
41. M: Class Str. Fr., in ME:SW 1:271f.
42. E: Wilh. Wolff, MEW 19:84; the references in the last paragraph to M and E by name were added in the 1886 revision.
43. Ltr, M to E, 10 Sept. 1862, in ME: Civ. War U.S., 255 [MEW 30:287].
44. M: Wage-Lab. & Cap., in ME:SW 1:150.
45. E: Hankering for State of Siege, MEW 6:472.
46. E: Ger. Camp. Const., MEW 7:196.
47. E: M & NRZ, in ME:SW 3:170.

10. BOURGEOIS AND PROLETARIAN REVOLUTION: BALANCE SHEET

1. ME: Review/May to Oct., MEW 7:421-38; part of this article later entered into Part IV of M: Class Str. Fr., but most of this economic section was not included in that work.
2. M: Class Str. Fr., Part IV, in ME:SW 1:289.
3. E: Intro./Class Str. Fr., in ME:SW 1:188.
4. E: Revol. & C.R. Ger., in ME:SW 1:300.
5. E: Real Causes, art. 1, p. 848.
6. See *KMTR* 1, Ch. 18, esp. 447-58.

7. M: Class Str. Fr., in ME:SW 1:192.
8. Ibid., 280f.
9. Ibid., 280.
10. Ibid., 281f; the thought is repeated in 283, 285.
11. Ibid., 282.
12. For the Chartist usage, see *Notes to the People,* London, no. 22, Sept. 1851 (Vol. 1, p. 433); for Marx's articles, see M: Chartists, in ME: Art. Brit., 117f, and M: untitled article, N.Y. Tribune, 25 Nov. 1852.
13. For a brief explanation of the S.U.C.R. program, see Draper: *Marx and Dict. of Prole.,* 34-37.
14. Hess: *Phil. Soz. Schriften,* 448, 453.
15. ME: Review/Mar.-Apr., MEW 7:294.
16. M: Class Str. Fr., in ME:SW 1:283.
17. E: Intro./Class Str. Fr., in ME:SW 1:189.
18. Ibid., 190-91.
19. M: Class Str. Fr., in ME:SW 1:214.
20. E: Revol. & C.R. Ger., in ME:SW 1:327.
21. M: Class Str. Fr., in ME:SW 1:277; M: 18th Brum., in ME:SW 1:401 [MEW 8:118].
22. E: Revol. & C.R. Ger., in ME:SW 1:332.
23. Ibid., 380f.
24. Ibid., 379.
25. ME: Addr. Com. Lg./Mar., in ME:SW 1:175.
26. For example, ltr, M to Freiligrath, 20 Feb. 1860, MEW 30:489; M: Herr Vogt, MEW 14:439f.
27. ME: Addr. Com. Lg./Mar., in ME:SW 1:175, rev. after MEW 7:244.
28. Ibid., 176.
29. Ibid., 182, 185.
30. Ltr, E to Bebel, 6 June and 11 Dec. 1884; in ME:SC, 374, 381 (esp. the second).
31. ME: Addr. Com. Lg./Mar., in ME:SW 1:177, rev. after MEW 7:246.
32. Ibid., 178.
33. Ltr, M to E, 13 July 1851, MEW 27:278; the context is given in Special Note E, p. 606f.
34. ME: Addr. Com. Lg./Mar., MEW 7:246f, rev. from ME:SW 1:177f.
35. Same, in ME:SW 1:178f.
36. Ibid., 179f.
37. Ibid., 180.
38. Ibid., 181.
39. Ibid., 185.
40. It may be useful at this point to look back at this material, in *KMTR* 1, esp. Ch. 14, sec. 10, and Ch. 15, sec. 5-9.
41. ME: untitled article, N.Y. Tribune, 23 Dec. 1858 (ascribed in MEW to Engels only); this was cited in *KMTR* 1:408, with continuation in 1:451f.
42. M: Prussia, in N.Y. Tribune, 5 May 1856.
43. H.: *Karl Marx/Interview,* 15f.
44. M: Revel. Com. Trial/Postscr., MEW 8:575 or MEW 18:569f.
45. E: Workingmen of Eur., art. 1. See also his summary description of the 1848 leaders in E: Wilh. Wolff, MEW 19:63 (footnote on 1886 text).
46. E: M & NRZ, in ME:SW 3:165f.
47. Ltr, E to Ernst, 5 June 1890, in ME:SC, 413.
48. E: Abdic. Bourg., in ME: Art. Brit., 395.

49. Ibid., 396.
50. E: Crisis in Prussia, MEW 18:291.
51. M: New Engl. Budget, N.Y. Tribune, 9 Mar. 1857.
52. M: Eng. Middle Cl., N.Y. Tribune, 1 Aug. 1854.
53. M: Berlin Conspiracy, N.Y. Tribune, 21 Apr. 1853.
54. M: untitled article, N.Y. Tribune, 4 Apr. 1853.
55. See *KMTR* 1, Ch. 23 passim.
56. M: Revol. in Spain, I, in ME: Revol. Spain, 147.
57. Ltr, E to Weydemeyer, 12 Apr. 1853, in ME:SC, 77.
58. M: Speech at Anniv. Ger. Ed. Soc., MEW 16:524.
59. Ltr, Zasulich to Plekhanov, 1 Jan. 1895, MEW 39:540 (Ger. tr. from Russian).
60. Ltr, E to Kautsky, 8 Nov. 1884, MEW 36:230.
61. Ibid., 230f.
62. Ltr, E to Bebel, 11-12 Dec. 1884; this is partly cited above, Ch. 3, p. 60, ref. n. 22, and below, Ch. 13, p. 385f, both passages touching on the question under discussion.
63. Ltr, E to Kautsky, 20 Feb. 1889, MEW 37:155.
64. E: Intro./Class Str. Fr., in ME:SW 1:190f; cited above, this chap., p. 256.
65. Connolly: *Workshop Talks*, 6.
66. M: Chartists, in ME: Art. Brit., 118.
67. E: Soc. Utop. Sci./Intro., in ME:SW 3:105; the next paragraph continues the thought.
68. Bernstein: *Cromwell & Comm.*, 86f.
69. M: Riot at Constantinople &c., N.Y. Tribune, 6 May 1853.
70. Ltr, E to M, 17 July 1851, MEW 27:285.
71. Ltr, E to M, ca.20 July 1851, MEW 27:287.
72. Ibid., 288.
73. Ltr, E to M, 11 June 1863, MEW 30:353.
74. M: Chartists, in ME: Art. Brit., 118.
75. See above, Ch. 7, p. 182.
76. See *KMTR* 1, Ch. 18, esp. sec. 6.
77. See above, Ch. 7, sec. 4-5.
78. E: Pruss. Mil. Ques., MEW 16:67.
79. Ibid., 68-71 (for the last three paragraphs).
80. Ibid., 72-73.
81. Ibid., 73-75.
82. Ibid., 76.
83. See above, Ch. 7, p. 196.
84. For the quotations from 1850, see ME: Review/May to Oct., MEW 7:446 and 434 respectively. For the reference to the English Freetraders, see ltr, M to Freiligrath, 31 July 1849, MEW 27:504. For other aspects, see the discussion of "Can the Bourgeoisie Do It?" in *KMTR* 1, Ch. 14, p. 336-38.
85. E: Pruss. Mil. Ques., MEW 16:76f.
86. Ibid.
87. M: Herr Vogt, MEW 14:450.
88. Ibid., 449f. One inaccurate reference is to Part I of the Manifesto (on p. 449). On p. 450, the reference to the *N.R.Z.-Revue* about England should have been to M: Revol. Movemt. in the *N.R.Z.*
89. For Marx's citation from his Class Str. Fr., M: Herr Vogt, MEW 14:449f; for the comment, ibid., 450.
90. See *KMTR* 1:436f.

91. M: Elections T. & W., in ME: Art. Brit., 110.
92. M: Pov. Phil., in ME:CW 6:137.
93. ME: Com. Manif., in ME:CW 6:486-89.
94. See *KMTR* 1, Ch. 17, esp. sec. 3.
95. M: Cap. 1:760, 757, 756, 753f.
96. ME: Com. Manif., in ME:CW 6:492.
97. E: Intro./Class Str. Fr., in ME:SW 1:191f.
98. ME: Com. Manif., in ME:CW 6:493.

11. THE PETTY-BOURGEOISIE IN REVOLUTION

1. M: Theor. S. V. 2:492f; cf. also 460. For the role of polar classes in analysis, see *KMTR* 1:15.
2. E: Pruss. Mil. Ques., MEW 16:67.
3. E: True Soc., in ME:CW 5:540.
4. E: Status Quo in Ger., MEW 4:45, 47 [ME:CW 6:79, 82] ; the picture of the petty-bourgeoisie weaves through 44-48 [ME:CW 6:78-82].
5. This is made explicit in ltr, E to M, 23 Sept. 1852, MEW 28:139.
6. For example, *Mittelstand* (listed along with *Kleinbürger* etc.) in M: 18th Brum., MEW 8:121 [ME:SW 1:404].
7. M: Theor. S. V. 1:395f.
8. Ibid., 106, rev. after MEW 26.1:80.
9. E: Pruss. Mil. Ques., MEW 16:67.
10. E: Pref./Pov. Phil., in M: Pov. Phil. (FLPH), 13.
11. Ltr, M to E, 26 Sept. 1868, MEW 32:167.
12. Ltr, M to Annenkov, 28 Dec. 1846, in ME:SW 1:527.
13. M: Pov. Phil., in ME:CW 6:178; see also 190.
14. Ltr, M to Schweitzer, 24 Jan. 1865, in ME:SW 2:30.
15. Ltr, M to Cluss, 7 Dec. 1852, in ME: Ltrs to Amer., 52. The richest evidence of Proudhon's idealization of the petty-bourgeoisie is in his notebooks, now published as his *Carnets;* they were of course unknown to Marx.
16. Ltr, M to Weydemeyer, 5 Mar. 1852, in ME:SC, 69f.
17. Ltr, M to Schweitzer, 24 Jan. 1865, in ME:SW 2:26.
18. ME: Com. Manif., in ME:CW 6:513.
19. Ibid., 509-13.
20. E: Anti-Dühr. (59), 430; E: Housing Ques., in ME:SW 2:326.
21. E: Housing Ques./Pref., in ME:SW 2:298; the reference is to Proudhon's *L'Idée Générale de la Revolution au XIXe Siècle,* 1851.
22. E: Pruss. Mil. Ques., MEW 16:67.
23. Ltr, E to E. Blank, 28 Mar. 1848, MEW 27:476f.
24. E: Ger. Camp. Const., MEW 7:112.
25. M: 18th Brum., in ME:SW 1:426.
26. M: Class Str. Fr., in ME:SW 1:221.
27. E: Revol. & C. R. Ger., in ME:SW 1:304f.
28. Ibid., 373.
29. Ibid., 380; a typographical error has been corrected.
30. Ibid., 386.
31. Ibid., 380f.
32. This development was touched on in *KMTR* 1:266f; and see the account of the period in Massing: *Rehearsal for Destr.,* Ch. 2-3. Massing insists on the

primarily urban base of this petty-bourgeois movement (p. 75), but the swell among the peasantry is evident from p. 88-90, 95f; for another aspect, p. 101f; on the Junkers, 64-66.

33. Ltr, E to Ehrenfreund, 19 Apr. 1890, MEW 22:49f.
34. M: Class Str. Fr., in ME:SW 1:228.
35. Ltr, E to Sorge, 6 Jan. 1892, in ME:SC, 440f.
36. Ltr, E to Bebel, 24 Nov. 1879, MEW 34:425f.
37. Ltr, E to L. Lafargue, 2 Oct. 1886, in E & Lafargue: Corr. 1:377f; for the other citations, 374-78.
38. E: Housing Ques./Pref., in ME:SW 2:298.
39. ME: Review/Daumer, MEW 7:203.
40. See above, Ch. 9, sec. 1-3.
41. E: French Work. Cl., MEW 6:560.
42. Ibid., 561.
43. See above, Ch. 10, sec. 5 (point 2).
44. E: Pruss. Mil. Ques., MEW 16:67f.
45. E: Ger. Soc. Dem., in *Newcastle Daily Chronicle*, 3 Mar. 1890 [MEW 22:5].
46. E: M & NRZ, in ME:SW 3:169.
47. Ltr, E to Bernstein, 24 Mar. 1884, MEW 36:128.
47a. But cf. Engels' attribution of the idea to Bakunin, in ltr, E to Sorge, 26 July 1873, MEW 33:598.
48. M: Crit. Gotha Prog., in ME:SW 3:21.
49. Same, in ME:SW 3:20.
50. Same, MEW 19:23, revised from ME:SW 3:20.
51. ME: Com. Manif., MEW 4:472, rev. from ME:CW 6:494.
52. Ltr, E to Bebel, 18-28 Mar. 1875, in ME:SC, 291.
53. Ibid.
54. M: Civil War Fr., in ME:SW 2:222, 224-26, 231, 233; also in the first draft of this work, in ME: Writings Par. Com., 139f, 155-60. Engels' introduction to this work does not mention this aspect. The issue will be discussed in Volume 4 with regard to the Commune state.
55. Ltr, E to Bebel, 18-28 Mar. 1875, in ME:SC, 291; this continues the passage indicated by ref. n. 53.
56. Ltr, E to Bebel, 28 Oct. 1882, in ME:SC, 354. For another passage in which the question is clearly put in terms of *parties*, see ltr, E to P. Lafargue, 19 May 1892, in E & Lafargue: Corr. 3:174.
57. Ltr, E to Kautsky, 14 Oct. 1891, in ME:SC, 432f.
58. Ibid., 433.
59. Ltr, E to P. Lafargue, 22 Jan. 1895, in E & Lafargue: Corr. (Fr.) 3:394 (English ed., 3:363).
60. E: Intro./Class Str. Fr., in ME:SW 1:198.

12. THE PEASANT QUESTION: SOCIAL SETTING

1. Mitrany: *M. Against Peasant*, 4-25 passim. I reviewed some of Mitrany's more ignorant statements in *Labor Action* (N.Y.), 11 Aug. 1952.
2. For Marx's agrarian theory, see, among other sources, M: Cap. 1:504-07, 673-712; Cap. 3:600-793 (Part VI); Theor. S.V. 2, Ch. 8-9, 11-14; and E: Anti-Dühr., 307-11. There is a considerable literature, for example, Kautsky: *Agrarfrage*; Cohnstaedt: *Agrarfrage in deut. S.D.*; Mandel: *Marxist Econ. Theory*, Ch. 9.

3. M: Cap. 1:761f.
4. M: Class Str. Fr., in ME:SW 1:275.
5. Prof. N. Rosenberg, review in *Political Science Quarterly*, Dec. 1952.
6. M: Cap. 3:792.
7. Ibid., 792f.
8. Ibid., 793.
9. M: Econ. Phil. Mss., in ME:CW 3:268.
10. See below, this chap., p. 329.
11. M: Cap. 3:119, rev. after MEW 25:131.
12. M: Econ. Phil. Mss., in ME:CW 3:264.
13. M: On F. List's Book, in ME:CW 4:289.
14. M: Cap. 3:786f.
15. ME: Ger. Ideol., in ME:CW 5:353f.
16. M: Cap. 1:761.
17. E: Mark, in E: Peasant War Ger. (56), 178.
18. M: Cap. 3:787; a more detailed analysis continues to the end of the chapter.
19. E: Peasant Ques., MEW 22:486 [ME:SW 3:458].
20. M: Wage-Labor & Cap., MEW 6:398 (see textual footnote); the tr. in ME:SW 1:151 is garbled in other ways besides making *Untergang* "destruction."
21. M: Cap. 1 in MEW 23:528; translations, including M: Cap. 1:505, omit the quote-marks without making any adjustment.
22. See, for example, E: Housing Ques./Pref., in ME:SW 2:302 [MEW 21:332]; E: Role of Force, in ME:SW 3:417 [MEW 21:450].
23. Cf. Mandel: *Marxist Econ. Theory*, 1:290-93.
24. Mitrany: *Amer. Interp.*, 5.
25. E: Lawyers' Soc., MEW 21:496f.
26. M: Inaug. Addr., in ME:SW 2:14.
27. ME: Ger. Ideol., in ME:CW 5:353.
28. M: Cap. 2:133.
28a. M: Thiers's Speech, in N.R.Z., 14 Oct. 1848, MEW 5:424.
29. M: Billion, MEW 6:355.
30. M: Class Str. Fr., in ME:SW 1:276.
31. E: Revol. & C.R. Ger., in ME:SW 1:306.
32. This phrase is from E: Mark, in E: Peasant War Ger. (56), 162.
33. E: Stock Exchange, in M: Cap. 3:885.
34. Cf. E: Peasant War Ger./Pref., in ME:SW 2:164; E: Housing Ques., in ME:SW 2:330; E: Workingmen of Eur., art. 4.
35. M: untitled article, in N.Y. Tribune, 12 Mar. 1858.
36. Session of 6 July 1869, in *G.C.F.I.* 68-70 [3], 123; see also the remarks of Jung on the preceding page.
37. M: Civil War Fr., 1st Draft, in ME: Writings Par. Com., 158.
38. M: Nationalization of Land, in *Labour Mo.*, 416f.
39. The phrases quoted are from M: Cap. 3:786f, quoted above, p. 323.
40. M: Civil War Fr., 1st Draft, in ME: Writings Par. Com., 158.
41. M: Cap. 3:635.
42. M: Econ. Phil. Mss., in ME:CW 3:264, 266.
43. M: 18th Brum., in ME:SW 1:481.
44. M: Cap. 3:853; the passage is quoted below, p. 336.
45. M: Grundrisse, 850.
46. M: Class Str. Fr., in ME:SW 1:276.
47. M: Cap. 1:505.

48. E: Peasant Ques., in ME:SW 3:460.
49. Ibid., 463.
50. M: Cap. 1:505.
51. Ltr, E to M, 1 Nov. 1869, in ME:SC, 224.
52. E: Peasant Ques., in ME:SW 3:459.
53. Ibid., 473.
54. M: Cap. 3:779.
55. See above, Ch. 11, p. 289. Engels makes the parallel explicit in E: Peasant Ques., in ME:SW 3:473.
56. E: Peasant Ques., in ME:SW 3:473.
57. E: Revol. & C.R. Ger., in ME:SW 1:306.
58. Ltr, E to M, 1 Nov. 1869, in ME:SC, 224.
59. See above, Ch. 11, p. 291, and this chapter, p. 331f.
60. M: Cap. 3:853.
61. Ltr, E to M, 1 Nov. 1869, in ME:SC, 224.
62. E: Cond. Wkg. Cl. Eng., in ME:CW 4:551f.
63. E: Status Quo in Ger., MEW 4:48 [ME:CW 6:83].
64. Slicher van Bath: *Agrar. Hist.*, 194.
65. Künzli: *K. Marx*, 68.
66. See *KMTR* 1, Ch. 2, esp. p. 75.
67. E: Herr Tidmann, MEW 16:34.
68. E: Peasant Ques., in ME:SW 3:457.
69. Mitrany: *M. Against Peas.*, 5.
70. The reference here is to the title of the book by Aimé Berthod, *P. J. Proudhon et la Propriété; un socialisme pour les paysans* (Paris, 1910).
71. The reference is to the 24 volumes of Proudhon's *Oeuvres Complètes* (Paris, 1867-69) plus the eight volumes of his *Oeuvres Posthumes* (Paris, 1866-75). Since no one now alive has read Proudhon's complete writings, I specify that I examined the detailed tables of contents of each volume, for any suggestion that it might contain writings devoted to peasant problems as such.
72. E: From Paris to Bern, MEW 5:471.
73. Ibid.
74. Ibid., 472.
75. Ibid., 473.
76. Ibid., 474.
77. Ibid., 475.
78. Ibid., 465.
79. Ibid., 475.
80. Ibid., 469f.
81. H. Paul: *Deutsche Wörterbuch* (Halle, 1960); F. Kluge: *Etymologisches Wörterbuch* (Berlin, 1957); A. J. Storfer: *Wörter und ihre Schicksale* (Berlin, 1935); P. F. Ganz: *Der Einfluss des Englischen auf den Deutschen Wortschatz 1640-1815* (Berlin, 1957); *Der Grosse Duden*, Bd. 17: *Etymologie* (Mannheim, 1963).
82. *Red Republican*, 9 Nov. 1850, p. 162.
83. In ME: Com. Manif./Ryazanoff, 31.
84. ME: Com. Manif., in ME:CW 6:488; cf. MEW 4:466.
85. M: Class Str. Fr., in ME:SW 1:237.
86. Cf. M: Cap. 3:793; ltr, E to M, 16 Dec. 1851, MEW 27:392; for another critical reference to the French peasantry (conditioned by the peasants' role as voting cattle for Bonaparte), ltr, M to E, 19 Oct. 1851, MEW 27:365.

87. ME: Ger. Ideol., in ME:CW 5:64 [MEW 3:50].
88. M: Cap. 1:361.
89. E: Housing Ques., in ME:SW 2:368.
90. E: Cond. Eng./18th Cent., in ME: Art. Brit., 19f [another tr. in ME:CW 3:478].
91. E: Cond. Wkg. Cl. Eng., in ME:CW 4:308f.
92. M: Crit. Heg. Ph. Rt./Ms., MEW 1:299 [ME:CW 3:94].
93. ME: Ger. Ideol., in ME:CW 5:66, 354 [MEW 3:52, 338].
94. Cf. E: Peasant War Ger. (56), 52; E: Revol. & C.R. Ger., in ME:SW 1:307; ltr, E to Bernstein, 30 Nov. 1881, MEW 35:237; E: Future Ital. Rev., in ME:SW 3:454; E: Peasant Ques., in ME:SW 3:457.
95. E: Switzerland, in N.Y. Tribune, 17 May 1853.
96. M: 18th Brum., in ME:SW 1:478f.
97. See, for example, E: Peasant Ques., in ME:SW 3:458, on landowners as "false protectors" of peasants' interests.
98. M: 18th Brum., in ME:SW 1:479.
99. See above, Ch. 2, p. 41 and fn.
100. E: Revol. & C.R. Ger., in ME:SW 1:318.
101. M: 18th Brum., in ME:SW 1:479; cf. MEW 8:198; *Convention* refers to the French National Convention of 1792-95.
102. E: Status Quo in Ger., MEW 4:48f [ME:CW 6:83].
103. E: Commun. & K. Heinzen, MEW 4:313 [ME:CW 6:295].
104. At this point the text in MEGA I, 6:394 has *noch* rather than *nicht:* ". . . profit the bourgeoisie still more than themselves." But in this context the negative makes no decisive difference.
105. E: Movemts. of 1847, MEW 4:499 [ME:CW 6:525].
106. E: Revol. & C.R. Ger., in ME:SW 1:307.
107. M: Class Str. Fr., in ME:SW 1:288f.
108. E: Mark, in E: Peasant War Ger. (56), 178; and in general throughout E: Peasant War Ger.
109. M: 18th Brum., in ME:SW 1:479.
110. Ibid., 482.
111. E: Foreign Pol. Russ. Cz., MEW 22:21 (for the sentence quoted, which is omitted from the *Time* version), and 20 (on Catherine).
112. Ltr, M to E, 14 June 1853, in ME:SC, 85.
113. M: Brit. Rule in Ind., in ME:SW 1:491.
114. M: Future Res. Rule, in ME:SW 1:494, 496.
115. Ltr, M to E, 14 June 1853, MEW 28:268 [ME:SC, 86]; cf. *KMTR* 1:527.
116. M: Brit. Rule in Ind., in ME:SW 1:492.
117. M: Ltr to Zasulich 8 Mar. 1881, 1st Draft, in M-E Archiv, 1:323f [ME:SW 3:157]; cf. *KMTR* 1:555.
118. E: On Social Rel. Russ., in ME:SW 2:394; for other statements along the same line, see *KMTR* 1:555f; about Java, ibid., 1:558-60. Also cf. Kautsky's article quoted in *KMTR* 1:662.
119. E: Peasant Ques., in ME:SW 3:457.
120. E: What Have Wkg. Cl., in ME: Russ. Men., 103.
121. M. I. Finkelstein: bk. rev. in *Studies in Philosophy and Social Science* (N.Y.), Vol. 9, no. 3, 1941, p. 507f.
122. Drennan: *B.U.F.*, 199.
123. This subject will be treated in a later volume; see Draper: *M. & E. on Women's Lib.*, 91f.
124. ME: Alliance S.D., 117.

125. Ibid., 112 fn.
126. On Bakunin and the peasantry, see Pyziur: *Doctrine Anarch. Bak.*, 61, 66, 72, 75, these pages esp. Cf. Bakunin on lumpen-class, below, Ch. 15, sec. 4; and on intellectuals, below, Ch. 18, sec. 6.
127. ME: Alliance S.D., 118. On Richard and Blanc's Bonapartism, see 49f; also ME: Alleged Schisms, in ME:SW 2:283-85; and incidental mention in ltr, E to Cuno, 24 Jan. 1872, in ME:SW 2:429, and in E: Freedom of Assembly, in ME: Scritti Ital., 93.
128. M: Conspectus of Bak., MEW 18:633.
129. See above, Ch. 3, sec. 8, p.78.

13. THE PEASANT QUESTION:
TOWARD A REVOLUTIONARY ALLIANCE

1. E: Peasant Ques., in ME:SW 3:459.
2. Ibid., 473.
3. Ibid., 474f.
4. Ibid., 475f.
5. E: Peasant War Ger./Pref., in ME:SW 2:164.
6. E: Cond. Wkg. Cl. Eng., in ME:CW 3:552f, 555f.
7. M: Defense—Finances &c., in N.Y. Tribune, 23 Feb. 1853.
8. Ltr, M to E, 10 Dec. 1869, MEW 32:416.
9. E: Strike Eng. Farm Workers, in ME: Art. Brit., 361 [ME: Scritti Ital., 107].
10. E: Pruss. Mil. Ques., MEW 16:74. Over three years later, E cited this passage in an "I told you so" article, E: On Dissolution Lass. W.A., MEW 16:327f.
11. M: Moralizing Crit., MEW 4:341 [ME:CW 6:322].
12. E: Peasant Ques., in ME:SW 3:459.
13. Ltr, E to M, 1 Nov. 1869, in ME:SC, 224.
14. Ltr, E to Cafiero, 1-3 July 1871, in ME: Corrisp. con Ital., 23 [MEW 33:659]; E's exact wording is uncertain—see note, MEW 33:654.
15. E: Peasant Ques., in ME:SW 3:465.
16. E: Housing Ques., in ME:SW 2:372.
17. Ltr, E to Bernstein, 9 Aug. 1882, MEW 35:349.
18. E: Peasant Ques., in ME:SW 3:457; likewise in E: Role of Force, in ME:SW 3:417.
19. E: Peasant Ques., in ME:SW 3:457.
20. Ibid., 458f.
21. The passages in the Manifesto mentioning the peasantry in some way occur in ME:CW 6:488, 491, 494, 498, 509.
22. Ltr, E to M, 14 Jan. 1848, MEW 27:109.
23. ME: Demands of C.P. Ger., MEW 5:4.
24. Ltr, E to Blank, 28 Mar. 1848, MEW 27:477.
25. E: On Hist. Pruss. Peas., MEW 21:245.
26. M/E: Patow's Memo, MEW 5:106f.
27. M: Bill on Abol. Feud., in N.R.Z., 30 July 1848, MEW 5:279-81.
28. Ibid., 282.
29. M: Bourg. & Counterrev., MEW 6:121; see above, Ch. 9, p.233.
30. M: K.M. Bef. Cologne Jury, MEW 6:251.
31. Ltr, M to E, 27 July 1854, in ME:SC, 87f.

32. M: Bill on Abol. Feud., MEW 5:283.
33. E: Debate on Redemp. Leg., MEW 5:311.
34. Ibid., 312.
35. E: Concil. Debates on Reg. Est.-Assy., MEW 5:272.
36. E: Debate on Redemp. Leg., MEW 5:312.
37. Becker: *K.M. & F.E. in Köln*, 122-25.
38. Hammen: *Red 48ers*, 260, 267.
39. Ibid., 267. There is a compact summary of the N.R.Z. group's peasant work in Hammen: *M & Agrar. Ques.*, 688-94, in this author's usual depreciatory style.
40. Hammen: *Red 48ers*, 267f.
41. Becker: *K.M. & F.E. in Köln*, 128.
42. Hammen: *M & Agrar. Ques.*, 689.
43. Becker: *K.M. & F.E. in Köln*, 127.
44. Ibid., 129.
45. Ibid., 130, quoting the issue of 7 Sept.; also see Hammen: *Red 48ers*, 260, 295.
46. Hammen: *Red 48ers*, 319.
47. Becker: *K.M. & F.E. in Köln*, 131f.
48. Hammen: *Red 48ers*, 295.
49. Becker: *K.M. & F.E. in Köln*, 133; Hammen: *Red 48ers*, 284.
50. Hammen: *Red 48ers*, 301.
51. Becker: *K.M. & F.E. in Köln*, 125-28; Hammen: *Red 48ers*, 301f.
52. Becker: *K.M. & F.E. in Köln*, 127-28 fn.
53. Hammen: *Red 48ers*, 303.
54. E: Uprising in Frankf., MEW 5:410.
55. Ibid., 411f.
56. Becker: *K.M. & F.E. in Köln*, 133f; Hammen: *Red 48ers*, 306f.
57. Hammen: *Red 48ers*, 319; and cf. Becker: *K.M. & F.E. in Köln*, 130.
58. For example, see appeal for a proletarian-peasant-petty-bourgeois bloc, in M: Köln. Ztg. on Elec., MEW 6:217, qu. in Ch. 9, p. 240.
59. E: On Hist. Pruss. Peas., in E: Peasant War Ger. (56), 193.
60. E: Wilh. Wolff, MEW 19:62f.
61. M: Billion, MEW 6:355.
62. Hammen: *Red 48ers*, 376.
63. E: Wilh. Wolff, MEW 19:67; Hammen: *Red 48ers*, 377; see also E: M & NRZ, in ME:SW 3:170f.
64. Ltr, M to Weydemeyer, 31 Oct. 1851, MEW 27:583.
65. E: Wilh. Wolff, MEW 19:63-81.
66. Ibid., 88.
67. E: Peasant Ques., in ME:SW 3:469.
68. Ibid., 457.
69. Ibid., 460.
70. Ibid., 458.
71. Ibid., 468.
72. E: Intro./Class Str. Fr., in ME:SW 1:200.
73. E: Ger. Camp. Const., MEW 7:134; cf. Hammen: *Red 48ers*, 400.
74. Ibid., 112; qu. in Ch. 9, p. 240, ref. n. 30.
75. E: Revol. & C.R. Ger., in ME:SW 1:379f; cf. also 306f.
76. ME: Addr. Com. Lg./Mar., in ME:SW 1:177f.
77. Ibid., 182f.
78. ME: Addr. Com. Lg./June, MEW 7:310.

79. E: Peasant War Ger. (56), 37, 155.
80. M: Crit. Heg. Ph. Rt./Intro., MEW 1:386 [ME:CW 3:182]; for remarks on the context, see *KMTR* 1, Ch. 6, sec. 5, esp. p. 141.
81. E: Progress Soc. Ref., in ME:CW 3:401; cf. also E: Cond. Eng./18th Cent., in ME:CW 3:474, and E: State of Ger., II, in ME:CW 6:27.
82. Ltr, M to E, 16 Apr. 1856, MEW 29:47 {ME:SC, 92].
83. Ltr, M to Lassalle, 19 Apr. 1859, in ME:SC, 116.
84. Ltr, E to Lassalle, 18 May 1859, in ME:SC, 119f.
85. For this theory, see above, Ch. 11, sec. 9.
86. Ltr, E to M, 5 Feb. 1865, MEW 31:55.
87. M: untitled article, N.Y. Tribune, 19 Oct. 1858.
88. M: Berlin Conspiracy, N.Y. Tribune, 21 Apr. 1853 (article misdated in ME: Cologne Com. Trial, 274).
89. Ltr, E to Kautsky, 8 Nov. 1884, MEW 36:230f.
90. Ltr, E to Bebel, 11 Dec. 1884, in ME:SC, 379f [MEW 36:251]. For a similar thought, not expressed in terms of the agrarian problem, see Zasulich's report of a conversation with Engels, MEW 39:540.
91. E: Housing Ques./Pref., in ME:SW 2:302f.
92. Ibid., 303.
93. Ibid., 304.
94. E: Peasant War Ger./Pref., in ME:SW 2:163.
95. Ibid., 164.
96. E: Mark, in E: Peasant War Ger. (56), 181; note also the 1883 addition, ibid.
97. E: Intro./Class Str. Fr., in ME:SW 1:201.
98. E: Peasant Ques., in ME:SW 3:457f.
99. E: Real Causes, in *Notes to the People*, 27 Mar. 1852, p. 949.
100. M: Class Str. Fr., in ME:SW 1:236f.
101. ME: Review/Jan.-Feb. '50, MEW 7:218.
102. M: Class Str. Fr., in ME:SW 1:241.
103. Ibid., 276f.
104. See *KMTR* 1, Ch. 18, sec. 6, 8.
105. Ltr, M to E, 19 Dec. 1868, MEW 32:238.
106. M: 18th Brum., in ME:SW 1:479f.
107. Ibid., 484.
108. Ibid., 484 fn.
109. Ibid., 482.
110. M: War Ques.—Brit. &c, in N.Y. Tribune, 24 Aug. 1853; and M: Russian Victory, in N.Y. Tribune, 27 Dec. 1853.
111. M: untitled article, N.Y. Tribune, 22 Nov. 1856.
112. E: Conditions & Prosp. for War, MEW 7:483.
113. Ibid., 488-91; the qu. is on 491.
114. M: Civil War Fr., in ME:SW 2:226.
115. M: Civil War Fr., 1st Draft, in ME: Writings Par. Com., 157f.
116. M: Notebk. Par. Com./Apr.-May, in *Arkhiv M-E*, 224.
117. The text of the manifesto is in Lanjalley & Corriez: *Hist. de la Rév.*, 248-50. Cf. also S. Bernstein: *Paris Com.*, 137.
118. Freymond, ed.: *Prem. Intle.*, 2:215.
119. Ibid., 216.
120. *G.C.F.I.* 70-71 [4], 443.
121. Freymond, ed.: *Prem. Intle.*, 2:217.
122. E: Workingmen of Eur., article 4.

123. Ltr, E to P. Lafargue, 13 Jan. 1895, in E & Lafargue: Corr. 3:355f.
124. E: Future Ital. Rev., in ME:SW 3:453f.
125. E: Position of Dan. Int., in *G.C.F.I.* 71-72 [5] , 291f.
126. Ltr, E to Pio, mid-Mar. 1872, in *Neue Zeit,* 1921, 1. Bd., no. 23, p.549; for date, MEW 33:428.
127. E: Workingmen of Eur., article 3; but see the discussion of the Danish peasant plan in Ch. 14, sec. 2, p. 415f.
128. M: Spain—Interv., in MEW 10:632f (retrans. from Ger.).
129. Ltr, M to E, 30 Nov. 1867, in ME:SC, 196.
130. Ltr, M to Kugelmann, 6 Apr. 1868, MEW 32:543. (ME:SC, 203, ruins the harmless pun.)
131. M: Record of Sp. Irish Ques. (as reported in an article by Eccarius), in ME: Ire. & Ir. Ques., 142 [MEW 16:552].
132. Ltr, M to Kugelmann, 29 Nov. 1869, in ME:SC, 230.
133. Ltr, E to M, 29 Nov. 1869, MEW 32:406.
134. M: Gen. Council to F.C. of Rom. Switz., in ME:SW 2:175 or in *G.C.F.I.* 68-70 [3], 403.
135. Ltr, M to Meyer & Vogt, 9 Apr. 1870, in ME:SC, 236.
136. Ibid., 235.
137. Ltr, M to E, 10 Dec. 1869, in ME:SC, 232 [MEW 32:414f] .
138. Ltr, M to Swinton, 4 Nov. 1880, in ME: Ire. & Ir. Ques., 325.
139. Ltr, M to E, 4 Dec. 1869, in ME: Ire. & Ir. Ques., 282 [MEW 32:408] .
140. Ltr, E to M, 9 Dec. 1869, in ME:SC, 231.
141. Ltr, E to Bernstein, 26 June 1882, MEW 35:337.
142. Ltr, E to M, 9 Dec. 1869, in ME:SC, 231.
143. Ltr, E to M, 23 May 1851, MEW 27:266.
144. M: Emanc. Ques., N.Y. Tribune, 17 Jan. 1859.
145. Ltr, E to M, 8 Apr. 1863, MEW 30:337.
146. Ltr, M to E, 1 Feb. 1865, MEW 31:50.
147. Ltr, E to M, 11 June 1863, MEW 30:354.
148. E: On Soc. Rel. Russ./Pref., MEW 18:586.
149. For Tkachov, see also *KMTR* 1:583-85.
150. E: On Soc. Rel. Russ., in ME:SW 2:390, 397f.
151. On this, see also E: Workingmen of Eur., article 5, written three years later.
152. Ltr, E to Faerber, 22 Oct. 1885, MEW 36:374.
153. E: On Soc. Rel. Russ./Afterword, in ME:SW 2:408, 409f.
154. Ltr, M to Liebknecht, 4 Feb. 1878, MEW 34:317.
155. Ltr, E to Bracke, 25 June 1877, MEW 34:279f; E: Foreign Pol. Russ. Cz., in ME: Russ. Men., 38.

14. THE PEASANT QUESTION:
PROGRAMMATIC PROBLEMS

1. M: Econ. Phil. Mss., in ME:CW 3:268.
2. ME: Com. Manif., in ME:CW 6:505; for the original, MEW 4:481.
3. M: Nationalization of Land, 416.
3a. Ltr, M to E, 14 Aug. 1851, MEW 27:314.
4. Ltr, M to E, 30 Oct. 1869, in ME:SC, 223 [MEW 32:380] .
5. *G.C.F.I.* 68-70 [3], 122.
6. Cf. Harrison: *Land & Labour League,* 171; Collins & Abramsky: *K.M. & Brit. Lab. Movemt.,* 164f.

7. Ltr, M to E, 30 Oct. 1869, MEW 32:381 [ME:SC, 223].
8. *G.Ç.F.I.* 68-70 [3], 123.
9. Ltr, E to M, 1 Nov. 1869, MEW 32:382 [ME:SC, 224].
10. E: Peasant War Ger./Pref., in ME:SW 2:164f.
11. Ltr, M to Lafargue, 19 Apr. 1870, in ME: Anarch. & A.S., 45 [M: Lettres et Doc., 174].
12. In ME:CW 6:505 (point no. 3).
13. Cf. above, Ch. 13, p. 381.
14. M: Conspectus of Bak., MEW 18:630-33 (no text on 631-32). For the same idea, see also E: Housing Ques., in ME:SW 2:372.
15. M: Nationalization of Land, 416f.
16. Ibid., 415, 417.
17. For example, see ltr, M to Sorge, 20 June 1881, in ME:SC, 342f.
18. M: Nationalization of Land, 417.
19. Freymond, ed.: *Prem. Intle.*, 1:379; ibid. for De Paepe's remarks in the Congress minutes; Marx's citation of De Paepe is in M: Nationalization of Land, 417.
20. E: Peasant Ques., in ME:SW 3:460f.
21. Ibid., 474.
22. See above, Ch. 13, p. 380f.
23. E: Peasant War Ger./Pref., in ME:SW 2:164.
24. Ltr, E to Meyer, 19 July 1893, MEW 39:103.
25. E: Peasant Ques., in ME:SW 3:469, 472, 473; see also below, p. 445.
26. E: On Anti-Sem. (ltr to Ehrenfreund, 19 Apr. 1890), MEW 22:49f.
27. Ltr, E to Bebel, 11/12 Dec. 1884, MEW 36:253f.
28. E: Peasant Ques., in ME:SW 3:474.
29. Ibid., 470f.
30. E: Amer. Food, in E: Articles fr. Lab. Standard, 30.
31. E: Mark (1883 add.), in E: Peasant War Ger.(56), 181 fn. See also ltr, E to Lafargue, 23 or 24 Aug. 1894, in E/Lafargue: Corr. 3:341; and E: Housing Ques., in ME:SW 2:372f, where the Danes' plans are mentioned as models.
32. M: Ltr. to Zasulich, 1st Draft, in ME:SW 3:157.
33. M: Civil War Fr., 1st Draft, in ME: Writings Par. Com., 157f.
34. Ltr, E to M, 1 Nov. 1869, in ME:SC, 224.
35. E: Peasant Ques., in ME:SW 3:469f.
36. For the Danish plan, see above, this chapter, p. 415f.
37. E: Peasant Ques., in ME:SW 3:471.
38. Ltr, E to Kautsky, 22 Nov. 1894, MEW 39:322. For another indication of this position, see the qu. cited below, this chapter, p. 439.
39. E: Peasant Ques., in ME:SW 3:474.
40. E: Housing Ques., in ME:SW 2:373.
41. E: Peasant Ques., in ME:SW 3:463.
42. On Kriege, besides ME: Circular Ag. Kriege (all), see: Schlüter: *Anfänge*, esp. 19-41; Wittke: *Refugees of Rev.*, 68; Wittke: *Utop. Comm.*, 102f, 115-20, 131, 160f; Kamman: *Soc. in Ger. Am. Lit.*, 20f, 36f; Weitling: *Guarantien*, pref. to 3d ed., 298f; and E: On Hist. C.L., in ME:SW 3:180f.
43. ME: Circular Ag. Kriege, MEW 4:8.
44. Ibid., 9f.
45. Ibid., 10.
46. ME: Com. Manif., MEW 4:492, rev. from ME:CW 6:518 (where the translation is so free as to be misleading).
47. M: Grundrisse, 473.
48. Ltr, M to E, 25 July 1877, MEW 34:59.

49. Beer: *Hist. Brit. Soc.*, 2:155f.
50. E: Agrar. Prog. Chart., MEGA I, 6:333 [ME:CW 6:358].
51. Schoyen: *Chart. Chall.*, 149.
52. E: Agrar. Prog. Chart., MEGA I, 6:333 [ME:CW 6:358].
53. Ltr, E to M, 25/26 Oct. 1847, MEW 27:98f.
54. Ltr, E to M, 14/15 Nov. 1847, MEW 27:102; the expression must refer to the land plan.
55. "Political and Social Review," *Kommunistische Zeitschrift*, in Grünberg, ed.: *Londoner Kom Zeitschr.*, 72-74.
56. ME: Review/May to Oct. [1850], MEW 7:445f.
57. Cf. Lenin on the Kriege case in "Marx on the American 'General Distribution,' " 1905, in his *Coll Wks.*, 8:323 et seq.
58. M: Vindication Moselle Corr., MEW 1:187f [ME:CW 1:346f]; see Cornu: *K.M. et F.E.*, 2:78f.
59. Cf. *KMTR* 1:79.
60. E: E. M. Arndt, MEW Eb.2:128 [ME:CW 2:147].
61. See above, Ch. 13, p. 396.
62. Ltr, E to Bovio, 16 Apr. 1872, in ME: Corrisp. con Ital., 177. This is part of a paragraph stricken from the letter as sent, but the reason appears to be that Engels decided not to go into this subject with his correspondent.
63. For Marx on Mazzini, see *KMTR* 1, Special Note C.
64. Ltr, M to Weydemeyer, 11 Sept. 1851, MEW 27:579.
65. Ibid.
66. Ltr, M to E, 13 Sept. 1851, in ME:SC, 59.
67. Ltr, E to M, 23 Sept. 1851, in ME:SC, 60.
68. M: untitled article, N.Y. Tribune, 4 Apr. 1853.
69. M: Cap. 1:765.
70. Ltr, E to Martignetti, 30 Mar. 1890, MEW 37:371.
71. For the words quoted, see above, Ch. 13 p. 399, ref, n. 134.
72. E: Interview N.Y. Volksztg., MEW 21:511f.
73. ME: Com. Manif., in ME:CW 6:518.
74. M: Speech on Poland 22 Feb. 1848, in MEGA I, 6:410f [ME:CW 6:549].
75. Ibid., 411 [ME:CW 6:549].
76. E: Speech on Poland 22 Feb. 1848, in MEGA I, 6:412f [ME:CW 6:550f].
77. E: Debate on Pol. in Fr., MEW 5:333.
78. Ibid., 345-46.
79. Ibid., 357.
80. E: Polish Proc., MEW 18:524, 526.
81. M: Ltr to Zasulich 8 Mar. 1881, 3d Draft, in *M-E Archiv*, 1:338f.
82. Ibid., 339f. (MEW 19:406 does not include the strike-outs.)
83. This echoes the passage cited from Engels above, p. 431.
84. M: Civil War Fr., 1st Draft, in ME: Writings Par. Com., 155f; for the final version, see ibid., 78-80, or ME:SW 2:225f.
85. Same, 1st Draft, in ME: Writings Par. Com., 157f; final version, in ME:SW 2:223.
86. *Boons*, instead of *loans*, is the reading suggested in the edited version in the Marx-Engels collection *On the Paris Commune* (Moscow, 1971), p. 160; although this edition is unreliable because it rewrites Marx's ms., I take this to be a new decipherment of Marx's handwriting.
87. M: Civil War Fr., 1st Draft, in ME: Writings Par. Com., 158.
88. M: Conspectus of Bak., MEW 18:633.
89. E: Peasant Ques., in ME:SW 3:460, 461, 469.

90. For Germany, see Hesselbarth: *Revol. S.D.*; for France, see Willard: *Guesdistes*, Ch. 18, and Landauer: *Guesdists & Sm. Farm.*
91. Ltr, E to Lafargue, 22 Nov. 1894, in E & Lafargue: Corr. 3:343.
92. Ltr, Lafargue to E, 5 Sept. 1893, in E & Lafargue: Corr. 3:290.
93. Ltr, Lafargue to E, 10 Oct. 1893, in ibid., 295f.
94. E: Peasant Ques., in ME:SW 3:461.
95. This was Charles Bonnier, for whom see Landauer: *Guesdists & Sm. Farm.*
96. Ltr, E to L. Lafargue, 17 Dec. 1894, in E & Lafargue: Corr. 3:349.
97. This is the theme of the article by Landauer: *Guesdists & Sm. Farm.*
98. Ltr, E to Lafargue, 22 Nov. 1894, in E & Lafargue: Corr. 3:344.
99. E: Ltr to Ed. Bd. Vorwärts, 12 Nov. 1894, MEW 22:480.
100. E: Peasant Ques., in ME:SW 3:471-72.
101. See above, Ch. 13, sec. 1.
102. E: Peasant Ques., in ME:SW 3:460.
103. Qu. in E: Peasant Ques., in ME:SW 3:464.
104. Qu. in ibid., 465. (The whole preamble is qu. on 462.)
105. Ibid., 467.
106. Ltr, E to Sorge, 10 Nov. 1894, in ME:SC, 476.
107. Ltr, E to Sorge, 4 Dec. 1894, MEW 39:334f; cf. also ltr, E to Lafargue, 22 Nov. 1894, in E & Lafargue: Corr. 3:343f.
108. Ltr, E to Lafargue, 22 Nov. 1894, in E & Lafargue: Corr. 3:343.
109. E: Peasant Ques., in ME:SW 3:462.
110. Ibid., 464.
111. Ibid., 469, 472, 473.
112. Ibid., 464, 463, 469, 473. See also ltr, E to Sorge, 10 Nov. 1894, in ME:SC, 475f; and ltr, E to Lafargue, 23 or 24 Aug. 1894, in E & Lafargue: Corr. 3:341.
113. E: Peasant Ques., in ME:SW 3:466f.
114. Ibid., 468.
115. Ibid., 467.
116. Ibid.
117. Ltr, E to Gorbunova, 5 Aug. 1880, MEW 34:452.
118. E: Peasant Ques., in ME:SW 3:468.
119. Ltr, E to Lafargue, 6 Mar. 1894, in E & Lafargue: Corr. 3:324, rev. after French edition, 3:353.
120. Ltr, E to L. Lafargue, 11 Apr. 1894, in E & Lafargue: Corr. 3:329. There is an allusion to this in E: Peasant Ques., in ME:SW 3:465.
121. Ltr, E to Lafargue, 6 Mar. 1894, in E & Lafargue: Corr. 3:324.
122. Goldberg: *Jaurès & Formul.*, 376.
123. Ibid., 388.
124. E: Peasant Ques., in ME:SW 3:461.
125. Ibid., 471.
126. Ibid., 465f.
127. Ibid., 469.
128. Ltr, E to Stumpf, 3 Jan. 1895, MEW 39:367.

15. THE LUMPEN-CLASS VERSUS THE PROLETARIAT

1. See *KMTR* 1, Ch. 6, sec. 1.
2. M: 18th Brum./Pref., in ME:SW 1:395 [MEW 16:359]; here (in 1869) Marx ascribes the thought to Sismondi's *Etudes sur l'Economie Politique* (1837); this passage of Sismondi's is more completely quoted in M: Cap. 1:595 fn [MEW 23:621 fn].
3. ME: Ger. Ideol., MEW 3:23; ME:CW 5:84, like previous translations, makes *lumpenproletariat* "proletarian rabble."
4. ME: Ger. Ideol., in ME:CW 5:202; cf. MEW 3:183; for the context, see Special Note G, p. 630.
5. Alfred Meusel, in *Encyc. Soc. Sci.*, 11:511.
6. M: Cap. 1:734 [MEW 23:762]; see also the end of its previous chapter and the beginning of the next.
7. E: Peasant War Ger. (56), 49 [MEW 7:337f].
8. Ltr, E to Kautsky, 21 May 1895, MEW39:482f; cf. ME:SC, 489. See also Engels' description of most of Italy as late as the 1890s, in ltr, E to Turati, 26 Jan. 1894, in ME: Corrisp. con Ital., 518, or ME:SW 3:453f [MEW 22:440].
9. ME: Ger. Ideol. in ME:CW 5:75.
10. Briefs: *Proletariat*, 62; Zaniewski: *Origine du Prol.*, 297.
11. According to Bronterre O'Brien: *Rise, Progress & Phases &c.*, 7, 84, which refers with disapproval to Guizot as the proponent of this fourfold classification.
12. In *KMTR* 1:132.
13. See above, Ch. 6, p. 152.
14. E: Ger. Socialism, MEW 4:219f [ME:CW 6:246f].
15. For the context, see above, Ch. 7, p. 181.
16. For the use of *Lump* here as virtual synonym for lumpenproletarian, see Special Note G, p. 631 fn.
17. E: Status Quo in Ger., MEW 4:49 [ME:CW 6:83f].
18. ME: Com. Manif., in ME:CW 6:494.
19. Same, MEW 4:472.
20. Hobsbawm: *Primitive Rebels*, Ch. 7 passim.
21. Ltr, E to L. Lafargue, 11 Mar. 1872, in E & Lafargue: Corr. 1:46 (Fr. ed., 1:28) [MEW 33:426].
22. E: Latest Feat, MEW 5:20.
23. E: June 25th, MEW 5:131f.
24. E: Antwerp, MEW 5:380.
25. M: Victory Counterrev. Vienna, MEW 5:457.
26. M: Counterrev. Berlin, MEW 6:10.
27. E: Ger. Camp. Const., MEW 7:126; also 129 for a similar account of the movement in Elberfeld. In ME: Great Men, MEW 8:320 [ME: Cologne Com. Trial, 216], the implication is that most of Willich's corps were lumpen, but it is dubious whether this is to be taken as history; in any case it does not jibe with the two accounts of the movement by Engels.
28. M: Class Str. Fr., in ME:SW 1:219f, rev. after MEW 7:26.
29. ME: Review/Conspirators, MEW 7:272.
29a. For an incidental and unenlightening use of *lumpenproletariat*, see ltr, E to M, ca. 11 Aug. 1851, MEW 27:310; also unclear or figurative uses in ltr, M to E, 31 Aug. 1851, MEW 27:330, and 13 Sept. 1851, MEW 27:339.
30. M: Class Str. Fr., in ME:SW 1:297 [MEW 7:105].
31. M: 18th Brum., in ME:SW 1:442, rev. after MEW 8:160f.

32. Same, in ME:SW 1:443 [MEW 8:161].
33. Ibid., 474 [MEW 8:194].
34. M: Revol. Spain, VII, in N.Y. Tribune, 1 Dec. 1854, in ME: Revol. in Spain, 71f [MEW 10:475f].
35. Ltr, M to E, 5 July 1861, in ME: Civil War U.S., 231; cf. MEW 30:186.
36. Ltr, E to M, 4 Sept. 1870, MEW 33:53 [ME:SC, 249].
37. M: Agitation Ag. Tight. Sunday Bill, MEW 11:343.
38. E: Peasant War Ger./Pref., in ME:SW 2:163 [MEW 16:398].
39. For Pyziur, see Bibliog.; in Mehring's biography, see esp. his Ch. 14.
40. ME: Alliance S.D., 71, 95, also 64-67 [MEW 18:407, 431, also 401-4]. Cf. Pyziur: *Doctr. Anarch. Bak.*, 72f, 82, 84.
41. ME: Alliance S.D., 136, previously mentioned on 104 [MEW 18:470, 440]; the emphasis is added in the pamphlet. The same passage is given in Pyziur: *Doctr. Anarch. Bak.*, 82. For the déclassé theory, see also Pyziur, 30, 72f, 82-84.
42. Pyziur: *Doctr. Anarch. Bak.*, 82.
43. Ibid., 82-84; for peasants and lumpen-elements as "barbarians," 61, 66, 72, 75; for Marx's different formulation, see above, Ch. 12, sec. 8. For more on Bakunin's view of the peasantry, see above, Ch. 12, sec. 11.
44. Ltr, E to Bebel, 15 Feb. 1886, MEW 36:445.
44a. Ltr, E to L. Lafargue, 9 Feb. 1886, in E & Lafargue: Corr. 1:334 (mostly in English but "Lumpenproletariat" is clearly used as a German word).
45. Ltr, Harney to E, 19 Feb. 1886, in Harney: *Harney Papers*, 308.
46. See Special Note G, p. 633f; the similar phrase in the Manifesto is mentioned in this chapter, p. 458.
47. M: Cap. 1:632, 633, 637 [MEW 23:661f, 666].
48. Ibid., 640, 641 [MEW 23:670].
49. Ibid., 643 [MEW 23:672].
50. Ibid., rev. after MEW 23:673.
51. Ibid., 644 [MEW 23:673].
52. Ibid. [MEW 23:673f].
53. Ibid., 653 [MEW 23:683].
54. M: Grundrisse, 623, 501; cf. also 498, 503.
55. See this chapter, p. 463f, ref. n. 29, 31. The forms *bohème* and *bohéme* are interchangeable.
56. M: Civil War Fr., in ME:SW.2:225, 230 [MEW 17:344, 350].
57. In this connection, see KMTR 1, Special Note D, on the phrase *state parasite.*
58. M: Civil War Fr., 1st Draft, in ME: Writings Par. Com., 158.
59. M: Rebuke, MEW 6:145.
60. M: Connections betw. IWMA, in *G.C.F.I.* 68-70 [3], 386 [MEW 16:333]. For a reference to another lumpen-journalist, Tellering, see ltr, E to M, 25 Apr. 1852, MEW 28:57.
61. Ltr, M to Lassalle, 22 Nov. 1859, MEW 29:629; ltr, M to E, 10 Dec. 1859, MEW 29:520. For M's opinion of Kinkel's organ, see esp. ltr, M tp E, 6 Jan. 1859, MEW 29:381; ltr, M to Weydemeyer, 1 Feb. 1859, MEW 29:571f.
62. Ltr, M to Lassalle, 6 Nov. 1859, MEW 29:619.
63. M: Class Str. Fr., in ME:SW 1:278 [MEW 7:85].
64. Ibid., 208 [MEW 7:14f].
65. M: Theor. S.V., 1:212 [MEW 26.1:189].
66. This is to be seen mainly in Marx's articles for the N.Y. Tribune; some examples occur in KMTR 1, Ch. 18, sec. 4-8.
67. Ltr, M to E, 12 Oct. 1853, MEW 28:303.

68. M: 18th Brum., in ME:SW 1:450 [MEW 8:169].
69. Ibid., 485 [MEW 8:205].
70. Same, MEW 8:154f [ME:SW 1:437].
71. E: Real Causes (art. 2), 949 [MEW 8:226].
72. M: 18th Brum., in ME:SW 1:483 [MEW 8:203].
73. Ltr, M to E, 30 Oct. 1856, in ME:SC, 95 [MEW 29:82].
74. E: Role of Force, in ME:SW 3:416 [MEW 21:450].
75. M: Econ. Phil. Mss., MEW Eb.1:523 [ME:CW 3:284].
76. M: Grundrisse. 183f.
77. Ibid., 198.
78. Ltr, M to E, 5 June 1882, MEW 35:68.
79. Ltr, M to Ed. Bd. Otech. Zap., Nov. 1877, in ME:SC, 313; cf. French original in ME: Ausgew. Briefe (53), 368.
80. Ltr, M to E, 6 May 1854, MEW 28:357.
81. Ltr, E to Bernstein, 22 Aug. 1889, MEW 37:260f; qu. at end of Ch. 4 above, p. 113.

16. INTELLECTUAL LABOR AND LABORERS

1. M: Cap./Afterword, Ger. ed., MEW 23:19 [M: Cap. 1:13]; for the loose use of *class,* see *KMTR* 1:16f.
2. E: Foreign Pol. Russ. Cz., MEW 22:37 [ME: Russ. Men., 46, or E: Foreign Pol. Russ. Cz/Time, 533]; for *enlightened classes,* see E: On Soc. Rel. Russ., MEW 18:567 [ME:SW 2:397].
3. This refers to the English version listed in the Bibliography; these passages have been silently corrected in this respect when cited here.
4. M: Cap. 1:178; cf. MEW 23:193, esp. for the omitted phrase.
5. M: Cap. 1:180.
6. E: Dialectics of Nat., 230.
7. M: Cap. 1:508.
8. M: Theor. S.V., 1:398.
9. Ibid., 399.
10. Ibid., 160.
11. ME: Ger. Ideol., MEW 3:46f, rev. from ME:CW 5:59f.
11a. Same, in ME:CW 5:45 [MEW 3:32]; see Marx's marginal note, in ME:CW 5:45 fn [MEW 3:31 fn].
12. On this, see *KMTR* 1, Ch. 14, sec. 4, esp. 322.
13. Cf. ibid., 324.
14. M: Theor. S.V., 1:298.
15. Ibid., 280.
16. M: Cap. 1:509.
17. M: Grundrisse, 212 fn [Nic. tr., 305-6 fn].
18. M: Theor. S.V., 1:148, 159, 167f; see also 380-84.
19. Ibid., 154.
20. Ibid., 278.
21. M: Grundrisse, 432 [Nic. tr., 533].
22. M: Cap. 1:509.
23. M: Grundrisse, 234 [Nic. tr., 328f]; cf. M: Theor. S.V., 1:161f.
24. Ibid., 184 [Nic. tr., 273].
25. M: Theor. S.V., 1:289.

26. Ibid., 153f.
27. Ibid., 389.
28. On this, see my introduction to ME: Articles N.A.C., esp. 13-16.
29. M: Theor. S.V., 1:397f.
30. Ibid., 279.
31. See *KMTR* 1:17.
32. M: Theor. S.V., 1:170f.
33. Ibid., 291f, rev. after MEW 26.1:274.
34. Ibid., 278, rev. after MEW 26.1:259.
35. Ibid., 276, rev. after MEW 26.1:257.
36. Ibid., 277, rev. after MEW 26.1:257.
37. M: Cap. 3:103; cf. MEW 25:113f.
38. M: Cap. 3:81.
39. M: Grundrisse, 651 [Nic. tr., 765].
40. Ibid., 479f [Nic. tr., 585].
41. Ibid., 428 fn [Nic. tr., 529 fn].
42. Ibid., 414 [Nic. tr., 515].
43. M: Theor. S.V., 1:343.
44. M: Cap. 3:103, rev. after MEW 25:114.
45. M: Theor. S.V., 1:280.
46. M: Cap. 2:410.
47. M: Theor. S.V., 1:281.
48. Ibid., 212.
49. Kautsky: *Die Intelligenz u. S.D.*, esp. 14, 44-46, 48, 74-76, 80.

17. THE SOCIAL ROLE OF INTELLECTUAL ELEMENTS

1. See above, Ch. 16, sec. 3.
2. M: Class Str. Fr., MEW 7:13 [ME:SW 1:206].
3. M: 18th Brum., in ME:SW 1:424.
4. Ibid., 421.
5. ME: Ger. Ideol., MEW 3:179 [ME:CW 5:196].
6. M: Moral. Crit,, MEW 4:357 [ME:CW 6:337].
7. For Marx on the "reciprocal influence," see the passage qu. above, Ch. 16, p. 495, ref. n. 35.
7a. E: Debate on Pol. in Frankf., MEW 5:360, rev. from ME:CW 7:378.
8. Ltr, M to Kugelmann, 13 Dec. 1870, in ME:SC, 252.
9. M: Second Addr. of G.C., in ME:SW 2:196.
10. M: Notes on Wagner, MEW 19:371.
11. M: Mazzini & Nap., N.Y. Tribune, 11 May 1858.
12. E: True Soc., in MEW 4:281 [ME:CW 5:572].
13. M: Civil War Fr., 1st Draft, in ME: Writings Par. Com., 160. See also the passage on scientific inquiry qu. below, this chapter, p. 530.
14. ME: Ger. Ideol., MEW 3:69 [ME:CW 5:52].
15. M: Moral. Crit., MEW 4:349 [ME:CW 6:330].
16. Ibid., 350 [ME:CW 6:330].
17. M: State of Brit. Manuf., N.Y. Tribune, 15 Mar. 1859.
18. Henderson & Chaloner: *F.E. in Manchester*, 25.
19. ME: Com. Manif., MEW 4:471 and ME:CW 6:493f.
20. In Special Note F, esp. sec. 5.

21. ME: Com. Manif., in ME:CW 6:494.
22. Ltr, E to Bernstein, 17 Aug. 1881, MEW 35:215.
23. Bernstein: *Es fehlt uns an Intell.*, article 2.
24. Ltr, E to M, 11 Feb. 1870, MEW 32:441.
25. Ltr, E to Bernstein, 13 Sept. 1882, MEW 35:361.
26. Ltr, E to Bernstein, 27 Feb./1 Mar. 1883, in ME:SC, 433.
27. Ltr, E to Bebel, 9-10 Nov. 1891, MEW 38:212.
28. See this volume, Ch. 16, p. 492, ref. n. 27.
29. M: Class Str. Fr., In ME:SW 1:278.
30. Ltr, E to L. Lafargue, 17 Jan. 1886, in E & Lafargue: Corr. 1:331f.
31. Ltr, E to Bernstein, 13 Sept. 1882, MEW 35:360.
32. For an account of the *Jungen* faction and its fate, see Lidtke: *Outlawed Party*, 305-19 (for more references, 319 fn); also Landauer: *Europ. Soc.*, 1:295-98.
33. E: Reply to Ed. Bd. Sächs. Arb.-Ztg., MEW 22:69f.
34. Ltr, E to Becker, 15 Sept. 1879, MEW 34:392.
35. Ltr, M to Sorge, 19 Sept. 1879, MEW 34:411-13.
36. Ltr, E to Sorge, 20 June 1882, MEW 35:333.
37. Ltr, E to Kautsky, 19 July 1884, MEW 36:176.
38. Ltr, E to Becker, 15 June 1885, MEW 36:328.
39. M: Frankfurt Assy., MEW 6:43.
40. Ltr, M to E, 10 Dec. 1864, MEW 31:39.
41. Ltr, M to Sorge, 4 Aug. 1874, MEW 33:636.
42. Ltr, M to Sorge, 19 Oct. 1877, in ME:SC, 309, rev. after MEW 34:302f.
43. Ltr, M to Kugelmann, 12 Oct. 1868, in M: Ltrs to Kugel., 77f, rev. after MEW 32:567. Cf. the similar statement in Annenkov: *Extraord. Decade*, 165f.
44. Ltr, E to Cuno, 24 Jan. 1872, in ME:SC, 274 [MEW 33:389].
45. Ltr, E to Turati, 28 June 1895, in ME: Corrisp. con Ital., 608.
46. Ltr, E to Kautsky, 19 July 1884, MEW 36:177.
47. In another context this pattern is noted in *KMTR* 1:440f.
48. M: Kossuth, Mazz. & L.N., in N.Y. Tribune, 1 Dec. 1852.
49. ME: Circular Ltr to Bebel et al., 17/18 Sept. 1879, in ME:SW 3:88. The trio's article appeared in August in Höchberg's *Jahrbuch für Sozialwissenschaft und Sozialpolitik*, 1. Jg., 1 Hälfte, 1879, p. 75-96, entitled "Rückblicke auf die sozialistische Bewegung in Deutschland," signed with a symbol, in fact written by Höchberg (pseud. L. Richter), C. A. Schramm and E. Bernstein, the last being then Höchberg's private secretary.
50. Ibid., in ME:SW 3:89.
51. Ltr, E to von Boenigk, 21 Aug. 1890, MEW 37:447 [poor tr. in ME:SW 3:486].
52. Ltr, E to Bernstein, 13 Sept. 1882, MEW 35:360f.
53. Ltr, E to P. Lafargue, 27 Aug. 1890, in E & Lafargue: Corr. (Fr.) 2:407f.
54. Ltr, E to Sorge, 24 Oct. 1891, MEW 38:182.
55. Ltr, E to Kautsky, 4 Sept. 1892, in ME:SC, 447.
56. Ltr, E to Sorge, 11 Nov. 1893, MEW 39:166 [ME:SC, 465].
57. Ltr, E to Sorge, 19 Apr. 1890, MEW 37:393 [ME:SC, 411f].
58. Ltr, E to Sorge, 20 June 1882, MEW 35:333.
59. Ltr, E to Bebel, 22-24 June 1885, MEW 36:335.
60. See e.g. ltr, E to L. Lafargue, 17 Jan. 1886, in E & Lafargue: Corr. 1:332.
61. Ltr, E to Becker, 22 May 1883, MEW 36:29.
62. Cf. this volume, Ch. 1, sec. 3.

63. Ltr, M to Bracke, 5 May 1875, in ME:SW 3:11.
64. See *KMTR* 1, Ch. 10, esp. sec. 4-5.
65. Ltr, E to M, 19 Nov. 1844, MEW 27:13.
66. Heine's long poem "Atta Troll," last section.
67. This will be taken up in *KMTR* 3.
68. See ltr, M to E, 5 Mar. 1856, MEW 29:27f.
69. Among other things, see Jenny Marx's account in *Reminisc. M.E.*, 234; ltr, M to Kugelmann, 23 Feb. 1865, in ME:SC, 167; the bulk of evidence is in the fine biography, Footman: *F. Lassalle*, at large.
70. Ltr, M to E, 9 Apr. 1863, MEW 30:340 [ME:SC, 140].
71. Qu. in Footman: *F. Lassalle*, 167f.
72. Ltr, M to Kugelmann, 23 Feb. 1865, in ME:SC, 168.
73. Marx's reference may have been modeled on Heine's use of this analogy in his poem "Georg Herwegh," *Neue Gedichte* (1844), where "Uckermark" is used in the same way.
74. Ltr, M to Lassalle, 19 Apr. 1859, in ME:SC, 117; see also ltr, E to Lassalle, 18 May 1859, ibid., 118-20. Lassalle's letters to M and E, before and after, are in Mehring, ed.: *Aus dem lit. Nachlass*, 4:132 et seq., 173 et seq.
75. On this, see Bernstein: *F. Lassalle as Soc. Ref.*, 35f, and again in his *F. Lassalle, eine Würdig.*, 56f. For Bernstein's discussion of the Sickingen correspondence, see the former title, 33-43; Lukacs analyzed it at some length in his *K.M. & F.E. als Lit.-hist.*, 5-62.
76. M: Cap. 1:518.
77. Ibid., 13f.
78. Ibid., 15.
79. Cf. this chapter, p. 506, ref. n. 13.
80. M: Cap. 1:15.
81. ME: [Review of] Guizot, in ME: On Brit., 350.
82. M: London Times & Lord Palm., in N.Y. Tribune, 21 Oct. 1861.
83. M: English Mid. Cl., in N.Y. Tribune, 1 Aug. 1854.
84. Ltr, E to Bebel, 22-24 June 1885, MEW 36:336.
85. Ltr, E to Bebel, 25 Aug. 1881, MEW 35:220.
86. Ltr, E to Becker, 11 Jan. 1878, MEW 34:316.
87. ME: Circular Ltr to Bebel et al., 17-18 Sept. 1879, in ME:SW 3:93.
88. Ltr, E to Bernstein, 10 May 1882, MEW 35:319.
89. Ltr, E to Kautsky, 19 July 1884, MEW 36:176f.
90. Ltr, E to Schmidt, 5 Aug. 1890, in ME:SC, 416.
91. M: Cap. 1:21.
92. Ltr, E to von Boenigk, 21 Aug. 1890, MEW 37:448 [ME:SW 3:486].
93. For ex., see ltr, M to E, 14 Sept. 1870, MEW 33:64; there is a similar reference in ltr, M to Beesly, 16 Sept. 1870, in London *Social-Democrat*, 15 Apr. 1903 [MEW 33:154].
94. See ME: Great Men, 230, and ME: Address Com. Lg./June, in ME: Cologne Com. Trial, 246 [MEW 7:307].
95. E: Revol. & C.R. Ger., in ME:SW 1:327f.
96. Ibid., 328.
97. Ibid., 351f.
98. Ibid., 379.
99. E: Ger. Camp. Const., MEW 7:154, 159.
100. Ibid., 182.
101. Ltr, M to E, 26 Dec. 1865, MEW 31:163; see also ltr, M to Becker, ca. 13 Jan. 1866, MEW 31:494.

102. Ltr, E to M, 4 Jan. 1866, MEW 31:167.
103. E: To Internatl. Cong. Soc. Stud., MEW 22:415.

18. INTELLECTUALS AND THE PROLETARIAN MOVEMENT

1. See this volume, Ch. 16, sec. 3, p. 489.
2. E: Cond. Wkg. Cl. Eng., MEW 2:452f [ME:CW 4:526f].
3. Ltr, E to Cafiero, 16 July 1871, in ME: Corresp. con Ital., 31.
4. Ltr, E to Bebel, 30 Aug. 1883, MEW 36:57f [ME:SC, 364f].
5. Ltr, E to Bebel, 18 Jan. 1884, MEW 36:88 [ME:SC, 367].
6. See this volume, Ch. 17, p. 538.
7. See this volume, Ch. 17, p. 534, ref. n. 91.
8. Ltr, E to von Boenigk, 21 Aug. 1890, MEW 37:447 [ME:SW 3:486].
9. Ltr, E to Bebel, 24-26 Oct. 1891, MEW 38:189.
10. Ltr, E to Bebel, 9-10 Nov. 1891, MEW 38:212.
11. Bernstein: *Es fehlt uns an Intell.*, article 2.
12. Ltr, M to Laura Marx Lafargue, 13 Apr. 1882, MEW 35:310f.
13. See *KMTR* 1:137f.
14. Qu. in this volume, Ch. 3, p. 76, and in Special Note H, p. 645; see ME: Edit. Note Eccarius, MEW 7:416.
15. ME: Review/ Conspirators, MEW 7:274.
16. See, for ex., ltr, E to M, ca. 23 Oct. 1846, in ME:SC, 33, or MEW 27:65 (sketch of the German *Straubinger* in Paris); on their anti-intellectualism, see ltr, E to M, Dec. 1846, MEW 27:70f.
17. Ltr, M to E, 16 Apr. 1856, MEW 29:47 [ME:SC, 91].
18. Rocker: *J. Most*, 14 (for the qu.); for Most's working career, Ch. 1-2.
19. Ibid., 56.
20. Ltr, M to Bracke, 11 Apr. 1877, MEW 34:264; for other remarks on Most as a Dühringite at this time, see ibid., 12-18, 54-55, 294.
21. Ltr, M to Sorge, 19 Oct. 1877, MEW 34:303 [ME:SC, 309f].
22. The qu. is from John Spargo's account of what Lessner told him, in Spargo: *Sidelights on Contemp. Soc.*, 82; the question is not mentioned in the excerpts from Lessner's reminiscences in *Reminisc. M.E.*, 142. For Lessner's background, see Kandel, ed.: *M. E. & erst. prol. Rev.*, 120 et seq.
23. Ltr, E to Bernstein, 25 Oct. 1881, MEW 35:229.
24. Kandel, ed.: *M. E. & erst. prol. Rev.*, 77-79.
25. E: On Hist. C.L., in ME:SW 3:175.
26. Ibid., 177.
27. Ibid., 178.
28. Schapper: *Intro./Komm. Zeitschr.*, in Bund. Kom., 1:503f; the qu. is on 504. (See this passage as qu. above, Ch. 7, p. 189.)
29. See this volume, Ch. 3, p. 78, and Special Note E, sec. 2.
30. Comm. League: *C.C. Session 15 Sept. 1850*, in ME: Cologne Comm. Trial, 252.
31. Comm. League, Cologne C.C.: *Address*, in ME: Cologne Comm. Trial, 254f.
32. Nicolaievsky & M.-H.: *K.Marx*, 156; Wittke: *Refugees of Rev.*, 353.
33. Comm. League, Cologne C.C.: *Address*, MEW 7:563 [ME: Cologne Comm. Trial, 255].
34. ME: Great Men, in ME: Cologne Comm. Trial, 198-201, 204f, 216, 220, 224-30; M: Revel. Comm. Trial, ibid., 108; and editor's intro., ibid., 21-25; also M: Knight Noble Consc., MEW 9:498, 507, 516f.

35. Comm. League: *C.C. Session 15 Sept. 1850,* in ME: Cologne Comm. Trial, 251.
36. Ltr, M to E, 10 Dec. 1864, MEW 31:39f.
37. Re Fox, see this volume, Ch. 17, p. 518f, and this chapter, p. 561 fn.
38. See Collins & Abramsky: *K.M. & Brit. Lab. Movemt.,* 101-3.
39. Ltr, M to E, 4 Nov. 1864, in ME:SC, 146; ltr, M to Klings, 4 Oct. 1864, MEW 31:417f; ltr, M to Philips, 29 Nov. 1864, MEW 31:432.
40. Ltr, M to E, 25 Feb. 1865, MEW 31:85.
41. M: Memo H. Jung, in *G.C.F.I.* 64-66 [1], 269.
42. *G.C.F.I.* 64-66 [1], 75-81, plus later echoes in the Council minutes; also ltr, M to E, 13 Mar. 1865, MEW 31:100f; ltr, M to Jung, 13 Mar. 1865, MEW 31:463f.
43. *G.C.F.I.* 64-66 [1], 77.
44. So reported in the account carried in the *International Courier,* in Freymond, ed.: *Prem. Intle.,* 1:55.
45. This is from the report drawn up by Tolain's cothinker, J. Card; in ibid., 80.
46. From the French report in ibid., 1:56; cf. Collins & Abramsky: *K.M. & Brit. Lab. Movemt.,* 123.
47. From the French report in ibid.
48. Ibid.
49. The extant minutes of the Council do not include the meeting devoted to electing its delegates to the congress; see *G.C.F.I.* 64-66 [1], 228.
50. Ltr, M to E, 26 Sept. 1866, MEW 31:254.
51. Ibid.
52. Ltr, M to E, 4 Oct. 1867, MEW 31:354; *G.C.F.I.* 66-68 [2], 161.
53. *G.C.F.I.* 66-68 [2], 36.
54. Ibid.; also ltr, M to E, 26 Sept. 1866, MEW 31:254; Collins & Abramsky: *K.M. & Brit. Lab. Movemt.,* 66. For Cremer's previous behavior, see also *G.C.F.I.* 64-66 [1], 146, 159.
55. Ltr, M to E, 25 Feb. 1865, MEW 31:85.
56. *G.C.F.I.* 70-71 [4], 80.
57. *G.C.F.I.* 71-72 [5], 166f.
58. Qu. from Woodhull's organ by Marx, in M: Amer. Split, in *G.C.F.I.* 71-72 [5], 324f.
59. E: International in Amer., MEW 18:97f. Engels based this article on Marx's notes (M: Amer. Split) for the case of Section 12; for other material, see *G.C.F.I.* 71-72 [5], 205-10, 250f; also S. Bernstein: *First Intl. in Amer.*
60. M: Resolutions on Split in U.S. Fed., in *G.C.F.I.* 71-72 [5], 412; I have edited the extract to omit references to other rules and to delete confusing commas.
61. *G.C.F.I.* 71-72 [5], 124, 206.
62. Ibid., 265; the awkward English is in the original.
63. This passage is given here as it appears in Marx's notes, in M: Conspectus of Bak., MEW 18:635f; the translation, based on Marx's German, has been checked for me against the original Russian as published in Bakunin: *Etat. et An.,* 148.
64. See this volume, Ch. 17, sec. 5, esp. p. 527f.
65. This information is scattered through Hümmler: *Oppos. gegen Lassalle,* and Footman: *F. Lassalle.*
66. Carr: *M. Bakunin,* 440.
67. See this volume, Ch. 12, sec. 11, and Ch. 15, sec. 4.
68. From Bakunin's "Confession," as qu. in Nomad: *Apostles,* 162.
69. Pyziur: *Doctrine Anarch. Bak.,* 83.

70. Qu. in ibid.
71. Bakunin, qu. in ME: Alliance S.D., 132.
72. ME: Alliance S.D., 48.
73. Ltr, E to L. Lafargue, 11 Mar. 1872, in E & Lafargue: Corr., 1:46, similarly in ltr, E to Liebknecht, 18 Jan. 1872, MEW 33:379.
74. Ltr, E to M, 29 Apr. 1870, MEW 32:489.
75. E: In Italy, MEW 19:91, 92, 95.
76. For the Weitling pattern, see Special Note I, p. 657f.
77. Carr: M. Bakunin, 146; see also passage from Bakunin's letter in Annenkov: Extraordinary Decade, 183.
78. Pyziur: Doctrine Anarch. Bak., 17.
79. ME: Alliance S.D., 63.
80. From Bakunin and Nechayev's "Revolutionary Catechism," as qu. in ME: Alliance S.D., 90.
81. ME: Alliance S.D., 106.
82. Ltr, E to Becker, 8 Sept. 1879, MEW 34:391.
83. Ltr, E to Bernstein, 18 Jan. 1883, MEW 35:426 [ME:SC, 357].
84. Ltr, E to Bernstein, 11 Nov. 1884, MEW 36:233.
85. Ltr, E to Bebel, 22-24 June 1885, MEW 36:335f.
86. Ltr, E to von Boenigk, 21 Aug. 1890, MEW 37:447f [ME:SW 3:486]. The Anti-Socialist Law lapsed in October but it had been clear since February that it would not be renewed.
87. Ltr, E to Schmidt, 5 Aug. 1890, MEW 37:437 [ME:SC, 416].
88. Ibid., 437f.
89. For Kautsky, see his article "Franz Mehring" in Neue Zeit, 22. Jg., 1903-04, 1. Bd., no. 4, p. 97-108, esp. 99-101; also the debate on the "Mehring case" and the role of intellectuals in the party at the 1903 congress in SPD: Protokoll . . . des Parteitages 1903, 158-264. Regarding Rosa Luxemburg, see Nettl: R. Luxemburg, 1:232-34.
90. SPD: Protokoll . . . des Parteitages 1903, 225.

Special Note A. MARX ON
THE ABOLITION OF THE PROLETARIAT BY AUTOMATION

1. Chase: Technocracy, 27.
2. See esp. Braverman: Labor & Monop. Cap., and Parker: Myth of Middle Class.
3. M: Econ. Phil. Mss., in ME:CW 3:257, including footnote [MEW Eb.1:495 and note].
4. Qu. by Marx in M: Pov. Phil., in ME:CW 6:189. Marx had quoted a similar sentiment of Ure's (in a different context) in 1845, in M: On F. List's Book, in ME:CW 4:285.
5. M: Wage-Lab. & Cap., in ME:SW 1:172.
6. Qu. in M: Grundrisse, 582, from a French tr. of Ure [Nic. tr., 690] ; partly qu. also in M: Cap. 1:418f.
7. M: Grundrisse, 482 [Nic. tr., 587].
8. Ibid., 584 [Nic. tr., 692].
9. M: Cap. 1:418f.
10. M: Theor. S.V., 1:379.
11. Ltr, M to E, 2 Apr. 1858, in ME:SC, 105.

12. M: Grundrisse, 587f [Nic. tr., 700].
13. Ibid., 589 [Nic. tr., 701].
14. Ibid., 592 [Nic. tr., 704f].
15. Ibid., 592f [Nic. tr., 705f].
16. Ibid., 593f [Nic. tr., 706].
17. M: Cap. 1:763.

Special Note B.
MARX'S CONVERSATION WITH HAMANN

1. De Leon in an editorial, reprinted in his *Industrial Unionism*, 37-39. —Laurat: *Marxism & Dem.*, 74-76. —Auerbach: *M. & Gewerksch.*, 51. —Lozovsky: *M. & Tr. Unions*, 152-55. —Enzensberger, ed.: *Gespräche mit M. & E.*, 1:337-39. —Most recently it has popped up in David McLellan's *The Thought of Karl Marx*, 175f, with the erroneous caption "Speech to a delegation of German trade unionists" and no mention of Hamann at all.
2. Ltr, M to E, 30 Sept. 1869, MEW 32:375.
3. For this background see Morgan: *Ger. S.-D. & F.I.*, 160-68.
4. On this letter, see this volume, Ch. 5, p. 122f, 134f.
5. The summary in sections 2-3 is based mainly on the following: Morgan: *Ger. S.-D. & F.I.*, Ch. 1, 2, 5; Opel & Schneider: *75 Jahre*, 51-55, 61-71; Müller: *Organisationen d. Lithog.*, 1:206-09, 249-54.
6. Ltr, E to M, 6 Apr. 1869, MEW 32:295.
7. Enzensberger, ed.: *Gespräche mit M. & E.*, 1:337. —Ltr, Dieter Schneider to Draper, 17 Aug. 1970.
8. For Schneider letter, see preceding note. For the photocopy, Opel & Schneider: *75 Jahre*, 69.
9. Translated here from *Volksstaat* (Leipzig), 27 Nov. 1869; this is the first complete English translation. The German text, lacking the *Volksstaat*'s introduction, will be found in Enzensberger, ed.: *Gespräche mit M. & E.*, 1:337-39; citations elsewhere are less complete.
10. See the Henderson-Chaloner edition of E: Cond. Wkg. Cl. Eng. (N.Y., Macmillan, 1958), ix, xx, 375f.
11. H.: *K.M./Interview*, 21.
12. Ltr, M to Nieuwenhuis, 22 Feb. 1881, MEW 35:159f.
13. Kisch: *K.M. in Karlsbad*, 62-72.
14. Ltrs, E to M, 24 Feb. 1865; M to E, 25 Feb. 1865, MEW 31:82, 83.
15. Ltr, E to M, 21 Sept. 1874, MEW 33:119.

Special Note C. PERMANENT REVOLUTION:
ON THE ORIGIN OF THE TERM

1. Dommanget: *Idées Politiques et Soc.*, esp. Ch. 3, 7; note his reference on p. 158.
2. Spitzer: *Revol. Theory Blanqui*, 171 fn.
3. Andler: *Introduction Hist.*, in his edition of *Manifeste Com.*, 2:129, 136.
4. Spitzer: *Revol. Theory Blanqui*, 168 fn, referring to Proudhon: *General Idea Revol.*, First Study, sec. 1.

5. See this volume, Ch. 8, p. 208f.
6. See this volume, Ch. 10, p. 253.
7. For more details on the inventive process, see Draper: *M. & Dict. of Prole.*, 15-19, 30-38.
8. Nicolaievsky: *Who is Distort. Hist.*, 219f.
9. See this volume, Ch. 8, p. 308 fn.
10. Seidler: *Gesch. d. Wortes Rev.*, 291.
11. Guérin: *Lutte de Classes*, 1:5-22 esp.
12. E: Intro./Class Str. Fr., in ME:SW 1:189.
13. M: 18th Brum., in ME:SW 1:398.
14. See this volume, Ch. 8, p. 206.
15. M: From Mem. Levasseur, in ME:CW 3:361 et seq.
16. M: On Jewish Ques., MEW 1:357 [ME:CW 3:156].
17. ME: Holy Fam., MEW 2:126 [ME:CW 4:119].
18. See *KMTR* 1:430f, also 182.
19. ME: Holy Fam., MEW 2:130 [ME:CW 4:122f].
20. E: State of Ger., I, in ME:CW 6:19.

Special Note D. HAIR!
or, MARXISM AND PILOSITY

1. *Reminisc. M. E. (Bax)*, 307.
2. ME: Great Men, in ME: Cologne Com. Trial, 166.
3. Ltr, E to Marie Engels, 29 Oct. 1840, MEW Eb.2:463f [ME:CW 2:511f].
4. Ltr, E to Marie Engels, 18 Feb. 1841, MEW Eb.2:477 [ME:CW 2:525].
5. Ltr, E to Marie Engels, 8 Mar. 1841, MEW Eb.2:481 [ME:CW 2:529].
6. Ltr, E to Marie Engels, ca. beginning May 1841, MEW Eb.2:486 [ME:CW 2:533].
7. M: Debates Freed. Press, MEW 1:59f [ME:CW 1:164]; qu. in *KMTR* 1:53 fn in context.
8. For the group portrait, see ME:CW 1, opposite p. 15; on the verso is a blowup of Marx's face alone (touched up).

Special Note E. THE ADDRESS TO
THE COMMUNIST LEAGUE OF MARCH 1850

1. Cf. Lichtheim: *Marxism*, 125.
2. The Pickwickian peccadillo will be found in Wolfe: *Marxism*, 182; a less enthusiastic version is on 152. For Marx's speech at this meeting, see this volume, Ch. 3, p. 78f.
3. This refers to ME: Circular Ltr to Bebel et al., for which see Bibliography.
4. Ltr, E to M, 23-24 Nov. 1847, in ME:SC, 45; for a fuller discussion, see this volume, Ch. 7, p.195 fn.
5. For the overview, Collins & Abramsky: *K.M. & Brit. Lab. Movemt.*, Ch. 4 (all); for the complaint, p. 51. For the Proudhonist position, see this volume, Ch. 4, p. 82 and footnote.
6. Ltr, M to E, 4 Nov. 1864, in ME:SC, 149.
7. Ltr, M to E, 14 Sept. 1870, MEW 33:64.

8. For the circumstances under which this work was written, see my Foreword to ME: Writings Par. Com., 10-16.
9. Ltr, Jenny Marx (daughter) to L. & G. Kugelmann, MEW 33:705 (retranslated).
10. *G.C.F.I.* 64-66 [1], 43f; Collins & Abramsky: *K.M. & Brit. Lab. Movemt.*, 43.
11. *G.C.F.I.* 70-71 [4], 204; also see my Foreword to ME: Writings Par. Com., 12-15.
12. For the paucity of documentation, see the explanation in Nicolaevsky: *Toward Hist. C.L.*, 235-40. So far the second volume of the document collection, *Bund Kom.*, has not been published; the first volume, which went up to 1849, was published in 1970.
13. See this volume, Special Note C, p.592.
14. Nicolaevsky: *Who Is Distort. Hist.*, 220.
15. For the "Blanquist" invention, see Bernstein: *Voraussetzungen d. Soz.*, 27-36. The translation *Evolutionary Socialism* omits all of Ch. 2, of which section (b) is titled "Marxism and Blanquism"; but the thesis itself is mentioned on p. 155.
16. Com. League: *C.C. Session 15 Sept. 1850*, MEW 8:598 [ME: Cologne Com. Trial, 251].
17. For the whole passage, see this volume, Ch. 3, p.78.
18. Com. League: *C.C. Session 15 Sept. 1850*, MEW 8:598f [ME: Cologne Com. Trial, 251].
19. For the incompatibility of Blanquism with permanent revolution, see this volume, Ch. 8, p. 208f; in this connection, cf. Dommanget: *Idées Polit. & Soc.*, 378.
20. Com. League: *C.C. Session 15 Sept. 1850*, MEW 8:599 [ME: Cologne Com. Trial, 252].
21. Ltr, E to Dronke, 9 July 1851, MEW 27:562.
22. Ibid., 600 [ME: Cologne Com. Trial, 253].
23. Com. League, Cologne C.C.: *Address*, MEW 7:562 [ME: Cologne Com. Trial, 254].
24. Ibid., 563 [ME: Cologne Com. Trial, 255].
25. Ltr, M to E, 13 July 1851, MEW 27:278.
26. Ibid.
27. Re Grün's "anarchistic" phrases, see the fragment, E: On Slogan Abol. State, MEW 7:417-20.
28. Ltr, M to E, 13 July 1851, MEW 27:279.
29. Ltr, E to M, 17 July 1851, MEW 27:284.
30. Ibid., 285.
31. Ltr, E to M, ca. 20 July 1851, MEW 27:288.
32. Ltr, M to Ebner, late Aug. 1851, MEW 27:577; see the note, ibid., 677 (note 426).
33. M: Revel. Com. Trial, MEW 8:414, similarly 461 [ME: Cologne Com. Trial, 64, 108].
34. Ibid., MEW 8:413 [tr., 63].
35. M: Knight of Noble Consc., MEW 9:507.
36. M: Revel. Com. Trial/Postscr., MEW 18:568-70 or 8:574-76 [tr., 131-33].
37. E: On Hist. C.L., MEW 21:220 [ME:SW 3:186f].
38. Nicolaevsky: *Who Is Distort. Hist.*, 220 fn.
39. The following reference works define *redigieren* as including the meaning of *abfassen* (draw up, write): J. H. Campe: *Wörterbuch zur Erklärung und*

Verdeutschung der . . . fremden Ausdrücke (Brunswick, 1801); J. F. Heigelin: *Allgemeines Fremdwörter-Handbuch* (Tübingen, 1838); J. H. Kaltschmidt: *Gesammt-Wörterbuch der deutschen Sprache . . . mit allen Fremdwörtern* (Leipzig, 1834); F. E. Petri: *Handbuch der Fremdwörter* (Gera, 1893); J. C. Schweitzer: *Wörterbuch zur Erklärung fremder . . . Wörter und Redensarten,* 2. ed. (Zurich, 1811). Heigelin even makes it mean *verfassen* in addition. Useful illustrative citations are given in J. Kehrein: *Fremdwörterbuch* (Wiesbaden, 1876, repr. 1969) and D. Sanders: *Fremdwörterbuch* (Leipzig, 1871). The Italian connection is explained in F. Seiler: *Die Entwicklung der deutschen Kultur* . . . (Halle, 1910), 3:304f, and mentioned in Kehrein. A 20th century work that still defines *redigieren* as *abfassen* is *Bachems Fremdwörterbuch* by J. Hitze (Cologne, 1949).

Special Note F. THE ALLEGED THEORY
OF THE DISAPPEARANCE OF THE MIDDLE CLASSES

1. See *KMTR* 1:622 et seq. on the "state parasite" nontheory.
2. Ltr, M to E, 13 Feb. 1863, MEW 30:324.
3. See Bernstein: *Evol. Soc.,* xi; Gay: *Dilemma Dem. Soc.,* 204f, 208, 213f.
4. See this volume, Ch. 11, p. 290.
5. M: Theor. S.V., 1:396f; Marx's square brackets are here replaced with parentheses.
6. M: Affairs in Prussia, in N.Y. Tribune, 1 Feb. 1859.
7. ME: Com. Manif., in ME:CW 6:485.
8. Ibid., 486.
9. Ibid., 487.
10. Same, in MEW 4:469f.
11. Same, in ME:CW 6:491f.
12. Ibid., 494; for the original, MEW 4:472.
13. Same, in MEW 4:484.
14. Same, in ME:CW 6:509.
15. M: Cap. 1:332.
16. M: Cap. 3:379f.
17. Ibid., 285.
18. Ibid., 287, 288.
19. Ibid., 293.
20. See this volume, Ch. 2, p. 34f.
21. M: Cap. 3:294.
22. Ibid., 295 fn.
23. M: Cap. 2:132, 134.
24. M: Theor. S.V., II, in MEW 26.2:576 [tr., 2:573].
25. Ibid., 563f [tr., 2:561].
26. Ibid., 564 [tr., 2:562].
27. Same, III, in MEW 26.3:57 [tr., 3:63].
28. M: Labor Parliament, in N.Y. Tribune, 29 Mar. 1854.
29. The *People's Paper* version is usually used in collections; see ME: Art. Brit., 216. The MEW translation, though purporting to be from the *People's Paper,* actually follows the *Tribune* text in using "radically"; cf. MEW 10:125.
30. M: Cap. 3, in MEW 25:892; the English version, in M: Cap. 3:862, uses "intermediate strata" for *Übergangsstufen.*

31. E: Pruss. Mil. Ques., MEW 16:69.
32. M: Labor Parliament, in N.Y. Tribune, 29 Mar. 1854; cf. M: Ltr to Labor Parl., in ME: Art. Brit., 216.
33. Mills: *White Collar*, 291.
34. Dahrendorf: *Class & Cl. Conflict*, 52.
35. Ltr, M to Kugelmann, 9 Oct. 1866, in ME:SC, 184.

Special Note G. ON THE ORIGIN
OF THE TERM *LUMPENPROLETARIAT*

1. Stirner's *Der Einzige und sein Eigentum* was published with the imprint 1845 but probably appeared at the end of October 1844. The English translation by Byington (*The Ego and His Own*, 1907) must be used with caution, since its terminology is sometimes peculiar (e.g., *commonalty* for *burghers* or *bourgeois*); unavoidably its English equivalents for the various *Lumpen*-words do not show the relationship. —For Stirner in general, see Hook: *From Hegel to M*, Ch. 5, or McLellan: *Young Hegelians*, 117 et seq.
2. See entries for *Lump, Lumpen* in Kluge & Götze: *Etymol. Wörterb.*, and in *Trübners Deut. Wörterb.*, 4:512-14.
3. This is confirmed also by the entry under *Lump* in Deutsche Akad. d. Wissenschaften: *Wörterbuch*, 2408.
4. See the entries in Ludwig: *Deutsch-Eng. Lexicon*, and in T. Heinsius: *Volksthüml. Wörterb.*, 3:216f.
5. One exception is Mackensen: *Deutsches Wörterb.*; there may be others, of course.
6. For example, see the entries in the Brockhaus encyclopedia for 1970, Grosse Duden-Lexikon for 1966, Meyers Enzyklopädisches Lexikon for 1975.
7. Bibliogr. Inst., Leipzig: *Fremdenwörter* (1964), 412; likewise in the 1954 edition, p. 364.
8. Andréas & Monke: *Neue Daten*, 26.
9. McLellan: *Young Hegelians*, 123.
10. Stirner: *Ego*, 119, revised after the German, *Einzige*, 123f.
11. ME: Ger. Ideol., in ME:CW 5:202 [MEW 3:183].
12. E: Status Quo in Ger., MEW 4:49, quoted in Ch. 15, p.457f.
13. E: Savoy, Nice & Rhine, MEW 13:598; this passage was quoted in *KMTR* 1:431 fn.
14. The page numbers cited by Marx are equivalent to about p. 125-26 in the Reclam edition of *Der Einzige* cited here.
15. ME: Ger. Ideol., in ME:CW 5:202.
16. See esp. Stirner: *Ego*, 121 [*Einzige*, 125f] for identification of "him who has nothing to lose" with *proletarian*. For other relevant passages in Stirner, see *Ego*, 123-25 [127-29], 137-38 [143-44], 266 [282], 271 [287], 277-78 [294-95], 286 [303], 288 [305], 330 [351], 332 [353-54].
17. ME: Ger. Ideol., MEW 3:23; cited in Ch. 15, p. 454.
17a. E: Lawyers' Soc., MEW 21:497; this article was written with Kautsky.
18. Schoyen: *Chartist Chall.*, 204; for more on Macfarlane, 202-04; for Harney's relation at this time, 129-31, 141ff, 154-56, 187, 202-05, 209.
19. Ltr, E to M, 8 Jan. 1851, MEW 27:164; and ltr, M to Weydemeyer, 16 Oct. 1851, ibid., 581f. Re the Tribune, see ltr, E to Jenny Marx, 18 Dec. 1851, ibid., 593, but it is unclear.

20. Gemkow et al.: *F. Engels*, 165 (Eng. ed.), 181 (Ger. ed.); MEW 5:566; Mayer: *F. Engels*, 1:300 (only the Eng. tr., p. 95, says he translated it "for Harney," but this is unreliable).
21. In *Red Republican*, 16 Nov. 1850, p. 171.
22. See *mob* in Oxford Eng. Dict., esp. but not only sense 2; also in Encyc. Brit., 11th ed., 18:635.
23. ME: Review/May to Oct., MEW 7:443.
24. Heine: *Lutezia*, dispatch of 25 Aug. 1840, in his *Works*, 8:137 (*Sämt. Werke*, 6:212).
25. Ladendorf: *Hist. Schlagwb.*, 206.
26. ME: Com. Manif., in ME:CW 6:494; cf. Ch. 15, p. 458.
27. M: Cap. 1:643; cf. Ch. 15, p. 469.
28. Chevalier: *Classes Lab. & Classes Dangereuses*, 58-72, 451-68, plus parts of next two chapters.
29. Stein: *Der Soz. & Komm.*, 9, as qu. in Silberner: *M. Hess*, 135.
30. For the passage in Stirner, see above, p. 630f.
31. M: Civil War Fr., 2d Draft, in ME: Writings Par. Com., 193.

Special Note H. TWO ADVENTURES
IN SOPHISTICATED MARXOLOGY

1. For Bakunin's priority, see Ch. 18, p. 564f.
2. Avineri: *Soc. & Polit. Thought*, 63.
3. M: untitled article, N.Y. Tribune, 27 July 1857 [MEW 12:235].
4. M: Indian Revolt, in ME: On Brit., 469.
5. Two of the main documents are available in English in ME: Cologne Com. Trial, 250-57 (including the minutes of Sept. 15, 1850); cf. MEW 8:597-601; of course a more voluminous documentation from dubious sources was put together by the government in the Cologne trial.
6. From the minutes, in ME: Cologne Com. Trial, 251.
7. The passage from Schapper's article is qu. in Ch. 2, p. 33.
8. From the minutes, MEW 8:600; in ME: Cologne Com. Trial, 253, *getrotzt* (gainsaid) is misleadingly tr. *defied*.
9. Avineri's reference is to MEW 8:598-600; the corresponding pages in the tr. in ME: Cologne Com. Trial are approx. 251-53.
10. Ltr, E to M, 23 Sept. 1851, MEW 27:344.
11. Drahn: *K.M. & F.E. über D. P.*, 29 et seq.
12. E: On hist. C.L., in ME:SW 3:180; ltr, M to E, 5 Dec. 1868, MEW 32:219.
13. Wittke: *Utop. Com.*, 120.
14. Ltr, M to E, 29 Jan. 1853, MEW 28:209.
15. Wittke: *Utop. Com.*, 250, 253, 259-74 passim.
16. Ltr, M to E, 20 July 1852, MEW 28:93.
17. For Mr. Deeds on pixillation, see KMTR 1:591.
18. Ltr, M to E, 9 May 1865, MEW 31:115.
19. Ltr, M to E, 24 Nov. 1857, MEW 29:218.
20. This exchange took place between Aug. 1976 and Jan. 1977.
21. Avineri: *M & Intell.*, 274-75; these two pages are the only ones offering the sort of documentation discussed and are the source of all citations.
22. See Ch. 17, p. 512, ref. n. 24.
23. Eccarius' article may be found in the *Neue Rh. Ztg.-Revue* reprint edition,

293-302. On Marx's help, see the editorial note, MEW 7:615, n. 277. For Marx's edit. note on Eccarius, MEW 7:416 (or in the reprint ed., 302f); the 2d paragraph was quoted in Ch. 3, p. 76, and referred to in Ch. 18, p. 546.

24. Ltr, M to E, 2 Dec. 1850, MEW 27:152; 11 Feb. 1851, ibid., 184.
25. See the various documents at MEW 7:414, 564 and MEW 8:602f.
26. See the various letters at MEW 27:594, 28:349, 354, 486, 492, 524, 528, 531, 583, 598, 635.
27. Ltr, M to E, 22 Jan. 1851, MEW 27:165.
28. Ltr, M to E, 9 Feb. 1859, MEW 29:393; see also Engels' comment in reply, 10 Feb. 1859, ibid., 395.
29. Ltr, M to E, 18 May 1859, MEW 29:437.
30. See letters during 1860, at MEW 30:77, 80, 86, 296f.
31. So we learn from ltr, Jenny Marx to Weydemeyer, 27 Feb. 1852, MEW 28:635.
32. Ltr, M to Cluss, 17 Apr., mid-Nov. 1853, MEW 28:583, 598.
33. M: Revel. Com. Trial, MEW 8:462 [ME: Cologne Com. Trial, 110].
34. M: Knight Noble Consc., MEW 9:510.
35. Cf. M: Correction (to a Zurich paper), *G.C.F.I.* 64-66 [1], 292 or 355 [MEW 16:96].
36. Ltr, M to E, 4 Nov. 1864, MEW 31:13 [ME:SC, 13].
37. Collins & Abramsky: *K.M. & Brit. Lab. Movemt.*, 67, 305f.
38. Ltr, M to E, 25 Feb. 1865, MEW 31:84.
39. Ltr, E to M, 3 May 1865, MEW 31:114.
40. Collins & Abramsky, 62.
41. Ltr, M to E, 24 June 1865, MEW 31:126.
42. Ltrs, M to E, 10 Feb., 24 Mar., 2 Apr. 1866, MEW 31:175, 194, 197; Collins & Abramsky, 67, 306.
43. Ltr, M to E, 2 Apr. 1866, MEW 31:197f.
44. For details on Eccarius' anti-Mill work, see Bibliography; note that it exists in three versions.
45. Ltr, E to Schlüter, 7 Dec. 1885, MEW 36:408. This probably applies to the *Commonwealth* series as well as the German brochure; cf. Marx's reference to "*his* critique of Mill" (with *his* meaningfully underlined) in ltr, M to E, 27 June 1867, MEW 31:316. For remarks on and summary of Eccarius' work, see Herrmann: *Kampf von K.M.*, 154-58; but Herrmann misinterprets Marx's phrase "moin Mill," p. 154.
46. See ltr, M to E, 27 June 1867, MEW 31:316, for how much the Comtists were impressed by Eccarius' work.
47. Ltr, M to E, 31 Aug. 1867, MEW 31:333.
48. Ltrs, M to E, 7, 11, 12 Sept. 1867, MEW 31:340, 344, 346.
49. Ltrs, M to E, 4, 9 Oct. 1867, MEW 31:354, 358; cf. *G.C.F.I.* 66-68 [2], 166f.
50. Collins & Abramsky, 130f; ltr, M to E, 9 Oct. 1867, MEW 31:358.
51. Ltr, M to E, 4 Sept. 1867, MEW 31:337f.
52. Ltr, M to E, 16 Sept. 1868, MEW 32:150f; see also Engels' comment, 18 Sept., 1868, ibid., 153.
53. Ltr, M to E, 19 Sept. 1868, MEW 32:155.
54. *G.C.F.I.* 68-70 [3], 38.
55. Collins & Abramsky, 148.
56. Ltr, M to S. Meyer, 14 Sept. 1868, MEW 32:561.
57. Ltr, M to Jung, 14 Sept. 1868, MEW 32:562.
58. Ltr, M to Meyer & Vogt, 28 Oct. 1868, MEW 32:574.

59. Ltr, M to Kugelmann, 12 Dec. 1868, MEW 32:582.
60. Ltr, M to E, 21 May 1869, MEW 32:320.
61. Ltr, M to E, 23 Sept. 1868, MEW 32:160.
62. Collins & Abramsky, 149 fn, quoting from *Baselski Kongress Pervovo Internationala, 1869* (Moscow, 1934), 147.
63. Ltr, M to E, 30 Oct. 1869, MEW 32:381; Collins & Abramsky, 165.
64. Ltr, M to E, 26 Nov. 1869, MEW 32:405; E to M, 22 Feb. 1870, ibid., 452.
65. Ltr, M to Eccarius, 3 May 1872, MEW 33:453f.
66. Collins & Abramsky, 250.
67. Ltr, Jenny Marx to Liebknecht, 26 May 1872, MEW 33:702; ltr, E to Liebknecht, ibid., 472-75 (the whole letter is a valuable summary; my citations are from 475).
68. The news is curtly stated in ltr, M to Sorge, 27 Sept. 1877, MEW 34:296.
69. Collins & Abramsky, 308f.

Special Note I. THE WEITLING MYTH:
HORNY-HANDED PROLETARIAN VERSUS INTELLECTUAL

1. Feuer: *M & Intell.*, 211.
2. Wittke: *Utop. Com.*, 101-04; McLellan: *K.M.*, 155.
3. Wittke: *Utop. Com.*, 85-89.
4. Ibid., 4-11, 309-12.
5. Ibid., 50, 109; see also summary on 53.
6. This is quoted by Weitling in his letter to Hess, 31 Mar. 1846, in *Bund Kom.*, 1:307.
7. M: Crit. Notes King of Pruss., MEW 1:404f [ME:CW 3:201f]; cf. *KMTR* 1:139.
8. Annenkov: *Extraord. Decade*, 168.
9. E: On Hist. C.L., in ME:SW 3:180.
10. Ltr, E to Bebel, 25 Oct. 1888, MEW 37:118.
11. Wittke: *Utop. Com.*, 300; cf. also 99f.
12. Sombart: *Soc. & Soc. Movemt.*, 34; Clark: *Neglected Soc.*, 82-84; Wittke: *Utop. Com.*, 57-63; Kautsky: *Dict. Prole.*, 18-21.
13. Clark: *Neglected Soc.*, 83.
14. Ltr, Weitling to Hess, 31 Mar. 1846, in *Bund Kom.*, 1:307f. See also ltr, E to Bebel, 25 Oct. 1888, MEW 37:118.
15. Hess: *Phil. Soz. Schriften*, 482.
16. Annenkov: *Extraord. Decade*, 169.
17. Ibid., 170.
18. M: Doct. Diss., MEW Eb.1:286 [ME:CW 1:54].
19. Wittke: *Utop. Com.*, 110, 298.
20. Ibid., Ch. 9-14 passim.
21. E: On Hist. Early Christ., in ME: On Relig., 318f.

Special Note J.
MARX'S COURSE IN APRIL-MAY 1848

1. Re Mehring, see his *Karl Marx*, 212. Re Mayer, see the references in Schmidt: *Der Bund d. Komm.*, 578 fn; Schmidt refers to the first edition of Mayer's biography. Re the Bernsteinian Max Quarck and others, see Schmidt, 578-80.
2. Hammen: *Red 48ers*, 216; cf. also 241; for 1849, see 375-80.
3. This fiction is considered in Ch. 8, sec. 5.
4. For the most part, this Special Note is based on information in Schmidt: *Der Bund der Komm. & die Versuche . . . im April und Mai 1848* (see Biblio.) and in Hammen: *Red 48ers*, 216-18; statements not otherwise ascribed will be found here. See also Dowe: *Aktion u. Organisation*, 140-42.
5. The Brussels period, and Marx's organizational policies in general, will be discussed in Volume 3 of *KMTR*.
6. Communist League, Central Comm.: *Decision of March 3, 1848*, in MEW 4:607 [ME:CW 6:651].
7. On Paris as German émigré center, see *KMTR* 1:137.
8. E: On Hist. C.L., in ME:SW 3:184.
9. Communist League, Paris Circle: *Minutes of 8 March 1848*, in MEW 4:608 [ME:CW 6:654f] ; *Minutes of 9 March 1848*, in MEW 4:609 [ME:CW 6:656f].
10. On the German Legion, see Nicolaievsky & M.-H.: *K. Marx*, 148-54; McLellan: *K. Marx*, 192f.
11. Ltr, Mrs. Jenny Marx to Weydemeyer, 16 Mar. 1848, MEW 27:604. For another statement by Marx, see ltr, ME to Bornstedt, 1 Apr. 1848, MEW 27:479 [ME:CW 7:10].
12. ME: Statement ag. Ger. Dem. Soc., in *Bund Kom.* 1:747 [ME:CW 7:8f].
13. Engels: On Hist. C.L., in ME:SW 3:184.
14. In Ch. 7, p. 199f.
15. For the background of Engels' visit to Barmen, the best account is in Gemkow: *Frederick Engels*, 165-67.
16. Ltr, M to E, before 25 Apr. 1848, MEW 27:124.
17. Ltr, E to M, 25 Apr. 1848, MEW 27:125f.
18. Ltr, E to M, 9 May 1848, MEW 27:127.
19. Ibid.
20. For Wolff's close relationship to Marx, see Ch. 13, sec. 7.
21. On the Mainz Appeal, see MEW 5:483 [ME:CW 7:535f] for the text; also *K. M. Chronik*, 49; Fedoseyev et al.: *K. Marx*, 161.
22. In Ch. 8, p. 207. For the Cologne "address," see *Bund Kom.* 1:755.
23. More detailed information on the organizers' itineraries will be found in Schmidt and Dowe (as listed in note 4 above). For Wolff's account of his tour, see *Bund Kom.* 1:759f. On Stephen Born, see Engels' summary in E: On Hist. C.L., in ME:SW 3:185f; also see *Bund Kom.* 1:1110f (note 199).
24. On Dronke's reports, see Kandel, ed.: *M. & E. & erst. prol. Rev.*, 376-78; for the reports themselves, see *Bund Kom.* 1:776, 779, 784, 785. On Dronke's recent recruitment, see ltr, E to M, 18 Mar. 1848, MEW 27:121f.
25. E: M & NRZ, in ME:SW 3:166.
26. In Ch. 8, p. 213f.

BIBLIOGRAPHY
(WORKS CITED)

This list provides bibliographic data for titles referred to in the Reference Notes or in the text. In the first three sections—writings by Marx and Engels, writings by Marx, writings by Engels—titles are given first in English, followed by the original language (in italics), or by a double degree sign (°°) if the original was in English. In these three sections, the form of citation is the same for different kinds of writings—articles, books, or whatever. The following information is provided for individual writings: date of writing (W) or dateline (D); date of first publication by the author (P); source of the original text cited in this book (S); and an English translation, if any, used in this book (Tr). The CAPITALIZED titles are for published books, mainly collections of writings. When two entries are given for the same title, the lower-case entry deals with the writing as such; the capitalized entry represents a book published with that title, but often containing other writings as well. In the fourth section of this list (books and articles by others), entries list the edition used in this book. For abbreviations, see the note introducing the Reference Notes.

WRITINGS BY MARX AND ENGELS

Address of the Central Committee to the Communist League, March 1850. *Ansprache der Zentralbehörde an den Bund vom März 1850.* (W) end of Mar. 1850. (P) in German bourgeois press, 1851; by Engels as appendix to 1885 ed. of M: Revel. Com. Trial (q.v.). (S) MEW 7:244. (Tr) ME:SW 1:175.

Address of the Central Committee to the Communist League, June 1850. *Ansprache der Zentralbehörde an den Bund vom Juni 1850.* (W) beginning of June 1850. (P) by Engels as appendix to 1885 ed. of M: Revel. Com. Trial (q.v.). (S) MEW 7:306. (Tr) ME: Cologne Com. Trial, 245.

Address of the German Democratic Communists of Brussels to Mr. Feargus O'Connor.°° Signed: The Committee / Engels, Gigot, Marx. (D) 17 July 1846. (P) 25 July 1846 in Northern Star. (S) ME:CW 6:58.

The Alleged Schisms in the International. *Les Prétendues Scissions dans l'Internationale.* (D) 5 Mar. 1872. (P) May 1872, as General Council brochure. (S) Mouvement Socialiste, Paris, July-Aug. 1913. (Tr) ME:SW 2:247, with an inaccurate title.

The Alliance of the Socialist Democracy and the International Working Men's Association. *L'Alliance de la Démocratie Socialiste et l'Association Inter-*

717

nationale des Travailleurs. (W) Apr.-July 1873, by Engels, Marx, and Paul Lafargue, with materials sent in by others. (P) end of Aug. 1873, as a General Council pamphlet, no personal signatures, London, A. Darson; Hamburg, Meissner, 1873. (S) The foregoing pamphlet. —The German translation published as a pamphlet in 1874 is reprinted in MEW 18:327.

ANARCHISM AND ANARCHO-SYNDICALISM. (Above title: Marx, Engels, Lenin.) New York, International Pub., 1972.

ARTICLES IN THE *NEW AMERICAN CYCLOPAEDIA.* Edited with historical introduction by Hal Draper. Berkeley, Independent Socialist Press, 1969.

ARTICLES ON BRITAIN. Moscow, Progress Pub., 1971.

AUSGEWÄHLTE BRIEFE. Marx–Engels–Lenin–Stalin Institut beim ZK der SED. Berlin, Dietz, 1953. —This edition gives texts in original language.

Circular Against Kriege. *Zirkular gegen Kriege.* (W) 20 Apr.-11 May 1846. (D) 11 May 1846. (P) May 1846, as circular; signed Engels, Marx, and four others; repub. in periodicals in June and July. (S) MEW 4:3. (Tr) ME:CW 6:35.

Circular Letter to Bebel and German Party Leadership. (In German) (W) 17-18 Sept. 1879; not dated. (S) MEW 34:394 or 19:150. (Tr) most, in ME: Corr. (35), 362; Part III of letter in ME:SW 3:88 or ME:SC, 321.

THE CIVIL WAR IN THE UNITED STATES. 3rd ed. New York, Citadel Press, 1961.

THE COLOGNE COMMUNIST TRIAL. R. Livingstone, ed. & tr. New York, International Pub.; London, L&W, 1971.

The Communist Manifesto. *Das Kommunistische Manifest* (originally *Manifest der Kommunistischen Partei*). (W) Dec. 1847-Jan. 1848. (P) brochure, Feb. 1848. (S) MEW 4:459. (Tr) ME:CW 6:477; ME:SW 1:98.

THE COMMUNIST MANIFESTO. D. Ryazanoff, ed. (including other writings). London, M. Lawrence, 1930.

CORRESPONDENCE 1846-1895. A SELECTION . . . (Binding title: *Selected Correspondence*). D. Torr, ed. & tr. (Marxist Lib., 29). New York, International Pub., 1935.

LA CORRISPONDENZIA DI MARX E ENGELS CON ITALIANI 1848-1895. A cura di G. Del Bo. (Istituto G. Feltrinelli. Testi e documenti di storia moderna e contemporanea, 11.) Milan, Feltrinelli, 1964.

Demands of the Communist Party in Germany. *Forderungen der Kommunistischen Partei in Deutschland.* (W) 21-29 Mar. 1848. (P) end of Mar. 1848, as leaflet; Apr. in some German papers. (S) MEW 5:3. (Tr) Struik: *Birth Com. Manif.*, 190.

The Downfall of the Camphausen Government. [German original not in MEW.] (M/E). (P) 22 June 1848 in NRZ. (Tr) ME:CW 7:106.

Editorial Note to Article by Eccarius. *Redaktionelle Anmerkung zu dem Artikel . . . von J. G. Eccarius.* (W) Oct. 1850. (P) 29 Nov. 1850 in NRZ Revue, no. 5/6, May-Oct. 1850. (S) MEW 7:416.

The German Ideology. *Die deutsche Ideologie . . .* (W) Nov. 1845-Aug. 1846. (S) MEW 3:9. (Tr) ME:CW 5:19, embodies new arrangement of Part 1, revising arrangement in MEW; for tr. of MEW arrangement, see next entry.

THE GERMAN IDEOLOGY. Moscow, Progress Pub., 1964. (Complete work.)

GESAMTAUSGABE (full title: *Historisch-kritische Gesamtausgabe . . .*) Marx-Engels Institute, Moscow, ed. Frankfurt/Berlin/Moscow, 1927-1935. Series (Abteilung) I comprises vols. 1-7 plus an unnumbered 8th; Series III comprises vols. 1-4 (correspondence); Series II, IV never published; others never completed. In Series I, vol. 1 comprises two volumes, here called vol. 1.1 and 1.2. (Abbrev.: MEGA.)

The Great Men of the Emigration. *Die grossen Männer des Exils.* (W) May-June 1852. (S) MEW 8:233. (Tr) ME: Cologne Com. Trial, 135, titled "Heroes of the Exile."

The Holy Family . . . *Die heilige Familie oder Kritik der kritischen Kritik . . .* (W) Sept.-Nov. 1844. (P) Feb. 1845, as book, Frankfurt. (S) MEW 2:3. (Tr) ME:CW 4:5.

IRELAND AND THE IRISH QUESTION. Moscow, Progress Pub., 1971.

LETTERS TO AMERICANS 1848–1895. L. E. Mins, tr. New York, International Pub., 1953.

ON BRITAIN. 2nd ed. Moscow, FLPH, 1962.

ON RELIGION. Moscow, FLPH, 1957.

Patow's Memorandum on Redemption. *Patows Ablösungsdenkschrift* (M/E). (P) 25 June 1848 in NRZ. (S) MEW 5:106.

Review [January-February 1850]. *Revue* [in German]. (D) 31 Jan. 1850. (P) end of Mar. 1850 in NRZ Revue, no. 2. (S) MEW 7:213. (Tr) M: Revols. of 1848, 265; part in ME: On Colon., 17.

Review [March-April 1850]. *Revue* [in German]. (D) 18 Apr. 1850. (P) mid-May 1850 in NRZ Revue, no. 4 (S) MEW 7:292. (Tr) M: Revols. of 1848, 281.

Review. May to October. *Revue / Mai bis Oktober.* (W) July-Oct. 1850. (P) Nov. 1850 in NRZ Revue, no. 5/6. (S) MEW 7:421.

[Review of] G. Fr. Daumer, "Die Religion des neuen Weltalters . . ." [in German]. (W) Mar. 1850. (P) end of Mar. 1850 in NRZ Revue, no. 2. (S) MEW 7:198. (Tr) ME: On Relig., 89.

[Review of] Guizot, "Pourquoi la révolution d'Angleterre a-t-elle réussi? . . ." [in German]. (W) Feb. 1850. (P) end of Mar. 1850 in NRZ Revue, no. 2. (S) MEW 7:207. (Tr) ME: Art. Brit., 89. —Probably by Marx.

[Review of] "Les Conspirateurs," par A. Chenu . . . [in German]. (W) mid-Apr. to mid-May 1850. (P) mid-May 1850 in NRZ Revue, no. 4. (S) MEW 7:266. —Probably by Marx.

REVOLUTION IN SPAIN. (Marxist Lib., 12) New York, International Pub., 1939.

THE REVOLUTION OF 1848-49. Articles from the Neue Rheinische Zeitung. S. Ryanzanskaya, tr.; B. Isaacs, ed. New York, International Pub., 1972.

THE RUSSIAN MENACE TO EUROPE. A COLLECTION . . . P. W. Blackstock & B. F. Hoselitz, eds. Glencoe, Ill., Free Press, 1952.

SCRITTI ITALIANI. A cura di G. Bosio. (Saggi e documentazioni, 1) Milan/Rome, Ed. Avanti, 1955.

SELECTED CORRESPONDENCE. I. Lasker, tr.; S. Ryazanskaya, ed. 2nd ed. Moscow, Progress Pub., 1965. (Abbrev.: ME:SC.)

SELECTED CORRESPONDENCE. Moscow, FLPH, n.d. [1955].

SELECTED WORKS IN THREE VOLUMES. Moscow, Progress Pub., 1969-70. (Abbrev.: ME:SW.)

SELECTED WORKS IN TWO VOLUMES. Moscow, FLPH, 1955.

Stein [in German] (M/E). (P) 18 Feb. 1849 in NRZ. (S) MEW 6:298.

The Turin *Concordia. Die Turiner "Concordia."* (M/E) (P) 25 July 1848 in NRZ. (S) MEW 5:260.

WERKE. Institut für Marxismus-Leninismus beim ZK der SED, ed. Berlin, Dietz, 1956-68. Thirty-nine volumes plus supplements; Vol. 26 (*Theories of Surplus Value*) in three parts, 26.1, 26.2, 26.3; supplementary volume (*Ergänzungsband*) in two parts, Eb.1, Eb.2.

WRITINGS ON THE PARIS COMMUNE. Hal Draper, ed. New York, Monthly Review Press, 1971.

WRITINGS BY MARX

Address to the National Labor Union of the United States.°° (W) Read to General Council 11 May 1869; dated 12 May. (P) soon afterward, as a General Council leaflet; also in several periodicals. (S) ME:SW 2:156 (without signatures), or G.C.F.I. 68-70 [3], 319 (with signatures).

Affairs Continental and English.°° (D) 23 Aug. 1853. (P) 5 Sept. 1853 in N. Y. Tribune.

Affairs in Prussia.°° This is the title of several articles in the N. Y. Tribune during 1858-1860.

The Agitation Against the Tightening of the Sunday Bill. *Die Aufregung gegen die Verschärfung der Sonntagsfeier.* (P) 5 July 1855 in Neue Oder-Ztg. (S) MEW 11:341. (Tr) ME: On Brit., 440.

American Split [mostly in Eng.]. (W) end of Feb. to end of May 1872. (S) G.C.F.I. 71-72 [5], 323.

The Belgian Massacres.°° (D) 4 May 1869. (P) May 1869, as a General Council leaflet. (S) G.C.F.I. 68-70 [3], 312.

The Berlin Conspiracy—London Police—Mazzini—Radetsky.°° (D) 8 Apr. 1853. (P) 21 Apr. 1853 in N. Y. Tribune. (S) part in ME: Cologne Com. Trial, 273 (misdated).

The Bill on the Abolition of Feudal Burdens. *Der Gesetzentwurf über die Aufhebung der Feudallasten.* (P) 30 July 1848 in NRZ. (S) MEW 5:278. (Tr) ME: Rev. 48/49, 71.

The Billion. *Die Milliarde.* (P) 16 Mar. 1849 in NRZ. (S) MEW 6:353. —Authorship not ascribed in MEW.

The Bourgeoisie and the Counterrevolution. *Die Bourgeoisie und die Kontrerevolution.* (P) 10-31 Dec. 1848, in 4 parts, in NRZ. (S) MEW 6:102. (Tr) ME: Rev. 48/49, 177; part 2 only in ME:SW 1:138.

The British Rule in India.°° (D) 10 June 1853. (P) 25 June 1853 in N. Y. Tribune. (S) ME:SW 1:488.

The Camphausen Ministry. *Das Ministerium Camphausen.* (P) 4 June 1848 in NRZ. (S) MEW 5:32. (Tr) M: Revols. of 1848, 118.

Capital. *Das Kapital. Kritik der politischen Ökonomie.* (W) Aug. 1863 to Feb. 1866; for vol. 1 as published, Feb. 1866 to Aug. 1867. (P) Vol. 1: Sept. 1867; vol. 2 (Engels, ed.): 1885; vol. 3 (Engels, ed.): 1894. (S) MEW 23, 24, 25. (Tr) next entry.

CAPITAL . . . Vol. 1: S. Moore and E. Aveling, trs.; Engels, ed. Moscow, FLPH, n.d.; vols. 2-3 (Untermann tr. revised): Moscow, FLPH, 1957-59.

Capital—Afterword to the Second German Edition [of Vol. 1]. *Nachwort zur zweiten Auflage* . . . (D) 24 Jan. 1873. (P) beginning of June 1873, in the book. (S) MEW 23:18. (Tr) published as preface to English edition of 1887 edited by Engels: in M: Cap. 1:12 or ME:SW 2:91.

The Chartists.°° (D) 10 Aug. 1852. (P) 25 Aug. 1852 in N. Y. Tribune. (S) ME: On Brit., 358.

The Civil War in France. Address of the General Council . . .°° (W) May 1871. (P) June 1871, as pamphlet. (S) ME:SW 2:202.

The Civil War in France—First Draft.°° (W) Apr.-May 1871. (S) ME: Writings on Paris Commune, 103.

The Civil War in the United States. *Der Bürgerkrieg in den Vereinigten Staaten.* (P) 7 Nov. 1861 in Die Presse. (S) MEW 15:339. (Tr) ME: Civ. War in U.S., 71.

The Class Struggles in France 1848 to 1850. *Die Klassenkämpfe in Frankreich*

1848 bis 1850. (W) Jan.-Nov. 1850. (P) Mar.-Nov. 1850 in NRZ Revue, nos. 1, 2, 3, 5/6, as series of articles. (S) MEW 7:9. (Tr) ME:SW 1:205.

The Communism of the Rheinische Beobachter. *Der Kommunismus des "Rheinischen Beobachters."* (P) 12 Sept. 1847 in Deutsche Brüsseler Zeitung. (S) MEW 4:191. (Tr) ME:CW 6:220.

Connections between the International Working Men's Association and English Working Men's Organizations. *Die Verbindungen der Internationalen Arbeiterassoziation mit den englischen Arbeiterorganisationen.* (P) 17 Oct. 1868 in Demokratisches Wochenblatt, untitled. (S) MEW 16:331, titled as above. (Tr) G.C.F.I. 68-70 [3], 384, titled as above.

Conspectus of Bakunin's Book *Statism and Anarchy. Konspect von Bakunins Buch "Staatlichkeit und Anarchie."* (W) 1874 to beginning of 1875, as notes. (S) MEW 18:597.

Correction. *Berichtigung.* (P) 22 Apr. 1865, in Der Weisse Adler, Zurich; signed by Jung, corr. secy. (S) G.C.F.I. 64-66 [1], 292, or MEW 16:96. (Tr) G.C.F.I. 64-66 [1], 355.

The Counterrevolution in Berlin. *Die Kontrerevolution in Berlin.* (P) 12-14 Nov. 1848, in 3 parts, in NRZ. (S) MEW 6:7. (Tr) ME: Rev. 48/49, 157.

Critical Notes on "The King of Prussia and Social Reform." *Kritische Randglossen zu dem Artikel "Der König von Preussen und die Sozialreform ..."* (P) 7-10 Aug. 1844 in Vorwärts, Paris. (S) MEW 1:392. (Tr) ME:CW 3:189.

Critique of the Gotha Program. *Kritik des Gothaer Programms. Randglossen zum Programm der deutschen Arbeiterpartei.* (W) Apr.-May 1875. (S) MEW 19:15. (Tr) ME:SW 3:13.

Critique of Hegel's Philosophy of Right: Introduction. *Zur Kritik der Hegelschen Rechtsphilosophie. Einleitung.* (W) end of 1843 to Jan. 1844. (P) Feb. 1844 in DFJ. (S) MEW 1:378. (Tr) ME:CW 3:175.

Critique ·of Hegel's Philosophy of Right (Manuscript). *Aus der Kritik der Hegelschen Rechtsphilosophie. Kritik des Hegelschen Staatsrechts ...* (W) Summer 1843. (S) MEW 1:201. (Tr) ME:CW 3:3.

Debates on Freedom of the Press. *Debatten über Pressfreiheit ... (Verhandlungen des 6. rheinischen Landtags. Erster Artikel).* (W) Apr. 1842. (P) 5-19 May 1842 in RZ. (S) MEW 1:28. (Tr) ME:CW 1:132.

Declaration. *Erklärung.* (P) 15 Apr. 1849 in NRZ, signed by Marx and fellow members of Democratic Assoc. (S) MEW 6:426.

The Deeds of the House of Hohenzollern. *Die Taten des Hauses Hohenzollern.* (P) 10 May 1849 in NRZ. (S) MEW 6:477.

Defense—Finances—Decrease of the Aristocracy—Politics.°° (D) 8 Feb. 1853. (P) 23 Feb. 1853 in N. Y. Tribune.

The Democratic Party. *Die demokratische Partei.* (P) 2 June 1848 in NRZ. (S) MEW 5:22. (Tr) ME: Rev. 48/49, 27. —Drafted by Bürgers, reworked by Marx.

Doctoral Dissertation: Difference Between the Democritean and Epicurean Philosophies of Nature. *Doktordissertation: Differenz der demokritischen and epikureischen Naturphilosophie.* (W) 1840 to Mar. 1841. (S) MEW Eb.1:257. (Tr) ME:CW 1:25.

Economic and Philosophic Manuscripts of 1844. *Ökonomisch-philosophische Manuskripte aus dem Jahre 1844.* (W) Apr.-Aug. 1844. (S) MEW Eb.1:465. (Tr) ME:CW 3:229.

The Eighteenth Brumaire of Louis Bonaparte. *Der achtzehnte Brumaire des Louis Bonaparte.* (W) Dec. 1851 to Mar. 1852. (P) May 1852 in Die Revolution,

New York. (S) MEW 8:111. (Tr) ME:SW 1:398. —Preface to the Second Edition. *Vorwort* . . . (D) 23 June 1869. (P) July 1869, in the book. (S) MEW 16:358 or 8:559. (Tr) ME:SW 1:394.

The Eighteenth of March. *Der 18. März.* (P) 18 Mar. 1849 in NRZ, untitled. (S) MEW 6:362.

The Election Results in the Northern States. *Die Wahlsresultate in den Nordstaaten.* (W) 18 Nov. 1862. (P) 23 Nov. 1862 in Die Presse, untitled. (S) MEW 15:565.

The Elections—Tories and Whigs.°° (D) 6 Aug. 1852. (P) 21 Aug. 1852 in N. Y. Tribune. (S) ME: On Brit., 351.

The Emancipation Question.°° (D) 29 and 31 Dec. 1858. (P) 17 Jan. 1859 in N. Y. Tribune; two articles under same head.

The English Middle Class.°° (W) probably by 31 Mar. 1854. (P) 1 Aug. 1854 in N. Y. Tribune, some parts rewritten by paper. (S) part in ME: Art. Brit., 218.

The Frankfurt Assembly. *Die Frankfurter Versammlung.* (P) 23 Nov. 1848 in NRZ. (S) MEW 6:43. (Tr) ME: Rev. 48/49, 169.

From the *Mémoires de R. Levasseur;* Notes. [In German and French.] (W) end of 1843 to beginning of 1844. (S) MEGA I, 3:417. (Tr) ME:CW 3:361.

The Future Results of British Rule in India.°° (D) 22 July 1853. (P) 8 Aug. 1853 in N. Y. Tribune. (S) ME:SW 1:494.

The General Council to the Federal Council of Romance Switzerland. *Le Conseil Général au Conseil Fédéral de la Suisse Romande.* (W) for adoption by the G.C. on 1 Jan. 1870. (P) excerpt in ME: Alleged Schisms, 1872. (S) G.C.F.I. 68-70 [3], 354. (Tr) ibid., 399; part in ME:SW 2:174.

General Rules and Administrative Regulations of the International Working Men's Association, 1871.°° (W) Sept.-Oct. 1871. (P) Nov. 1871. (S) G.C.F.I. 70-71 [4], 451; the Rules only in ME:SW 2:19.

Grundrisse [commonly so called in English]: Fundamentals of the Critique of Political Economy. *Grundrisse der Kritik der politischen Ökonomie (Robentwurf).* (W) 1857-58. (S) next entry. (Tr) see below for Nicolaus tr.

GRUNDRISSE DER KRITIK DER POLITISCHE ÖKONOMIE (ROHENTWURF) 1857-1858. ANHANG 1850-1859. Marx–Engels–Lenin Institute, Moscow. Berlin, Dietz, 1953, 2d ed.

GRUNDRISSE. FOUNDATIONS OF THE CRITIQUE OF POLITICAL ECONOMY (ROUGH DRAFT). Translated with a Foreword by Martin Nicolaus. (Pelican Marx Library) London, Allen Lane, 1973.

Herr Vogt. *Herr Vogt.* (W) Jan.-Nov. 1860. (P) Dec. 1860, as book. (S) MEW 14:381.

Inaugural Address of the Working Men's International Association.°° (W) 21-27 Oct. 1864. (P) 5 Nov. 1864 in Bee-Hive; then in pamphlet *Address and Provisional Rules* . . ., London, 1864; German tr. by Marx in Social-Demokrat, 21-30 Dec. 1864. (S) ME:SW 2:11; German version, MEW 16:5.

The Indian Revolt.°° (D) 4 Sept. 1857. (P) 16 Sept. 1857 in N. Y. Tribune. (S) ME: On Brit., 469.

Indifference to Politics. *L'Indifferenza in materia politica.* (W) end of Dec. to beginning of Jan. 1873. (D) Jan. 1873. (P) in Almanacco Repubblicano per l'anno 1874, Lodi, ed. E. Bignami. (S) ME: Scritti Ital., 98. (Tr) ME: Anarch. & A.-S., 94.

The June Revolution. *Die Junirevolution.* (P) 29 June 1848 in NRZ. (S) MEW 5:133. (Tr) ME: Rev. 48/49, 45.

Karl Marx Before the Cologne Jury. *Karl Marx vor den Kölner Geschworenen.* (W) Marx's defense speech at trial, 8 Feb. 1849. (P) 25-27 Feb. 1849 in NRZ;

pamphlet titled as above, 1885. (S) MEW 6:240. (Tr) ME: Rev. 48/49, 227.

The King of Prussia's Insanity.°° (D) 2 Oct. 1858. (P) 23 Oct. 1858 in N. Y. Tribune.

The Knight of the Noble Consciousness. *Der Ritter vom edelmütigen Bewusstsein.* (D) 28 Nov. 1853. (P) Jan. 1854, as pamphlet, New York. (S) MEW 9:489.

The Kölnische Zeitung on the Elections. *Die "Kölnische Zeitung" über die Wahlen.* (P) 1 Feb. 1849 in NRZ. (S) MEW 6:214.

Kossuth, Mazzini and Louis Napoleon.°° (D) 16 Nov. 1852. (P) 1 Dec. 1852 in N. Y. Tribune, as letter to the editor.

The Labor Parliament.°° (D) 10 Mar. 1854. (P) 29 Mar. 1854 in N. Y. Tribune.

Letter to the Labour Parliament.°° (D) 9 Mar. 1854. (P) 18 Mar. 1854 in People's Paper. (S) ME: Art. Brit., 216.

Letter to V. I. Zasulich of 8 March 1881: Drafts. [Original in French.] (S) Marx–Engels–Archiv, Frankfurt. D. Ryazanov, ed., Bd. 1, p. 318-42, incl. four drafts and final version. (Tr) first draft only in ME:SW 3:152; final version in ME:SC, 339.

LETTRES ET DOCUMENTS DE KARL MARX 1856-1883. (Texts in original languages.) In Istituto G. Feltrinelli, Milan, *Annali*, Anno I, p. 149.

The London Times and Lord Palmerston.°° (D) 5 Oct. 1861. (P) 21 Oct. 1861 in N. Y. Tribune. (S) ME: Art. Brit., 309.

The March Association. *Der Märzverein.* (P) 11 Mar. 1849 in NRZ. (S) MEW 6:334.

Mazzini and Napoleon.°° (W) 30 Mar. 1858. (P) 11 May 1858 in N. Y. Tribune.

A Meeting. *Ein Meeting.* (P) 24 Mar. 1855 in Neue Oder-Ztg. (S) MEW 11:135. (Tr) ME: Art. Brit., 229.

Memorandum to Hermann Jung Apropos of the Conflict in the Paris Section.°° (W) 16-18 Mar. 1865. (S) G.C.F.I. 64-66 [1], 265.

The Militia Bill. *Der Bürgerwehrgesetzentwurf.* (P) 21-24 July 1848, in 3 parts in NRZ. (S) MEW 5:243. —Authorship not ascribed in MEW.

MISÈRE DE LA PHILOSOPHIE. Réponse à La Philosophie de la Misère de M. Proudhon (Oeuvres Complètes de Karl Marx) Paris, Ed. Sociales, 1968.

Montesquieu LVI. [In German.] (P) 21-22 Jan. 1849 in NRZ. (S) MEW 6:182.

Moralizing Criticism and Critical Morality. *Die moralisierende Kritik und die kritisierende Moral. Beitrag zur deutschen Kulturgeschichte gegen Karl Heinzen* ... (P) 28 Oct.-25 Nov. 1847 in Deutsche Brüsseler Ztg. (S) MEW 4:331. (Tr) ME:CW 6:312.

The Nationalization of the Land. (W) Mar.-Apr. 1872. (S) Labour Monthly, Sept. 1952, p. 415, but erroneously identified. Revised version of Marx's draft by Dupont published 15 June 1872 in the International Herald, titled as shown, repr. in ME:SW 2:288.

The New English Budget.°° (D) 20 Feb. 1857. (P) 9 Mar. 1857 in N. Y. Tribune.

Notebook on the Paris Commune. Press Excerpts, April-May 1871. (S) original text, mostly French, in Arkhiv Marksa i Engel'sa, Moscow, vol. 15, 1963, p. 22.

Notes for the Report on Wages, Price and Profit.°° (W) June 1865. (S) G.C.F.I. 64-66[1], 272.

Notes on Adolph Wagner's *Lehrbuch der politischen Ökonomie. Randglossen zu Adolph Wagners "Lehrbuch der politischen Ökonomie."* (W) second half of 1879 to Nov. 1880. (S) MEW 19:355.

On Friedrich List's Book *Das Nationale System der Politischen Ökonomie.* (Draft of an Article). [In German] (W) Mar. 1845; unfinished ms. (S) none as yet. (Tr) ME:CW 4:265.

On the Jewish Question. *Zur Judenfrage.* (W) Autumn 1843. (P) Feb. 1844 in D.F.J. (S) MEW 1:347. (Tr) ME:CW 3:146.

Peuchet: On Suicide. *Peuchet: vom Selbstmord.* (W) second half of 1845. (P) Jan. 1846 in Gesellschaftsspiegel, Elberfeld, Bd. 2, Heft 7. (S) MEGA I, 3:391. (Tr) ME:CW 4:597.

The Poverty of Philosophy. *Misère de la Philosophie. Réponse à La Philosophie de la Misère de M. Proudhon.* (W) First half of 1847; foreword d. 15 June 1847. (P) July 1847, as book, Paris/Brussels. (S) see entry under French title. (Tr) ME:CW 6:105.

Proudhon's Speech Against Thiers. *Proudhons Rede gegen Thiers.* (P) 5 Aug. 1848 in NRZ. (S) MEW 5:305. —Authorship not ascribed in MEW.

Provisional Rules of the Association.°° (W) 21-27 Oct. 1864. (P) 1864, as pamphlet. (S) G.C.F.I. 64-66[1], 288. (See also M: General Rules . . .)

Prussia.°° (W) 15 Apr. 1856. (P) 5 May 1856 in N. Y. Tribune.

The Prussians (That Canaille). This is an unpublished manuscript, held by the Marx-Engels–Lenin Institute, Moscow, from which quotations are given in the pamphlet *Reactionary Prussianism* (which see in fourth section of Bibliography).

Rebuke. *Abfertigung.* (P) 27 Dec. 1848 in NRZ. (S) MEW 6:145. —Authorship not ascribed in MEW.

Record of a Speech on the Irish Question Delivered by Karl Marx to the German Workers' Educational Association in London on December 16, 1867. *Aufzeichnung eines Vortrages von Karl Marx zur irischen Frage . . .* (S) MEW 16:550. (Tr) ME: Ire. & Ir. Ques., 140. —This report of Marx's speech was written by J. G. Eccarius for *Vorbote* but not published; for Marx's speech, see MEW 16:445 and ME: Ire. & Ir. Ques., 126.

Report of the General Council to the Fourth Annual Congress . . . *Bericht des Generalraths . . . an IV. allgemeinen Congress in Basel.* (D) 1 Sept. 1869; signed by the G.C. (P) Delivered 7 Sept. 1869 in German and French; published in German as pamphlet, titled as above, Basel, 1869; in English and French, published in pamphlet *Report of the Fourth Annual Congress* etc., Basel, 1869, and then in periodicals. (S) G.C.F.I. 68-70 [3], 326, for English version; MEW 16:370, for German.

Report on Marx's Speech Against Weitling at the Cologne Democratic Association. *Bericht über das Auftreten von Karl Marx gegen Wilhelm Weitling . . .* (W) speech delivered 4 Aug. 1848. (P) report of speech published in Der Wächter am Rhein, Cologne, 23 Aug. 1848. (S) Photocopy of Wächter am Rhein article; part in Bund Kom. 1:827; but second part is relegated to notes, p. 1122, on ground it is distorted; under German title as above. (Tr) ME:CW 7:556f.

Resolutions on the Split in the United States' Federation Passed by the General Council . . .°° (W) about 5 Mar. 1872; adopted by G.C. 5 and 12 Mar. (P) in Apr.-May in periodicals. (S) G.C.F.I. 71-72 [5], 410.

Revelations on the Communist Trial in Cologne. *Enthüllungen über den Kommunisten-Prozess zu Köln.* (W) Oct.-Dec. 1852. (P) Jan. 1853, as pamphlet, Basel. (S) MEW 8:405. (Tr) ME: Cologne Com. Trial, 57. —Postscript. *Nachwort.* (D) 8 Jan. 1875. (P) 27 Jan. 1875, in Volksstaat, then in 1875 edition of book. (S) MEW 18:568 or 8:574. (Tr) ME: Cologne Com. Trial, 131.

Revolution in Spain—I.°° (W) 25 July 1856. (P) 8 Aug. 1856 in N. Y. Tribune. (S) ME: Revol. in Spain, 141.

The Revolutionary Movement. *Die revolutionäre Bewegung.* (P) 1 Jan. 1849 in NRZ. (S) MEW 6:148. (Tr) ME: Rev. 48/49, 203.

Revolutionary Spain.°° (Series of eight articles) (P) 9 Sept.–2 Dec. 1854 in N. Y. Tribune. (S) ME: Revol. in Spain, 19.

THE REVOLUTIONS OF 1848. (Pelican Marx Library. Political Writings, vol. 1) D. Fernbach, ed. Penguin Books, 1973.

Riot at Constantinople—German Table Moving—The Budget.°° (D) 22 Apr. 1853. (P) 6 May 1853 in N. Y. Tribune.

Russian Policy Against Turkey.°° (D) 1 July 1853. (P) 14 July 1853 in N. Y. Tribune.

The Russian Victory—Position of England and France.°° (D) 13 Dec. 1853. (P) 27 Dec. 1853 in N. Y. Tribune.

Second Address of the General Council of the International Working Men's Association on the Franco-Prussian War.°° (W) 6–9 Sept. 1870. (D) 9 Sept. 1870. (P) bet. 11–13 Sept. 1870, as leaflet. (S) MEW:SW 2:195.

Spain—Intervention. *Spanien—Intervention.* (W) about 21 Nov. 1854; drafted for the N. Y. Tribune but not published; only German version in MEW has been published. (S) MEW 10:631.

Speech at the Anniversary of the German Educational Society for Workers in London . . . *Aufzeichnung einer Rede von Karl Marx auf dem Stiftungsfest des Deutschen Bildungsverein für Arbeiter in London* . . . (W) delivered 28 Feb. 1867; this report written by F. Lessner as part of an article on the affair. (P) Lessner's report published in *Der Vorbote*, 3 Mar. 1867. (S) MEW 16:524.

Speech at Workers Association Committee Session of 15 January 1849. *Komiteesitzung des Arbeitervereines vom 15 Januar 1849.* (P) 21 Jan. 1849 in Freiheit, Arbeit, organ of the Association. (S) MEW 6:578.

Speech by Mr. Karl Marx [on the Polish question]. *Discours de M. Karl Marx.* (W) delivered 22 Feb. 1848, in French. (P) March 1848 in brochure, *Célébration, à Bruxelles, du deuxième anniversaire de la Révolution Polonaise* . . . (S) MEGA I, 6:409. (Tr) ME:CW 6:545.

Speech on the Question of Free Trade. *Discours sur la Question du Libre Echange. Prononcé à l'Association Démocratique de Bruxelles* . . . (W) delivered 9 Jan. 1848, in French. (P) Feb. 1848, as pamphlet, Brussels. (S) M: Misère de la Phil./68, 197. (Tr) ME:CW 6:450; "printed according to the Amer. edition of 1889 . . ."

The State of British Manufactures.°° (D) 25 Feb. 1859. (P) 15 Mar. 1859 on N. Y. Tribune.

Theories of Surplus Value. *Theorien über den Mehrwert.* (W) Jan. 1862–July 1863 in notebooks. (P) in 1905-10 as edited and revised by Kautsky. (S) MEW 26.1, 26.2, 26.3, newly edited version. (Tr) next entry.

THEORIES OF SURPLUS VALUE (VOLUME IV OF CAPITAL). Three vols. by various translators, called Parts I to III; Moscow, FLPH (vol. 1) and Progress Pub. (vol. 2-3), n.d., 1968, 1971.

To the Workers of Cologne. *An die Arbeiter Kölns.* (P) 19 May 1849 in NRZ, signed by the Editorial Board. (S) MEW 6:519. (Tr) ME: Rev. 48/49, 266.

The Turkish War—Industrial Distress.°° (D) 2 Dec. 1853. (P) 16 Dec. 1853 in N. Y. Tribune.

Value, Price and Profit. *See* M: Wages, Price and Profit.

Victory of the Counterrevolution in Vienna. *Sieg der Kontrerevolution zu Wien.* (P) 7 Nov. 1848 in NRZ. (S) MEW 5:455. (Tr) ME: Rev. 48/49, 146.

Vindication of the Moselle Correspondent. *Rechtfertigung des ††-Korres-*

726   Bibliography of Works Cited

pondenten von der Mosel. (P) 15-20 Jan. 1843 in RZ. (S) MEW 1:172. (Tr)
ME:CW 1:332.
Wage-Labor and Capital. *Lohnarbeit und Kapital.* (W) articles based on lectures
delivered in Dec. 1847, but (P) 5-11 Apr. 1849 in NRZ, series unfinished;
revised ed. by Engels 1891. (S) MEW 6:397; Marx's original version of 1849 in
MEGA I, 6:473. (Tr) ME:SW 1:150, Engels' revised version.
Wages. *Arbeitslohn.* (W) end of Dec. 1847, ms. notes for lectures later written up
as M: Wage-Labor & Cap. (S) MEW 6:535.
Wages, Price and Profit.°° (W) end of May to 27 June 1865; delivered as lectures
to General Council 20 and 27 June 1865. (P) first posthumously, 1898, as
brochure titled *Value, Price and Profit,* ed. by Eleanor Marx Aveling; first
German tr., titled *Lohn, Preis und Profit,* in Neue Zeit. (S) ME:SW 2:31.
The War Question—British Population and Trade Returns—Doings of Parliament.°° (D) 12 Aug. 1853. (P) 24 Aug. 1853 in N. Y. Tribune.
The War Question—Financial Matters—Strikes.°° (D) 7 Oct. 1853. (P) 21 Oct.
1853 in N.Y. Tribune. .
War—Strikes—Dearth.°° (D) 1 Nov. 1853. (P) 15 Nov. 1853 in N. Y. Tribune.

WRITINGS BY ENGELS

The Abdication of the Bourgeoisie. *Die Abdankung der Bourgoisie.* (P) 5 Oct.
1889 in Sozialdemokrat. (S) MEW 21:383. (Tr) ME: Art. Brit., 395.
The Agrarian Program of the Chartists. *Le programme agraire des Chartistes.* (P) 1
Nov. 1847 in La Réforme, untitled. (S) MEGA I, 6:333. (Tr) ME:CW 6:358.
American Food and the Land Question.°° (P) 2 July 1881 in Labour Standard.
(S) E: Art. Lab. Stand., 28.
Anti-Dühring (full title: Herr Eugen Dühring's Revolution in Science). *Anti-
Dühring (Herrn Eugen Dührings Umwälzung der Wissenschaft).* (W) Sept. 1876
to June 1878. (P) Jan. 1877 to July 1878, as series in Vorwärts; 1878 as book.
(S) MEW 20:1 (Tr) next entry.
ANTI-DÜHRING. HERR EUGEN DÜHRING'S REVOLUTION IN SCIENCE.
2nd ed., Moscow. FLPH, 1959.
The Antwerp Death Sentences. *Die Antwerpner Todesurteile.* (P) 3 Sept. 1848 in
NRZ. (S) MEW 5:378. (Tr) ME: Rev. 48/49, 110.
ARTICLES FROM THE LABOUR STANDARD (1881). Moscow, Progress Pub.,
1955, 1965. —This edition contains 12 articles.
The Bakuninists at Work. *Die Bakunisten an der Arbeit. Denkschrift über den
Aufstand in Spanien in Sommer 1873.* (W) Sept.-Oct. 1873. (P) 31 Oct. to 5
Nov. 1873, in 3 parts, in Volksstaat; then as a pamphlet; in 1894 included in
the pamphlet *Internationales aus dem "Volksstaat" (1871-75),* slightly revised.
(S) MEW 18:476. (Tr) ME: Revol. in Spain, 211.
Berlin Conciliation-Debates. *Berliner Vereinbarungsdebatten.* (P) 7 June and 7
July, 1848. (S) MEW 5:44 and 178. —Two separate articles with same title.
The Berlin Debate on the Revolution. *Die Berliner Debatte über die Revolution.*
(P) 14-17 June 1848, in 4 parts, in NRZ. (S) MEW 5:64. (Tr) first part in ME:
Rev. 48/49, 35.
The Communists and Karl Heinzen. *Die Kommunisten und Karl Heinzen.* (P) 3-7
Oct. 1847, in 2 parts, in Deutsche Brüsseler Ztg. (S) MEW 4:309. (Tr) ME:CW
6:291.
The Conciliation-Assembly of 15 June. *Die Vereinbarungsversammlung vom 15.*

Juni. (P) 18 June 1848 in NRZ. (S) MEW 5:79. (Tr) M: Revols. of 1848, 124.
—Authorship not ascribed in MEW; ascription to Engels is my opinion.
Conciliationist Debates on the Regional Estates-Assemblies. *Vereinbarungs-debatten über die Kreisstände.* (P) 26 July 1848 in NRZ. (S) MEW 5:271.
The Condition of England: 1. The Eighteenth Century. *Die Lage Englands: 1. Das achtzehnte Jahrhundert.* (W) Feb. 1844. (P) 31 Aug.-11 Sept. 1844, in 4 parts, in Vorwärts, Paris. (S) MEW 1:550. (Tr) ME:CW 3:469.
The Condition of the Working Class in England. *Die Lage der arbeitenden Klasse in England.* (W) Sept. 1844 to Mar. 1845. (P) May 1845, as book, Leipzig. (S) MEW 2:225. (Tr) ME:CW 4:295; the tr. listed in the next entry is not recommended. —Preface to English Edition, 1892.°° (D) 11 Jan. 1892. (P) in London 1892 edition. (S) ME:SW 3:440.
THE CONDITION OF THE WORKING CLASS IN ENGLAND. W. O. Henderson & W. H. Chaloner, eds. & trs. New York, Macmillan, 1958.
Conditions and Prospects for a War by the Holy Alliance Against a Revolutionary France in 1852. *Bedingungen und Aussichten eines Krieges der Heiligen Allianz gegen ein revolutionäres Frankreich im Jahre 1852.* (W) Apr. 1851, memo not for publication, untitled. (S) MEW 7:468, titled as above.
CORRESPONDENCE / FREDERICK ENGELS / PAUL AND LAURA LA-FARGUE. Three vols. Moscow, FLPH, 1959-1961?.
CORRESPONDANCE / FRIEDRICH ENGELS / PAUL ET LAURA LA-FARGUE. E. Bottigelli, ed.; P. Meier, tr. Three vols. Paris, Ed. Sociales, 1956-1959.
The "Crisis" in Prussia. *Die "Krisis" in Preussen.* (P) 15 Jan. 1873 in Volksstaat. (S) MEW 18:290.
Critical Notes on Proudhon's *L'Idée Générale de la Révolution.* [In German] (W) 1851, ms. notes. (S) Russian tr. in Arkhiv Marksa i Engel'sa, vol. 10 (1948), p. 5-39; as far as I know, the only version so far published.
Critique of the Erfurt Program. *Zur Kritik des sozialdemokratischen Programm-entwurfs 1891.* (W) 18-29 June 1891, for German party leadership. (S) MEW 22:225, titled as above. (Tr) ME:SW 3:429, "Critique of the Draft Social-Democratic Programme of 1891."
The Debate on Poland in Frankfurt. *Die Polendebatte in Frankfurt.* (P) 9 Aug. to 7 Sept. 1848, in 9 parts, in NRZ. (S) MEW 5:319. (Tr) part in ME: Rev. 48/49, 82.
The Debate on the Poster Law. *Die Debatte über das Plakatsgesetz.* (P) 22-27 Apr. 1849, in 2 parts, in NRZ. (S) MEW 6:434.
Debate on the Redemption Legislation in Force up to Now. *Debatte über die bisherige Ablösungsgesetzgebung.* (P) 6 Aug. 1848 in NRZ. (S) MEW 5:309.
Details about June 23rd. *Details über den 23. Juni.* (P) 26 June 1848 in NRZ. (S) MEW 5:112.
Dialectics of Nature. *Dialektik der Natur.* (W) 1873-82, 1885-86, unfinished mss. (S) MEW 20:305. (Tr) next entry.
DIALECTICS OF NATURE. C. Dutt, tr. Moscow, FLPH, 1954.
England in 1845 and 1885.°° (W) mid-Feb. 1885. (P) 1 Mar. 1885 in Common-weal, London. (S) ME: Art. Brit., 388.
The English Elections. *Die englischen Wahlen.* (D) 22 Feb. 1874. (P) 4 Mar. 1874 in Volksstaat. (S) MEW 18:494. (Tr) ME: Art. Brit., 366.
The English Ten Hours Bill. *Die englische Zehnstundenbill.* (W) Mar. 1850. (P) mid-May 1850 in NRZ Revue, no. 4. (S) MEW 7:233. (Tr) ME: Art. Brit., 96.
An English Turnout. Postscript on the Condition of the Working Classes in England. *Ein englischer Turnout. Nachträgliches über die Lage der arbeitenden*

Klassen in England. (W) summer-autumn 1845. (P) Jan.-Feb. 1846 in Das Westphälische Dampfboot. (S) MEW 2:591. (Tr) ME:CW 4:584.

Ernst Moritz Arndt. [In German] (W) Oct.-Dec. 1840. (P) Jan. 1841 in Telegraph für Deutschland. (S) MEW Eb. 2:118. (Tr) ME:CW 2:137.

A Fair Day's Wages for a Fair Day's Work.°° (P) 7 May 1881 in Labour Standard. (S) E: Art. Lab. Stand., 5.

The Festival of Nations in London. *Das Fest der Nationen in London . . .* (W) end of 1845. (P) 1846 in Rheinische Jahrbücher zur gesellschaftlicher Reform, vol. 2. (Tr) ME:CW 6:3.

The Foreign Policy of Russian Czarism. *Die auswärtige Politik des russischen Zarentums.* (W) Dec. 1889 to Feb. 1890. (P) May 1890 in Neue Zeit. (S) MEW 22:11. (Tr) ME: Russ. Men., 25. —A tr. made with Engels' collaboration (Ch. 2-3 probably by Engels) in Time, London, Apr. and May 1890, p. 353, 525. (*Abbreviated* E: For. Pol. Russ. Cz./Time.)

Freedom of Assembly and Organization in England—Repercussions of the Hague Congress. London Letters [4]. *Libertà di riunione e di organizzazione in Inghilterra.—Le ripercussioni del Congresso dell'Aia. Lettere Londinesi* [4]. (P) 14 Dec. 1872 in La Plebe, Lodi, untitled. (S) ME: Scritti Ital., 113 plus 91.

The French Commercial Treaty.°° (P) 18 June 1881 in Labour Standard. (S) E: Art. Lab. Stand., 19.

The French Working Class and the Presidential Election. *Die französische Arbeiterklasse und die Präsidentenwahl.* (W) beginning of Dec. 1848, for NRZ; unpublished ms. (S) MEW 6:557.

From Paris to Bern. *Von Paris nach Bern.* (W) end of Oct. to Nov. 1848, unfinished ms. (S) MEW 5:463.

The Future Italian Revolution and the Socialist Party (Letter, Engels to Turati, 26 January 1894) [In French] (D) 26. Jan 1894, letter in French. (P) Italian tr., 1 Feb. 1894 in Critica Sociale, Milan. (S) French original in ME: Corrisp. con Ital., 518; Italian tr. in ME: Scritti Ital., 170. (Tr) ME:SW 3:453, titled as above (tr. of Critica Sociale title).

The German Campaign for the Reich Constitution. *Die deutsche Reichsverfassungskampagne.* (W) Aug. 1849 to Feb. 1850. (P) Mar.-Apr. 1850 in NRZ Revue, no. 1-3. (S) MEW 7:109.

The German Social Democrats.°° (W) 21 Feb.-1 Mar. 1890. (P) 3 Mar. 1890 in Newcastle Daily Chronicle. (S) photocopy supplied by Newcastle Daily Chronicle.

German Socialism in Verse and Prose. *Deutscher Sozialismus in Versen und Prosa.* (W) 1846 and early 1847. (P) 12 Sept. to 9 Dec. 1847, in 8 parts, in Deutsche Brüsseler Ztg. (S) MEW 4:207. (Tr) ME:CW 6:235.

Hankering for a State of Siege. *Belagerungsgelüste.* (P) 6 May 1849 in NRZ. (S) MEW 6:471.

"Herr Tidmann," an old Danish Folk Song. *Herr Tidmann, altdänisches Volkslied.* (P) 5 Feb. 1865 in Social-Demokrat. (S) MEW 16:33.

The Housing Question. *Zur Wohnungsfrage.* (W) May 1872 to Jan. 1873. (P) 26 June 1872 to 22 Feb. 1873, in 11 parts, in Volksstaat; then as pamphlet, in 2 parts, 1872-73; complete in pamphlet, 2nd ed., 1887, Zurich. (S) MEW 18:209. (Tr) ME:SW 2:295. —Preface to Second German Edition. *Vorwort . . .* (D) 10 Jan. 1887. (P) 12-22 Jan. 1887, in 2 parts, in Sozialdemokrat; March 1887 in the pamphlet. (S) MEW 21:325. (Tr) ME:SW 2:295.

How Not to Translate Marx.°° (P) Nov. 1885, in The Commonweal, London.

The Hungarian Struggle. *Die Magyarische Kampf.* (P) 13 Jan. 1849. (S) MEW 6:165. (Tr) M: Revols. of 1848, 213.

In Italy. *Aus Italien.* (P) 16 Mar. 1877 in Vorwärts. (S) MEW 19:91. (Tr) ME: Anarch. & A.-S., 154, titled as above.

In the Matter of Brentano versus Marx re Alleged Falsification of Citations; narrative account and documents. *In Sachen Brentano contra Marx wegen angeblicher Zitatsfälschung; Geschichtserzählung und Dokumente.* (W) Dec. 1890 to Feb. 1891. (P) April 1891, as brochure, Hamburg. (S) MEW 22:93.

The International in America. *Die Internationale in Amerika.* (P) 17 July 1872 in Volksstaat. (S) MEW 18:97.

Interview in the London Daily Chronicle.°° (W) date of interview: end of June 1893. (P) Daily Chronicle, London, 1 July 1893. (S) E / Lafargue: Corr. 3:394, "Frederick Engels and the German Elections."

Interview in the New Yorker Volkszeitung. *Interview der "New Yorker Volkszeitung" mit Friedrich Engels.* (W) date of interview, with T. Cuno: 19 Sept. 1888. (P) 20 Sept. 1888. (S) MEW 21:511.

Introduction to Marx's "The Civil War in France." *Einleitung zu Karl Marx' "Bürgerkrieg in Frankreich."* (D) 18 Mar. 1891. (P) 1891 in Neue Zeit, then in 3rd German edition of book. (S) MEW 22:188 or 17:613. (Tr) ME:SW 2:178.

Introduction to Marx's "The Class Struggles in France 1848 to 1850." *Einleitung zu Marx' "Klassenkämpfe in Frankreich 1848 bis 1850."* (W) Feb.-Mar. 1895. (D) 6 Mar. 1895. (P) in bowdlerized form, Mar.-Apr. 1895 in Neue Zeit, then in book. Engels' original text first published 1930. (S) MEW 22:509. (Tr) ME:SW 1:186.

Irish Internationalists' Meeting in Hyde Park. London Letters [no. 3]. *Gli Internazionalisti Irlandesi in Favore del Condannati Politici e per il Diritto di Riunione. Lettere da Londra [3].* (P) 17 Nov. 1872 in La Plebe, Lodi, untitled. (S) ME: Scritti Ital., 110, titled as above. (Tr) ME: Art. Brit., 363, "Letters from London, III [Meeting in Hyde Park]."

June 23rd. *Der 23. Juni.* (P) 28 June 1848 in NRZ. (S) MEW 5:118.

June 25th. *Der 25. Juni.* (P) 29 June 1848 in NRZ. (S) MEW 5:128.

Karl Marx. [In German] (W) mid-June 1877. (P) 1878 in Volks-Kalender, Brunswick, an almanac. (S) MEW 19:96. (Tr) ME:SW 3:78.

The Kölnische Zeitung on the June Revolution. *Die "Kölnische Zeitung" über die Junirevolution.* (P) 1 July 1848 in NRZ. (S) MEW 5:138.

The Late Butchery at Leipzig.—The German Working Men's Movement.°° (P) 13 Sept. 1845 in Northern Star. (S) ME:CW 4:645.

The Late Trial at Cologne.°° (D) 1 Dec. 1852. (P) 22 Dec. 1852 in N. Y. Tribune. (S) ME:SW 1:389.

The Latest Feat of the House of Bourbon. *Die neueste Heldentat des Hauses Bourbon.* (P) 1 June 1848 in NRZ, untitled. (S) MEW 5:19, titled as above.

Lawyers' Socialism. *Juristen-Sozialismus.* (W) planned by Engels; written Nov. to beginning of Dec. 1886 by Engels and Kautsky. (P) 1887 in Neue Zeit, unsigned. (S) MEW 21:491. (Tr) ME: On Relig., 267, "Juristic Socialism."

Letter to the Editorial Board of Vorwärts. *Brief an die Redaktion des "Vorwärts."* (D) 12 Nov. 1894. (P) 16 Nov. 1894 in Vorwärts. (S) MEW 22:480.

Ludwig Feuerbach and the End of Classical German Philosophy. *Ludwig Feuerbach und der Ausgang der klassischen deutschen Philosophie.* (W) beginning of 1886. (P) 1886 in Neue Zeit; 1888 as booklet, with Foreword dated 21 Feb. 1888. (S) MEW 21:259. (Tr) ME:SW 3:335.

The Manifesto of M. de Lamartine.°° (P) 13 Nov. 1847. (S) ME:CW 6:364.

The Mark. *Die Mark.* (W) Sept.-Dec. 1882. (P) 1882, as appendix to German edition of E: Socialism Utop. Sci. (S) MEW 19:315. (Tr) E: Peasant War Ger. (56), 161. Included is the 1883 addition by Engels for a separate printing

entitled *Der deutsche Bauer* &c. (*Abbreviated* E: Mark/1883.)
Marx and the Neue Rheinische Zeitung. *Marx und die "Neue Rheinische Zeitung"
1848-1849.* (W) Feb.-Mar. 1884. (P) 13 Mar. 1884 in Sozialdemokrat. (S)
MEW 21:16. (Tr) ME:SW 3:164.
May 4 in London. *Der 4. Mai in London.* (P) 23 May 1890 in Arbeiter-Ztg.,
Vienna. (S) MEW 22:60. (Tr) ME: Art. Brit., 402.
Mediation and Intervention. *Vermittlung und Intervention; Radetzky und
Cavaignac.* (P) 1 Sept. 1848. (S) MEW 5:376. (Tr) ME: Rev. 48/49, 108.
The Movements of 1847. *Die Bewegungen von 1847.* (P) 23 Jan. 1848 in
Deutsche Brüsseler Ztg. (S) MEW 4:494. (Tr) ME:CW 6:520.
Anti-Semitism (letter to Ehrenfreund, 9 Apr. 1890). *Über den Antisemitismus
(Aus einem Brief nach Wien).* (P) 9 May 1890 in Arbeiter-Ztg., Vienna, as
excerpt from a letter to an unnamed correspondent; reprinted in German press
same month. (S) MEW 22:49, titled as above. (Tr) ME: Corr. (35), 469.
On Social Relations in Russia. *Soziales aus Russland.* (P) 16-21 Apr. 1875,.in 3
parts, in Volksstaat, titled *Flüchtlingsliteratur, V.*; as pamphlet, titled as shown,
Leipzig, 1875; in book *Internationales aus dem "Volksstaat" (1871-1875),*
1894. (S) MEW 18:556. (Tr) ME:SW 2:387, titled as shown. —Afterword to
1894 Edition. *Nachwort (1894) zu "Soziales aus Russland."* (W) Jan. 1894.
(P) Jan. 1894 in the book *Internationales* &c. (S) MEW 22:421. (Tr) ME:SW
1:398. —Preface to the 1875 Edition. *Vorbemerkung zu der Broschüre
"Soziales aus Russland."* (W) May 1875. (P) 1875, in the pamphlet. (S) MEW
18:584. (Tr) ME: Russ. Men., 274, 203-5.
On the Dissolution of the Lassallean Workers Association. *Zur Auflösung des
Lassalleanischen Arbeitervereins.* (P) 3 Oct. 1868 in Demokratisches Wochen-
blatt. (S) MEW 16:326.
On the History of Early Christianity. *Zur Geschichte des Urchristentums.* (W) 19
June-16 July 1894. (P) about Sept.-Oct. 1894 in Neue Zeit. (S) MEW 22:446.
(Tr) ME: On Relig., 313.
On the History of the Communist League. *Zur Geschichte des Bundes der
Kommunisten.* (D) 8 Oct. 1885. (P) Nov. 1885 in Sozialdemokrat; then in
1885 edition of M: Revel. Com. Trial. (S) MEW 21:206. (Tr) ME:SW 3:173.
On the History of the Prussian Peasants. *Zur Geschichte der preussische Bauern.*
(D) 24 Nov. 1885. (P) 1886, as part of introduction to Wilhelm Wolff's
pamphlet *Die schlesische Milliarde.* (S) MEW 21:238. (Tr) E: Peasant War Ger.
(56), 182.
On the London Dock Strike.°° (W) 20-26 Aug. 1889. (P) 31 Aug. 1889 in Labour
Elector, London, untitled. (S) ME: Art. Brit., 401, titled as above. —This was
an excerpt from a letter by Engels, apparently addressed to union organizer
Eleanor Marx.
On the Slogan of the Abolition of ·the State and the German "Friends of
Anarchy." *Über die Losung der Abschaffung des Staates and die deutschen
"Freunde der Anarchie."* (W) Oct. 1850, for NRZ Revue; unfinished ms. (S)
MEW 7:417.
The Peasant Question in France and Germany. *Die Bauernfrage in Frankreich und
Deutschland.* (W) 15-22 Nov. 1894. (P) Nov. 1894 in Neue Zeit. (S) MEW
22:483. (Tr) ME:SW 3:457.
The Peasant War in Germany. *Der deutsche Bauernkrieg.* (W) summer 1850. (P)
Nov. 1850 in NRZ Revue, no. 5/6; Oct. 1870 as brochure with preface,
Leipzig; another edition in 1875. (S) MEW 7:327. (Tr) E: Peasant War Ger.
(56), 37. —Preface. *Vorbemerkung . . .* (W) Feb. 1870. (P) 2-6 Apr. 1870 in
Volksstaat; Oct. 1870 in the pamphlet. (S) MEW 16:393. (Tr) ME:SW 2:158,

or E: Peasant War Ger. (56), 15. —Supplement to Preface (*abbreviated* Peasant War Ger./Pref. '75). (D) 1 July 1874. (P) 1875, added to the 1870 preface. (S) MEW 18:512. (Tr) ME:SW 2:165, or E: Peasant War Ger. (56), 26.

THE PEASANT WAR IN GERMANY. Moscow, FLPH, 1956.

A Polish Proclamation. *Eine polnische Proklamation.* (W) May-June 1874. (P) 17 June 1874 in Volksstaat, as *Flüchtlingsliteratur, I.* (S) MEW 18:521. (Tr) ME: Russ. Men., 109.

The Position of the Danish Internationalists in the Agrarian Question. Report by Engels at the General Council Meeting of December 5, 1871.°° (P) 9 Dec. 1871 in Eastern Post. (S) G.C.F.I. 71-72 [5], 291.

Preface to *Capital*, English Edition of 1887.°° (D) 5 Nov. 1886. (P) Jan. 1887, in the book. (S) M: Cap. 1:3.

Preface to the Communist Manifesto, German Edition of 1883. *Vorwort . . .* (D) 28 June 1883. (P) 1883, 3rd German ed., Hottingen-Zurich. (S) MEW 21:3 or 4:577. (Tr) ME:SW 1:101.

Preface to the Communist Manifesto, English Edition of 1888.°° (D) 30 Jan. 1888. (P) 1888, in 1st English ed., London. (S) ME: Selected Wks (55), 1:25.

Preface to "Karl Marx Before the Cologne Jury," *Vorwort zu "Karl Marx vor den Kölner Geschworenen."* (D) 1 July 1885. (P) in the pamphlet. 1885, q.v. (S) MEW 21:198.

Preface to Marx's "The Poverty of Philosophy," First German Edition. *Vorwort . . .* (D) 23 Oct. 1884. (P) Jan. 1885 in Neue Zeit and in the book, Stuttgart. (S) MEW 21:175 or 4:558. (Tr) in any English ed. of Marx's work.

Principles of Communism. *Grundsätze des Kommunismus.* (W) end of Oct. 1847; ms. draft, untitled. (S) MEW 4:361. (Tr) ME:CW 6:341; ME:SW 1:181.

Progress of Social Reform on the Continent.°° (W) late Oct. to early Nov. 1843. (P) 4-18 Nov. 1843, in 2 parts, in New Moral World; reprinted but shortened in Northern Star, 11-25 Nov. 1843. (S) ME:CW 3:392.

The Prosecution of Montalembert.°° (D) 6 Nov. 1858. (P) 24 Nov. 1858 in N. Y. Tribune.

Protective Tariff or Free Trade System. *Schutzzoll oder Freihandels-System.* (P) 10 June 1847 in Deutsche Brüsseler Ztg. (S) MEW 4:58. (Tr) ME:CW 6:92.

The Prussian Constitution.°° (P) 6 Mar. 1847 in Northern Star. (S) ME:CW 6:64.

The Prussian Military Question and the German Workers Party. *Die preussische Militärfrage und die deutsche Arbeiterpartei.* (W) Jan.-Feb. 1865. (P) Feb. 1865, as a pamphlet, Hamburg. (S) MEW 16:37.

Rapid Progress of Communism in Germany.°° (W) Nov. 1844 to Apr. 1845. (P) 13 Dec. 1844 to 10 May 1845, in 3 parts, in New Moral World. (S) ME:CW 4:229.

Real Causes Why the French Proletarians Remained Comparatively Inactive in December Last.°° (P) 21 Feb.-10 Apr. 1852, in 3 parts, in Notes to the People. (S) reprint edition of the periodical, q.v.

Reply to the Editorial Board of the Sächsische Arbeiter-Zeitung. *Antwort an die Redaktion der "Sächsischen Arbeiter-Zeitung."* (D) 7 Sept. 1890. (P) 13 Sept. 1890 in Sozialdemokrat. (S) MEW 22:68.

Revolution and Counterrevolution in Germany.°° (W) Aug. 1851 to Sept. 1852; drafted by Engels, then went through Marx's hands. (P) 25 Oct. 1851 to 23 Oct. 1852, in 19 articles, in N. Y. Tribune, signed by Marx; published as book by Marx in 1896, ed. by Eleanor Marx Aveling. (S) ME:SW 1:300.

Revolution in Paris. *Revolution in Paris* [in German]. (P) 27 Feb. 1848 in Deutsche Brüsseler Ztg. (S) MEW 4:528. (Tr) ME:CW 6:556.

The Revolutionary Uprising in the Palatinate and Baden. *Die revolutionäre*

Erhebung in der Pfalz und in Baden. (P) 3 June 1849 in Der Bote für Stadt und Land, untitled. (S) MEW 6:524.

The Role of Force in History. *Die Rolle der Gewalt in der Geschichte.* (W) end of Dec. 1887 to Mar. 1888; unfinished ms. (P) posthumously, 1896 in Neue Zeit, and as book, 1946. (S) MEW 21:405. (Tr) ME:SW 3:377.

The "Satisfied" Majority—Guizot's Scheme [etc.] ...°° (P) 8 Jan. 1848 in Northern Star. (S) ME:CW 6:438.

Savoy, Nice and the Rhine. *Savoyen, Nizza und der Rhein.* (W) Feb. 1860. (P) Apr. 1860, as brochure, Berlin; unsigned. (S) MEW 13:571.

Socialism in Germany. *Der Sozialismus in Deutschland.* (W) 13-22 Oct. 1891 in French; in Dec. 1891-Jan. 1892, the German version, enlarged. (P) the French version in *Almanach du Parti Ouvrier pour 1892*, Lille, entitled "Le Socialisme en Allemagne"; the German version in Neue Zeit, 1891-92, Jg. 10, Bd. 1. (S) MEW 22:245.

The Socialism of Herr Bismarck. *Le Socialisme de M. Bismarck.* (W) end of Feb. 1880. (P) 3-24 Mar. 1880, in 2 parts, in L'Egalité, Paris. (S) photocopy from L'Egalité.

Socialism, Utopian and Scientific. *Socialisme utopique et socialisme scientifique.* (W) Jan.-Mar. 1880, as revised version of chapters from *Anti-Dühring* for France. (P) 20 Mar.–5 May 1880, in 3 parts, in Revue Socialiste; then as pamphlet, Paris, 1880. (Tr) ME:SW 3:115, reproducing Aveling tr. of 1892. —Introduction to the English Edition of 1892.°° (W) Feb.-Apr. 1892. (D) 20 Apr. 1892. (P) in the book. (S) ME:SW 3:95.

Speech by Mr. F. Engels [on the Polish question]. *Discours de M. F. Engels.* (W) delivered 22 Feb. 1848, in French. (P) Mar. 1848, in brochure *Célébration, à Bruxelles, du deuxième anniversaire de la Révolution Polonaise* ... (S) MEGA I, 6:412. (Tr) ME:CW 6:549.

The State of Germany.°° (P) 25 Oct. 1845-4 Apr. 1846, in 3 parts ("letters"), in Northern Star. (S) ME:CW 6:15.

The Status Quo in Germany. *Der Status Quo in Deutschland.* (W) Mar.-Apr. 1847; unfinished ms. for pamphlet. (S) MEW 4:40, titled as shown. (Tr) ME:CW 6:75, "The Constitutional Question in Germany."

The Stock Exchange; Supplementary Notes to the Third Volume of *Capital.* *Die Börse. Nachträgliche Anmerkungen zum 3. Bd. des "Kapital."* (W) Apr.-May 1895; unpublished ms. (S) MEW 25:917. (Tr) M: Cap. 3:884.

Strike of English Farm Workers. London Letters [no. 1]. *Sciopero dei Lavoratori Agricoli Inglesi. Lettere Londinesi [1].* (P) 24 Apr. 1872 in La Plebe, Lodi. (S) ME: Scritti Ital., 105. (Tr) ME: Art. Brit., 360.

The Swiss Civil War. *Der Schweizer Bürgerkrieg.* (P) 14 Nov. 1847 in Deutsche Brüsseler Ztg. (S) MEW 4:391. (Tr) ME:CW 6:367.

Switzerland. Political Position of this Republic.°° (D) 1 May 1853. (P) 17 May 1853 in N. Y. Tribune.

Three New Constitutions. *Drei neue Konstitutionen.* (P) 20 Feb. 1848 in Deutsche Brüsseler Ztg. (S) MEW 4:514. (Tr) ME:CW 6:540.

To the International Congress of Socialist Students. (D) 19 Dec. 1893. (P) 25 Mar.-10 Apr. 1894 in L'Etudiant Socialiste, Brussels, untitled, in French. (S) MEW 22:415; cited here in retranslation from German.

To the Spanish Federal Council of the International Working Men's Association. *Al Consejo Federal de la Region Española de la Asociación Internacional de Trabajadores.* [In French except for this heading] (D) 13 Feb. 1871. (S) G.C.F.I. 70-71 [4], 346. (Tr) ibid., 479.

Trades Unions, I.°° (P) 28 May 1881 in Labour Standard. (S) E: Art. Lab. Stand.,

11. —Trades Unions, II.°° (P) 4 June 1881 in Labour Standard. (S) E: Art. Lab. Stand., 15.
The True-Socialists. *Die wahren Sozialisten.* (W) Jan.-Apr. 1847; unfinished ms. (S) MEW 4:248. (Tr) ME:CW 5:540.
The Uprising in Frankfurt. *Der Aufstand in Frankfurt.* (P) 20-21 Sept. 1848, in 2 parts, in NRZ. (S) MEW 5:410. (Tr) ME: Rev. 48/49, 134.
The Wages System.°° (P) 21 May 1881, in Labour Standard. (S) E: Art. Lab. Stand., 8. ·
What Have the Working Classes to Do with Poland?°° (W) Jan.-Apr. 1866. (P) 24 Mar.-5 Apr. 1866, in 3 parts, in Commonwealth. (S) ME: Russ. Men. 95.
Wilhelm Wolff. [In German] (P) 1 July–25 Nov. 1876, in 11 articles, in Neue Welt, Leipzig; in 1886, revised, as part of Engels' introduction to reprint of Wolff's *Die schlesische Milliarde.* (S) MEW 19:53.
A Working Men's Party.°° (P) 23 July 1881 in Labour Standard. (S) E: Art. Lab. Stand., 35.
The Workingmen of Europe in 1877.°° (P) 3-31 Mar. 1878, in 5 parts, in Labor Standard, New York. (S) Cited here from photocopy from Labor Standard.
The Zeitungs-Halle on the Rhine Province. *Die "Zeitungs-Halle" über die Rheinprovinz.* (P) 27 Aug. 1848 in NRZ. (S) MEW 5:373. (Tr) ME: Rev. 48/49, 105.

BOOKS AND ARTICLES BY OTHERS

Adler, Max. *Démocratie et Conseils Ouvriers.* Yvon Bourdet, tr. (Bibliothèque Socialiste, 10) Paris, Maspero, 1967. (Bourdet's notes are cited here.)
Andler, Charles. Introduction historique et Commentaire, *in* Marx et Engels: *Le Manifeste Communiste,* II (Bibliothèque Socialiste, 9-10) Paris, Cornély, 1910.
Andréas, Bert. *Le Manifeste Communiste de Marx et Engels; histoire et bibliographie 1848-1918.* (Bibliographies par l'Institut G. Feltrinelli) Milan, Feltrinelli, 1963.
Andréas, Bert, and W. Mönke. *Neue Daten zur "Deutschen Ideologie"* ... Sonderdruck aus dem Archiv für Sozialgeschichte, Bd. 8, 1968, Hannover.
Annenkov, P. V. *The Extraordinary Decade. Literary Memoirs.* A. P. Mendel, ed.; I. R. Titunik, tr. Univ. of Michigan Press, 1968.
Auerbach, N. *Marx und die Gewerkschaften.* Berlin, Vereinigung Internationaler Verlagsanstalten, 1922.
Avineri, Shlomo. "Marx and the Intellectuals," *Journal of the History of Ideas* (Apr.-June 1967), p. 269.
———. *The Social and Political Thought of Karl Marx.* Cambridge, University Press, 1968.
Bakunin, Michael A. *Etatisme et Anarchie, 1873.* (Archives Bakounine, I. I. S. G., Amsterdam, 3) A. Lehning, ed. Leiden, Brill, 1967. (Russian texts plus French tr.)
Becker, Gerhard. *Karl Marx und Friedrich Engels in Köln 1848-1849. Zur Geschichte des Kölner Arbeitervereins.* Berlin, Rütten & Loening, 1963.
Beer, Max. *A History of British Socialism.* Introduction by R. H. Tawney. 2 vols. London, Bell, 1923.
Bernstein, Eduard. "Die Briefe Johannes Miquels an Karl Marx," *Neue Zeit* (3-10 Apr. 1914, Jg. 32, 2. Bd.), p. 4 and 65.
———. *Cromwell and Communism. Socialism and Democracy in the Great English*

Revolution. H. J. Stenning, tr. London, Allen & Unwin, 1930. (Tr. of his *Sozialismus und Demokratie in der grosser Englischen Revolution,* 1895.)

——. " 'Es fehlt uns an Intelligenzen,' " *Sozialdemokrat* (28 July—11 Aug. 1881).

——. *Evolutionary Socialism: A Criticism and Affirmation.* E. C. Harvey, tr. (Socialist Library, 7) New York, Huebsch, 1909. (Tr. of his *Voraussetzungen . . .,* q.v.)

——. *Ferdinand Lassalle as a Social Reformer.* Eleanor Marx Aveling, tr. London, Swan Sonnenschein, 1893. (Tr. of his introduction to Lassalle's works.)

——. *Ferdinand Lassalle; eine Würdigung des Lehrers und Kämpfers.* Berlin, Cassirer, 1919.

——. *My Years of Exile.* Trans. by B. Miall. London, Parsons, 1921. (Written 1915)

——. *Der Sozialismus einst und jetzt.* 2nd ed. Berlin, Dietz Nachf., 1923. Vorwort d. Nov. 1921.

——. *Die Voraussetzungen des Sozialismus und die Aufgaben der Sozialdemokratie.* Stuttgart, Dietz Nachf., 1902. (First pub. 1899.)

Bernstein, Samuel. *The First International in America.* New York, A. M. Kelley, 1962.

——. "The Paris Commune," *Science and Society* (Spring 1941).

Bibliographisches Institut, Leipzig. *Fremdenwörter.* The Institute, 1964. —Another ed., 1954.

Blake, William J. *An American Looks at Karl Marx.* New York, Cordon Co., 1939.

Braverman, Harry. *Labor and Monopoly Capital; the degradation of work in the twentieth century.* New York, Monthly Review Press, 1974.

Briefs, Goetz A. *The Proletariat; a challenge to Western civilization.* New York, McGraw-Hill, 1937.

Brisbane, Albert. *A Mental Biography.* Boston, Arena Pub. Co., 1893.

Der Bund der Kommunisten; Dokumente und Materialien. Institut für Marxismus-Leninismus beim ZK der SED; Institut für Marxismus-Leninismus beim ZK der KPdSU. Band 1: 1836–1849 (no more pub. so far). Berlin, Dietz, 1970.

Cabet, Etienne. *Voyage en Icarie.* Paris, Populaire, 1845.

Carr, E. H. *Michael Bakunin.* New York, Vintage, 1961, c1937.

Chase, Stuart. *Technocracy—an Interpretation.* New York, John Day, 1933. (John Day Pamphlets, 19)

Chevalier, Louis. *Classes Laborieuses et Classes Dangereuses à Paris pendant la Première Moitié du XIXe Siècle.* Paris, Plon, 1958.

Clark, Frederick C. "A Neglected Socialist," *Annals* of the American Academy of Political and Social Science (Mar. 1895), p. 718.

Cohnstaedt, Wilhelm. *Die Agrarfrage in der deutschen Sozialdemokratie von Karl Marx bis zum Breslauer Parteitag.* Munich, Reinhardt, 1903.

Cole, G. D. H. *History of Socialist Thought.* Vol. 1: *The Forerunners 1789-1850.* London, Macmillan, 1955.

Collins, Henry, and C. Abramsky. *Karl Marx and the British Labour Movement. Years of the First International.* London, Macmillan, 1965.

Communist League. *Central Committee Session of September 15, 1850; Minutes.* In: MEW 8:597. Tr in ME: Cologne Com. Trial, 250.

Communist League, Cologne Central Committee. *Address to the Communist League, Dec. 1, 1850.* In: MEW 7:561. Tr. in ME: Cologne Com. Trial, 254.

Connolly, James. *Workshop Talks.* Dublin, Repsol, n.d. [1909] .

Coser, Lewis A. *Men of Ideas: a sociologist's view.* New York, Free Press, 1970.

Dahrendorf, Ralf. *Class and Class Conflict in Industrial Society.* Stanford Univ. Press, 1959.

De Leon, Daniel. *Industrial Unionism; selected editorials.* New York Labor News Co., 1933. (First pub. 1920.)

Deutsche Akademie der Wissenschaften zu Berlin. *Wörterbuch.* Berlin, 1967.

Dommanget, Maurice. *Les Idées Politiques et Sociales d'Auguste Blanqui.* Paris, Rivière, 1957.

Dowe, Dieter. *Aktion und Organisation.* Hanover, Verl. f. Lit. u. Zeitgeschehen, 1970.

Drahn, Ernst. *Karl Marx und Friedrich Engels ueber die Diktatur des Proletariats.* (Der Rote Hahn. Doppelband 51/52) Berlin-Wilmersdorf, Verlag "Die Aktion," 1920.

Draper, Hal. "Marx and Engels on Women's Liberation," in Salper, Roberta, ed. *Female Liberation,* New York, Knopf, 1972, p. 84.

———. "Marx and the Dictatorship of the Proletariat," *Etudes de Marxologie* (Cahiers de l'I.S.E.A., Série S), no. 6, Sept. 1962, p. 5.

Drennan, James [i.e., W. E. D. Allen]. *B.U.F.; Oswald Mosley and British Fascism.* London, J. Murray, 1934.

Dutt, R. Palme. *Fascism and Social Revolution.* New York, International Pub., 1934, 1935.

Eccarius, J. George. *Eines Arbeiters Widerlegung der national-ökonomischen Lehren John Stuart Mill.* Berlin, Verlag A. Eichhoff, 1869. [Expanded revision of author's article-series in *Commonwealth,* London, 1866–1867, under somewhat different title.]

———. "A Workingman's Refutation of the Political Economy of J. Stuart Mill," *Labor Standard,* New York (30 Dec. 1876 to 26 May 1877, 18 installments). —This is a translation of most of the preceding entry; left incomplete.

Enzensberger, Hans Magnus, ed. *Gespräche mit Marx und Engels.* 2 vols. (Insel Taschenbuch, 19-20) Frankfurt, Insel Verlag, 1973.

Fedoseyev, P. N. et al. *Karl Marx; a biography.* Tr. from Russian. Moscow, Progress Pub., 1973.

Feuer, Lewis S. *Marx and the Intellectuals.* Garden City, N.Y., Anchor Books (Doubleday), 1969.

The First International. Minutes of the Hague Congress of 1872 with related documents. Hans Gerth, ed. & tr. Madison, Univ. of Wisconsin Press, 1958.

Footman, David. *Ferdinand Lassalle, Romantic Revolutionary.* Yale Univ. Press, 1947. [Brit. ed. titled *The Primrose Path: A Life of . . .,* 1946.]

Freymond, Jacques, ed. *La Première Internationale; recueil de documents.* (Publications de l'Institut Universitaire de Hautes Etudes Internationales, no. 39) 2 vols. Geneva, Droz, 1962.

Gay, Peter. *The Dilemma of Democratic Socialism. Eduard Bernstein's Challenge to Marx.* New York, Columbia Univ. Press, 1952.

Gemkow, Heinrich, et al. *Frederick Engels; a biography.* Institute for Marxism-Leninism. Dresden, Verlag Zeit im Bild, 1972.

———. *Friedrich Engels; eine Biographie.* Institut für Marxismus-Leninismus beim ZK der SED. Berlin, Dietz, 1970.

The General Council of the First International . . . (Series: *Documents of the First International*) Five unnumbered volumes published, each beginning as above, followed by the years covered. Moscow, FLPH (for vol. 1) or Progress Pub., n.d. —Vol. [1] G.C.F.I. 1864-1866. The London Conference. Minutes. [2] G.C.F.I. 1866-1868. Minutes. [3] G.C.F.I. 1868-1870. Minutes. [4] G.C.F.I. 1870-1871. Minutes. [5] G.C.F.I. 1871-1872. Minutes.

General Council of the I.W.M.A. "To the Working Men of Great Britain and Ireland," *Miner & Workman's Advocate*, 2 Sept. 1865. —In: G.C.F.I. 64-66 [1], 299.

Goldberg, Harvey. "Jaurès and the Formulation of a Socialist Peasant Policy, 1885-1898," *International Review of Social History*, Amsterdam, vol. 2, 1957, part 3, p. 372.

Grünberg, Carl, ed. *Die Londoner Kommunistische Zeitschrift und andere Urkunden aus den Jahren 1847/1848*. Leipzig, Hirschfeld, 1921.

Guérin, Daniel. *La Lutte des Classes sous la Première République; Bourgeois et "Bras Nus" (1793-1797)*. (Collection La Suite des Temps, 16) 6th ed. 2 vols. Paris, Gallimard, 1946.

Guillaume, James. *L'Internationale; Documents et Souvenirs (1864-1878)*. 4 vols. Paris, 1905-10.

H. "Karl Marx. Interview with the Corner-Stone of Modern Socialism . . . ." *Chicago Tribune*, 5 Jan. 1879, p. 7. (Datelined London, Dec. 18, "Special Correspondence of the Tribune.") Cited here from pamphlet reprint, *An Interview with Karl Marx in 1879* [sic: read 1878], T. W. Porter, ed. (American Inst. for Marxist Studies, Occas. Papers, 10), New York, 1972.

Hammen, Oscar J. "Marx and the Agrarian Question," *American Historical Review*, 1972, p. 679.

———. *The Red '48ers; Karl Marx and Friedrich Engels*. New York, Scribners, 1969.

———. "The Spectre of Communism in the 1840's," *Journal of the History of Ideas* (June 1953), p. 404.

Harney, George Julian. *The Harney Papers*. F. G. Black & R. M. Black, eds. (Publications on Social History, 5) Assen, Van Gorcum, 1969.

Harrison, Royden. *Before the Socialists. Studies in Labour and Politics 1861-1881*. London, Routledge & K. Paul, 1965.

———. "The Land and Labour League. (Some new light on working class politics in the eighteen seventies)," International Institute of Social History *Bulletin*, Leiden (vol. 8, 1953, no. 3), p. 169.

Heine, Heinrich. *Sämtliche Werke*. Hrsg. von Ernst Elster. (Meyers Klassiker-Ausgabe) 7 vols. Leipzig/Wien, Bibliographisches Institut, n.d. [1890].

Heinsius, Theodor. *Volksthümliches Wörterbuch*. Hanover, 1820.

Heinzen, Karl. *Erlebtes*. 2. Theil: *Nach meiner Exilirung*. (Gesammelte Schriften, Bd. 4) Boston, The author, 1874.

Henderson, W. O., and W. H. Chaloner, "Friedrich Engels in Manchester," *Memoirs and Proceedings*, Manchester Literary and Philosophical Society (1956-57, vol. 98).

Herrmann, Ursula. *Der Kampf von Karl Marx um eine revolutionäre Gewerkschaftpolitik in der I. Internationale 1864 bis 1868*. Berlin, Verlag Tribüne, 1968.

Hess, Moses. *Philosophische und Sozialistische Schriften 1837-1850. Eine Auswahl*. A. Cornu and W. Mönke, eds. Berlin, Akademie-Verlag, 1961.

Hesselbarth, Hellmut. *Revolutionäre Sozialdemokraten, Opportunisten und die Bauern am Vorabend des Imperialismus*. Berlin, Dietz, 1968.

Hobsbawm, E. J. *Primitive Rebels*. New York, Norton, 1965, c1959. (Originally titled *Social Bandits and Primitive Rebels*.)

Hook, Sidney. *From Hegel to Marx. Studies in the Intellectual Development of Karl Marx*. New York, Humanities Press, 1950.

———. *Towards the Understanding of Karl Marx. A Revolutionary Interpretation*. New York, John Day Co., 1933.

Hoyt, J. K. *The Cyclopedia of Practical Quotations*. New edition. New York, Funk & Wagnalls, c1896.

Hümmler, Heinz. *Opposition gegen Lassalle*. Berlin, Rütten & Loening, 1963.

Hutt, Allen. *British Trade Unionism; a short history*. New York, International Pub., 1953.

Jaeckh, Gustav. *Die Internationale. Eine Denkschrift* . . . Leipziger Buchdruckerei Aktiengesellschaft, 1904.

Johnson, Christopher H. *Utopian Communism in France. Cabet and the Icarians, 1839-1851*. Cornell Univ. Press, 1974.

Kamman, William F. *Socialism in German American Liteature. A thesis* [Ph.D.] . . . (Univ. of Pennsylvania. Americana Germanica series) Philadelphia, Americana Germanica Press, 1917.

Kandel, E. P., ed. *Marx und Engels und die ersten proletarischen Revolutionäre*. Berlin, Dietz, 1965.

Karl Marx; Chronik seines Lebens in Einzeldaten. Marx–Engels–Lenin Institute, Moscow, 1934.

Kautsky, Karl. *Die Agrarfrage*. 2nd ed. Stuttgart, Dietz, 1902.

———. *The Dictatorship of the Proletariat*. H. J. Stenning, tr. (ILP Library) 2nd ed. Manchester, National Labour Press, n.d. [1920].

———. *The Economic Doctrines of Karl Marx*. H. J. Stenning, tr. New York, Macmillan, 1936.

———. "Die Intelligenz und die Sozialdemokratie," *Neue Zeit* (1894-95, Jg. 13, Bd. 2), p. 10.

Kisch, Egon Erwin. *Karl Marx in Karlsbad*. Berlin/Weimar, Aufbau Verlag, 1968.

Kluge, F., and A. Götze. *Etymologisches Wörterbuch*. Berlin, 1951.

Kommunistische Zeitschrift, Probeblatt, nr. 1 [Sept. 1847]. Reprinted in: *Bund Kom.* 1:501 (incomplete), and in Grünberg, ed.: *Die Londoner Kommunistische Zeitschrift* . . ., q.v.

Künzli, Arnold. *Karl Marx; eine Psychographie*. Vienna, Europa Verlag, 1966.

Ladendorf, Otto. *Historisches Schlagwörterbuch. Ein Versuch*. Strassburg, Trübner, 1906.

Landauer, Carl. *European Socialism*. 2 vols. Berkeley, Univ. of California Press, 1959.

———. "The Guesdists and the Small Farmer: Early Erosion of French Marxism," *International Review of Social History* (vol. 6, 1961, part 2), p. 212.

Landor, R. "The Curtain Raised. Interview with Karl Marx, the Head of L'Internationale [etc.]," *New York World*, 18 July 1871 (datelined London, July 8). —Cited here from *New Politics* (Fall 1962), p. 128.

Lanjalley, Paul, and Paul Corriez. *Histoire de la Révolution du 18 Mars*. Paris, Lib. Internationale, 1871.

Lassalle, Ferdinand. *Franz von Sickingen; a tragedy in five acts*. Daniel De Leon, tr. N. Y. Labor News Co., 1904.

Laurat, Lucien. *Marxism and Democracy*. E. Fitzgerald, tr. London, Gollancz, 1940.

Laveleye, Emile de. *The Socialism of Today*. G. H. Orpen, tr. London, Leadenhall Press, n.d. [1884]. —Tr. of *Le Socialisme Contemporain*, 1881.

Lenin, V. I. *Collected Works*. 45 vols. Moscow, FLPH/Progress Pub., 1960-70.

Lichtheim, George. *Marxism; an historical and critical study*. New York, Praeger . 1962, c1961.

Lidtke, Vernon L. *The Outlawed Party; Social Democracy in Germany, 1878-1890*. Princeton Univ. Press, 1966.

Lozovsky, A. *Marx and the Trade Unions*. New York, International Pub., 1935.

Ludwig, C. *Deutsch-Englisches Lexicon.* Leipzig, 1716.
Lukacs, Georg. *Karl Marx und Friedrich Engels als Literaturhistoriker.* Berlin, Aufbau-Verlag, 1948.
Mackensen, Lutz. *Deutsches Wörterbuch.* Munich, 1967.
McLellan, David. *Karl Marx; his life and thought.* London, Macmillan, 1973.
——. *The Young Hegelians and Karl Marx.* London, Macmillan, 1969.
Manale, Margaret. "Aux origines du concept de 'marxisme.' " *Etudes de Marxologie,* No. S.17, Oct. 1974.
——. "La Constitution du 'marxisme.' " *Etudes de Marxologie,* No. S. 18, Apr.-May 1976.
Mandel, Ernest. *The Formation of the Economic Thought of Karl Marx; 1843 to Capital.* B. Pearce, tr. New York, Monthly Review Press, 1971.
——. *Marxist Economic Theory.* B. Pearce, tr. 2 vols. London, Merlin Press, 1968.
Massing, Paul W. *Rehearsal for Destruction; a study of political anti-Semitism in Imperial Germany.* New York, Harper, 1949.
Mayer, Gustav. *Friedrich Engels; eine Biographie.* 2nd ed. 2 vols. The Hague, Nijhoff, 1934. —A one-volume translation in a somewhat revised condensation was published as *Friedrich Engels; a biography.* G. and H. Highet, trs.; tr. ed. by R. H. S. Crossman. New York, Knopf, 1936.
Meek, Ronald L. *Studies in the Labour Theory of Value.* London, Lawrence & Wishart, 1956.
Mehring, Franz, ed. *Aus dem literarischen Nachlass von Karl Marx, Friedrich Engels and Ferdinand Lassalle.* 4 vols. Stuttgart, Dietz Nachf., 1902. [Vol. 1-3 = *Gesammelte Schriften von K.M. und F.E.*]
——. *Karl Marx; the story of his life.* E. Fitzgerald, tr.; R. & H. Norden, eds. New York, Covici Friede, 1935. [Original was pub. 1918.]
Mills, C. Wright. *White Collar; the American middle classes.* New York, Oxford Univ. Press, 1951.
Mitrany, David. *American Interpretations; four political essays.* London, 1946.
——. *Marx Against the Peasant.* Univ. of North Carolina Press, 1951.
Morgan, Roger. *The German Social Democrats and the First International 1864-1872.* Cambridge, University Press, 1965.
Müller, Hermann. *Die Organisationen der Lithographen, Steindrucker und verwandten Berufe.* Bd. 1. Berlin, Sillier, 1917.
Nettl, J. P. *Rosa Luxemburg.* 2 vols. London, Oxford Univ. Press, 1966.
Neue Rheinische Zeitung; politisch-ökonomische Revue, redigiert von Karl Marx. [Reprint of the magazine] Eingeleitet von Karl Bittel. Berlin, Rütten & Loening, 1955.
Nicolaievsky, Boris, and O. Maenchen-Helfen. *Karl Marx, Man and Fighter.* G. David & E. Mosbacher, trs. Philadelphia, Lippincott, 1936.
Nicolaievsky, Boris. "Toward a History of 'The Communist League' 1847-1852," *International Review of Social History* (vol. 1, pt. 2, 1956), p. 234. [Note that Nicolaevsky's name is spelled two ways.]
——. "Who Is Distorting History?" *Proceedings* of the American Philosophical Society (vol. 105, no. 2, 21 Apr. 1961), p. 209.
Nomad, Max. *Apostles of Revolution.* Boston, Little Brown, 1939.
Notes to the People (London), May 1851–May 1852, edited by Ernest Jones. [Reprint of the periodical] 2 vols. London, Merlin Press, 1967.
Noyes, Paul H. *Organization and Revolution. Working-class associations in the German revolutions of 1848-1849.* Princeton Univ. Press, 1966.
O'Brien, James Bronterre. *The Rise, Progress, and Phases of Human Slavery . . .*

London, Reeves, 1885. —First published as a series of articles beginning 17 Nov. 1849.

Opel, Fritz, & Dieter Schneider. *Fünfundsiebzig Jahre Industriegewerkschaft 1891 bis 1966 . . .* Hrsg. I. G. Metall. Frankfurt a.m., Europäische Verlaganstalt, 1966.

Pankhurst, Richard K. P. *William Thompson (1775-1833); Britain's pioneer socialist, feminist, and co-operator.* London, Watts, 1954.

Parker, Richard. *The Myth of the Middle Class.* New York, Liveright, 1972.

Proudhon, P. J. *Carnets.* P. Haubtmann, ed. 4 vols. published so far. Paris, Rivière, 1960-74.

———. *De la Capacité Politique des Classes Ouvrières.* Nouvelle éd. (Oeuvres Posthumes) Paris, Lib. Intle.; Bruxelles, Lacroix, Verboeckhoven & Co., 1868.

———. *General Idea of the Revolution in the Nineteenth Century.* J. B. Robinson, tr. London, Freedom Press, 1923.

Puech, Jules L. *Le Proudhonisme dans l'Association Internationale des Travailleurs.* Préface de Charles Andler. Paris, Alcan, 1907.

Pyziur, Eugene. *The Doctrine of Anarchism of Michael A. Bakunin.* Milwaukee, Marquette Univ. Press, 1955. (Marquette Slavic Studies, 1)

Reactionary Prussianism. (Above title: Karl Marx and Frederick Engels.) New York, International Pub., n.d. [194-]. —This pamphlet is an essay about Marx and Engels, not by them; a note states: "prepared by the Marx–Engels–Lenin Institute on the basis of the writings of" Marx and Engels; contains quotations from unpublished manuscripts.

Reminiscences of Marx and Engels. Moscow, FLPH, n.d.

Robertson, Priscilla. *Revolutions of 1848; a social history.* New York, Harper, 1960, c1952.

Rocker, Rudolf. *Johann Most; das Leben eines Rebellen.* Berlin, Verlag 'Der Syndikalist,' 1924.

Rosdolsky, Roman. *Zur Entstehungsgeschichte des Marxschen 'Kapital.' Der Rohentwurf des 'Kapital' 1857-58.* 2nd ed. Frankfurt/Vienna, Europäische Verlaganstalt, Europa Verlag, 1969, c1968. —Contains Bd. I and II in one volume.

Rubel, M. "La Charte de l'Internationale." *Le Mouvement Social,* No. 51, May-June 1965.

Sabine, George H. *A History of Political Theory.* Rev. ed. New York, Holt, Rinehart & Winston, 1960.

Saville, John. *Ernest Jones: Chartist. Selections . . . with introduction and notes.* London, Lawrence & Wishart, 1952.

Schapper, Karl. "Der Auswanderungsplan des Bürgers Cabet [Citizen Cabet's Emigration Scheme]," *Kommunistische Zeitschrift* (q.v.), in *Bund Kom.,* 1:508. [Unsigned; Schapper is the probable author.]

———. "Einleitung [Introduction]," *Kommunistische Zeitschrift* (q.v.), in *Bund Kom.,* 1:501. [Unsigned: Schapper is the probable author.]

Schlüter, Hermann. *Die Anfänge der deutschen Arbeiterbewegung in Amerika.* Stuttgart, Dietz Nachf., 1907.

Schmidt, Walter. "Der Bund der Kommunisten und die Versuche einer Zentralisierung der deutschen Arbeitervereine im April und Mai 1848," *Zeitschrift für Geschichtswissenschaft,* Berlin, Jg. 9, Heft 3, 1961, p. 577.

Schorske, Carl E. *German Social Democracy 1905-1907; the development of the great schism.* Harvard Univ. Press, 1955.

Schoyen, A. R. *The Chartist Challenge; a portrait of George Julian Harney.* New York, Macmillan, 1958.

Seidler, Franz W. *Die Geschichte des Wortes Revolution.* Unpublished dissertation, Ludwig-Maximilians-Universität zu München, 1955.

Silberner, Edmund. *Moses Hess; Geschichte seines Lebens.* Leiden, Brill, 1966.

Sismondi, J. C. L. Simonde de. *Etudes sur l'Economie Politique.* 2 vols. Paris, 1837.

Slicher van Bath, B. H. *The Agrarian History of Western Europe, A.D. 500–1850.* O. Ordish, tr. London, Arnold, 1966, c1963.

Sombart, Werner. *Socialism and the Social Movement.* Tr. from 6th German ed. by M. Epstein. London, Dent; New York, Dutton, 1909.

Somerhausen, Luc. *L'Humanisme Agissant de Karl Marx.* Paris, Richard-Masse, 1946.

Sozialdemokratische Partei Deutschlands. *Protokoll über die Verhandlungen des Parteitages der Sozialdemokratischen Partei Deutschlands . . . Dresden . . . September 1903.* Berlin, Vorwärts, 1903.

Spargo, John. *Sidelights on Contemporary Socialism.* New York, Huebsch, 1911.

Spitzer, Alan B. *The Revolutionary Theories of Louis Auguste Blanqui.* (Columbia Studies in the Social Sciences, 594) New York, Columbia Univ. Press, 1957.

Stirner, Max [Johann Kaspar Schmidt]. *The Ego and His Own.* S. T. Byington, tr. New York, Modern Library, n.d. [originally pub. 1907]. —Tr. of next entry.

———. *Der Einzige und sein Eigentum. Mit einem Nachwort.* Hrsg. von Ahlrich Meyer. Stuttgart, Ph. Reclam Jun., 1972. —Originally published Oct. 1844, with 1845 imprint; written in 1843–Apr. 1844.

Struik, Dirk J., ed. *Birth of the Communist Manifesto.* With full text of the Manifesto, all prefaces . . . early drafts . . . and other supplementary material. New York, International Pub., 1971.

Thompson, William. *Labor Rewarded . . . By One of the Idle Classes.* London, 1827 (reprinted, New York, A. M. Kelley, 1969).

Trotsky, Leon. *Permanent Revolution.* Calcutta, 1947.

Trübners Deutsches Wörterbuch. Berlin, W. de Gruyter, 1943.

Uroyeva, A. *For All Time and All Men.* Moscow, Progress Pub., 1969.

Villetard, Edmond. *History of the International.* S. M. Day, tr. New Haven, Conn., G. H. Richmond, 1874. —Tr. of his *Histoire de l'Internationale,* Paris, 1872.

Weitling, Wilhelm. *Garantien der Harmonie und Freiheit.* B. Kaufhold, ed. Berlin, 1955.

Willard, Claude. *Les Guesdistes.* Paris, Ed. Sociales, 1965.

Wittke, Carl. *Refugees of Revolution; the German Forty-eighters in America.* Univ. of Pennsylvania Press, 1952.

———. *The Utopian Communist; a biography of Wilhelm Weitling, nineteenth-century reformer.* Louisiana State Univ. Press, 1950.

Wolfe, Bertram D. *Marxism; one hundred years in the life of a doctrine.* New York, Dial Press, 1965.

Wolff, Wilhelm. "Der Preussische Landtag und das Proletariat in Preussen wie überhaupt in Deutschland [The Prussian Diet and the Proletariat in Prussia . . .]," *Kommunistische Zeitschrift* (q.v.), in *Bund Kom.,* 1:511. [Unsigned; Wolff is the probable author.]

Zaniewski, Romuald. *L'Origine du Prolétariat Romain et Contemporain; Faits et Théories.* (Université de Louvain, Collège de l'Ecole des Sciences Politiques et Sociales, 153), Louvain and Paris. 1957

INDEX

This Index does not cover the Reference Notes or Bibliography. There is no listing for *Marx, Engels,* and a number of geographical terms and subject headings which occur so abundantly that a long list of page numbers would be of little use. Topics under these subjects should be sought under headings of narrower scope. Titles of writings by Marx and Engels are indexed only for substantive references, not if merely quoted or mentioned as a source. The same applies to names of periodicals. Reference to a page includes footnotes on that page; reference to a footnote only is indicated by *n*. The following abbreviations are used:

n = note (footnote); hence 119n = footnote on page 119.

f = following page; hence 119f = pages 119-20.

... means *passim;* hence 107...119 means that the subject is explicit or implicit on pages 107-19.

741

LIST OF ERRATA FOR VOLUME I

The Special Notes should have subtitles giving their reference to the text; add these as follows. (A) p. 591, A Note to Chapter 5, page 123. *(B) p. 609,* A Note to Chapter 9, page 196. *(C) p. 619,* A Note to Chapter 18, page 460. *D), p. 622,* A Note to Chapter 20, page 514. *(E) p. 629,* A Note to Chapter 21, page 545.

The following are corrected spellings and phrases: Page 44, line 6, haled; *p. 99, line 1,* Buonarroti's; *p. 137, line 8,* about 100,000 Germans; *p. 152, line 12,* on your golden throne; *p. 210, line 19,* nor to yield; *p. 213, line 1,* Promethean; *p. 690, line 43,* Programs; *p. 709, line 1,* G. David; *p. 711, last line,* et Sociales; *p. 715, under Chang, delete comma after* Sherman; *p. 720, in alph. order,* Lelewel.

On pages 337 and 385, the asterisk in the last line applies to the footnote on the next page.

The following errata involve numbers and source information especially:

343, note 101. The second sentence should read: Also see MEW 27:646 (note 170), 680; and Rubel *etc.*

348, note 23 (last line). The page reference should read: 3:6 fn.

349, note 5a. The second line of this note should read: Freiligrath, 29 Feb. 1860, passim, MEW 36:489f.

354, note 9, line 1. ME:SW (55) *should read:* ME: Sel. Wks. (55).

356, note 40, should read: E: Orig. Fam., in ME:SW 3:327, rev. after *etc.*

358, note 37. The reference should read: MEW 5:245.

359, note 45 and 52. In both notes, the correct date of the article is: 5 Nov. 1853.

359, note 60. The correct date of the article is: 12 June 1854.

360, note 32, should read: Ibid., 356.

412, Sec. 1, line 5. Date should be 1866, *not* 1886.

499, last line of footnote should refer to Chapter 23.

592. Two lines of type were dropped from the bottom of this page, as follows: Christ, like the mystery of the *ancient Jewish blood-worship,* finally appears quite unmasked as the *mystery of the beast of prey.*" There is

610. The first stanza of the poem "The Minstrel" was dropped from the bottom of the text (blank space above the footnote). As it happens, this first stanza is exactly the same as the last, which see.

615. In the poem numbered VI, there should be no space between lines 5 and 6.

671, note 50, should read: M: France, in N. Y. Tribune *etc.*

672, note 44. The reference should read: ME:SW 1:110.

673, note 19. The reference should read: MEW 1:185; cited in Ch. 2, p. 65.

678, note 8, should read: E: Anti-Dühr. (59), 247, 248.

709, under Proudhon. The publication dates should read: 1960–1974.

www.ingramcontent.com/pod-product-compliance
Lightning Source LLC
Chambersburg PA
CBHW060016030426
42334CB00019B/2065